D0372606

THE
PRACTICAL
NOMAD

How to Travel Around the World

E D W A R D   H A S B R O U C K

FIFTH EDITION

www.practicalnomad.com

AVALON
TRAVEL

Liberty of movement is an indispensable condition for the free development of a person.
—United Nations Human Rights Committee

Contents

Preface

WHO IS THIS BOOK FOR?

If you've ever dreamed of a trip around the world, this book is for you. It's a unique, comprehensive "how-to" handbook of advice and tips for independent, on-your-own travel anywhere in the world. It's especially suitable for anyone planning—or dreaming about—the "big trip" or trip of a lifetime around the world.

Perhaps you're a student thinking about a "gap year" or semester or summer abroad, someone contemplating a midlife "wander year" sabbatical or career break, a parent wanting to give your children first-hand experience of the world while they are young enough to get the most lifelong benefit from it, a business traveler who needs to find your own way in foreign places without a tour group or guide, or a retiree with a pent-up dream of exploring the world. Whatever type of trip you are planning, this book offers concrete tips, advice, and guidance for planning your trip and for use while you are on the road.

If your fantasy is a trip around the world, you're not alone and you're not crazy. More and more people from all walks of life are finding ways to make that fantasy real. If you make it a priority, you can too.

But this book isn't just for people whose journeys will take them all the way around the world. It's for *anyone* considering, planning, or preparing for long-term, complex, multistop, or multicountry international travel;

first-time international travelers; travelers new to different regions of the world; and would-be travelers interested in learning more about travel planning than any guidebook to a specific destination can or does say. Even experienced travelers will find new and useful advice in the chapters that follow.

The Practical Nomad: How to Travel Around the World answers questions like, "How can I afford the time and money to travel? How can I find my way around and find places to eat and sleep if I don't know the language and haven't made reservations in advance? How can I figure out which places to visit will be best for me? What visas will I need, and how do I get them? How can I get the best prices on complicated and confusing international airline tickets? Are there alternatives to flying for long-distance travel in other parts of the world, and what are they like?" Also included is a 100-page guide to print and Internet resources for independent international travel.

In writing this book and compiling this advice, I've drawn on the experiences of thousands of travelers I've worked with over the years as they planned their trips as well as thousands more who've come to my seminars, sent me letters and email messages, or left comments on my blog after reading previous editions of this book. The opinions expressed here are my own, of course, but they are informed by the individual and collective experiences of an extended worldwide community of fellow travelers.

This book gives tips that all travelers can use to enhance their next trips: about choosing destinations and planning your route; obtaining visas and permits; money, budgeting, and finances; safety and health; what to bring; how to find your way around; rail, road, and water transportation; the often-misunderstood inside world of international airline tickets, fares, and discounts; and much more to ease and enhance your travels and travel planning.

WHY I WROTE THIS BOOK

For 15 years, I worked full-time as a travel agent in addition to my writing. More than anything else, this book grew out of my dissatisfaction with my job; or, to be more precise, my dissatisfaction with the limitations of my job.

As a travel agent, I specialized exclusively in around-the-world and other multicountry international trips for independent, do-it-yourself travelers. I was never a peddler, much less a pusher, of cruises, tours, or package holidays. Rather, I've always done my best to encourage and empower people to travel independently and to make as many of their arrangements locally as is possible.

Nonetheless, even the most experienced and independent travelers often want and need advice about how to plan and prepare for their journey. Rarely do they have access to any independent source of professional travel advice other than that of guidebooks and travel agents. As more people turn from human travel agents to online travel agency robots, personal travel advice from an expert gets harder and harder to find.

Most travelers, even those planning extensive, long-term journeys, come to a travel agent primarily to buy airline tickets. And they tend to do so only after they have made (or failed to make) most of their other commitments and advance arrangements, when it is already too late to take advantage of whatever suggestions a travel agent might offer.

Although many travel agents call themselves, some more accurately than others, "travel consultants," most of them make their money selling cruises, packages, and tours, which gives them little incentive to help you figure out how to travel on your own without advance reservations.

Even at an agency specializing in independent travel, I simply couldn't afford to spend as much time with each traveler who consulted me, or give them nearly as much advice and assistance, as I would have liked.

Of course, some of the most important questions are those that aren't asked at all, because people either don't realize they are important or assume they already know the answers, especially when the conventional wisdom is a myth.

Destination guidebooks focus on specific information about particular places or regions, not the things that are common to international or long-term travel in diverse places. Even most compendia of general travel advice are intended for short-term travelers on package tours or those who only travel on their own and unescorted in the wealthy, "Westernized" countries most like their homelands.

This book is my effort to fill that gap: to provide a how-to guide to independent world travel, to answer the most frequently asked questions about this sort of travel, to debunk the most widespread myths, and to share some advice compiled from my own trips, my colleagues, my clients, and other travelers. I've also tried to include the most important things you need to know to be your own do-it-yourself travel agent on the Internet, should you choose that route. It's the desire to empower and facilitate independent travel—and the learning, communication, and understanding between different peoples and parts of the world that it leads to—that kept me in the travel business for so long despite the low pay, long hours, high stress, deadlines, and (contrary to myth) the limited time and opportunities it left me to travel myself.

This book began as a series of short answers to travel questions on the Internet—posted anonymously because my employer at the time thought my explanations of international airline ticket discounting revealed too many trade secrets! Later, when I changed employers and began answering questions in my own name, some of my tips came to be widely known and archived, prompting more people to call, write, and email me with questions, suggestions, and issues on which they sought advice.

"I Couldn't Take a Big Trip Like That Because . . . "

You say want to travel around the world, but you haven't done it? What's your excuse for not fulfilling your travel dreams?

"I couldn't get that much time off."

If you think, *No one in my situation could get six months off,* you're wrong. Whatever your age, occupation, and stage in your career, people like you are finding time to travel. Once you really resolve to travel, you'll find a way to make the time.

"I have a job and a career."

Your job and career may be the best reasons for world travel: There's no better investment in your skills and future earning potential than a year or two of international travel.

"I have children."

Children are another great reason to take a trip around the world. Few other gifts you could give your children could match the lifelong value of international experience and exposure to global diversity as a child. No one I know who traveled abroad as a child would think of trading a year of world travel for a year of conventional schooling. Experience living abroad as a child is the single best predictor of success in an international career as an adult.

"I don't have that much money."

You can't extrapolate from short vacations to long-term travel, or from package

Later, I began leading seminars on how to plan and prepare for long-term and around-the-world travel at hostels, colleges and universities, travel-gear stores and bookstores, and travel shows and events throughout the United States, Canada, and the U.K. This has given me even more understanding of what travelers seek in the early stages of their preparations, long before they talk to a travel agent.

Eventually, all of this information came together, much revised and expanded, as the first edition of this book. After more than a decade in print through four previous editions, it's been thoroughly updated once again in early 2011, incorporating changes in the world, changes in travel, and feedback and suggestions from readers.

tours to independent travel. Most people who follow the principles in this book find that their total costs, including airfare, for an extended international trip are less than their living costs are at home. If you can afford to spend a summer or a year sitting around your backyard doing nothing, you could afford to spend the same amount of time traveling around the world—for less than the cost of staying home.

"The places you talk about are too far away."

Europe isn't the closest other continent to North America. From San Francisco or Seattle, Tokyo is closer than London. From Miami, São Paulo and Santiago de Chile are closer than Madrid. From New York, Senegal is closer and a shorter flight than Switzerland. And the Third World is, of course, right next door to the United States in Mexico and much of the Caribbean.

"It would be too difficult and uncomfortable."

Because services are so much cheaper in poorer places, independent budget travel in the Third World can be much easier and more comfortable than in the First World. It's travel in wealthy, expensive places like the United States or Western Europe that's most difficult on a budget and takes the most travel savvy.

"I don't speak a foreign language."

Never before has any language had the truly global hegemony that English has today. You'll learn much more if you know more languages, but there is almost nowhere that you can't get around on English. You speak English: you're lucky and privileged. Make the most of it—you can go wherever in the world you want.

HOW TO USE THIS BOOK

This is not a menu, a list of choices, or a guide to specific routes around the world or anywhere else. There aren't many specific prices in this book, and those that appear are only examples. (Except as otherwise noted, prices are based on available information as of early 2011, and all prices have been converted to U.S. dollars.) This book is intended to direct you to resources, information, and advice that will help you prepare for and plan the trip *you* want to take.

I'll discuss some things that can happen along the way, but mainly in terms of what you can do in advance to prepare for them. The emphasis is on what to do *before* you leave.

In the following sections I give some basic suggestions on how to plan your trip, answer some frequently asked questions, and suggest sources of answers to a variety of other questions. Although the stages of planning and preparation overlap and can vary from trip to trip, I've tried to present topics in the general sequence in which I recommend that you deal with them.

I begin with the most basic question, "Where do you want to go?" and some sources of information—in print and on the Internet—to help you choose.

Next, you're ready to start figuring out how to get there. I first survey the possibilities and limitations of rail, road, and water travel, with an emphasis on where they are and aren't feasible and affordable, and when you need to make decisions before you leave home. Then I'll explain how to get the best set of airline tickets for your trip, with a particular emphasis on international airline ticket discounting and how best to find and work with the travel agent who's right for you. (I include, of course, information about travel agents and other Internet ticket sellers, although I also made the Internet and travel the subject of a separate book a few years ago, *The Practical Nomad: Guide to the Online Travel Marketplace.* Specific websites have changed, but most of the general strategies and consumer advice in that book remain applicable today.)

Then I'll review some of the other essential things you'll need to do before you leave and how to go about them: obtaining necessary travel documents, making health and insurance preparations to protect yourself while traveling, deciding what to bring with you, planning your budget, and dealing with money.

Then I'll talk about some of the nitty-gritty of traveling life: accommodations, food, tours, guides, and sightseeing. Even if you plan to deal with these things on your own as you go, you may want to start thinking about them in advance.

To put it all in perspective, throughout the book I share general advice about what makes for good and bad trips, and what you can do both before and during your trip to improve your chances of enjoying your trip.

Don't feel you have to read the whole book. I'll probably repeat some things that seem obvious, especially if you're an experienced international traveler. And I'll probably leave some of your questions unanswered, or raise new ones. Where I've deliberately left information out, it's because it has already been compiled elsewhere or it changes too often to be kept up to date in a book like this. I've tried to include references (in the text, in the *Resource Guide* at the back of the book, and on my website, www.hasbrouck.org) to sources where this sort of information can be found. I'll be happy if each traveler who reads this book finds something in it of value.

I especially hope this book will serve the needs of people who don't like package tours, or can't find one they like, but who aren't confident that they can do what they want on their own, or just don't know how. If there is one thing I want to get across, it's that anyone can do it. Independent travel isn't for everyone, but it is *possible* for anyone who wants to try it.

An Introduction to Travel Around the World

"Is This for Me?"

INDEPENDENT WORLD TRAVELERS

Long-term, independent world travelers are a far more diverse lot than anyone would imagine. If you think this sort of travel is only for students, hippies, and other broke young people willing to put up with bad food and bedbugs, think again. I've seen everyone from gray-haired pensioners to middle-aged upper-class financiers to 20-something dot-commers take off around the world for a year or two at a time.

DEMOGRAPHICS

People who buy tickets around the world are far more diverse than most people would imagine. When I worked at Airtreks.com, our customers' average age was 35, but 15 percent were younger than 20 (including children of all ages), 8 percent were in their 50s, and 5 percent (and rising) were older than 60. Women traveling alone made up 24 percent of all our customers, a percentage that has been increasing.

INDEPENDENT TRAVEL DEFINED

By "independent" travel, I mean travel that isn't done as part of a tour, and for which most accommodations and other services are arranged locally, on

Key Advice About Travel Around the World

- World travel is fun. World travel is sexy. World travel is the ultimate trip.
- Independent world travel is the world's best learning experience. It's the best possible investment of time and money you can make in your own career or your children's education.
- World travel will change you, and change your life, for the better.
- World travel is easier than you think.
- Getting time for travel is easier than you think.
- World travel is more affordable than you think.
- Traveling affordably doesn't take magic and doesn't require giving up comfort or convenience. The keys to affordable world travel are traveling independently and concentrating on more affordable regions of the world.
- Independent world travelers include women, men, and children of all ages, occupations, backgrounds, and careers.
- World travel can be for you if you want it to be. Making your travel dreams come true is mostly just a matter of deciding to do it.

This book will hold your hand and help show you how you can explore the world easily, safely, and affordably. For more information on the topics in this chapter, see the *Resource Guide* in the back of the book and the links on the Practical Nomad website at www.practicalnomad.com.

arrival, as you go along, rather than reserved in advance. It is travel on your own, by yourself or with only one or a few traveling companions (perhaps people met along the way), not with a group following a common itinerary. It's travel that involves direct, unmediated, daily interactions with local people and involvement with local ways of living and doing.

WHO IS INDEPENDENT TRAVEL FOR?

This sort of travel isn't for everyone. Impatient, intolerant, inflexible, or closed-minded people; worriers; and those without a sense of humor aren't likely to enjoy it unless they are transformed by this travel into people with different traits. Control freaks either love it or hate it, sometimes simultaneously. Be honest with yourself. (Self-awareness is a key travel skill, in many ways.) Are you ready to learn new things and to experience the unexpected? Don't travel independently just to save money. Travel on your own only if you truly want to travel that way and are open to the possibility and potential benefits of the unexpected, including the possibility that you will come home a different person. Take for granted that you don't know, and can't be sure, in advance what your trip will be like. If you don't like that idea or need to know in advance just how things will go, take a tour. That's what tours are for.

What long-term independent travelers have in common is not their age, race, wealth, or social status but simply their taste in travel: they take more time to travel; they prefer to arrange things on their own as they go, leaving themselves maximum flexibility to change their plans en route; and they put a relatively low priority on money spent on accommodations as opposed to other travel activities. These tastes reinforce each other: it's hard to afford to travel for a long time unless you are careful about your budget, and the best way to cut the cost of travel is to stay in locally booked budget accommodations, making any tour arrangements locally.

Reasons to Travel

Anthropologist and travel researcher Klaus Westerhausen, who studied long-term travelers in Asia (see the *Resource Guide*), came up with this partial list of common motives for extended international travel.

The Long-Held Dream: travel as the fulfillment of a lifelong aspiration

Journey into Adult Life: travel as a rite of passage, personal growth, and empowerment

The Final Fling: travel before "settling down" to career, family, or other involvements

The Escape: travel as part of, or as a response to, a career break or life transition

STEREOTYPES

The image of independent long-term travelers as undesirables is, fortunately, much less prevalent than travelers often expect, or than it was some years ago. "Starving" First World students are rich by local standards in the rest of the world, and their spending is the backbone of the economy in many places where few package tourists go. These days most poorer countries welcome backpackers and their money.

Prejudice against independent travelers remains widespread in the First World, especially in the travel industry itself. When I mention "independent" travel to travel agents, airlines, and government tourist promotion offices, they usually assume that I am talking about customized but prearranged inclusive tours ("FIT" travel, as this type of travel is called in industry jargon). They find it incomprehensible that people would prefer to arrange things for themselves, or that I would want to facilitate their doing so.

"They're going to stay somewhere," is the industry adage, "so why not make sure it's somewhere that gives you a commission?" The last thing most travel agents want travelers to realize is that cheaper places are cheaper *because* they aren't paying commissions to travel agents or having their prices marked up by overseas tour operators.

BACKPACKER FACTS

Factual research about independent travelers supports neither the demographic stereotypes of them as students and youth nor the economic stereotype of them as poorer than other tourists. Those who bother to learn who backpackers really are find out what experienced travelers have always known: almost every type of person likes to travel. For example, Australia's former Minister of Tourism, Michael Lee, described the results of that country's first serious study of international backpackers as follows: "Despite their reputation as travelers on a shoestring budget, backpackers actually pour more money into our economy than almost any other type of traveler."

The Australian Bureau of Tourism Research found that despite spending an average of only A$51 (approximately US$40 at that time) per day (compared with A$78/US$60 for all visitors to Australia), backpackers stayed so much longer (almost three times as long as the typical visitor) that the average backpacker spent almost twice as much in Australia as the average for all visitors.

Only one-fourth of "backpackers"—defined as tourists who spent at least one night of their stay in Australia in a hostel—were students. Fully one-third were employed in professional or technical occupations, and 7 percent were executives and managers.

Contrary to the widespread presumption that long-term visitors take jobs away from locals, the Australian Department of Employment, Education, and Training estimated that backpackers—the category of tourists most likely to seek paid jobs while on holiday—generate two-thirds more jobs for locals per visitor than other tourists, both because of their greater total spending and because more of their spending on travel goes directly to local businesses as opposed to foreign tour operators and agents. In addition, "Backpackers spend much more than they earn, since they work only to supplement their funds and to travel further."

Further, the report recommended that visa restrictions be eased and procedures simplified, long-term visas made less expensive, and visa extensions made easier and cheaper. "Such changes could encourage travelers to stay longer and to spend more tourist dollars in Australia, instead of having to curtail their holidays simply because their visas have expired."

Introduction

The Australian report was, according to Minister of Tourism Lee, "The first time any national government anywhere in the world has developed a specific strategy for this sector of the tourism industry." Implementation of that strategy has lagged even in Australia. Most tourism organizations still ignore independent travel entirely.

My experience in Australian hostels—and hostels elsewhere—supports the conclusions of this research. A study of foreign backpackers in North America, or many other regions, would find similar figures. Perhaps countries such as the United States, where the government does the least to facilitate inbound international tourism, will eventually recognize the values of making it easier for foreigners, especially independent travelers, to come here and spend their money.

FINDING TIME TO TRAVEL

Don't rule out long-term travel just because you have a full-time job. I don't mean to make light of unemployment, job insecurity, and the student-loan and credit-card debts that burden so many North Americans. Nonetheless, my impression is that the key reason more people don't get more time to travel is that would-be long-term travelers are afraid even to ask for additional time off for fear of losing their jobs.

I regularly ask other travelers, "How did you get the time for this trip?" No one has ever answered, "I asked for time off, so they fired me."

TRAVEL IS A BUSINESS ASSET

Over the 20 years since my own first trip around the world, I've noticed that far more—and far more diverse—people are taking extended trips abroad. A variety of trends are making it easier for people to justify travel to themselves, their friends and families, and their employers: the trend from permanent to contingent employment; the globalization of the economy, one major corollary of which is the enormous demand in all economic sectors for workers

REAL LIFE

Workers in the United States get very short paid vacations compared to those in Europe. Unlike a typical two-week U.S. vacation, a standard four- to eight-week European vacation is long enough to give significant freedom for independent exploration within one region or large country, if not for a trip around the world. In the United States, only students and teachers and union members with a lot of seniority have annual vacations long enough for that sort of travel. But that doesn't mean other Americans have to feel limited to short-duration tours, or can't get additional unpaid leave if they ask for it.

Introduction

"How Can I Get Time to Travel?"

I continue to be amazed at the diversity of people I hear from about their plans for months-long trips. How do they get the time? Here are some of the ways:

Educate, agitate, and organize for more time off.
Everywhere in the world, mandatory allowances of time for rest and limits on working hours have been the result of extended political struggle. Laws and union contracts entitling workers in Europe to 4–8 weeks of vacation have come about through the same processes that led to the eight-hour day and the 40-hour week in the United States. North American workers will get the same vacation rights as Europeans only if the labor movement, individual workers, and voters make this an issue.

Work as a temporary, freelancer, or contractor.
So-called "contingent" workers make up at least 10–15 percent of the workforce in the United States. It's now possible for people in almost any occupation or career to reorganize their work — if they haven't been forced to already — on a freelance or contract basis that leaves them regular opportunities to travel after finishing one job or assignment and before starting the next. You might even be able to do some paid work, remotely, for clients back home while you're on the road (although finding new clients can be hard when you're abroad).

Work in a seasonal job or occupation.
Seasonal jobs may be more diverse than you think, including those in agriculture, the building trades, tourism, etc. Some seasonal jobs, such as those at resorts or in national parks and forests, include employer-provided housing. I've known ski-resort workers who travel every summer and national park workers and foresters who travel every winter without having to pay to maintain a home while they're on the road in the off-season.

Work for a school, college, or university.
Many jobs in educational institutions are seasonal. Part of the trade-off for teachers' low wages (although far from a sufficient one) is their long summer vacations. What many people don't think about is that schools, colleges, and universities employ all sorts of workers for the academic year. Academic-year

jobs include everything from food service to computer support to building maintenance. For much of the time that I was growing up, my mother did office and administrative work for a college, rather than some other employer, in order to have long summers off with her children. Others do the same thing in order to have time to travel. And even nonacademic educational staff are often eligible for paid sabbaticals.

Take a sabbatical.

Periodic yearlong paid sabbaticals are standard for professors and exist for some teachers even at the elementary and secondary level. During my most recent trip around the world, my partner was on a partially paid sabbatical from her high school teaching job. But sabbaticals aren't limited to academia anymore. More and more employers have formal or informal programs for granting paid or unpaid extended leave. (See the *Resource Guide* for some surveys and examples of corporate sabbatical and leave programs.) Sabbaticals improve employee skills, productivity, morale, and loyalty. If your employer doesn't already have such a program, why not suggest it (or find an employer who does)?

Take an unpaid leave of absence.

Even if your employer doesn't have a formal leave program, you can always ask. Pitch it to your employer as a no-lose proposition: you are willing, entirely at your own expense, to take an unpaid leave to acquire some of the skills they need most to succeed in a global economy. If it's not going to cost them anything, why would they say no? Even if they think travel is irrelevant to your job, they'd probably rather you come back to work for them after your travels than go to work for someone else.

Quit your job. Get a better one when you get back.

Even if you have to quit your job, there's a good chance you'll actually get it back — if you want it — when you return. If not, you'll have international travel experience under your belt and on your résumé. With that, you should be able to find a new job a step up the career and salary ladder from your old one. If you are out of work anyway, international travel will look much better on your résumé — and cost less — than idle unemployment at home.

with international experience; and the growing cultural and ethnic diversity of the United States, with its similar corollary of demand for cross-cultural communication and business skills. Travel—*especially* the sort of independent, international travel that necessitates interaction and communication with diverse local people—is increasingly recognized as a valuable experience, with cultural and educational immersion leading to personal growth and self-improvement. This kind of travel is no longer thought of as a frivolous, self-indulgent, or escapist vacation—not that this sort of trip isn't also the most fun and excitement you could ever hope for.

JUST ASK

Don't be afraid to ask for time off. Your boss may never have gotten such a request before and may not know what to do. The most common response from management seems to be a mix of mild jealousy and "I wish that I'd had the courage to do that when I was your age." The most common answer is "Yes." Even if the boss says "No, I won't guarantee you a job when you get back," you haven't lost anything by asking.

BUT WHAT ABOUT MY RÉSUMÉ?

Some people are afraid to have a gap in their résumé. Don't worry about it: put your travels on your résumé. Having taken a trip around the world means far more than having taken the Grand Tour of Europe ever did. More and more I hear from returned travelers who are putting their travel experience at the top of their résumés: "A year spent traveling the world, familiarizing myself with the diversity of world cultures, and learning how to understand and deal with people from backgrounds different from my own." Prospective employers may smile, they may laugh, they may be jealous—but they will offer you the job.

TRAVEL BECOMES A JOB CREDENTIAL

Businesses today can't find enough qualified employees with international experience. International travel will teach you new skills and improve your ability to do almost any job. If your old job isn't waiting for you, travel will be a credential that will help you get another job.

    "But I'm just going to travel, not work abroad. That's not the sort of international experience that businesses want." Maybe, but consider the competition: 75 percent of all U.S. citizens don't have a passport, and among native-born U.S. citizens the percentage is even higher. That means they've never left North America—and couldn't even if a free ticket fell in their lap. If you've ever been overseas, you have more international experience than three-fourths of the people in the United States. If you've spent six months traveling around the world, you have more bona fide international experience than almost all competing job seekers.

Even in the shrinking number of industries where the global marketplace isn't yet perceived as relevant to job skills, "I quit my last job because I wanted to travel around the world" is a strong line to use in a job interview when you get back. It's a good opening for describing the things you've done that will set you apart from other candidates for the job.

I've come to the conclusion—one that has surprised me as much as it has surprised most of the people whose experiences have brought me to it—that the greatest barrier to long-term travel by American workers is the perceived disempowerment that leaves them unable to bring themselves even to ask for time off.

Just do it.

HOW MUCH DOES A TRIP LIKE THIS COST?

Too many people abandon all hope of world travel because they assume that it must be very expensive. I'll return to the question of travel costs and budgeting in much more detail later on in the chapter *The Bottom Line.* But I want to give you a sense of just how affordable independent world travel can be.

So how much does it cost for a trip around the world? One way to predict your expenses is to look at how much other travelers have spent.

SURVEY DATA

The best data on international travelers from the United States comes from an annual survey by the U.S. Department of Commerce of several tens of thousands of passengers on intercontinental flights departing from the United States. The most recent available

REAL LIFE

The most important factor in being able to afford to travel is not being in debt. If you want to be able to travel, start living within or below your means (if you aren't already), and pay off your credit cards and student loans as fast as possible. That may not seem easy, but let your wanderlust be your motivation to keep your spending under control. You don't need huge savings to cover your expenses on the road in the more affordable parts of the world. It's another story if you are trying to service preexisting debt as well.

comparison of short-term and long-term travelers' budgets is from 1998, when Airtreks.com commissioned an analysis of this data by trip length.

The average traveler on a coach-class air ticket (excluding first- and business-class travelers) taking a 60–100 night trip overseas from the United

"How Can I Afford to Travel?"

Lots of travelers seem to want a magic bullet for travel costs: "How can I go on fancy tours or cruises, or go to big cities or major tourist destinations in expensive countries like those in Western Europe, stay in five-star hotels, and have everything be cheaper?"

There are some money-saving tips that can cut the cost of this sort of travel to these sorts of places, but let's not lose the forest for the trees. Two things, above all else, will determine how expensive or how affordable your travel will be. Compared to these, other strategies for cutting costs, and their impact on your travel bottom line, are trivial.

Do you travel to rich, and therefore expensive, places? Or do you travel to poor, and therefore cheap, places?

Travel is a "service industry." When you travel, most of what you're paying for is for people to do things for you: cook and serve your food, clean the rooms and make the beds in the hotel, drive or guide you around, and so forth. Most of the cost of travel services is the cost of labor. What this means is that the cost of local travel services in a particular country is almost purely a function of local wage scales. And the differences between First World and Third World wages are so extreme that which world you travel in makes much, much more difference to your costs than how thriftily you travel.

Do you prearrange services through intermediaries in the First World? Or do you arrange as little as possible other than air tickets in advance, and arrange and pay for accommodations and other services locally, as close as possible to the people by whom and the places where those services are actually provided?

The premium you have to pay to arrange things in advance is highest for travel in countries where local services are cheapest. That's because the foreign intermediaries (tour operators, travel agents, etc.) in the First World have U.S. dollar or other hard-currency, high-wage costs and expenses to cover: rent and overhead for an office in the United States, salaries for staff in the United States to handle your reservations, commissions in U.S. dollars to travel agents in the United States to represent them, a guide based in the United States or Europe to accompany the tour, and so forth. These are real costs inherent in making it possible for you to make reservations in advance from the United States. But these transaction costs far exceed the actual costs of services provided by local people at local wages in a Third World destination country.

In addition, only the more expensive local Third World tour companies and accommodations providers can afford to be connected to a computerized reservation system, maintain a foreign hard-currency bank account, or pay commissions to foreign travel agents. Even in wealthy First World countries there is usually an entire layer of local hostelries, guesthouses, and freelance guides who aren't set up to take reservations through travel agencies or tour companies from abroad and who have fundamentally lower costs and prices as a result. The cheapest hotel room in a major city that can be reserved through agents abroad may be five or 50 times the cost of the cheapest bed available locally.

States in 1998 budgeted a total of US$3,418, including airfare, prepaid tours and hotels or other services, and planned expenses on the road. Because longer trips are so much less expensive per day, that's less than 50 percent more than the average cost of the typical two-week overseas trip (US$2,396). The average budget for a six-month trip was US$7,092, only about three times as much as for the typical two-week trip overseas.

Per diem cost declined steadily with increased trip length: the typical American overseas budgeted US$68 per person per day, but this fell to US$29 per person per day for trips of two months or more. And these figures would have been even lower if business travelers were excluded. On the other hand, because the survey was conducted on outbound flights, the survey measured expected—not actual—spending. In my experience, most people spend somewhat more than they expected. The numbers produced in this survey are averages: some travelers spent more and some spent less. Prices have increased since then with inflation, but the relationship between (high) short-term travel costs and (low) long-term travel costs has remained the same.

CONSIDER THE VALUE

Your mileage may vary. Overall, though, these survey results show that people like you can and do travel for months for less than you might spend on a new entertainment system, a typical honeymoon, or the down payment, much less the monthly bills, for a new car or SUV. (Chris Balish saved enough to take a trip around the world by selling his SUV and living without a car, first in St.

Louis and then in Los Angeles, where most people think a car would be "essential" to a comfortable life. He has an excellent analysis of the often unnoticed total cost of car ownership, and how living without a car can save you enough money to afford to travel more, in his personal finance book, *How to Live Well Without Owning a Car.*) Think about other things you might spend this kind of money on, and compare the value.

PACKAGED TRAVEL COSTS

If you don't want to travel independently, it's another story. Escorted around-the-world group tours come and go. Various tour operators have scheduled them from time to time, but they are infrequent. A few tour operators have offered monthlong around-the-world packages by chartered private jet for US$40,000–50,000 per person. Each year several cruise ships steam around the world; prices for 2011 sailings ranged upward from about US$20,000 (per person, double occupancy, not including any activities or excursions on land at ports of call) for 3–4-month cruises. Details vary, but these prices and durations are typical of what has been offered.

Most people, however, prefer to travel on their own without a group or escort. Most have smaller budgets than would be required for these tours. And many want to travel for much longer periods of time. Few happen to want exactly the itinerary of one of these tours or cruises.

TYPES OF TRIPS

A trip around the world, or any long-term international trip, is, at the very least, a significant step on anyone's journey through life. Many (perhaps most) of those who take such a trip do so only once in a lifetime. It's a major undertaking, one in which you may be investing as much as a year or more of your life and on which you may be spending most of your accumulated savings or using all the vacation time you've accumulated at work. The check I wrote for my own first set of tickets around the world was the largest check I had written in my life. A trip like this means a lot to anyone who takes one.

There are different sorts of travelers, trips, and reasons for multistop and long-term journeys. You obviously have your own reasons, or you wouldn't be reading this book.

ONE EXTREME—SHORT ON TIME

At one extreme are travelers who combine specific business trips or visits to friends and relations in different places that are more quickly and cheaply reached as multiple stops on a single trip than as separate roundtrips from home.

Trips like this tend to be shorter. In 2006 I arranged a successful trip for a *USA Today* reporter from the Unites States around the world and back home in eight days, with stops in Asia, Africa, the Middle East, and Europe. Travelers like this tend to have more specific requirements for their travel dates and the sequence in which they visit the cities on their itinerary. Moreover, those who are short on time tend to put a higher priority on direct flights and routings. They often prefer to travel by air whenever possible, to fix their exact travel dates in advance, and to have all their tickets in hand before they leave.

THE OTHER EXTREME

At the other extreme are those whose trips are extended explorations, adventures, or even just very long vacations. These travelers tend to have more time than money, and some are traveling for more than a year at a time.

These sorts of travelers tend to be more flexible in choosing a set of destinations and a sequence in which to visit them, to be more willing to change their itinerary to save money, and to want to use surface transportation wherever possible. They often welcome the opportunity for additional stopovers or layovers en route, even in places they may not originally have thought to visit. They usually want tickets that will permit them to change their travel dates as they go. Finally, some of them deliberately buy tickets for only part of their trip so that they can change their onward routing and itinerary. They decide along the way whether to take optional side trips or to travel some sections by air, land, or water, or to extend their travel for more than a year.

BETWEEN EXTREMES

Many trips combine several purposes and have aspects of both these extremes: "I'm going to my cousin's wedding in Delhi on September 5. I need to arrive by September 3 at the latest, and to stay for at least one full week. On the way there I want to stop for 2–3 business days to meet with my business contacts in Shanghai, and before returning home I'd like to spend about two weeks on vacation in Greece." Or whatever. Each trip is different, and each traveler has different priorities.

CUSTOMIZING YOUR TRIP

Smart travelers and good travel agents customize each trip around the world. You should try to find the best route and tickets for what you want, not which "standard" package more or less approximates what you want.

When travel agents question you about your plans, they do so not to pry but in order to find the itinerary and the set of tickets that will best meet your needs. The more the agents understand your purposes, the better they can help you to fulfill them. And before you call a travel agent or start clicking on "buy tickets now," you need to be clear in your own mind on your own goals and destinations. In the next chapter, I'll guide you through some of the major sources of information you can use to figure out where you want to go.

Choosing Destinations

"Where in the World . . . ?"

IT'S A BIG WORLD AFTER ALL

It may seem obvious, but the first step in planning a trip is deciding where to go.

We're often told that we live in the Jet Age on a planet that modern technology has made a small world. There's a certain truth to all of that. By scheduled airliner, most major world cities are no more than two or three days' travel time apart, if money is no object, space is available, and you pick the right day of the week on which to leave. There aren't many countries where people aren't watching CNN and (if they are literate) exchanging email. But information technology has a way of making physical distances seem shorter than they are. Earth is still as big a world as ever, and, fortunately, is still a pretty varied one.

Six months, a year, two years, or a lifetime aren't long enough to "see it all." There's much more of the world that you won't see than that you will. Color in all the places you've seen with your own eyes on the largest globe you can find, and all you'll see will be a few dots for the broadest views from tall buildings and mountains, and intermittent hairlines marking routes you flew over in cloudless daylight while looking out the airplane window.

Some people seem (and claim) to have been everywhere. What does that mean? Has someone who once spent a day in New York or Miami "seen" the United States? Someone who "did" the entire United States in two or

Key Advice About Choosing Destinations

- The world is big. You can't see it all in a lifetime, much less a few months or years. Narrow your choices. Most people try to do too much in too little time.

- Contrary to what you might think, the best way to start your planning may be to choose a list of specific destinations, not to draw lines on a map.

- Make your own choices. Don't go somewhere just because someone else liked it or told you to go there.

- Your daily activities and the people you meet have more influence on the quality of your travel experience than the sites you visit or sights you see.

- Travel in the present. Use the Internet and other resources to learn about contemporary life and current affairs in the places you are going.

- Think about who is giving you advice and what their knowledge is based on. Many resources for travelers are propaganda designed to sell travel "products" rather than to inform. Many of the most useful resources for choosing destinations aren't intended primarily for travelers.

- Look to resources from and by people in the places you are thinking of going for the most accurate picture of what travel in those places will really be like.

For more information on the topics in this chapter, see the *Resource Guide* in the back of the book and the links on the Practical Nomad website at www.practicalnomad.com.

three weeks, the way a foreigner might "do" a country of comparable area like China? Some people are country collectors, and there's a club exclusively for those who have visited at least 100 countries. Yet, even the rare globetrotter who reaches that threshold has been to fewer than half the world's sovereign nations.

I'd go a day out of my way to get a glimpse of any country I hadn't been in before. (Admittedly, I've also declined the chance to step across a border into a new country when it would have cost me US$100 for a visa.) But I try not to kid myself about the significance of merely setting foot somewhere. One of my conscious goals for my first trip around the world was to learn the meaning of my ignorance: to get a better sense of just how much allowance I should make, in drawing conclusions about things, for how little I knew about the world. I came back having been many places, and learned many things, but with a much-heightened sense of how much I don't know and never will.

No matter what the length of the trip, it's tempting to try to go too many places and to see and do too much. Paradoxically, people who realize that they'll never be able to see everything and who fear that they may never get back to a country or region again are sometimes those who feel most driven to complete their mental "must-see" checklist on their first visit to an area. When I talk to travelers after a big trip, most of them say they wish they had chosen fewer places to try to visit, or that they had narrowed their explorations to smaller regions.

Even places that seem small in our conventionally Eurocentric North American worldview can be huge. Getting a less distorted mental map of the world is one of the potential benefits of world travel. If the trains are on time and you make the best possible connections, it's a journey of three days and nights across the full width of the territory governed by the People's Republic of China. (Chinese trains have gotten so much faster that it's the same journey time as when I did it 20 years ago, even though the railroad has been extended another 1,000 miles to the west from Urumchi to Kashgar across Chinese-ruled East Turkestan.) It's 2–3 weeks by ship from one end of the Indonesian archipelago to the other, if you time your departure just right. It's 1,300 km (800 miles) from Capetown to Johannesburg, and South Africa is only a small piece of the tip of Africa. The entire distance across Europe from London to Istanbul is shorter than the distance across just a part of Brazil, from Rio de Janeiro to Manaus in the center of the country.

Within the United States, we're accustomed to being able to travel long distances quickly and easily to places with wildly different landscapes (no other country is geographically more diverse then the United States, although China and perhaps India come close), but with only minimal variation in culture, language, or way of life. Elsewhere in the world, be prepared to find much more extreme variations in lifestyle even within smaller countries or regions—which makes it important to research and choose specific destinations, not just general regions or countries.

Choosing Destination Points

It's natural to start planning a trip around the world by drawing lines on a map. But my strong recommendation, unless your plans require otherwise, is to start planning any multistop trip by choosing a set of destination points, not a route. Or start with a set of experiences you want to have or activities you want to engage in, even if you don't yet know in what part(s) of the world you might best pursue those interests.

Once you know where you want to go, the ways to get there will follow, as will other incidental places that happen to be along the way. Think about points first, not lines. Resist the temptation to try to connect the dots until you've gotten airfare estimates (as discussed in the *Air Transportation* chapter

Efficiency and Independence

Capital vs. Labor

In the United States and many other Northern countries, we are rich in material possessions, while our very wealth (and restrictions on immigration) makes labor expensive. So we measure efficiency in terms of maximizing what can be done with a given amount of human labor, and regard labor-saving devices as improvements. Poor countries, where the greatest problems are often unemployment (a surplus of labor) and national debt (a shortage of capital), measure efficiency in how much can be accomplished with fixed material and capital inputs. People in these countries often regard more labor-intensive methods as improvements if they reduce the need for material and capital inputs.

Southerners regard us as wasteful of capital for using elaborate gas-guzzling machines to do things that could be done by a sufficient number of people with hand tools, while we regard them as inefficient in labor expenditure for using so much human energy to keep old vehicles and machinery running.

Many Southern ways of doing things that Northerners are tempted to dismiss as backward look different when they are evaluated in terms of labor efficiency rather than capital efficiency. Worldwide, labor is a plentiful and all-too-rapidly self-renewing resource; metal and petroleum — the main constituents of capital goods — are not. Capital-intensive ways of living cannot be sustained. A large part of the definition of "appropriate" or "intermediate" technology is that it uses a more appropriate balance of capital and labor inputs than "high" technology.

Northerners may have something to teach Southerners about technology, but we also have a great deal to learn. The world's most skilled mechanics aren't the Northerners who can afford to throw something away and buy another if it's "too much trouble" to repair it. Southerners are — by necessity — the world champions of ingenuity, improvisation, repair, rebuilding, scrounging, adapting, and making do. These are all alternative names for recycling. Forced to make a long journey in an unreliable, randomly chosen old vehicle, with few tools or spare parts, I would unhesitatingly choose a team of Vietnamese, say, or other Third or Fourth World mechanics as most likely to get me where I wanted to go.

Independence vs. Interdependence

Northerners, especially those from the United States and Australia, with our frontier settler cultures of self-reliance, tend to define "independence" as freedom from other people. So we think of driving our "own" car as more independent, an interpretation derived from the following, often unconscious, underlying cultural assumption: machines are more reliable than people, and with them we can live our lives in splendid isolation from dependence on other people.

However, machines can't be relied on in most of the world. And "interdependence" — a recent buzzword in the North — has always been taken for granted as a fact of life for those just barely getting by, whether they describe it in terms of ritual or religious obligation or as "the solidarity of the oppressed."

People who know this, and whose marginal survival depends upon other people's willingness to help them when they are in need, can often be relied on to a degree that surprises Northerners. (For some travel examples, see the anthology *The Kindness of Strangers,* listed in the *Resource Guide.*) In places where few people can afford machines, security and independence often depend more on human relationships. Southerners, in fact, may interpret Northerners' desires for "independence" and "doing things for themselves" as a sign of distrust and disrespect. Why would you insist on doing it yourself unless you felt the local people couldn't be relied on to do it properly?

Insist on going it alone, and they will conclude you think them untrustworthy or incompetent, or that you are too snobbish or antisocial to associate with them. If things then go wrong, you can count on the minimum of sympathy and assistance at the maximum price.

later on in the book) and thoroughly researched the expense, time, difficulty, and political feasibility of any overland travel (as discussed in the chapter that follows, *Surface Transportation*). Unless you really have to follow a particular route, it is the set of destinations you want to go to that will determine the best and cheapest route, not the other way around. Lots of lines you could draw on maps, on the other hand, don't correspond to any possible, much less affordable, travel routes.

Reasons to Choose a Tour

If you have little time and a long agenda of specific sites, sights, and highlights that you'd be heartbroken if you didn't get to, especially a list derived from tour brochures, you may really be better off on a tour. Perhaps the biggest reason to travel on a tour, rather than independently, is that you can cover more ground in a short time. On your own, you'll spend a significant amount of your time arranging things that others arrange in advance for people on tours, and you won't be able to make as "efficient" use of your time for sightseeing. Try to remember this when you budget your time for independent travel, and don't plan a schedule as fast and busy as that of a tour. During a longer trip, you can often arrange tours locally, for anything from a few hours to a week or two at a time, thus combining the efficiency of escorted and guided travel with the flexibility of independent travel.

Pace

Different people prefer different paces. Some people are eager to go on after a few days in one place, always wanting to keep moving. Others would rather settle into each place they visit and are always reluctant to move on. Often, as people gain more travel experience and learn to travel more quickly, they begin to desire to travel more slowly. The most frequent mistakes of people planning their first long-term trip are either not planning at all (assuming that "We'll work it out as we go") or planning to do too much in too little time. If you are inexperienced or at all unsure, my recommendation is to err on the side of planning to visit fewer places more slowly.

From the start you have to make choices; no one else can tell you where you should go. This chapter is about how to figure out where you want to go, and—together with the *Resource Guide*—about resources to help you decide.

DIVISIONS OF THE WORLD

When thinking about where to travel, most people think in terms of a map or globe. So you might expect me to start by surveying the world in continental or other physical regions. In the broadest terms, however, it makes more sense for purposes of overall travel planning to think first in terms of different economic, rather than cartographic, worlds. There is considerable cultural similarity within some continents and physical regions, of course, although far less than is generally assumed by inexperienced travelers. But there are even greater commonalities in the nature of travel, especially when it comes to logistics, within even physically distant parts of the same geopolitical region. Travel in interior Borneo may have more in common with travel on other continents—in the Amazon, say, or in Central Africa—than with travel elsewhere in Southeast Asia, such as in Singapore or Peninsular Malaysia. There are continental patterns of wealth, but the world's most fundamental divisions are not between continents, per se, but between rich and poor.

The division of the world by political economists into the First, Second, Third, and Fourth Worlds, or the North and South, may require some explanation. This terminology is less familiar in the United States, where there is little discussion using these labels, than to the majority of the world's people.

And many Southerners would say that "North-South dialogue" between the world's peoples has largely been a Southern monologue ignored by the North. But I think that these crude categorizations of world regions are helpful for purposes of travel planning and budgeting. Since these terms may not be familiar to some readers and are used in different ways by different writers, let me explain what I mean by them.

First World

The "First World" refers to the "developed" (i.e., wealthy and industrialized) capitalist or market economies (including social democracies and most mixed economies): the United States, Canada, Western Europe, Israel, Japan, Australia, Aotearoa/New Zealand, and perhaps the less populous and wealthier oil-exporting countries such as Saudi Arabia and the Gulf states. A few countries sometimes described as "middle income" are borderline First World states: for example, Singapore, South Korea, and Taiwan have been moving into this category, while Argentina may be falling out of it.

REAL LIFE

In more and more countries, the First and Third Worlds coexist side by side. South Africa and Brazil are perhaps the most obvious examples, although certainly not the only ones. In such places, both the local elite and First World travelers can live and travel in a technologically enabled "bubble" of comfort and convenience, almost completely isolated—unless they seek it out—from how the majority of the people live.

Second World

The term "Second World" originated during the Cold War when the United States divided the world into our side and their side. The "Second World" now refers to "developed," centrally planned (or formerly so) economies, mainly Russia and the former Soviet Union—now referred to as the Commonwealth of Independent States (CIS)—and to a lesser extent the rest of Eastern and Central Europe. Despite Westernization, these countries retain a certain commonality in the nature of their tourist and other infrastructures, the appropriate and feasible modes of budget travel and types of budget accommodations, and the costs of travel relative to the other main world regions.

Third World

The "Third World" was a term originally used to identify those countries neither in the First nor the Second World by virtue of political nonalignment

Choosing Destinations

with either the capitalist or communist blocs. It has since come to mean those that are in neither of the first two worlds by virtue of not being "developed"—the "developing," or poor, countries. The Third World includes countries with capitalist, communist, and mixed economies as well as those trying to pursue independent economic paths.

Fourth World

The "Fourth World" is the most recently coined and least precisely defined of these terms. As distinct from the "developing" Third World, Fourth World countries are those poor countries that are not "developing" economically. These are marginalized poor countries that have been deemed peripheral to the world's centers of power and trade and have been written off by those centers of power.

While some Asian countries (Bangladesh, Afghanistan, Myanmar/Burma, Cambodia, Laos, and Nepal are most often cited) are regarded as Fourth World, most of the Fourth World is in Africa, and almost all of sub-Saharan Africa is in the Fourth World. (Of the 49 countries categorized as least developed by the United Nations, 33 are in Africa, 15 are in Asia, and only one—Haiti—is in the Americas.) One reason for the dearth of flights to, from, and within Africa (especially other than between African cities and their former colonial capitals in Europe) is that airline routes follow trade routes, and less than 1 percent of the total value of international trade is to, from, or within Africa.

Prior to the adoption of the term *Fourth World,* there was much controversy over how to refer to these countries without stigmatizing them. Various euphemisms remain in use but are often disliked; the United Nations calls them "least developed countries" while the World Bank calls them "low-income" countries.

The differences between the Third and Fourth Worlds, and between Third and Fourth World travel, are mainly differences in degree. Fourth World infrastructure is, as a rule, bad to nonexistent. Unlike in the Third World, where almost anything is available for a price, many things we take for granted—from clean water to reliable motorized transport—are not available in much of the Fourth World, particularly outside the largest cities, at *any* price.

To confuse matters further, some people use "Fourth World" to denote indigenous and "traditional" peoples and tribes. Although definitions are essentially arbitrary, and this concept does need a word to identify it, this alternate usage of "Fourth World" muddies the meaning of an already well-defined term, and I have declined to adopt it.

Choosing Destinations

East and West

During the Cold War, the First World was referred to as "the West," and the Second World was referred to as "the East." Nowadays "the West" is more often used to refer to Europe and the Eurocentric world of white-skinned people (including the United States, Canada, Australia, Aotearoa/New Zealand, and Asian Russia), and "the East" is used to refer to those parts of Asia inhabited primarily by nonwhite people (i.e., Asia except Russia). But many people see the former usage as obsolete and the latter as Eurocentric and racist.

In any case, the two very different sets of meanings make any usage of the terms "the East" and "the West" hopelessly ambiguous and subject to misinterpretation. I try to avoid any use of these terms; if you want to be understood around the world, you will too.

Asians do not think of themselves as living in "the East." And, in relation to the Pacific Ocean, I live in the East in San Francisco, while Japan lies in the West. "The Orient," "the East," "the Far East," and "the Middle East" are labels that people in the regions thus referred to often find offensive, except in the Russian Far East, where people insist on using that label to distinguish their region from Siberia, which is farther west.

What Europeans and Eurocentrists call the Far East is a group of quite different, geographically separated regions, variously referred to locally as East or Northeast Asia, Southeast Asia, and South Asia. What Europeans call the Middle East is usually described by others as the Eastern Mediterranean, West Asia, or North Africa, depending on their perspective.

North and South

Use of the terms "North" and "South" has increased as use of the old Cold War labels "East" and "West" has declined. "North" is the term commonly used to describe the wealthy countries that dominate the world economy, most of which are located north of the world's poorer countries, the "South." Most of the people and countries of "the South" are in South America, sub-Saharan Africa, and South and Southeast Asia. Those who are represented on top of most standard maps (with north "up") also tend to be on top of the world's economic and power relationships. But the point of the terms is to describe the strata of economic, political, and military power, not cartography.

There are obvious exceptions to the geographical division between North and South. Australia and Aotearoa/New Zealand are unambiguously Northern countries in the southern hemisphere. The most populous Southern countries are India and China, both in the northern hemisphere and the latter almost entirely north of the northern tropics. Some Northerners argue that the terms *North* and *South* are inaccurate or confusing, but some of the same people seem to have no problem using *East* and *West* in their traditional, non-geographic yet widely understood senses.

The term *North* has never been as widely used as *South,* and both terms are heard much more in the South than the North. A distinction is not always made between the Third and Fourth Worlds, and in casual usage "the Third World," "the Third and Fourth Worlds," and "the South" are equivalent terms.

There is no consensus on which usage is best. Kofi Buenor Hadjor, in the essay on the meaning of "Third World" that introduces his *Dictionary of Third World Terms,* argues that, "To use the terminology of North-South…contains the danger of converting a social, economic, and political division into a geographic one." On the other hand, Paul Harrison said in his introduction to an updated edition of his *Inside the Third World* that, "If this book were appearing for the first time today, it would be called *Inside the South.*"

Were this a book about politics rather than travel, my strong preference would be to use "South" except where making specific distinctions between the Third and Fourth Worlds. The danger of "South" being misunderstood by nonspecialists in a geographic or directional sense has induced me to refer instead, in many cases, to "the Third and Fourth Worlds," and where I'm talking about something that is similar in both I have often, for conciseness, used "Third World" as shorthand for "Third and Fourth Worlds." I beg the indulgence of political scientists, economists, and other academics, offering in my defense that readers will undoubtedly hear all of these terms used somewhat interchangeably, without definition, in books, newspapers, and conversations throughout the regions thus described.

The former Soviet Union is sometimes said to have "become a collection of Third World nations." While Russia has lost most of its empire, it's still its own world for travelers with its own ways. Whatever the merits of the academic argument that the former Second World should now be considered Third World or Southern in view of politics or economics, such claims have limited basis in travel conditions. When I say "the North" I mean both the First World and the Second World. Feel free to read this as, "the former Second World," if that makes you happier. There are some similarities to travel anywhere outside the First World; in such cases, I use the ungainly "the Second, Third, and Fourth Worlds" for want of any clear, concise alternative.

Finally, I must stress that these generalizations, while useful, all have their exceptions. In particular, keep in mind that variations within a country or region—between rich and poor, center and periphery, urban and rural, black and white—can be as great as those between regions. Life on Native American ("First Nations") reservations in the United States and Canada is often reminiscent of the Third World, while urban elites in many a Third World capital have access to the latest First World consumer goods and services.

Which World's for You?

The preceding categorizations may have struck some readers as irrelevant. Aside from defining terminology, what's the point?

The longer your trip, the more likely you are to be limited by your budget. Most employed middle-class North Americans, if they choose to make it their highest priority and have three weeks' vacation a year, could fly to almost any major city in the world and spend two weeks happily and comfortably there. But even if they had the time, most of the same people wouldn't want to spend what it would cost for two or three comfortable months, much less a year, in Western Europe or Japan, no matter how carefully they planned.

TIME VS. MONEY

Per day, as I've already mentioned, long-term travel is cheaper. As you spend more time in a place, you figure out how to do things more cheaply, and you can spread out the cost of getting there over more days. But the total expenses for a months-long trip tend to enforce constraints even on people who wouldn't have to pay much attention to prices in planning a two-week vacation.

So what does how much you spend have to do with which "world" you go to? Not everything, but a lot. Yes, there are lots of ways to save money on travel wherever you go. Staying in hostels or camping, and traveling around by train or bus rather than by plane or rented car, can drastically reduce the price of travel in Western Europe, North America, or Japan. But as long as you don't

> ### REAL LIFE
>
> When I hear that the value of some foreign currency has crashed, I immediately start investigating travel possibilities. An economic crisis for locals is typically a window of opportunity for foreign budget travelers.

Choosing Destinations

insist on intercontinental standards of luxury and make a minimal effort to travel economically, the differences between travel costs in the different worlds are much greater than the differences between more and less expensive styles of travel in the same world.

So the longer your trip, the larger the proportion of it that you may need to spend in cheaper places if you are going to stay within your budget. Nothing wrong with that. Doesn't everyone like places where everything is cheaper?

Occasionally everything is cheap for some artificial reason, such as that the exchange rate doesn't reflect the real buying power of the local currency. More often, travel in a place is cheap for a single, simple reason: the people there are poor. The all-too-often overlooked corollary to affordable, long-term travel is that it means spending the majority of your time in places where most people are poor.

Nothing wrong with that either; most places are poor. The majority of the world's people make less than US$5 a day. Some of the most interesting, educational, beautiful, and enjoyable places in the world are among the poorest. But you need to be honest with yourself: if you aren't prepared to confront the reality of the world, you aren't prepared to try to travel around the world.

When people come home from a trip around the world, the most enduring memories are usually not of museums, monuments, or famous sights but of encounters with the reality of everyday life for the ordinary people of the Second, Third, and Fourth Worlds. This is the dominant reality of human life, and seeing it face-to-face is the aspect of world travel that most often changes people's lives.

This doesn't mean you need to live or travel like the poor to travel cheaply. It's often the reverse: in a rich country on a budget, you have to travel like the poor; in a poor country, you can live like a king (or at least like an upper-middle-class local business traveler). Where people are poor, labor is cheap, and you may be able to afford labor-intensive services and ways of doing things that are considered great luxuries, or have disappeared entirely, in the First World.

REAL LIFE

If you so choose, you can travel around South and Southeast Asia in first-class sleeping cars, occasionally hiring a private guide for a tour of a city or a car and driver for an out-of-town excursion, staying in comfortable hotels (not the best, but upper-class), having your laundry professionally cleaned and pressed, and eating catered meals at restaurants and food stands, for less than you'd spend to travel around Western Europe sitting up all night on second-class trains, staying in hostels, washing your clothes in the sink, and subsisting on bread and cheese.

TYPICAL ITINERARIES

On the whole, around-the-world and other long-term travelers spend more time in Asia than any other continent, mostly in East and Southeast Asia (though the proportion of travelers' time spent in Latin America is growing rapidly). Those who stay in Africa for anything more than a weeklong safari or Nile cruise usually spend at least a couple of months. An overland trip entirely across Africa in either direction, if you can complete it, takes six months to a year or more. More and more travelers to Europe are going farther and farther east. As for trends within the First World, if you're curious, the biggest ones for

Population Centers

The most populous countries of the South, according to estimates as of 2010 from the United Nations, are:

- China (1.4 billion people)
- India (1.2 billion people)
- Indonesia (230 million; next most populous country after the United States)
- Brazil (200 million)
- Pakistan (180 million)
- Bangladesh (160 million)
- Nigeria (160 million)
- Mexico (110 million)
- Philippines (94 million)
- Vietnam (89 million)
- Ethiopia (85 million)
- Egypt (84 million)
- Turkey (76 million)
- Iran (75 million)
- Thailand (68 million)
- Dem. Rep. of the Congo (68 million)
- Myanmar/Burma (50 million)
- South Korea (48 million)
- Colombia (46 million)

Together these 19 countries — roughly 10 percent of the membership of the United Nations — have about two-thirds of the world's population. The most populous seven contain more than half the world's people. China (larger in area than the United States, including Alaska), Brazil, India, Congo, Mexico, and Indonesia are also among the world's dozen largest countries by area. Two-thirds of these most populous Southern countries are in Asia.

So there are more than just financial reasons why a journey around the world is likely to be, more than anything else, a journey through the Third and Fourth Worlds — especially those parts of them in Asia. If you find yourself wondering why so many of the examples in this book are from Asia, and to a lesser extent Africa and Latin America, it's because that's where most of the world's people are and where most long-term independent budget travelers spend the most time.

independent travelers continue to be away from Western Europe and toward the Americas (except the United States, which is widely thought to be inhospitable to foreigners), Australia, and Aotearoa/New Zealand.

Your fantasy of seeing the world may start out with the classic image of a months-long grand tour of a long list of cities in Western Europe, followed perhaps by a few weeks in Central or Eastern Europe, and ending with a week or less in each of a few more "exotic" places in Africa and "the East" to round out the trip: perhaps Cairo to see the pyramids, somewhere in East Africa for a wildlife-viewing safari, India for the Taj Mahal, and Japan for some shrines and temples.

I don't mean to denigrate such a trip, if you want it and you can afford it. But trips that begin from this fantasy often end up consisting of a fast few weeks' glimpse of Western Europe, a more leisurely month or two in Central or Eastern Europe, and six months or more in Africa and Asia, ending with a few days in Japan. Or reversing the whole order, with Western Europe last.

NEW WORLD ORDER

Inexperienced travelers often think they aren't "ready" for the South, and defer Third World travel until after they have had a chance to gain experience at overseas travel within the First World, where they figure it will be easier. Depending on your budget, the best strategy may be the other way around.

In the first place, it takes much more skill and experience, if it is possible at all, to travel on the same budget in the First World as in the Third World. Traveling on the same budget, you may actually have to put up with lower standards of comfort and cleanliness of accommodations in a rich country where you have to stay in hovels and dives (or don't yet know how to find the few good, cheap places) than in a poor country where you can easily afford to stay in places catering to the local gentry.

In the second place, budget travelers in the First World have to figure out how to do things for themselves that they could afford to pay local people to do for them

Choosing Destinations

REAL LIFE

If you don't want to deal with mass transit from the airport to downtown New Delhi and instead take a taxi directly to your hotel, you're out US$5. If you can't find the local bus from Ezeiza Airport to downtown Buenos Aires, you can hire an immaculate private chauffeured car ("remise") for US$30. Arrive at Charles de Gaulle airport in Paris after the buses and trains have stopped running, and a cab downtown will cost you US$75 or more. If you arrive at Narita Airport and take a taxi to central Tokyo, it could set you back US$200.

in the South. You have to be more self-sufficient in the First World. You can't afford to hire an English-speaking private translator and guide to show you around a city if you can't find your way on your own, or to pay someone else to go down to the train station and buy your tickets for you. Each of these might cost you only a couple of U.S. dollars, maybe only pennies, in the Third World.

In the third place, mistakes, misunderstandings, and misjudgments in the First World are apt to be expensive. Learning by experience is cheaper in cheaper places. Budget travelers can more easily afford to solve problems and rectify mistakes by throwing money at them in the South, where costs are lower.

All else being equal, I'd definitely put as much as possible of the First World traveling at the end of my first big trip, not at the beginning where it might blow my budget. I'd make somewhere in Latin America or Southeast Asia my shakedown trip to prepare for Western Europe, not the reverse.

TRY BEFORE YOU GO

If you want to find out what independent travel is like in a place where it will be easier, consider a trip in your home country or region, where presumably you know the language and how things are done. I'm always surprised how few people in the United States have ever spent a few months or more exploring North America, a destination that draws tourists from around the world.

FOURTH WORLD TRAVEL

Fourth World, as opposed to Third World, travel sometimes requires more logistical self-sufficiency and skill. If my first trip abroad was a trip around the world, I wouldn't go first to New Guinea. But I wouldn't be too worried about planning to include it later in a first trip. After a few months in the Third World, you'll be as ready for the Fourth World—if you still want to go there—as you'll ever be. At the same time, don't kid yourself: as First World services follow the tourist money trail, Third World travel is getting easier all the time, but the hassles of truly Fourth World travel, especially outside the most cosmopolitan and connected cities, are changing much less.

TRAVEL IN THE PRESENT

An important point to keep in mind, wherever you consider going, is that you will be traveling in the present, not the past. The farther you get from the First World, the smaller your budget, and the more you know about the history, traditions, or past of your destination, the more important this idea becomes.

You may be interested in a destination because of its "classical" history or culture, and the sights you want to see may be primarily ancient monuments or archaeological sites. These are all good and sufficient reasons to travel. But for every spine-tingling moment spent in a place whose history you've read and dreamed about, you'll also spend days or weeks dealing with the present-day reality of the place.

You may have learned a country's language to read its classical literature, but most people who speak that language may be illiterate, the most popular publications in that language may be film-star gossip magazines and soap-opera digests, and the most popular contemporary music in that language may be rap. You can ask locals if they have read the Ramayana, or where to find a concert of classical music, and they may even humor you. But they may be much more interested in asking you about American pop stars or World Bank structural adjustment programs, or finding out if you have seen the latest Hollywood movies (bootlegs of which are often available worldwide before they open in theaters, much less are released on video, in the United States).

In my experience, people who are ignorant but who are aware of their ignorance, are open-minded, and genuinely desire to learn are less likely to suffer from "culture shock" than those who think they know the most about where they are going but who know only or primarily about its past and have paid inadequate attention to the present. Some extremely naive people are remarkably successful travelers. Other travelers, extremely knowledgeable about the past, are utterly disoriented by their inability to reconcile the modern reality of their traveling life with the context and setting they had imagined from the literature.

These latter travelers are also some of the people who, because they fail to pay attention to their surroundings, do the most dangerous things, usually without even realizing the risks they are taking. The best insurance against getting into trouble is to keep your eyes open, keep thinking about what you see and what it means, read the newspapers, and talk to local people about what is going on.

Sourcing Real-Life Information

For a variety of reasons (see the references on the world information order in the *Background Reading* section of the *Resource Guide*) we in the First World get very little information about contemporary Second, Third, and Fourth World life. English-language newspapers, magazines, and novels from these countries are published throughout the world, and many of them are available on the Internet. Television channels from other countries, including some in English, are available on many satellite (and some cable) TV services. You can get movies from around the world, with English subtitles, through Netflix or from your local library as well as on DVD from "ethnic" specialty shops catering to immigrants. Local people and resident expats are blogging, some of them in English, about their daily lives in pretty much any place you might think of visiting. But few First Worlders pay attention to any of these. Our impressions of the other worlds are shaped by the more accessible literature about them: classics, histories, travelogues (by foreigners), and tourist brochures and websites. None of these focuses on, or gives much indication of, contemporary real life. It's well worth making an extra effort to seek out a reality check in websites, news and entertainment videos, and recent literature, fiction and nonfiction, *by*, not just about, people in the places you plan to visit.

REAL LIFE

One extreme example of tourism propaganda is Africa south of the Sahara: it's difficult to find *any* pictures or even mention of Black African urban life. Presumably tour operators think that tourists want to come to Africa to see animals, not Africans, and that enough of the potential tourists are racists, or scared of Southern cities, that it would be bad for business to remind people that the "big game" animals coinhabit Africa with a billion (mostly nonwhite) humans. Sad to say, the brochure writers are probably all too correct in their assessment of the attitudes of too many tourists.

Choosing Destinations

PITFALLS OF TOURISM PROPAGANDA

Tourist literature, whether from tour operators or government tourist boards, often glosses over the less attractive aspects of contemporary reality, or avoids them entirely, for fear of scaring away potential tourists.

Even the attractive features of contemporary local culture and life—things that will be immediately apparent to any visitor—may not be mentioned in tourist propaganda if the people writing the websites and brochures think this would conflict with the *image* of the country that attracts foreign visitors, no matter how distorted or out-of-date that image may be. The flip side of this is that you can always find what you expect, if you're willing to pay for it. The customer is always right: if people go somewhere in search of something, locals will (for a price) attempt to fulfill the tourists' fantasies, even if that means dressing in costumes and performing "rituals" or "traditional" music, arts, or other activities that have been created solely to satisfy the tourist market (perhaps even by copying pictures in tour brochures).

THE TROUBLE WITH TRAVELOGUES

Reading lists in guidebooks, even in otherwise-sensitive guidebooks for independent travelers, tend to be heavy on narratives by First World travelers about their visits to the destination. These are often entertaining reading, but don't take them too seriously as a guide to what your trip will be like. Travelogues are written to entertain, and a good deal of artistic license is permitted to spice up a narrative. You also need to pay attention to the authors' attitudes. Did they dislike a place because of their racism or because the "natives" were insufficiently servile, for example?

A notable exception to all this is the excellent series of anthologies for travelers published by Whereabouts Press, which feature writing by people from different countries, selected in most cases by editors from those places. (See the *Resource Guide* for details.)

THE PACE OF CHANGE

It's obvious that things may have changed greatly since a Victorian travelogue was written. It may be less obvious, and must be stressed, that things may have changed completely since something was written 20, 10, or two years ago. In making allowances for dated information about other "worlds," it would be a mistake to apply the same standard that you would to information about the First World.

Northerners are taught to think of the South as "backward" (i.e., living in the past), "underdeveloped," or "developing" (as though they were somewhere "behind" us on a timeline of development). We compare aspects of Southern ways of life (such as subsistence agriculture) with those the North has "left behind" in our past, and we compare Southern averages of wealth and health with those of Northerners a century or more ago.

It's entirely natural, but entirely wrong, to infer from this (not all of which is true in the first place) that poor countries are traditional and "living in the past," and from there to jump to the conclusion they are "timeless" and unchanging, or that what was written about them in the past will still be true to a greater extent than would dated information about Northern places that are "making progress," "moving forward," "going places."

Nothing could be further from the truth. The world, and *especially* the Third World, is changing fast. Life is changing much more rapidly in "developing" countries than it is in those that have already been highly "developed" for some time. The pace of change may be greater today in parts of the Third World than it has ever been in what is now the First World.

Travel-specific matters are not exempt from the winds of Second, Third, and Fourth World change. It would be easier to get to, or get around, New York or San Francisco with a guidebook 25 years old than to get around Guangzhou with a guidebook five years old. Almost none of the landmarks I remembered from my first visit to Doha in 2005 were even recognizable when I came back less than three years later in 2008.

CONTEMPORARY LOCAL LIFE

The reality of contemporary local life matters much more to long-term, independent, and budget travelers than to escorted or group tourists, or to people with larger budgets. Travelers in groups interact mainly with each other and may scarcely speak with any local people. This holds true even for budget groups, such as overland group camping "expeditions." Escorted travelers, even "independent" ones (i.e., on personalized private tours) interact mainly with their guides and translators, who as speakers of English or another foreign language and in regular contact with foreigners (and their money) are almost by definition part of the local upper-middle class or elite. With enough money, you can insulate yourself from Third World reality in an Intercontinental Hotel or hire enough servants to travel in the same way as the gentlemen and ladies who wrote Victorian travelogues.

On your own, on a budget (long-term travel puts almost everyone on a budget, as I've mentioned already), you have to deal with local people, here and now, many times every day. Your life on the road will resemble the lives of local people, at least local resident expats or local travelers of similar means, except to the extent that you pay extra to have things done differently for you than they are for locals.

You won't have to live like the local poor. Southerners migrate North in the belief, confirmed by the judgments of their acquaintances who have gone before them, that they will be materially better off as poor people in the North than as middle-class people (those who have passports and can afford passage North, much less get a visa, are usually at least middle class) in the South. Even as a "budget" First World traveler you can afford to travel more comfortably in any other world than you could for the same money in the First World. But neither can you entirely avoid experiencing the reality of the places you go. After all, that's the point of travel. I just recommend that you "Be prepared."

EVALUATING TRAVEL ADVICE

A common problem with any set of sources is conflicting advice or information of uncertain reliability. Here are some general principles you can use to assess destination information and other travel advice. This advice is applicable to information in all media and from all sources, including books and word-of-mouth. But it's especially important on the Internet, where one often knows little or nothing about who has provided a particular piece of information.

How Recently Did They Visit?

As I've already pointed out, things can change overnight. People often give undue weight to the experience of a friend, or someone from a place, even if they visited or emigrated some time ago. Ask someone what year they were there. Ask an immigrant when they emigrated, and when they last went "home" to visit. A further useful question in evaluating what an immigrant says about their "mother country" is, "Where is home now? Here or there?"

Disregard excessively vague answers. Obsolete advice, delivered in an authoritative tone and relied on, can lead to worse surprises than total ignorance. If the information is second (or third) hand, discount it heavily and don't assume it is current. "My friend was just there," may mean that they were there last week or five years ago; you won't find out which, or if the intermediary knows, unless you probe carefully.

How Long Did They Stay?

This is kind of a trick question. You'd think that people who had been in a place longer would know more about it, and they generally do. On the other hand, people who spent a long time in a place—especially if they lived there, rather than just traveling through—may have lived very differently than you will as a transient. Things that were "no problem" for someone who knew at least some of a local language, had local connections, perhaps had their own car (and driver) and friends to stay with along the way might be very much harder for a new arrival to arrange. If they were there a long time, ask them how easy or difficult things were when they first arrived, and how long it took them to figure out how to get things done and get around.

Don't assume that travel writers (including guidebook writers) spend a lot of time getting to know each place they write about. Professional travel writers are experts at collecting the essential information about a place quickly so that they can move on to the next. Someone who writes a book about a country or region probably spent at least several months there doing research. But they may only have spent a day in a provincial town, even a large provincial city, if it's not especially popular with tourists. Some guidebook publishers seek to hire authors with destination expertise. But others (notably including Lonely Planet) prefer writers with little or no prior experience in the destinations they are writing about so that they will describe them from the perspective of the first-time visitor who's the likely reader of the guidebook.

People who seem to have been everywhere probably weren't anywhere for very long. If their purpose in travel is to collect countries or sights so as to be able to say, "Been there, done that," they probably don't make it a priority to hang around. Ask them specifically how long they spent in the particular place or country you are interested in. They may have very useful nuggets of practical information, but don't count on subtlety or depth of understanding.

How Does Their Style of Travel Compare to Yours?

This is probably the most important question to ask in evaluating why someone else did or didn't like a place.

The experience of travel for someone in a group, or on a tour, has little in common with that of an independent traveler. How did they travel? If they liked or didn't like the hotels, are they talking about the US$300 a night hotels? The US$30 a night hotels? The US$3 a night hotels? The US$30 hotels are great value in some places where the US$3 and US$300 hotels are a terrible value. Did they stay in places you'd want to stay? Did they do things you'd want to do? What was the purpose of their trip?

If they thought there was nothing to do, was that because there were no beaches? No museums? No discotheques? No street markets and bazaars? No air-conditioning? What is their picture of an ideal day of traveling? (If they take photographs while traveling, they can probably show you.) If they loved the place, was it because of the food? The conversations? The music? The scenery? The social structure? The pattern of daily life? Even independent budget travelers with similar travel styles may be interested in very different aspects of places, and find the same place exciting or boring, wonderful or awful.

The reasons some people would choose a destination are reasons other people would shun it, and vice versa. This is one of the strongest reasons not to rely on experts, no matter how well traveled

REAL LIFE

Every guidebook I've read describes Tashkent, Uzbekistan, as completely without touristic interest—a big, industrialized city. Too civilized. Too modern. Not quaint. Too fast-moving. Too aware of the rest of the world. Too much of an ethnic mix to give one a proper sense of "pure" Uzbek culture. All accurate descriptions. Most tourists don't like Tashkent, for just these reasons.

Reading the guidebooks' denunciations, I knew immediately that Tashkent was the place for me. I found it was everything I had hoped for. I didn't find a mythic past in Tashkent, but I wasn't looking for the past. Tashkent is the future of Central Asia, all brought together in one bustling, cosmopolitan, accessible mélange: an intellectual and ideological center; the largest and richest city north of the Himalayas between Beijing and Moscow; a magnet for the best, brightest, and most ambitious people of a dozen nationalities from 1,000 miles around. As of this writing, U.S. citizens no longer need a sponsor (as they still do for Russia) in order to obtain a visa for Uzbekistan, although the U.S. military presence since 2001 has altered attitudes toward U.S. visitors.

Choosing Destinations

and knowledgeable, in deciding where *you* should go. Travel writers often adopt a pseudo-objective voice that gives too little information about themselves for readers to judge whether they would prefer the places writers love or the ones they pan. The perfect trip is different for everyone, and there's nothing like travel itself for making one aware of the diversity of humanity and our multiplicity of tastes and styles. It's your trip; make your own choices.

EDUCATING YOURSELF ABOUT DESTINATIONS

A wide variety of resources can help you decide where you want to go, and when: the Internet, libraries, bookstores, guidebooks, tourist boards, embassies and consulates, governments, immigrants, friends, other travelers, bloggers, tour operators, and travel agents. Specific references and contact details are given in the *Resource Guide* at the back of this book and on the Practical Nomad website. What follows is only a general introduction to some of the major types and sources of destination information.

Tour Operators and Travel Agents

Tour brochures and travel agents are usually the first places people turn when figuring out where to go. In my opinion as a former travel agent, they should be the last.

TRAVEL AGENTS

People always ask me, "I want to go around the world. Where should I go?" I can't give that sort of advice. Not only may someone end up not liking the places I suggest, but more importantly, people often can't preface this question with enough information about themselves, their goals, and their desired style of travel to provide a meaningful basis for a recommendation.

REAL LIFE

"Where should I go for a month in Southeast Asia?" is not a question anyone can answer for you without a great deal more information about what you want. If you want a lazy beach holiday, maybe you should go to Ko Samui. If you want scenic landscapes and romantic cities, maybe you should go to Vietnam. If you want to sit around talking politics with the local intelligentsia, maybe you should go to Bandung. If you want a diversity of cultures, ethnicities, and cuisines in one country, or want to speak English with middle or lower-class people, maybe you should go to Malaysia. If you want sex with prostitutes, maybe you should go to Bangkok or Manila (but don't ask me for help if that's your goal). And if you are scared of Asia and are willing to prop up the local authoritarians to get a sanitized glimpse of Europeanized Asia with all the comforts of home (at the same prices), maybe you should go to Singapore.

A good travel agent can be a great help in facilitating and organizing your trip and helping you to get places, once you have decided where you want to go. Trying to do it all yourself, particularly dealing with airlines directly, is likely to lead you to spend much more on transportation than you would have with the assistance of an agent. And a specialist agent, or one who happens to have a lot of knowledge or experience about a particular small country or region, may be able to refine your choices of precise places: "In which of these three cities am I likely to find fewer tourists?" "In which of these two neighboring countries will it be easier to get out of the cities into the countryside and talk to villagers?" Do see a travel agent, but do so *after* you decide, at least preliminarily, where you want to go and what kinds of things you want to do.

Travel agents spend less time traveling than many of their clients. You can't expect any travel agent to have been to every country, much less city, that you are going to. But good travel agents solicit, and pass on, recommendations from their clients. It's worth at least asking whether they happen to know a place to recommend, of a particular type, in a particular price range.

The better agencies that specialize in around-the-world travel know where to find things like visa applications and instructions, guidebooks, maps, and the like. Most travel agents get paid to sell tickets, not to do research, but you should be suspicious of the qualifications of an agent who can't or won't help provide pointers for these sorts of references.

TOUR OPERATORS

Printed and online brochures from tour operators can sometimes be useful even if you plan to travel independently: they'll give you a quick idea of which are the most popular times to visit and the "must-see" attractions, so that you can either avoid them entirely or approach them with an awareness that they are certain to be more crowded, more expensive, and more dominated by foreign tourists than other places that aren't featured in tours and times when the groups are gone.

The alternative to a tour is another tour. But the alternative to *all* tours is independent travel. For tour operators, the very possibility of do-it-yourself travel is the ultimate competition. All tour operators share a collective interest in persuading tourists that it is too difficult or dangerous to go it alone. They showcase in their brochures things you genuinely can't do by yourself, because they require special permits granted only to tour groups, admission is rationed with the quotas held by tour operators, or individual transportation is prohibitively expensive.

Don't look to brochure itineraries to give you *any* picture of what travel is like for independent travelers. "After breakfast, you will be transferred to the train station . . ." in a tour brochure might instead be summarized as follows for the independent traveler: "On the morning of day one, you start looking for the railway ticket office. It's moved, and by the time you get to the new location (after various interesting and educational sights and encounters along the way), it is closed. Eventually, you find someone who tells you that it is only open in the mornings. So you come back on the morning of day two, have a long conversation over several cups of tea with the stationmaster, and buy a ticket. After breakfast on day three, you board the train. . . ."

One of the worst mistakes you can make is to try to replicate an itinerary from a brochure or guidebook, day by day, on your own. If you actually want to follow that itinerary, take the tour. If you can follow a brochure itinerary on your own, you can expect it to take at least twice as much time, anywhere in the world, as it would on a tour. In the Third World, it will probably take longer and/or require hiring a private car, driver, and guide. In the Fourth World, it may not affordably be possible at all. Budget your time accordingly. If you *must* see or do certain things in a certain amount of time, either give yourself a generous additional allowance for delay (the more so the less experienced you are in that part of the world or type of country) or take a tour. Outside the First World, trying to travel independently on a fixed schedule that allows only a few days in each place is a recipe for frustration and disappointment.

On the whole, tour operators avoid giving out (much less including in their brochures) the sort of information that would enable you to replicate their tours on your own. Don't be discouraged if tour brochures imply that independent travel is impossible or prohibitively expensive, as that is rarely the case.

A more common situation is that there is no middle ground between an expensive and efficient tour and a challenging independent trip. In a fair number of countries (Russia is at present the outstanding example, and has changed surprisingly little in this regard since the early 1990s) there is very little infrastructure for independent travel. You can either travel more or less smoothly, quickly, comfortably, and expensively on an escorted tour—or you can find your own way, cheaply but not without difficulty.

I've been in big cities where all the hotel rooms cost over US$100 or under US$10 a night, nothing in between. It's particularly common to find that only (relatively) expensive "international" hotels can easily be reserved in advance from overseas, even in places where comfortable, midrange local hotels exist.

Offices of Foreign Governments
TOURIST BOARDS

Most countries have some sort of national tourist board or government ministry for the promotion of tourism. Most of these have a presence on the Internet. Some are larger and better funded than others, but all of them exist precisely to serve potential visitors like you: to inform you about why you might want to visit their country and to give you information that will help you have an enjoyable trip.

Some of the less helpful tourist board offices do no more than refer you to operators of package tours, but the services of the tourist boards themselves are free. The best of them provide mountains of useful free maps; weather tables; train, bus, and ferry schedules; hotel, restaurant, sightseeing, and shopping guides; schedules of holidays, festivals, and special events; peculiarities of local modes of travel, accommodations, customs, religious practices, and taboos; cultural and historical background information; suggested itineraries; and practical tips for independent travelers.

It can be surprisingly hard to track down some tourist board offices, especially those that aren't on the Internet. In the United States, few tourist boards have toll-free numbers. The only quasi-comprehensive listings of them are in expensive specialized references for travel agents. A travel agent should be able to give you the telephone number and address or URL of a country's tourist board office, if there is one in your country.

If you can't find a travel agent who knows, and you can't locate the tourist board's office or website, try asking the national airline of the country (many airlines have offices even in countries to which they don't fly, and in the United States even these "offline" offices almost all have toll-free telephone numbers). If they don't know, or there's no such airline or office, ask any embassy or consulate of the country. If there is a national tourist board office, they will be able to refer you to it. Virtually every country in the world has either or both an embassy to the United States in Washington, D.C. (directory assistance +1-202-555-1212, or the list of accredited foreign embassies on the U.S. State Department website) and/or a mission to the United Nations in New York (directory assistance +1-212-555-1212).

NATIONAL AIRLINES

Whether or not it's the airline on which you will fly, the national airline of the country you wish to visit can often provide literature promoting that country as a destination.

Airline literature tends to be more marketing and package-tour oriented and less objective and informational than that of tourist boards, but for some small countries the national airline is the only source (and may even share an office with, or be officially designated to represent, the national tourist board).

CONSULATES AND EMBASSIES

Consulates and embassies of larger countries generally serve a purely diplomatic role, but ambassadors of smaller countries often interpret their role more broadly. If there isn't a separate tourist board office, try the embassy or a consulate.

Don't be too surprised if they aren't too helpful. Maintaining offices in the United States is expensive for poor countries, and consulates are often understaffed and overworked. Some countries have had particularly bad experiences with culturally insensitive foreign tourists, and many have official policies against "hippies."

Remember also that some countries get few visitors from the United States at all, and that independent travel in some places is genuinely difficult, or possible but quite unheard-of by the embassy. Some countries try hard—sometimes with good reason—to steer would-be visitors toward organized, escorted group tours.

But consular staff can be astonishingly helpful and supportive to independent travelers who are polite—not demanding—and who evince genuine interest and respect for their country. Ask for a visa, and you might get pages of handwritten notes from the ambassador on his favorite nooks and crannies of his country, as I once did (even without identifying myself as a travel agent or journalist)!

U.S. Department of State Publications

Don't count on too much from the U.S. government. On the whole, State Department publications (and the U.S. government as a whole) are less helpful to travelers than most U.S. citizens expect. I list various State Department publications in some detail here, not because they are especially useful but because many travelers from the United States ask about some of them (not necessarily the most useful ones) and give them undue weight in deciding where to go. These are available on the State Department's travel or general websites at either http://travel.state.gov or www.state.gov.

BACKGROUND NOTES

Country-specific *Background Notes* for almost every country in the world are available at www.state.gov/r/pa/ei/bgn. These are produced for the use of travelers as well as soldiers, diplomats, and other U.S. government personnel or contractors who may be sent to a country on short notice, and as a starting point for Americans considering doing business in or with the country. They focus on the most basic questions: "What is it most essential for an American to know before getting off a plane in Country X?" For travelers, they include tips from the U.S consular staff in the country on visas, health, crime, safety, political instability, communications, banking, internal transportation, etc. If U.S. citizens routinely experience trouble in a country or seek help from an embassy or consulate, the field staff there will eventually warn travelers about these problems. While they are, perhaps, overly cautious, and certainly have their biases, these background notes have been considerably improved in recent years.

TRAVEL WARNINGS

The U.S. State Department issues *Travel Warnings* when it recommends that U.S. citizens avoid travel to a certain country. All *Travel Warnings* are available at http://travel.state.gov/travel/warnings.html.

Travelers from countries other than the United States often find themselves consulting U.S. government travel advisories and warnings, even while they complain about their biases. A favorite sport of foreigners, on the Internet and elsewhere, is writing parodies of what the advisory for travel to the United States would look like if there were one.

Whether or not you're a U.S. citizen, U.S. travel advisories can be useful as long as you read them with an awareness of the perspective from which they are written. They can be counted on to stress the hazards of countries whose governments are in disfavor with the U.S. government, and to minimize problems that would embarrass governments friendly or subservient to the U.S. government.

Many people decide where it is safe enough to go solely on the basis of *Travel Warnings* (or the absence thereof). You shouldn't ignore them: they provide much useful information on which countries, and which areas within them, may be less safe, and why. But the desire to protect itself against liability, as a rule, makes the U.S. State Department err on the side of caution. Most people traveling around the world travel quite happily through at least one country for which a *Travel Warning* is in effect, as I've done myself on several occasions without feeling that I was in any great danger.

Books, Periodicals, Websites, and Videos

If it's worth spending US$1,000 or more on transportation and a month of your time on a trip somewhere, it's certainly worth spending a day before you leave home on the Internet, in a library, or visiting bookstores to learn about where you are going. You don't have to become an expert, and you shouldn't be intimidated into not traveling because you haven't prepared enough. But if you can, take the time to do some reading. These small investments in extra effort will be repaid with generous interest.

Dig a little further down in the results of an Internet search to find some of the less-prominent sources from—not just about—the place you are thinking of visiting. Request a few books on interlibrary loan or special-order them from the publisher. Take out a subscription to a regional magazine from or about the place(s) you plan to go next year. Visit a research library with a regional studies collection you can browse through. Or take your own little "field trip" to an immigrant neighborhood to track down some immigrant or imported print publications or videos. Many specialized and local publications, including English-language newspapers and, of course, blogs by both locals and resident expats from around the world, are available online. But enough aren't that the Internet still isn't a complete substitute for books, periodicals, or libraries. (For more on using the Internet for travel research, including using the Internet to find offline travel resources, see my other book, *The Practical Nomad: Guide to the Online Travel Marketplace*.)

Unfortunately, most people start their research too late, reading up on places only *after* they decide to go there. A little research earlier on can be crucial in helping you make choices of destinations that you'll be happy with when you get there. Doing your homework can also help you travel in a more culturally and politically responsible manner. It won't eliminate all the surprises: encounters with the unexpected are among the inevitable joys (and annoyances) of travel. If you could know in advance exactly what you'd find, you wouldn't need to travel to find it.

REAL LIFE

The Kashmir Valley has been unsuitable for tourism since the current phase of the Kashmiri struggle against Indian occupation began in 1989. But for more than a decade after that, the valley was still described as "idyllic" in some "current" guidebooks—despite martial law enforced by half a million Indian troops; 24-hour curfews; torture, "disappearances," and assassinations of suspected nationalists and sympathizers by Indian death squads; machine-gunning of nationalist street demonstrations; razing of inner-city neighborhoods suspected of harboring anti-Indian militants; attacks on Kashmiri religious shrines; and the murder, rape, and kidnapping of foreign tourists by Indian soldiers and renegade Kashmiris (condemned by mainstream Kashmiri nationalists) alike.

INFORMATION SHELF LIFE

Feature articles in the travel sections of Sunday newspapers usually have a lead time of at least a couple of months between acceptance of an article and publication. Articles about seasonal destinations and activities, however, are often held for publication in the same season, a full year after the research on which they are based, often without any serious updating. Lead times for glossy magazines are considerably longer, with the same problem of seasonal articles being published a year after they were researched.

SEARCH FOR SOURCES

Some of the publications in the *Resource Guide* may seem obscure, and you may be tempted to dismiss them out of hand as impossible to find. But the most obvious and accessible publications are sometimes the least useful. With a few exceptions, noted as such in the listings and included nonetheless because of their exceptional usefulness, all of the books in the *Resource Guide* should be readily available from your local library, and many are as close as the Internet. Your local library will probably have to request a few of them on interlibrary loan from a big-city or university research library, but don't let that hold you back. Interlibrary loan services are available, usually for free, at almost all U.S. public libraries. Borrowing books this way is a simple process.; ask your local librarian. Libraries are improving interlibrary loan procedures, and integrating their catalogs, in order to save money by eliminating duplicate holdings with other nearby libraries.

I've tried to include information on publishers and distributors wherever possible (particularly for periodicals not stocked by ordinary newsstands and magazine dealers) to facilitate orders and subscriptions. Regular bookstores are sometimes reluctant to place special orders with obscure or foreign publishers, and may not be familiar with importers of books from the South. For most of the imported books and most of the periodicals in the *Resource Guide,* you'll find it easier to order directly from the publishers or the listed specialty distributors.

GUIDEBOOKS

Independent travelers tend to buy guidebooks only after they've chosen their general destination, and to use them primarily as directories of recommended places to stay (and perhaps secondarily for choosing specific places or routes to go within a country or region).

I use guidebooks very little for choosing specific hotels. In my opinion—and, I've discovered, in the opinion of most other guidebook writers—the greatest value of guidebooks intended for independent travel is in the early stages of deciding where to go.

Properly used, good guidebooks for independent travelers can be some of the best tools for getting a feel for what travel in a place will be like. Resist the temptation to skip the front or back matter. The first things I read in any guidebook are the introductory "how-to" sections. These things change less from edition to edition than hotel ratings, so it's a good idea to buy an inexpensive used or remaindered copy of the previous edition to help you decide if you want to go to a place, then a new copy of the latest edition just before you leave, if you do go. (If it's worth carrying a guidebook with you, it's worth paying for the latest edition.)

The guidebooks that have the least to say about the sights and attractions of a place—which churches, temples, or mosques to visit, when monuments were built, the literary or historical associations and significance of sites—sometimes have the most to say about what life is like for independent travelers. "Practicalities" aren't a side issue for independent travelers: they are daily life. As you read the descriptions of the things you'll have to deal with while traveling—how you'll get around, how you'll communicate, what you'll eat, where you'll sleep—try to visualize the sort of day that you might spend in such a place. When you get there, it will be real, not a fantasy. The more you can make the day-to-day reality of your destination real in your mind, before you leave, the better you'll be able to chose where to go and the more prepared you will be when you get there.

There's a fine line, of course, between being adequately prepared and being unable to adapt. Temper your expectations with an awareness of the possibility that things will be different. The less you count on, the less disappointed you'll be, and the better able you'll be to enjoy, rather than be frustrated by, the inevitable surprises.

The better guidebooks are written in the hope that you'll read them well in advance, and they include extended bibliographies of suggested further reading about the countries or regions they cover. Your tastes may differ, but I rarely find the sorts of things I'm interested in on these booklists. There are exceptions, but guidebook bibliographies tend to overemphasize travelogues by foreigners. It's rare to find listings or ordering information for contemporary publications from the destination, or by emigrants from it, even though these almost always exist and often are available on the Internet. This is a pity, as this information can be difficult to track down, and guidebook writers and publishers would be the people best able to provide it.

IMPORTED AND IMMIGRANT PUBLICATIONS

If you can find them in English or a language you know, current publications, websites, movies, or television programs from the place you are thinking of visiting, or by or for emigrants from there, are the single best window into current events in their home country. Scanning the headlines in a newspaper, reading a contemporary popular novel, or watching a hit movie or TV show can give you a better picture of life than anything else. The greatest value of the Internet for would-be world travelers is the access it gives to contemporary news, analysis, and other writing from and by people in even the most obscure parts of the world.

Most people assume that English-language publications don't exist in places where English isn't a major local language, or that they aren't available in First World countries. They are sometimes expensive (though by no means always) or hard to find in print, but they do exist. And even if they aren't on the Internet, they are worth great effort and cost to track down. I've gone on some wild-goose chases looking for English-language books, and I've wasted some money on boring tracts, but I've never regretted having sought out local writing in English.

I have yet to visit a country without: at least one English-language newspaper or magazine, fiction and nonfiction books published or translated in English, and some blogs in English. Current English-language versions of local newspapers or newsmagazines from more than 100 countries, including ones from all seven continents (including the only Antarctican newspaper) and from all major world regions are available for free on the Internet.

No language has ever dominated the world the way English does today. Other languages (see the sidebar *Most Useful Languages for World Travel* in the *Practicalities* chapter) are widely used in particular regions or groups of former colonies. You'll find some speakers of most of these languages almost anywhere you go. But no other language reaches the worldwide listenership or readership of English. Like it or not (most of the world doesn't like it, and English is not especially easy to learn as a foreign language), anything intended for a truly global audience perforce must be—and is—published in English. The Internet has greatly accelerated this trend, and some newspapers translate their entire daily content into English solely for posting on the Internet for international consumption.

Native speakers of English, and to a lesser extent anyone who has learned English, are the beneficiaries of this linguistic hegemony. English speakers can get away with speaking only English in most of the world. But if we don't learn the local languages—which isn't really possible for all but the most adept of short-term visitors—the least we can do to make up for making others speak to us in our language is to make some effort to read what they have to say to us in our language. In today's world, literacy in English is a privilege that opens windows into every part of the world. Take advantage of it. You'll shortchange yourself if you waste the opportunities that knowledge of English gives you.

Most long-term travelers spend most of their travel time outside the wealthy "developed" North, in part because poorer countries are usually cheaper to travel in for long periods of time. Regardless of your own perspective on North-South relations, it's important to understand the perspectives of those with whom you'll be dealing. Gandhian, Maoist, and Nehruvian analyses of imperialism and the history of the Non-Aligned Movement and the North-South conflict have been as central to political discourse in most of the world as anti-Communism, the history of the Cold War, and the East-West conflict have been in the United States. Editorials in Southern newspapers, for example, take for granted familiarity with Southern terminology, ideologies, and world views that First World travelers may not have learned about in school.

I've been in numerous countries where Al Jazeera television news—marginalized in the United States and available only online—was looked upon as the epitome of mainstream objectivity, the "standard" view of the world in relationship to which all other journalism and interpretation was judged. Meanwhile, some of the most widely watched and read U.S. news sources are taken for granted in much of the world to be one or another sort of imperialist propaganda, the mouthpieces of their corporate owners. My point isn't that either worldview is right. One reason to travel is to see and hear for yourself, and form your own opinions. But you are more likely to understand what people are saying to you as a traveler if you already have some familiarity with their terminology, assumptions, and frame of reference.

Fortunately, the kinds of materials of most relevance to travelers are among those most likely to be published in English. English speakers, much less readers, are the educated and internationalist elite. Southern publications in English, including websites and blogs, are consciously directed to an international and educated audience, often going out of their way to clarify local terminology and ideas that might be unfamiliar to foreign readers. That makes sense. If they were intended for the local masses, they'd be published in the vernacular. In a country such as India, for example, of which it is often falsely said that "everyone speaks English," only a small percentage of the population is literate in English, with publishing in Hindi, Urdu, and the so-called "regional" languages larger and faster growing than English-language publishing.

English is particularly used for academic materials and as a link language between native speakers of different languages from different world regions. Three of the most common kinds of nonfiction books to find in English in any country are all excellent starting points for a traveler wanting to learn about the country: histories of the country by local scholars, texts on the national culture and arts, and contributions by local thinkers to debates on global issues. Especially interesting are those publications directed to readers in other regions of the South rather than to Northerners.

English fiction is less reliably useful. The most common fiction to find in English includes translations of national classics (sometimes ones that few locals actually read in any language, and not necessarily of much use in understanding current events) and short stories and novels by the foreign-educated elite. On the other hand, the standard of living of First World budget travelers, on the road in the South, may be most similar to that of the local upper-middle class; i.e., the sort of locals who are educated in English-medium schools and write in English. And foreign-educated bloggers and other local writers may be able to serve as cultural interpreters, in both directions, between local and First World points of view.

All this is interesting, you may say, but of little use in planning if you can't find these publications at home before you leave. True enough. But with some effort you can find English publications from all over the world. Places to look for them include ethnic and immigrant cultural, religious, and community centers and neighborhoods; academic departments of ethnic and regional studies and languages; and region-specific Internet sites.

Included in the *Background Reading* section of the *Resource Guide,* under the heading of *Southern Perspectives on the World,* is a selection of pan-Southern publications and examples of some leading strains of Southern thought, all of which are available in First World libraries or online. Also included in the *Resource Guide* are some general world references from the South (*The World Guide* is the most outstanding), a few of the leading First World distributors of English-language books imported from the South, and regional English-language websites and magazines distributed in the First World, from and about each of the Southern continents (South America, Africa, and Asia).

Those newspapers printed in English from the South that aren't available on the Internet are hard but not impossible to come by in the North. You'll find them in major academic libraries, especially those with regional studies centers or departments; in consulates and embassies (whenever I visit a consulate, I pause to browse the home-country papers in the waiting room or library); and sometimes in immigrant community centers.

An increasing number of foreign newspapers—to which print subscriptions by airmail would be prohibitively expensive—now publish online international editions in English translation. On the Internet, in English, you can read what was considered the top of the news in Tokyo, Rio de Janeiro, Taipei, Chennai (Madras), or Melbourne. You don't need access to the Internet to read a newspaper that you could have delivered to your door for 50 cents. But it's a great way to browse through a sample copy of a paper from the other side of the globe.

Where you can't get an imported newspaper, you may be able to find a local periodical or website for emigrants from the place you are going. The smallest ethnic and immigrant communities have some sort of journal for networking and news from home. These are distributed anywhere immigrants congregate: ethnic and immigrant neighborhoods, restaurants, cafés and bars, sports clubs, places of worship, community centers, foreign-language video-rental shops, imported-food shops, and businesses run by members of the im-migrant group. Ask anyone you know who is from the place you are going where they get news from home, or ask around in appropriate ethnic neighborhoods or businesses, if you can find them.

Movies and videos don't even have to be in English to be useful. Consider renting or borrowing a few DVDs or videotapes of recent TV or movie hits from your destination. They are likely to include contemporary street scenes, interiors of homes and workplaces, and images of clothing, body language, and social interactions. The picture they give of ordinary life will probably be as distorted as the picture of ordinary American life that the world gets from Hollywood movies and TV shows. Still, movies and soap operas are in some respects more realistic in depicting ordinary life than CNN, which only shows pictures of the most extreme and unusual ("newsworthy") events.

Finding English books while you are traveling in a non-English-speaking country is a hit-or-miss affair. Resign yourself to spending a lot of time searching through English textbooks (English as a foreign language, business and management, science and engineering) to find the locally written social science, humanities, and fiction books. Don't despair, and don't be put off by locals and expatriates alike who say they don't exist. But buy local books that interest you when you find them; you aren't likely to see the same book twice.

English-language newspapers are easy to find while traveling. In some cases they have a substantial local audience and are sold all over. There are more English-language daily newspapers in New Delhi, for example, than in any city in the United States. In other places English-language newspapers are read almost exclusively by expatriate foreigners and local people who are studying English. Look for them where such people might congregate: in the arrival area of the international airport (many such publications give away free copies to arriving international airline passengers), in expensive hotels catering to foreign business travelers, or local English-language schools. Or ask any English-speaking expatriate or local English-language teacher.

Word of Mouth

It scarcely needs mentioning that you can learn from any friends or acquaintances who hail from your expected destination. They'll probably be happy to give you advice. But be aware that things may have changed greatly in their home country since they emigrated. And remember that accepting invitations to visit their friends or relatives incurs an expectation of reciprocal hospitality should your hosts later come to your country.

Once you start talking about going around the world, or mention specific destinations, you'll probably get lots of suggestions from friends. You'll hear even more tales from fellow travelers along the way. Some will be firsthand, some fourthhand, some entirely unfounded rumor. Use common sense, a modicum of skepticism, and the guidelines for evaluating advice in the previous section.

Travel Events

If you get a chance, go to events where you can meet other travelers, and people from the place(s) you are thinking of going, in person. Most travel trade shows are marketing events dominated by sales pitches for tours. But others, such as the annual TNT Travel Show in London (successor to Independent Traveller's World), and the annual "Meet, Plan, Go" events in cities across the United States (www.meetplango.com) offer resources for do-it-yourself travelers. Nonprofit membership organizations such as Hostelling International affiliates worldwide and the REI cooperative in the United States are more likely to emphasize education and empowerment at their events. HI-USA (www. hiusa.org) sponsors a variety of "World Travel 101" workshops at hostels, as well as highly recommended but infrequent "International Travel Day" events at which you can meet people who are from, or who have lived in, dozens of countries (a mix of tourist board representatives, diplomats, foreign students, returned Peace Corps volunteers and other former expatriates, etc.). See the *Resource Guide* for contact details.

Internet Information Sources

Travel and the Internet go hand-in-hand. That should be no surprise: the movement of information has always paralleled the movement of people, power, and money. Historically, global electronic networking was pioneered by the travel industry long before the Internet existed. Travel reservations, especially airline ticket sales, remain the leading edge of e-commerce.

Online information sources—especially Internet editions of local newspapers and magazines, blogs from and about your destinations, local websites for people from the places you are going, and discussion forums—can be a great source of information on current conditions in other parts of the world, and a good way to make contact in advance with people in or from countries you are going to.

Gathering travel information on the Internet is not without its pitfalls. The Internet is rife with obsolete, misleading, self-serving, and simply wrong information. And the glut of information available on the Internet makes it essential to find efficient tools and strategies for selecting what's relevant, credible, and accurate—and avoiding scams, shills, and stupidity.

This section and those in other chapters of this book on the Internet are only an introduction to the uses of the Internet for travelers. For additional information and consumer advice on how you can best use the Internet for travel planning, reservations, and purchasing, see my companion book in this same series, *The Practical Nomad: Guide to the Online Travel Marketplace,* and the Practical Nomad website at www.practicalnomad.com.

ONLINE DISCUSSIONS

People talk about travel on a wide variety of online forums, newsgroups, mailing lists, and bulletin boards. If there's a detail crucial to your trip, chances are

What the Internet Is and What It Isn't

A Communication Medium, Not a Source

The Internet is not, strictly speaking, a source of information. The Internet is a communication medium through which you can gather information from millions of sources.

That may sound like semantic nitpicking. It's not. The single most important thing to keep in mind when you're doing research about anything on the Internet is that, "I found it on the Internet" says nothing about where it came from, who provided it, why, or — most important of all — whether or not there is any truth to it.

So what? you may ask. The same could be said about books or television. But books, TV, and other media are not the same. Books, television programs, and the like are relatively expensive to produce. That cost serves as a screening mechanism: If you read something in a book, it means that someone thought it was important enough to spend thousands of dollars on printing. And before they spent that much money, they probably took some care to check their facts. Unless a book is self-published, it generally reflects a publisher's judgment — corroborating the author's own — that the book has some truth and value.

Not so with the Internet. Because it's so quick, easy, and cheap to post, much more information is available on the Internet. Anyone can do it, no matter how ignorant or thoughtless they may be. They can do it on their own, with no need for anyone else to check their "facts." Since it doesn't cost them much, there's less reason to consider whether they're saying anything worthwhile. The volume of information placed online, even by commercial publishers, precludes the degree of fact-checking that's the norm in print.

Too Much of a Good Thing

The biggest problem with Internet research is data glut. And the Internet has at least as much bad information as good. Worse, how something looks on the Internet is little indication of its accuracy. An expensively produced book or fancy-looking tour brochure isn't necessarily accurate, though it does indicate a substantial investment probably made with some care. A fancy-looking website, on the other hand, could be produced by a skilled graphic designer who knows nothing about travel. Our instinct to "judge a book by its cover" is nowhere else as dangerous as on the Internet. Slick-looking design is a poor indication of credibility and accuracy.

Similarly, books normally indicate the author, publisher, date, and place of publication. They don't have to, but most bookstores won't carry them if they lack this information. Web pages usually say little or nothing about their authorship or vintage.

Don't get me wrong: I'm not an advocate of Internet censorship. I'm glad that anyone can say anything online. But the anarchy and ease of Internet access requires a higher level of individual judgment and choice than do other media. It's not hard to find some information online about any given topic or destination. The difficulty is in figuring out which information to believe.

Advice or Advertising?

Most travel websites are basically online brochures: advertising and propaganda, with all the same problems as printed brochures. If you aren't sure who is behind a travel website, assume it's a paid advertisement. The Internet is full of advertisements masquerading as journalism or personal stories. Travel companies have offered to pay me to write about them favorably in my blog. I've said no, but others have accepted. And I've heard a major advertising agency boast to an audience of travel industry executives that they have an entire division (offshore where labor is cheap, of course) of people who spend months establishing fake online identities from which to post secretly paid reviews and "personal" messages in blogs, chat rooms, and online bulletin boards promoting their clients' products and services. Every day I delete obvious promotional spam like this masquerading as comments in my blog. Favorable reviews of hotels or restaurants are often posted by friends of the owner or manager, or by paid publicists. Negative reviews are often posted by competitors.

Choosing Destinations

someone is sitting at a computer somewhere who was there last month and has just the information you need. The problem is finding where to ask and how to figure out which answer is correct for your situation—and which are rumors, ancient history, or sales scams.

If you can find the right forums in English, "community" discussions among people in and from destination countries are less likely to be plagued by shills and travel braggadocio. They tend to be quite welcoming to would-be travelers to their home countries, and quite generous with their time in educating them. Just reading the postings and the topics of the threads in one of these discussions can be an informative introduction to the country. These are also a good place to find out about immigrant newspapers or sources of imported books or other printed information about a country.

REGIONAL WEBSITES AND BLOGS

As in print, the more useful websites for travelers tend to be those that aren't intended primarily for travelers: English-language blogs, English-language Web editions of local newspapers, and sites that cater to people in or from the places you are thinking of going. The latter include news sites for people in other countries and regions like www.rediff.com in India, as well as sites for immigrants and expatriates looking for news from home (which are more likely to be in English than portals for locals).

Almost anywhere you go, there are people blogging in English. Travel blogs are the online equivalent of stories told by strangers in a bar or café. You know only what the blogger chooses to tell you, and you may have nothing in common. I read blogs from places I'm thinking of going, but I always read them skeptically and don't rely on them.

Blogs and bloggers are a fascinating slice of life. English-language blogs reflect some of the demographics of who reads English, who knows how to read and write (many people in other countries aren't literate in any language), who has adequate access to the Internet, and which countries allow access to which blogging websites. Many repressive governments use their national firewalls and Internet censorship mechanisms to block access to Blogger.com, Blogspot.com, and other blogging sites. Ask locals or immigrants which sites are popular with, and accessible to, local English-language bloggers.

English-language blogs from the Second, Third, and Fourth Worlds are a mix of the local intelligentsia and technocracy, "travel blogs" by backpackers passing through the place, and foreign expatriates who live there. Expat bloggers include missionaries (a particularly large proportion of the blogs about expat life with children in poorer parts of Africa and Oceania), foreign students and visiting academics, diplomats and government employees and their families, workers for multinational corporations and their families, English teachers, and volunteers, paid staff, and contractors for international organizations and nongovernmental organizations (NGOs, or what in the United States are called "nonprofit organizations" or in the U.K. "charities"). "Trailing spouses" and partners of corporate expats and diplomats often have difficulty getting work permits or finding professional jobs wherever their partner is stationed and have more time to blog than their partners.

EVALUATING TRAVEL INFORMATION ONLINE

The Internet is an invaluable resource for travel planning. Remember, though, to treat advice without an identifiable source (a ".gov" host is probably a real

U.S. government agency, for example) as skeptically as advice from a stranger. Your respondent may have very different tastes and interests, a budget of a different order or magnitude, and may travel very differently than you. The Internet is a powerful medium for the rapid global dissemination of information; it is also an effective medium for the rapid global propagation of rumor, myth, and false information. Internet travel bulletin boards and wikis are filled with authoritative-sounding false information and bad advice.

Newspapers and magazines traditionally separate "editorial" content from advertising. There's no comparable norm on the Web. Does a website give the opinions of independent writers who are paid to say whatever they really think, or is it just propaganda for the chamber of commerce, government ministry of tourism promotion, or a particular tour operator or travel agency? You can't always tell. Does a Web page of hotel "recommendations" list the places a knowledgeable independent writer inspected and thought were best, or those that pay the highest commissions if you clink on the links to them? Does the website even tell you if it is getting paid when you click on those links? In 2009, the U.S. Federal Trade Commission issued a public reminder that websites and blogs, like all publishers and broadcasters, are legally required to disclose these sorts of commercial relationships with products or services they endorse, but few travel websites have made any visible effort to comply.

Personal blogs usually don't have hidden commercial motives. Often, however, they lack perspective. Treat them as a source of individual anecdotes: don't assume they are carefully researched, that they mention all the factors relevant to their opinions, or that you will like the same places.

If a printed guidebook is no good, it likely won't stay in print for long. But on the Web, anyone can say anything and keep saying it, no matter how many other people tell them that it's wrong. There's no way for a browser to tell what's true, and very little way to tell the real source of the information on a website, or what hidden agenda its author or publisher may have. Some websites are designed to appear to have been produced by someone other than their real sponsor. Some of the best-looking, best-written travel websites are full of false or misleading information: political propaganda, dangerous advice, thirdhand rumors.

Even websites from otherwise-reputable guidebook publishers sometimes mix excerpts, updates, and stories from their own writers with unverified information from readers' letters. The largest travel bulletin board, the "Thorn Tree" section of the Lonely Planet website, is probably the largest single repository of travel rumor, misinformation, and bad advice on the Internet. Some reader contributions are useful news, some are exaggerated boasting, some are simply inaccurate or incomplete. There's no way to tell how knowledgeable any contributor was, or how careful their research and reporting. The same is true of any "user generated" site of travel advice or reviews.

CLIMATE, WEATHER, AND WHEN TO GO

Most of the sources I've already mentioned include information on when to go as well as what to do. The best single reference on world weather is the *World Weather Guide* (see *Logistics* in the *Resource Guide*). Many websites give current weather, but fewer give good information on climate patterns and typical weather at different times of the year. Keep in mind that variations in climate within the same country can be extreme, and that even seemingly small countries can be more climatologically diverse than many Americans realize.

National tourist boards and guidebooks have information on other seasonal factors that affect travel. It's particularly worth checking whether the dates you plan to visit correspond with a local holiday or festival (Diwali, Ramadan, Lunar New Year) that would either enhance or interfere with your other plans. If you're trying to do business on a tight schedule, remember that days as well as hours of business vary: are they closed for the local day of prayer on Friday, Saturday, Sunday, or even some other day?

Resist the temptation to try to arrange to be in each place at the time that the books say is best. Experienced travelers generally prefer to avoid peak season (August in Europe, October in Nepal, etc.) anywhere. Better weather is rarely enjoyable enough to offset the extra crowding and higher prices.

Most of the time, in most places, the weather isn't perfect. Most of the time, if you let your budget determine your schedule, you'll find yourself in places at sometime other than peak season. That's reality. If you want to engage in some specific activity that isn't possible all year-round, it's usually more important to avoid the worst weather than it is necessary to be there in the absolute best weather.

For a long, multistop trip, my advice is first to figure out which (if any) of the things you want to do absolutely must be done, or cannot be done, at certain times of the year. Let those requirements determine the overall direction of your trip, but let the timing and sequence of the rest of your stops be determined by whatever will make the airfare cheapest (or is necessary for visa purposes), with minor adjustments in your schedule to avoid any really intolerable seasons.

On a long-term trip around the world, airfare for the sequence of stops that will put you in each place at the "perfect" time of year is likely to be at least twice the airfare for the cheapest sequence of stops. Even if you like crowds and can afford to pay peak-season prices everywhere, it's rarely worth it. Once you've chosen your set of destinations, and perhaps a general direction, use information about local climates as a guide to what weather to expect at the times that you'll be in places rather than to determine exactly when to go where.

Surface Transportation

Even for those who prefer surface travel, air travel is usually the only realistic and affordable option for long-distance international travel. Even if you set out to travel around the world as much as possible overland or by sea, you will probably end up covering 90 percent or more of the distance by air, assuming you have the typical budget of time, money, patience, and tolerance for delay, discomfort, danger, and uncertainty.

It remains possible, though, to travel entirely around the world without flying: A handful of people have done it recently, with considerable difficulty and great patience and commitment to their goal. They did it to prove it could be done, and at least one of them wrote a book about it, Jeff Greenwald's *The Size of the World* (see the *Resource Guide*). More people accomplish around-the-world surface travel on luxury cruises for prices far beyond most of our budgets.

I happen to like airplanes; they are the fastest, safest, and, considering the shorter time one has to spend cooped up in them, most comfortable way to cover long distances. But airplanes have their drawbacks. They are incredibly unecological; they isolate you from the places you pass over; if you aren't really in a hurry, speed may be not be a good thing; and a lot of people are, irrationally, afraid of flying.

Key Advice About Surface Transportation

- Don't plan on any means of surface travel — or even assume it's possible — until you've carefully checked out conditions on the route, current services, and the rules for any border crossings or restricted areas. You could draw a lot of lines on maps that don't correspond to feasible surface travel routes.

- Don't try to convert distances into times without knowing something about local conditions and conveyances. Mass transportation is often more readily available in places where fewer people have their own cars. But surface transportation in most of the world is slower and less reliable than in the First World.

- For safety's sake, travel by train rather than by road when you have a choice. The biggest difference between rail and road travel is the greater safety of rail travel.

- Avoid driving at night or taking night buses outside the First World when there's an alternative. Road travel in general, and night road travel in particular, are overwhelmingly the most dangerous things that ordinary travelers regularly do.

- Treat the journey as part of the experience and the adventure, not as an interruption in your trip. Thinking of a trip by rail, road, or boat as just a way to get from point A to point B is an excellent recipe for impatience and frustration.

- Be prepared for surprises. (Some of them will be pleasant!) Be prepared for delays. Be prepared to change your plans. Do your homework to get an idea of what to expect, but don't take schedules, prices, or other information in guidebooks or on the Internet as gospel. If you want things to be predictable, take a guided tour. There will still be surprises on a tour, but someone else will be responsible for deciding what to do about them.

- Don't punish yourself or take unnecessary risks just to earn a merit badge for hard traveling. Overland travel isn't usually an expedition, but it isn't usually a picnic either. There's no shame in going first class if you can afford it; most local people would think you crazy not to. Bad trips may make for good stories, but that doesn't mean they're fun while they're happening, or worth the discomfort or danger.

For more information on the topics in this chapter, see the *Resource Guide* in the back of the book and the links on the Practical Nomad website at www.practicalnomad.com.

However, there is often no functional alternative to air travel. To understand why requires a survey of surface transportation options, with particular reference to where they are and aren't likely to be available and when they are likely to be good or bad choices.

That survey of surface transportation makes up the balance of this chapter. We'll return to a much more detailed discussion of air travel in the chapter that follows.

RAIL TRANSPORTATION

Trains are the safest, most energy-efficient, and often the fastest and most comfortable means of motorized land transportation. Trains are almost always cheaper than planes, but can still constitute a sizable portion of your budget. Planning ahead is helpful, sometimes essential, in making the best use of the railways.

Railroad History

Unfortunately, building and equipping a railroad on most terrain requires a larger initial investment than building a minimally passable road. Many poor countries—particularly those that don't produce their own locomotives, railroad cars (coaches), and other equipment—have found it hard to come up with enough capital to expand their rail systems or link them to those of neighboring countries.

Third World countries have often lacked the resources to extend or connect the railroads left behind by the colonialists. Most railroads in the South were originally intended and designed for military defense or to carry raw materials and other export commodities—minerals, agricultural products, slaves—to ports where they could be shipped to the ruling colonial country.

Local needs, internal commerce, and most of all regional ("South–South") linkages are typically ill-served by these ex-colonial railways, especially where neighboring countries had different colonial masters. Competing colonialists had every interest in not coordinating their railroads, and usually imported their equipment, and differing gauges (widths between the rails) and technical standards, from their different homelands.

So trains—my favorite way to cover distances too great for a bicycle— are mainly useful for transportation within certain countries, within certain international regions, and on certain particular transcontinental routes. Outside of Europe, relatively few trains cross continents or international borders. Many desirable rail links and routes just don't exist. While railroads are generally being extended and improved in wealthier and developing countries, they continue to decline in poorer countries where investment in roads seems a quicker, cheaper fix.

For planning purposes, it's important to work out whether a train can take you where you want to go; whether train information will be available locally, or what schedules you should bring with you; and whether you need to make reservations or buy tickets before you leave.

Transcontinental Train Routes

There are many rail routes across Europe, several east–west routes across North America, two across Eurasia, one across Australia in each direction (east–west and north–south), and none across Africa or South America. There are no railroads in Antarctica, though there are some other things in Antarctica that you might not expect. (For a while the United States had a nuclear reactor there, for example, despite having signed a treaty making Antarctica a nuclear-free zone.)

EUROPE

Railroads go almost everywhere in Europe. Where trains don't go, ferries and buses are integrated with the rail system, usually on the same tickets.

Western Europe: Unless you are touring by bicycle, have a whole lot of money to rent and operate a car, or are traveling with a family or other small group to share the cost of a car, I can't think of a good reason to travel in Western Europe by any means but train.

Americans are more likely to have heard of Japan's "bullet trains," but the pace-setters in fast long-distance rail service are the French Trains à Grande Vitesse ("Very Fast Trains"), known by their acronym as the TGV. The name is appropriate: TGVs operate reliable scheduled services at well over 300 km/h (185 mph). Minimally modified TGV locomotives and cars have been tested with carloads of dignitaries at speeds exceeding 570 km/h (350 mph).

Two types of passenger trains now operate in the Chunnel under the English Channel. Automobiles are carried on special rail cars, while walk-on passengers are carried through the Chunnel on Eurostar trains using TGV technology. The TGV network continues to be extended into neighboring countries. Eurail Passes are valid on the TGV (although not for passage through the Chunnel). Don't miss a chance to try the TGV or other fast Western European trains.

Central and Eastern Europe: I recommend the choice of rail travel even more strongly in Central and Eastern Europe. Central and Eastern European roads are much worse, and the risks of automobile theft and vandalism are much higher, than in Western Europe. A car in most of this region is more hindrance and hazard than help.

Planners in the Second World of Central and Eastern Europe and the former USSR, and centrally planned Third World economies such as China, all made the same decision: railroads are the appropriate technology for long-distance passenger and freight transportation; roads aren't. Railroads and associated industries (e.g., locomotive and passenger-car construction) were accordingly expanded and improved while roads languished in mud.

Long-distance trains in the former Second World are only a bit slower than in the First World, and much faster than Second World buses. Comparable classes of service may be slightly less comfortable than in Western Europe, perhaps more on a par with the oldest Amtrak cars; however, you can usually afford a much higher class, enabling you to travel in greater comfort on the same budget. For the price of a seat on a Western European or other First World train—sometimes much less—you can get a berth in a sleeping car, or even a private compartment, on a Second World train in Central or Eastern Europe or ex-Soviet Asia.

I once paid US$3 for a berth in a first-class compartment on a 12-hour overnight train from Kiev to Moscow. At prices like that, single foreign tourists or couples on ex-Soviet trains routinely bought all four tickets to a sleeping compartment for privacy and security. Prices have risen, but Second World trains are likely to remain a good value.

Railroads are also useful in Second World cities. Quiet, energy-efficient, low-pollution urban underground railways (subway, metro, underground) and electric street railways (streetcars, trolleys, trams) were the Second World's chosen means of urban mass transportation. At the time of the breakup of the USSR, 88 percent of urban passenger trips in the USSR were by public transport, compared to 19 percent in the U.K. and 3 percent in the United States, putting Eastern and Central Europe in the enviable position (one that is now, unfortunately, being lost) of not being dependent upon the automobile.

ASIA

There is no clear geographic break between Europe and Asia—only in culture are they really two continents rather than one—and there are many routes across Eastern Europe and into Asia. But only two through routes cross the center of Eurasia, both of which require advance planning for visas to Russia.

The Trans-Siberian Railway and Its Branches: The most famous transcontinental train is, of course, the Trans-Siberian Railway. Since the 1991 opening of the city of Vladivostok it's been possible, as it hadn't been for 50 years before that, for foreigners to travel the full length of the Trans-Siberian between European Russia, Siberia, and the Russian Far East.

Some cities have little to recommend them but the allure of the formerly forbidden. Vladivostok is another story. It's a natural sister city to San Francisco, the other most-European city of the Pacific Rim, with splendid prerevolutionary Victorian architecture. It includes the Trans-Siberian terminus, itself a monument to the czars' manifest destiny to extend their rule to the Pacific. All this in a spectacular setting on steep hills overlooking the narrow mouth of the Golden Horn Bay.

In the early 1990s, Vladivostok was transformed from a military city closed even to Soviet citizens without special permits to a "Wild East" free port and center of smuggling and black-market trade. There are now direct international flights to Vladivostok, most popularly via Seoul, permitting air travel to or from the United States and other countries without having to go through European Russia.

The "Russia," train #1 (westbound) and #2 (eastbound), is the train usually known outside the former USSR as the "Trans-Siberian Express." These through Vladivostok–Moscow expresses (seven days and nights' journey time, if you don't stop over anywhere along the way) operate daily in both directions. Many other expresses and local trains operate on shorter sections of the route, which is double-tracked and electrified for its entire 9,200 km (5,700 miles).

There are also branches from the middle of the Trans-Siberian south through Mongolia and Manchuria to Beijing. Fares on these branches are much higher, and service less frequent, than on the Russian main line. Only one Moscow–Beijing train each week operates over the respective Trans-Mongolian and Trans-Manchurian branches, making it almost impossible to get reservations on short notice, especially in the summer.

The longest continuous through train in the world is the weekly train on the least-known branch from the Trans-Siberian. Diverging from the main line less than 100 km (60 miles) north of Vladivostok, it continues for another day and a half into the Democratic People's Republic of Korea (DPRK), or North Korea, for which, I regret to say, U.S. citizens are generally not being given visas. Russia and the DPRK have a land border along the coast so short that it shows on only the most detailed maps. If you leave Moscow on day one, and the train is on time, you arrive in Pyongyang, North Korea, on day nine. It's truly the end of the line.

I've enjoyed several three-to-four-day train trips across both the United States and China. The diversity of scenery kept me enthralled each time, and I rarely felt the need to open a book or leave the window. The Trans-Siberian Railway is a longer route through less diverse scenery. Russian and other ex-Soviet railways were engineered for freight, and Russian and ex-Soviet passenger trains still move at speeds set by freight. Bring plenty of books and diversions for the long ride.

The Central Asian Rail Route: Fewer people have heard of it, and it's more recent—the last rails on the Northern Xinjiang Railway were only laid in 1990, and passenger service began in 1991—but there is now a more diverse and scenic through rail route all the way across Asia. It is well south of the Trans-Siberian, although it's possible to make connections between the two.

Some Chinese literature calls it the "Eurasian Railway," but this new route has no single consistently used name, nor are there yet through passenger trains. You have to change, at a minimum, in Urumchi, East Turkestan (occupied by China as what it calls "Xinjiang Province"), and Almaty, Kazakhstan. From Almaty there are connections on the Turkestan-Siberian (Turksib) Railway north to the Trans-Siberian mainline at Novosibirsk, and southwest to Tashkent, Uzbekistan, and thence to Samarkand, Bukhara, and on to European Russia. In the other direction from Urumchi there are direct trains east to Beijing and Shanghai or southwest to Kashgar, as well as connections to the entire Chinese rail network.

As with the Trans-Siberian, this is a route to take only if you are interested in and have appropriate visas for some of the intermediate stops. Some of the visas required for U.S. citizens and most other nationalities cannot be arranged on arrival or at the borders. If you are just trying to get from eastern China to Europe, it makes more sense to fly.

NORTH AMERICA

North America is the next best region for transcontinental train travel. Until World War II the United States had by far the world's largest passenger rail system. So dense was the U.S. rail network that you could get from New York to Chicago entirely by electric streetcars and interurban railways. American trains declined steadily after World War II until the creation of the National Railroad Passenger Corporation (Amtrak) in 1971. Since nationalization, service on U.S. railroads has steadily improved, with almost all Amtrak passenger cars being replaced or completely refurbished to modern (if not, by world standards, contemporary) standards.

Most Amtrak trains run at capacity, and one of Amtrak's biggest problems is getting funds to buy enough rolling stock (cars and locomotives) to handle peak-season demand. Amtrak's future depends on whether the U.S. government will offer a more secure source of long-term funding or anything comparable to the U.S. government subsidies for air, road, and barge transportation.

Canadian trains were similarly but more recently nationalized as VIA Rail Canada. Despite drastic cutbacks in the extent and frequency of operations, Canadian train services remain first-rate and a justifiable point of national pride.

Speeds of trains in the United States and Canada lag behind Western European averages but usually exceed those of cars or buses, particularly on longer routes. Prices for sleeping car accommodations typically exceed airfares, but North American long-distance coach or economy (chair-car) accommodations are designed for overnight and multiday journeys. They have more spacious and comfortable seating than business class on an airplane, at prices often less than those of buses. It's sad that so many foreign visitors and locals alike overlook the opportunity to ride the railroads of North America. There is simply no comparison between the view from a train and the view from a highway, or the fast-food restaurants where buses stop versus the dining-car food on the railroad. There's no better or easier way to see the scenery of the continent than by train.

Amtrak and VIA Rail don't go everywhere, but feeder buses, with coordinated schedules and guaranteed connections, greatly extend their networks. Major tourist destinations, such as Yosemite and Grand Canyon National Parks, are linked to the rails by Amtrak buses and are included in Amtrak ticketing and passes.

Limited routes do mean that touring North America by train is likely to require careful planning. For example, there are surprisingly few connections between the U.S. and Canadian rail systems, and no north–south routes in the United States between those along the Mississippi River and along the West Coast. Get timetables and route maps in advance, and start studying them early.

AFRICA

No rail line, or even road, in any North American or European sense of the word, crosses Africa from south to north or west to east.

East–West: Operations on the Benguela Railway, which used to provide connections between the Atlantic coast and Zambia, eventually linking to Dar es Salaam on the Indian Ocean, by way of Angola and southern Congo, were interrupted in the 1990s by the fighting in Angola. Even if local service resumes, it seems unlikely foreigners will be permitted to travel through that part of Angola anytime soon due to the millions of land mines left buried along the road and railway.

North–South: You can cover most of the distance across the the Sahara by rail from Alexandria through Egypt and Sudan, but you have to transfer to a combination of buses and/or boats (along the Nile) to cover major gaps before you can get back on the rails in Kenya. One friend recently traveled roughly this route by bus on a research trip; after hearing his stories, I wouldn't recommend it to tourists unless the situation in southern Sudan stabilizes.

Between eastern and southern Africa, there is a single almost-continuous north–south rail route from Kenya to Zimbabwe, by way of Tanzania and Zambia. The key link in this route is the TAZARA Railway, built with Chinese aid to provide the front-line southern African states with an alternative to dependence on South African ports. Now that it has lost that raison d'être, service on the TAZARA (never known for comfort or speed) has declined even more.

Railroads in Botswana and Namibia are still linked to this system, but international service that used to connect Zimbabwe to the still-functioning South Africa railways has been discontinued, necessitating yet another bus connection.

SOUTH AMERICA

South and west of the Amazon, South America had at one time an unusually well-connected network of railroads. As in North America, the railroads have suffered from the diversion of wealthier passengers to planes, private cars, and even buses. Passenger service on most lines, including almost all international and trans-Andean routes, has been discontinued. Services on many of the remaining routes are infrequent or erratic, sometimes limited to certain seasons, one train a week, or only unscheduled special trains for tour groups. As in North America, the ecological advantages of railroads will probably in time be rediscovered. But in the near future, possibilities for South American rail travel are quite limited.

AUSTRALIA

There is rail service across Australia both from north to south (Darwin–Alice Springs–Adelaide) and east to west (East Coast–Adelaide–Perth), for prices comparable to flying. The transcontinental trains run only a couple of times a week in each direction, and you still need a car to get to many of the attractions of the interior. Most independent travelers take the train only between Adelaide and Perth, if at all, and take buses elsewhere. The Australian government can't figure out why, because trains are potentially more useful in the more densely populated eastern and southeastern part of the country.

Most people who want to see the whole country end up taking at least a few planes, or renting or buying a car. Flights within Australia are often cheaper when purchased in conjunction with your international ticket, before you leave for Australia. Minimal advance planning of your inter-Australian itinerary, before you leave home, can save you a substantial amount of money.

Rail Travel Within Countries and Regions

Even if you aren't crossing a continent, there are many countries and regions within which trains are your best long-distance transportation choice.

ASIA

Trains are the primary means of long-distance passenger transportation in all the largest countries of Asia.

China and India: Railroads in much of the Third World have to import locomotives, signals, and other significant parts from Europe (or the United States: much of the rolling stock taken out of service in the United States remains in use by Third World countries that bought it). Railroads take a lot of capital and tend to receive low priority in the allocation of scarce hard currency for economic development. India and China, however, have developed the capability to produce everything their railroads need, including locomotives. This is not surprising, as both countries also produce atomic bombs, satellites and launchers, and intermediate-range missiles.

India and China continue to build new rail lines, electrify existing ones, and increase speeds and capacity, unlike countries where whatever the colonialists left behind is gradually rusting away, despite the best efforts to patch it up and keep it running.

Railroads already go pretty much everywhere within India, while China continues to extend its railways to the farthest borders of its rule. In 2000, China opened a US$700 million new rail line to Kashgar, the center of East Turkestan's resistance to Chinese rule, 1,000 km (620 miles) of almost uninhabitable desert beyond the previous railhead at Urumchi. In 2006, passenger service began on a new billion-dollar rail line from China proper to Tibet, in cars partially pressurized on account of the altitude. For what it's worth, as of 2011 the fastest rail service in the world is the 430 km/h (265 mph), 30-km (19-mile) "maglev" train between central Shanghai and Pudong Airport.

It's worth noting that there is no railroad or road *between* India and China, or between South Asia (India and the "Subcontinent") and Southeast Asia. With rare exceptions (the most important of which are the Karakoram Highway through Pakistan and the rail links between China and Vietnam), travelers between India, China, and Southeast Asia have to fly at least part of the way. Land transit of Myanmar/Burma is strictly forbidden, road transit of Laos is arduous and of Cambodia dangerous, and the border between Tibet and Nepal opens and closes unpredictably, at the whim of the Chinese authorities.

Malaysia and Thailand: Two linked small and excellent national railroads frequently used by foreign travelers are those of Malaysia and Thailand. It costs about US$100 to go the 1,500-km (930-mile) length of the Malay Peninsula in an air-conditioned sleeper, depending on which route and trains you take, and how often and where you stop. Although expensive by Third World standards, the service is worth every penny. The equipment, on most lines in both countries, is clean, comfortable, and well maintained.

There are railroad tracks on the mile-long causeway between Johore Bahru, Malaysia (often referred to as JB), and Singapore, so one could technically include Singapore with the Thai and Malaysian railways. But prices for through train tickets to or from Singapore are almost 50 percent higher than those to or from Johore Bahru. For that matter, just about everything is cheaper in Malaysia than in Singapore. That's why downtown JB is dominated by malls catering to transborder shoppers. So spend a dollar or two on the bus between central Singapore and JB, and get on or off the train in Malaysia. The new JB train station is about 400 meters (0.25 miles) from the bus stop for customs and immigration at the Malaysian end of the causeway.

Japan: Japan's railways are best known for the Shinkansen, or bullet trains, that signaled Japan's post–World War II return to world technological and industrial leadership. In 1964, the bullet trains began running start-to-stop scheduled service at 125 km/h (80 mph). Since then, the trains' speeds have doubled, although they have now been surpassed by the French TGV. Even the original, 30-year-old Shinkansen technology still compares favorably with almost any train outside Western Europe.

The larger engineering miracle is simply the existence of a truly national Japanese rail network: linking all the main Japanese islands by rail has involved the construction of the world's longest tunnel—53 km (33 miles) under a deepwater ocean shipping channel in an active earthquake fault zone—and some of the longest bridges over deepwater channels.

Even the slowest Japanese trains aren't cheap, with highway buses costing about as much as the slowest local trains. Faster trains with fewer stops have progressively higher supplemental charges. Shinkansen fares are only slightly cheaper than domestic airfares, although if you include the time and expense of getting to the airport, the Shinkansen has a bigger edge, being somewhat cheaper, much easier, and almost as fast for all but the longest journeys. Traffic makes buses far slower and less reliable than trains, and everything about automobile travel in Japan—car rental, gasoline, parking, repairs, and tolls for roads, bridges, and tunnels—is prohibitively expensive. Japan probably has the world's highest density of passenger rail traffic. Most travelers, like most Japanese, travel by train. If you can't afford the trains, you probably can't afford to travel in Japan.

Other Asian Countries: Some other Asian countries within which trains are particularly useful to travelers:

Vietnam: There is basically just one slow single-track narrow-gauge line (with a few short branches), which follows the main tourist route, but the roads and buses are appallingly slow, dangerous, and uncomfortable, so the train is still the best choice if you are traveling along that main line.

Taiwan: It's a small island compared to continental Asia, but it's bigger than you might think, and the most scenic parts are away from the big cities. The train is the best bet for longer distances. A high-speed line the length of the island between Taipei and Kaohsiung based on Japanese Shinkansen technology opened in 2007.

South Korea: Likewise, this is a bigger country than many people think, with an excellent, dense rail network. Massive upgrades to rail and other transport and tourism infrastructures began with the 2002 soccer World Cup and have continued since. A high-speed line using French TGV technology runs the length of the country between Seoul and Pusan.

Indonesia: There is a remarkably good, insanely cheap rail system throughout the island of Java, although almost none anywhere else in the archipelago.

Pakistan: Trains are safer than buses, although Pakistan's railroads cover less of the country than India's railroads.

Turkey: There are trains between Europe and Turkey (I took the overnight between Istanbul, Turkey, and Thessaloniki, Greece, on my last trip), but few think to take trains within Turkey. Distances in Turkey are long, and trains are more comfortable than buses, especially on routes where sleeping cars are available. Even in a sleeping berth, the best trains are cheaper than buses. On some routes trains are slower than buses, but as of 2011, parts of the Istanbul–Ankara line had already been upgraded to high-speed operation at 250km/h (150 mph) with new track and rolling stock.

Myanmar/Burma: The trains are bad, but the buses are worse. Where there is one, take a train.

Where not to take a train:

Cambodia: Several foreign tourists have been kidnapped from trains, purely for ransom and not for any political reasons. I recommend against tourist travel in Cambodia in general, but if you must go, try to fly.

As for countries without railroads, it is perhaps worth noting, given the frequency with which people tell me they plan to travel to Nepal by train, that Nepal is far too mountainous, not to mention poor, for railway construction. You have to take a long, slow, uncomfortable bus on dangerous mountain roads, fly, or walk to get from India to Nepal, or to get anywhere within the country, although I've read there are 50 km (30 miles) of narrow-gauge railroad trackage somewhere in the Nepalese lowlands.

OCEANIA

Australia: The railroads of this continent-country-island are discussed above in the section on transcontinental routes.

Aotearoa/New Zealand: One rail line runs the north–south length of the country, with a ferry connection between the rails of the North and South Islands.

THE AMERICAS

Railroads in the United States and Canada are discussed in the sections above on transcontinental rail routes of North America. Through the end of the 20th century, Mexico still had a functional national passenger rail system, but since then most long-distance services have been discontinued, including those to and from Juárez on the U.S. border (across from El Paso).

There are small, mostly disconnected (but sometimes useful) pieces of railroad in several Central and South American countries, including Peru, Bolivia, and Argentina. Service deteriorates except for special (and specially priced) tourist services, however. Most investment goes toward road-building rather than railroad maintenance. Only Argentina seems to prioritize plans to revive and modernize its once-excellent national passenger rail system, although these have been set back by the economic crisis.

AFRICA

There are limited but useful domestic services in South Africa, although their future is uncertain and they don't reach many parts of the country or operate on some of the most obvious routes. Where they do go, the long-distance services offer excellent comfort and value. (Urban commuter trains in South Africa are another story. These are plagued by crime, some of it violent, and are not recommended for foreign tourists.) In Kenya, there is good overnight sleeping-car service between Nairobi and Mombasa. In addition, there are isolated but very good domestic rail systems in Egypt and Morocco. Two detached and deteriorating but potentially useful rail lines—if service is operating, which has been somewhat intermittent in recent years—run inland from the West African coast to the Sahel between Abidjan (Côte d'Ivoire) and Ouagadougou (Burkina Faso), and between Dakar (Senegal) and Bamako (Mali).

Timetables

Except in First World countries, rail timetables—even in local languages, much less in English—can be hard to find. It is frequently easier to find good local maps than local timetables. Train timings, frequencies, trip durations, and fares in even the best guidebooks are usually much less accurate than those in timetables, even much older ones. Schedules posted online are often outdated and obsolete. I pack the best rail timetables I can find, and I've never regretted their volume or weight in my luggage. Even in the First World, many national railroads have been broken up into separately privatized pieces, making it harder and harder to find comprehensive, integrated timetables.

Don't be intimidated by timetables in a foreign language, such as Spanish or Portuguese in Central and South America, or French or Portuguese in Africa. All you need to be able to understand are the station names, times, and codes for the days of the week (usually 1–7 for Monday–Sunday). On the other hand, a Chinese timetable without pinyin transliterations will do you no good if you can't recognize any of the characters in the place-names. In such circumstances be grateful for any timetable in the Latin alphabet.

"Inquire Locally"

There are some routes you'll never find unless you inquire locally.

On our last trip around the world, we spent six weeks making our way from Lisbon to Rome. We had Eurail Passes and made reservations a day, or a few days, before each leg of the trip. But we also stopped off in some places on impulse — or got on the next local train and moved on earlier than we had planned.

Our railway route map showed — somewhat cryptically — a rail line through the middle of the Pyrénées, between Zaragoza (Spain) and a town in France I'd never heard of called Pau. It looked like part of a logical main route between Madrid and Paris. But we couldn't find it in either the French or Spanish or Eurail timetables, which all showed only slow trains between Spain and France around the Pyrénées, along the coast through Barcelona or Bilbao. Even at the station in Bilbao, the ticket agents assured us there was no train between Zaragoza and Pau. Which were we to believe: the staff, website, and printed timetables of the national railway, or our map?

In Zaragoza itself, we asked again, and discovered that there was indeed such a rail line, although part of it had been "temporarily" out of service since a viaduct was damaged by a freight train whose brakes failed in 1970, and we would have to change to a bus — included in the rail fare or, for us, our Eurail Passes — over the pass between Canfranc and Oloron, instead of going through the Somport Rail Tunnel (currently being used as a scientific laboratory, and not to be confused with the newer, separate Somport Highway Tunnel). The extra transfers from train to bus to train were apparently why the through trans-Pyrénéen service didn't show up in any timetable or online route planner. On the Spanish side, between Zaragoza and the tunnel, the line passes through Huesca and its environs, an area perhaps best known abroad as the scene of the Spanish Civil War fighting in the 1930s which was participated in and recounted by George Orwell in *Homage to Catalonia*.

We liked Pau and we liked the trip through the Pyrénées. Along the way, the former border station at the Spanish end of the tunnel is a tourist attraction in its own right, even in its dereliction, and slated to be restored as a luxury hotel. This was once, and may someday be again if grassroots activists on both sides of the border are successful, the main line between Spain and France.

Just as our map suggested. But you can never count on that.

Treat all published timetables, especially those published other than by the railroads themselves, as no more than suggestions. These tables contain many sometimes glaring errors, and all schedules can change overnight.

Building a railroad takes a while, so you are unlikely to happen upon an entirely new major route, except in China. You may find more or fewer trains, though. Allow room in your plans for the possibility that a daily service has been cut back to weekly, a weekly service changed to a different day of the week, a night train changed to a day train, or vice versa.

Beware of train timetables posted on the Internet. If the site provides on-line reservations, the schedule is probably reasonably accurate (albeit subject to change between when you buy your ticket and when you plan to travel). Otherwise, the information was probably taken from a printed timetable collected by or sent to the webmaster, or from notes someone took at a station—possibly long ago, or badly translated. Treat any timetable that doesn't specify its date and source with extreme skepticism. I've seen schedules at least 10 years out of date posted on otherwise authoritative-looking websites.

Even if you have reservations and tickets, always check the schedule of your next train locally, as soon as you get to the departure point. The most current, but still not guaranteed, schedule is usually posted in the station. If the lines aren't too long, try to confirm the posted schedule with the local railway staff as well.

Outside Western Europe and Japan, allow substantial time for any train to be late. If the journey is scheduled to take more than a day, or operates less often than daily, allow at least a day for delays en route. Better to be pleasantly surprised by an on-time arrival at your destination than to have your plans frustrated by counting on it.

NORTH AMERICA

Amtrak and VIA Rail Canada (see the *Transportation* section of the *Resource Guide*) publish similar complete national timetables for the United States and Canada, respectively, which you can download from their websites. These are also supposed to be available at all staffed Amtrak and VIA Rail stations (some stations are actually unattended flag stops), but they are often out of stock. Be sure to request a fare and pass guide at the same time, as the timetables have no information on fares. You can get schedules and fares for specific routes from the Amtrak or VIA Rail websites, but for overall planning the printed timetables are much more useful.

Whether or not you bring timetables with you to North America, it's worth looking at them in advance to get an idea of the routes. Routes are somewhat limited, requiring fairly careful itinerary planning if this is to be your primary means of exploring the continent, and travel times, like the

Surface Transportation

distances, are long by European standards. The frequencies of the transcontinental United States and Canadian trains are particularly susceptible to change, and whether they operate twice a week or daily can be critical to the availability of summer seats and sleeping compartments.

WESTERN EUROPE

Eurail Pass buyers are given the best English-language timetable, summarizing express trains between major cities, for Western European train travel. Even if you don't get a Eurail Pass, try to find someone to give you a copy of the timetable. Main-line European train schedules change surprisingly rarely, so even a two-year-old schedule can be valuable.

Complete Western European timetables are available only from private publishers; they are too big, heavy, detailed, and expensive for the needs of ordinary travelers. Locally available free European timetables are usually produced by national tourist boards or national railways, and are limited to single countries or at most regions, such as Scandinavia or Benelux. You'll need a thick pile of these if you're crossing borders often, and it may be difficult to figure out routes and times of through international trains between regions (for which the Eurail Pass timetable is best). Up to 85–90 percent of European rail travel is domestic, so there's been little motivation for the development of good planning, booking, or ticketing tools for international rail journeys. See the sidebar *Tips for Train Travel in Europe* for some coping strategies.

REAL LIFE

In 1992 I held in my hands a copy of the last edition of the Soviet national railway timetable. It was the size of a telephone directory, in Russian only, and for the eyes of railroad employees only. Those who showed it to me refused all my entreaties and proffered bribes. I think they would have given it to me, maybe even for free, if they hadn't feared that doing so would cost them their jobs. So far as I can tell, nothing like it has been published since.

EASTERN EUROPE AND THE FORMER USSR

The USSR had the world's largest rail system, and Russia's remains among the world's three largest, along with those of India and China. It's hard for foreigners to navigate, however, because there's no comprehensive printed timetable in any language and the schedule information on the Russian railways' official website is in Russian only. Some Russian travel agencies provide rail schedule information for tourists in English or other languages. It's not always accurate and any prices include their markup.

Railroads in Central Europe used to base their operations on Soviet models but have been becoming much more "Westernized." Printed timetables are now available locally in most Central European countries. As of 2007, Romania, Hungary, and, of course, the former East Germany have even joined the Eurail Pass program, and their mainline trains are included in the Eurail Pass schedules.

ASIA

Because there are few international trains in Asia, most of your train travel in Asia is likely to be within countries. And because these countries are mostly much larger than European countries, using separate timetables in different countries is less likely to be an inconvenience. The following are some suggestions for the Asian countries with the largest rail systems, except for the former USSR.

Note: I've included the former USSR above with Eastern Europe for conventional and cultural reasons, though geographically it's mostly in Asia.

Japan: As in the U.K. and Australia, Japanese railways have been privatized and broken up into competing regional fragments. Most printed information is published by individual companies, making it hard to figure out which company operates a given route. Printed national timetables for Japanese trains are available only in Japanese, so far as I can tell. The Japan National Tourist Organization (JNTO) has an excellent English-language guide to the rail system on their website (www.jnto.go.jp). Both the JNTO and Hyperdia.com (apparently a technology demonstration project of Hitachi) offer English-language online rail fare and schedule search tools.

India: There are two privately published English-language timetables of Indian trains. *Trains at a Glance* is a compact but still quite detailed summary of mainline expresses, which are the only trains most foreigners ever take. *Newman's Indian Bradshaw* is a book listing every train in India. It's sold at newsstands on railway platforms in major cities. Oddly, it is not available at ticket offices, even those for foreigners.

Neither of these books is readily available anywhere outside India. Indian government tourist offices have little information on train routes, schedules, or fares, except for the Palace on Wheels, an ultraluxury chartered train of former private cars of the maharajas that costs a minimum of almost US$300 per person per night in a double compartment. Online fare and schedule tools are difficult to navigate without understanding train classes, accommodations types, and which trains operate between multiple stations in a given pair of cities. If you are planning far enough ahead, ask an Indian friend who's going home for a visit to bring you back a recent copy of *Trains at a Glance*. Some schedules are seasonal, but Indian railway services aren't changing nearly as fast as those in China. Any copy from within the last couple of years should be adequate for planning purposes.

China: Foreign-language train timetables are hard to find within China. The rapid pace of railroad improvement and construction of new rail lines in China makes most foreign publications based on second-hand information obsolete. The most up-to-date English-language timetables are privately produced by Duncan Peattie and are available at www.chinatt.org. The summary timetable of the fastest trains between the largest cities is free, while the comprehensive national timetable is available as a paid PDF download or a printed book. It's essential for any independent traveler in China, although it would be better if it were fully bilingual instead of having most listings only in English.

If you can't read Chinese or speak Mandarin, equip yourself with a good bilingual map showing railroads. Like a bilingual timetable, it's a tool for communicating with ticket clerks and train attendants. You point at the English and they read the corresponding Chinese. And vice versa. Because one of the great accomplishments of communism in China has been the achievement of near-universal literacy, this is a surprisingly effective, if limited, means of communication.

AFRICA

Printed timetables are hard to come by anywhere in Africa, and accurate online timetables are hard to find except for South Africa. In much of Africa, schedules are sufficiently elastic that timetables are of limited usefulness, but anything is better than no schedule at all, at least in giving you a vague idea of where trains might exist and the approximate frequency of trains on particular routes.

CENTRAL AND SOUTH AMERICA

Chances of finding timetables are a bit better in South America than in Africa, although where they exist they are likely to be limited to single countries or routes.

AUSTRALIA

The Rail Australia marketing consortium has links on their website to timetables for all long-distance trains. Since the actual timetables are provided by the individual railroads, the formats vary considerably and somewhat confusingly, and should be read with care. Within Australia, there's no single office where you can make reservations or buy tickets for trains throughout the country. (I was quoted wildly inaccurate prices at the train stations in Sydney and Melbourne when I inquired about prices for trains departing from Adelaide or from Alice Springs.) Only the operating railroad for the specific train has correct information about current fares and discounts.

Passes, Tickets, and Reservations

The most important thing to find out about the trains you intend to take is whether you need to make reservations or buy tickets in advance, either to get seats on the schedule you want or to get a better price. Except within Europe, there is no standard format for train tickets, and unlike airline tickets there is no international payment clearinghouse to permit an agent in any country to issue tickets for travel in any other. Most train reservations and tickets are best obtained locally (or in a minority of cases, online). But there are some significant exceptions that require advance booking or ticketing, particularly for train travel in Japan, Western Europe, or North America.

If advance reservations or ticketing is not required and if you are unsure of your plans, don't tie up your money or foreclose other options unless you have to. It's worth getting an idea, if you can,

REAL LIFE

In my experience, there is a remarkable worldwide spirit of professionalism among railroad workers. Even in countries where nothing else seems to work, they take pride in doing their jobs well. Let them help you. They know the schedules better than you or I ever will. If the ticket clerk says, "There is a better train to where you want to go," they are probably right.

how much tickets for the trains you want to take are likely to cost. But for the Second, Third, and Fourth Worlds it's almost always easier and cheaper to make reservations and buy tickets locally. Arranging reservations and/or tickets in advance for Second, Third, or Fourth World train travel generally means paying an agent in your country to pay an agent in the destination country to send a person down to the local booking office or station in the city from which the train will depart to make reservations and buy you a ticket.

The countries where it is most difficult and expensive to do this tend to be the poorest countries or those where the currency has collapsed. Not coincidentally, this is also where tickets bought locally are likely to be cheapest. Communications, funds transfer, and other transaction costs (not to mention the agent's time) are likely to be expensive in relation to the ticket price. It wouldn't be unreasonable for an agent to charge US$50 or more to have a US$5 ticket waiting for you. Unless you are on a rushed and critical schedule, or you want to take a train that is likely to be sold out weeks in advance, that's not worth it.

First World rail travel is another story. All of the First World countries in which you are most likely to travel by train have special passes or fares for foreign visitors. These are often cheaper than tickets purchased locally. An unlimited travel pass may cost only a fraction of what you would pay locally for separate tickets, and it is often less restrictive. The common feature of these passes is that they can only be purchased outside the country in which they are to be used, so you have to decide in advance whether you will want them. The Canrailpass and the USA Rail Pass are exceptions; either can be purchased on arrival. But advance reservations (available through the Amtrak and VIA Rail websites, by phone or email, or through local agents in some countries overseas) are strongly recommended for travel on Amtrak or VIA Rail Canada, especially for sleeping car, peak-season, or transcontinental travel.

You can often buy a rail pass even before you know your exact route, although the better sense you have of your plans, the better you can judge which pass or ticket will be best for your trip. You also need to make a realistic assessment of the degree of uncertainty in your plans: if they are likely to change, getting cheaper fixed-route tickets, rather than a somewhat more expensive but flexible pass, may be a false economy.

RAIL PASSES

Of the passes described below, all except the highest classes of Indian ("Indrail") rail passes are for coach or economy (chair-car) service. With any of the other passes, upgrades to various categories of "couchettes," berths, and private compartments may be available at additional, per-night charges. If you expect to travel in sleeping cars, be sure to check before you buy a pass how much extra this will cost.

In some countries there are supplements or surcharges in addition to the basic fare for travel on faster or more luxurious trains. Check whether the pass you are considering covers these.

Also check whether all trains have cars (coaches) of the class for which you are buying a pass. You can't use a second-class pass on a train that has only first-class cars. You can't use a chair-car pass, without paying sleeping car charges, on a train that has only sleepers and no chair cars.

> ### REAL LIFE
>
> I once wanted to take four overnight trains in little more than a week during Diwali, a big Indian holiday. All the trains I wanted were sold out. What to do? "Buy an Indrail Pass," I was told. I did, and space materialized on every train. I didn't have to take any time out of the couple of days I spent at each stopover to arrange onward reservations; it had been taken care of all at once back in Mumbai. I simply went down to the train stations in Ahmedabad, Abu Road, and Jaipur at the appointed hours, and there was my name on a berth-assignment list by the door of the car when the train pulled in. Quite a testament for those who think nothing works in India.

EUROPEAN RAIL PASSES AND TICKETS

The best-known of all rail passes is the Eurail Pass. There is actually no one Eurail Pass or single price. Instead, there is a confusing multiplicity of Eurail Passes at widely varying prices.

The most expensive Eurail Passes allow unlimited travel for a certain period of time by train and certain buses and ferries, such as those between Ireland and France and between Brindisi, Italy, and Patras, Greece. Note that they do not include any trains or ferries to or from the United Kingdom. Eurail Passes may be used for unlimited travel within a specified validity period within Western Europe excluding the U.K., the Chunnel, and Turkey.

Some but not all Central European countries have joined the Eurail Pass program. Some (but not all) of these participate in a separate "European East Pass." Rail ticket prices in most of these countries remain low, however. As of 2011, point-to-point tickets, purchased locally, usually remain cheaper than these passes. There are as yet no passes for rail travel in Russia or Ukraine.

> ## REAL LIFE
>
> You can often find clerks in smaller European cities or suburbs who are less busy, equally competent, less jaded by tourists, and thus more helpful than those at the biggest stations or downtown ticket offices most crowded with foreigners.

For those traveling more slowly, there are Eurail Flexipasses. If you aren't on a train every day, these are usually a better deal than the continuous-travel Eurail Passes. Flexipasses allow varying numbers of days of travel within a longer validity period. The Flexipass expires either when all the travel days have been used or the overall validity period expires, whichever comes first.

Both unlimited Eurail Passes and Eurail Flexipasses are available at different prices for travel in first and second class; for adults, youth, and children; and for groups of as few as two or three people traveling together. Prices and rules of some categories vary between peak season (April–Sept.) and off-season (the rest of the year). Pass rates are adjusted at the start of each Christian calendar year. Check approximate prices early in your planning. Eurail Passes are an excellent deal, but still cost more than many Americans expect.

There are a variety of other Eurail Passes for specific countries and regions, as well as passes combining various numbers of days of train travel and car rental. It is also possible to mix and match combinations of specified numbers of countries from certain groups. (See the *Transportation* section of the *Resource Guide* for sources of detailed Eurail Pass information and pass selection advice.)

Tips for Train Travel in Europe

European Railway Route Maps

For now, most timetables and schedules are oriented toward point-to-point trains. Connection information, especially if you're crossing borders or need to change trains more than once, is spotty at best. The best way to figure out for yourself which are likely to be the best routes and connections is to study one of the specialized maps that not only show the rail lines but clearly distinguish high-speed lines, normal-speed main lines (which in European usage can mean up to about 200 km/h or 125 mph), and slower branch lines. The network of high-speed service is expanding rapidly throughout Europe, so make sure you get an up-to-date map. Omni Resources (Omnimap.com) and other map dealers stock several such maps, including those from ITMB. The laminated Streetwise map, the map given out with Eurail Passes, and Rick Steves's Europe map are too small and selective in which places they show. If you can find it, my favorite for its combination of legibility and detail has been the Kümmerly + Frey rail map of Europe, available from Stanford's.

Continental European Rail Timetables

It's getting harder and harder to find printed timetables at all, and when you do find them, they generally only cover routes within the country you are in, or at most a few international trains to and from that country. The best summary of express services between major cities in Europe, including through international trains, is distributed free to each Eurail Pass purchaser (but, annoyingly, isn't available for purchase at any price). You're short-changing yourself, though, if you only visit the biggest cities.

National railroads' websites have the same problems as their printed timetables. Better for international connections, although far from perfect and often showing only more expensive fares, is the point-to-point timetable services from RailEurope.com. A recent trip from Geneva to London was typical: Only one website came up with the best route (with same-station connections in Lyon and Lille), and only after I went through a long list of slower and/or less convenient routes. That site, however, was entirely unable to price the journey. Rail Europe was able to calculate prices, but could only suggest slower (in total journey time) and more awkward routes with a tedious transfer by RER (commuter train) between the Gare de Lyon and the Gare du Nord in Paris.

Pricing and Tickets

Point-to-point train tickets for simple domestic trips within any single country are usually cheapest from the railroad's own website. For trips with stopovers, especially multistop one-way international journeys at through fares, you may need to go to a ticket office in Europe in person. Point-to-point tickets purchased through agents in the United States or elsewhere outside Europe, whether online or in person, are usually more expensive. Price point-to-point tickets for your intended journey (or the one you think is most likely) before buying a pass, so you'll know how much of a premium you are paying for the extra flexibility of a pass. Remember to include the cost of required reservations, sleeping berth surcharges, and supplements for high-speed trains in your calculations of the total cost of both point-to-point and pass ticketing.

Continental European Rail Reservations

If you already have a ticket (most likely because you have a Eurail Pass), and just need reservations, it's generally easier and the same price (or cheaper) to make reservations in person at a train station rather than online. I've almost always found railway clerks at smaller stations, in the suburbs or in the provinces, more willing to take the time to help me, and to put up with my inability (or limited ability) to speak their language, than those at main stations in big cities. Even with a pass and even in low season, try to make your reservations at least a couple of days in advance, as the number of seats on the fastest trains allocated for pass holders is limited. In peak season or around holidays, especially for high-speed trains or berths in sleeping cars, you may need to book further in advance (although a couple of weeks is usually sufficient for the best price on almost any trains except the Eurostar).

British Rail Timetables and Tickets

The privatization and breakup of British Rail have recreated the situation that existed decades ago before nationalization, with multiple railways competing between the same cities. The U.K. National Rail Enquiries website (www.nationalrail.co.uk) will tell you which railway companies operate between any two towns or cities in Britain, and link you to the railways' own websites to make reservations and purchase tickets. Tickets are either electronic or can be picked up at the station on departure. (Be sure to leave extra time in case you have to stand in line at the ticket collection window: Many ticket-collection kiosks only read credit cards with "chip and PIN" authentication. Cards issued in the United States, which don't contain a compatible chip, are accepted for payment but have to be processed manually by a ticket agent.) Last-minute walk-up fares can

(continues on next page)

Surface Transportation

Tips for Train Travel in Europe *(continued)*

be 10 times the lowest advance-purchase fares. Nowhere else in Europe is it as important as it is in Britain to fix your rail itinerary and purchase your tickets at least a couple of weeks in advance, even in low season. For typical itineraries, BritRail Passes are reasonably priced compared to full fare, but outrageously expensive compared to the cheapest advance-purchase prices.

Channel Tunnel Trains (Eurostar)

No rail pass includes the Eurostar trains through the Channel Tunnel between England and France or Belgium. But if you are also buying a Eurail or BritRail Pass, you can buy a Eurostar ticket from the same place you bought your pass, at a pass-holder price that's less than the full Eurostar fare. Most other Eurostar discounts (including some sale fares that are cheaper than the pass-holder prices) are available only on the Eurostar.com website, just like "Web fares" for flights that are available only from the airlines' own websites. You can pick up your tickets from a check-in kiosk (or, if your card was issued in the United States and doesn't have a chip, at the ticket window) when you get to the station, so there's no need to pay for ticket delivery. The difference between the cheapest tickets and the full fare is substantial, and the cheapest tickets sometimes sell out weeks in advance, but the cheapest tickets are also nonchangeable. How certain are you that your plans won't change?

Within the U.K., a similar range of pass options is offered under the BritRail Pass scheme. These include passes for travel throughout the U.K., for various regions, and for combinations of U.K. rail travel with ferries to and from the Irish Republic, rail travel in Ireland, and/or car rental.

Neither Eurail nor BritRail Passes are valid for any means of transport between the U.K. and the Continent, across or beneath the English Channel. Special fares are available on Eurostar services in conjunction with BritRail or Eurail Passes. Eurostar prices for pass holders are less than the unrestricted fares, but restricted nonchangeable advance-purchase tickets are often cheaper still. The best deals are usually on the Eurostar.com website.

Eurostar trains carry passengers only. There are separate trains for transporting automobiles through the Chunnel, although they are more likely to be useful to Europeans than to overseas visitors. Unless you have a car on a long-term lease, it's not likely to be worth the expense to take a rental car across the channel by train or ferry.

Surface Transportation

All but the most expensive Eurostar tickets (which are more expensive than flying) and the special Eurostar fares for pass holders have fixed dates and change penalties that make them inappropriate for travelers without set schedules. Buy tickets only once you are sure of your dates. By comparison, there are so many channel ferries that finding space, especially for walk-ons or bicycles as opposed to cars, is scarcely ever a problem.

All Eurail Passes and BritRail Passes must be used within six months of being issued.

Eurail Passes and BritRail Passes are sold only outside Europe. Eurail. com, BritRail.com, and possibly some other vendors will ship them to you in Europe (or anywhere else) if you have a non-European passport with no indication of residency in Europe.

By now you should have gotten the message that there is no simple answer to the frequently asked question, "How much does a Eurail Pass or BritRail Pass cost?" Fortunately, various agencies and websites that sell these passes (see the *Resource Guide* for details) publish annual summaries of pass options and prices.

Adding up point-to-point fares in Western Europe may lead you immediately to conclude that some form of pass will be cheaper for any multistop long-distance rail journey. This isn't always so. A little-known fact is that full-fare one-way point-to-point tickets within Western Europe (and in some other places) allow unlimited stopovers within certain route restrictions. If you plan a continuous, more or less direct one-way journey across Europe, in whatever direction, a one-way ticket between your starting and ending points may permit all or most of the stops you want for less than the price of a pass. Try to find a ticket agent who will price out such a through-fare option for you before buying a whole series of separate one-way tickets.

Most Western European trains require advance reservations, for which, even if you have a Eurail Pass, you have to pay a nominal fee. Most European services are frequent, and it's usually sufficient to reserve seats a day or two in advance for off-season travel. For holidays or other busy times, or if you want sleeping berths, allow more time. Holiday trains in Europe, like holiday flights in the United States, can be fully booked months in advance.

Unless you are extremely short on time or trying to cover many destinations very quickly, it's probably an unnecessary extra hassle to make reservations before you get to Europe. In marked contrast to the situation in most of the world, you can make reservations at any Western European train station or ticket office for trains throughout the region, even for trains leaving from other countries. So it often saves time and effort to book several legs of your trip at a time, particularly if you are spending only a few days in each city.

Surface Transportation

JAPAN RAIL PASSES

Like point-to-point tickets on Japanese trains, Japan Rail Passes seem expensive but offer good value for the money. Prices are fixed in yen, unlike Eurail and other passes with fixed foreign-currency prices, so prices in your home currency will fluctuate with the yen.

Japan Rail Passes allow unlimited travel for 7, 14, or 21 days in second-class (ordinary car) or first-class (green car) seating. This includes travel to and from the train stations at all international airports. Ordinary class is more than adequate. The price of a seven-day ordinary-class Japan Rail Pass is comparable to the cost of a roundtrip domestic airfare or Shinkansen (bullet train) fare between Tokyo and Osaka.

Japan Rail Passes cannot be purchased on or after arrival in Japan, and must be used within 90 days of purchase. If you are traveling for a long time before getting to Japan, you may have to buy yours along the way. Passes can be purchased from designated agents in many countries. Check with the Japan National Tourism Office (JNTO) or www.japanrailpass. net for a list of pass agents in your country, or wherever you will be within 90 days before arriving in Japan. Japan Air Lines (JAL) and All Nippon Airways (ANA) sell Japan Rail Passes, but in most cases only to passengers holding JAL or ANA tickets.

AUSTRALIAN RAIL PASSES

Australia is one country where it pays to plan your route ahead and to enlist the help of a specialized travel agent in figuring out which transportation options will be best.

Rail Australia offers several varieties of rail passes, including the nation-wide rail-only Austrail Pass, regional rail-only passes, and combination passes for bus and train travel. The plethora of air, rail, and bus passes for Australian travel, most of which must be purchased outside the country and are valid only on specific routes, make it quite challenging to figure out which variety of passes—if any—are right for you.

It's difficult to make reservations for most specific trains from outside Australia, but it's best to make them as far in advance as possible, or as soon as possible after your arrival. This is especially true for the Adelaide–Perth "Indian Pacific" and the Adelaide–Alice Springs–Darwin "Ghan."

NORTH AMERICAN RAIL PASSES AND SPECIAL FARES

USA Rail Passes: USA Rail Passes are available for 15, 30, or 45 days of travel. Unlike most of the passes discussed in this section, the USA Rail Pass is available at the same price to U.S. citizens, residents, or foreign visitors, and can be purchased even after you arrive in the United States.

Surface Transportation

Amtrak agents outside North America are few and often hard to find, so you may be tempted to wait until you get to the United States. But a pass is useless if no space is available, and the pass-holder quotas on many trains are fully booked days or weeks in advance in peak season. Book as far in advance as you are sure of your plans, and don't buy an Amtrak pass without first making reservations for all the trains you want to take that require them. You can buy a pass and make reservations for specific trains, either at the time of purchase or afterward, by phone, or by email as well as through the limited number of Amtrak agents abroad. See the *Transportation* section of the *Resource Guide*.

If you can't get reservations in advance, don't risk the money on a pass you may not be able to use. Wait and make reservations and buy your pass as soon as you arrive in North America. If space turns out to be available, you can still buy a pass at the same price as if you had bought it abroad.

USA Rail Pass holders must pay a supplement for travel on Acela expresses (the fastest trains on the northeast corridor between Boston, New York City, and Washington, D.C.) or for sleeping compartments or berths. But there are plenty of conventional chair-car trains on the same corridor route, and you may find sleeping-car travel less essential than you had expected. Europeans, in particular, may be pleasantly surprised at the comfort level of North American long-haul chair cars. Most Americans can't afford sleepers. Amtrak and VIA Rail chair cars are about as well designed as possible for multiday rides.

Canrailpasses: The Canrailpass may be bought upon arrival by Canadians and foreign visitors alike. However, it is subject to most of the same caveats as the Amtrak passes: difficulty in finding overseas agents, limited capacity, and the need to make reservations well in advance and before buying tickets. Unlike the USA Rail Pass or most other passes, Canrailpass prices are seasonal: 60 percent higher June 1–October 15 than the rest of the year.

Don't assume that a pass will be the cheapest ticket, especially for a one-way transcontinental journey with stopovers. A Canadian rail journey, even one with stops, is likely to follow a single continuous through route. A full one-way fare allows unlimited stopovers along the way. Full fare (the highest, least restricted, nondiscount price) isn't cheap, but it's usually cheaper than buying separate tickets for each leg of the journey and more economical than one-way plane fare. Good rail tariff agents are even harder to find than good air tariff agents; you'll probably have to go to a train station or VIA Rail ticket office to get a ticket with multiple stopovers.

TRANS-SIBERIAN TICKETS AND RESERVATIONS

I noted earlier that it is rarely necessary or desirable to make reservations for rail travel before leaving home for the Second, Third, or Fourth World. There

Surface Transportation

is an important exception: the two branch lines between the Trans-Siberian Railway and China, one of which passes through Mongolia as well.

The only trains on these routes are the weekly through trains on each branch in each direction between Moscow and Beijing, and a few other trains on the Trans-Mongolian branch that terminate at Ulan Bator and on which one is not allowed without a visitors visa (not just a transit visa) for Mongolia.

The trains to and from China were popular with foreigners who wanted to get a glimpse of Russia. But changes in Russia, and the opening of the full length of the true Trans-Siberian main line to foreigners, have made it unnecessary and indeed more costly to go through China just to ride part of the Trans-Siberian. There are now easier ways to see more of Russia. Many people erroneously think of the branch lines to China as being the Trans-Siberian. But more than 3,500 km (2,200 miles) of the Trans-Siberian main line, including some of the most interesting cities and scenery, lie east of where either of the branches to and from China diverge.

There are no chair cars on the through China trains, only sleeping cars. In the summer, all berths are often booked months ahead. Foreigners need foreign-price tickets, as passports are checked repeatedly, which are higher than for Russian or Chinese domestic trains.

So you have three options: pay an agent in your country a high price to arrange through train tickets between China and Russia well in advance; risk a considerable wait (several weeks, possibly longer) in Beijing or Moscow arranging tickets and transit visas; or jump through the Russian "visa support" hoops to take the Trans-Siberian within Russia. The last option does require a Russian visa, but it's worth it. Even at the prices scalpers charge foreigners, you'll pay less than you would for a ticket to or from China. (However you do it, in either direction, it's likely to cost more than it would to fly between the Pacific Rim and Europe. But the point of a week-long train trip isn't to save money.)

OTHER RAIL PASSES AND TICKETS

Indrail Passes: For foreigners in India, the advantage of an Indrail Pass is not the price but the priority it gives you for otherwise unavailable space on sold-out trains. An Indrail Pass is extremely unlikely to be cheaper than separate tickets.

The Indian railways provide special foreigners' booking offices in Delhi, Mumbai (Bombay), Kolkata (Calcutta), and Chennai (Madras). (The official names for these cities have been changed, but the older names remain recognized and in widespread parallel use.) These offices are comfortable, air-conditioned (when the power is on), and relatively uncrowded—a near-miraculous respite from the norms of Indian bureaucracy and the hubbub and confusion of Indian train stations, which may have literally dozens of different windows for tickets in different classes on different rail lines, and where you may have to wait in half a dozen different queues to find out on which trains space is available, make reservations, pay for tickets, collect your tickets, and reserve and pay for bedding. (Yes, in India you sometimes have to reserve bedding separately, or do without. It's a small additional charge and a large additional nuisance.)

Use the foreigners' booking offices whenever possible. If buying an Indrail Pass is the only way to get space on the trains you want, or that will be best for your desired itinerary, the staff at the foreigners' booking office will tell you so. Take their advice. In my experience, the staff at these offices are efficient, helpful, and knowledgeable. I've never heard of anyone being given bad advice, or asked for a bribe, at any of these offices.

The final reason to use the foreigners' booking offices is that they can arrange reservations even for trains leaving from other cities. Normally, in India (as in China, Russia, and most other countries in the Second, Third, and Fourth Worlds) you can confirm reservations only for journeys originating from wherever you make the reservations. So if you break your journey, you can't make reservations for your next onward leg until you reach each stopover point. The foreigners' booking offices in India provide the exception. Before you leave one of the four cities where they are located, book your trains as far ahead as you know your plans. You'll be spared a great deal of hassle and wasted time in each intermediate city from which you prearrange your departure.

The Indian Airlines "Discover India" Airpass, which is far less of a bargain than the Indrail Pass, can also be purchased by foreign passport holders even within India. So whether you will use a pass or separate tickets, there is no need to commit yourself to either flight or train tickets before you get to India and see what both are like.

The only reason to prepay transportation within India is if domestic flights can be included in your through international tickets for less than the likely price of transportation purchased on arrival.

OTHER SECOND, THIRD, AND FOURTH WORLD RAIL TICKETS

A few other Third World countries offer rail passes, but all the ones I know of can be bought once you are in the various countries. You can decide when you get there if they will be worthwhile or not.

Both Thailand and Malaysia offer passes for unlimited domestic rail travel, but almost no one but rail fans who spend all their time on trains would travel enough within either country in the allotted time to make either pass pay off.

In most of the rest of the Second, Third, and Fourth World you will need to make your reservations and buy train tickets locally, in each place

REAL LIFE

I was once on a 4,000-km (2,500-mile) trip on an express train across China when a man riding hard-seat class pulled the emergency cord, bringing the train to a screeching halt from 100 km/h (60 mph) in the midst of a rice paddy far from even a village, much less any scheduled stop. The conductor and attendants booted him unceremoniously out into the mud. As he threw mud on their starched white uniforms while they yelled at him, one didn't have to understand Mandarin to imagine the peasant's denunciation of the train crew's class prejudice.

you stop, for the next leg of your journey. The easiest time to do so is as soon as you arrive, while you are still at the station, unless, as is not unknown, especially for ticket purchases by foreigners, you have to go to a ticket office at some remove from the station.

Whether or not you buy your onward tickets immediately upon arrival, at least try to do so as far as possible before your intended departure, up to several weeks ahead if you know when you will want to leave. In my experience, you have a much better chance of getting on the trains you want, in the class of service and accommodations you want, if you book each leg at least a few days in advance.

On shorter notice you may have no choice but to pay for a higher class of service or accommodations than you want or need, such as air-conditioning; to travel in a lower class of service than you want, such as sitting up overnight or for several days; or to take a slower train than the one you want.

Truly local trains can be excruciatingly slow in countries where even the fastest expresses may go only 50 km/h (30 mph). Passengers on local trains routinely pull the emergency cord to stop the train wherever they want to get off. Slow trains may only have third-class (or 10th-class) cars; few foreign tourists willingly take such a train more than once.

URBAN MASS-TRANSPORTATION PASSES

Urban passenger rail systems—subways, elevated trains, streetcars, trams, and suburban and commuter trains—are more common in the rest of the world than they are in the United States. Most large world cities, from Beijing to Buenos Aires to Cairo, have some sort of intraurban railroad. (Note that outside the United States the word *subway* is generally used only in its British sense of "pedestrian underpass." What is called a "subway" in the United States—an underground intracity railway—is more often called an "underground" or "metro" in the rest of the world.) You'll find excellent subways/undergrounds/metros in some places you may not expect: the engineers of the San Francisco BART train systems took their lessons in how to build an earthquake-resistant subway from the engineers of the fine modern metro in Tashkent, Uzbekistan.

Especially where you don't speak the language, urban railways are almost always much easier to navigate, and harder to get truly lost on, than buses. Trains are more likely than buses to follow fixed routes and to be marked with their route or their final destination. Rail stations and stops are more likely to be marked, and easier to find, than bus stops. Even if there are no announcements, if you have even a crude schematic map, you can usually tell how far to go and when to get off by counting stations or stops. Within urban areas, railways are invariably faster than buses, often faster even than taxis in big cities with slow-moving traffic. And electric trains are, of course, much less polluting than buses. For all these reasons, it makes sense to make urban rail transportation your first choice, and to take buses around town only where there are no trains or rail cars, or when you don't want to get anywhere in particular but just want to sightsee on random streets.

REAL LIFE

One evening out on my last trip to Berlin, I realized too late that my pass had expired. I tried half a dozen downtown U-Bahn and S-Bahn (subway and elevated train) stations before realizing that it was going to be impossible to buy a ticket back to my hotel: None of the attended ticket windows were open at night, and none of the machines would accept my credit or debit cards. I had to choose between walking 8 km (5 miles) across town or risking a €40 (US$55) fine for ticketless travel.

There's a good chance you can save by using some sort of daily or weekly pass or multiride ticket almost anywhere you're using mass transit. Check for passes used by locals as well as those for tourists: mass-transit passes marketed to tourists are often more expensive than mass-transit passes for local commuters. Watch for commuters showing passes or coupons to conductors and ticket-takers, or using tokens or proximity cards at turnstiles. Ask the passengers how they got them and how much they cost.

Even if the price is the same, buying a pass, prepaid farecard, or book or strip of tickets for multiple rides can save you hassles paying for bus or subway rides. Many subway and commuter-train stations are unattended, especially at night and on weekends. Ticket machines may accept only exact change, only certain denominations of coins or paper money, or worse, only credit or debit cards. If you're in Europe with a U.S.-issued card without European-style "chip and PIN" authentication, your card probably won't work in these or any other vending machines. Buy a pass or a batch of single-ride tickets or a prepaid farecard at an attended station at your first opportunity, typically at the airport or a mainline train station.

Surface Transportation

Paper tickets often have to be "validated" by swiping, scanning, punching, imprinting, or a proximity-reading device at the entrance to the station (usually when you board, sometimes also when you exit). Stored-value farecards almost always have to be validated both when you enter and exit, so that you can be charged according to distance. Watch what other passengers are doing, and follow their example.

Don't assume that you can wait to pay your fare onboard just because there are no turnstiles and nobody checks tickets at the station entrance. That might be true in a Third or Fourth World country where even a minibus has a conductor or fare collector as well as a driver, but in a wealthier or more automated country, fares may be collected on an "honor system." In many places, you are required to buy and validate a ticket or pass before you cross a specified line at the entrance to the station or platform, or before you board the transit vehicle. Spot checks are made by ticket inspectors or controllers, and if you are caught beyond the line or onboard without a properly validated ticket, you may have to pay a fine many times greater than the fare, sometimes on the spot.

Rail Ticket Prices

Don't be fooled by ticket prices in guidebooks. Expect them to have increased substantially with inflation. The poorer, more remote, and less visited a country is, the longer the lead time and the less frequent the revisions of guidebooks are likely to be, and the more you should expect prices to have increased from those in current guidebooks.

REAL LIFE

Don't buy a through train ticket with stopovers—even if it is a cheaper and, in theory, allows stopovers—unless you can make seat or sleeping berth reservations beyond the stopover point(s). If you get off, and later get back on another train to continue your journey, you may have to stand for the rest of your trip. If "the rest of your trip" is several days, or even just overnight, the savings on the through ticket was probably a false economy.

Aside from surcharges for faster trains, more comfortable seating, and sleeping accommodations, there used to be a few prices for tickets between two points: a one-way ("single journey" in British usage) fare, a roundtrip ("return") fare with an open return, and perhaps a lower excursion ("day-tripper") fare for a same-day return. Not any more. In regions with more sophisticated rail reservation systems, including Western Europe and North America, rail fares are becoming more and more like airfares, with different prices for refundable and nonrefundable tickets, tickets with or without change fees, tickets purchased further in advance, and tickets on less heavily booked dates or specific trains.

LOCAL VS. FOREIGNERS' PRICES

In some countries foreigners have to pay more, sometimes much more, for train tickets (and sometimes other things) than locals have to pay. Foreign travelers in such countries spend a lot of their time complaining—to each other and to locals—that the higher prices for foreigners are unfair.

Rarely do foreigners take time to consider the rationale for the dual-price system. In communist and socialist countries, and even most "social democracies," local people subsidize transportation and other services with their labor. Whether they officially "pay" taxes, or whether these fringe benefits are simply reflected in low salaries, they receive only part of their earnings in take-home pay. The rest of their earnings goes to support public services such as transportation. It would be grossly unfair to local workers if foreigners—who haven't paid local income taxes or contributed labor—were allowed to travel for the same nominal ticket price as locals.

Foreigners who demand to be allowed to buy tickets at the local price are, in effect, demanding that local people subsidize tourists who are already many times richer than most of them can ever hope to be. To claim this as your right is to set yourself up for accusations of exploitation, imperialism, and, depending on your skin color and theirs, racism as well.

Foreigners' prices seem quite logical and fair to those who charge them. Arguing will only anger them, make you lose face, and reinforce their low opinions of rich capitalist foreigners.

Part of what may tempt foreign travelers to argue is that a country doesn't generally set up a separate price schedule for foreigners unless the price difference is substantial. Where they exist, foreigners' prices can be 50 percent, 100 percent, or 1,000 percent more than local prices. Still, they are usually cheap compared to the prices of similar services or goods in capitalist countries, even Third World capitalist countries.

It's hard to predict just where you'll find a "dual-price" system with higher prices for foreigners. In a declining number of countries with government-controlled pricing, it's official policy, the way it used to be for First World tourists throughout the communist Second World. In other places, it is just standard operating procedure, not law, to quote foreigners higher prices for everything from souvenirs and food to accommodations and transportation.

In some countries such as Russia and Vietnam where foreigners prices have been officially abolished, the result is that tickets (especially for first-class sleeping births on the fastest long-distance express trains) have been cornered by scalpers. Foreigners still get charged a premium (since they

Tourist Class

Foreign tourists often have to pay more for air and train tickets than locals, but they usually get treated differently as well, both when buying tickets and while traveling.

In India, foreigners who pay in hard currency (precluding buying on the black market, where they might save slightly on the price) get to buy train tickets in special air-conditioned offices, with guards at the door to keep out the pickpockets and touts. Instead of standing in line, you relax in comfortable upholstered armchairs while being waited on by the most expert few dozen of Indian Railways' 1.2 million employees.

In China, foreigners who buy train tickets at special foreigners' prices, at special ticket offices for foreigners, or through travel agencies, are spared the scrum at the regular ticket windows or the problems of communicating in Chinese. At a travel agency or through the concierge at your hotel, you pay a service charge of a few U.S. dollars — well worth it, I think — for them to send a messenger to spend a day fighting through the reservation and ticket lines at the station, while you go about your sightseeing. At the station, your soft-class ticket gives you entrée to the soft-class waiting room, with comfy couches, bright lighting, and refreshments available. Meanwhile, in many stations, local passengers crowd each other for squatting space on the floor of the cavernous hard-class waiting hall.

Nowhere, though, were the differences more dramatic than on domestic flights in the USSR and (until the special foreigners' prices were abolished) in post-Soviet Russia. Foreigners — whether or not they were on Intourist tours — checked in at the Intourist desk at the airport, where they got the sort of special service — even if they were flying in coach — that only business- and first-class passengers get in most countries.

You went to a separate check-in area (sometimes in a separate building), which was often air-conditioned, clean, and spacious with comfortable chairs or couches. An attendant came to your seat to collect your tickets, saving you from having to stand in any lines. When your flight was ready for boarding (in most cases, after all other passengers had boarded, so that you waited on the plane as little as possible before takeoff) an attendant came to your seat to tell you that your plane was ready and to escort you and any other foreigners onto the plane.

On arrival, you went not to the main arrivals area but, again, to the Intourist desk or building. (This could actually be a bit hard to find if you were the only foreigner on the plane and Intourist, not expecting anyone on an Intourist tour, hadn't known to send a representative to meet the plane and escort you to its building or office.) Again, you waited in a separate, more comfortable area for your luggage to be delivered. In both arrival and departure areas you had access to foreigners-and-VIPs-only restaurants and bars.

When one of my flights was delayed, we were told that we could wait in the bar with US$1 bottles of champagne and 50-cent platters of bread and caviar, among other refreshments. When the flight was ready, Intourist sent someone to the bar to fetch us.

Fewer people would complain about the higher fares for foreigners — even aside from the question of tax subsidies by locals — if they thought twice about the fact that the higher price got even coach-class foreigners dramatically higher-quality VIP treatment and amenities on the ground. Too many foreigners, unfortunately, take such special privileges and amenities for granted (or never even notice that they are being treated differently from the locals), even while they demand to be allowed to travel for the local price.

usually don't know the language and have less ability to bargain), but now the difference goes to the scalpers instead of the government to operate and maintain the railroads.

Life on Board

Some trains have only one sort of car for all passengers, while others have many different classes with several gradations even within each class. You may find second class more luxurious than necessary in some countries, and first class intolerably uncomfortable in others. As with hotels, the key to happiness is figuring out which of the available options best suits your particular standards and budget.

A good destination guidebook should explain the types of trains, classes of service and accommodations, and the surcharges for faster trains (fast, rapid, special, express, or mail trains), higher classes, air-conditioning, sleeping berths, private compartments, meals, bedding, etc.

This is where you will learn that in India first class is actually the fourth-best of a great many classes, with three air-conditioned classes above it—only someone who grew up in a caste society can fully comprehend the nuances of the class system of the Indian railways. You will learn that a Japanese Kodama makes more stops than a Hikari; or that a mail train in India

REAL LIFE

I've crossed the border between India and Pakistan by rail, road, and air, and the train is unquestionably the worst of these means. The train stops on one side of the border for everyone to get off, with their luggage, for departure customs and immigration formalities. Only after everyone and everything has completed and passed these inspections are you allowed back on to continue across the border and repeat the process on arrival on the other side. I recommend splurging on taxis to and from the border, so you don't have to wait for a whole trainload of local people to be shaken down, twice.

is faster than an express. But what all this means is hard to judge without some context.

It's hard to learn much about train classes from other travelers unless you can find some country in which you have both ridden the same class of train, as a basis of comparison. "First class here is a little more comfortable than second class in Country X" is only helpful if you know Country X. "I found second class intolerable" is of little use without a sense of the other person's standards. Also, don't count on people to remember accurately in which class they traveled.

The best way to learn about the different classes and types of equipment is actually to look at them. If you've already gone to the station to buy your tickets, it should be easy to check out whatever trains are passing through. At most you'll have to pay a trivial price for a platform ticket to look at the trains.

Ticket clerks and other locals will often suggest the class that they think is appropriate for foreigners. Unless a lot of foreigners are traveling in lower classes, this is generally the highest class, the one that probably used to be exclusively for the former colonial masters.

You might find a lower class acceptable, but don't dismiss their advice out of hand. If they are seriously reluctant to sell you a lower-class ticket, there may be a good reason. Last-class Third World train travel, and anything but top-class Fourth World train travel, can be more than most First World travelers are prepared for. If you haven't ridden a rail line before, and haven't been able to inspect the cars, err on the side of a higher class.

Train-station restaurants are generally poor, and train passengers—a captive market—are generally overcharged severely for the fruit, drinks, and snacks offered through the windows or on platforms by vendors at stations. If you don't want to pay for this convenience, bring your own food with you. In Japan, for example, you can buy "bento box" meals packed for this purpose.

If every vendor at a station is offering the same fruit or dish, give it a try. It's probably a distinctive local delicacy of the place or region that you're passing through. I didn't get off the train in Hami, but I'll never forget the taste of the Hami melons—renowned for a thousand kilometers—that were sold to us through the train windows when we stopped there for a few minutes.

Dining cars, where they exist, tend to overcharge even more. Good sleeping cars are common in the South, but good dining cars rare. Sometimes you'll get lucky and get a wonderful cheap meal on board, but don't count on it. Always bring enough food and water to see you through to your destination. Most trains have some sort of toilet, but don't expect much more than a hole in the floor. Bring your own toilet paper. Availability of washing up facilities, and of water for washing and drinking, varies greatly. Sometimes you'll be brought hot moist towels after every meal, and thermos bottles of boiled water. Sometimes there will be no water to drink or wash with unless you bring it yourself.

International Trains

Procedures for crossing borders by train vary greatly. In some cases customs and immigration inspectors carry out their work on board while the train travels between the stops on either side of the border. This is true of all rail border crossings within Western Europe. In other places, the train stops for a tedious car-by-car check at the border before it proceeds. When Amtrak trains between the United States and Canada switched from in-motion customs and immigration formalities to a customs and immigration halt at the border, more than two hours had to be added to the schedule of each international train.

In the worst cases, everyone has to disembark at the border. This is unusual; one reason people pay more to take a through international train, rather than two domestic trains that connect on either side of a border, is precisely to avoid this delay. But it does happen, sometimes unexpectedly.

It's common to have to stop at a border, or even within a country, for a change of locomotive from diesel to electric, or vice versa, or between third-rail and overhead electric power, or between electric locomotives operated on different types of current (AC or DC), frequencies, or voltages.

There are no real standards for any of these things, although some electric locomotives, including those of the French TGVs, can operate on more than one type of power.

RAILWAY GAUGES

The most common reason not to connect two adjacent railways is that they have been built to different gauges. The gauge is the width between the rails, specified as the distance between the outer flanges.

For travelers, variations in rail gauges could mean a transfer between trains, and perhaps between stations on different rail lines, even when the rails appear on a map to be seamlessly connected across a border or through a

Surface Transportation

> ### REAL LIFE
>
> Rarely is a route so important as to justify dual-gauge cars or other expedients, but there is at least one notable exception: on the branch lines from the Trans-Siberian to China, each car is lifted by a crane while the wheel and axle assemblies ("bogies" or "trucks") are changed between those for the Chinese and the Russian gauges.

city. It's common for a single city to have many train stations, so always make sure to ask which station your train leaves from. On the other hand, within rail networks on the same gauge—such as the main lines within most of Western Europe—through cars can be switched from train to train as often as necessary. The same train often includes cars bound for different destinations, so that if you get on the wrong car, even if you're on the right train, you can wake up on the wrong branch line, or in the wrong country!

Train gauges are also one of the clearest and most conspicuous examples—set in steel—of how differing colonial legacies have hampered postindependence efforts to promote trade, travel, and cooperation between Third and Fourth World countries.

Most countries that could afford it have tried to convert their railroads to a single national gauge. Australia has invested particularly large amounts in converting from other gauges, both wider and narrower, to standard gauge. Where this hasn't been financially feasible or when crossing borders between countries with different standards, a change of gauge usually requires a change of train.

ROAD TRANSPORTATION

Road travel has a seductive appeal: get on the road and you can go anywhere. But as the song goes, "It ain't necessarily so."

Roads themselves cover far more territory than railroads, although still not everywhere. No such elaborate geographic survey as I conducted in the previous section on railroads is needed here: pretty much anywhere you can go by rail, you can also go by road, and then some.

There are significant regional differences, however, in the desirability and (dis)advantages of road travel relative to other options. The appropriate mode of road travel differs from region to region as well.

In the following sections on private and public road vehicles, I'll try to give some sense of the factors to consider in choosing whether to go by road.

Road or Rail: "Comfort, Safety, Speed"

Where there is a train, take it. Don't think twice about the choice. In comparison with rail travel, road travel is dangerous, polluting, and expensive.

"Comfort, Safety, Speed" was the slogan of the Pacific Electric Railway, the Los Angeles and Southern California streetcar and interurban system that was once, believe it or not, the world's largest. Comfort, safety, and speed are the advantages of trains over road vehicles. Even where cars or buses are faster, comfort and safety—especially safety—are the reasons I still travel by rail wherever and whenever I have a choice.

COMFORT

With few exceptions, road travel is less comfortable than travel by rail. Don't be misled by the apparent comfort of the interiors of luxury buses. Luxury or even ordinary-class long-distance buses in many other countries make Greyhound coaches look like cattle cars by comparison. (Argentina is perhaps the gold standard, with flat-bed sleeper seats and four-course meals on the fanciest buses.) But no matter how well-appointed their interiors, they are limited by the conditions of the roads on which they are operated. Even the best bus will bump and bounce slowly and painfully over an unpaved, potholed, rutted road.

SAFETY

Railroads use relatively mature and forgiving technology. Even human errors are less likely to be disastrous. If the engineer or motorman of a train falls asleep, he (female professional drivers are unknown in most of the world) will probably wake up before any damage is done. If a bus or truck driver, who may drive for 24 hours, or 72, with no more than brief meal breaks, falls asleep, the

REAL LIFE

"Rail travel in the United States, per passenger-kilometer, is 18 times as safe as private car travel…. The risk of being injured or killed in a road accident is 29 times as great as that for rail in the former West Germany and the Netherlands, and 80 times as great in France."—Worldwatch Institute

vehicle will probably run off the road within a few seconds. The safety advantages of trains over road travel are even greater in areas where both are less safe than they are in the United States.

It may be obvious that Third and Fourth World countries with limited resources have put a lower priority on road than rail development, because the same investment in rail can build a system that can carry many times as many people as the same investment in roads. It may be less obvious that roads in even the most industrialized Second World countries are almost as bad as Third and Fourth World roads, central planners having decided that roads were not appropriate technology.

Surface Transportation

In most of the world, rail travel is probably at least 10 times safer than road travel. Given that surface transportation is already the most dangerous aspect of almost any trip, this is a compelling reason to ride the rails rather than the roads.

SPEED

Some bus rides are so difficult, dangerous, slow, or uncomfortable that even the stingiest travelers, if they can at all afford it, make it a monetary priority to fly or take a train. The cost for flying may be large in comparison with your daily budget in a poor country, but it may be a price worth paying to avoid two or three days on a bus through deserts, mountains, rain forests, or mud holes. On the other hand, the scenery makes some truly scary bus trips worthwhile, if nothing goes wrong. Let both your budget, your tolerance for danger and discomfort, and what transportation is available to the particular places you want to go be your guides in choosing whether to use road transport.

NORTH AMERICA AND AUSTRALIA VS. THE REST OF THE WORLD

North Americans and Australians travel by road, rather than rail, more than anyone else in the world. North Americans are thus accustomed to an extreme imbalance between the availability and convenience of road and rail transport. Coming from the United States, Canada, or Australia, your first instinct may be to rent a car or take a bus, even in a place where neither makes any sense.

Conversely, first-time visitors to North America typically expect such a wealthy country as the United States to have a modern public transportation system. Even if they are forewarned about the 20th-century decline of North American intercity trains, they are often unprepared for the near-total abandonment of urban public transit by all but the poorest people in many major U.S. cities. (Australia, by contrast, has few intercity passenger trains but excellent local public transit within urban areas.)

The difficulties this causes are compounded by the tendency of visitors from smaller countries to underestimate the scale of the United States, Canada, or Australia. It's almost impossible for people who grew up in Western Europe, Japan, or Taiwan, and who haven't traveled to big countries before, to imagine just how far it is between different places in any of the largest countries. A bus trip across North America or Australia may seem less of a bargain when you realize that it will take at least 72 mostly sleepless hours.

Road vs. Air

Where there is no railroad, you may have no choice but road travel. Don't rule out air travel, particularly if local roads are horrible. Domestic airfares in some countries are very cheap. Some international fares are quite low too, and customs and immigration formalities are usually less of a hassle at airports than at land borders.

The bottom line is that the appropriate mode of transportation depends greatly on local conditions. You can make life pretty hard for yourself by choosing the wrong way to get around.

Where There Is No Road

Good or bad, roads are almost everywhere, so in a sense road travel is the most widely available choice. Other than Antarctica, there is no continent that can't be crossed (albeit with difficulty) by some sort of land vehicle on something called a "road."

Severe logistical difficulties, however, are presented by road travel across the Sahara, the Congo basin, the Amazon basin, and between Europe and East, South, or Southeast Asia. None of these crossings should be attempted without careful planning and preparation.

THE SAHARA

From west to east, there is a continuous band across the continent of countries posing problems for would-be north-south travelers.

Western Sahara: As of 2011, there was an uneasy ceasefire between Morocco's army of occupation and the nationalist Polisario Front, although no sign of an end to the conflict. The Polisario Front's government-in-exile is recognized as the rightful government of the Saharan Democratic Arab Republic (RASD) by dozens of other countries, the International Court of Justice, and the Organization of African Union. But documents associating a traveler with the RASD, even if one of its offices-in-exile could be persuaded to issue a "visa," would only brand a traveler a subversive in the eyes of the Moroccan soldiers who wield power at gunpoint in most areas.

Algeria: Widespread assassinations of those accused of being agents of European secularism and cultural imperialism, including foreigners, make this an area to travel with extreme caution, if at all. It's probably still an OK route for Muslims, but only for those who are very sensitive and careful not to offend local sensibilities.

Libya: As of 2011, Libya is embroiled in civil war. Roads across the Sahara in Libya are actually *relatively* good, compared to those in neighboring countries, so this could become a viable transit route if the political situation stabilizes and tourist travel becomes feasible again.

Sudan: The only public transit across the Sahara has been on buses through Sudan. There's a very serious danger of land mines, however, especially in southern Sudan, and it's unclear whether this route will remain open once the south becomes fully independent as the world's newest country following the plebiscite held in 2011.

CONGO

There are roads across the Democratic Republic of Congo (DRC or Congo-Kinshasa, formerly Zaire), but they are among the world's worst. Going between East and West Africa, there is no way around the DRC: go north or south, and you have to cross minefields and war zones of Sudan or Angola, respectively. No road across the DRC is paved, and the only vehicles on many stretches are lumber trucks (or military vehicles). You have to pay for rides, when you can find them. When the trucks stop—whether for rest or because they have bogged or broken down—you have no choice but to stop where they do. If you're lucky, you'll be allowed to sleep under a truck, giving you some protection from the rain. Conditions were bad already, but got much worse during the civil and international war in the Congo that began in 1998 and was still going on in 2011.

It's possible to get stuck in the middle of the rain forest for weeks, and if you decide you want to give up it could be a long way to an airport, railhead, or major river port.

Domestic flights in Congo, when they operate at all, are also among the world's worst and most dangerous, so there's no readily available alternative if you give up on overland travel.

AMAZONIA

There are east–west and north–south roads (of a sort) across Amazonia, and even a bridge over the Amazon itself at Manaus (the first over the Amazon or any of its major tributaries) that opened in 2010. I've heard from fewer people who have taken these roads than those across the Congo basin, but my impression is that they are a bit better. Certainly Brazil is spending more money than is Congo on building roads to open up, exploit, and clear-cut the land. On the other hand, crossing Amazonia between north and south requires a much longer distance by road than does crossing Congo. It's not for the timid.

EURASIA

Until 1979, it was possible to travel by road between Europe and Asia by way of Turkey, Iran, and Afghanistan. There were regular through "hippie buses" via Pakistan and India as far east as Nepal. The Iranian revolution in 1979 and the war in Afghanistan closed that route through the 1980s. It reopened in the 1990s, and as of this writing U.S. citizens are welcomed in Iran, but the through route closed again with the start of the U.S.-Afghan war in 2001.

It's theoretically possible to take buses across Central Asia via Russia, Kazakhstan, East Turkestan (Chinese-occupied "Xinjiang Province"), and China, following essentially the same route as the rail route described earlier. Buses as well as trains run between Almaty and Urumchi. But it's peculiarly difficult to get permission to bring foreign vehicles across Chinese borders, and given the conditions of roads in Russia and China, much less Central Asia, I can't think of any reason to forsake the comforts of the trains. *Red Odyssey* (see *Background Reading* in the *Resource Guide*) is the narrative of a well-connected Soviet citizen who tried to drive the Soviet section of this route around 1990 and gave up halfway.

> ### REAL LIFE
>
> For what it's like for U.S. tourists to visit Iran, see Rick Steves's videos at www. ricksteves.com/iran/ showing the "overwhelming friendliness of the people" he experienced on his 2009 trip, and Geoff Greenwald's article about watching the total eclipse of the sun in Isfahan in 1999, available as "Total Eclipse" on Salon.com and as a chapter in his book, *Scratching the Surface*. Isfahan is near the top of my personal "wish list" of places I haven't been to yet.

Private Road Transport

It's not always easy, and rarely simple or cheap, to bring, buy, or rent any private vehicle larger or more elaborate than a bicycle. Before we get to the bicycle question, though, let's work down through some of the more grandiose possibilities, in descending order of power, independence, and expense: taking a car with you, buying a car locally, renting a self-drive car, hiring a chauffeured car, bringing or buying a motorized two-wheeler, and hiring a motorized two-wheeler.

BRINGING YOUR OWN VEHICLE

Taking a car with you makes sense only if you either already have a car and are going to a nearby destination that you can get to by road (e.g., within North and Central America, or within Europe) or by relatively short and affordable ferries (e.g., from Europe to North Africa), or you are going to a more distant place where suitable vehicles are either utterly unobtainable

> ### REAL LIFE
>
> Even people who don't steal a car you've imported from abroad will still readily identify you as a rich person who can afford to travel in the luxury not just of a private car, but of a foreign car. Short of a yacht, a private airplane, or a private railroad car, I can't think of any more conspicuous sign of a traveler's wealth.

or so much more expensive as to warrant the costs of shipping your own car from home (e.g., for trans-African travel).

If you are going to somewhere nearby, with a similar level of wealth and technology and similar cars and roads (such as between the United States and Canada, or within Western Europe), then the only things different from driving within your home country will be dealing with different legal and regulatory requirements and possibly different languages, signage, and driving on the opposite side of the road.

If you are going somewhere farther afield, you'll have to deal with additional costs and complications of shipping. Unless there's a ferry that carries both vehicles and passengers, as is the case across the Strait of Gibraltar, you'll have to send your vehicle by cargo ship.

Because you won't be there to expedite its arrival and passage through customs, it's important to triple-check all the papers and procedures before you consign your vehicle to the shipping line. Even so, you'll probably want to plan your own arrival for shortly before the ship with your vehicle is scheduled to dock and unload, to keep an eye on things. If you can't, you may have to hire a customs broker or shipping agent to push the papers and perhaps grease palms in your absence.

The minimum legal and regulatory requirements are registration of your vehicle in your home country, a driver's license in your home country, an international driver's license, and liability insurance valid in each country in which you operate the vehicle. If you are driving between very different countries, you'll need to be prepared for considerable, and perhaps unexpected, additional logistical as well as legal and regulatory hassles.

OPERATOR LICENSING

To operate a motor vehicle in any country, you need either a valid local driving license or both a license to drive in your home country and an International Driving Permit (IDP).

An IDP is a certified translation of your driver's license in standard format into English, French, Arabic, Chinese, German, Italian, Japanese, Portuguese, Russian, Spanish, and Swedish.

An IDP is valid only in conjunction with your license to drive in your home country. The permit has no independent validity and should always be carried, and shown, with your local license. Most travelers, and even many traffic police, don't realize this. But if you carry only an IDP, and not your driving license from home, there's always a risk of being stopped by an officer who knows and enforces the requirement that you carry both documents.

International Driving Permits are issued either by local governments or by driving clubs or organizations designated and authorized by the government to perform this function. If you want an IDP, you have to get it before you leave home. An IDP is valid for one year from the date of issue, provided that the local license in conjunction with which it is issued and used remains valid.

In the United States, International Driving Permits are issued by the American Automobile Association (AAA) and its local affiliates. You don't have to be an AAA member to get an IDP from the AAA. Just bring your current driver's license and a passport photo to any AAA or affiliate office, and for a nominal fee they will issue you an IDP on the spot.

The permit is endorsed to be valid only for the class(es) of vehicle(s) for which your regular license is valid. If you want to be able to operate a truck, bus, or motorcycle, you must already have a license to operate such a vehicle in your home country before you apply for your IDP.

VEHICLE LICENSING AND INSURANCE

As I said above, the minimum requirement is that a vehicle you take abroad be legally registered in your home country (or the country you are coming from). Many countries have additional requirements, from minor fees and taxes to mandatory insurance, massive duties, or requirements for a *carnet de passage.*

At each border crossing you can expect to be asked for proof of ownership, registration, and insurance of your vehicle. Bring extra copies (if possible, notarized) of the title, registration, and insurance certificates, as you will have an extremely hard time if you lose them.

If the owner of the vehicle isn't traveling with you, you may also need to produce written permission from the owner (preferably notarized) to be using and crossing borders with their car. This is for good reason: many cars and trucks stolen in the United States end up in Mexico or Central America, and even more cars stolen in Western Europe end up in Central or Eastern Europe or ex-Soviet Asia.

Often you'll be required to display a standard emblem identifying what country your car is registered in. You're probably already familiar with these white oval stickers with a black border and a one-, two-, or three-letter abbreviation for the country of registration (i.e., the country that issued your license plates). You'll need one to cross most borders.

Many countries impose more-or-less minor taxes or fees on incoming vehicles of foreign registration. If they put a tax or registration sticker on your car when you pay the fee to take it into the country, at least you know the money probably went to the government, not in the tax collector's pocket.

Standard automobile insurance policies are valid only in the country in which the vehicle is registered and insured. Check with your regular automobile insurance agent and/or automobile association for the vehicle insurance rules of each country to which you might bring your vehicle.

Supplemental insurance policies to cover U.S.-registered vehicles taken into Mexico are available through U.S. insurance brokers or in storefront insurance sales offices in most U.S. border towns. Get it *before* you cross into Mexico. Most U.S. auto insurance policies cover driving in Canada, but typically you need to get a special certificate from your U.S. insurance provider, in advance, to prove that you are insured in Canada.

You should get insurance valid wherever you are going, even if it's not required. Those who engage in activities as dangerous as driving have, I believe, a moral obligation to ensure that those whom they might injure will be provided for. If that doesn't move you, consider this: if you don't have insurance and are in a collision in many countries, you can be jailed until liability is determined and all claims are settled.

IMPORT DUTIES

A fair number of poor countries have decided that importing private cars is inappropriate and a waste of scarce foreign exchange. Either regarding a private car as inherently a luxury and deserving of being taxed as such, and/or trying to protect the development of an indigenous automobile manufacturing industry, they impose duties on imported cars. These duties may be as much as several times the value of the car.

Obviously, this is prohibitive for a tourist, especially one who wants to drive through a whole series of such countries, as one must do to cross Africa or Central or South America.

In theory, it is possible to pay the duty and to get it refunded after one can prove that one has taken the vehicle back out of the country ("reexported" it). In practice, nobody in their right mind would pay thousands of dollars in duties to most of these governments and ever hope to see their money again.

CARNETS DE PASSAGE

The other way to avoid the automobile import duties is to have a *carnet de passage*. (It's a French term but is used worldwide, including in English-speaking countries.) A *carnet* is a sort of reexport performance bond: it's a document guaranteeing that you will pay the import duty if you fail to reexport the vehicle that you are bringing into the country. The point is to allow you to drive your vehicle *through* a country, while preventing you from evading the import duty by bringing a vehicle in as a tourist and then selling it or giving it away locally.

If you bring a vehicle in, then don't take it out again and don't pay the duty, the issuer of the *carnet* will pay the duty and collect it from you. If the issuer of the *carnet* has to pay duty for your vehicle, you are liable to them for the duty in addition to what you had to pay for the *carnet* in the first place. They can sue you, if necessary, to collect it from you.

Because few people take cars through countries that require a *carnet*, it can be quite hard to find someone to issue one. A bank or insurance company can issue them, but they are most often arranged through automobile organizations. You must get a *carnet* in advance; it isn't something you can arrange at the border.

Because a *carnet* is a financial commitment by the issuer, you have to pay something for it and provide your own guarantee to the issuer that you'll reimburse them if need be. Usually this means you have to post a deposit equal to the possible duties, or buy a bond. If you post a deposit, you can get it back when you've taken the vehicle out of any country that requires the *carnet* and have had the *carnet* canceled.

Carnets are most often needed for trans-African travel; most people planning to drive their own vehicles across Africa arrange for *carnets* in the U.K. or France before they leave for Africa. Insurance companies in the United States rarely are called upon to issue a *carnet de passage* and thus tend to be unfamiliar with the procedures.

Most countries in the Americas no longer require a *carnet* as long as you certify via specific paperwork that you are a tourist and will take your vehicle back out of the country when you leave. Even if they don't require a *carnet*, however, they can still charge you import duties if you fail to take the car back out of the country.

LEAVING WITHOUT YOUR CAR

Carnet or no, it will be noted in your passport, visa, or other documents if you enter a country with a vehicle. Unless you leave the country with that vehicle, you are liable for duty.

If you sell the vehicle (most people who drive across Africa start from Europe and sell their vehicle in a distant part of Africa at the end of their trip, or when they decide to stop driving), make sure you have the purchaser pay the duty.

If the vehicle breaks down and has to be abandoned (common in the Sahara and elsewhere), or is stolen, or if you can't find a buyer for it at the end of your road and can't afford or find a way to ship or drive it back home, you are liable for duty for having imported it. This is a cost that can be hard to predict, and one more reason not to bring a vehicle. If you can't afford this risk, you can't afford to take your own vehicle abroad.

LOGISTICS

A surprising number of roads cross directly from the First World to the Third World, the outstanding examples being between the United States and Mexico, or from the First World to the Second World, mainly between Western or Central and Eastern Europe, through the former Iron Curtain. The ease of the crossing itself makes it all too easy to forget just how different things can be a short distance over a border. Learn as much as you can about the current conditions where you are going, and be prepared.

The Association for Safe International Road Travel (ASIRT), listed in the *Resource Guide,* publishes country reports on local driving practices, peculiarities, and hazards in countries around the world. The largest number of Northerners driving their own vehicles into the South are those from the United States and Canada driving into Mexico; some of the best general advice on driving into the Third World is found in *The People's Guide to Mexico.* Fourth World road trips, mainly across Africa, are the stuff of a whole subgenre of travel books.

If you are bringing your own vehicle because suitable vehicles aren't available locally, that's a good indication that parts and repair services, maybe even fuel, won't be easy to find either. Be prepared to be self-sufficient.

VEHICLE TYPES

Not all First World vehicles are suitable for extensive travel on rough or unpaved roads. It's one thing to drive a pickup truck to Mexico; it's quite another to drive a subcompact car. Both are possible, but different.

Most people planning extensive overland journeys in more remote areas, especially in the Second or Fourth World, start with a four-wheel-drive light truck or SUV and invest considerable time and money in modifications such as skid plates under the body; rock screens for the headlights, windshield, and perhaps other windows; extra fuel and water tanks; interior or secure rooftop luggage enclosures; enclosed sleeping accommodations; etc.

If you're buying a vehicle specifically for such a trip, it's worth considerable effort to find out what sort of suitable vehicle (if any) is in most common local use, and get one of that model. This will maximize your chance of finding parts and repairs, although parts for even the most common models may still be scarce and expensive. For example, if the most common local private vehicle is a Toyota Landcruiser (the standard vehicle of United Nations and NGO fieldworkers in the Fourth World), that's what you want too.

While you are at it, think about whether you'd be better off buying such a local vehicle on arrival, rather than trying to bring one with you. (See *Buying a Car at Your Destination,* below.) Sometimes suitable vehicles, or ones that could be made suitable with locally available materials, are unlikely to be available, or are terribly overpriced because of import duties. In such cases, the only feasible way to have a vehicle may be to bring your own vehicle with you.

FUEL

Try to get current information on what sort of motor fuel is most widely available: unleaded gasoline, leaded gasoline, diesel, or gasohol. Vehicles made for leaded gas require fuel additives if operated exclusively on unleaded gasoline. Gasohol (common only in Brazil, although available elsewhere including at some gas stations in the United States) requires specially built or at least re-tuned engines.

Unleaded gasoline is entirely unavailable in some countries, while a single tank of leaded gasoline will irrevocably ruin the catalytic converter on any vehicle made for unleaded gasoline. You'll have to replace the catalytic converter if you ever want to operate the vehicle again in the United States, Canada, or another country with emission limits for vehicle licensing.

Diesel cars are uncommon in the United States, but common in many other places, including Western Europe. (Why? Diesel engines are more fuel-efficient than gasoline engines, but produce more of some types of air pollution. Government regulations in the United States have put a higher priority on low emissions than on high fuel efficiency. Some other countries have made the opposite choice, or don't have such regulations at all.) Don't put fuel in any motor vehicle, even a passenger car, without being sure if it needs gas or diesel.

There are diesel trucks even in places where there are no cars, so a diesel vehicle may be most versatile in the extreme back of beyond. But trucks have large fuel tanks and a long range, so places to buy diesel can be spaced farther apart (especially in the back of beyond). If you are headed to such a place, you'll probably need to equip your vehicle with auxiliary fuel tanks.

Notice that I said "tanks," not "cans." Fuel is precious in the Third and Fourth Worlds, particularly in the back of beyond. Cans of gasoline (petrol) or diesel fastened to the exterior of your vehicle may swiftly be removed by thieves.

THEFT

Of course, your vehicle itself is vulnerable to thieves. Car theft is the most compelling reason not to drive a car from Western Europe into Eastern Europe, or for that matter from the United States into Mexico. Again, if you are bringing your own car because such cars are excessively expensive where you are going, that's strong evidence that cars such as yours will be prized by local thieves. Foreign makes and models of cars, foreign license plates and other insignia, and visibly foreign gear or accessories (not to mention foreign faces) all help to single you out as a target.

INCREASED COSTS

The kinds of vehicles favored by hard-core overland travelers with their own vehicles tend to be the favorite vehicles of the highest levels of the local elite.

Surface Transportation

Traveling in such a vehicle, you'll get plenty of attention—maybe more than you want. You'll be treated like a king, and you'll be charged a king's ransom for anything you need to buy along the way.

As a rule, outside the First World, people who arrive in a place by any sort of private car or truck will be charged more for everything, at least by people who see or hear about their vehicle, than people who arrive by any form of nonmotorized or public surface transportation. In the United States, where "everyone" has a car, it's easy to forget that in most of the world any sort of good or service related to automobiles—fuel, parts, repairs, towing out of mud holes—is, by definition, a luxury, and priced accordingly. Even elsewhere in the First World, such as in Western Europe and Japan, cars are often treated as a luxury, and things such as road tolls and parking are priced accordingly.

In places where officials and functionaries expect to supplement their income by fees, fines, or bribes, drivers are the first target. If you can afford a car, they think, you can obviously afford to share some of your great wealth with a soldier or village policeman whose life's dream may be to save enough to buy a moped. They may have a point, but that doesn't mean you'll be happy to pay them what they want.

BUYING A CAR AT YOUR DESTINATION

By now you may have decided that I'm inflexibly anticar. Not so. In a few countries, I'd even recommend buying a car. Buying a car locally may make sense for an extensive trip across a region where public transport is poor or nonexistent, but where foreign cars may be hard to repair or attract undue attention.

REAL LIFE

It may be better to buy a used car of a locally common variety on another continent than to have a foreign car shipped in by sea. Sure, a locally made car may break down more often. But it's much less likely to get stripped or stolen for parts than an "exotic" and locally rare make, and when it breaks it'll be much easier to find a mechanic with the skills, tools, and parts to fix it if it's a more common model.

Another time to purchase a car is for a long stay in a place where a very high proportion of the local people have cars, so there is no other effective mode of transportation. Be sure you are staying long enough for the cost savings of buying over renting to offset the much greater hassles of buying (and selling again when you leave). If you will be traveling away from places where there are hotels, especially if you are traveling with a small group of friends or family with a common itinerary, having a vehicle allows you to camp where the facilities and the climate permit it.

Surface Transportation

Where does this mean? Mostly, this means stays of at least a couple of months in the United States, Canada, Australia, and perhaps Argentina, Chile, Mexico, or South Africa.

In Australia, in particular, some dealers specialize in selling used cars to arriving travelers and buying them back at the ends of their trips. You have to watch out, of course, especially if you don't know a lot about cars or local conditions. Caveat emptor (let the buyer beware) is never as appropriate as when buying used cars. But at least these specialists are somewhat familiar with the special difficulties foreigners face in licensing, insurance, etc., and can offer at least some assistance, for a price, as well as a network of affiliates in other cities who will later buy back cars, suitably depreciated for wear and tear.

I know of no such specialists in the United States or Canada. Bureaucracies in the United States are set up with no consideration whatsoever for the needs of foreigners. If at all possible, get a local friend or acquaintance to assist you with the paperwork and formalities of purchase, registration, taxes, and insurance, or at least to refer you to their automobile insurance agent. If the agent values your friend's business, they may take more time to help you than would an agent who stood to sell you only a short-term policy. Be aware that vehicle licensing and insurance rules vary greatly between U.S. states, so advice or experience from another state is at best useless and at worst misleading.

Joining the American Automobile Association (AAA) may also be worthwhile. For the price of annual dues you get all the road maps you want; emergency road service and towing; helpful publications and advice on questions like insurance and international road travel; and hotel, campground, and sightseeing guides.

The AAA guidebooks are poor, but their campground guides are much better. That an organization for motorists publishes one of the most comprehensive sets of campground guides—they're better for most government campgrounds on public land than any publications from the government itself—is not surprising; most campgrounds in the United States can be reached only by private car. (Of course, AAA guides aren't the only privately published campground guides. Other campground guidebooks, such as those in the *Moon Outdoors* series, also published by Avalon Travel, give more detail and list hike-in campgrounds not listed in the AAA guides.)

One tow, or a complete set of maps of the United States and Canada, could cost you more than a year's AAA membership, currently priced at approximately US$50 per person. Unfortunately, the AAA uses a portion of each member's dues to support its lobbying in support of road-building and in opposition to railroads and mass transit. If you join the AAA, consider contributing an offsetting or larger amount to railroad or transit advocacy groups, such as the National Association of Railroad Passengers (see the *Resource Guide*).

One alternative in the United States to buying or renting a car for a cross-country road trip is a "driveaway" company. These companies serve as intermediaries between car owners who are relocating long distances but don't want to drive their own cars, and freelance drivers, often foreign tourists. The usual deal is that the owner (through the driveaway company) pays for insurance and sometimes gas, and the driver pays the rest of the expenses. As a driver, you don't get paid, but you get the equivalent of a free car rental with a specified allowable maximum of time and miles to get from where you pick the car up to where you deliver it.

In the United States, look for ads for these companies in hostels (a major source of their drivers), or under "auto transportation" in the phone book. Auto driveaway companies are a product of the peculiar transience and auto-dependence of life in the United States, however, and don't seem to exist on a large scale anywhere else I've visited.

RENTING A SELF-DRIVE CAR

If you aren't in a country long enough to warrant buying and selling back a car, need a car in only some of the places you will visit, or don't want the time, work, or inconvenience of long-distance driving, it probably makes more sense to rent (hire) a car locally, where and when you need it.

> **REAL LIFE**
>
> I've never seen so much roadkill as in Australia, much of it kangaroos large enough to wreck a car. Rural Australians don't drive at night except in emergencies, and then at substantially reduced speed. Proprietors of motels and bed-and-breakfasts were shocked to have guests arrive after dark, even when we had reservations, and warned us with gruesome cautionary tales about the hazards of night driving in rural country or the outback.

Western Europe and Japan: It makes sense to rent a car in places with car-oriented transportation systems (if private cars can be called a "system") and poor public transit; good roads; readily available vehicle services; available and affordable parking (a strike against driving in Western Europe or Japan); free or low-toll roads (strike two); and affordable fuel prices (strike three).

Despite generally good roads and (unfortunately) increasingly automotive cultures, renting a car in Europe or Japan just to get from one city to another is rarely worth the expense and hassle, unless you have a carful of people traveling together, such as a family, and are experienced at driving in the region in question. It makes more sense in these and many other regions to limit car rental to day trips to places inaccessible by mass transit. There may be fewer places you need a car than you expect, as mass transit systems extend to more of even the rural parts of Europe and Japan than of the United States.

Australia and Aotearoa/New Zealand: Both are reasonable places to rent cars, especially if you combine car rental with public transit for the longer legs in Australia. Don't underestimate the distances. If you are coming from the United States, be aware that only a few Australian outback roads are paved. There's no limited-access or divided road across the country north-south or east-west. One transcontinental route in each direction is now paved, but they are only two lanes and they are not fenced. Kangaroos and other wildlife dot the road and require constant alertness; driving between dusk and dawn is inadvisable, which limits the distance you can drive in a day. Settlements along the main highways can be 200 km (120 miles) apart, and roadside services and facilities are extremely limited. I've driven across Australia, and in many respects it's more like driving the Alaska Highway than like driving across the continental United States.

North America: Car rental is particularly likely to make sense on this car-crazy continent. It's possible to get around greater Miami or Phoenix by public transit, but you'll spend as much time on buses as Lagos or Jakarta slum-dwellers spend commuting to their jobs. I hate cars and driving, but I'd get together a few fellow travelers to rent a car if I wanted to go sightseeing anywhere in the United States or Canada except the "ecotopian" West Coast cities from San Francisco to Vancouver, and the largest and densest cities of the Northeast and Midwest (Boston, New York, Philadelphia, Washington, Chicago, Toronto, Montréal, and Québec). Los Angeles is a special case. There's a surprisingly good, but still limited, subway system, and I've been able to have a good time without a car when I could stay close to the subway. Whether you need a car in LA depends on what you want to see and do as a tourist, although you certainly need a car if you want to see it like a local.

Foreigners may be afraid of the United States, and have probably heard of carjackings and murders of foreign tourists. These fears are to some extent well founded; in comparison to many other countries, the United States is a violent country and guns are prevalent. Many ordinary-seeming Americans keep guns in their houses, cars, and offices and carry concealed guns on their persons on public streets. All U.S. police officers carry guns; indeed, when I see guns being brandished on my street, they are usually in the hands of police.

But fear of violence shouldn't be a reason not to rent a car in the United States. Because the upper and middle classes have abandoned public transit to the poor and the under-class, public buses (the only urban mass transit in most of the United States) may be even more dangerous than travel by rental car. Driving in most places in the United States is, as driving goes, extremely safe.

If anything, foreigners may be frustrated by how slowly and carefully North Americans (except Québécois) drive, especially by comparison with Europeans. That's not a slur against Québec, just a note that it has, in many respects that include driving style, a distinctly European culture and way of life. If you drive at European autobahn speeds on U.S. interstate highways, you are likely to be arrested.

The most unpleasant surprise for foreign drivers in the United States is that not only are distances on road signs in English units (miles, yards, and feet) rather than metric, but U.S. road signs are in words only. English words. International-standard symbolic road signs are almost entirely unheard-of in the United States, greatly complicating life for non-English-speaking drivers. A profusion of peculiar abbreviations, unique to U.S. highway signage, makes the problem even worse.

Both the cause and effect of U.S. auto-mobility is that the danger of violence is largely confined to certain ghettoes of the urban, nonwhite poor. Wealthier people with cars simply never go near such areas, or whiz through on highways at 105 km/h (65 mph).

Your visit to the United States would be incomplete without a visit to such an area, but driving by yourself, especially in a conspicuously rented car, is an inappropriate way to do so. If you are going to explore a slum anywhere in the world, try to do so with a local guide.

South Africa: With the continent's best roads, this is the only country in Africa where self-drive car hire makes any sense. Fuel isn't cheap, and there are other ways to get around. But renting a car gives you a chance that you won't get elsewhere in Africa to explore the countryside. By renting a car in South Africa, I got to many scenic places that would otherwise have been inaccessible. If you plan to drive into poor black South African urban neighborhoods, a local guide is even more essential than it is for white people driving into similar neighborhoods in U.S. cities. Anywhere else in Africa, if you hire a car, hire a driver too. (See *Costs of Renting a Self-Drive Car,* below.)

Argentina, Chile, and Uruguay: These neighboring countries are important anomalies in Latin America. The overall levels of industrialization and infrastructure are borderline First World, and the middle class is large and wealthy enough for most families outside the largest cities, and some within them, to own a family car, truck, or SUV. With a sparsely distributed population almost entirely descended from European immigrants and an economy centered on agricultural exports, Argentina compares itself to Canada and Australia more than to other Latin American countries. Roads in these countries aren't quite up to U.S. or Canadian standards, and a truly superlative bus system serves the cities and major towns, but many interesting and scenic rural areas are hard to get to without a car. I've rented a car in Chile, and would do so in Argentina or Uruguay as well if I wanted to explore the countryside.

Central and Eastern Europe: Carjacking, car theft, vandalism, and assault or extortion of motorists are major reasons not to drive in Central or Eastern Europe. I'd consider hiring a car and driver if I could afford it, or take trains and urban mass transit, rather than trying to drive myself.

COSTS OF RENTING A SELF-DRIVE CAR

When calculating the cost of renting a car, be sure that you consider the following costs:

- Daily, weekly, or monthly rental fees
- Additional per-mile or per-kilometer charges
- Taxes: Value-added tax (VAT) and other taxes may be 20 percent of the pretax price. Quoted prices usually do not include tax.
- Insurance: Absolutely essential even if not legally required. Depending on the country, it can cost US$20–50 per day or more. The places where insurance is most expensive are the ones where it's most needed. In the United States, even a nonfatal collision could easily leave you liable for hundreds of thousands of dollars in medical costs for someone who is injured.
- Fuel: U.S. and Canadian gas prices are still exceptionally low by world standards. Gasoline can cost twice as much in Western Europe or Japan.
- Road, bridge, and tunnel tolls: Japanese highway tolls often exceed train fares for similar distances; Western European road and bridge tolls are encountered more frequently, and are several times higher, than U.S. tolls.
- Parking: Especially in cities, finding parking can cost you time as well as money; once again, Western European and Japanese urban parking lots and garages often charge several times as much as their counterparts in even the densest U.S. cities.

Make sure to get copies of all essential documents before you set off in a rented car. Don't leave them in the car when you aren't in it: keep them with you, with your most important papers, in your money belt at all times. Losing them could cost you thousands of dollars, especially if you have traveled across international borders, can't get back without proper papers, and have to pay for weeks of additional rental charges while proper replacement documentation is procured.

You'll need proof of the car's registration (licensing) with the proper governmental authorities, proof of ownership (title) by the rental company, proof of your permission to operate it (usually provided by the rental contract), and proof of insurance (sometimes in the rental contract, sometimes in a separate insurance contract and/or certificate).

Each person who will be driving a rented car must be listed on the rental and insurance contract, which usually means that all potential drivers must be personally present when the car is rented, and each must sign the contract. Don't ignore this rule. If an unauthorized driver gets into an accident, the renter who let that person drive could be liable not merely for damages (unprotected by insurance, which doesn't apply to unauthorized drivers) but also for breach of contract in allowing someone else to drive.

In addition to the general licensing and border-crossing requirements for privately owned vehicles discussed earlier, you'll need the permission of the car rental company (as the owner of the car) to take it across any international border.

CROSSING INTERNATIONAL BORDERS

It is imperative that the rental car contract explicitly give you permission to take the car into any country that you will pass through, no matter how briefly, and that the insurance policy explicitly cover operation of the car in each country.

If you plan to take a rented car across an international border, that should be the first thing you tell the car rental company or travel agent when you inquire about renting the car. Rates for international rentals may be much higher than domestic rates, and international rentals may be subject to very different rules.

For example, car rental companies generally allow their cars to be taken back and forth across the United States–Canada border, although one-way transborder rentals may be prohibited or severely surcharged. But almost none will allow cars rented in the United States to be taken into Mexico, at any price.

Similarly, most car rentals in Western Europe have substantial surcharges, if not outright prohibitions, on travel out of the European Union, especially into Eastern Europe. Rental contracts in South Africa generally prohibit travel into any other country.

If there are restrictions like this, there's a reason, and you should think twice about what it might be. Are road conditions much worse or more dangerous across the border? Are repair services harder to find, or more expensive? Are cars (perhaps especially foreign cars) more likely to be stolen, vandalized, or stripped of easily removed but essential parts?

REASONS TO HIRE
A CAR AND DRIVER

In most of the Second, Third, and Fourth Worlds, it makes more sense to hire a chauffeured car rather than to drive a car yourself. In many countries, it's the only way to hire a car, and if you ask to rent a car it will be assumed that you want to hire a driver as well.

This is a strange idea to many First Worlders. If you've never been in a chauffeured car other than a taxi, you might never even think of hiring one. This is actually the predominant form of car rental in much of the world, and I've hired chauffeured cars in places as diverse as Ethiopia, Syr-

> ### REAL LIFE
>
> "Self-sufficient" First Worlders think it a sign of incompetence to ask directions from people along the way. People in the rest of the world think it symptomatic of arrogant First Worlders' "superior" knowledge that they insist on following their map—even if ambiguous, potentially out of date, or simply wrong—when there are plenty of local people around who actually know exactly where local places are and would be happy to tell them if asked.

ia, Vietnam, Pakistan, China, and Russia. But it seems so outlandish, to those unfamiliar with it, that a somewhat detailed explanation of its rationale is in order. "I know how to drive," you may be tempted to say. "Why would I want or need a chauffeur?" There are many reasons.

A Local Driver's Most Important Role May Be as Navigator.

They may already know the way, especially if yours is a nearby or a common destination. If not, they may be better able than you to read and interpret cryptic road signs, ask directions in local language(s) from passersby, figure out which people are best to ask, and—perhaps most important—know how to interpret the directions they are given. They are more likely than you to know which routes are apt to be faster, less crowded, or more scenic, or which are apt to be impassable in the current season and weather.

In rich countries, there are detailed maps of even small streets and roads in less-traveled areas. In poor countries, there are usually fewer, less-detailed, and less-frequently updated maps—if you can find any maps at all. The best available maps may be the mental maps of local residents. A day's wages for a driver may be less than you'd willingly pay in your home country for a good map.

In addition to navigating the roads, a local driver can navigate the local bureaucracy and deal with officials. Roadblocks, police and/or military checkpoints, and document checks are more common in countries outside the First World. Private cars, being most rare (and thus most suspicious) are

Surface Transportation

most likely to be stopped. A local driver is more likely than you to know the appropriate things to say and do in such situations, and to be able to maximize your chances of being allowed to proceed without having to pay too much. In places where hijackers and extortionists often masquerade as officials, a driver is more likely than you to be able to recognize the real Mc-Coy, and to know when it is best to stop, when and how much to pay, and when to drive on without stopping.

A Chauffeur Can Often Be Helpful as an Interpreter and Guide.

Presumably, you are driving around in a strange country because you want to experience it and learn about (and from) it. Why spend your time in a car in silence, or talking to yourself or fellow travelers, when you could spend it talking with a local informant? Even a chauffeur who doesn't speak a word of your language can point out things to look at, take you to places that you wouldn't have found or noticed on your own, or indicate places that you shouldn't go or things you shouldn't do.

A driver's less-carefully constructed presentation may give you a more accurate perspective on local opinion than that of a professional guide who is trained and paid to say what they think tourists want to hear. A driver gets paid to drive, no matter what they think or say, and taxi drivers the world over are rightly known for speaking their minds. There's a reason cabbies are quoted so often by foreign journalists as the mouthpieces of local public opinion.

A Driver Buys Fuel and Arranges for Any Necessary Repairs or Services, Sparing You Much Work, Worry, and Responsibility.

In some countries it is expected that professional drivers will also be professional mechanics, scroungers, and hoarders of scarce parts. Even in countries where "driver" and "mechanic" are distinct jobs, a local driver will probably be more knowledgeable than you at finding fuel, parts, and services, and knowing how much they ought to cost. And your driver may be able to take care of some of these tasks while you are sightseeing, so you don't have to waste your time on them. If your self-drive car breaks down, you'll have to stay with it until it is fixed. With a driver to look after the vehicle, you can do other things while it is repaired, or settle your bill, abandon car and driver, and continue your travels without them.

Having a driver thus gives you, perhaps paradoxically, more freedom and flexibility. It's possible, for example (I've done it several times) to hire a car and driver for a one-way journey—provided you are willing to pay the cost for the driver to return without you—in many places where one-way self-drive car rental would be impossible.

Hiring a Driver Greatly Reduces Your Legal and Financial Liability.

Hiring a driver is, in a certain sense, the most effective and often the cheapest form of insurance. If you are driving a car, you are responsible for complying with all the local ownership, licensing, tax, and insurance requirements, and for having all the related paperwork in order.

In your own country, where you know the language and are familiar with the rules, this may be a straightforward task. In other countries, even your best efforts to comply with the law may be unsuccessful. If you are told that your vehicle's documents aren't in order, you may have no way of knowing whether or not you have actually committed a crime, or whether you are simply being shaken down for a bribe. Unfortunately, both inadvertent law-breaking and attempted extortion are common road hazards in most of the world—even if you are lucky enough never to be involved in a collision. You are far less vulnerable to fine, arrest, or extortion, whether for real or pretend violations, if you aren't driving.

If you are in a collision (assuming you survive unhurt), whether you are the driver can make all the difference in the world. In the United States, motor vehicle collisions are presumed to be accidents unless there is proof of negligence, drunkenness, or violation of the rules of the road. Hitting someone or something with a motor vehicle is not, per se, a crime.

In less automotive societies, where cars are a luxury, a nuisance, and a danger, people operating automobiles are responsible for any damage caused by their cars. Laws in many countries require fatal or injury car crashes to be treated like any other incidents of killing or wounding of people by other people. Suspects—that is, any surviving drivers—are automatically arrested on assault or murder charges. At the very least, you can expect to be held for questioning until the police have completed their investigation. You may be held until it is known if the injured people will survive or how extensive or permanent their injuries are. This could mean days, weeks, or months of incarceration, even if you are eventually acquitted. As a foreigner who is rich enough to afford a car, you are obviously likely to be motivated and able to flee, and thus are unlikely to be released on bail.

Drivers blamed for fatal crashes in some other countries are likely to be lynched, or at least severely beaten, by mobs of survivors, victims' families, and other passersby.

Passengers, on the other hand, are likely to have no liability, and (unless they are injured) little inconvenience in such cases. You may be delayed, even held briefly by the police for questioning, but if you aren't hurt, it probably won't ruin your trip or delay you more than a few days, possibly not at all.

A Driver Will Look After the Vehicle When You Aren't in It.

You still can't be too cavalier about leaving valuables in a vehicle, or too unconcerned with where it is parked, but a driver is the best security for a vehicle and its contents that would otherwise be left unattended.

Security is the main reason hiring a car and driver can even be cheaper, as well as easier, than hiring a self-drive car. In a country where labor is cheap, it may be entirely reasonable for someone who hires out a car without an accompanying driver to charge more—on the basis of the justifiable expectation that renters on their own are more likely to get into costly trouble or to damage the car or allow it to be damaged.

Paying to protect a rented car shouldn't be an unusual concept. After all, we are accustomed to paying more per day for theft and vandalism insurance on a car rented in the First World than would equal the wages of a semiskilled Third World worker. We are just accustomed to capital-intensive approaches to security—locks, alarms, garage doors—rather than labor-intensive ones like a full-time watchman, lookout, and vehicle guard. This is only one example of a much larger pattern of how things are done, and how people expect them to be done, in different worlds. (See the sidebar *Efficiency and Independence* in the *Choosing Destinations* chapter.)

HOW TO HIRE A CAR AND DRIVER

You can hire a car and driver by the hour, by the day, or for a specific journey. In places where chauffeurs' wages are very low and visitors rich enough to hire cars are relatively wealthy, the chauffeur's wages are usually included in prices quoted for the hire of a car. But it never hurts to ask.

The longer the journey or term of the rental, the more everything is negotiable. Be sure whether you will have exclusive use of the vehicle. If you charter a car to take you from point A to point B, there will typically be one price for a ride shared with as many other riders as the car's owner or driver can find, and a higher price to ride alone. Also settle whether you will be expected to pay for fuel (usually yes) and/or food and lodging for the driver (usually no) in addition to

REAL LIFE

More than one person I know has been charged with murder in a foreign country for having been the driver of a car involved in a fatal collision. One friend's car was hit head-on by a car driven by a drunk speeding down the wrong side of the road. The drunken driver was killed; my friend and his wife were both injured. He was well-connected and lucky, and he spoke a locally understood language: he bribed his way out of the local jail after only six months, although he still faces criminal charges if he ever returns to that jurisdiction.

Surface Transportation

the agreed-upon price. Never get in any vehicle except a metered taxi without agreeing in advance on a precise price.

If need be, don't hesitate to tell the driver to slow down, or to drive more safely. (The Association for Safe International Road Travel, ASIRT, listed in the *Resource Guide,* produces multilingual pocket "cheat sheets" for this purpose.) You'll probably only be laughed at if you ask a reckless or speeding public bus driver to slow down, but if you've chartered the vehicle and hired the driver, you are perfectly entitled to insist that they satisfy your standards of safe driving. Don't assume that "they must know what they are doing" if you feel they are driving recklessly or too fast.

Drivers often make the assumption that you have chartered a car because you wanted to go faster than you could by bus. If this isn't the case, make that clear before you start. It can be hard to get across that you are willing to pay for the privilege of going more slowly, less directly, and stopping more often. If the driver doesn't speak your language, and you can communicate more easily through the person with whom you have arranged the rental, have that person explain this to the driver before you set off.

Private companies in Russia and some other countries routinely offer bonuses to drivers if their foreign passengers don't complain about their speed or safety. Chartering a car on your own, you can take their example: if the driver knows they will be paid a few extra dollars at the end of the day if they don't exceed a certain speed, or simply if you are pleased with how they have driven, they will be much more willing to humor your desire to survive the ride.

Sometimes an archaeological, historical, or scenic site is accessible only by slow, painful, and unreliable buses, or a game park admits visitors only in motorized vehicles. If you can't afford to hire a vehicle on your own, a solution is to gather a group of travelers to share the rental of a car and driver for a few hours or days. At times like these "travelers' ghettos" come in handy: ask around at places where travelers hang out, or post notices on guesthouse bulletin boards. Put out the word that you'll give a small tip to anyone who finds you people to share a ride, and soon the word will be all over town.

MOTORIZED TWO- AND THREE-WHEELED VEHICLES

Most of the world's motorized vehicles are two-and three-wheeled: mopeds, scooters, and motorcycles.

As with a car, you can bring such a vehicle with you, buy one locally, rent one, or even hire someone to drive you around on one. As with a car, each has its pitfalls. And two-wheelers have a few special dangers of their own, even aside from the intrinsically greater danger of riding them than riding in cars.

Licensing, registration, tax, and insurance requirements are fundamentally similar for two-wheelers and four-wheelers, although somewhat cheaper

REAL LIFE

Author Bill Dalton's comments in his *Moon Indonesia* could be applied to anywhere in the Third or Fourth World: "Indonesia is no place to learn to ride a motorcycle. Ride one with great caution as serious motorcycle accidents on Indonesia's madcap roads are common. Chickens, dogs, and children dart out unexpectedly into the road, there are giant potholes, big trucks lumber down the road straddling both lanes, and cars travel at night without using their headlights. Boulders, small rivers, and landslides on the road in the rainy season are other hazards.... You should possess at least a crude knowledge of motorcycle mechanics if you plan to rent a bike here. It's also advisable to bring a few simple tools."

for two-wheelers. Not that much cheaper, though: even a moped, much less a four-stroke motorcycle, is still a luxury in most of the world, and taxed and dutied as such. There's about the same amount of paperwork and bureaucracy regardless of the size or type of vehicle.

Transoceanic shipping charges are likewise not that much less for big motorcycles than for small cars. You can, however, sometimes bring a small motorbike or scooter in the baggage car of a passenger train. Some ships and ferries that won't carry cars will carry motorcycles.

Roads are a mixed bag. A car's higher wheels (especially compared to a small-wheeled scooter) can get through deeper mud and larger potholes. But many Third and Fourth World roads are too narrow for cars. And a motorbike is easier than a car to carry or push through or over obstacles, or to carry on a raft or small boat across floods or waters that simply aren't bridged.

There's less reason to bring a motorbike with you (except perhaps if you want the largest of motorcycles) than to bring a car, since mopeds and scooters are in wider use in the South than the North. You're likely to find more types of mopeds and scooters available where you are going than at home. Vietnam takes the prize, with every conceivable variety of Russian, Chinese, Japanese, Indian, Western and Central European, and U.S. motorbike in use. Several large Southern countries, such as India, not only produce but export large numbers of motorized two- and three-wheelers. (For a while you could even get Indian scooters in the United States, modified and certified to meet California emissions limits!)

As with a locally purchased car, it's usually easiest to find parts and repairs for a locally purchased bike, especially a locally made one.

You are probably more likely to be tempted to rent a small moped or motor scooter than to bring, buy, or rent a big motorcycle. However, don't be lulled into complacency by the small size and weight, small engine, and relatively low speed of a moped or scooter. Even small motorbikes are much more dangerous than bicycles. Motorized two-wheeler crashes are the leading cause of death among Peace Corps Volunteers, for example.

The legal requirements to own and/or operate any motorized vehicle are essentially the same, with the additional requirement that both your local and international driving licenses must be specially endorsed for motorcycles for them to be valid for any motorized two-wheeler. You probably wouldn't even think of renting a motorcycle unless you were an experienced rider already. But you might not realize that operating even a small scooter or moped legally requires, in most countries, both a regular license and a motorcycle endorsement. If you want to be able to rent a moped or scooter anywhere along the way, get a proper motorcycle license in your home country before you get your international driving permit. Even if you don't care about the law, do it for your own safety.

People who rent small scooters and mopeds to foreigners would lose most of their business if they rented only to riders with valid motorcycle licenses. So they don't check. But that doesn't mean the police won't check your license, either at routine roadblocks or traffic stops or if you're in any kind of crash. You can probably bribe your way out of a charge of riding without a license, but it could be expensive. Getting into an injury crash while operating a motorbike without a valid motorcycle license could have more serious legal consequences.

Outside the First World, I wouldn't ever drive more than a couple of miles at night, in any motor vehicle. The best book on Third World travel by car, Carl Franz's *The People's Guide to Mexico,* has this simple advice on night driving: "Don't." I'd say the same for riding motorbikes or buses at night.

It's all too easy to get in trouble on mopeds or scooters. We tend to think of them as just like bicycles: "child's play." But what is only a fender-bending crash in a car can leave a motorbike rider with scrapes, gashes, broken bones, and the possibility of serious infection from the wounds. Foreign travelers often use two-wheelers to get to remote or rural areas where medical treatment is a long way away. If you went by motorbike because cars can't get through (because the roads are too narrow or muddy, or the ferries or fords are too small to carry cars), getting back on the bike may be the only way out, no matter how badly you are hurt.

People who rent out motorbikes by the day in the Third or Fourth World don't usually even pretend to offer insurance. If you get hurt while operating a vehicle illegally, no insurance will cover you anyway. If someone else gets hurt, and you are operating your vehicle illegally (without a proper license), you will be presumptively at fault.

Surface Transportation

Keep a close eye on any motorbike, bought or rented, and always leave it securely locked and, if possible, guarded or watched. In rich countries, where there are more cars than motorbikes, thieves prefer cars. In a poor country, a stolen car is conspicuous and can be hard to sell or make use of. A stolen motorbike is easy to ride away, yet widely coveted. Even a small moped may still cost the average worker a years' wages—enough to motivate thieves to pretty extreme measures. Don't count on collision or theft insurance for a rented motorbike. If you rent a bike, and it's stolen or destroyed in a crash, you'll have to buy the owner a new one. Find out before you rent one how much it will cost if it's stolen or wrecked. If you couldn't afford to pay for it if you had to, don't take the risk of renting it. Or rent something cheaper, like a nonmotorized bicycle.

WHICH SIDE (OF THE ROAD) ARE YOU ON?

If you operate your own vehicle, of any sort, you may have to deal with doing so on the opposite side of the road. There is no world standard, but, at the risk of offending the British, I will say that the practice of the majority of the world is to ride and drive on the right-hand side of the road. For up-to-date country-by-country listings, see the online article by Brian Lucas listed in the *Resource Guide.*

Outside the First World, of course, roads are more often than not one lane or less wide, and any vehicle drives down the middle of the road. But when they pass, they keep to the right. They drive on the right in all of the Americas (except some former British colonies in the Caribbean and northern South America), continental Europe, northern and western Africa, Madagascar, and Asia north of the Himalayas except Japan and Hong Kong. They drive on the left in the British Isles, South Asia, southern and most of eastern Africa, Australia, and Aotearoa/New Zealand.

Southeast Asia and Oceania are a complex patchwork. They drive on the right in Taiwan, the Philippines, Vietnam, Laos, Cambodia, and (rather strangely, given its history and neighbors) Myanmar/Burma. They drive on the left in Papua New Guinea, East Timor, Indonesia, Malaysia, Brunei, Singapore, and Thailand. The smaller Pacific Ocean island states and colonies are likewise a mix.

Your first experience of driving or riding on the opposite side of the road is not an easy situation. Use extreme caution. On a bicycle, go slowly and keep to the edge of the road. In a car, it can be harder to go more slowly than the rest of the traffic. Keep reminding yourself that your instinct in an emergency will be to swerve the wrong way, into the path of oncoming traffic. If you start to panic and don't know which path to follow through an intersection, which way to turn, or which lane to use, follow the vehicle in front of you. It is always better to take a wrong turn than to turn the wrong way down a one-way street, around a rotary/roundabout/traffic circle, or onto a highway, and cause a head-on crash. (See the sidebar *Advice for the First Time You Drive on the "Wrong" Side of the Road*.)

There are remarkably few roads across borders between left- and right-hand-drive countries. Most of them are on extremely lightly traveled roads between central and eastern or southern Africa. You are unlikely ever to drive yourself across such a border. By far the busiest crossing is between Hong Kong and the rest of China, but it's mostly a crossing for local and professional drivers; few visitors drive themselves in China.

Bicycles

Bicycles are the world's most common vehicles and most common form of mechanized transportation. With good reason: they are also the most energy-efficient form of human transportation now known, or likely to be developed in the foreseeable future. The whole point of a bicycle, after all, is to enable you to go farther, with more cargo, with less work, than you could on foot.

Bicycles are also the most environmentally friendly form of short-distance mechanized transportation. Except for protection against the weather, they are everything one could hope for. They produce very little chemical pollution, essentially only that required for their manufacture and occasional maintenance. And bicycles are essentially silent; the first thing most people used to notice on a city street in China, before motor vehicles began to dominate the traffic mix in the 1990s, was the absence of noise pollution.

Because bicycles make such efficient use of even narrow streets, they require very little land for roads. Bicycle roads also require smaller (or no) bridges and

REAL LIFE

One might think that bicycles have too short a range and too small a cargo capacity to displace motor vehicles. But one would be wrong, not least because motor vehicles have yet to displace human-powered walking and cycling as most of the world's primary means of transportation. Most of the world's people never go beyond a day's bicycling distance from the place of their birth. In the United States, most travel—for commuting, shopping, socializing—is within bicycling distance of travelers' homes. Even for longer commutes, most people are within bicycling distance of mass transportation. Until just a few years ago, far more people in the world relied on bicycles than motor vehicles for daily transportation. And the big change of late has been from bicycles to motorized two-wheelers, more than to cars.

Surface Transportation

Advice for the First Time You Drive on the "Wrong" Side of the Road

Don't do it when you are fresh off a long-haul flight.

This is most likely to be a temptation for people from countries where they drive on the left, coming for the first time to parts of America where it's hard to get anywhere without your own car. No matter what the circumstances, and no matter how great the expense, spend the night at the airport, or take a taxi or public transit into town, before trying to drive on the "wrong" side for the first time. Come back to the airport the next morning, if necessary, to pick up your car. Airports — which generally have relatively well-signed access roads — are typically better places to start out on the "wrong" side than downtown car rental locations, so this may be a worthwhile strategy anyway.

Don't do it alone. No matter what.

If you are traveling by yourself, and can't find anyone you know and trust to accompany you, arrange for an initial lesson from a driving school. If you make a mistake, and don't notice it in time, the odds are that your companion will.

Minimize distractions in the car such as music, telephone calls, and navigation.

Driving on the "wrong" side for the first time demands your complete attention, even on a quiet country road. This is another very strong reason to have someone else with you in the car to handle navigation and other tasks.

Expect to make mistakes.

Be conservative, and give yourself more room for error than you usually would. Everyone makes at least a few mistakes. The issue is whether you (or your traveling companion) notices them, and you correct your course, in time.

Avoid doing it in a city.

You aren't likely to wander across to the wrong side of a country road, even if there's no traffic to remind you which side to keep to. The big hazards are intersections and, to a much lesser extent, narrow roads or roads without shoulders. When you are sitting on the opposite side to what you are used to, it takes quite a while to get used to judging where the edges of the car are, and the clearance to the edge of the road or traffic alongside. Complex intersections, or suburban "strips" with lots of entering, exiting, crossing, and turning, are the most difficult and dangerous places.

Avoid night driving if at all possible.

There's a good reason why learners' permits are often valid only for daytime driving. Night driving is harder, especially at first. Your first time on the opposite side of the road, you're a student driver. Do it in daylight. For similar reasons, avoid starting out in rain or snow, if you can.

Pick a time and day with as little traffic as possible.

Avoid rush hour. If you have a choice, pick up your car on a Sunday morning, or the equivalent ebb in the local schedule and traffic pattern, when other drivers will be in less of a hurry and will give you more slack.

Try to find an automatic-transmission car, at least at first.

This is another reason to consider a driving-school lesson, if your rental car will have a manual transmission. One of the most common errors of "wrong-side" learners is to start to turn into oncoming traffic, realize your mistake, and stop short — stalling the car before you can turn back to the correct path. I'm more ambidextrous than most people (it often goes along with being left-handed), but I still found that shifting with the "wrong" hand was one more thing to get used to. I also found it hard to get used to having the pedals in the same arrangement while the hand controls were all reversed. I made many more mistakes with the pedals, including the clutch, than with the stick shift. The fewer things you have to learn and remember at once, the safer you will be.

Don't get overconfident.

The most dangerous time is when you have begun to think you have gotten the hang of it (and have, mostly), but your reactions in an emergency, when you have to swerve without conscious thought, are still wrong. Go more slowly and carefully than you usually would for at least your first couple of weeks of wrong-side driving, and the first few days every time you switch sides after that.

Surface Transportation

less elaborate engineering and construction of roads than for any other type of vehicle. We think of bicycles more as urban vehicles, but they are even more dominant in rural areas where there is little or no mass transportation and roads are little wider than paths. A family bicycle is the mechanical workhorse of the world's peasantry.

As the only land vehicle readily portaged by a single person, a bicycle can go almost anywhere a pedestrian can—only faster, and with less work. As for cargo, minimally modified bicycles or pedal tricycles can carry up to half a ton of cargo at jogging speed on smooth level pavement. Foreigners think of pedal tricycles as "bicycle rickshaws" for passengers, but local people use them more as light trucks for hire by the load. "In Bangladesh, trishaws...transport more tonnage than all motor vehicles combined," notes the Worldwatch Institute. In short, the bicycle is already the world's primary means of mechanized short-distance personal transportation and will be the primary medium-distance (between walking and trains) vehicle of any "green" or sustainable human future.

BICYCLING IN ALL WEATHER

A bicycle rider is exposed to the weather, and I won't try to persuade you to emulate the millions of people who ride their bicycles through the heaviest snowstorms in Beijing. But I will point out that in all but extreme cold, exercise and a warm coat may keep you warmer on a bicycle than riding the typical Third World unheated but drafty bus. And it's difficult to imagine any circumstances in which bicycling could be less comfortable than some Fourth World buses, no matter what the weather.

It's also worth noting, for those of you who remain skeptical, that places far from the tropics, such as Copenhagen, Denmark, and Basel, Switzerland, have a year-round average of 20 percent of daily passenger trips made by bicycle, with the figure climbing to as much as 50 percent in some Dutch cities.

In a hot climate, relaxed pedaling can create a pleasant breeze. I'm more comfortable bicycling in the tropics than walking, especially if there's little or no wind. If it's hot, rain can also be quite enjoyably cooling.

If it rains, you'll get wet, but so what? In tropical areas subject to heavy rainstorms, it's better to dress for a soaking and enjoy the free shower if it happens, rather than to make a futile attempt at dressing to stay dry that will only ensure that you stay too hot. Any attempt to stay dry in a tropical downpour is futile, no matter what means of transport you use.

BRINGING A BICYCLE BY AIR

As with cars and motorcycles, you can bring a bicycle with you, buy one locally, or rent one. Given the cost and hassle of shipping a bike by air, and the greater availability of parts for locally purchased models, bringing a bicycle from home makes sense only if you'll be spending a long time in one place, or in a region within which you won't need or want to travel much by air but will still need to cover as much distance as possible.

As part of their increasing reliance on "ancillary fees" as a profit center, airlines have greatly increased their prices for taking a bike with you. Fees for bikes and other excess or oversize baggage are also much less standardized than they were a few years ago. Some airlines charge a flat rate per bike, some charge by weight (which usually costs more), and some "low-fare" airlines don't want to carry bikes at all. Regardless of the system used, the fee is rarely nominal. The same airline may use different

REAL LIFE

A snapshot I took in Shanghai 20 years ago shows a trishaw carrying two people and a full-size refrigerator. They went by faster than I could walk. None of the locals thought it an unusual sight. If they looked at anything, they looked at the electric refrigerator-freezer—a sign of considerable wealth—not the mode of its transport.

systems on different routes. Check with the specific airlines, individually, about their bike charges on the specific routes you are interested in.

If you plan to take many flights, it may make sense to take your bike only as far as you can on the piece rule, and then sell it, rather than trying to take it all the way around the world. The same principle applies for other heavy items such as surfboards, collapsible kayaks, or heavy camping or trekking gear.

Shipping such things home isn't usually much of an option. Unaccompanied air cargo costs even more than excess accompanied baggage—one reason for the use of air couriers to accompany express cargo on passenger flights. Sea-freight shipping is moderately expensive and an enormously time-consuming pain to arrange in most foreign countries.

Getting a bike through customs is generally no problem, except in places where *everyone* gets hassled at customs. If you are entering the country as a tourist, it's usually taken for granted that you will take the bike away with you when you leave. If you are considering or planning to sell the bike or give it away before leaving the country, don't say so. But be sure to take note of

Surface Transportation

whether the bike is recorded in your customs declaration or any other document you'll have to show when you leave the country. If it is, the game is up, and you'll probably have to pay some sort of duty or fee to leave the country without the bike.

Tires, components, and parts to fit a foreign bike may or may not be available locally. Standard rim and tire sizes, frame tubing diameters, etc., vary. If possible, check with someone who has toured that country with a bike similar to the one you are considering bringing. Before you go, locate mail-order suppliers who will, if necessary, ship you replacement parts in an emergency, or make arrangements with your local bike shop to do so if needed. Find out how long shipping is likely to take, how much it is likely to cost, and whether bike parts are likely to be subject to customs delays or duty on arrival.

As long as you say you intend to take the bike with you when you go, you'll rarely be charged duty or need a *carnet,* proof of ownership, or any documentation. Tourists are rarely forced to register their bikes with any government agency, even if bicycle registration requirements are strictly enforced on local people.

BUYING A LOCAL BIKE

Buying a bike locally makes sense if you're staying in one place for a while and are interested in local transportation rather than cross-country touring. (Local bikes outside the First World are apt to be heavier and slower, but less and less so as the same bikes come to dominate the midrange market worldwide.)

Buying a bike may also be a good choice if you are traveling by train or bus through an area where, although bicycles are effective local transportation, bicycle rental is little known and thus time-consuming to arrange in each town.

One way to look for a used bike is to ask around among shorter-term expatriate residents, such as teachers at language schools or NGO workers. Many buy new bicycles when they arrive, even for stays as short as a few months, and sell them when they leave. They may be able to help spread the word that you are looking for a

REAL LIFE

If a steel-frame bike crashes or gets damaged by heavy cargo stacked on top of it on top of a bus, it's usually possible to bend it (or, in the worst case, weld or braze it) back to rideable condition using simple, locally available tools. Aluminum or carbon-fiber frames, forks, and other components are sometimes lighter, but when they fail, they do so catastrophically and irreparably.

used bike, suggest places you could post "wanted to buy" notices, advise you on how much to pay, or suggest bike dealers who speak your language and are accustomed to dealing with foreigners.

Don't count on getting much back, if anything at all, by selling your bike before you leave. Buyers will know you are leaving, can't take the bike with you, and have to take whatever you can get. You might get more in barter than in cash. Many foreigners simply give their bikes away when they move on, sometimes as a "tip" to someone who has been particularly helpful or generous to them during their stay.

RENTING A BIKE

In the South, renting is usually the simplest way to get the use of a bicycle when you need one. If you are taking more than a few flights, and not staying more than a month in one place, renting will probably be cheaper than buying a bike or bringing one with you.

The ease of arranging to rent a bicycle varies enormously from place to place. In tourist centers in China and Vietnam, for example, bikes are a standard means of local transportation for foreign travelers as well as expatriates, and the rental of bikes to foreigners is a well-established trade. Elsewhere in Asia, except in the former USSR, bikes are common, and with a little effort you can always find someone willing to rent you a bike, even if there is no organized system of bicycle rental.

Bikes make perfect sense in smaller Second World cities, weather permitting. But Soviet people, like North Americans, are so infatuated with automobiles and so over-protective of foreigners that you may have trouble persuading them to let you travel by bicycle. It's certainly not the Intourist way to go. Fortunately, you may not need a bike in Second World cities, as most have good mass transit alternatives. At the time of its breakup, the Soviet Union had the world's best urban rail transportation systems, even in provincial cities.

Bicycles are a less-dominant transportation form in most countries in Africa and Central and South America than in Asia. People too poor to afford motorized transportation in these parts of the world are more likely to walk, except in a few countries—notably Cuba—where central economic planners have decided to emphasize providing bicycles for the masses. That doesn't mean bikes are unknown—there are bicycles everywhere—but it does mean your request to rent a bike may be unusual. Most people will assume at first that you want a motorbike; be prepared to explain "no motor" and to pantomime pedaling.

Unfortunately, destination guidebooks tend to mention bicycle-rental services only in the few cities where many foreigners rent bikes, and where

All in a Day's Ride

You never know just what will happen when you ask for a bike. Consider how it went for me some years ago in Ahmedabad, India (at the time the world's 52nd-largest city, population about 3.5 million — slightly more than Sydney, Australia). My traveling companion was sick in bed and wanted a room with a private, clean, flush toilet. So we stayed at a downtown hotel, more expensive than my norm. At 250 rupees (then about US$15) per night, it was insufficiently upscale for most foreigners, but a fairly high-class place by the standards of the domestic business travelers who seemed to make up most of its clientele.

When I told the desk clerk I wanted a bicycle, he first offered to arrange the hire of a car and driver for the day. This was a big city, he made clear, with roads wide enough for cars, where big-city services like cars for hire could be had. He took it for granted that no one would choose a bicycle if there were "better" options.

When I insisted I wanted a bicycle, he tried to hail a cycle rickshaw for me. Finally I got across that I wanted to pedal a bicycle myself.

Still trying to set me straight, he insisted that this just wouldn't do. As tactfully as possible, he warned me that pedaling a bicycle just wasn't appropriate for a sahib. He could have said, but didn't, that it violated the rules of the caste-like special status of a white person, and thus offended his sense of caste. He did say that I would be embarrassed and that people might mistake me for a commoner. He really felt that he was trying to help me, in my obvious ignorance, avoid an inadvertent faux pas and loss of face. Had I been traveling on business and trying to keep up a "respectable" appearance, I would have been grateful for his advice.

But it would have been impossible to get him to understand that I wanted to be able to talk to people that I met as an equal, not to have the conversation limited to, "Yes, sahib," "No, sahib," and "What you want, sahib?" I simply insisted that I wanted to pedal myself. Finally he gave up trying to dissuade me and gamely got to work getting me what I wanted.

He might have come to the conclusion that I was a crazy sahib, but I was still a sahib, and a rich one (by local standards) at that. As everywhere, rich lunatics are humored, and Indians, like most once-colonized peoples, have a long tradition of being forced to provide for the desire of rich white foreigners for bizarre-seeming styles of living. If I was willing to pay 250 rupees a night for a room, he was willing to do his best to accommodate my eccentricities. Just as, if you order peanut-butter sandwiches from a US$250-a-night Ritz Hotel, the chefs will do their best, and the waiter will bring them with a smile.

The clerk summoned one of the hotel servants and gave him instructions in Gujarati. "You go with our man here," he said to me in English.

I followed him down a side street and through the maze of the bazaar to a bike shop I would never have found on my own, where he argued for a while with the man in charge. Neither the servant nor anyone in the shop spoke any English, but I assume that he was vouching for me on behalf of the hotel.

Presently I was shown a fine new bike and a sum to pay for the day (50 rupees, about US$3), asked to sign a chit (presumably acknowledging responsibility for the bike), and without having to hand over my passport or a deposit I was on my way. The hotel's man showed me the best way out of the bazaar before he left me, and the hotel never tried to charge me extra for their services.

It was a fine day full of experiences I wouldn't have had without the bike. I rode through the countryside to the museum and library at Gandhi's ashram, 6 km (4 miles) out of town, stopping to watch the bathing and laundry ghats by the river along the way. Returning, on the other side of the river, I kept stopping to watch the street life and shrines in a series of exceptionally diverse neighborhoods. My snapshots from that day include the roof lines, towers, and minarets of Muslim, Hindu, Sikh, Buddhist, Jain, and Parsi mosques, temples, and gurdwaras.

Few people paid me any special notice or interrupted what they were doing to stare back at me. In local clothes, I was just another bicyclist. When I stopped to have a look at the exterior of one temple, however, I was noticed as a foreigner and good omen, invited in for tea (pressed upon me by a fasting acolyte), and not allowed to leave until I had joined them for the annual ritual blessing of the temple's financial account books, which happened to be going on that day.

you'd have little trouble finding a bike to rent. They rarely include general information about bike rental rates or availability, or bicycling conditions, in their summaries of transportation options. You'll probably be on your own in finding a bike, or dependent on tips or help from local expatriates, other foreign travelers (if you see another foreigner on a bike, don't hesitate to stop her or him and inquire), or the staff of your hotel, hostel, or guesthouse.

You might get lucky, but you are more likely to find a rental bike suitable for low-speed city sightseeing than one suitable for long-distance touring or fast riding for sport.

Bike shops or people who rent bikes will usually demand some sort of deposit. Either they want cash equal to the replacement cost of the bike (i.e., the price of a new bike, even if you are renting an old one), typically US$50–200. Or they want your passport or some other essential document without which you wouldn't be able or willing to abscond if anything happens to the bike.

If the bike is wrecked or stolen while under your care, you're responsible. Unconditionally. Never mind that you don't consider yourself at fault for the wreck, or that you were careful to lock the bike. That won't repay the former owner, nor will it get her or him another bike. Nor is anyone in a poor country likely to have theft or accident insurance.

Get the damaged bike restored to as good condition as it was when you rented or borrowed it, or better. Or buy another bike, as good or better. Don't try to scrimp, even if it costs US$500 for a proper replacement. The value of the bike—perhaps someone's life's savings—means more to its owner than the money does to you. This is one more reason to rent a bicycle rather than a motorbike, as the cost of even the smallest motorbike can be much higher than that of the best bicycle.

Try to avoid having to leave a cash deposit. Having so much cash in hand creates a great temptation for even the most honest poor person to find some way—such as inventing or exaggerating a claim of damage to the bike—to hold onto some of it when you bring the bike back. If you have so much money for a deposit, you obviously can afford to lose a small part of it. Given a choice, I'd rather leave my passport than cash. But the best solution is to leave some other document that is less essential, but sufficiently official and important-looking to be acceptable as security. An International Driving Permit, printed in nine or more languages with your photograph and official-looking seals, fills the bill well. In fact, I've used my IDP more often as security for renting bicycles and other things than for actually driving motor vehicles. Airline frequent-flyer cards embossed with your name and identification number—easily mistaken for some sort of credit card—sometimes work as well. Be creative: I've sometimes used a library card.

The best place to start looking for a bike to rent is wherever you are staying. Renting a bike from, or arranging the rental through, the place you are staying usually obviates any need for a deposit. After all, they have your luggage as security for the safe return of the bike. Point this out if your hotel, hostel, guesthouse, or whatever asks for a deposit.

Some guesthouses and hostels keep bikes for the use of their guests, sometimes including bicycle usage in the services provided for the basic nightly or weekly room rate. In destinations where renting a bike can cost as much as a night's stay, it's worth searching out such a place to stay. Others add a small charge to their bill for bicycle use. Still others may loan or rent their personal bike, or that of one of their employees, relatives, friends, or neighbors.

Ask, "Do you have a bicycle I can use today? Do you know where I can find one?" There's a good chance you won't be charged anything if you don't mention "renting" or "hiring" a bike. If you aren't charged, give a tip when you return the bike, or when you leave. Try to give the tip to the person who actually loaned the bike, particularly if it wasn't the proprietor of the hotel.

If you do have to pay, rates in Southern cities vary from 50 cents to US$5 per day, depending on the place and the bicycle. Ask other travelers on bicycles what they have paid, or ask disinterested local people how much you should have to pay. You can bargain, as always, but if you push too hard for the cheapest price you're likely to get stuck with a lemon of a bike and come back the next day willing to pay the original asking price for a better one. Rates are usually specified by the day, but you can sometimes rent a bike for half a day, and you can usually negotiate a substantial discount for longer-term rentals.

CHOOSING A BIKE

In more bicycle-friendly places, you'll be offered several types for rent. Three-fourths of the world's bicycles, listed here in order of production volume, are made in China, Taiwan, Japan, the United States, the former USSR, and India. All of these countries export bikes.

I've ridden cargo and city bikes as a professional bicyclist for courier services in Boston and San Francisco. I own road, touring, and city bikes as well as a long-wheelbase recumbent. And I've ridden every common type of foreign bike while traveling. For a short distance around town, any bike will do.

Japanese, Western European, and U.S. bikes are of high quality but so expensive as to be rare in the South. If you want one, bring it with you. Former Soviet bikes are typically the only choice in the Second World, but rare elsewhere. In most Third and Fourth World countries, the choice is between a more expensive Chinese export-grade or Taiwanese low-end lightweight multispeed mountain or road bike, or a cheaper Chinese domestic-style, Indian, or comparable locally made heavy one-speed "cruiser."

Lightweight 10-speeds may seem more modern, but all else being equal, I'd choose heavy one-speeds unless I needed to cover long distances. One-speeds are more versatile, more resistant to damage, and more easily repaired. They are more suitably equipped (wide low-pressure tires and padded spring seat for bad roads and trails, cargo rack and/or basket, etc.), and for most riders more comfortable, stable, and easy to ride. Their weight, for example, makes them track better over ruts and bumps. They are slower, but speed isn't usually the highest priority.

You may think of mountain bikes as best suited to mud, but on a wet or unpaved road you'll stay much cleaner and drier on a bike with mudguards and an enclosed chain, both rare on mountain or road touring models.

Never rent a bike without a lock. Never leave it unless it's locked or in an attended parking area. If there is a guarded parking area, use it, both for security and because parking a bicycle elsewhere may not be allowed. Watch where and how other people park their bikes, and be considerate of other users of the roads and sidewalks when you park a bike. In Asian cities, you can be ticketed and fined for parking a bike in a prohibited area, or obstructing passage.

Chinese, Indian, and Russian one-speed bikes come with integral frame-mounted wheel locks. To lock one, push down the lever to bring a pair of steel fingers together through the spokes, preventing the wheel from turning. To unlock it, turn the key and a spring pulls the fingers out of the spokes and secures the key in the lock. You can't lose the key while you are riding, and you can't remove it unless the lock is locked. It doesn't look that secure, but I've never heard of anyone having their bike stolen while it was locked with one.

Some people prefer Chinese to Indian bikes, or vice versa, but between similar models the condition of the individual bike makes more difference than the manufacturer. Inspect a bicycle closely before you rent it. The first priority is working brakes. (The performance of caliper brakes can often be improved greatly by a quick adjustment to take the excess slack out of the cables, and by oiling the pivots, if oil is available.) The second is main bearings—headset, hubs, cranks, and pedals—that don't stick. The third is a working lock. In addition, there's no point renting a multispeed bike if it doesn't shift easily.

You can't count on finding a well-fitting frame, but at least check the seat and handlebar height, and insist that they be adjusted to fit you as well as possible. Don't be hasty. Check for broken spokes, cable housings, cables, other broken parts, or cables that are frayed close to the breaking point. Tighten any loose nuts and bolts. Pump up the tires. Not too far—they may be tires designed for a lower pressure than those to which you are accustomed, and you may want somewhat less pressure on bumpier roads than on smooth pavement.

Ride the bike up and down for a hundred meters (yards). Listen for unusual sounds, especially of anything rubbing against the tires. Swerve back and forth. Try a few panic stops. Lock the bike. Remove the key. (Sometimes a lock opens and closes but is useless because the key sticks and can't be removed.) Put the key back in and open the lock. If you're not satisfied with anything, ask to look at another bike, or to have better adjustments and lubrication done.

GETTING AROUND BY BIKE

If you plan on bicycling during your travels, and you don't already bicycle regularly in conditions similar to those where you are going, practice before you go. Try both to get in physical shape for riding (and walking) and to learn how to ride in heavy mixed city traffic and on unpaved paths.

Good practice for riding rented bikes in, or on excursions from, Southern cities would be to find or borrow a one-speed "clunker" and try riding it downtown in the nearest big city and on some mountain-bike trails or old dirt roads in the woods.

Don't be too intimidated by city traffic. Most of the danger to bikes in traffic comes from cars, and the more bikes there are, the fewer cars there are likely to be. If you can bicycle through suburban U.S. strip-mall developments, where traffic is heavy and fast and the roads are planned with nil concern for bicycles, you can handle bicycling anywhere, even an Indian city street where bicycles mix it up with pedestrians, bullock carts, and buses, while auto-rickshaws dart around them like bumper cars.

It surprises inexperienced riders to find that the most crowded U.S. cities—thought of as having the worst traffic—are actually the best U.S. cities for bicycling. Distances aren't large, and the traffic slows the cars down to a safe bicycling pace (or slower).

REAL LIFE

Bicycling makes you seem accessible. Other good ice-breakers include: squatting on your heels while eating, conversing, waiting, or resting (people who can't afford chairs and tables are accustomed to squatting and to using the floor or ground as their work surface); joining in pickup football (soccer) games or other sports; flying a kite (you can get very small backpackers' parafoil kites without any sticks); washing and mending clothes (I save my sewing for trains, planes, and waiting rooms, where it helps break through women's fear of me as a man); playing with infants or children; and sharing food, especially foods known to be scorned by foreigners and/or the privileged (sometimes the best local food is looked down on by the local elite). In Yemen, where most foreigners dismiss qat-chewing with contempt, joining in at least once (it did nothing for me, and tasted like chewing grass) was essential to show that we weren't holding ourselves aloof from local culture.

City drivers, especially in the most traffic-choked downtown areas that depend on bicycle messengers for urgent deliveries, are more accustomed to bicycles and know to watch for them on the streets. Washington, D.C., seems as though it was designed for bicyclists. New York City (especially Manhattan) may be the next-best major U.S. city for bicycling. Boston, San Francisco (if you have adequate gears for the hills, or stick to the flats), and Seattle are pretty good as well. Bicycle-rental services, catering increasingly to foreign tourists, are springing up rapidly in all these cities.

In the South, day trips by bicycle are an excellent way to see the countryside while staying in the city. In the United States, we are accustomed to sprawling automotive cities where it takes at least an hour of driving, at 100 km/h (60 mph), to get beyond the city and its residential suburbs. Land use patterns are denser and different in poor cities where most people and goods move by nonmotorized means. Start in the center of a Southern city of a few million people, and a half day of bicycling may take you into villages of farms and market-gardens supplying produce to the city.

One of the greatest advantages of riding a bicycle is that it brings you closer to local people. "Most people in the Third World will never sit inside—let alone own—an automobile," according to the Worldwatch Institute. Most people honestly have no idea what they might have in common with someone who rides around in a car. Even when you have stopped and gotten out of the car, it's hard to escape from being seen as an alien being from the foreign world of the automobile. Sure, some local people ride in cars—politicians, police, landlords, and the like. Friends of the peasantry or the slum-dwellers don't ride in cars, even if they could afford to, for exactly the same reasons I'm advising you not to if there's another way to get where you are going. Sightseeing by car introduces a major barrier to communication with ordinary people.

Riding a bicycle isn't enough for you to pass as a local. But it brings you into contact with local people while engaged in, or at least identified with (if they see you arriving by bike) an activity to which they can relate. It's amazing how much difference this can make. On a bicycle, you become a participant in things that you could only observe as external scenes from a car. On a bicycle, you will be perceived as a fellow human being before you're perceived as a foreigner or a tourist.

TRANSPORTING BIKES ON TRAINS, BUSES, AND BOATS

It's possible to take a bicycle with you, at minimal cost, on almost any other means of surface transportation, including buses, trains, and boats. Procedures vary with the place and the conveyance; you'll have to ask and/or watch what other cyclists do. (Taking bikes on *planes* is another, more expensive story, as discussed earlier under "Bringing a Bike.")

In addition to checking my bike as airline luggage, I've been poled across a river in a canoe while holding my bicycle upright (with half a dozen other people and sundry animals), taken it on subways and long-distance trains, and seen hundreds of bikes tied on the roofs of long-distance buses in diverse countries.

Urban rail systems—subways, elevated trains, streetcars, and commuter trains—have erratic rules and procedures for bicycles, and some try to prohibit them entirely. No matter what the rules, a foreign tourist can usually get let off with only a lecture, once, by being apologetic and pleading ignorance.

On long-distance trains, bikes are usually carried in the baggage car but sometimes in special hanging racks. Sometimes you ride your own bike up to the car and put it in yourself, or hand it over at trackside when the train arrives. In other places you have to check it in at the baggage office in advance. On arrival, you claim your bike the same way you checked it in. You can also ship a bike as unaccompanied rail freight.

Between major stations with baggage service in the United States, shipping a bike by Amtrak, either with you or as unaccompanied "Amtrak Express" freight, is cheaper and easier than bringing it with you on a plane or shipping it by air freight. A bike shipped by Amtrak is less likely to be damaged in transit than one shipped by air.

Check at the train station in advance to see what is required. Bikes may be allowed only between certain stations or on certain trains. You might or might not have to remove the pedals, turn the handlebars, or box your bike to take it on trains with you. In any case, you should take all your panniers and gear off before you check it. You may not be allowed to lock it, as the baggage handlers need to be able to wheel it on the platform. Get to the station well before the train is scheduled to depart to allow for last-minute mix-ups or changed instructions and to be sure you have time to find the baggage office or the right place on the platform to wait.

On ferries, you can usually just ride on and be directed to where to put your bike. On car ferries bikes are sometimes carried with the other vehicles and sometimes on the passenger deck. Securing your bike with bungee cords and even a bit of padding on each side (e.g., a couple of large scraps of cardboard) can help keep it from getting too badly scraped if a bunch of bikes are stacked in a heap, as they often are, or if the crossing is rough. You can't usually stay within sight of your bike, so lock it and take everything portable away from it with you.

Whether you can take a bike on an intercity or long-distance bus depends on the bus, and where luggage is stored. On streamlined high-speed buses, such as those in the United States, luggage is stored in enclosed compartments below the passenger space. If the bus company will accept an unboxed bike, they will do so at your own risk. The bike will be lying on its side, and there's a fair chance of damage from bumps and bangs and other luggage.

Most Third World and almost all Fourth World buses lack cargo holds. Luggage is piled and tied to the roof. Passengers may ride on the roof too, often sitting on the luggage. On buses like these, you are welcome to put your bike on the roof. It's up to you, though, to carry it up the ladder to the roof and tie it on. Secure it well against the jolts from rocks, bumps, and potholes taken at too high a speed: pad it as best you can, and try to load it last, so it will be on the top of the pile. And keep a close eye on it whenever the bus stops and especially when other luggage is being loaded or unloaded.

Urban buses don't generally like to take bikes unless they are equipped with special bike racks. But that's not a problem, because if you have a bike you don't generally need local buses.

IF YOUR BIKE BREAKS DOWN

If your bike breaks down, you may (with a fair amount of grumbling) be allowed to bring it on an ordinary bus, or tie it on the roof of a bus. But you may be better off locking up the broken-down bike and going for help, tools, or parts by bus, or taking the bike away in a taxi or trishaw. I've seen a surprising number of bicycles being carried by trishaw, sometimes half a dozen or more at a time.

In a poor country, a bike mechanic may well be willing, for a minimal surcharge, to come back with you to where you locked up your broken bike. A bike mechanic in a poor country probably doesn't have an elaborate workshop or too many tools to carry anyway. In poor countries where bikes are common, you'll find bike mechanics and tire patchers everywhere, so you won't have far to look. In some countries, when you get a flat tire, you can be accosted by rival tire patchers before you've even figured out why your bike has come to a stop.

Buses

Buses, of diverse sorts, are the most widespread form of public transportation. They are always dangerous, usually uncomfortable, often slow, sometimes an ordeal, and only rarely appropriate where there's any other mass transit choice. But in their many forms they go more places than any other form of mass transit.

As a general rule, the worse the transportation infrastructure is in a country, the greater difference it will make to your comfort to avoid long bus rides. Trains can be pretty bad, but they are almost never as bad as the worst buses. Use buses only where there's no other choice. If you can go partway by train, do so; take a bus only beyond the railhead.

VARIETIES OF BUSES

There are buses ("coaches" in British usage), and then there are buses. They aren't all alike.

In the United States, until the recent emergence of competition from "Chinatown buses" and upstart companies like Megabus, there was essentially only one major long-distance bus company: Greyhound. Bus systems in most other countries are more diverse, with many different companies operating buses of different levels of quality between the same cities, often from completely different bus stations.

The difference in comfort between the cheapest local bus and a luxury "executive" or "tourist-class" express bus can be greater than that between a third-class train ticket on an unreserved train and a private sleeping compartment on a premium-fare mainline express. Locals are, naturally, most familiar with buses. Drivers often have little information about buses, even where they are plentiful. To find out about a mode of transit, ask someone who uses the type and class of conveyance you are interested in.

Middle-income countries with large numbers of people wealthy enough to travel long distances but too poor to own their own family cars, and which for historical or geographic reasons don't have good, comprehensive rail systems, tend to have the best, and most complicated, long-distance bus systems. Among these are Brazil, Argentina, Chile, Mexico, Turkey, and Iran. Major bus stations in any of these countries rival the largest airports in passenger numbers and have a comparably wide array of services.

> ## REAL LIFE
>
> The extreme case of bus stratification is probably still South Africa. Overcrowded (and typically extremely unsafe) minibuses for Black people operate between Black townships or "locations." Greyhound operates buses comparable to those of its namesake in the United States between wealthy, mostly White suburbs. For the population groups in the middle, "Asian" South African bus companies using new Brazilian coaches operate between the traditional downtown city centers. Ask about where the bus leaves from, how much it costs, how long it takes, what company operates it, or how and where to buy tickets, and the answer will depend on your informant's skin color (and your own).

Bus reservation systems can be highly sophisticated, with Internet ticket sales, touch-screen seat selection kiosks, and other features. Unlike airlines that mostly outsource their reservations, most bus lines operate their own reservation systems. There's no way a travel agent or traveler can search for or compare routes, schedules, fares, or availability for multiple bus companies the way they can with traditional airlines. (See the sidebar *How to Find a Bus in Córdoba.*)

CONDITIONS ON BUSES

In Australia, the United States, and Canada, there are many places where the only alternatives to buses are private cars or airplanes, either of which are much more expensive. This does mean that buses are regarded as the vehicles of the poor, especially in the United States, and bus services are often less frequent in the United States than between Third World cities of comparable size, where few people have cars and more people ride the buses. Long-distance buses in these countries are reasonably comfortable (air-conditioned, with toilets, cushioned reclining seats, individual reading lights, overhead racks for carry-on luggage, etc.), and the roads are good, although even main highways in the Australian outback and the Canadian far north are sometimes unpaved.

Outside the First World, it's another story. You hear tales of bus rides from hell at any gathering of people who've traveled in the Third or Fourth Worlds. Second World buses can be as bad, but Second World trains are so good that bus travel is rarely necessary.

Some buses are the other extreme, which can be deceptive. It's easy to be fooled by high-class buses—if you forget about the roads. Ultra-deluxe *ejecutivo* buses in Mexico, or sleeper buses in Argentina, look far more luxurious than Greyhound buses in the United States or Canada. Inside, they are. First-class buses in many cheap-labor countries have onboard attendants to bring you hot towels and serve you meals (included in the ticket price) at your seat.

So where's the rub? The limiting factor in the comfort and safety of road travel is as likely to be the quality of the road itself as the condition of the vehicle. A ride on a truly bad road can be torture for the passengers (and, for that matter, the driver), even on the best of buses.

Your first long bus ride in the South can be a shock. I don't want to exaggerate—a bus ride isn't an expedition. Many things that look intolerable aren't. But you should do what you can to find out what you're in for, and prepare for it.

RESERVATIONS

It amazes me how often people who insist on knowing what type of aircraft is usually used on a particular flight before they make reservations, and on reserving their preferred seats on planes in advance, will buy bus tickets without checking out the equipment and without asking for preassigned seats.

Variations in equipment, and in the comfort of different seats, are much greater on buses than planes. Because you are often on buses for longer than the longest flight, and since they are less comfortable than airplanes in the first place, it's much more important to choose your bus and seat carefully than to worry about which type of plane or which seat you have when you fly.

Don't buy a bus ticket from an agent without first looking at the company's buses. I always try to go down to the bus station or bus yard to check things out before I buy my ticket. There are often several companies and/or different types of buses operating between the same places. Different bus companies, with different terminals and ways of operating, may market their services to different ethnic or racial communities, just as "Chinatown buses" compete with Greyhound between Boston and New York (and increasingly among other U.S.

cities). Guidebooks and information sources intended for one community may not even mention the bus services targeted at other communities. If someone tells you about "the bus," assume they mean, "the bus that people like me ride." Keep in mind that there may be other options. Or there may not—sometimes there's really only one bus that follows a little-used route, or no through long-distance bus at all, only local buses that stop every few minutes.

You may want to reconsider the other possible ways of getting there if the buses look intolerable. Southern buses are cheap and uncomfortable enough that I usually take first-class buses when there's a choice, even though I often take second-class trains and fly third class.

For people in the United States who haven't traveled outside the First World and want to know what to expect of buses elsewhere, start by thinking about a standard U.S. school bus. Lots of decommissioned U.S. school buses are, in fact, sold south and used as public buses in Mexico and Central America. Other Third and Fourth World buses are often similar, although generally a bit smaller overall, with harder seats and the addition of a rooftop luggage rack and a ladder welded onto the back to reach it. No, the seats aren't moved any farther apart for carrying adults than for carrying children in the United States, and there are often more adults on each seat. Many bus bodies are locally built onto truck chassis.

Another common form of "bus" is a minibus that carries 12–15 passengers in the United States, but with as many people packed in as will fit. In Mozambique, I was in a 15-seat van with at least twice that many people (I couldn't see them all to count) as well as their goods and chattels.

Unless you are really desperate and can't wait for a better seat on the next bus, never take a seat behind the rear wheels. (Remember bouncing up and down in the back of the school bus?) The farther forward your seat, the smoother the ride. The seats in the front row (behind or next to the driver and conductor) are the best because they are the least affected by road bumps and have the best view. On a double-decker bus, the front-row seats above the driver and conductor have a great (if sometimes alarming!) view, but may have substantially reduced legroom.

Outside the United States and Canada, you usually reserve a specific seat when you buy a long-distance bus ticket. If tickets aren't sold in advance or seats aren't preassigned for a long bus trip, that's a tip-off that most people aren't taking the bus very far (and thus that it's a local bus that stops a great many times), that there are going to be more passengers than seats, and/or that all the seats, such as they are, will be equally excruciating. Be very suspicious of long-distance buses with open seating. Do yourself a favor and take a more expensive bus with reserved seats, if there is one.

If you care, check if videos will be shown on the bus. It gets harder and harder to find a "luxury" bus without a VCR or DVD player. The novelty of continuous high-volume, low-fidelity videos, movies, and TV shows—ranging from the local equivalent of MTV to Hollywood, Bollywood, or Hong Kong shoot-'em-up films or soap operas dubbed into a language you don't understand—wears off quickly. If you haven't experienced a video bus before, and don't know if you'll like it, bring an eyeshade and earplugs (not a bad idea on any bus, train, or plane).

BUS SCHEDULES AND ROUTES

Outside the First World, I've rarely found much use for long-distance bus schedules or route maps. Bus routes, unlike railroads, can change overnight. Some buses don't even follow fixed routes. If buses are well-used, and thus frequent, there's little need for a schedule. If you want a schedule to know when a bus will run, that's generally because there is little traffic and buses are infrequent. But bus services under such conditions are unreliable anyway, prone to be suspended or changed, and may operate only "on demand," meaning they depart only when and if there is a full (overflowing) load of passengers and/or cargo.

Even a "schedule" may not be precise. If local people say, "There will be a bus here tomorrow," that may well mean—as it has in some places I've been—that you are expected to be waiting by the side of the road at dawn for a bus that may pass by any time between then and dusk—and quite possibly won't stop unless the driver sees you waving.

Guidebooks are even less use. If a guidebook says, "A bus leaves A for B every Tuesday and Thursday," that's a fair indication that it will be possible for you to get from A to B by bus, probably at least once a week. But you certainly shouldn't turn up in A on Monday, counting on there being a bus the next day. Nor should you blame the guidebook writer if there isn't.

One of the most useless things to say to anyone is, "But it says here in this guidebook that . . ." The outsider who argues with reality, on the basis of a book—including this one!—will be interpreted only as stupid, closed-minded, unwilling to learn, and/or contemptuous of local people.

TRIP DURATION

Try to find out in advance how long the bus trip normally takes. In most of the United States, "It's about 60 miles (100 km)," and "It's about an hour," are used as synonyms. It's assumed that one travels by car, that distance is measured along a highway, and that distance is converted into time, and vice versa, at or close to the highway speed limit (currently 65 mph in most states, equivalent to 105 km/h). This equivalence becomes deeply ingrained and unconscious, causing people from the United States automatically to underestimate the time required for road trips in other countries with less elaborately engineered highways.

Thirty km/h (20 mph) is good time for a bus on level dirt, exclusive of meal and rest stops, loading and unloading of passengers and cargo, and other delays. Speeds can be much slower on sand, mud, or hills, or where buses are underpowered and/or overloaded. In mountainous terrain on the Karakoram Highway, I've been on a 24-hour express through bus that averaged 25 km/h (15 mph) on smooth traffic-free pavement wide enough for other buses or trucks to pass.

> **REAL LIFE**
>
> The ride to Kashgar from Turpan cost 38 kuai—US$10.50. When inquiring at the station how many days the trip would last, we received only the reassurance that however many it did take, the price would be the same.
>
> —Stuart Stevens,
> *Night Train to Turkestan*

So it's common for a trip across a country that looks small on the map to take several days by bus. For example, it takes more than 72 hours on the road (plus any stops) to go the length of the trans-Sumatra highway in Indonesia, traversing just one of the islands of that archipelago, even now that the road has been paved.

NIGHT BUSES

Some buses travel straight through, day and night, or are scheduled to travel only at night. Because traffic is lighter at night, it is possible (albeit suicidal) to drive faster at night. If the road is smooth enough, and the bus comfortable enough, you can sometimes sleep. In hot climates, it cools down at least a little at night. Night buses, where they exist, are thus often the most luxuriously equipped "premium" choice, recommended by everyone including guidebook writers who ought to know better.

For safety's sake, avoid night buses and any other night road travel. There are all kinds of obstacles and hazards on Third and Fourth World roads: pedestrians, bicycles, herds of livestock, carts, and broken-down vehicles. They are as likely to be squarely in the middle of the road as to either side. Most of the roads and the vehicles are poorly lit, if at all. Poor countries can't afford elaborate markings of blind curves, hazards, potholes, rock slides, and the like. Roads typically lack any shoulders or guardrails. Both collisions and single-vehicle accidents are far more common at night. If you must make a multiday journey by bus, try to find a bus that stops at night.

PACKING FOR BUS TRIPS

You need to pack with more care for a trip by bus than for one by plane. Unless you've seen that the bus has interior luggage compartments, assume that your

How to Find a Bus in Córdoba

by Ruth Radetsky

Argentina is the mother of the open road. The road here cries out for a car, a tank of gas, and a wallet. It beckons as much as any American road, perhaps more, because the distances are as vast and the country much emptier.

But sometimes you don't have a car, and there are no trains between most cities. So you take a bus.

At least in Córdoba there's only one long-distance bus station. It's huge and modern, with about 55 *boleterías* (ticket windows) and 70 *andenes* (platforms). Each *boletería* is a different *compañía*. All the *compañías* have different route systems. None of them know the others' route systems.

So you feel increasingly desperate, until you find the *Información Turística*. You tell them where you want to go, and they tell you which companies have buses that go there, and which *boleterías* are for each company. (No, this information isn't available anywhere online, even though there are *locutorios* or cybercafés everywhere.) It turns out that there are four different bus companies that go from Córdoba to Rosario.

So you go to each *boletería* and ask the schedule and price, and whether there are seats, and whether the seats are *semi-cama* (about like Greyhound, but maybe a little better), *coche-cama* (better than business class on an airplane, with only three seats across which open to 180 degrees but not flat), or first class (three seats across, privacy panels, flat seats — better than the pictures I've seen of airlines' intercontinental first class). All vary by company and aren't posted anywhere.

Then, once you've decided what you want, you go back and find out the seat you wanted was sold since you asked, so you go to your second choice. You're not surprised, since it is the July 9th long weekend in a country where every town has an Avenida 9 de Julio.

You buy your second choice: 28 pesos (ARS28), about US$10, to go six hours in the front row seat *semi-cama* from Córdoba to Rosario, from the second-largest city in the country to the third, halfway to Buenos Aires. You have an hour to make the bus, most of the trip will be in the daytime, and you'll get to your destination not too late at night.

Great! Now you figure you'd better buy your onward ticket, since you have to be in Buenos Aires Monday morning rested and ready to work, and it is still the July 9th weekend. You go back to the *Información Turística*, and they don't know anything about that. They only know the buses from Córdoba. You can take potluck when you get to Rosario, but you really do have to be in Buenos Aires, so that doesn't feel safe.

You go to the larger windows with lists of cities all over the country over their windows, and you start asking. "No, we don't go there, try...company." "Yes, but we don't have any seats, try...company." "Yes, we have seats." "What's the schedule?" "Oh. It gets into the main bus station in Buenos Aires, Retiro, at 2 A.M." For me, scary. "Why don't you try...company." "Yes, we have seats. We leave at 2 A.M. No, it's *semi-cama*, not *coche-cama*." Yuck. "Why don't you try...company." "Yes, we have a bus, we have seats, we leave at 10:30 A.M. and get in at 4:30 P.M." Perfect. You ask for a ticket. "Go back to Window 10; they'll sell it to you." "But I already asked there, and they told me they didn't have any daytime buses with seats." "They don't, we do." "But . . ." "They'll sell you a ticket on our bus."

And wonder of wonders, they do.

But at least there is a great network of long-distance buses that go everywhere, and there's certainly no monopoly. Even if it could be a little easier to use.

luggage will be tied on the roof, exposed to the elements. Pack your bag to withstand having heavy boxes piled on top of it or people sitting on it.

On the best buses, baggage goes into a luggage space under the passenger compartment, where it's relatively secure and stays mostly dry. On lesser classes of buses, baggage may be tied on the roof. If there is no roof rack, or there is but you want to keep all your baggage with you inside the bus, you may have to pay for an extra seat for your pack. That's only fair, especially if you have a large piece of luggage on a bus where the capacity is determined not by how many seats there are but by how many people can be crammed in.

If it might rain, pack everything you want to stay dry in waterproof bags. A sturdy, cheap cover that goes over your bag, such as a large plastic or burlap sack, can be a worthwhile investment for a trip where your bags will be tied on the roof. A cover can provide some protection against dust and dirt and makes your bag less conspicuous to thieves. Use something that looks like whatever locals use for this purpose. Even air travelers in many countries routinely sew cloth covers over their suitcases, or have them wrapped in multiple layers of the sort of plastic used as "pallet wrap," as added protection against damage and pilferage. Vendors may offer this service at major bus stations.

Unless your pack is extremely small, and you are prepared to hold it on your lap the whole way, what to carry onto a bus is a dilemma. No matter how long the trip lasts—even several days—you can't count on being able to get luggage down from the roof anywhere en route. You have to carry on everything you'll need for the ride and any night halts. On the other hand, you can't count on having any room to put luggage inside the bus anywhere but in your lap, so you don't want to carry on any more than is essential. Organize your carry-on bag before you board: once you are on, you may be so crowded you can barely move.

FACILITIES ALONG THE WAY

Provisions for meals and night halts vary. On luxury buses, attendants may bring hot meals and drinks to your seat. Alternatively, road-house meals and beds for the night at intermediate stops may be included in the price of the bus ticket.

Ordinary buses stop periodically at places where some sort of meal (generally overpriced and from a limited menu) is available at your own expense. If you don't speak the language, just follow the lead of the other passengers when the bus stops.

You can't count on finding anything particularly edible at bus stops, so it's wise to bring your own food if you can, enough to get you through the entire trip if necessary. For a price, most hotels or guesthouses will pack box meals for you, if you ask a day in advance. At the very least, bring plenty of water and some snacks.

Keep a close eye on when other passengers get back on the bus, but don't worry too much about being left behind as long as you stay in sight. As a foreigner, you're probably pretty conspicuous, and people will probably notice and yell or beckon if you're not back on the bus when it's ready to leave.

Very few buses in the South have toilets. Toilets at bus stops around the world are frequently among the filthiest of public toilets. As always, bring your own toilet paper.

Don't be surprised if a bus stops in the middle of nowhere for people to answer the call of nature. You can always ask the driver to stop—pantomiming the urgency of your need will help, and will usually be understood—but you'll have to be prepared to do your business in full view of everyone on the bus. In open country, when everyone on the bus gets off to relieve themselves, the usual custom is for men to go off on one side of the road and women on the other, pretending not to see each other.

Other Public Road Transportation
LONG-DISTANCE TAXIS

Intercity or other long-distance shared taxis are a convenient alternative to buses. "Taxi" denotes a type of service: the actual vehicles used may be sedans, station wagons, pickup trucks, or (most common) vans, and may go by many names. These often operate on fixed routes from a central taxi stand. If it's not far out of the way, they will usually drop you at the door of your destination before going to the taxi stand to pick up return riders. There is usually a standard price and sometimes a standard number of passengers for a given route. Other times taxi operators cram in as many people as they can, even if they are sitting in each others' laps. A taxi leaves when there are enough passengers to fill it. If you want to leave sooner, or have the taxi to yourself, you can pay for any empty places and it will leave right away. If you don't want to pay extra, but no one else gets into the taxi with you, make sure there isn't a misunderstanding, and that you aren't going to be charged for chartering the entire vehicle.

> **REAL LIFE**
>
> The most terrifying moments on my last trip around the world were in a rattletrap shared taxi coming down out of the Andes from Potosi to Sucre, Bolivia, with dubious brakes, worn tires, and the speedometer topping 140 km/h (87 mph). We would have taken a slower, safer bus, but the bus conductors on the route had been on strike for several days.

Fares for shared taxis can be lower or higher than bus fares, depending on how crowded they are and the quality and comfort of competing buses. A full carload starting for the same destination won't have to stop, so a bus trip that would take six to eight hours on a local bus, with frequent stops, may take only four hours by taxi. Unfortunately, taxi drivers often feel they are being paid extra for speed (in a sense they are, because the faster they go the more runs they can make in a day) and drive in an accordingly more dangerous fashion.

SPECIAL BUSES FOR TOURISTS

In areas with lots of tourists, travel agencies and tour companies have been offering more and more private intercity bus, minibus, and van services specifically for foreigners, especially backpackers. These seem attractive because tickets are sold by agents who speak English or other foreign languages and have offices at or near tourist hotels, hostels, or guesthouses—you don't have to go down to the bus station—and they usually leave from tourist districts, or even pick passengers up at their hotels or hostels. They go straight from one tourist center to the next. They are air-conditioned. Sometimes they are cleaner and more comfortable than local buses. But they are much more expensive than local buses or even shared taxis. They ensure that your traveling companions will be other foreigners, not local people, depriving you of the chance for a leisurely chat with a local seatmate. And minibuses and vans—top-heavy and poorly protected in a crash—are the most dangerous of four-wheeled vehicles. I've taken these sorts of buses—I couldn't find any other decent through buses on part of the route of the Baz Bus from South Africa to Swaziland—but only as a last resort.

CITY BUSES

Bus travel within cities takes many forms, with two main flavors: full-size buses (again, visualize the vintage U.S. school bus), often run by public entities, and a plethora of private, often informal and unlicensed, smaller vehicles. Public buses are often easier to find and more likely to be marked with their route and/or destination. Private buses are much harder to deal with, especially if you don't speak the language of the bus conductors, but they are often faster, more frequent, and more direct. Outside the First World, all buses have both a driver and a conductor.

Private and informal bus lines make use of every conceivable sort of light vehicle: vans, open or closed large and small pickup trucks with benches or seats in the bed, jeeps, and custom bodies built on car or truck chassis. They go by an equal diversity of names: wagons, jeepneys, jitneys, matatus, bemos, tempos, "bush taxis," colectivos, etc.

> **REAL LIFE**
>
> Two of the four times in more than 25 years of travel together that my traveling companion or I have had pockets picked were on city buses. Once was on the way from the train station to our hotel in Urumchi, East Turkestan, and the other was while boarding a bus on Oxford Street in London. In the latter case, I knew it was happening, but was hemmed in so tightly by the crowd (so much for dignified English queuing!) that I couldn't do anything about it.

Informal buses often have fixed routes but no fixed stops. You have to watch other passengers to see how they signal when they want to get off. In some places you shout to the conductor or driver. In others, such as when you're in the back of a closed truck out of their sight, you may need to stamp—hard—on the truck floor to get the driver's attention.

You can expect local buses of any sort to be cramped and hideously overcrowded. Getting a backpack on and off a bus can be a real challenge. Before you board, try to arrange your valuables and hold your luggage so that it will be difficult for pickpockets to take anything important, as you may not be able to move to stop them once you are onboard or in the boarding scrum.

LOCAL TAXIS

All sorts of vehicles are used as local taxis, from cars to motorized three-wheelers to pedal tricycles. The cardinal rule is to agree on a price and make sure the driver understands where you want to go before you get in.

The most dangerous form of public transportation is the motorcycle taxi. This is just what it sounds like: you pay someone to carry you behind her or him on a motorcycle or moped. Don't try to carry too much luggage this way. This mode of travel is encountered in rural areas where roads are unfit for four-wheeled vehicles and in crowded cities without rail systems where it is the fastest way through gridlock. Motorcycle taxis in Bangkok, for example, charge as much as taxis, and are the fastest way to get across town. But the greater speed comes with less comfort and more danger.

BEASTS OF BURDEN

Animal-drawn carts are still used for local public transportation in more remote places. I've been in a city of half a million people where the public buses were pulled by ponies and the taxis were chartered donkey carts. If you ride, you can rent horses in rural parts of the South for much less than they cost in the North, because much of the cost of maintaining animals is the cost of human labor to care for them. Likewise, trekkers who don't want to carry all their own gear, or who want to have provisions for a longer stay in an area without villages, stores, or provisions, may be able to afford pack animals (mules, llamas, yaks, etc.) or porters that they couldn't afford at home.

HITCHHIKING

You might think that where there's a road, there's a bus. There's a certain truth to that, but it's not entirely so. You can't count on a bus to come along if you wait by just any road. If you need to get somewhere, and haven't been told by local people to expect a bus on a particular day, be prepared to ask for a ride from any vehicle that passes. Beggars can't be choosers. You may be crowded into an open truck full of livestock (one of my favorite snapshots is of some other riders wrestling with a truckload of goats trying to clear enough space to unload their bicycles) or expected to sit on top of other passengers or piles of cargo (a loose pile of coal, say) or on the roof of a truck's cab or bus. The poorer the place, the more likely you are to have to hitch rides with whomever passes, even on vehicles not designed for passengers.

Surface Transportation

Ask local people how you should signal to passing vehicles that you want a ride. In some places, all vehicles stop for anyone standing by the road. In Russia, you hold your arm out at a downward angle, palm down, with your fingers extended and waving as though beckoning passing traffic in toward you at the roadside. In North America, you either hold up a sign with your destination (or the big city nearest it) or you extend your arm with your fingers curled in and your thumb pointed up. Don't try this anywhere else unless you see others doing it: in many places this, and similar gestures (such as pointing or beckoning with a single extended finger), have obscene, rude, or insulting connotations. In a new place, it's safest not to point at all and to beckon Asian-style, with your fingers together, palm down. People everywhere will understand, even if they think you a little strange, and this gesture rarely gives the sort of offense that finger-up gestures often do.

PAYING FOR RIDES

Outside the First World, riders are expected to pay. Agreeing to pay is implicit in soliciting a ride. If you accept a ride, you are morally and maybe legally obligated to pay the customary price for the ride. Most often this is what the fare would be for the same or a comparable trip by bus or shared taxi, although sometimes riders in private cars are expected to be willing to pay more for a faster, more comfortable ride than in a bus.

North Americans, accustomed to the presumption that people who stop for hitchhikers are offering free rides, unless they say otherwise, may feel uncomfortable initiating negotiations about prices with passing drivers (who, if they decide they don't like you, can always just drive off without you). But if you say nothing, you are agreeing to pay and will be assumed to know how much is normally expected from riders on that route.

TRUCKS

In some locations there are no purely passenger vehicles, only trucks. In the Congo and Amazon River basins, Borneo, and New Guinea, for example, only the mining and logging companies are making enough money to afford to build roads. They build them no better than is necessary for their lumber and ore trucks, and they often have such deep ruts and mud holes as to make them impassable to smaller vehicles. Hitchhikers in such places are expected to be willing to pay for their rides on trucks.

Rides on trucks aren't necessarily cheaper for being less comfortable. As Geoff Crowther pointed out in *Africa on a Shoestring*, "The price of lifts often reflects the difficulty of getting there rather than the distance." In such places, you can count on nothing by way of accommodations at night. Mud, fallen trees, washouts, landslides, and the like can close a road for a week at a time, and there may be no other way around. You need to be pretty self-sufficiently equipped and prepared for delays. Once you start out into the bush by bus or truck, you are committed. There may be no way to turn back for days or weeks.

Most travelers never get this far off the beaten track, and don't really want to. Of course, there's a silver lining: cross a region like this on the ground, and you can impress people for years with your stories. More importantly, you will see places and meet people you could encounter no other way. Proximity to a railroad or a good road is a significant local advantage in a Fourth World country where most people live a days' walk or more from a road (i.e. a jeep track). Whatever you see along a highway in such a country, even in a rural area, isn't typical of life "in the bush."

Walking

In most places where you could take a bus, you could also walk, provided that water and places for lodging or camping are available at adequate intervals. Few people choose to walk across continents, of course, or even countries. But you could, if you have enough time and money and are physically up to it.

In some ways, it seems faddish that so many people include treks from village to village in Nepal and so few ever walk through the countryside or villages anywhere else, even in the Himalayas. Certainly there is more infrastructure for trekking in Nepal, but that doesn't mean it's not possible, or even that it's difficult, to arrange elsewhere.

But most people have other priorities. They don't want to work that hard, don't have enough time, don't have enough money, or prefer to travel more quickly through some regions in order to linger longer in others. Walking creates a unique immersion in a place, but it also enforces its own pace.

Walking to get from one place to another, rather than on sightseeing or recreational excursions, is actually most common to bridge small gaps in motorized transportation routes. But where there isn't a road, there's usually a reason, and you can't expect walking to be easy.

For example, there is no road, railroad, or ferry service between North and South America. A stretch of hilly, roadless jungle in southern Panama breaks the continuity of the Pan-American Highway. Foot travel might seem an obvious means across, and in some sense it is. But "possible" doesn't always mean "practical," much less a good choice.

It is possible to trek across the Darien Gap between North and South America, particularly if you are in good physical condition, well equipped but only very lightly burdened, and can afford to hire a guide. But most people choose other routes and means once they realize what this overland trip entails, and how arduous it is likely to be. Everyone I've known personally who has set out to cross the Darien Gap by land and/or water has changed his or her mind and turned back or decided to fly.

On the other hand, in many cases where there aren't through international trains or buses, it is nonetheless possible to take a train or bus to one side of the border, walk across, and catch another train or bus on the other side. I think I've crossed almost as many international borders on foot as by any other means except flying. Stepping from one country to the next, on my own two feet, gives me a satisfying feeling of accomplishment.

At such places there are often porters, bicyclists, or motorcyclists willing, for a price, to carry your luggage across the no-man's-land between the borders. At crossings with only light traffic you may have no choice but to carry all your belongings on your back. This is when you'll be most glad to have kept your luggage light and easily carried. I've encountered border posts and train or bus stations anywhere from 50 meters (50 yards) apart to 5 kilometers (3 miles).

You can expect to do a lot of walking, even if you plan no trekking. Most of the physical work ("exercise") of long-term budget travel is in walking around cities and towns, either seeing the sights, getting logistical things done, or getting to and from motorized transportation (often on the way to or from hotels or places where you are staying, and therefore often carrying all your luggage with you).

Try to be in the best physical condition for walking that you can be in before you leave, and try to get regular (or if need be irregular) exercise while traveling even when you are in situations where you don't have to do a lot of walking. You'll be glad you're in shape when you arrive in an interesting but sprawling town without a good bus system, or when you discover that the sight you came to see is a three-km (two-mile) walk up a trail only fit for foot traffic. Every day in San Francisco, I see tourists whose visits have been ruined by their lack of preparedness for extensive walking on the city's hills.

WATER TRANSPORTATION

If you have enough time, if the price is right, and if the ship is sufficiently comfortable and safe, most people would rather take a ship than fly. So why don't more people do it?

Sad to say, water transportation is less of an option than many people think or hope, particularly across oceans and other long distances. Long-distance water travel requires either good luck or careful planning and research to know what will be possible. Some things that look easy are impossible, yet there are other possibilities that have probably never occurred to you.

Cruise Ships

Cruising may be an enjoyable vacation experience. But cruise ships aren't intended as pure transportation and aren't an affordable means of transportation for independent travelers.

Cruise ships do go around the world. Typically, these cruises last three to four months with minimum prices (per person, double occupancy, sharing one of the worst cabins) ranging from US$20,000 to US$50,000 exclusive of taxes, fees, and shore excursions. If you don't have that much time or money, it's possible to meet most of these ships for just part of one of their routes around the world. But you're still looking at a minimum of US$200–400 per day.

Around-the-world cruises schedule at most a day in each port, except perhaps for a couple of two- or three-day dockings for passengers to take added-cost excursions to inland points (e.g., two days in Mumbai so people can fly to Agra and back to see the Taj Mahal, three days in Mombasa so people can drive to a game preserve).

REAL LIFE

When cruise lines have misjudged demand or overpriced a cruise, or when other unexpected circumstances cause them to have space unsold at the last minute, their last recourse is to offer the remaining cabins very cheaply through local travel agencies in the port from which the cruise departs. The lowest prices are when the cruise sails from a small city, or one with few wealthy locals, and when it is too late for bargain-hunters to fly in from elsewhere or the port is too remote and expensive to reach by air. You can't count on finding cruises like this, but you can sometimes find last-minute deals for US$75 or less per person per night, double occupancy, including meals but excluding taxes. The best deal I've ever seen was in Valparaiso, Chile, in 2007, where flyers in the windows of local travel agencies were advertising a 20-night cruise-of-a-lifetime to Antarctica, departing in about a week, for US$1,000 plus taxes per person, double occupancy.

If you like cruising, like the route one of these ships will take, and have the money, one of these cruises may be for you. Plenty of people think so. These cruises are popular and generally are fully booked months in advance. There are more cruises around the world than escorted tours around the world by air.

Cruises are not for independent travelers. The appeal of cruises is precisely that everything is decided and arranged in advance—the ultimate package holiday. You know many months ahead exactly where you will be each day. You dine with the same fellow travelers every day. You sleep in the same bed in the same cabin every night. You have to pack and unpack only once, at the start and end of the cruise. You never have to arrange anything on your own with local people.

Whether this is your idea of a good time, much less of active, independent, or experiential travel, is probably irrelevant. Most around-the-world travelers simply don't have that much money to spend, and wouldn't choose to spend it that way if they did.

Even if you have the money and want to do it, the chances that there will be a cruise ship going where you want to go, when you want to go, are slim. And the chances that you'll be able and willing to commit to the cruise ship's schedule for that leg of your trip, months in advance, are probably even smaller.

I'm not a cruiser, as you might have guessed. If you want to do this sort of thing, you need expert advice. Imagine choosing your hotel room, months in advance, sight unseen, and committing yourself to stay there for three months. Plan far in advance; see a travel agent who specializes in cruises and really knows the ships.

Freighters

Some transoceanic cargo ships have cabins for a few passengers in addition to those for their crew. Those that carry paying passengers generally provide a high standard of comfort, accommodations, and food, although not, of course, the diversity of entertainment that you'd find on a cruise ship.

Travel on cargo ships has advantages over cruising. Freighters sometimes spend more time in each port to load and unload cargo and tend to visit less touristed, although, of course, bigger, busier, and more industrial ports than cruise ships.

The market for long-distance freighter travel is mainly among retired or independently wealthy people with lots of time and ample means: people who could choose a cruise around the world, but who prefer a more personal and contemplative shipboard experience.

Unfortunately, the total passenger capacity of freighters is tiny compared to that of the world's cruise ship fleets. Cargo ships charge less than cruise ships, but

REAL LIFE

One reader, Michael Hodson, made it entirely around the world without flying. "I am a notorious nonplanner," he wrote, but "I never could have made my trip" without planning the ocean crossings well in advance, and being flexible about dates and routes. "Those four freighter crossings ended up being basically the only reservations I made in my entire trip: 16 months, 6 continents, 44 countries."

Surface Transportation

they aren't cheap: few charge less than US$75–100 per person per day. Even at that, they are often fully booked many months in advance.

You have to make an advance commitment, but the shipping line doesn't. As a supernumerary, you are at the ship's mercy. A scheduled sailing can be canceled, advanced, delayed, or its ports of departure and arrival changed, at any time including while at sea, all without explanation or obligation to you. If you aren't willing to accept these conditions, shipping lines don't want you as a passenger. They can find plenty of other, more flexible, people to fill their cabins many times over.

The chances of finding a freighter willing to take you across the ocean, with space available when you want to go, are poor unless you can plan your dates long in advance. And your chances of finding all this for a price competitive with flying, even if you plan far ahead, are essentially nil.

If you want to take a freighter for one leg of a long trip, it probably makes the most sense to do so for your first transoceanic leg, because it's usually easier to fix the date of your initial departure than of any intermediate stages or your return. In this niche, demand far exceeds supply. You'll need to plan and commit yourself longer in advance than for almost any other form of common-carrier transportation. Several agencies, websites, and newsletters for passenger travel on cargo ships are listed in the *Resource Guide*. They can give you an idea of what's possible, on what routes, and at what prices.

As for "working your way" as a member of a ship's crew, forget it unless you already have seamen's papers to prove your qualifications and experience. Unskilled crewmembers are not hired on working oceangoing ships.

Yachts

Hitching rides on yachts is sometimes possible but not to be relied on. Your chances are best if you have sailing experience (credentials, letters of reference, or names to drop will improve your chances) and have contacts in the yachting community to give you leads on times and places to look for rides.

To find rides, ask yachting friends where to look. If you are already at your intended port of departure, go down to the harbor and ask yachties or the harbormaster, "If you were looking for crew, where would you advertise? Who would you talk to?" Ask the staff and hangers-around and look for bulletin boards at yacht marinas, harbormasters' offices, and businesses serving yachts and yachties. Ask yachties what publications carry "crew wanted" ads.

Don't expect to find rides right away. Budget for the possibility that finding a ride may take a month or more even if you are qualified and know where to look, and that you may not find a yacht at all and may have to fly.

Small-boat traffic even on the most common transoceanic routes is highly seasonal, often concentrated during a brief window of optimal weather during just a few weeks or months of the year. Finding an owner or skipper making an out-of-season crossing may be impossible.

Crewmembers on pleasure yachts normally share in the work and the running expenses. Work out an explicit understanding, in advance, of what is expected.

Space on yachts is always cramped; privacy ranges from limited to nonexistent. Personality conflicts are the bane of yachting. Take time to get to know everyone who will be traveling with you before you commit yourself to living with them for weeks in the middle of an ocean in a space smaller than a studio apartment.

A short shakedown and get-acquainted cruise will give you a chance to judge the ship's condition, the skipper's competence, and familiarize yourself with the people and routine on board. A ship at sea, even a yacht, is a paramilitary dictatorship, not a democracy. If you aren't ready to trust the skipper completely and take orders without question, don't go.

Even in this best of circumstances, be prepared to have potential rides fall through. The skipper changes plans at the last minute, the boat needs work, another member of the crew falls in love, falls out of love, doesn't show up, or decides to leave. Yachts are an incestuous little world, and anything can happen. Yachting isn't for people with a fixed agenda, itinerary, or schedule. As with cruising, the point is the experience and way of life more than the destination.

About the only people who can readily find rides on yachts, without boating experience, are young women (and sometimes men) willing to provide sexual services to yachtsmen in exchange for passage. Thinly veiled "female traveling companion wanted" ads abound in the classified pages and on bulletin boards. Similar ads for male companions show up regularly in the gay press. Expectations of sex aren't always explicit until you're at sea. If there's a shadow of doubt in your mind, ask point-blank before you sail if you're being taken along for sex.

Seagoing Ferries

There are ferries across every significant channel, strait, sea, and narrows in Europe and the Mediterranean, although perhaps not as many trans-Mediterranean ferries as one might expect. European ferry services are highly developed in safety, speed, convenience, and comfort. Whether or not they actually carry rail cars (many do), European (and Turkish) ferries are extremely well coordinated with the railroads. Ferries between railheads are timed to connect with trains, and some within the Eurail zone honor Eurail Passes.

In other parts of the world, it's hard to tell where you'll find ferries operating, or to get good information about prices, schedules, or services.

Surface Transportation

Japan, the world's richest archipelago, has invested extraordinary amounts of money and engineering skill in bridges and tunnels that obviate the need for ferries between any of the major islands. Excellent public ferries continue to operate, however, and provide the only alternative to air travel to the smaller islands of the Ryukyu chain in the south. Several international ferries operate between Japan and neighboring countries: Russia, South Korea, China, and Taiwan. It should be noted, however, that the cheapest and most-used of these, between Japan and Pusan, South Korea, are something of a dead-end as a way out of Japan to anywhere else, as South Korea has no open land borders.

Indonesia and the Philippines are the most extensive and (along with Japan) most populous archipelagic nations. They also possess the world's most extensive interisland ferry services. Some of the ships are in terrible condition, uncomfortable, overloaded, and dangerous. Others are safe, modern, and comfortable, with air-conditioning, staterooms with private baths, and restaurant-quality dining rooms. These are some of the best chances you'll ever have anywhere for affordable long-distance ocean voyages.

It's typical of the disparity everywhere between domestic (common) and international (not) ferry services that there are no ferries *between* Indonesia and the Philippines, or Malaysia and the Philippines. There are ferries between Malaysia, Batam Island (Singapore), and Indonesia. But the international ferries to Indonesia land in Sumatra or the Riau Islands. It's a long tedious journey between any of these ports and the population and tourist centers of Java or Bali.

Most populated offshore islands—even in countries where water transportation is generally poor, such as the United States—have ferry service to somewhere on the mainland. Multi-island countries may or may not be linked by ferries, depending on how wealthy and how far apart the islands are. There are ferries between the Australian mainland and Tasmania and between the North and South Islands of Aotearoa/New Zealand, for example. But there are no ferries between Australia and Aotearoa/New Zealand (flights aren't cheap either), and no ferries link many poorer, more spread-out Pacific island nations.

Good destination-specific guidebooks for low-budget independent travelers are the best source of information on domestic ferry services. If service, comfort, or amenities are anything less than international-class, the national tourist board or guidebooks for upmarket travelers may gloss over, or not even mention, ships and ferries. Moon Handbooks, Footprint Handbooks, Rough Guides, and Lonely Planet all make a particular effort to give information on public water transport, but no guidebook can have complete or up-to-date information.

Routes operated by sizable ships, once established, don't suddenly change without strong reason (such as that the ship breaks down or sinks). As a rule of thumb, I wouldn't plan a trip, without a backup plan, that depends on a ferry or shipping service so new that it hasn't made it into a guidebook yet. If a guidebook says that service on a route is "uncertain," "erratic," "endangered," or the like, heed the warning. If it was on its last legs when the book was researched, it may well be gone by now. Have a more reliable alternative worked out in case it is. Don't just assume that you will fly if there is no ferry. If the reasons for the absence of ferry service are political, there may be no flights either. You may have to backtrack for hundreds of kilometers to get a flight, and a short flight on an obscure route flown by only a single airline can cost as much as a discounted flight across a large ocean between major air hubs.

International ocean ferry services are much less common than domestic ones. Oddly, their very rarity makes them conspicuous by their mere existence.

Unless I had a recent printed timetable, schedule, or brochure from the shipping company in hand, or had spoken directly with someone who had personally traveled on (not merely heard of) the ship in question within the last few months, I would evaluate with great skepticism rumors of international passenger shipping services. Abandoned and unmaintained websites can linger for years, so a website describing a ferry service can't be relied on unless you are *sure* it is not just authoritative but also up to date.

In particular, there are persistent false rumors—seen most recently on the Internet—of ships carrying passengers between Australia and Indonesia (don't get me wrong: this would be a good thing, and may someday happen, but it hasn't yet) and between South and Southeast Asia (there apparently once was a ferry from Penang to Chennai (Madras), but no such service has operated for many years). There are less frequent rumors of ships between India and eastern or southern Africa (Mumbai–Dar Es Salaam–Durban or the like). As of 2011 there was no truth to any of these rumors. You have to fly or get lucky and get a ride on a yacht (unlikely, as discussed above) to travel between these places.

The Greater and Lesser Antilles islands of the Caribbean Sea appear to form an almost-continuous chain between North and South America. This is among the most popular cruise routes, and some islands make most of their money from cruise ships' port calls. One might expect to find a passenger ferry plying the same through route, more cheaply, for island-hopping local traffic. Alas, there are no through ferries around the Antilles, and not even local ferries between many of the adjacent islands. The flights between these islands cost more than direct flights across the Caribbean between Miami and Caracas or other cites on the north coast of South America.

Coastal Ships and Ferries

Coastal shipping or ferry services along the edges of, rather than across, bodies of water have become rare. The usual reason for their existence is that the coastline is either too steep or too swampy for a road or railroad; in the former case they are invariably highly scenic. Some of the outstanding remaining ones are along the Norwegian and Chilean coasts, between Hong Kong and Shanghai, and in northwest North America.

The ferries along the coast of Norway are somewhat cheaper than a cruise, but still too expensive for most people on a budget.

The least scenic of the routes listed here is along the coast of China between Hong Kong and Shanghai. Although it's no cheaper than a train, it's an interesting and novel experience all the same.

The Washington State Ferries (www.wsdot.wa.gov/ferries), British Columbia Ferries (www.bcferries.bc.ca), and Alaska Marine Highway (actually ferry) System (www.dot.state.ak.us/amhs) all have extensive routes connecting offshore islands and mainland ports in the Pacific Northwest, British Columbia, and southeast Alaska. The longest through journey is on the Alaska Marine Highway, from Bellingham, Washington, through the Inside Passage to Skagway and Haines, the southernmost road heads in Alaska. The 1,700-km (1,050-mile) trip takes four to five days if you don't stop over at any of the half-dozen intermediate ports. These public ferries carry automobiles as well as passengers, and they cost a fraction of the price—even for a private stateroom—of any of the cruise ships that follow the same spectacular route.

There are few passenger ships along most of the coast of Chile, the most obvious place in the world to expect to find them. The longest stretch with regular passenger ferry service is from Puerto Montt to Puerto Natales. That's just over 1,000 km (600 miles), and a great 3–4 day journey, but still only a small fraction of the 5,000-km (3,000-mile) length of Chile. Some ferries in the south of Chile operate only seasonally for tourists in the southern-hemisphere summer.

Lake and River Boats

River travel has declined less than ocean travel. It remains the dominant mode of inland transportation along most of the great rivers outside the First World. You can ride riverboats for long distances along the Nile, the Congo and some of its tributaries, sometimes the Niger, the Yangtze, the Yellow (Huang), the Irawaddy, the Paraná, throughout Amazonia, and from coastal ports into the interiors of Borneo and New Guinea.

Water transport is the obvious mode of travel in river deltas. There are excellent ferry services, for example, in the Pearl River Delta between Hong Kong, Macau, and Guangzhou (Canton), and the River Platte estuary between Argentina and Uruguay. Virtually everywhere in Bangladesh lies in the Ganges-Brahmaputra Delta, and there are many riverboats. There are trains in Bangladesh, but trips by train are apt to be interrupted by ferry crossings, washouts, or floods, so you might as well take a boat in the first place. Strangely, there are few long-distance passenger riverboats in most other South Asian countries. Most tourists drive through the Mekong Delta in Vietnam, but boats are available and give a better feel for the region.

There are ferries on all of the world's inland seas and great lakes. The one major exception is the Aral Sea, from whose tributaries so much water has been diverted for irrigation that it has shrunk to half its original size, leaving vast flats of blowing salt. There are a few lake ferries in the sparsely populated northern parts of Canada. There are also public passenger ferries on Lake Titicaca, some of the lakes of the east African rift valley, and on the Great Lakes of North America. (The Great Lakes once had the world's largest car ferry fleet. At least two major ships still operate across Lake Michigan—see www.ssbadger.com and www.lake-express.com—in addition to others to various Great Lakes islands.)

Third and Fourth World riverboats and lake steamers vary enormously. You may find yourself in a luxurious cabin on an aging colonial steamship, in a high-speed catamaran with airplane-style seats, in a village of huts on top of a barge, or in an open canoe with an outboard motor. As with trains or buses, try to get a look at the vessel, or at least talk to people who've been on it, before you book your passage.

Water transport—more energy efficient and, perhaps more importantly, requiring less investment than roads—was favored by Second World economic planners and remains well developed throughout the former USSR. There are both slower large ships and smaller fast hydrofoils on the Volga, Dnieper, Amur, and Angara, among other rivers. There is a ferry across the Caspian Sea between Baku and Krasnovodsk. Long, narrow, enclosed hydrofoils with aircraft-style cabins and seating go the 650-km (400-mile) length of Lake Baikal in 12 hours. Many other countries use Soviet hydrofoils for their fast long-distance river, lake, and coastal ferries. These are generally comfortable vessels, but Soviet engines are fuel-inefficient and loud; bring earplugs.

First World river transport, where available, is generally more expensive than trains or buses. There are ferries on most rivers in Europe, although more of them are designed for sightseeing than for transportation. Except for a few Mississippi River cruises (at typical cruise prices) and a few short sightseeing rides, there are almost no river boat services in North America.

Folding Kayaks

I debated whether to head this section *Portable Boats* or *Folding Kayaks*. In the end, I decided it didn't matter, because folding (also known as "collapsible") kayaks are the only seaworthy portable boats. Sure, an inflatable raft is portable. But what can you do with it? A folding kayak, on the other hand, is the most seaworthy of all small boats. Its structure just happens to be such that you can take it anywhere—on the plane, on a train, on a bus, in a car, or maybe even on a bicycle.

Assembled, a folding kayak consists of a framework of wood, aluminum, fiberglass, or composite ribs and stringers (longerons), covered with a skin of rubberized fabric, vinyl, or plastic.

Disassembled, it consists of a big folded piece of heavy fabric and a bunch of rib and strut pieces and fittings. It can all be portaged in one or two duffel bags that look like they might hold an old-fashioned canvas tent. It takes from 10 minutes to an hour, depending on the model and your practice, to put one together or take it apart.

Folding kayaks have the same basic skin-and-bones structure, with lighter and stronger materials, as the original kayaks used for hunting, fishing, and transportation in the harshest conditions of the open Arctic. Folding kayaks have been sailed across the Atlantic, paddled around Cape Horn, and are regularly used by wilderness explorers, expeditions, and military commandos. White-water paddling races in the Olympics used to be exclusively for folding kayaks.

I say all this only to dispel the false image of fragility often created by the term *folding kayak*. It's actually impossible for one to "fold" in the water, and unlike rigid kayaks they flex when stressed rather than cracking in half.

Lightweight single (one-person) folding sea kayaks weigh 14–18 kg (31–40 lb). Double (two-person) folding kayaks weigh 30–40 kg (66–88 lb). If you pack carefully, you can fit a single or half a double, and the rest of your gear, within the two pieces of luggage allowed on flights to and from North America. On flights subject to the 20-kg limit, the boat alone will use up your free baggage allotment. If you're bringing anything else at all, you'll have to pay for excess baggage.

Sale prices for new folding sea kayaks made in the United States or Western Europe start at about US$1,500 for a single and US$2,000 for a double. If you feel competent to assess the condition of a used boat, you can find them used for significantly less through Craigslist or paddlers' bulletin boards. My partner and I got our first one used, for free, from a friend—to whom we will always be grateful—who hadn't used it in years. Even the more expensive makes and models are surprisingly cheap when you consider what they can do and how long they last. Our Folbot was more than 30 years old before we had to replace it with a new one of similar design but more modern materials.

Soviet and Eastern European folding kayaks are cheaper. Most of those now being exported were originally designed for military use and, like other Second World products built to "milspec" quality-control standards, offer excellent value for the money compared with First World goods.

Imagine a boat that can be flown in with you by the smallest bush plane, or carried by pack animal, to the most remote lake or river. A boat that you can take anywhere there's a train, bus, or taxi (they'll fit in the trunk of most cars). A stable, seaworthy, capacious boat you can use for paddling, sailing, sightseeing, nature- and bird-watching (kayaks are wonderful in shallow wetlands), camping (a two-person folding kayak can carry almost as much gear as a full-sized canoe, enough for a week's camping trip), snorkeling, diving, and fishing. For pictures and descriptions of the cheapest and most popular U.S.-built models, see www.folbot.com.

Still, a folding kayak is a sizable investment, and transporting it isn't trivial. Carrying one, and your regular pack, on foot is at the limit of most people's ability, and only possible for short distances. A folding kayak is too expensive for most travelers to be willing to abandon, and too exotic for you to recover much of your investment if you have to sell it in a hurry. So you'll have to pay to ship it home separately if you are going on to places where you won't want to lug it around. Only a hard-core paddler, for whom paddling was the point of the journey, would want to take one around the world.

Folding kayaks are the original and optimal modern sea kayaks. But most people paddle them in flatter, safer waters: rivers, lakes, and protected bays and estuaries. Don't take one on the open ocean unless you are sure you know what you are doing.

Some sense of the possibilities opened up by a portable boat can be obtained from Paul Theroux's travelogue, *The Happy Isles of Oceania: Paddling the Pacific,* about a lengthy trip with a folding kayak. I don't like Theroux's attitude toward most of the places he writes about, and he doesn't say too much about his boat as such, but he uses it, matter-of-factly, to get to places and do things that would be impossible without it.

Folding kayaks are best known in Europe. Although awareness of folding kayaks is growing, paddling organizations and publications in the United States are dominated by paddlers of rigid canoes and kayaks. Limited to transporting their boats on cartops or trailers, they pay little or no attention to paddling opportunities overseas, or to the information relevant only to folding kayakers, such as the proximity of train stations to suitable launch sites. General-purpose guidebooks, even for independent active sports and outdoor travelers, are written by people who've never heard of folding kayaks. The only general guidebooks in which I've seen them mentioned are David Stanley's *Moon South Pacific* (Avalon Travel, www.southpacific.org) and *Eastern Europe on a Shoestring* (Lonely Planet).

I hope I've piqued your curiosity. Ralph Diaz's *Complete Folding Kayaker* will tell you everything you need to know if such a boat is right for you (see the *Resource Guide*). These technically elegant but simple boats have a worldwide appeal to technophiles, making Internet communication ideal for such a globally dispersed lot. The best place to find them is the Usenet newsgroups "rec. boats.paddle" and "rec.boats.paddle.touring," which are also the place to post queries about paddling possibilities in particular places.

Air Transportation

"The Plane Truth"

This chapter explains how to plan your air travel itinerary and get the best available combination of the right tickets and the right price for your trip.

Air transportation isn't the largest part of the cost of most long trips. But it's the largest part of the *transportation* budget and the largest single *up-front* expense for most independent travelers. As such, air tickets are the focus of many people's financial concerns when they start planning a trip, and many people think solely about price when they are buying air tickets.

Air transportation is about more than prices, though: finding the set of tickets that will be best for your trip is at least as important as getting the lowest price for them. Especially for around-the-world and other multistop itineraries, it's rarely obvious what will be the best or cheapest route, so buying airline tickets is very different from shopping for a known commodity.

Airline ticket prices, rules, and procedures are complicated and confusing. That's deliberate. Prices are set by the airlines, whose goal is to get each traveler to pay as much as possible. Airlines use increasingly sophisticated technological tools to limit and reduce the information available to travelers or intermediaries who might use it for comparison shopping.

The information imbalance between airlines and ticket buyers is getting worse. Despite the illusion of comprehensiveness presented by websites that "search" millions of possibilities, no one site has access to all air ticket prices.

Key Advice About Air Transportation

- Don't assume that you'll get lower prices on the Internet, or directly from the airlines. No single source has comprehensive airline ticket price information, no matter what they claim. Some prices are available only directly from the airlines, some only from travel agents, some only online, some only offline.

- Plan ahead. To get the best price on a complex multistop international flight itinerary, you need to buy your tickets at least a month in advance, preferably sooner. Start planning even earlier to leave time to work out your itinerary.

- Know where you want to go before you start shopping for tickets to get there. There is no standard route or fixed-price "go anywhere" ticket around the world. Before you can begin to get price estimates you need a list of specific desired destinations.

- If you want help from a travel agency, find one that specializes in air tickets for independent world travelers. Around-the-world and multistop airline tickets are a small and esoteric specialty. Don't expect much help from airlines or all-purpose travel agencies, online or offline.

- Choose a travel agent as you would choose any professional consultant. You're buying service and advice, not a commodity. Differences between good and

Even travel agents who want to help consumers have dramatically less information about prices than they did 20 years ago. Fewer ticket prices, not more, are being made available in any standardized or searchable format.

Airlines used to be required by government regulations to file all their fares with the government in a "tariff" of prices and corresponding rules, and publish them electronically through centralized computerized reservation systems (CRSs). The CRSs, in turn, were required to deliver unbiased search results and rankings to their travel agency subscribers. These rules insured that comprehensive, unbiased fare information was available to travel agents, if not directly to travelers.

The first online travel agencies, starting with Eaasy Sabre on Compuserve in the 1980s, relied on these CRSs for comprehensive, unbiased price information. But that's no longer possible. As a result of deregulation in the United States of both fares and CRSs, airlines no longer have to file most fares with the government or provide them equally to travel agents or CRSs. Airlines could have been freed from government price-fixing but still required to publish their tariffs. Instead, they successfully lobbied for the gradual elimination bad agencies in quality of service — especially after you've paid for your tickets and hit the road — are far greater than differences in price.

- If your travel agent won't customize your route and tickets to suit your desires, find one who will. Buying tickets from a limited menu of "standard" options, or that don't include all the flights you will need, is likely to end up costing you more by the time you get to your real destination(s).

- Be aware of the risk you take if you buy tickets on a "low-fare" airline. If they cancel the flight, they'll probably just give you back your money. They won't be able to put you on another airline's flight.

- If you are certain of your route, include as many of your flights as possible in the package of tickets you buy in advance. The more tickets you have to buy at the last minute, the higher your total ticket cost is likely to be.

- Insist on confirmed reservations for all flights before you pay for any tickets. So-called "open date" tickets have many hidden drawbacks, including the possibility that no seats will be available when you want to fly.

For more information on the topics in this chapter, see the *Resource Guide* in the back of the book and the links on the Practical Nomad website at www.practicalnomad.com.

of the requirements to publish fare tariffs and make them available to the public and, through CRSs, to travel agencies.

Freed from any legal requirements for fare transparency, airlines are treating information about their prices as confidential and proprietary. Airlines are withholding more and more of their fares from both CRSs and travel agencies (including online travel agencies and fare search engines), so that you can only find their prices by searching airlines' individual websites, one at a time. Some airlines provide only a subset of their fares to CRSs and travel agencies, or provide some of their fares only to certain "preferred" agencies. Many new "low-fare" airlines don't participate in CRSs or accept bookings through travel agents at all.

As this edition goes to press, airlines are fighting it out in court with the CRSs and online travel agencies those same airlines originally founded (before they were spun off as separate companies) over access to airline ticket pricing information. It's likely to be a long legal war, but consumers' interests aren't represented in those lawsuits. The lack of a publicly disclosed tariff seems to me to be contrary to the essential idea of what it means to be licensed as a "common carrier," but governments haven't chosen to make that argument against opaque or personalized airline ticket pricing.

Where does that leave travelers? Worse off than ever, and with fewer and fewer places to turn for help. It's harder and harder to find a travel agent who will work for you against the airlines, trying to find what's best for you rather than trying to sell you whatever is best for them.

If it's hard to get good advice about airfares, it's even harder to know who to believe. Most published advice about airfares is written either by people who work in the travel industry or by writers of destination guidebooks, neither of whom are usually a good source of consumer advice for air ticket purchases.

The less you know, the easier it is for travel companies to get you to pay more than necessary. Almost everywhere I worked as a travel agent, I got complaints from bosses and coworkers: "Why do you spend so much time educating people rather than selling? Why do you want to educate potential customers anyway?"

Guidebook writers are hired for their expert knowledge of destinations, not airfares. No matter how experienced they are as travelers or writers, they rarely have an inside knowledge of the air transportation industry, because that is almost impossible to acquire without working for an airline or discount travel agency. Forced to analyze the system from the outside, they (like many ordinary travelers) engage in what amounts to reverse engineering: theorizing about what is inside a sealed black box by observing its behavior and what inputs produce what outputs. In fact, much of the published advice about air ticket discounting is speculation based on this sort of reverse engineering, not description of fact. Some clever and plausible, but false, inferences have been widely reprinted and have become commonly accepted airfare myths. Much of what you think you know about airfares may not be correct.

I'll start with a quick overview of the three basic ways to arrange airline tickets for a trip around the world, and their pros and cons. Then I'll debunk some of the most widespread and misleading of the popular myths about airfares, with a particular eye to what mistakes people make on the basis of those myths. For those who want to understand the reasons for my advice, I'll next explain how airfares and ticket discounting really work in the section titled *The System of Airfares*. This section is rather technical because there's no way to explain discount airfares both simply and accurately. If you don't really care about the "whys" and just want to know how to go about getting the best tickets and price, skip ahead to the final section of this chapter, *Arranging Your Air Transportation*.

THREE WAYS TO BUY TICKETS FOR A TRIP AROUND THE WORLD

Before you even begin thinking about routes or fares, you should have at least a preliminary starting and ending point and a set of desired destinations. As a general principle, think about where and when you want to go before you start searching the Web for airfares, or calling airlines or travel agents. It's impossible for an airline, a travel agent, or you as a do-it-yourself travel agent to assess whether what you want is possible or what it might cost until you have formulated at least a tentative wish list of destinations.

Once you know where you might want to go, there are three basic ways to arrange tickets for a trip around the world, each with its own pros and cons.

A Single Ticket at an "Around-the-World" (RTW) Fare

Pros: You only need to deal with one airline, once, to buy your tickets. Your tickets can all be arranged before you leave, so unless you want to make changes you don't have to waste any time dealing with airlines or travel agents while you are on the road. There are only three major airline alliances to choose among, so comparison shopping is relatively straightforward. You can change the dates of your flights relatively easily and cheaply, if space is available. You might be able to change your route as you go, although only within the routes of that airline alliance and the rules of that ticket. You can accrue frequent-flyer miles with one airline for all or most of the trip. You can buy your ticket directly from the airline, so you don't have to put any effort into finding a travel agent or searching for the best airlines or sources of tickets.

Cons: You are limited to flights on the member airlines of a single marketing alliance, ruling out almost all "low-fare" airlines as well as any other nonallied airlines that might have more frequent or direct service between your destinations. Airline RTW rate desks are notoriously unhelpful and difficult to deal with (unless you don't care at all about how much you have to pay). It can be complicated and/or expensive to add separate tickets for flights that can't be included in the RTW fare. Some destinations can only be reached on awkward routings or with lengthy and inconvenient backtracking through the hubs of participating airlines. Depending on the destinations, the total price including any necessary side trips or extra tickets can be substantially more expensive than other alternatives. You have to use all your tickets within a year—or throw away the portion of your tickets that's unused after a year. Not an option for trips that don't fit the airline's definition of "around the world." Overland travel legs are included in the "flown" mileage used to calculate the price. An RTW fare isn't an option at all if your route exceeds the maximum allowable number of flights, miles, or stopovers.

A Package of Tickets Assembled by a Specialist Travel Agent

Pros: Because you aren't limited to a single alliance, you have many more options than with an RTW ticket. Often you can get more direct routes on better airlines. The total price is often, if not always, lower than with either of the other two options. You can arrange all your tickets before you leave, to satisfy onward ticket or other visa requirements and to avoid having to deal with buying more tickets on the road. Or you can buy your tickets in several stages, to leave yourself flexibility as to your onward route and so that your trip doesn't have to be completed within a year. You may be able to save money by combining several legs of your journey—even if they are on different airlines—into a single through ticket with stopovers. You don't actually have to go entirely around the world, and there are no restrictions on backtracking, numbers of flights, numbers of continents, miles, discontinuities, land or sea travel, etc. You can take advantage of an agent's advice in planning your trip, and you have your agent as a single point of contact to help you with any changes to your tickets or problems with airlines while you are traveling.

Cons: This isn't always the cheapest option. Some low-fare airlines don't sell tickets through travel agents at all. You'll probably have to pay fees if you want to change the dates of your flights. Some airlines don't like travel agents, and will refuse to deal with you directly to make changes if you bought your tickets from an agent. If you have problems making connections between airlines for which you have completely separate tickets, neither one may be willing to take responsibility. (This happens routinely even between members of the same alliance, but it's slightly less common between "partners" than between unrelated airlines.)

Individual One-Way Tickets Purchased on Your Own

Pros: Maximum flexibility. Minimum commitment. If you haven't bought tickets yet, you can always change your plans. Sometimes you can find tickets on your own that work out cheaper than any other option.

Cons: Maximum complexity and time and effort required, including time and effort while you are traveling. Maximum *potential* cost and uncertainty as to how much your tickets will end up costing. Sometimes works out much, much more expensive than either of the other two options. Sometimes you can get into a place cheaply, only to find that any ticket out is expensive, or that all seats at any price are sold out on the dates you want to travel. Onward ticket requirements in some countries may force you to buy full-fare tickets on the spot to avoid being refused entry, if you don't already have your next ticket. If you need to make changes after you bought your tickets, you'll have to deal with each airline individually, on your own, from wherever you are in the world. You'll have to pay to change almost all flight dates, once you've bought your tickets.

MYTHS ABOUT AIRLINE PRICES AND ROUTES

Myths about what routes are, and are not, permitted by affordable airfares lead many people to spend unnecessary time and energy trying to choose a route that conforms to "rules" that don't really apply to them, or to plan their trips in ways that result in needless inconvenience and/or expense. Because these myths are so widespread, I'll deal with them and their implications for destination planning here, even at the risk of getting ahead of myself.

The near-infinity of airline route and price possibilities is a good thing, but can make it difficult to make a choice. Advertised air ticket prices and routes around the world are just that: examples. If you buy a cheap set of tickets that don't go to the places you actually want to go, and then spend more money later to get to your real destinations, you might end up spending more, at the end of the day, than if you start with a slightly more expensive initial package of tickets that will get you to more of the places you actually want to visit.

Each of the major myths detailed in this section leads people not to put enough effort into planning and choosing their route in advance, either because they don't realize how many choices they have or because they don't realize the financial benefits of planning ahead rather than deciding as they travel, one flight at a time. As a result, they spend more than they need to, miss out on options to improve their trip, or find they can't afford things they could have afforded had they planned ahead.

Some people conclude, as an outgrowth of one or more of these myths, that airline fare rules dictate and limit the possibilities and affordability of travel routes, and thus their destinations. As a result, they try to plan their trips by choosing a *route* before they have really settled on *destinations*. Often, the result is that they plan a route that isn't what they really want, doesn't get them where they really want to go, isn't optimized for their needs and desires, or isn't affordable or feasible at all.

Myth 1: "The Price Around the World Will Be the Same, No Matter What Route I Follow"

There is no ticket that will let you go anywhere in the world, visit any destinations, or follow any route for a single fixed price. Tickets can be issued with "open" dates but not with "open" places.

Most people are more or less aware of these basic generalizations. The problem is that there are exceptions, and people who know a little about the exceptions often think that the exceptions are much broader than they really are, largely because of misleading advertisements by the airlines. As a result, people who plan on using an "air pass" or an around-the-world (RTW) ticket, in particular, frequently count on buying a general-purpose ticket and deciding later on, as they go, where to fly. In practice, almost all affordably priced tickets require you to choose your route (although not necessarily your dates) before you buy your tickets.

Certain air passes for travel within particular countries, and published RTW fares, do allow *some* changes of routes and destinations. These fares are marketed with sweeping claims about being able to "go anywhere we fly," and people mistakenly assume that these special fares have special prices that are cheaper than the alternatives. But that's not usually true.

WHY PLAN YOUR ROUTE IN ADVANCE?

"Fixed-price" or reroutable tickets, where they exist, are rarely the cheapest. Fewer routes qualify for air passes or published RTW airfares than people think. There is no airline counterpart to the Eurail Pass—a pass that you can just flash to get on any plane, going anywhere, within a region. Where they exist, air passes are priced and ticketed for a specific route.

Around-the-world tickets purchased from an airline in the United States, for a journey starting and ending in the United States, start at a minimum of about US$4,500 (US$3,700 in "base fare" plus another US$500–1,000 in fare "surcharges" and taxes) for the simplest routes, with the fewest flown miles, in coach/economy class. But these tickets permit only a limited number of stops and routing choices, and actual itineraries—when they can be ticketed at an RTW fare at all—generally require higher tiers of RTW fares that go up to US$8,000 or more in coach class depending on the numbers of flights, miles traveled, and/or continents visited. Alternatively, you might be able to get tickets to a simple set of destinations for US$2,500 or less from a discount agency or on your own.

REROUTABLE TICKETS: NOT AS FLEXIBLE AS THEY SEEM

Airlines will tell you that you can change the route of an RTW ticket, within the allowable routes. But they don't tell you that because most airlines have "hub and spoke" route systems, from any given "spoke" city reached on such a ticket there is often only one city to which you can continue on an allowable route. It's rare enough that a given itinerary can be ticketed on any published RTW fare. It would be truly stellar good luck if a desired en-route change to such an itinerary were actually allowed on the same fare.

Similarly, an air pass on a particular airline is only good where that airline flies. You can't use a Thai Airways Discover Thailand air pass to get to Ko Samui, for example, because only Bangkok Airways flies there. It doesn't generally make sense to buy any ticket unless you have already decided where you are going. And if you do know where you are going, there are likely to be cheaper fixed-routing tickets for it.

If you want to get the best price for your airline tickets, you need to decide, before you buy your tickets, all of the specific places you will fly during the time that those tickets are valid. You can save a significant amount of money if you make those decisions as far in advance as possible.

Myth 2: "I'll Have to Follow a Specific Route Around the World"

There is no standard or usual around-the-world airline route, nor is there a standard ticket price. People who have heard about the routing restrictions of published RTW fares often think that their choices are limited to these fares. They waste large amounts of time and energy in a misguided effort to shoehorn the itinerary they want into one that will qualify for such a fare. Or they assume that any destinations not on such a routing will have to be ticketed as separate side trips.

In reality, advertised around-the-world prices are almost never published RTW fares that are limited to specific routes. Advertised prices from travel agencies are usually just examples of combinations of consolidator tickets that can be modified and customized almost endlessly. Most actual around-the-world itineraries cannot be ticketed on any of the limited number of published RTW fares.

There is thus no point in restricting your consideration of possible destinations to ones that you think qualify for such fares or that you have seen advertised as examples of around-the-world prices.

As long as you don't limit yourself to published RTW fares, the key facts about packages of tickets that will get you around the world are as follows:

- You do not have to start and end your tickets in the same place.
- Your route does not have to be continuous.
- You do not have to travel in any particular or continuous direction or on any particular combination of airlines.
- You do not have to travel only on airlines that are part of the same marketing "alliance."
- You are not limited to any maximum number of miles, flights, continents, or stopovers.

Nor are any of these things particularly likely to make your tickets more or less expensive. The majority of tickets sold by specialist around-the-world travel agents, or that travelers piece together on their own, include backtracking, discontinuities, and combinations of airlines other than those that publish joint RTW fares. Most of those ticket packages cost less than published RTW fares to the same destinations would cost.

Myth 3: "It Will Always Be Cheaper to Buy a Roundtrip Ticket"

People who are traveling entirely within one country or region often overlook destination planning because they assume that roundtrip fares to a single destination and back to the starting point are much cheaper than any multistop or discontinuous tickets. This leads them to choose a single city to use as a "base," to which they buy a roundtrip ticket. They figure they don't need to decide until they get there which other cities they'll visit as side trips.

Similarly, people traveling around the world will often include just one stopover on their long-haul tickets in a region or continent such as Europe or Australia, to use as a base for side trips to many other "nearby" places.

This approach is usually a mistake for an extended journey. Most destinations can more cheaply be reached as part of a through journey without backtracking, rather than as a side trip from a local or regional "hub." And roundtrip tickets are rarely cheaper than tickets into one city and out of another, as long as both are served by the same airline. So-called "open-jaw" tickets generally cost the average of the roundtrip fares for the two halves (outbound and return) of the journey.

An open-jaw ticket to fly into a city at one geographic extreme of the country or region, and out of the other, can save you from circling back to your arrival point to catch your return flight. But you can't realize those savings unless you have enough idea of where you are going to choose appropriate arrival and departure cities before you buy your tickets.

Every few days in the summer, for example, foreign visitors who bought roundtrip tickets from home to the East Coast of the United States would show up in my office on the West Coast, wanting last-minute transcontinental one-way tickets to connect with their return flight to Europe. Even if they took a bus or train, their total cost would end up higher than if they had known they would travel to the West Coast and had gotten an open-jaw ticket in the first place, arriving somewhere in the east and returning from the west.

Airlines and travel agencies advertise roundtrip (or "half roundtrip") airfares without mentioning the possibility of open jaws at similar prices. If you ask about roundtrip fares, they'll only tell you about roundtrip fares. It sometimes takes extensive probing for me to find out that someone asking about roundtrip prices actually plans to visit many places and would be better off with an open-jaw ticket. Awareness of open-jaw ticketing is the single simple thing that could save most travelers exploring a region the most money and time.

Myth 4: "Tickets Will Be Cheaper If I Wait Until the Last Minute"

Many people have heard they can get a cheaper ticket if they wait until the last minute, when "airlines sell off blocks of unsold seats cheaply to consolidators, who sell them for whatever they can get." This is not true.

Discounters don't pay the airlines up front to buy seats. So you are wasting your time if you try to bargain with travel agents on the assumption that they have already paid for a ticket and that they would rather get any money for it at all than have it go unsold. Neither a retail agent nor a wholesale consolidator pays a penny for a seat until a ticket has been sold to a specific person.

Last-minute fares or fares that will allow you to stand by for any available seat are set for business travelers and other desperate passengers who have to go, no matter what the price. The walk-up or standby fare is the highest fare. Airlines are quite willing to leave three seats empty that could have been filled had the walk-up fare been set at US$500, if that enables them to extract US$2,500 from one last-minute business traveler. Not only does the airline get more money, but those who do travel are less crowded and happier.

The Internet has made it easier for airlines to offer discounted "Web fares" directly to the public at the last minute, if lots of seats remain unsold. But these are rarely as cheap as the prices offered further in advance, through consolidators, for those same low-season flights that the airline knows will be hard to fill.

The situation is somewhat different for tour packages or cruises. Many of a tour operator's or cruise line's costs are paid in advance. They may be willing to discount the land or cruise portion of a package very deeply, at the last minute, if they are already committed to costs for hotel rooms or cabins that will otherwise be empty. But inclusive tours are rarely the cheapest option for people willing to travel on their own, especially more adventurous, experiential, or long-term travelers.

Myth 5: "Tickets Will Be Cheaper If I Buy Them Locally, As I Travel"

Many people have heard (correctly) that tickets in some places are cheap, and conclude (mistakenly) that it will be cheaper to buy parts of their tickets en route than to buy them before they leave.

In fact, those same tickets can probably also be obtained cheaply in advance, sometimes more cheaply than if bought en route.

Deliberately not buying tickets to places you know you will go, and buying them separately en route, is usually a mistake. Most of the people who buy air tickets en route could have gotten tickets to the same places, at a lower total cost, had they bought them before they left.

An especially common, unnecessary, and costly mistake is to

REAL LIFE

Check out your transportation options before you make definite commitments: I've heard from people who had already made arrangements to arrive in a city on a day when no flight arrived or no seats were available at any price, to get from one place to another more quickly than any scheduled service operated, or to follow itineraries for which they could not afford the tickets.

buy a ticket to one place for the sole purpose of buying a ticket there to some other place. Buying a ticket to Bangkok for a month is a mistake if your goal is to spend a month in India; likewise buying a ticket to London or Paris just to get to Africa. Through tickets from A to B and on to C are almost always cheaper than the combined cost of tickets from A to B and from B to C, even when B is a good place to get cheap tickets onward and even if you want to stop over and spend time in B on your way.

Flexibility, plans to use surface transportation, wanting the ability to make decisions on the spot, or wanting to travel for more than a year are good reasons not to buy air tickets in advance for particular portions of your trip. Saving money is not. Plan to pay a premium for the flexibility of buying tickets en route.

The shorter your trip, the more true this is, because if you are in a hurry you have to buy tickets at whatever price is available—if they are available at all. Unless you stay somewhere for several weeks or months, you'll have to buy tickets on short notice, when the cheapest tickets are gone.

Even if you have the time to wait around in London, Bangkok, or wherever for seats on the cheapest onward flight to become available, your expenses there are likely to offset whatever financial savings you expected on the air tickets.

If a separate ticket is appropriate for some part of your trip, a good agent can probably get it for you for less than you'd pay for it separately, or tell you which low-fare airline to go to for it (if it's an airline that doesn't sell tickets through travel agents). Travel agencies that specialize in long-haul and around-the-world travel buy and sell tickets from each other—at preferred wholesale rates, from suppliers whose reliability and value they have had time to establish—in every major world city where you would be likely to consider buying a ticket en route.

Some people are misled by the air ticket prices in guidebooks or advertisements. Like other prices in guidebooks, these costs are typically at least a year or two out of date. Even on routes without discounting (e.g., domestic fares within most countries), inflation alone is likely to make current fares at least 20 percent higher than those in up-to-date guidebooks.

Airlines have learned that they will go bankrupt if their planes are half empty, or if they sell too many tickets below cost in order to fill them. The only way airlines will stay in business is if they raise average prices. If they have to, they will deliberately reduce capacity, as they have been doing since 11 September 2001, so as to be able to raise prices even with reduced demand. One way or another, the long-term trend in airfares is likely to be upward.

Nor can you rely on advertisements as a guide to how much you can expect to have to pay. Despite chronic complaints from consumer advocates, most airlines advertise "bait and switch" prices. Surcharges (which are really just a differently labeled part of the fare) and taxes can double or triple the price of a cheap ticket for a short flight, and can add US$100–200 or more to the price of a longer flight. Deceptive airline price advertisements are an especially severe problem in the United States, where federal law exempts airlines from most state and local truth-in-advertising laws.

Discount prices given as examples in guidebooks for budget travelers are typically the lowest advertised prices: i.e., the lowest conceivable prices for tickets purchased well in advance for the cheapest seats for low-season travel on the cheapest airlines, exclusive of taxes, etc. Few people ever pay as little as the advertised prices—even among the experienced travelers who write guidebooks, who are familiar with the place and probably know some of the local language.

Some of the greatest cost savings in planning ahead can be on domestic tickets within other countries. First, domestic flights can often be included in through international fares at less additional cost than if ticketed separately, and often without liability for domestic ticket taxes. Second, special fares are available to foreign visitors for domestic flights within many countries, generally only on condition that tickets be issued prior to arrival in the country and in conjunction with international tickets. Once you arrive in such a country and find out the local fares, it's too late to take advantage of the discounts for tickets purchased abroad.

Whenever you can, make reservations and buy tickets for domestic flights within other countries at the same time as your international flights. Often they are cheaper that way, and that way you can lock in reservations and the price up front.

Occasionally—if none of the local airlines sells tickets online, or if none of their websites accept credit cards issued in your country, for example—you may have no choice but to wait until you get to another country before buying tickets for some domestic flights. If you can't make reservations or buy tickets from outside the country, either through your travel agent or directly from the airline, you probably won't be able to get reliable schedule or fare information either. Don't count on any information about air service if you don't have a confirmed reservation or ticket. Low-fare airlines are especially quick to discontinue routes that don't prove profitable. I've seen people get into real trouble by counting on the existence of a particular flight mentioned in a guidebook or that was advertised on the Internet months earlier when they were planning their trip, especially if it's on a route not served by any other airline, or any affordable one, or if they count on it to operate on a particular day of the week.

Myth 6: "Tickets Will Be Cheaper If I Piece Them Together Myself on the Internet"

Can you do better as a do-it-yourselfer than by going to a travel agency? Maybe, but maybe not—and certainly not always. Some prices, especially for tickets on "low-fare" airlines and some "Web fares" offered by traditional airlines, are only available online. But other prices, including most consolidator prices, are only available offline though travel agencies. (You might be able to find some consolidator ticket agencies online, but few of them make all their prices available on their websites.) And even those prices available online aren't all available or searchable through any single website.

Consumers think of airline ticket websites as search engines for prices from all possible sources, but they aren't. As I noted at the start of this chapter, airlines are making it harder and harder—deliberately—for anyone to build an airfare search engine. As airlines seek to centralize control of retail selling prices for their tickets, they are making less and less information available to travel agencies, computerized reservation systems, search engines, and other intermediaries or aggregators of price information.

Airlines' own websites show no consolidator prices at all. Aside from published fares, major online travel agencies like Travelocity.com and Expedia.com only list prices from their own consolidator contracts directly with the airlines—not those from the thousands of other consolidators around the world. As I'll explain in the following section, there's an entire global market of discounted "consolidator" prices for international tickets set by travel agents, not by airlines. For every published international fare, tickets can be available at hundreds of different, lower prices from different consolidators. These prices—the majority of international air ticket prices—are not shown in any computerized reservation system (CRS), are not available directly from the airline, and are not available from any Internet site that depends on airlines and/or CRSs as its source of fares.

Writing software to make consolidator ticket prices available on the Internet is a huge task. It's taken airlines decades and many billions of dollars to develop the current CRSs for published fares. Even the wealthiest Internet travel agencies would take many years to develop comparable systems—if they wanted to, which they don't. Their goal is to get you to pay as much as possible, not to save you money. (See the sidebar *Which Side Is a Travel Agent On?*)

Most Internet travel agencies only sell simple one-way and roundtrip tickets. Most air tickets sold in the United States are for domestic travel, and even most international tickets are simple roundtrips. So most Internet travel agencies don't really care about the itineraries they can't price, and they aren't about to spend the money to develop the ability to deal with them.

Advice for the Do-It-Yourself Travel Agent

"Why should I have to learn all this?" I hear some of you saying. "Isn't the Internet supposed to make it easy? Aren't there websites that will find the best deals for me?"

To make a long answer short, "No." The single most common and costly mistake in buying tickets on the Internet is to rely on a single website or "best-fare finder" robot to find you the best deal or to protect your financial interests.

The Internet makes it technologically possible for you to make your own reservations and purchase tickets without ever talking to a ticket clerk or travel agent — just as the Internet makes it possible for you to place your own "buy" and "sell" orders for stocks without talking to a human stockbroker. But the Internet no more eliminates the need to understand airline pricing and ticketing than it eliminates the need to understand the stock market — at least if you don't want to waste your money or risk getting scammed.

Many people think that travel websites are designed to help them get the best deals and find the lowest prices, but that's not true. With rare exceptions, they are designed to maximize the profits of airlines and travel agents by getting you to pay as much as possible for your tickets. It's possible to use them to find good deals, but only if you know enough about what you're doing to beat the designers at their own game.

"So what?" may be your retort. "I don't want to be a travel agent — I want to have the computer do it for me. How much skill does it take to be a travel agent, or to be my own travel agent? Don't travel agents rely on computers for all their information, anyway?"

Travel agents get much, though not all, of their information about airline prices from computerized sources — just like currency traders, air traffic controllers, librarians, and stockbrokers, to name a few. However, that doesn't mean that any of these jobs are unskilled or could easily be done by robots, or that you could do them yourself successfully as long as you had the same tools. Few people would set out to be their own carpenter, plumber, or electrician without first learning some of the skills those professions require. Yet few travelers appreciate the complexity of travel agents' work or the skills their work requires. Good travel agents are skilled information technology professionals.

The bottom line is this: if you don't understand what is going on, you have no way to tell when you're being ripped off. Much of this chapter is therefore a primer on how to be your own travel agent or to understand what is going on behind the scenes when you are working with a travel agency or airline, online or offline.

When the stars are aligned, piecing together your own tickets sometimes works out very well. But it entails some risks you may not have realized. Piecing tickets together on your own, especially online, you're apt to rely extensively on tickets on "low-fare" airlines, since these are the carriers that publish the lowest one-way point-to-point fares. This can deprive you, unwittingly, of potentially greater savings through consolidator tickets or through tickets that combine multiple flights and stopovers. Perhaps more importantly, it exposes you to the greater risk that a low-fare airline will cancel a route without being able to protect you on another airline, because low-fare airlines don't participate in traditional airlines' extensive networks of interline agreements. Before you buy tickets on a low-fare airline for a flight more than a month or two in the future, read the section later in this chapter about their drawbacks under *Types of Fares and Tickets*.

THE SYSTEM OF AIRFARES

Like the rules of chess or of a computer programming language, airfares are an artificial and formal system, with an essentially arbitrary set of rules. Little about the system is natural, obvious, or intuitive. There are historical, political, and economic explanations for some aspects of it, but much of it could just as well have been set up differently. The system has its own jargon, in which some words are used to mean quite different things than they do in common usage. It's no surprise that most people find airfares confusing.

This is an inherently complex subject. I'll try to be as clear and straightforward as I can, but I'm describing a complex closed system that is protected by participants who have an interest in keeping you uninformed. There is little accurate public information about the airline industry, and most readers are likely to have, for understandable reasons, false preconceptions about it.

Experienced travelers, business travelers, and others who are reading this book mainly for inside information on airfares may find this the most useful part of the book. People who are mainly interested in general travel planning advice, or who just want to know how to get the best and cheapest tickets, may want to skip this part and go directly to the following section, *Arranging Your Air Transportation*. If it all seems too complicated, by all means move on. But the reasons for some of the advice I give later will be more apparent if you understand how airfares and discounting work. If you find yourself asking, "Why does he say that?" about things in the later sections of this chapter, you may want to refer back to this part of the book.

"Published" Airfares

For many years the U.S. government—like most others in the world—treated airlines like public utilities. The government regulated which routes each airline could fly, fixed their prices, and guaranteed them a profit.

The rules that govern airlines and other "common carriers" originated with laws designed to protect travelers against exploitation and price-gouging by innkeepers when they arrived on foot or horseback and had no other place to stay, since the next nearest inn might be too far away. The successors to those innkeepers laws are why even today hotels and motels in most of the United States are forbidden to charge more than the maximum "rack" rate posted in each room. Over time, similar consumer protection rules evolved, for similar reasons, to govern transportation companies: first public stagecoach services, then railroads (which often had a local monopoly, especially for transporting farmers' crops to market from rural areas), and eventually airlines.

The basic idea behind the pricing rules established for airlines in U.S. law and international aviation treaties was that airfares should be fair, i.e. nondiscriminatory and the same for everyone, and that full transparency of fares was necessary to ensure oversight and nondiscrimination. Airlines were required to "publish" a tariff of fares: to file it with the government and make it available to the public. Airlines were required to sell a ticket to anyone offering to pay the fare in the tariff and comply with its rules, and forbidden to sell tickets except at the prices in their published tariff.

Computerized reservation systems (CRSs) were developed by the airlines to enable them to make schedule, fare, and seat availability information available to their own ticket offices and to travel agencies around the world. Because airlines were required to file complete tariffs with the government in standardized form, and needed to make them available at all of their own ticket offices, it was relatively easy for the CRSs to make the details of all published fares available to travel agents as well. Eventually, the CRSs themselves became subject to government regulation on antitrust (antimonopoly) grounds in the United States, Canada, and the European Union. To prevent the relatively small number of airlines that owned the original CRSs from exploiting their oligopoly against smaller airlines, those airlines were required to provide the same information to all the CRSs. And the CRSs were forbidden to bias their displays of fares and options to favor certain airlines. For a brief while, any travel agent who subscribed to any of the major CRSs could get a comprehensive, unbiased display and ranking of all published fares, almost instantly, from a single source.

In 1978, domestic airfares and routes in the United States were deregulated. While the government continues to subsidize air travel (see the sidebar *Government Subsidies for Deregulated Airlines*) and to license and certify airlines for operational competence and safety, airlines are now free to fly any routes, charge any fares, and make any profit they please. Airlines are now restricted only by the requirement that as common carriers they transport all would-be customers on a nondiscriminatory basis, and by antitrust laws that

Government Subsidies for Deregulated Airlines

Airlines in the United States whine about "regulations" and "freedom of the skies." In fact, they receive a wide range of subsidies, tax preferences, and other forms of special treatment from federal, state, and local governments.

How? Let me count the ways:

- Airports and air-traffic-control infrastructure are built and operated by tax-exempt government entities (consider the real estate and other taxes that would be paid by privately owned airports on huge tracts of land in prime urban and suburban locations) with below-market capital costs (tax-exempt government bonds).

- Employee training for pilots, mechanics, and other skilled employees is provided by the military at no cost to airlines. (Ex-military pilots and mechanics may require additional training and certification for specific civilian aircraft types, but they've already logged thousands of very expensive hours of jet aircraft experience.)

- Air traffic control (ATC) and other services to airlines are provided by the government. (Airlines will claim that they pay for this in user fees, but that ignores the taxes that would be paid on private ATC infrastructure, and the artificially depressed labor costs: as government employees, air traffic controllers and many other civil aviation workers are forbidden to strike, enabling the government unilaterally to impose below-market wages.)

- U.S. airlines are paid all the time, even when their aircraft aren't being used, for agreeing to make their planes available on demand to the government as part of the "Reserve Air Fleet." But the times when they are needed — times of war — are generally times of reduced civilian air travel, when they would otherwise be idle. And when the "Reserve Air Fleet" is used, airlines are paid market rates for government charters.

- Government funding for military aircraft subsidizes production and operation of civilian aircraft: manufacturers of aircraft and associated equipment pay nothing for knowledge transfers from government-funded military aircraft research and development to civilian aircraft. Military aviation provides critical support for economies of scale and continuity of operations during cyclical declines in civilian aircraft demand. Many civilian aircraft types are sold directly to the military, and these sales are often essential to enlarging production runs to the break-even point.

- Under the preemption clause of the Airline Deregulation Act of 1978, airlines are exempt from state and local truth-in-advertising and other consumer protection laws. (This wouldn't matter if the federal government enforced similar rules, but, as state Attorneys General have pointed out, the feds allow many practices that enhance airline profits but would be forbidden under state and local antifraud laws.)

- Airlines based in the United States, like those in most other countries, are protected by law from all foreign competition: No airline based anywhere else in the world is allowed to carry passengers between points in the United States, and no foreign entity is allowed to own more than 25 percent of the voting stock in any airline based in the United States. It's illegal, for example, to buy a through ticket on a foreign airline between Guam (a U.S. territory) and the U.S. mainland via Seoul or Taipei (even though travel agents occasionally issue such tickets by mistake), no matter how much cheaper that would be than a ticket on Continental Micronesia, the only U.S. airline with service between those places. You have to buy two separate tickets, and claim and recheck your luggage at the transfer point. U.S. airlines prattle about wanting "freedom of the skies" to operate within other countries. But as long as they continue to support these protectionist rules against foreign competition within the United States, their rhetoric about "free trade" must be dismissed as merely a lobbying ploy to get the government of the United States to intervene on behalf of their economic interests vis-à-vis those of foreign airlines with which their service wouldn't otherwise be competitive.

- Under "Buy American" rules, all travel funded even in part by the U.S. government must be on a U.S.-flag airline, no matter how much more it costs than a foreign-flag competitor. Where, as is often the case, there is often only one U.S.-flag airline serving a given destination, this gives them a de facto monopoly on government-funded travel, a large and often high-revenue portion of the traffic on some routes.

The situation is similar elsewhere in the world, even if the details vary from country to country. If airlines really want to be free of government regulation and oversight, they first should have to agree to give up their government subsidies and special privileges and protections.

prohibit them from collaborating to fix prices. On deregulated routes, airlines can set any fares they like, and can change fares as often as they like, without prior approval from the government or anyone else.

The theory behind deregulation was supposedly that air service would improve if airlines were not required to prove that their operations were in the public interest, but instead were allowed to operate purely in their own profit interest. Whatever one thinks of this theory, deregulation in the United States has been a mixed blessing for travelers and airlines alike. Fares on the busiest and most competitive routes have gone down. Fares have increased and service has been reduced, in some cases eliminated entirely, in many smaller cities. There are fewer nonstop flights and more hub-and-spoke operations, so a higher percentage of air travelers have to change planes. For better or worse, deregulation is spreading to more and more of the world.

Obviously, consumers benefit from lower fares. But they don't benefit from a system that precludes government oversight of unfair or monopolistic practices, which is why the requirement to publish tariffs was initially retained when domestic fares were deregulated in the United States.

Deregulation of airfares, so that they were no longer set by the government, was at least arguably a good thing. The later stages of deregulation have been unarguably bad for travelers. Since the first edition of this book was published in 1997, CRSs have been completely deregulated in the United States, so that even travel agents have no reliably unbiased or integrated source of fare information. And most of the requirements for airlines to publish tariffs have been eliminated, frustrating would-be comparison shoppers and making oversight of nondiscrimination in pricing all but impossible. Today, the airlines' goal is just the opposite: "personalized" prices. There's an urgent consumer protection need to reregulate the CRSs and to once again require airlines to publish and abide by a tariff of fares available in its entirety at their offices, on their websites, and to travel agents. Without that, effective comparison shopping or oversight of airlines' price advertising is impossible.

Even leaving aside personalized, off-tariff, and consolidator prices, finding the best fare is still a complex task for a traveler or travel agent. There are several million different published fares in effect at any given time just between points within the United States. Each fare has 2–10 pages of associated rules. Airfares have a bewildering variety of weird conditions. Travelers often ask their travel agents, "Doesn't the computer tell you what the best price is?" These people, and some computer programmers, may be surprised to learn that there is as yet no infallible computer algorithm for determining the lowest available published fare between two points on given dates, despite the best efforts of airlines using some of the world's largest commercial computer centers and most sophisticated artificial intelligence techniques. Human beings

Match the Price or Match the Rules?

Because it's easier for potential customers to compare advertised fares than rules, most airlines closely track, and match, competitors' fares. Often even the most mainstream airlines will offer at least a few highly restricted tickets at the same price as a competing "low-fare" airline. The average fare on American, United, or Delta is much higher than the average on JetBlue, Southwest, or Virgin America. But because people looking for cheap tickets look first at "low-fare" airlines, these are the first airlines to sell out their cheapest seats on any given route. And the cheapest seats actually available are often on a less-full flight on what is, on average, a more expensive airline.

Similar fares do not, however, necessarily have the same rules. An easy way for an airline to attract business at the expense of its competitors, without having to reduce its fares, is to make its rules slightly less restrictive. The airlines most likely to do this are ones that passengers would be less likely to choose if all else were equal.

If you are looking to find a way around some rule of a cheap fare that you can't comply with, check the rules of other airlines. Start with the least known or least popular airlines serving the route, especially those that don't have nonstop or direct service, have only infrequent schedules, and/or have the worst reputations for in-flight service (especially if it's a long flight). If there are many airlines in the market, there's a good chance that at least one of them has matched the others' fares but with a less restrictive set of rules.

For what it's worth, differences in airlines' actual quality of service are smaller than, and only weakly correlated with, differences in their reputations. Some of my favorite airlines are ones that just aren't well known, or that have poor reputations based largely on mistaken assumptions by people who haven't actually flown on them. I've had terrible experiences on other airlines that spend a lot of time and money successfully burnishing their images, and not nearly enough on living up to the expectations they create.

(travel agents or airline rate desk staff) still have to read the rules to figure out which fares apply. You can't do it yourself even if you want to, since the public no longer has access to the airlines' tariffs.

WHY ARE FARE RULES SO WEIRD AND UNFAIR?

At first glance, fare rules seem to have no rhyme or reason. "Why does the price depend on whether I fly only on Tuesdays, at 2 A.M., or when the moon is full?"

Which Side is a Travel Agent On?

It should be obvious that, when you want to buy a ticket (and pay as little for it as possible), the airline is not your friend. What about the travel agent? Which side are they on, yours or the airlines'?

An "agent" is someone who works on someone else's behalf. A travel agent can be a "seller's agent" (working for the airlines, for a commission paid by the airline), a "buyer's agent" (working for the traveler, for a consulting or service fee), or a "dual agent" (working for and paid by both the supplier and the consumer).

Traditionally, travel agents have been exclusively seller's agents, answerable exclusively to the airlines and other suppliers of travel services. Such an agent's sole goal, and legal duty, is to get you to pay as much as possible. All agencies, offline or online, who sell tickets at published fares without charging additional service fees are strictly seller's agents. They are not on your side. Most even tell you so, explicitly, if you read the fine print: "This travel agency acts solely as an agent for suppliers of travel services," or words to that effect. Even some agencies that charge fees still choose to declare themselves as seller's agents.

everyone asks. Try to look at the rules from the point of view of the people who make the rules—the airlines—and they will begin to make sense.

Airlines start with the highest fare that they conceivably hope to get anyone to pay, which they define as the full or normal fare. The "normal" coach or economy roundtrip fare from New York to Los Angeles and back, as the airlines define it, is thus more than US$2,000, or four to five times what most people would consider to be the norm. The full fare is unrestricted: fully refundable, freely changeable, available at any time, long in advance or at the last minute, on every seat of every plane. Anything cheaper than the full fare is considered a discounted fare, and has rules restricting its use.

The airlines' goal in discounting is to fill seats that would otherwise go empty, without diverting passengers who would be willing to pay higher prices. Fare rules have, in most cases, little or nothing to do with the airlines' costs (and certainly nothing to do with fairness) and everything to do with airlines' perceptions of passengers' willingness to pay.

Airlines are neither irrational nor stupid. They spend huge amounts of money on market research and on sophisticated computer hardware and software for "yield management" (profit maximization). Viewed from the customer's perspective, or a cost perspective, fare rules seem bizarre and arbitrary. They are not. From the airlines' perspective, they are part of a highly

Buying airline tickets from an agency that is solely an agent of the airlines is like buying a house from a real estate agent who works exclusively for the seller. Don't do it if you can avoid it, at least if you care about price and value.

The way to insure that a travel agency has accepted at least some obligation to work for you, and not just against you, in dealing with the airlines, is to insist on using an agency that charges service fees or sells discounted tickets (making them either a buyer's agent or, more often, a dual agent). Travel agents who sell discounted tickets include a de facto fee for their services in the mark-up from their wholesale costs to their retail prices. They are thus either buyer's agents, dual agents, or not agents at all but "principals" to the sale. Their exact legal status is unclear, but they certainly aren't purely seller's agents.

It shouldn't be surprising that if you want an agent to work for you, you need to pay them to do so. Agency law also affects what rights you have if you have problems with a travel company. You have far more rights in a dispute with a buyer's agent, or a dual agent, than in a dispute with a seller's agent.

developed, and largely successful, system for identifying exactly how much each passenger is willing to pay, and getting them to pay that full amount. One workshop at a conference for airline pricing managers I was invited to a few years ago was entitled, "Measuring your customers' willingness to pay."

For example, it costs the airline the same amount to fly you from A to B and back, regardless of how long you stay in B. But most cheap fares—in many cases all but the most expensive fares—have both minimum and maximum stay requirements. Airlines have found that how long you want to stay is one of the best indicators of how much you are willing to pay, and set their fare rules accordingly.

The airlines' perception (probably a correct one) is that people who don't want to spend a weekend at their destination are business travelers who are able and willing to pay extra to come home sooner to spend the weekend at home with their friends or family. Airlines therefore use the requirement that you spend a Saturday night at your destination as a way to identify people who are willing to pay more, and to make them do so. If you aren't willing to stay over a Saturday night to qualify for a lower fare, the airlines infer that you aren't really that price-sensitive, and they charge you more for the privilege of coming home sooner.

Similarly, the airlines' perception is that people who are staying only a

Do It Yourself or Use a Travel Agent?

Whether you are working with published fares, consolidator prices, or both, how do you find the ticket that's best for you?

You can try to sort through all the fares and rules yourself on the Internet, although almost no airline ticket website shows the complete fare and rule information you'd need to make an informed choice. Or you could call every airline, although the airline with the best fare may be one you've never heard of and wouldn't think to call. But you have little practical chance of actually finding the best fare and schedule without professional help from a travel agent. Would you know to look to Jet Airways of India for prices from Newark to Brussels, or Malaysian Airlines for prices from Buenos Aires to Capetown — nonstop inter-continental routes flown by airlines based on different continents altogether? Even if you did, these airlines wouldn't sell you tickets at the prices some travel agents offer on those airlines. It's offline travel agents' consolidator prices, not the airline-direct prices or any prices available online, that put these airlines among the price leaders in their respective markets.

I'm often asked what the easy way is to find the best travel deals. The easy way? Go to a travel agent, and pay them to do the research for you, using their expertise and access to specialized knowledge and data sources.

You can't expect doing it yourself to be quicker or easier than paying a professional to do it for you. Learning the skills of a travel agent takes a sub-stantial investment of time and effort as well as access to specialized knowl-edge. Much of the essential information is proprietary, such as the information available through computerized reservation systems but not on the Internet. It's not a substitute for on-the-job training and mentorship, but you might want to look at my other book in this series, *The Practical Nomad Guide to the Online Travel Marketplace*. It's intended in part as an introductory textbook for do-it-yourself travel agents.

There are reasons to do things yourself, but you should expect it to be slower and harder than having them done for you. Unless you have both natural aptitude and substantial experience as a do-it-yourself travel agent, you can expect to make mistakes — some of them expensive. And arranging a com-plex international trip is quite different from arranging a simpler domestic trip, whether for a professional or a do-it-yourselfer.

If you go to a travel agent, expect to pay a fee for their consulting services, whether or not you buy anything from them. Travel agents are no longer paid commissions by most airlines. Even robotic Internet travel agencies charge service fees, or include the cost of their services in the prices they set. Only by buying directly from an airline — forgoing a travel agent's advice and possibly their discounted consolidator ticket prices — can you avoid service fees.

Unless travelers are willing to pay a consulting fee, travel agents can no longer afford to take the time to give advice or search for the best deals. If travelers refuse to pay a fee, they have no one to turn to for airfare advice but the airlines themselves. This is a recipe for getting ripped off, or at least for paying more than would otherwise be necessary.

week or two are vacationers, for whom travel is discretionary and who might not travel at all, or might go someplace else, unless they are offered a low price. Travelers who want to stay longer, on the other hand, are likely to be people with jobs or other strong ties to the place, and compelling reasons to go, who can amortize the cost of their tickets over a longer period, and who thus can be expected to be willing to pay more. So roundtrip fares for longer stays are higher, often much higher, than short-stay fares. The cheapest fares on U.S. domestic routes typically allow a maximum stay of 30 days, while the cheapest "tourist" roundtrip fares on international routes have maximum stays varying, depending on the route, from as short as seven days to as long as six months.

WHY BUYING DIRECTLY FROM AN AIRLINE MAY NOT BE THE BEST DEAL

Airlines want consumers to think that if they sold all their tickets directly to travelers—either over the phone or via the Internet—and paid no commissions to agents, they would reduce their costs for distributing tickets. In reality, since they no longer pay commissions to most travel agents, it almost certainly costs an airline more to issue a ticket than to have a travel agent issue it for them. And that's as true on the Internet as offline. Most service providers would be delighted to outsource their distribution, at no cost, the way the airlines have.

The real reasons airlines want to get rid of travel agents—in spite of the money they save the airlines in ticketing and customer service costs—are to make it harder for new airlines to break into the industry and to make it easier to raise fares. Established airlines want to eliminate the role of the travel agent as an impartial consultant who might find a way to offer the passenger a cheaper fare on their flights, or who might (God forbid) recommend the competition.

Air Transportation

The last thing Air Established wants is for a frequent flyer to call a travel agent who might tell them, "Did you know that Air Upstart is now offering a lower fare? You may not have heard of Air Upstart, but we've sold tickets on Air Upstart to several of our customers, and they said the service was good." Were it not for the travel agent, the travelers might never have heard of Air Upstart, or wouldn't have known what to think of them. They would simply have called Air Established, bought a more expensive ticket, and never known that they had an alternative. That's just what Air Established wants them to do.

DOMESTIC FARES WITHIN OTHER COUNTRIES

There is no international regulation of any aspect of domestic (internal) airline operations within any given country, including domestic airfares. Each country can make its own rules, and nothing can be inferred from how things work in one country about how they work in any other. Countries have a wide range of domestic airline choices and fare structures. In some countries domestic airlines and fares have been deregulated, as in the United States. National airlines have been privatized, fare structures have become more complex, and visitors are confronted with a choice between various start-up airlines they've never heard of. Most of them will get you where you are going just fine, if you buy a ticket for today's flight, but some of them will probably be out of business next month, let alone next year. It's hard to predict, and buying tickets on airlines like these for travel months in the future is definitely a risk.

REAL LIFE

At one point during a Cebu Pacific Air flight I was on in the Philippines, the flight attendants came through the aisle hawking T-shirts with the airline's logo and route map, like vendors on a Third World long-distance bus. I bought one as a souvenir.

Travelers often presume that domestic tickets can only, or most cheaply, be purchased within the country. This is not usually true. As I discussed earlier in this chapter, domestic tickets can be issued abroad for flights in more countries than most travelers imagine. And when it is possible to buy tickets abroad it is generally cheaper to do so than to buy them locally, if only because that enables you to buy them further in advance, when the cheapest seats are still available.

Tickets for domestic flights don't necessarily have to be issued as separate tickets. Some of the greatest savings on domestic flights are when they can be issued as stopovers or add-ons to through international tickets.

Stopovers are fairly straightforward, although not everyone thinks to ask for them. On a ticket from Europe to Australia via the United States, for example, it may be possible to make stopovers in New York and Los Angeles, and to include the flight between New York and Los Angeles as part of the international ticket, at no additional fare or for much less than a separate ticket would cost.

Add-ons are less well known or understood, but equally valuable. Most international flights operate only between capital cities or other big international gateway cities. But lots of people want to fly between airports not served by direct international flights. To attract their business, airlines provide discounts on domestic flights to the gateway cities where their flights originate and from the destination cities where they arrive.

If the same airline operates the connecting domestic and international flights, the add-on may be little or nothing (a so-called zero add-on between common-rated cities).

Competition forces some airlines to common-rate cities even when they have to pay another airline to carry passengers between them. For example, several Asian airlines fly to Los Angeles but not San Francisco, and to compete with airlines that fly from San Francisco most of them charge the same price for passengers starting from San Francisco as they do for passengers who board their flights directly in Los Angeles. They include the connecting flight on a U.S. airline between SF and LA at no extra charge.

Add-ons are typically less costly, and less restricted, than separate domestic fares. When a foreign airline contracts with a domestic airline to carry through passengers to and from its gateway(s), it is in a position to steer a large volume of business to the add-on carrier, with little or no marketing or sales effort on the part of the airline that gets the domestic business. So foreign airlines can, and do, negotiate extraordinarily low add-on prices per kilometer of domestic flying.

Because the United States forbids foreign airlines to carry passengers entirely within the United States, most flights by foreign airlines make only one stop at a single U.S. gateway. Almost all foreign airlines serving the United States, and not just those that have "codeshares" with U.S. airlines, have add-on agreements with one or another U.S. airline to carry people to and from their gateways. Roundtrip transcontinental U.S. add-ons are typically about US$350–500—as cheap as the cheapest transcontinental tickets on the busiest routes, and much less than the cheapest tickets between smaller cities.

From a point in the United States to a destination abroad, it's usually cheaper to get a through ticket with an add-on than to get one domestic ticket to a U.S. gateway city and a separate international ticket from there. It's a particularly poor choice to use a "free" ticket obtained with frequent-flyer mileage to connect to an international flight, where all it will save you is what the add-on would have been. Price through tickets, with an add-on, before committing yourself to use frequent-flyer mileage credits to get to an international gateway from somewhere else in the United States or Canada.

The bottom line on domestic flights in any country: do yourself a favor and at least ask your travel agent, before you buy any of your international tickets, if domestic flights you plan to take can be included in your package of tickets, or for the agent's recommendation as to which local or low-fare airline you should try to get tickets from directly if the agent can't.

Consolidator Air Ticket Prices

If fares are published at all, government rules officially prohibit selling tickets for lower (or higher) prices, even when the fares are deregulated. Those rules are intended to allow government oversight of possible illegal practices and to ensure that, as common carriers, airlines are treating all customers equally. But airlines don't want to make their prices public. Thus, even where bilateral aviation agreements between countries have been revised to permit airlines to set their own fares, most airlines still choose to publish fares substantially higher than some of their actual selling prices, in order to conceal their real price structure from their competitors and the public.

Airlines like having the "official" fares high, so they can get more money out of price-insensitive travelers who have to buy tickets at the last minute because of family emergencies, urgent business, and so forth. But if tickets were sold only at these high published fares, the airlines would have too many empty seats.

The goal of the airlines is to maximize revenue, not necessarily to fill every seat. If they can fill more seats while still getting each passenger to pay the most they are willing to pay, they make more money. The problem for the airlines is how to get as much money as they can for filling seats that would otherwise be empty, without destroying the system that keeps prices high for those for whom price is no object, and while diverting as few passengers as possible from official-price tickets to lower-revenue discounted tickets.

Travel agents are the essential element in the scheme of "consolidator" prices that airlines developed during the period of regulated fares, and still use even after deregulation, to deal with this revenue-maximization problem.

Rules that regulated fares placed no limit on the size of the commissions that airlines paid to travel agents. Airlines no longer pay normal travel agents any across-the-board "base" commission, but they still pay "incentive," "override," or "bonus" commissions on certain tickets. These commissions are, theoretically, intended to increase the incentive for agents to sell tickets on those airlines and routes.

The easiest way for an agent to use a commission to increase sales is, of course, to give part of the commission back to the customer as a rebate or discount, making the effective price (after the rebate) less than the official fare. The result is what is called a "consolidator" ticket.

In practice, it works like this: An airline contracts with certain travel agencies ("consolidators") and authorizes them to issue tickets for a net whole-sale price that is lower than the official fare. Sometimes the net remit from the agency to the airline is specified as a fixed amount, and sometimes as a percentage of the published fare. In either case, the difference between the wholesale price paid by the agency to the airline, and the official fare, is con-sidered a "commission."

Some consolidators sell tickets directly to the public, online and/or of-fline. Others are wholesalers who issue tickets only for other travel agencies who in turn mark them up to retail customers.

Some consolidator tickets show the official fare (regardless of how much either the agency or the traveler actually paid). Others show no price at all, or the misleading legend "FREE" or "BULK" in place of a price. That has led to a widespread misunderstanding that consolidator tickets are issued "in bulk," and that consolidators actually have buckets of tickets with no names on them that they have already paid the airlines for. In reality, tickets aren't and can't be issued, and consolidators don't pay airlines for them, until they are sold to specific named passengers whose names are printed on them when they are is-sued. Don't make the mistake of assuming that a consolidator has already paid for some number of tickets, and will lose their investment if they go unsold.

The airline fixes the wholesale price it charges a consolidator for a ticket. But the airline neither knows nor controls the price at which the consolidator (or the retail travel agent who buys a ticket through a wholesale consolidator) sells the ticket to a traveler. Once an airline has set its wholesale prices, the air-line gets the same amount of money regardless of how much the agent marks that ticket up to a retail customer. The airline neither knows nor cares how much you pay an agent for a ticket.

Actual consolidator selling prices for airline tickets are set by, and are known only to, those individual consolidators. Consolidators' prices are valu-able trade secrets. Neither any airline, any individual consolidator, any one website, or any single intermediary or data aggregator has access to compre-hensive information about all the prices offered by consolidators worldwide, even for tickets on a single airline. That isn't a technological limitation or one that could be eliminated by sufficiently clever ticket price search software. That's inherent in the nature of consolidator ticket pricing.

Airlines continue to use consolidators, even in markets where fares have been completely deregulated, in order to hide their prices. Airlines could simply publish lower fares, or offer lower prices directly on their own website. But if they do so, their competitors will immediately know exactly which flights they are having trouble filling, and how much they have had to lower their prices. And those lower prices will immediately be obvious to any potential customer who visits their website, even someone who might be willing to pay much more. By dumping their "distressed inventory" of seats they can't otherwise fill through consolidators, instead of directly and publicly, airlines deprive competitors and the public of information about their prices. Prevention of comparison shopping is a desired feature (from the airlines' point of view), not a bug, of the consolidator pricing and ticketing system.

The airline ticket consolidator industry developed as a way for airlines to sell tickets for less than officially fixed prices. Now that airlines are free to set their own prices, airlines' desire for price opacity is the sole raison d'être for the persistence of consolidator tickets.

FINDING THE RIGHT TYPE OF TRAVEL AGENCY

Asking an airline how much they want you to pay for a ticket is like asking the IRS how much tax they want you to pay. They will give you an answer, but probably not the one that's in your best interest. Why should you expect airlines' salespeople, or the websites they have designed, to tell you about their cheapest product rather than to try to sell you their most expensive one? If you want independent comparative advice about different airlines and their prices, you'll either need to go to a travel agency (online or offline) or rely on your skill as a do-it-yourself travel agent.

There are travel agents, though, and there are travel agents. Not all travel agents are skilled at interpreting fare rules, advising on routes, or finding discounts. On the other hand, given how little travel agents are paid, it's remarkable how many competent agents there are. In the United States, most travel agents are women, and the wage scales for travel agents are further reduced by its being regarded as "women's work." But as those travel agencies that served only as remote ticket offices for the airlines have gone out of business, those that have survived have tended to be those that are able to offer advice and services that justify their fees. As the numbers of travel agents have gone down, agents' average competence in their fields of expertise has gone up. The problem is finding an agent with the right specialization: discounted airline tickets for independent international travelers.

In the United States and most other countries, there are no meaningful professional standards for people who call themselves travel agents. Whether there should be is a topic of hot debate within the profession. My own opinion is that travel agents have such different specializations, requiring such different skills and bodies of knowledge, that no single set of criteria could distinguish competent agents from incompetent. I considered myself an expert travel agent in my specialty, but I'd have flunked any travel agent qualification test that asked about the travel services most U.S. agents sell: cruises, package tours, Disneyland, and all-inclusive resorts.

Different agents are best for different travelers. Few people from the United States travel abroad, compared to the numbers who travel within the United States, and most who do travel to a very limited number of places in Western Europe or the Caribbean. Most U.S. agents have limited experience with international travel, and no experience with multistop or long-term travel or travel outside the First World. Thus, finding the right agent may take some effort.

Don't hesitate to ask a travel agent, "What kind of travel services do you specialize in?" If the answer is cruises, tours, or "We can do anything," look elsewhere. You want to hear two magic phrases: "international airline tickets" and "independent travelers." And "independent" travel should mean "do it yourself" travel rather than "customized tours" or "FIT travel."

Few travelers anywhere appreciate the diversity of skills required of travel agents, and if you've never worked with a good agent you may not know how much help they can be. But a good travel agent can offer prices you couldn't have gotten directly from the airlines and can advise you about routes and airlines you would never have thought of on your own.

Travel agencies have been leaders in computer use and networking for decades. The local travel agency in your town was probably the first local business to have a real-time connection to a global computer network, and travel agents were the first professionals to all have computers on their desks. The first local area network in most towns was at the travel agency office. Only sometime in the 1990s was the network of airline computerized reservation systems (CRSs) surpassed by the Internet as the world's largest interconnected computer network.

Experiences with bad travel agents can lead travelers to conclude that travel agents know less than travelers themselves know about airline routes and fares, that agents have little to offer by way of deals or advice, and that travelers could do better for themselves by dealing directly with the airlines and cutting out the intermediary. Websites that claim to give "direct" access to CRSs tempt travelers by promising to provide all the information travel agents have, and to enable travelers to do anything a travel agent can do. But the CRS access provided by these gateways is actually indirect, through quite restrictive interfaces. And as I've discussed earlier, the information available through these channels is increasingly incomplete and fragmented.

Even for published fares, the interpretation of airfare rules is as specialized a skill as the interpretation of legal statutes, requiring experience, knowledge of specialized terms of art, and access to interpretive resources that travelers who aren't travel agents and haven't worked for airline rate desks aren't likely to have.

Airlines have made determined efforts to automate the interpretation of fare rules, and airfare search software has long been a leading goal of artificial intelligence researchers. But no computer program can yet reliably determine the price applicable to a particular itinerary (specific set of flights), much less which alternatives might better suit a traveler's desires. No airline has been able to replace its "rate desk" with machines. Every airline maintains a staff of highly skilled human beings solely to interpret the rules of its own fares, and it's not uncommon even for rate desk employees to disagree with each other as to the fare that should be charged, according to the myriad rules, for a particular set of flights.

The problem is, of course, all the more complex when you are dealing with the fares not of one airline but of every possible airline. And the Internet gateways to CRSs don't give access to more than a small fraction of the software tools that travel agents who use the full-featured versions of the CRSs have for searching for, analyzing, and comparing fares and rules.

The CRSs (Sabre, Galileo, Worldspan, Amadeus, etc.) contain only official published fares. For consolidator tickets, actual selling prices are set by agents, not airlines. Agents' contracts with airlines determine what commissions are paid to them on which fares, and with what conditions. Agents' commissions in turn determine how far below the published fares they are able to set their selling prices. The real structure of consolidator ticket selling prices is determined by each airline's discount agreements with each of its agents, read in conjunction with its published fares and rules.

Consolidator agreements are, by nature, confidential contracts between agents and airlines, which both parties agree not to disclose to anyone else. All commission contracts contain confidentiality clauses. Airlines offer discounts only to selected agents. Airlines don't want other agents to find out what deals they have agreed to, lest other agents ask for the same thing. Agents likewise don't want competing agents to find out what deals they have been offered, lest they ask for and get them too. You will never see consolidator contracts or their terms published in CRSs, on the Internet, or anywhere else. They are compiled (and in some cases indexed by computer) only internally by individual discount agencies, and occasionally by consortia of discount agencies or by wholesale consolidator ticket price aggregators and brokers.

The discount airfare market is not a perfect or open market. Discount agents spend much of their efforts trying to find out which agents for which airlines in which places are being offered which discounts on which tickets on which airlines, with what rules, so that they can buy each ticket wherever and from whichever wholesale agent it will be cheapest, or issue it under their own contract with the airline.

Airlines' local offices sometimes have a high degree of autonomy. An office in a particular obscure place may have decided to give a local agent a better deal than any of that airline's offices in other places, enabling that agent to sell tickets more cheaply than any agent elsewhere. Differences in prices of tickets on the same route when bought in different places are usually mistakenly attributed to currency fluctuations. But the airlines' standard system for calculating price equivalents in local currency is fairly effective in limiting the impact of all but the most rapid changes in exchange rates. Most variations of ticket price from place to place are due to differences in the wholesale prices offered to consolidators, and the markups set by those consolidators, in different places.

Demand for tickets between A and B (and willingness to pay, which is the airlines' measure of how much to charge) is generally highest in either A or B. It's harder to drum up customers for flights between A and B in other places. So there's often some other place C where a consolidator is given a lower wholesale price on tickets between A and B than is any agent in A or B. For the airline, discounting in C has the advantage that it isn't likely to depress the market for tickets in A or B, where people are willing to pay more.

For these reasons, tickets for flights between two places can be cheapest in some third place far away from either. Most agents aren't set up to import tickets from other places. Those specialized discount agents who shop the global ticket market can offer much better prices on certain tickets than agents familiar only with ticket suppliers and suppliers in the local market.

Over the last decade, airlines have begun major efforts to centralize their pricing, and have dramatically reduced the autonomy of their local sales offices to approve different consolidator prices. That has significantly reduced the frequency and extent of differences between consolidator prices for the same tickets on the same airline in different parts of the world. Nonetheless, there are still times when you can get significant advantages by buying tickets from an agency that sources consolidator tickets globally, not just locally, and far enough in advance of your departure for them to have time to import paper tickets from the other side of the world if necessary.

Airlines' and agents' collections of information about the terms of their own and other airlines' and agents' discount agreements are their most important trade secrets. An agent's competitive edge in a particular market may depend on his or her knowledge of a particular supplier of especially cheap tickets on a certain airline and route. Industrial espionage and intelligence-gathering in the discount travel industry focuses on finding out who has what deals with whom, or which airline is offering what wholesale prices to which agent where. Agents use all kinds of tricks to find new suppliers. Airlines use agents to find out what competing airlines are offering. Agents use customers to find out what competing agencies are offering. No one has complete information about ticket prices worldwide, but the traveling public has less information than any of the other players (airlines and agents).

The terms *price* and *fare* are often used as though they were interchangeable, but they aren't. Only those prices in published tariffs are properly considered "fares." If you call the airline directly, and ask about a price that an agent or a friend told you about, the airline may well say, "We don't have a *fare* like that. If you want to get a *price* like that, you'll have to talk to one of our agents," which is technically true but sounds like double-talk if you don't know the code.

There is no necessary correlation between which airline publishes the lowest fare, or offers the lowest prices on its own website, and which airline offers the lowest consolidator prices. Because the whole point of consolidator prices is to hide the extent of discounting, it's quite common for the airline that is cheapest through consolidators to have the highest published fares.

AIRLINES AND DISCOUNT AGENCIES

Airlines have a love-hate relationship with consolidator ticket agencies. Airlines themselves created and perpetuate the consolidator ticket market, as a way to preserve the benefits of (high) regulated fares while still enabling them to offer prices that maximize their profits. Airlines handpick the agents to whom they offer special discount agreements, and the terms of those agreements are determined and subject to change by the airlines, not the agents. But airlines are reluctant to talk openly about consolidator prices, lest wider awareness of their availability and legitimacy undercut the willingness of most passengers to pay the official fares.

Some airlines deliberately foster the image of disreputability and unreliability of discount agents and consolidator tickets as part of their revenue-maximization (yield management) strategy. People who are truly price-sensitive, and couldn't afford to buy tickets at the official prices, will probably buy consolidator tickets even if they think of them as somehow tainted or of dubious legitimacy. The airlines are unlikely to lose these people's business. People who are afraid to buy tickets from discounters are usually people who are able and willing to pay more for the perceived greater security of getting tickets directly from the airlines, or from full-price agents.

Frequently, airlines' contracts with consolidators restrict how those agencies can advertise. For example, the agency might be forbidden from mentioning the name of the airline in advertising (they are still allowed to show it on itineraries) or allowed to advertise or market only to a particular geographic or ethnic market. That doesn't mean, however, that you should pay for a ticket without knowing on what airline you are going to fly.

An agent should always tell you on what airline an advertised price is available; a price for tickets on a scheduled airline from an agent who refuses to name the airline before taking your money is presumptively a fraud. The only two exceptions are tickets for charter flights—no guarantees are usually made as to which airline will actually operate a charter flight—and the "opaque" or "white label" prices offered through some Internet travel agencies (such as Hotwire.com and Priceline.com). In no other case should you buy tickets on a scheduled flight without knowing on what airline you hold reservations.

All airlines' contracts with agents I've ever seen are subject to change at the sole discretion of the airlines, with minimal or no notice. While some airlines maintain fairly stable long-term contracts, many airlines revise their wholesale prices continuously in response to current load factors, advance booking levels, and competitive pressures. If an agent starts selling too many tickets at a discounted price, the airline will conclude that people are willing to pay more, and that it doesn't need to discount so heavily. The airline will therefore raise the wholesale price, forcing the agent to raise the selling price, or will terminate the contract and cease to offer any discounts below its published fares on that route.

It's not common, but more than once I've seen airlines raise consolidator wholesale prices on a particular route by more than US$500 per ticket, overnight. There are many "bait-and-switch" agents who quote low prices and then charge higher ones, but many price changes by agents are due to wholesale price changes by airlines. Because agents are forbidden to disclose the terms of their agreements with the airlines, and wouldn't want to anyway, it's hard for travelers to know what's really going on. The result is that agents often take the rap when airlines raise prices, and that passengers find it harder to tell good agents from bad or to know whom to blame for price increases.

Types of Fares and Tickets

"That's all well and good," some of you are probably saying by now, "But what kinds of ticket and airfare options does this leave us?" Within the framework described in the previous section, there's a complex structure of different types of published fares, including published RTW fares as well as one-way, round-trip, and "open-jaw" fares. There are also consolidator tickets sold for prices set by travel agencies, "Web fares" offered only online, "low-fare" airlines, charter flights, subsidized tickets for courier travel, and an illegal black market in brokered frequent-flyer tickets.

See the *Types of Fares and Tickets* chart for a comparative summary of the advantages, disadvantages, and attributes of the different types of fares and tickets described in the following pages.

Air Transportation

Types of Fares and Tickets

(For a more detailed explanation of each category, see the appropriate text sections)

TYPE OF FARE OR TICKET	Biggest Advantage	Biggest Drawback	Price Range (for comparable routes)	Flights Typically Available: From	Flights Typically Available: To	Available for Flights Originating Outside Country Where Tickets Are Bought?
Tickets You Have Earned As A Frequent Flyer	Free, if you didn't have to pay (or pay extra) for your tickets to earn the frequent flyer mileage	Your airline may may not go where you want; tickets on airlines with frequent flyer programs usually cost more, by more than the credits are worth.	Free–Moderate	Places served by one airline (or, for more miles, by a few of its marketing partners)	Places served by one airline (or, for more miles, by a few of its marketing partners)	If the airline has local traffic rights on such a route (or for more miles on a "partner" airline)
Courier Travel	Where available, this is often the cheapest option	Not available on most routes, and getting less common and more expensive	Low	Major international business centers only	Major international business centers only	Yes, but in practice it's very difficult to arrange
Charter Flights	Where available, this is often the cheapest option	Only available on limited routes, usually only at limited times of year	Low	Major population centers	The busiest holiday and resort destinations only	Yes, but in practice it's difficult to arrange
Student Fares	Available for one-way and long-stay round trips	Limited routes; not always the cheapest	Low–Moderate	Most major airports, sometimes also minor ones	Most major airports	Sometimes
Group and Tour Fares	Often the cheapest airfare, if available, if you are taking a cruise or tour or booking a hotel or resort package"	Limited routes and flexibility. If you don't want a package, it's only occasionally worth buying one just to qualify for the airfare.	Low–Moderate	Charters: big cities; scheduled airlines: most airports	Major resort, holiday, and package tour destinations	Only through tour operators in the country where flights originate
Airpass and Foreign Visitor Fares	Usually more flexible and sometimes cheaper than separate tickets	Not always cheapest. Sometimes available only if your international flights are on the airline of the destination country	Very Low–Moderate	Airports within certain countries served by particular airlines	Airports within the same countries served by the same airlines; occasionally between countries in a region	Yes. Usually must be bought outside the country of travel, and not available locally

TYPE OF FARE OR TICKET	Biggest Advantage	Biggest Drawback	Price Range (for comparable routes)	Flights Typically Available: From	Flights Typically Available: To	Available for Flights Originating Outside Country Where Tickets Are Bought?
Published Routing-Based RTW Fares	Few other legitimate discounted tickets are available in Business or First Class	Extremely limited routes; actual routes often require many expensive side trips	Low–Moderate	Most airports, often even minor ones	Only certain destinations permitted by the routing rules	Yes
Published Mileage-Based RTW Fares	Few other legitimate discounted tickets are available in Business or First Class	Limited routes; actual routes often require expensive side trips; not always the cheapest option	Moderate	Most airports, often even minor ones	Only certain destinations permitted by the routing rules	Yes
Consolidator Tickets	Greatest flexibility and widest range of routes of any discounted tickets	Available only from specialized travel agents, many of whom give only minimal service or advice	Very Low–Moderate	Anywhere	Anywhere	Yes
Low-Fare Airlines	Cheap, when and where available.	No interline agreements with other airlines. Limited and changeable routes, sometimes to or from inconvenient secondary airports.	Very Low–Moderate	Limited and changeable routes, often to or from secondary airports	Limited and changeable routes, often to or from secondary airports	Sometimes, depending on ticketing and payment systems
"Web Fares" and Published "Sale" Fares	When and where available, these are often among the cheaper options	Limited routes and unpredictable availability; no changes	Low–Moderate	Most airports, often even minor ones	Most major airports; sometimes also minor ones	Only when there's a sale or "fare war" in that market
Regular Published "Discount" Fares	Most widely available "discounted" tickets.	Most expensive "discounted" tickets	Moderate–High	Most airports, often even minor ones	Most airports, often even minor ones	Yes
Published Normal, Walk-Up, or Standby Fares	Most widely available type of tickets	Extremely expensive	Very High	Anywhere	Anywhere	Yes
Brokered (Purchased) Frequent-Flyer Tickets	Only discounted business or first class tickets available on many airlines and routes	Illegal; costs can include fines and jail, plus additional fare, if you get caught	Moderate (if you get away with it)–Extremely High (if you get caught)	Places served by certain airlines	Places served by certain airlines	Usually No

Types of Fares and Tickets (continued)

TYPE OF FARE OR TICKET	Likelihood of Availability: Low Season	Likelihood of Availability: High Season	Likelihood of Availability: Holidays	Refundable If Entirely Unused?	Minimum Stay	Maximum Stay	Date Changes Permitted?
Tickets You Have Earned As A Frequent Flyer	Fair	Bad	Bad–Nil	Usually, but with penalties	Usually none	Varies (30 days–1 year)	Often free, usually for a smaller fee than for changes to most paid tickets
Courier Travel	Poor to any specific destination; Fair if you don't care where you go	Poor–Bad, even if you plan far ahead	Nil	No	3–7 days	7–21 days, rarely longer	No
Charter Flights	Often not operated at all	Fair	Bad	No	Until the next charter flight back (typically 3–7 days)	30 days or more (or until the last charter flight back of the season)	Sometimes, for a fee
Student Fares	Excellent	Fair	Bad	Usually, but with penalties	None	1 year	Yes, for a fee
Group and Tour Fares	Excellent, if tours are operating year round; nil if not	Good, especially if you book several months in advance	Poor–Bad	Sometimes, with penalties	2–10 days	7–45 days (often may extend longer than the duration of the tour)	Sometimes not; sometimes for a fee
Airpass and Foreign Visitor Fares	Excellent	Good, if your schedule is fairly flexible or you book in advance	Bad	Usually, but with penalties	Usually none	14 days–1 year (usually 30–60 days)	Usually, sometimes for free and sometimes for a fee

TYPE OF FARE OR TICKET	Likelihood of Availability: Low Season	Likelihood of Availability: High Season	Likelihood of Availability: Holidays	Refundable If Entirely Unused?	Minimum Stay	Maximum Stay	Date Changes Permitted?
Published Routing-Based RTW Fares	Excellent	Good if you're not in a hurry and your dates are flexible	Fair	Yes, sometimes with penalties	14 days	1 year	Yes (Free)
Published Mileage-Based RTW Fares	Excellent	Good if you're not in a hurry and your dates are flexible	Fair	Yes, sometimes with penalties	14 days	1 year	Yes (Free)
Consolidator Tickets	Excellent	Good; Very Good if you're not picky about airlines, routes, or exact dates	Poor; Fair if you book several months in advance	Usually, with penalties	None–7 days	Up to 1 year; no limit if you buy your tickets in stages	Yes, sometimes for free or for a low fee
Low-Fare Airlines	Good (but routes can change, and some are seasonal)	Poor; Fair if you buy tickets long in advance	Bad	Sometimes	Usually none	Usually none	Usually for a fee, sometimes not (especially for the lowest fares)
"Web Fares" and Published "Sale" Fares	Good but erratic	Poor and erratic	Bad and erratic	No	0–14 days	14–30 days	No
Regular Published "Discount" Fares	Excellent	Fair	Poor	Sometimes, with penalties	3–14 days	7 days–90 days (up to 6 months or 1 year only in certain markets)	Usually for a fee
Published Normal, Walk-Up, or Standby Fares	Excellent	Excellent	Fair–Good	Yes	None	1 year	Yes (Free)
Brokered (Purchased) Frequent-Flyer Tickets	Excellent	Coach: Poor; Business/ First Class: Fair	Bad–Nil	No	Usually none	Varies (30 days–1 year)	Usually for a fee, sometimes free

Air Transportation

Types of Fares and Tickets (continued)

TYPE OF FARE OR TICKET	Open Jaws Permitted?	Stopovers Permitted?	Advance Purchase Required?	Allowable Time Between Reservation and Payment	Available in Coach/ Economy (Third Class)?	Available in Business/Club Class (Second Class)?
Tickets You Have Earned As A Frequent Flyer	Sometimes	Sometimes, especially at that airline's hubs	None–14 days	1–3 days	Yes	Yes
Courier Travel	No	No	Highly variable (None–6 months)	Short but variable (no more than a few days)	Yes	No
Charter Flights	Only if the route is flown by the same charter operator	No	Highly variable (None–6 months)	Short but variable (no more than a few days)	Yes	Rarely
Student Fares	Yes	Sometimes	None, if space is available	1–7 days	Yes	Yes
Group and Tour Fares	Sometimes, mainly with open-jaw tours or cruises	Rarely	None–90 days	None–several months (but deposit required immediately)	Yes	Occasionally, with expensive luxury tours or cruises
Airpass and Foreign Visitor Fares	Yes	Yes (usually limited in number, or charged for)	Before you leave your home country	1–7 days or more, if tickets are bought before leaving home	Yes	No

TYPE OF FARE OR TICKET	Open Jaws Permitted?	Stopovers Permitted?	Advance Purchase Required?	Allowable Time Between Reservation and Payment	Available in Coach/ Economy (Third Class)?	Available in Business/Club Class (Second Class)?
Published Routing-Based RTW Fares	No, with very few specified exceptions	Yes	None–21 days	Up to 14 days	Yes	Yes
Published Mileage-Based RTW Fares	Yes, but surface mileage counts toward mileage limit	Yes	7–21 days	1–7 days	Yes	Yes
Consolidator Tickets	Yes	Yes	None, if space is available and there is time for ticket delivery	1–7 days	Yes	Occasionally (rarely on airlines business-class travelers want)
Low-Fare Airlines	Yes	If the plane stops (most flights are nonstop)	None	None (instant purchase required)	Yes	Rarely
"Web Fares" and Published "Sale" Fares	Usually No	No	None–6 months	None (instant purchase required)	Yes	Rarely
Regular Published "Discount" Fares	Usually	Sometimes (often at substantially higher fare)	7–21 days	None–7 days	Yes	Rarely
Published Normal, Walk-Up, or Standby Fares	Yes	Yes	None	Variable but relatively long	Yes	Yes
Brokered (Purchased) Frequent-Flyer Tickets	Sometimes	Sometimes	None–14 days	Short but variable (no more than a few days)	Yes	Yes

Types of Fares and Tickets (continued)

TYPE OF FARE OR TICKET	Available in First Class?	Available Roundtrip?	Available One-Way?	Range of Routes Available	Best Suited For
Tickets You Have Earned As A Frequent Flyer	Yes	Yes	Sometimes (varies by airline)	Poor; Fair if you have enough miles for tickets on partner airlines	People who've earned miles on business trips they didn't have to pay for
Courier Travel	Yes	Yes	Sometimes (varies by airline)	Poor; Fair if you have enough miles for tickets on partner airlines	People who've earned miles on business trips they didn't have to pay for
Charter Flights	No	Yes	Rarely	Bad	Short high-season holidays to the most popular destinations
Student Fares	Yes	No (round trip must be issued and priced as two one-way tickets)	Yes	Fair	Certain one-ways and long-stay roundtrips, if you qualify.
Group and Tour Fares	Occasionally, with expensive luxury tours or cruises	Yes	No	Poor–Bad	People who are reserving hotels, package tours, or cruises in advance
Airpass and Foreign Visitor Fares	No	Usually (but may only be allowed to transit or stop in each city once)	Yes	Very good in countries where available	People taking many flights within a large country without domestic low-fare airlines, especially if within a short time

TYPE OF FARE OR TICKET	Available in First Class?	Available Roundtrip?	Available One-Way?	Range of Routes Available	Best Suited For
Published Routing-Based RTW Fares	Yes	No (must continue on around the world)	No; must return to starting point	Bad–Poor	If your plans fit within the allowable routes, and there's no cheaper option; flexible dates
Published Mileage-Based RTW Fares	Yes	No (must continue on around the world)	No; must return to starting point	Fair	If your plans fit within the allowable routes, and there's no cheaper option; flexible dates
Consolidator Tickets	Occasionally (rarely on airlines first-class travelers want)	Yes	Yes	Excellent	Complex, multistop, or discontinuous long-haul routes; one-ways; tickets originating in other countries; long stays
Low-Fare Airlines	No	Yes	Yes	Fair (depending on country or region); changeable	One-ways, if your route matches theirs and you're willing to fall back on surface transport if they discontinue the route
"Web Fares" and Published "Sale" Fares	No	Yes	No	Fair (when there's a fare war or system-wide sale)	Short-stay impulse travelers
Regular Published "Discount" Fares	Rarely	Yes	Rarely (except on routes competing with low-fare airlines)	Good	When nothing cheaper is available, or when matching the price of a low-fare airline
Published Normal, Walk-Up, or Standby Fares	Yes	Yes	Yes	Excellent	Not recommended if any cheaper alternative is available, unless you need a fully refundable ticket to satisfy onward-ticket requirements
Brokered (Purchased) Frequent-Flyer Tickets	Yes	Yes	No	Fair	Not recommended ever.

PUBLISHED DISCOUNT FARES

Airlines call the highest fare the "normal" fare and consider anything less than that a "discounted" fare. Advertised discount amounts or percentages are calculated from the highest possible fares. What you consider a normal price is probably described by the airline as a 50–80 percent discount from what the airline calls the "normal" fare.

The cheapest published fares offered directly by the airlines, published-fare websites, or offline travel agencies are almost invariably roundtrip fares; even when airlines advertise what looks like a one-way fare it usually turns out when you read the fine print to be a "half roundtrip" fare or "fare for one-way travel, based on roundtrip purchase." I agree with you: these sorts of ads are misleading and should be prohibited. In the United States, the federal government has "preempted" regulation of the airlines, so state and local authorities are powerless to stop these deceptive practices. In 2006, 44 of the 50 state Attorneys General jointly petitioned the Department of Transportation, to no avail, in support of an end to the preemption of their ability to enforce state truth-in-advertising and consumer fraud laws against airlines.

There are too many types and names of fares (APEX, Super APEX, PEX, Superpex, Super Discovery, etc.), and too little standardization in how airlines use these and other names and assign fare basis codes, to make it useful to try to categorize or describe particular types of discounted published fares. Don't waste your time trying to figure out what the best fare for your itinerary will be called. The names are essentially arbitrary, and the same general principles apply to cheap published fares by any name or with any fare code.

During the occasional and short-lived "fare war," when some airline lowers fares dramatically and others are forced to match the special fare, published roundtrip fares for short stays with fixed dates can be quite a bit lower than the cheapest consolidator ticket prices. But cheap published fares, especially during short-duration sales, are invariably among the most highly restricted of all tickets. The advantage to consolidator tickets is not that they are necessarily much cheaper than the cheapest published fares but that, because consolidator tickets are less restrictive, more travelers' desired itineraries qualify for them than qualify for the cheapest published fares.

For all but the simplest trip for a brief visit to a single destination, the cost of backtracking or circling to other destinations from the single turn-around point of a roundtrip ticket is likely to more than offset the additional price of a ticket with stopovers, or an open jaw, that will take you to or from more than one destination.

An airline will only publish an especially low fare, much less initiate or join a fare war, when it has or expects to have an unusually large number of empty seats. In such circumstances, lots of seats are likely to be available for consolidator tickets as well, often with more flexibility: one-way tickets, stop-overs, open jaws, discontinuities, longer stays, etc.

WEB FARES

The lowest prices offered directly by the airlines are "Web fares" offered exclusively on the Internet.

These deals are almost always limited to roundtrip travel for short stays within limited ranges of fixed dates. And these deals are short-lived and deliberately unpredictable. If there's a Web fare available for your itinerary, great. But you can't count on one being offered when you want it. Like fare-war tickets, they are extremely inflexible and of little, if any, value for longer stays or more complex or multistop itineraries.

Ultimately, Web fares do not serve consumer interests. Airlines could easily elect to publish their "Web fares," include them in CRSs, and allow them to be sold by all travel agencies. But airlines don't want to publish their lowest fares; this would make them too widely available and would frustrate the airlines' goal of price discrimination (getting different people each to pay as much as they are willing). So what do airlines do instead? They offer unpublished fares, but only on the Internet, where they seem to have assumed that no rules apply. And they've gotten away with it, despite accusations by consumer advocates, CRSs, and offline travel agencies that the major high-fare airlines are using the non-transparency of Web fares to hide oligopolistic and strong-arm pricing tactics against start-up and low-fare competitors. Refusing to make Web fares available through CRSs does nothing to lower prices. It serves only to distort the market, frustrate government oversight of antitrust laws, and reduce the availability of low fares and the ability of travelers to comparison shop.

If you're going to buy a ticket at a Web fare, buy it directly from the airline's own website. Participating airlines may also offer their Web fares through one or more of the big online travel agencies, so their websites can be useful tools for finding Web fares. But airlines often give bonuses, such as extra frequent-flyer mileage credits, for buying tickets on their own websites rather than through intermediaries. And some of the largest low-fare airlines—including Southwest Airlines in the United States and Ryanair in Europe—don't sell tickets through any online travel agencies, so it's important to check their websites individually.

CONSOLIDATOR TICKETS

If a travel agency—offline or online—offers a lower price than is available directly from the airline, it's for what is called a "consolidator" ticket.

Because a consolidator ticket is sold for less than the published fare, there is no such thing, strictly speaking, as a consolidator *fare,* only a consolidator's

How Around-the-World Airfares Have Changed

You're taking your trip now, so it might seem irrelevant to talk about how things used to be. But to the extent that you might get advice from people who have taken similar trips in the past, or from older publications, it may be worth highlighting the major changes in around-the-world airfares since the fourth edition of this book was published in 2007. The balance has shifted sharply away from published around-the-world (RTW) fares in business class, and less dramatically away from consolidator tickets in coach/economy class, relative to other types of fares and tickets.

Business Class

Published RTW fares used to be the best deal for most business-class RTW trips. For decades, published business-class RTW fares were far cheaper per mile flown than almost any other business-class prices, including consolidator business-class prices. And they were as little as 25 percent more expensive than comparable coach-class published RTW fares. Not any more, on either count.

In the last few years, airlines finally figured out that they had been grossly underpricing these business-class RTW tickets. Many published business-class RTW fares have doubled in the last few years, and they are now typically twice the price of comparable coach-class published RTW fares. At the same time, airlines have introduced more complexity into their business-class pricing, making available more discounted one-way and roundtrip business-class fares in addition to the traditional unrestricted "normal" fares.

The result of all this? It's much more likely than ever before that the lowest business-class price, especially for simpler routes with only a few stops, will be some combination of published-fare or consolidator point-to-point tickets, rather than a single ticket at a published RTW fare. And business class is no longer an inexpensive upgrade form a published coach-class RTW ticket.

Coach/Economy Class

Published coach-class RTW fares haven't gone up nearly as much in price as have published business-class RTW fares or, more importantly, as have other published or consolidator coach-class one-way or roundtrip tickets. The expansion of the three major global airline alliances (Skyteam, Oneworld, and Star Alliance) to include more member airlines — especially members based on more continents and in more regions of the world — means that you can reach more places on the routes of each of these alliances with less backtracking and fewer total miles than before. And all three of the alliances have replaced rules in these fares that used to require travel in a continuous direction with more flexible rules based primarily on total route mileage and/or numbers of continents visited.

At the same time, prompted by competition from low-fare airlines, even traditional airlines have started offering discounted one-way fares on routes where the only discounts from prohibitively high "normal" one-way fares used to be on round-tip tickets.

When all of the previous editions of this book were published, in the heyday of airline ticket consolidators, the cheapest way to get tickets for the vast majority of RTW routes was to buy a package of one-way tickets put together buy a travel agency specializing in international consolidator tickets. That's still true in many, perhaps most, cases. But there's a much larger proportion of routes than previously for which the cheapest option is either a published coach-class RTW fare or a package of one-way published-fare tickets that you could, if you are sufficiently skillful at tracking them down, buy directly from the airlines without going through a travel agent.

selling *price.* This is how airlines or published-fare Internet sites can misleadingly guarantee that they have "the lowest fare" even when they know they don't have the lowest price.

As discussed earlier, almost all airlines—except those low-fare airlines that don't work with travel agents at all—give at least some of their agents, somewhere, special deals that allow them to sell tickets for less than the lowest published fare. Consolidator tickets are available on almost all airlines (again, except some of the low-fare carriers) and routes, with two caveats:

First, you have to find the consolidator outlets. It's not surprising that the greatest discounts are often found through the most obscure and unlikely seeming agents in the last places you would think to look. That's perfectly consistent with the airlines' goal of discounting only through distribution channels that won't divert customers or depress prices in their primary markets. Retail travel agents who specialize in selling consolidator tickets are constantly tracking wholesale ticket prices and searching for new suppliers around the world. Their business success depends on it. Unless you get really lucky, you'll do better to go directly to a specialist who already knows where to find the best deal for your route than to beat the bushes on your own for every conceivable source of tickets.

Travel Agency Profits?

Profit margins for travel agencies are thin. Airlines have eliminated most of their commissions to travel agencies. Today, travel agencies make money only through service fees on published-fare tickets, or through their markup on discounted tickets, neither of which usually matches the 10 percent commission they used to get as standard. That's why so many storefront agencies have gone out of business. Those that remain typically focus on selling other travel services (cruises, tours, etc.) that still pay commissions, and/or charge service fees for issuing airline tickets at published fares.

Some people think that travel agents won't recommend the cheapest airlines because the agents will make less money on their tickets. It doesn't really work that way. The service fees travel agents charge travelers for issuing tickets are generally the same amount per ticket, regardless of the fare. Travel agents compete with each other, and their competitive success depends on finding their customers the lowest fares that will suit their wants. Travel agents will only sell more expensive tickets if they can give customers good reasons not to buy cheaper tickets. This is part of the service they provide: who else will know how to decipher the fine print to tell you the hidden defect in the advertised special that really is too good to be true?

If you think I'm saying this just because I used to be a travel agent, think again: I'm urging you to seek the advice and assistance of a travel agent in buying tickets that cost an agent more to issue, in labor and overhead, than most travelers are willing to pay in service fees. Among themselves, travel agents talk constantly about how not to waste time on money-losing published-fare airline tickets, without alienating people who might later be in the market for tours, cruises, or other more profitable (for the agent) services. For the typical travel agency in the United States, airline tickets are now a loss leader, not a profit center, even with service fees. I could serve travel agents' interests by telling you that you could do just as well, just as easily, by yourself on the Internet, rather than asking a good travel agent for help. But most of the time, it wouldn't be true.

What I will say is that in asking an agent to issue tickets at published fares, you are asking them to provide you with consulting and ticketing services — the more so the more time they spend searching for the best fare for you. If you want a travel agent to work for you, and not for the airlines, you have to be prepared to pay them for their services in finding you the best fare. If you don't pay your travel agent a service fee, you can scarcely be surprised if they don't have your interests at heart.

Second, consolidator tickets are usually available only on flights on which the airlines expect that they would have empty seats if they didn't offer some tickets at less than the published fares. People who expect that discounts will always be available on all flights have missed the point of why airlines give discounts: to fill seats that would otherwise be empty.

For appearances' sake, the airlines generally offer a few reservations on each plane at consolidator prices even for travel at the busiest times (just as they usually offer a couple of seats on even the most popular flights for frequent-flyer mileage redemption, or at the lowest published fares). But those few tickets may be sold within a few days of being offered, months before the flight. Some flights in peak season, especially flights around Christmas everywhere in the world and some other holidays in particular regions, routinely sell out months in advance. Some Christmas flights to Africa sell out by July at any price, much less consolidator prices.

"Yield management," the process by which airlines determine how many people to confirm on each flight, at any given time, in each booking class, is extraordinarily complex. I'll leave it as a topic for advanced classes in operations research. For our present purposes, it's an adequate approximation to conceptualize yield management as the allocation of the seats on each plane among "booking classes" that correspond to different fares. One (or more) of those booking classes is used for consolidator ticket bookings. Once the seats allocated to that class are reserved, no more consolidator tickets are available on that flight, even if seats allocated to higher-fare booking classes remain available.

Airlines' wholesale prices to consolidators often aren't fixed until the airlines have enough of an idea of advance booking levels to know how much of a discount they need to offer to fill their planes. Some airlines fix wholesale prices to their consolidators a year at a time, based on past experience of seasonal variations in load factors (percentage of seats filled). Other airlines set commissions one or two seasons (six weeks to six months) in advance, which is why you will sometimes be told that discount prices for your travel dates haven't been set yet. That doesn't necessarily mean that discounts will be offered later, especially for peak-season travel. If flights are filling up on schedule, or are already fully booked, consolidators may never be offered any deals for those flights or dates.

Most flights aren't full, and consolidator tickets are usually available if you buy them at the right time. Airlines vary in the sophistication of their yield management algorithms. In low season, when there are lots of empty seats, you are likely to have several choices of airlines at similar prices. In high season, you're more likely to find that fewer airlines have discounted seats available.

With those caveats about seasons and seats, consolidator tickets are available between more places than any other kind of discounted tickets, even on some lightly traveled routes between obscure places. Except on routes flown by low-fare airlines, consolidator tickets are often the only affordable choice for journeys other than short roundtrips, or for long stays. Unlike any other type of discounted ticket, consolidator tickets are available for long-stay roundtrips and for one-way, multistop, and discontinuous travel. If you are prepared to import tickets from a country where they can be issued and sold at a discount, consolidator tickets are available for travel originating in more places than any other kind of discounted tickets, even places where fares are high and few, if any discounts are available locally.

Some online consolidators, including Hotwire.com and Priceline.com, offer even lower prices if you are willing to pay for a ticket before you know what airline or flights you'll be on. These "opaque" or "white label" deals, limited to short-stay roundtrip tickets, are a special case, and should be clearly disclosed as such before you are asked to pay. Otherwise, you should receive a confirmed itinerary showing specific airlines, flight numbers, and times, before you pay for your tickets.

FARES FOR STUDENTS AND TEACHERS

Student fares are the best known and most widely available of a class of fares called "status" fares. By restricting eligibility for these fares to people who can prove they have a certain status indicative of limited willingness to pay—such as students or professors—airlines are able to offer these discounts with little risk that they will be used by people who would otherwise have paid higher fares.

Not all airlines offer student fares, and the rules and their prices vis-à-vis consolidator tickets vary. On most airlines, you must have a current, valid International Student Identity Card (ISIC) at the time of ticketing and when traveling on tickets at a student fare.

Being published fares, student fares should, in theory, be available directly from the airlines. In practice it's almost impossible to buy a student-fare ticket at an airline ticket counter or on an airline website. Most student fares aren't programmed into the computerized databases and CRSs used by ordinary online and offline travel agencies. Almost all student-fare tickets are sold by specialized travel agency chains specializing in the student market such as STA Travel (originally Student Travel Australia, but now operating in many countries including the United States, the U.K., and Ireland) and Travel CUTS (owned by the Canadian Federation of Students, Canada's national student organization, but now with subsidiaries in the United States as well).

Student fares are distinct fares, with distinct rules. You can't combine two different kinds of discounts; there is no such thing as a student discount from any other fare. I know of no agency that will sell student-fare tickets for less than their face value.

Student fares are not necessarily the lowest fares, much less the tickets sold at the lowest prices. Consolidator tickets may be cheaper and/or more flexible.

Because student travel agencies often deal only with student fares, and are often less familiar with the full range of other discounted tickets, it is not necessarily the case that a student will get the best price, particularly on an around-the-world ticket or multistop ticket, from a student travel specialist. Student fares are excellent values in some cases and relatively poor values in others. Before buying a student-fare ticket, I would always get an estimate on tickets to the same destination(s) from an agency whose expertise isn't limited to student fares.

Because they are intended for students studying abroad for a semester or a school year, student fares are generally available for longer stays (up to a year) than most other cheap roundtrips. This makes them the only cheap long-stay (more than three months) roundtrip tickets available on some, though by no means all, trans-Atlantic and North America–South America routes. Long-stay consolidator fares are much more widely available on trans-Pacific and other long-haul routes.

Many airlines have made teachers at postsecondary educational institutions eligible for the same fares as students, although rules on faculty eligibility for student fares vary from airline to airline. Like their students, professors may find student fares better or worse than consolidator tickets, depending on their itinerary.

I know of no airline that allows elementary or secondary school teachers to use student fares. The exclusion of teachers in lower grades is unfortunate and unfair (fairness being of course irrelevant in setting fares), because teachers often get paid less than college or university professors for higher-stress work, with few compensations except for the longest vacations of any major job category in the United States. A pity, because it's the academic calendar, and the opportunity it allows for travel, that attracts some people to teaching in the first place, or keeps them in it; certainly students would benefit if their teachers had more international travel experience.

FARES FOR PACKAGE TOURISTS

Airlines have long offered special prices for tickets purchased as part of a package in conjunction with a tour, cruise, prepaid accommodations, or other travel services. As with all other discounts, the point is to ensure that the rules of these tickets preclude their use by the sorts of people who would be willing to pay higher fares. The harder it is to figure out how much of the price of the package is the price of the airline ticket, the more willing the airline is to offer a discount in exchange for keeping its pricing opaque.

Obviously, you have to be in a place where other fares are high, and other discounted tickets hard to find, for a package that includes the required minimum value of land services to cost less than other tickets would cost by themselves. There are times and places, though, when a package can be cheap enough that it is worth buying a package tour even if you don't plan to take the tour. That's begun to be true even in the United States: I've seen some cases, mainly for short domestic roundtrips without a Saturday-night stay, where adding the cheapest available hotel or a rental car to make up a "package" lowers the total price on Expedia.com or Orbitz.com below what the airfare alone would have been.

Some air-inclusive tour packages are designed and marketed with this in mind, with the full awareness and understanding of seller and buyer alike that most buyers of the package will throw the tour vouchers away and go off on their own once at the destination. If a proffered air-inclusive tour seems suspiciously cheap, or the seller of the tour seems surprised that you even ask about the accommodations or services to be provided, be alert to the possibility that it may be a tour of this sort.

The biggest problem with tour or package fares is that, to ensure they are used only by package tourists, they generally are available only on a roundtrip basis for fixed dates with quite a short maximum-stay limit, usually 45 and sometimes only 21 or fewer days. Otherwise they work just fine, where they are available and suit your schedule.

GROUP FARES

Some airlines publish "group fares" fares available to any group traveling on the same itinerary, sometimes with a minimum of as few as seven people traveling together on the exact same flights throughout their trip.

There's nothing wrong with group fares if you are actually traveling in a group with a fixed and qualifying itinerary, although they aren't necessarily less than consolidator prices for tickets at other fares, and most groups (especially larger groups of 20 or more) don't use group fares. But they are obviously not suitable for independent travelers, and like package or tour fares they are limited to roundtrips for short stays with fixed dates.

If you do have a qualifying group and itinerary, it's worth going through an agent, rather than directly to the airline. Prices for groups are negotiable, the more so the larger the group, and an agent is likely to have more expertise in knowing what to ask for. Some agents are given special commissions, and give discounts through rebating, on group as well as individual fares. If a "group fare" will be the best price for your group, a good agent will have every reason to tell you about it and to offer to sell you tickets at that price, or less.

Beyond a certain point, as the size of a group increases, airlines want more per person from groups than from individual passengers. An airline can sell a few seats cheaply to fill the plane, and still make money on the flight as a whole if there are enough high-fare travelers. But if a group fills enough of the plane to displace those who would otherwise pay enough to cover the cost of the flight, the group has to pay its own way.

LOW-FARE AIRLINES

So-called "low-fare" airlines operate on a growing number of domestic and international routes in every region of the world: Southwest, JetBlue, and Virgin America in the United States; WestJet in Canada and between the United States and Canada; Volaris in Mexico; EasyJet, Ryanair, and Wizz Air in Europe; Spicejet in India; Air Asia throughout Southeast Asia; Air Arabia and Flydubai in the Middle East; GOL and Azul in Brazil and to and from other South American countries; 1time and Kulula in South Africa and to and from other African countries; Virgin Blue, Jetstar, and Tiger Airways in Australia and between Australia and Asia; and many others. I've flown on low-fare airlines on six continents. (No airline flies scheduled public service to Antarctica.)

A few low-fare carriers are experimenting with long-haul transoceanic and intercontinental flights, but their "sweet spot" has been on domestic flights within larger countries and on short-haul regional routes between nearby countries.

Low-fare airlines don't necessarily have lower fares. Especially on routes where they compete directly, other airlines often match their prices. The main difference between low-fare and "traditional" airlines is that low-fare airlines usually have opted out of some or all of the industry norms. In particular:

- Each low-fare airline does things their own way. Anything and everything about how they operate—baggage rules, ticketing and check-in procedures, and so forth—may be different from what you are used to. Take nothing for granted. Read the fine print. If it's in a language you don't understand, try to get a fellow traveler to translate it for you, or at least to tell you if there is anything special you need to know. Show up at the airport early.

- Many low-fare airlines don't sell tickets through travel agents, so the only way to deal with them is directly, usually through their websites.

- Most low-fare airlines have no interline baggage agreements with other airlines (so you can't check your bags through if you are making connections with a different airline, but will have to claim and recheck them).

- Most low-fare airlines have no interline ticketing agreements with other airlines (so they can't put you on another airline's flight, or honor tickets from another airline).

The *Resource Guide* lists some websites with unofficial, incomplete, but nonetheless useful lists of low-fare airlines that you might not know about. Once you figure out which low-fare airline serves a route you are interested in, you can usually get schedules and prices on their website. Buying tickets on their websites from a different country can be more of a problem: some won't accept a credit card with a billing address in a different country (just as many e-commerce companies in the United States won't accept foreign credit cards, to reduce the risk of fraud). Badly designed airline websites sometimes won't allow you to enter a phone number or address that doesn't match the format of addresses in the country where they operate, doesn't have a valid postal code in their country, or the like. (See the sidebar on *Using Foreign Websites* in the *Life on the Road* chapter.) And if a low-fare airline uses paper tickets, they may not be set up to ship them out of the country. You can usually work something out, at the price of an international call to their reservation center. If that fails, you may have to wait until you get to a city where they fly, and buy a ticket the old-fashioned way, over the counter from their office at the airport.

The good thing about low-fare airlines is that they typically price tickets on a one-way basis, and require little or no advance purchase as long as seats are still available. You may get a better price further in advance, or with a roundtrip purchase, but their last-minute one-way fares are still much less than the prohibitive "walk-up" fares of traditional airlines.

The bad thing about low-fare airlines is that you can't count on them. Unlike national "flag carriers," they are operated to make a profit, not for national prestige. If they don't make money for their investors, they will be quick to shut them down. Governments are less likely to bail them out than they would be with a national airline, even a nominally privatized one. Similarly, if a particular route or flight isn't making money, they are quick to discontinue it.

One reason there is less difference between the highest and lowest fares of "low-fare" airlines is that they operate with fewer empty seats. Traditional airlines try to charge business travelers enough that they can make money even if what they refer to derisively as "the back of the bus" is empty. Low-fare airlines only fly where, and when, they think they can get enough passengers to fly full. Many of their flights operate only in the busy season for the route (whenever that is). They are willing to try out odd-seeming routes where they think traditional airlines have overlooked a profitable opportunity, but they are equally willing to dump them unceremoniously if they don't work out, or if something causes traffic on a previously profitable route to flag. The routes where they are offering the largest discounts, in order to try to fill their planes, may be the ones most in danger of imminent discontinuation of their service. Conversely, they may be entirely sold-out at short notice on a successful route, even in the off-season.

As discussed in more detail in the later section on cancellations and refunds, low-fare airlines typically have no interline agreements, and can't put you on another airline if they cancel a flight or cease service to a destination. All flights on low-fare airlines (or any airline without interline agreements to protect you in case of a flight cancellation) should therefore be considered to be subject to cancellation at will by the airline at any time, without prior notice or any obligation to get you to your destination. All they owe you if you have a ticket is a refund.

What this means is that if you are planning to use a low-fare airline for part of your trip, you should always have a backup plan. You need to be prepared either to use surface transportation, if it's possible, or to pay for a ticket on a competing airline. If the low-fare airline picked the route because it was poorly served by traditional competitors, or their fares were high enough to create what the low-fare airline thought would be a profit opportunity, a walk-up replacement ticket could cost many times what the low-fare airline originally charged.

Low-fare airlines are thus most suitable for "impulse purchases" of tickets bought while you are traveling, and least suitable for tickets planned or purchased long in advance. If you had planned to use surface transportation, and there's a cheap flight with seats available that you'd rather take, great. Maybe you want to linger someplace longer than you had expected, or people coming in the other direction report that the bus or ferry you'd planned to take is slower or more uncomfortable or dangerous than you had realized. If you know that you will have to fly, though, don't count on a low-fare airline. Know that you are taking a risk, and know the cost of your contingency plan. Keep checking with the airline at intervals, to make sure your flight is still scheduled to operate.

Some low-fare airlines operate from secondary airports, where their landing fees and other costs are lower. Often these are farther from city centers and tourist districts, and less well served by public transport. Before you buy a ticket to or from an airport with which you aren't familiar, check out how easy it will be, and how much time and money it will take, to get between the airport and the place you really want to go. If you're a foreign tourist without a car, it may be worth paying considerably more to fly into La Guardia Airport in New York City rather than MacArthur Airport in Islip, Long Island, or

Heathrow Airport on the London Underground (subway train) rather than suburban/exurban Luton Airport. Transportation to and from secondary airports can be especially poor late at night. Find out what time the bus or train stops running, and how frequently it runs, not just whether it exists.

AROUND-THE-WORLD AND MULTISTOP TICKETS

Hearing there are special around-the-world (RTW) or "circle-the-Pacific" fares, or seeing advertised prices for such routes, is what starts many people thinking about the possibility of such a trip. But when it comes time to actually plan their itinerary, many people are misled and disempowered by published RTW fares and advertisements. They conclude they have to stop in certain places, or follow a certain route, because "all the [advertised] flights go that way." Or they ask, "Where can I stop on an around-the-world ticket?"

Airlines offer very limited RTW fare options. If you get an RTW ticket from the airlines, you have to start and end in the same country and are limited to a certain maximum distance, maximum number of flights, and maximum number of stopovers, on the routes of a specific small group of "allied" airlines. On the less expensive of these RTW tickets, you must travel in a continuous east–west or west–east direction, without backtracking.

Very few people want to follow routes that satisfy these rules. Many long-term, multistop travelers don't happen to be going entirely around the world. In any event, many RTW travelers get a better price by buying a set of discounted tickets put together for them by a travel agent, or assembled themselves, based on their desired destinations. Most advertised RTW or other multistop ticket prices are actually prices for sets of tickets like this, and it's usually a waste of time to try to shoehorn the route you want to follow into one of the routes permitted by a published airline RTW fare.

With a customized set of discounted tickets, you don't have to start and end in the same place; your route does not have to be continuous, go in any particular direction, or be limited to any particular combination of airlines, number of stops, or maximum distance traveled; nor will you necessarily or usually save money by complying with any of those "rules." There is no standard or usual route or price. Prices vary greatly, depending primarily on the starting and ending points and specific set and sequence of stops you want, and to a lesser extent on the starting season and duration of your trip. You can piece together your own set of tickets, before you leave or as you travel. You can have a travel agent put together a package of tickets for you. Or you can combine these options by buying your tickets in two or more large (but less than RTW) bundles, or by buying some of your tickets before you leave and the rest along the way. With a published RTW fare, it's all or nothing: There's no "half-RTW" or "partial RTW" fare.

The first thing many people do when they start to plan a trip around the world is to try to work out a route that satisfies the rules of a published RTW fare. For budget travelers, this is a complete waste of time. Regardless of what sort of tickets or fare you use, you have to know what route you plan to follow before you can buy your tickets. Settle on a tentative set of destinations before you start to look for tickets or study fares. If an RTW fare will be the best deal for that set of destinations, great. If not, you have other options. But you can't tell which is best until you've decided where you want to go.

PUBLISHED AROUND-THE-WORLD (RTW) FARES

No one airline currently flies around the world. (The most recent airline to do so was Aeroflot Russian International Airlines, which discontinued service on part of its previous around-the-world route in early 2000.) Various partnerships of airlines publish joint around-the-world (RTW) fares.

Published RTW fares vary greatly by country of origin. So you can't assume anything from what a friend paid for a ticket, or was able to do, if that friend's flight started from another country—even if you want to travel on the same airlines. Trips originating in some other countries are substantially cheaper, and a better deal, than those starting in the United States, even if they're on the same airlines.

> ### REAL LIFE
>
> Published RTW fares from Canada have sometimes been substantially lower than those from the United States. The price difference is sometimes enough to make it worth driving or taking a bus or train to Canada, in order to start your flight tickets from north of the border.

(No, you can't buy an RTW ticket for a journey starting in one country, and use it for a journey starting in another. Travel agents who try to sell you tickets like that, with the order of the flight coupons rearranged, are scammers trying to defraud both their customers and the airlines. Flight coupons are valid only in the sequence issued. I've heard from people who've gotten caught halfway through a trip they tried to take with tickets like that, and had to pay thousands of dollars for new tickets.)

In order to keep them from being used by business travelers, most published RTW fares also require a minimum number of stops (most often at least three, of at least 24 hours each), a minimum trip duration (most often 14 days), and 21 days' advance purchase.

Within these constraints, published RTW fares are of two distinct types: those restricted primarily by routing specifications and those restricted primarily by a limitation on total distance flown.

ROUTING-BASED PUBLISHED RTW FARES

The cheapest, but most restricted, published RTW fares are "routing-based" RTW fares offered by partnerships of two, three, or occasionally four airlines. Several hundred partnerships offer fares of this general type, each with its own peculiarities and prices. The same airline often has several routing-based RTW fares in conjunction with different partners. Many airlines have different sets of partners for RTW fares originating from different countries.

Regardless of the number of airlines involved, these fares are valid only for continuous travel on those airlines and those airlines only, beginning and ending in the same city, without breaks in the air itinerary to be traveled by land or sea, proceeding always in the same direction (east or west), without backtracking or transiting any city more than once.

Published routing-based third-class (coach or economy) fares around the world start at about US$3,000 for routes entirely within the northern hemisphere, beginning and ending in the United States. Fares including the southern hemisphere (Africa, South America, Australia, Aotearoa/New Zealand, or the South Pacific) are at least US$1,000 higher.

All these prices are deceptively low, because ticketing most RTW trips at these fares would require multiple additional side trips, or sectors on other airlines, at additional fares. Most around-the-world itineraries require travel on more than just two or three airlines and at least some backtracking through the participating airlines' hubs, neither of which is permitted by most of these fares. Similar routes can usually be ticketed more cheaply as a series of one-way consolidator tickets, as discussed in the following section.

Airlines will tell you, "Our RTW fares let you go anywhere we fly." But stopovers are limited in number and are allowed only within the permitted routes. The routing rules of this type of RTW fares are far more restrictive than they appear at first glance.

The routes of two airlines that offer a joint RTW fare may only fit together to circle the globe in two or three ways. Except for minor variations such as which domestic stops you make within the countries where the airlines are based, you can usually count on one hand the alternative routes permitted on any given routing-based RTW fare. Most of the cities shown on any given airline's international route map cannot actually be reached on any of that airline's and its various partners' routing-based RTW fares! They are dead-end spokes, not points on any through route.

Most airlines have hub-and-spoke route systems centered on the capital city or biggest airport(s) in their home country. Few airlines have extensive rights to carry people between other countries, except by way of their hub(s). Longer-range planes mean more and more nonstop flights from hub to spoke and back, with ever fewer intermediate stops in places along the way. If an airline serves many cities in a region, it probably serves most of them only from a hub that you are forbidden to pass through more than once without paying extra for separate side-trip tickets.

Routing-based RTW fares were the first and for a long time the only published RTW fares. They've largely lost favor with the emergence of the more flexible but more expensive mileage-based RTW fares described in the next section, and they are rarely advertised. Their continuing advantage, however, is that if one of them fits your desired route, they can be as little as half the price of a mileage-based alliance RTW fare to the same destinations.

If you call an airline to ask about their RTW fares, they will probably tell you only about their mileage-based alliance RTW fares. To find out about the others, you will need to ask very specifically, "Do you participate in other RTW fares with other airlines or groups of airlines? What are those?" The list may be longer than you think, and a travel agent may be able (for a fee) to help you figure out which, if any, might work for your desired destinations.

MILEAGE-BASED PUBLISHED RTW FARES

Mileage-based RTW fares are more expensive but usually more flexible than the routing-based RTW fares described above. Most fares of this type are offered by the brand-name airline marketing consortia ("alliances") such as the Star Alliance, Oneworld, and Skyteam. Starting and ending in the United States, these fares start at over US$4,000, more often US$5,000, including required surcharges and taxes, for coach/economy (third-class) travel.

Mileage-based RTW fares permit unlimited backtracking and retransiting of hub cities, as long as you confine yourself to the participating airlines, don't exceed a specified total allowance of kilometers or miles for the entire trip, and don't stop over in the same city more than once. You can usually change planes in the same city any number of times as long as you don't stop there for more than 24 hours. If you use separate tickets (at an additional fare), or travel overland between two points on such an RTW ticket, the mileage between those points is still included along with the flown mileage in calculating the total mileage for the RTW fare. Most have three or four tiers of higher prices for additional flights, stopovers, miles, or continents visited beyond the basic allotment (up to some maximum number of flights, stopovers, and miles).

These fares are an improvement over routing-based RTW fares, but not nearly as much of one as they might seem. You can often do more on one of these tickets, but you have to pay quite a bit more for it. And because you are still restricted to only a few airlines, you still have to follow their limited routes or buy additional tickets to bridge the gaps. Most cities are still reachable on such a fare only as side trips from one or maybe two of the participating airlines' hubs.

If you want to go from South Africa to Senegal on a Oneworld RTW fare, for example, you'll have to go by way Europe, thousands of miles out of the way, using up a huge portion of your mileage allotment. And you'll have a change of planes (no big deal) and perhaps an overnight layover (more of a nuisance and expense in an expensive European hub city) to make connections. To continue on to anywhere from Senegal on this fare, you'll have to go back to Europe again. The same goes within South America on the Skyteam alliance: to get from Rio de Janiero to São Paulo, 350 km (220 miles) away, you'd have to go more than 15,000 km (9,000 miles) to Atlanta and back. The specifics could change as the alliances add members, but all of the major alliances have major gaps in their route systems within one or another region, and/or in domestic coverage within some major countries. At the moment, the Star Alliance has the largest and most widely distributed membership, but still has no member that flies within Australia or India, among other missing links. To get between Delhi and Mumbai, you'd have to fly to Bangkok and back and go through Indian customs and immigration, and to get between Melbourne and Adelaide you'd have to go through either Singapore or Auckland, wasting many hours and eating up your mileage allotment. You can make side trips, but you can only make so many without exceeding the limits on miles and/or on numbers of flights.

For those who want to fly in second class (business or club class) or in first class, however, published around-the-world fares are often the cheapest choice. Fewer discounts are available on business- and first-class one-way tickets than on coach tickets on most airlines and routes. But it's not an inexpensive upgrade from coach to business class, and not nearly as good a deal as some business-class RTW fares used to be. Don't even ask about published mileage-based alliance RTW fares in business class, originating in the United States, unless you have at least US$10,000 per person to spend on airfare. Prices for higher mileage tiers in business class go up to as much as US$15,000.

That seems pricey to ordinary travelers, and it is, but it compares favorably with regular one-way or roundtrip business-class fares if you want to visit multiple destinations scattered around the globe.

HOW TO BUY A TICKET AT A PUBLISHED RTW FARE

If you call an airline to make reservations or buy tickets at one of their RTW fares, you'll be referred to a special RTW desk. Airlines' RTW specialists are experts in figuring out what price applies to a particular itinerary, once you've told them what you want to do. But they work for the airline, and their job is not to help you figure out how to spend less. So they are unlikely to point out what might be cheaper alternatives. And they are solely airline ticket sellers, not consultants who can advise you on where you might want to go. Many people find it extremely frustrating not to be able to get any price from an airline RTW desk until they have chosen specific flights and dates.

The alternative is to go through a travel agent who can help you choose which RTW fare, from which alliance or combination of airlines, will be best for you. Not all travel agents are knowledgeable about RTW fares, however, and even those that aren't experts will probably still charge you a substantial service fee for arranging such a ticket. Working with you to find the best option, making reservations, calculating the exact price (which typically requires the agent to work with the airline's rate desk), and issuing tickets entails at least a couple of hours of work. If you go to an agent, expect to compensate them accordingly for their time. Travel agents get no commission from airlines on most sales of RTW tickets at published fares.

Published RTW fares are fixed by the airlines, and are the same throughout the year. Airlines don't have sales or offer discounts or specials on these tickets, either directly to the public or through travel agents. The reason to go to a travel agent is not to get a discount on a published RTW fare but for help in figuring out which (if any) published RTW fare might fit your itinerary, or to see if there is a better and/or cheaper alternative to such a fare.

An agent who tries to tell you that you have to follow the routes or rules of published RTW fares probably isn't the sort of specialist from whom you should buy your tickets. If your routing happens to fit the route of a published RTW fare, and would be cheaper that way, a good agent will tell you so. In most cases your routing won't fit such a fare. Many routes actually flown around the world, much less those that travelers would like to follow, do not satisfy the rules of any airline's published RTW fare. Even those that do can often be more cheaply ticketed as a combination of one-way tickets, as discussed in the following sections.

DISCOUNTED AROUND-THE-WORLD AND MULTISTOP TICKETS

Essentially all RTW and other multistop ticket prices advertised by travel agents are combinations of discounted one-way tickets strung together. Such a set of tickets permits you to use any number of airlines, to begin and end your trip in different cities or on different continents, to travel some portions by land or sea, and to backtrack at will.

Depending on the route, prices for tickets like this start at less than US$2,000 from the United States—half the price of the cheapest published RTW fares. At additional cost, you can go any place any airline flies, in any order. The shorter and more direct your path, the cheaper it is likely to be. But even small changes in an itinerary can greatly change the price, and there are few general principles behind these price differences (other than the general rule that the farther you fly, the more it will probably cost).

Because one ticket with stopovers can cover several legs of your journey, and because good agents can offer a wide range of discounts on diverse routes, you can pay much less for these tickets from a skilled discount agency than you would pay if you bought separate tickets, even separate discounted tickets at the best possible prices, for each flight. Because consolidator prices are only available through travel agencies, you can't get tickets like this directly from an airline.

On the other hand, most agents rarely sell tickets for any sort of multistop, long-haul, long-term, or around-the-world travel. Because nondiscounted one-way fares on most routes are prohibitively expensive, constructing a set of tickets around the world at a competitive price requires access to a comprehensive network of discount contracts and wholesale suppliers of discounted tickets on one-way flights worldwide. Agents who don't sell tickets like this regularly have no reason and no way to negotiate discount contracts with airlines, or to keep track of prices from wholesalers, for one-way tickets between other countries. This is one type of travel where you have to go to a specialist to get any useful advice or a decent deal. See *Arranging Your Air Transportation* later in this chapter.

AIR PASSES AND OTHER SPECIAL FARES FOR FOREIGN VISITORS

Air passes, special fares, or discounts are offered to foreign visitors for travel within many countries. These fares are usually substantially less restrictive and sometimes (not always) cheaper than tickets available for purchase locally on the same routes.

Sometimes these are special published fares; sometimes these are consolidator prices offered through travel agencies. In some cases you can buy stand-alone tickets at these prices, but more often they have to be ticketed in conjunction with international tickets to the country or region. Some airlines give discounts of 50 percent, or more, on domestic or short-haul regional travel in conjunction with long-haul travel on the same airline. This is one reason it is often advantageous to use a country's own national airline to fly to a country where you plan extensive domestic air travel.

Some air passes and visitor fares apply only to domestic flights within a single country. Others such as the LAN "South America Airpass" and the "ASEAN Airpass" offered by a group of Southeast Asian airlines include specified international flights within a particular region. Some visitor passes and prices are available only directly from the airlines, others either from airlines or travel agents, and still others such as those listed at AllAirpass.com are available only from specific travel agents.

The common denominator is that, with few exceptions, tickets at these prices must be purchased outside the country, in conjunction with your international tickets. If you don't find out about them (or how expensive tickets are locally) until you arrive in the country, it's too late to do anything about it. This is one of the strongest reasons to plan even domestic air travel before you buy international tickets, and to include it in the wish list you give to a travel agent when you request a price estimate or use when you start shopping for tickets on your own.

Compare prices of ordinary tickets before you buy a ticket at a visitor fare. Some visitor fares (such as the 14-day Indian Airlines airpass and the 60-day Visit USA and Visit North America fares) have maximum stay limits too short for many long-term travelers, so be sure to check the maximum permissible stay before you buy such a ticket.

Even where prices are comparable to the cheapest local prices for fixed-date tickets, it may be worth buying tickets ahead at a visitor fare to get tickets with (typically) more easily changeable dates and more flexible rules. In particular, these tickets often allow you to put together a circuit or discontinuous itinerary composed of one-way flights, without needing to fly roundtrip to get reasonable prices.

Not all visitor fares require you to reserve space on specific flights or even fix your routing, but it's advisable to do both, whenever possible, so as to be sure that the special fare is really a better deal than any alternative and that the flights and seats you want are available.

Special fares or passes like these are available in the United States, Canada, Australia, Aotearoa/New Zealand, South Africa, India, Indonesia, Thailand, Russia, Brazil, and many other countries. Air passes for each country have different rules. Some are confusing, and many are little known to nonspecialist travel agents. Almost none of them can be purchased online, although you can find information about some of them on airlines' own websites. Travel agents who specialize in a particular destination are most likely to know the ins and outs of foreign visitor fares.

It's worth noting here that the reverse is equally often true, and airline ticket prices for foreigners in some countries such as (currently) Argentina are higher than those for locals. Where that's the case, accept it—like it or not—and plan accordingly. Complaining won't change other countries' rules. Trying to cheat by using a fake local ID to buy a ticket at the local fare is unlikely to succeed, and could get you kicked off the plane and heavily fined, or land you in jail. That's not worth the risk. If you're a foreigner, pay the foreigner's price or don't fly.

SUBSIDIZED TICKETS FOR COURIERS

Travel as a courier can be the cheapest way of all to travel. Sometimes couriers get their transportation provided for free. If you can get hired to travel as a courier on an itinerary that suits, courier travel is an unbeatable deal.

Obviously, there's a catch, or more budget travelers would fly this way. The catch is that most people's itineraries don't correspond to courier routes and schedules, and the few opportunities for courier travel on routes and schedules of greater interest to the general traveler are snatched up quickly, far in advance.

Courier travel works like this: in exchange for your agreement to accompany their cargo, a company that ships high-priority air freight (usually documents) subsidizes the price of your ticket. In effect, they hire you as a courier, but they don't pay you in cash. Rather, you pay them: they buy a ticket for you, and they charge you only part of what the ticket cost them. In return, they use your allotment of "free" checked baggage, and check additional cargo as your excess baggage.

The main reason for this arrangement is that baggage accompanying passengers is, so as not to delay travelers, given priority over unaccompanied cargo in customs inspection lines. In practice accompanied baggage is usually cleared within minutes or hours, while unaccompanied cargo can wait for days or weeks. In addition, airline rates for transporting excess baggage accompanying passengers (high though they may seem) are less than the rates for unaccompanied priority air cargo. By subsidizing a ticket for a courier to check their cargo as the courier's accompanied luggage, a shipping company gets their urgent shipment to the destination and through customs more quickly and cheaply than if they sent it without a courier.

As a courier, you are permitted only whatever luggage you can carry on, including a manifest of what has been checked in your name. You never see the checked cargo; you just get the manifest from the courier company's agent before you depart. Usually you get your ticket at the same time. You deliver the manifest to an agent on arrival, usually along with your return ticket, which is given back to you with the return manifest when it's time for your flight home.

There is no such thing as a courier fare or courier ticket. Couriers travel on whatever tickets, at whatever fare, the courier or express shipping company buys for them. Usually they travel on cheap consolidator tickets, although courier companies are more concerned with schedules, routes, and cargo rates than with passenger ticket prices, so couriers often travel on some of the more expensive airlines. Couriers often mistakenly believe they are traveling on full-fare tickets because, like most consolidator tickets, theirs have a high face value and look, to the untrained eye, like full-fare tickets. This frequently leads couriers to think that their tickets have been more heavily subsidized than is actually the case. Whether couriers are eligible for frequent-flyer mileage and other such amenities depends on the rules of the particular consolidator agreement. The courier company doesn't care about such things and won't want to bother to research them for you in advance.

Because an agreement to travel as a courier is more in the nature of an employment contract, you have to deal directly with courier and express companies to arrange for work as a courier. (Couriers are technically freelance contractors of the courier companies. Fortunately, the IRS doesn't yet require shipping companies to report the ticket subsidy as "income" for the courier's labor in accompanying the cargo, although legally they could.) Travel agents can't sell "courier tickets" or arrange courier travel.

Whatever their procedures for signing up couriers, the companies doing the hiring want their money's worth. Typically, this means you must travel roundtrip (because a roundtrip ticket for one courier costs less than two one-way tickets for different couriers) and come back soon. The more time you have at the destination, the more likely you are to wander off and fail to show up for the return flights, which can be disastrous for the courier company. A courier is often required to put up a deposit of several hundred dollars before the trip. If you don't show up for your scheduled flight home, you forfeit your deposit and will never again be hired as a courier. To simplify their scheduling, some companies want all their couriers to a destination to stay for the same amount of time. They might, for example, automatically assign each courier to the return flight 7 or 14 days later.

One-way courier assignments are rare. Open-jaw or multistop courier assignments (except on a few routes with a mandatory one-night intermediate layover) are essentially unheard-of. The most common lengths of stay for courier assignments are 7, 14, or 21 days. A few companies have begun to offer longer stays, particularly on trans-Pacific routes, because they have found that couriers allowed to stay longer are willing to pay a greater share of the price of their ticket, so the courier company can get away with paying less of a subsidy toward the ticket price.

Longer assignments, peak-season assignments, and assignments to more touristic and less business-oriented destinations (when they exist) are likely to be highly coveted and to be awarded to experienced couriers. These are people who travel as couriers several times a year, are willing to go to unpopular and expensive places when a courier is needed on short notice (such as when a new freelancer flakes out and doesn't show up), and who have the right contacts for winning plum jobs.

Air courier opportunities are limited, and getting more so all the time as more businesses switch to express cargo carriers like FedEx and DHL. Couriers are needed only on routes where there is a large volume of high-value urgent cargo. Most of this cargo is business documents, and the main courier routes are trade routes between business and banking centers within the First World. There are few couriers to anywhere in the Third World, and essentially none to the Fourth World. It's easiest to get a courier assignment, and your ticket will be most heavily subsidized, to places where local costs are high and during seasons when the destination is least attractive.

What does this mean? If a week in a cold, expensive place such as London or Zurich or Tokyo in midwinter, for perhaps half the price of a low-season consolidator ticket, is attractive enough to be worth a moderate amount of extra effort to arrange, courier travel might be the way for you to go. Friends and lovers of expatriates, or anyone with a standing offer of a place to stay whenever they might get to some big business center, might also find it appropriate to their interests.

You may luck into something else that suits your fancy, or a company with more flexible options. But courier travel is of little or no use to most long-term, multistop, budget, or Third World travelers, simply because there are no courier assignments appropriate to their needs. As a travel agent, I got calls all the time from would-be couriers who, unable to go where they wanted as couriers, had turned to other sources of discounts such as consolidator tickets.

If you can't get a courier assignment to where you want to go, you are unlikely to be able to piece together courier travel and onward transportation for a total price less than what discounted through tickets to your ultimate destination would have cost you in the first place. Even if you can get a free ticket as a courier to Tokyo, for example, a ticket from Tokyo (or wherever) to your ultimate destination elsewhere in Asia may cost you more than you would have paid for a ticket from home to your destination.

The best sources of information and advice on courier travel are subscription-based directories, newsletters, and websites listing which companies use freelance couriers on which routes, and giving advice on how to contact and get hired by them. Some of these call themselves "clubs," but they are really all just listing services. Some are legitimate, but others make their money selling worthless membership cards and deliver little of real value.

CHARTER FLIGHTS

A charter flight works like this: a charter operator "charters" a plane by contracting with an airline to fly a planeload of people from one place to another, and contracts with passengers to provide them with transportation between those places. Charter prices are almost entirely unregulated: charter operators can charge whatever they think the market will bear. At times, and on routes where charter flights are available, they can be the cheapest way to go. But they are rarely available or suitable for long-term or multistop travel.

The terminology is confusing: the charter operator doesn't actually "operate" the plane. Some charter flights are operated by airlines that specialize exclusively in charter flights, and some charter flights are operated by the same airlines that also operate regularly scheduled services. The "charter operator" is an intermediary between the passengers and the airline. Some charter operators sell tickets directly to the public, while others sell tickets through retail travel agents and/or tour operators. Some sell tickets for air transportation only, some sell tickets only as part of an air-inclusive package, and some offer both options.

Charter-only airlines are subject to the same safety, airworthiness, maintenance, and certification requirements as scheduled airlines. The only difference in the planes used for charters is that some (not all) charter airlines use planes with single-class seating (no business or first class) and a shorter seat pitch (distance between seats from front to back) to maximize the number of passengers they can fit on a plane. Some charter airlines actually provide very good service, meals, etc., though most offer no-frills transportation.

Regular flights operate on the same schedule, with the same frequency, even when many seats are empty. Charter operators make money even with lower prices by filling every seat. Charter operators won't charter a plane somewhere unless they are confident of being able to fill it.

Most charters operate only to popular resort and tourist destinations in peak tourist season, when charter operators can count on regularly scheduled flights being full. Scheduled airlines can't readily add extra flights to accommodate peak or overflow demand. Most charter operators are either tour operators (who can count on filling charter flights with people on the tour they run) or wholesale consolidators (who charter planes on routes and schedules where they expect demand to exceed the supply of seats on scheduled flights).

Transportation on charter flights is generally sold only on a roundtrip basis for short stays between specific dates. A few of the largest charter operators sell tickets with options to return on flights from different places or on different dates, but few charter operators have extensive enough schedules to offer these choices. Charters are thus most likely to be a good choice if you are going from a big city to a single, popular destination for a known short period of time during a peak holiday season.

Trying to construct a more complex trip by combining charter flights with onward transportation on scheduled flights carries a serious risk of missed connections. A "ticket" on a charter flight may show a departure time or operating airline, but contracts for charter transportation invariably reserve the right to substitute airlines or means of transportation and to alter schedules by at least 24, often 48, and sometimes 72 hours. No compensation is due to passengers on account of such changes. All that a charter operator is contractually obligated to do is to arrange to have you transported, somehow or other, between the points specified, within a few days, one way or the other, of the date contracted. Some charter operators reserve the right to cancel the charter if not enough people sign up. You'll get your money back if that happens, but it might be too late to find alternate tickets for a decent price.

Operating charter flights requires lots of working capital. Chartering a plane is a gamble: if not enough seats can be sold, the operator's costs to the airline for the flight may greatly exceed the amount paid by passengers. Airlines average these things out over many flights and routes, year-round, but charter operators are often smaller and their business is by nature seasonal and focused on a more limited set of routes. An abrupt decline in tourism to a particular destination—such as from a widely publicized natural disaster or incident of political or criminal violence—can put a charter operator focused on a particular destination or region out of business. Bankruptcy of charter and tour operators is much more common than bankruptcy of airlines, and is the leading reason for travelers to be stranded abroad without transportation home. Operators specializing in a single destination are, of course, most vulnerable to any unexpected change in the volume of tourism to that place.

It's important to read the fine print of a charter contract carefully, and to understand clearly exactly what you can and can't expect. Do not purchase a ticket on a charter flight without buying trip cancellation and interruption insurance that covers you against bankruptcy of the charter operator. Do not buy your travel insurance from the charter operator: if it goes bankrupt without paying the airline that was supposed to transport you, it'll probably turn out not to have paid the insurance company either.

Prices of tickets on charter flights aren't usually subject to government price-fixing, even in countries where fares on scheduled airlines are. So charters are the only cheap option available locally for travel out of some countries where fares for travel on scheduled airlines are kept high to protect the profits of the national airlines. However, there are usually other ways to get tickets out of such a country: buy consolidator tickets elsewhere before you arrive, make that country a stopover on a set of through tickets, or (if you live there) import tickets from a discount agency abroad.

COLLECTING AND USING FREQUENT-FLYER MILES

The cheapest tickets for all or (more often) part of some itineraries are eligible for credit in some frequent-flyer program or other. The number of miles the tickets will earn you depends on the specific itinerary. As a rule, though, tickets eligible for frequent-flyer mileage credit cost more than the mileage credits are worth. Either you have to pay more for tickets on an airline with a popular frequent-flyer program than for tickets on a cheaper airline, or only higher-priced tickets on a particular airline are eligible for frequent-flyer mileage credits. Frequent-flyer programs are, in effect, kickbacks to motivate business travelers to steer their business, and their employers' money, to more expensive airlines. It rarely makes sense for people like you, who are paying their own way, to buy tickets just to earn frequent flyer miles. All you're doing is paying more for your tickets in order to get part, but not all, of the price increase back as a kickback.

You don't get something for nothing. Frequent flyer programs are a profit center for airlines. Airlines would eliminate them if they weren't. Airlines that provide "free" transportation pay for it by charging more for tickets. Airlines wouldn't offer these programs if they weren't confident that the promise of "free" travel would induce people to pay more for tickets to earn those miles than the "free" travel members earn is actually worth.

Airlines charge their "partners" US$0.05–0.10 per passenger-kilometer or mile for mileage credits. One way or another, this has to be reflected in prices. For most itineraries, the additional cost for tickets on "preferred partners" eligible for frequent-flyer mileage credit with major airlines is more than the likely value of the frequent-flyer mileage.

Don't count on frequent-flyer mileage credit unless you have specifically asked, and been told in writing on your itinerary, that specific flights will be eligible for a mileage credit in a particular frequent-flyer program. Tickets at different fares, or tickets from different travel agencies, even on the same airline, may differ in their eligibility for frequent-flyer mileage credit.

Rather than joining one airline's frequent-flyer reward program, and then always flying on that airline even when it's more expensive, I recommend signing up for the frequent-flyer program of any airline you fly on, and buying tickets purely on price.

Before you pay extra for tickets just to get miles, calculate whether the miles are worth the price. How many miles do you need for a "free" ticket? How much would that ticket probably cost if you had to buy it? Compare how much extra it will be for the ticket that's eligible for miles, and how many miles you would earn.

For example, suppose you need 30,000 miles to get a "free" ticket that you would use on a route where you would otherwise pay US$450 for a ticket. That means mileage credits are worth 1.5 cents per mile. If it would cost you US$100 extra to earn miles on a roundtrip to someplace 2,500 miles away (5,000 miles roundtrip), you'd be paying 2 cents per mile of credit. That's a bad deal. Do the math for your own situation: the typical value of mileage credits is 1–2 cents per mile, and their effective cost in higher ticket prices on airlines with name-brand mileage programs is often twice that.

BROKERED FREQUENT-FLYER TICKETS

There are few legitimate discounts on second-class (business- or club-class) or first-class tickets. Most front-cabin travelers' tickets are paid for by their employers, not out of their own pockets, so they choose airlines on service, not price. Airlines don't regard them as price-sensitive—probably rightly—and thus don't feel the need to offer discounts to attract their business. The airlines that offer legitimate discounts on business- or first-class tickets are, almost inevitably, those on which business- and first-class travelers don't want to fly.

The only way to get business- or first-class tickets on the most prestigious airlines for less than full fare is in exchange for frequent-flyer mileage you or a friend has earned, or to use frequent-flyer mileage or other coupons to upgrade a coach ticket. Some people travel so much that they accumulate more frequent-flyer mileage credits than they can use and are willing to request "free" tickets or upgrades for other people in exchange for cash compensation, though this is in violation of airline rules.

Some black-market ticket brokers make their living by "selling" frequent-flyer tickets and upgrades. A would-be traveler pays the broker for a ticket, and the broker pays a frequent flyer to request a "free" ticket for the would-be traveler. A high proportion of the advertisements for heavily discounted business- or first-class tickets, especially on U.S. and Western European airlines, are from these brokers.

These are not legitimately issued or traded tickets. Buying and selling frequent-flyer coupons or tickets is illegal and dangerous for buyers and sellers alike. Both the frequent flyer who requests the ticket and the traveler who uses it must sign statements that no money has changed hands; both are liable for the full fare and additional penalties if it did.

Selling frequent-flyer upgrade certificates, or most other upgrades, is equally illegal. If someone tries to sell you an upgrade certificate, or a coach ticket with an upgrade coupon attached, read the fine print on both sides of the coupon carefully. If it says "void if sold," don't buy it.

If you buy a ticket from someone who obtains it for frequent-flyer mileage, the airline gets no money at all. Airlines go to great lengths to protect themselves against losing revenue this way. Airline employees get bounties for catching people traveling on brokered frequent-flyer tickets. If the airline finds out that a frequent-flyer ticket was sold, both buyer and seller (and intermediary broker, if there is one) are equally liable.

No matter what coupon brokers may tell you, there is no safe or legal way to buy someone else's frequent-flyer mileage or tickets. Buyers of frequent-flyer tickets are, in the eyes of the airlines and the law, committing a crime, construed in different jurisdictions as theft of transportation and/or fraud. If you are caught, you are subject to having the ticket confiscated as void, having both the ticket buyer and seller expelled from the airline's frequent-flyer program, losing any mileage credits in your accounts, and having to pay the full fare for any portion of the ticket that you have already used, in addition to any applicable criminal penalties.

Restrictions on Tickets

Only the most expensive tickets at the full "normal" fare are unrestricted. Few people can afford to pay full fare for any flight, much less for each flight of a trip around the world. You can only get a reasonable price by buying what the airlines consider a "special" (restricted) fare, or by buying consolidator tickets that are sold for less than the official fare. All special-fare and discounted tickets, whether purchased through a travel agency or directly from the airline, have important restrictions and penalties.

One of the most widespread myths about consolidator tickets is that they are highly restricted. This is, in some sense, true, although the restrictions don't necessarily matter to most budget travelers, as long as they know in advance what they are. The real question is which tickets are more restricted, and in what ways.

Consolidator tickets used to be, in general, significantly less restricted than tickets sold directly by airlines for similar prices. But that's no longer necessarily true. The only valid generalization is that *all* discounted tickets are significantly more restricted than they used to be, making it more important than ever to investigate the details of each ticket before you buy it.

Once a ticket is issued, it is governed by the rules of the fare shown on the ticket, except as specifically endorsed (notated on its face) to the contrary. But endorsements can make the ticket either more or less restricted than it would otherwise be, and in either case may be in coded jargon. Without an understanding of the codes and access to the complete rules implicit in them, it's impossible to tell from the face of a ticket exactly what restrictions it has.

It's even harder, of course, with an electronic ticket than with a paper ticket. E-ticket receipts show only a fraction of the essential information on the ticket itself, and omit some things that can be critical to your rights. The only way to know what your e-ticket really says, or means, is to get a printout from the airline of the "passenger receipt" coupon, and then decode it the way you would a paper ticket.

A common mistake is to call an airline to ask about its lowest published fare and its rules, then call agents for prices of discounted tickets on that airline, assuming that the agents' lowest prices will be subject to the same rules as the airline's lowest published discount fares. Any or all of the rules of consolidator tickets may be more or less restrictive than those of any published fares. No assumption whatsoever about the rules of discounted tickets—such as permitted routes or stopovers, minimum or maximum stay limitations, or fees for changes to date(s), destinations, or routes—can be made on the basis of published fare rules. Different agents may have contracts with the same airline with different terms.

The only way to find out any meaningful information about the rules

REAL LIFE

Airlines make the rules, and they can waive them on a case-by-case basis. A sufficiently high-level airline manager can waive advance purchase, minimum or maximum stay, stopover, change fee, or cancellation penalty rules. Travel agents can't waive any of these rules, but can only relay your request to the airline. If you can give the airline a good reason to grant a waiver, you're usually better off pleading your case directly with the airline. Just keep in mind that airlines waive rules only when they think it is in their interest to do so. If you can't make a case for why the airline would benefit from giving you a waiver, it's probably a waste of time to ask for one.

of your ticket is to ask the specific agent from whom you intend to buy that ticket about the specific rules, restrictions, and cancellation or change penalties that will apply if you buy those particular tickets from that particular agent. If some particular rule or condition is really critical to your decision to buy a ticket, get the agent to put it in writing before you pay. Assume nothing.

Following is a list of some of the restrictions that can be placed on tickets. I'll try to note which are likely to apply to which sorts of tickets, but in general any or all of these restrictions may apply to any discounted ticket, whether you buy it directly from the airline or from an agent.

VALIDITY DATES

The most important and widely misunderstood restriction applies to all airline tickets at any price: no ticket can be valid for more than one year. The key question is whether that means "one year from the date the ticket is issued" or "one year from the date of departure on the first flight." The answer depends on what sort of ticket it is.

One-way tickets for a single flight can be valid no more than one year from the date of issuance. Roundtrip tickets can have a first departure date up to one year from the date of issue, and, in certain cases at certain fares, a return date up to one year after the date of first departure. If you are sure of your plans, ready to commit your money, and want to lock in a price long in advance of your departure—and thus more than one year before your intended return—this is an advantage to roundtrip tickets.

Published RTW fares are considered roundtrip fares, and thus can be valid (if issued with open dates) for up to one year from the date of departure. Tickets constructed as a combination of several one-way tickets, on the other hand, can be valid only up to one year from the date of issuance.

If you want to travel for longer, you'll have to buy tickets for only part of the trip at a time. This is rarely a real problem, because few people are actually sure of their plans more than a year in advance. But it's important to understand how the system works, especially if you find work, fall in love, or settle down somewhere along the way, but still want to get home without having to buy new tickets. Unused tickets can sometimes be submitted for refund after the expiration of their validity, but discounted tickets may have little or no refund value.

Not all tickets, even if they are issued with open dates (i.e., without reservations for any specific flights or dates), are valid for as much as a year. Roundtrip tickets may be valid for one, two, three, four, or six months, one year, or some other period. Most one-way tickets are valid either for a specific and fixed date, or for one year, but there are other possibilities as well. If you are unsure when or how long your tickets will be valid, ask before you buy.

The cheapest published fares generally permit only relatively short (but not too short) roundtrip stays. If you want one-way tickets or tickets for an especially short (less than a week) or long (more than three months) stay, consolidator tickets, tickets from low-fare airlines that price all tickets on a one-way basis, and, if you qualify, student fares are usually your only options at a reasonable cost.

DATE CHANGES

More and more tickets are valid only on the specific dates for which they are issued. If you want to travel on a different date, you have to buy a whole new ticket, and you can throw the original one (and the money you paid for it) away. Some tickets can be changed, but only on payment of a fee. I've seen date-change penalties ranging from US$25 to US$250 to 50 percent of the face value of the ticket, although there aren't necessarily any upper or lower limits.

Some tickets permit changes from one date or time to another at no charge, as long as the same airline has space available on a flight between the same cities as originally ticketed. Tickets with freely changeable dates have become vastly less common, however, since the change from paper tickets to e-tickets made it possible for the first time for airlines to enforce date change fees. Now that airlines can charge date fees and stop travelers from evading them, they do. Airlines that want to make money see everything—including date changes, cancellations, sickness and death of ticketed passengers, and family emergencies—as a potential profit center.

Date-change rules are not always apparent, even to an expert, from the actual tickets, and certainly not from the more limited information on a typical itinerary. In theory, under most airlines' general rules of fare construction, dates are changeable at no charge unless stated otherwise somewhere in the rules, but in practice it is best to assume the reverse: tickets are valid only on specific dates, and cannot be changed, unless you are told otherwise. If there is any chance that you might want to change the dates of some or all of your

REAL LIFE

The dates on paper tickets can be changed by "revalidating" them with a paper sticker. In practice, once there's a sticker on the tickets with the new dates, it's almost impossible for the airline to tell whether any required change fee has been paid. In practical terms, this made it possible for frontline ticket counter or travel agency staff to give on-the-spot waivers of change fees to other travelers or themselves. Any savvy travel agent or airline employee always used to keep a few blank revalidation stickers stashed in the back of their wallet, to spare themselves and their traveling companions from date-change fees. I can talk about this now because the window of opportunity has closed. I still have some stickers somewhere, but now they're worthless. E-tickets have to be reissued to change flight dates, giving airlines centralized knowledge and control over whether change fees have been paid.

flights, or if an agent tells you that date changes will be free, get it in writing, on your itinerary, before you pay for your tickets.

Watch out if your tickets are supposed to be changeable but they have an endorsement like "CHANGE SUBJECT TO FEE," "CHG SUBJ FEE," or "CHG ONLY THRU AGT." Such an endorsement doesn't necessarily mean what it seems, but at minimum it probably does mean you will be charged for any changes unless they are made through the issuing agent. This can be quite inconvenient when you are abroad. If the price isn't much higher, try to get tickets that will permit you to make changes yourself directly with the airlines, without having to deal with the original issuing agent.

Most consolidator one-way tickets allow date changes for a reissue fee, but the fees are all over the map from nominal (US$25, say, or occasionally still free) to as much as, or more than, a new ticket for that leg would cost. The change penalty sometimes depends on how far in advance of the originally scheduled and/or the new date you make the change, as well as on the availability and price of seats on the new date. So it's usually best to make changes as far in advance as possible.

One of the most common explanations for differences in price estimates for long-term or multistop travel, even on the same airlines, is that the cheaper estimate is for fixed-date tickets and the higher estimate is for changeable tickets. Most around-the-world and long-term travelers end up changing at least some of their flight dates. If you end up changing the dates of even one or two flights, date-change penalties are likely to more than offset any up-front cost savings to fixed-date tickets, making them a false bargain. Even small date-change fees can add up if you reschedule each leg of a trip on multiple airlines, and have to pay a change fee to each airline. It's hard to draw any firm generalizations about which types of tickets will have lower change fees. (In particular, it's a myth that consolidator tickets are always more restricted, in this or any other respect, than tickets purchased at published fares directly from airline.) But it's worth asking a travel agent or an airline whether there are more easily changeable tickets available for not too much more money up front. I took two trips around the world without changing the dates of any of my flights, but on my third (and longest) trip around the world I needed to change the dates of several of my flights.

ADVANCE BOOKING AND ADVANCE PURCHASE

Tickets for the cheapest fares generally must be purchased at least two to three weeks prior to departure on the first leg of the journey, further in advance in high season when the cheapest seats may be sold out months in advance. Once you make reservations, you usually have only 24 hours to buy your tickets, or your reservations will automatically be canceled.

As if that weren't bad enough, the trend—in order to pressure travelers into impulse ticket purchases—is toward instant-purchase fares that require what their rules describe as "simultaneous reservations and ticketing."

Airlines want to get you to pay as far in advance as possible, because they get the use of your money at no charge between the time you pay and the time they have to spend money to transport you. By buying tickets in advance, you're making what is in effect an unsecured interest-free loan to the airline. The average time between ticketing and travel is critical to airlines' cash flows.

If airlines offered lower prices at the last minute than in advance, potential passengers would be tempted to wait until the last minute, in the hope of a better price. In the meantime, they might decide not to go at all, or to choose a different airline. Airlines don't want people holding reservations who haven't paid. What if they don't ever pay, but don't cancel their reservations until it is too late to sell their seats to someone else? Cheap last-minute fares or long holds on unticketed reservations go against the airlines' long-term interests. Airlines have an interest in getting people to plan and pay far ahead, and their fares and discounts are structured accordingly.

It's widely known that many consolidators' agreements with the airlines include waivers of the normal advance-purchase requirements for cheap fares. When they get desperate and have misjudged demand, airlines offer cheap (but very highly restricted) Web fares at the last minute. Many people misunderstand what this means, and think that consolidator tickets or Web fares will *always* be available for less if they wait until the last minute.

Cheap tickets of any sort can be issued at the last minute only if space allocated to those cheap prices is available at the last minute. In fact, the seats allocated to the cheapest tickets on many airlines are routinely sold out earlier than the advance-purchase deadline. At the last minute, no cheap seats may be available, or you may have much less choice of airlines if you want a discount.

TRANSFERRING TICKETS FROM ONE PERSON TO ANOTHER

You cannot transfer any airline ticket from one person to another, or change names on reservations or tickets once they are made or issued. All airline tickets are "nontransferable." They can be used only by the person to whom they are issued. Passports or government-issued identity documents are checked against names on tickets at check-in for all international flights, as well as on domestic flights in most countries, including the United States. You cannot give or sell an unused ticket to someone else to use.

You may read or hear about various scams used to travel on other people's tickets. They are all illegal, and risk both civil and criminal penalties for both the person whose ticket is used and the person who tries to use it. Don't try it. It's increasingly likely that both the ticket buyer and seller will be caught and fined and the ticket confiscated. If you've already traveled when the scam is uncovered—tickets are sometimes, unexpectedly, checked and compared with passports on arrival—either or both of you could have to pay the full, non-discounted fare for the transportation used. In the present climate of concern for terrorism and airline security, either or both of you could be arrested not merely for theft of transportation but on suspicion of terrorism or espionage if the ticket doesn't match the passenger's travel documents at all times.

CANCELLATIONS AND REFUNDS

Only full-fare tickets are entirely refundable if they aren't used. All cheap tickets have cancellation penalties. Cancellation penalties can vary from US$25 to 100 percent of the fare or price paid (i.e., totally nonrefundable). It's generally cheaper to buy discounted tickets with cancellation penalties, and buy trip cancellation insurance, than to buy full-fare tickets with no cancellation penalties. (See the *Safety and Health* chapter and the section of the same name in the *Resource Guide* for more information on trip cancellation insurance and other types of travel insurance.)

Cancellation penalties and rules can be extremely complex. The refund value of a ticket can depend on which portion or portions, if any, have already been used; when the ticket is submitted for refund relative to the ticketed flight dates (the sooner the better); the rules of the fare shown on the ticket; the rules of a consolidator's contract with the airline; and the travel agent's cancellation policies and fees.

If you bought the ticket from a retail travel agent who bought it from a wholesale consolidator, both the retail agent and the wholesaler may impose cancellation penalties. If the ticket was issued in another country, the refund value can depend on the relative value of that country's currency and the currency in which your refund is paid at the time the refund is received. Each ticket that makes up a set of multistop tickets can have its own cancellation penalties, influenced by each of these factors.

It's impossible to say, in advance, exactly what the refund value of part of a set of tickets might be, unless you know exactly when and in what circumstances you might submit which portion(s) for refund. Any notice of cancellation penalties on a complex set of tickets is of necessity incomplete.

In some jurisdictions the law requires a full disclosure of cancellation penalties, but compliance would be impossible for even the best-intentioned travel agent or airline. (For what it's worth, travel agents generally do a better job of disclosing penalties than the airlines themselves.) A "full" disclosure would require dozens of pages of rules, conditions, and contingencies, couched in jargon incomprehensible to most travelers, and incorporating lengthier and less comprehensible general rules. I assume that the legislators who enacted these requirements had no idea what they really meant.

It's important to identify whether stated cancellation penalties are those of the airline, the agent, or both. "Cancellation penalty 25 percent of refund value of tickets" on an agent's itinerary probably means that the agent will keep 25 percent of any refund, after the airlines' penalties, as the agent's fee for processing the refund. But it doesn't say what the airlines' penalties may be. Processing refunds is much more labor-intensive and costly for agents than issuing tickets, and this is quite a reasonable fee for an agent's services in processing a refund.

Don't try to judge the refund value of a ticket from its face value. Because the face value of a consolidator ticket may be the higher official fare, even if you bought it for less at a discount, you can't necessarily get the full face value back if you don't use it, even in the absence of any penalties. You can only submit such a ticket for refund through the agent who issued it, because only the agent knows how much you actually paid for it. The endorsement "REFUNDABLE ONLY THROUGH ISSUING AGENT," usually abbreviated "REF ISS AGT ONLY" or just "REF AGT ONLY," is used to prevent you from submitting the ticket for refund directly to the airline and getting more money back than you actually paid. This endorsement is the most common clue that a ticket was issued by a consolidator and sold for less than its face value.

Don't throw an unused ticket away just because it says "NONREFUND-ABLE" or "NONREF." Such a ticket is not necessarily completely nonrefundable. These endorsements are sometimes used, like "REF AGT ONLY," merely to preclude your submitting the ticket directly to the airline for refund, or to indicate that it is not *fully* refundable. It may still have some, occasionally substantial, refund value, or be exchangeable for some amount of credit toward another ticket on that same airline. The only way to find out is to submit it for refund to the agent from whom you bought it.

Cancellation penalties are one of the more surprising advantages of consolidator tickets over cheap published fares. The cheapest published fares, including virtually all rock-bottom "fare war" tickets, are completely nonrefundable or have refund penalties so high as to make them effectively nonrefundable. Consolidator tickets generally have substantial cancellation penalties, and some are entirely nonrefundable, but most consolidator tickets have at least some refund value if entirely unused.

CHANGING AIRLINES

Almost all tickets are, in airline jargon, "nonendorsable." This means that they are valid only on the specified airlines. If you want to change your flight or dates, you may change only to another flight on the same airline. Unless an agent specifically promises you otherwise, you should not expect to be able to use your tickets on any airlines other than those on which you are booked. Nonendorsable tickets usually say "NONEND," "XX ONLY," "VALID XX ONLY," or "VLD XX ONLY," where XX is the two-letter code for the airline.

The exception is full-fare tickets, which may be the only ones available for certain flights. Full-fare tickets can be endorsed to any other airline with which the issuing airline has a joint ticketing agreement.

Some commentators point to the inability to change to another airline if your flight is canceled or delayed as a particular drawback of consolidator tickets. This makes no sense. Nonendorsable tickets can be, and often are, endorsed in such circumstances. And there is no real difference between the endorsability of consolidator tickets and tickets at discounted published fares. *All* discounted tickets are, in theory, nonendorsable. Unless you are traveling on business, or someone else is footing the bill, you probably can't afford full-fare endorsable tickets. The cheapest endorsable tickets on most routes are at least twice the price of discounted tickets, often much more. The cheapest endorsable tickets across the United States start at over US$2,000 roundtrip. Unless you've traveled on business, or had to pay the full fare in an emergency, you've probably never seen an endorsable ticket.

In practice, the notation "NONEND" on a ticket means only that an airline isn't required to endorse the ticket to another airline. But airlines may endorse nonendorsable tickets if there is a good reason for doing so. That you have changed your mind, or don't like the schedule, or that the flight has been delayed, are not good reasons. In these cases, it's still worth asking the airline if it will endorse the ticket you already have before you break down and buy an entirely new ticket on another airline—airlines have been known to endorse ticket under these circumstances. Just realize that if your ticket says "NON-END," you are asking a favor, not claiming a right.

That a flight has been canceled entirely might be good enough reason for the airline to endorse a nonendorsable ticket, though it depends on how many days it is until that airline's next flight and whether it will be cheaper for the airline to pay another airline to fly you or to put you up until their own next flight. (The airline isn't required to do either, but in most cases will do one or the other.) That the airline has discontinued service on the route entirely since you bought your ticket is almost always sufficient reason for it to endorse your nonendorsable ticket to another airline. In my experience, even airlines with poor reputations for customer service will do the right thing and endorse even very cheap, nonendorsable tickets in most cases when it is appropriate to do so.

Paper tickets are much easier to get endorsed to another airline than e-tickets. If you have a paper ticket, all the issuing airline has to do is stamp or sticker it with the endorsement. To endorse an e-ticket to an airline that uses a different computer system, the original airline first has to convert it to a paper ticket and print it out, then endorse the paper ticket. Because e-ticket interlining is more technically complex and costly than paper-ticket interlining, airlines typically have many fewer e-ticket interline agreements than they used to have paper ticket interline agreements. Conversion from paper tickets to e-tickets has been accompanied by withdrawal of major airlines from hundreds of long-standing interline agreements, especially with smaller international airlines in other parts of the world. That gives them, and you, far fewer choices if they cancel your flight or it's overbooked. The abandonment of formerly near-universal interline capability between competing airlines has been one of the major drawbacks for travelers in the switch to e-tickets.

The biggest difference in endorsability is not between consolidator tickets and full-fare tickets but between tickets on "traditional" airlines and tickets on low-fare airlines. Most low-fare airlines have no interline agreements with any other carriers. If they cancel a flight or discontinue service on a route, they have no way to put you on another airline's flight, even if there is one about to leave with empty seats. All they can do is give you back your money, which probably won't be enough to buy a ticket at the last-minute walk-up fare on another airline.

CHANGES OF DESTINATIONS OR ROUTE

Many discounted tickets are nonrerouteable ("NO RERTE"). This means that once the tickets are issued you cannot change the sequence of connection and stopover points specified on the tickets, even if the same airline also flies between the end points of your ticket by way of other places.

Tickets without stopovers are more likely to be reroutable, because if you aren't allowed to stop anywhere, the airline has less reason to care where you change planes. That's sometimes helpful if you want to change your travel date, and the only available seats on your desired new date are by way of an alternate transfer point. But a change to a different connection point, even without a stopover, is still considered rerouting, and is sometimes subject to a fee or prohibited entirely.

In some cases additional stops on the same airline can be added or other changes made simply by paying a reissue fee and an additional stopover charge or the difference in fare. If you want to make a change, or discover that the airline has another route by way of a place in which you'd rather change planes or stop over, it's worth asking before you buy an entirely new ticket.

Changes of destinations are considered routing changes, and are likewise largely discretionary with the airlines. Some airlines allow destination changes for a reissue fee, as long as the price to the new destination would have been the same as to the original one. It never hurts to ask if you want to make changes, but you shouldn't buy tickets until you are sure of which places you want to fly to. You can't count on changing destinations without having to buy new tickets.

Both discounted published-fare tickets and consolidator tickets are, officially, equally nonreroutable. Rerouting is rarely an issue with low-fare airlines, since most of their routes are direct "point to point" flights rather than connections through a hub.

Tickets at published RTW fares are, within limits, supposed to be reroutable. Rerouting such a set of tickets requires the whole package to be reissued, however, and you may be limited to one such change in your entire journey. Because of the multiple airlines involved and the complexity of the fare, getting tickets at an RTW fare reissued isn't likely to be possible on the spot. You'll need to confer with one of the participating airlines, then wait at least overnight and more likely several days for them to consult their rate desk and the other airlines involved to confirm that the change you want is possible and to figure out how much you have to pay for the change.

Keep in mind that if you ask an airline whether a change is possible, they will consider only whether space is available. "Yes, you can make that change," means, "Yes, you can make that change—for a price." Find out exactly how much you will be charged before you authorize any change.

STOPOVERS

If you fly from A to B, spend some time in B, and then fly from B to C, B is considered a stopover. It is usually cheaper, when possible, to get a ticket from A to C, with a stopover in B, than to get one ticket from A to B and a second ticket from B to C. It's sometimes possible to combine a dozen or more flights in this way on a single through ticket with multiple stopovers, at an enormous savings over separate tickets for each flight.

If you want to fly from A to C, with a stopover in B, the obvious (although not necessarily the only) choice is an airline based in B. An airline based in B probably flies between A and B, and between B and C. Flying the airline of B between A and C probably requires a change of planes in B anyway, and some of the fares of the airline of B probably permit a stopover there. Distance permitting, the airlines of A and C probably fly nonstop between A and C, not stopping in B or anywhere else.

One of the ways an expert can use his or her skill in finding you the best tickets is to figure out where to break the tickets and start a new fare. Suppose you want to fly from A to B, B to C, and C to D. Is it cheaper to get one ticket A-B-C, and a second ticket C-D? Or is it cheaper to get one ticket A-B, and a second ticket B-C-D? Or is there some through fare that will permit the whole trip A-B-C-D on a single ticket? It's unlikely to be obvious to you, and only an expert is likely to find the right answer without a lot of tedious trial and error, if at all.

Stopover rules are not synonymous with flight routes. Flights sometimes make "technical" stops for refueling at places where they are not allowed to take on or discharge passengers. And airlines can forbid stopovers at other points or charge whatever they think the traffic will bear for them. So don't assume that because an airline's route involves a refueling stop in City X or requires a change of planes in City Y, all fares on that airline allow stopovers in X and/or Y, or that those stopovers will be free. Conversely, some airlines have interline agreements with other airlines that permit you to include a short flight on one airline on a through ticket on another airline, thus making possible stopovers that aren't on the routes of any one airline.

For example, many people assume that all or most tickets between Europe and the West Coast of the United States will permit a free stop in New York or elsewhere on the East Coast. But most flights between Europe and the West Coast follow nonstop polar routes. Even those airlines that offer service via connection points on the East Coast rarely permit stopovers of more than 24 hours without charging separately for each leg.

As a legacy of the occupation of Japan after World War II, U.S.-based airlines have retained preferential rights to carry traffic between Japan and other countries. As Japan became one of the world's most profitable airline markets, attempts by airlines in the United States to expand their inter-Asia services from Japan prompted increasingly strong opposition from Japanese airlines and the Japanese government. The United States has accused Japan of protectionism, even though the United States protects its domestic airline market—the world's largest and most profitable domestic market—by strictly forbidding Japanese or any other foreign airlines to carry local traffic within the United States.

U.S. airlines are under heavy pressure to increase the percentage of passengers on their inter-Asia flights from Japan who make connections directly from the United States, rather than originating in Japan, so as to prove that their Japan–Asia flights are intended to serve the U.S. market and not just (as it appears at present) to poach the lucrative Japan-originating market. As a result, many fares on U.S. airlines between the United States and mainland Asia require a change of planes in Japan but forbid stopovers there.

Most airlines consider stops of less than 24 hours as connections rather than stopovers, and don't charge for them. Depending on the schedules it's sometimes possible to circumvent the stopover rules by arranging as long a connection as is possible without exceeding 24 hours, if such a short stop will be of use or interest to you.

The cheapest published fares on most routes prohibit stopovers even at places where you have to change planes. One of the big advantages to consolidator tickets is that they usually permit stopovers at the airlines' hubs, sometimes elsewhere along the way as well, at least for a fee. All routes on Air France from the United States to Europe, Asia, and Africa, for example, require a change of planes in Paris. But only the most expensive Air France published fares permit stopovers in Paris, while almost all Air France consolidator fares permit stopovers in Paris at minimal additional charge.

DISCONTINUOUS ROUTES

Tickets for discontinuous routes are not necessarily more expensive than tickets for continuous ones. It's possible to use a single through air ticket even if part of your trip between points in the middle will be made by surface transportation, or to get a roundtrip fare even if you fly into one place and back from another and/or return to someplace other than where you started from.

The airline term for any of these sorts of discontinuities is an "open jaw," shown on tickets by "SURFACE" (for "permitted surface transportation not included in airfare") and on itineraries and airline computer displays by "ARNK" (for "arrival to the point of origin of the next flight by means unknown," pronounced "a-runk"). If you plan an ARNK in your itinerary, make sure that the "means unknown" are actually possible: I've heard people propose sectors by surface transportation that would have required walking on water where there are no ferries, through minefields, across closed and fortified borders, and over roadless mountains.

There are four different kinds of open jaws, and different fares permit different ones. The four types, as illustrated in the diagrams, are: open jaw at the origin, open jaw at the destination, double open jaw at origin and destination, and internal open jaw.

Many published roundtrip fares permit at least a single open jaw at either the origin or the destination, although some especially low "fare war" tickets prohibit all open jaws. Domestic roundtrip fares in many countries permit open jaws. In the United States, most year-round discounted fares permit open jaws, and most sale and Web fares don't. This is one of the biggest drawbacks to the cheapest published fares, domestic or international.

Most roundtrip consolidator tickets permit a single or double open jaw at

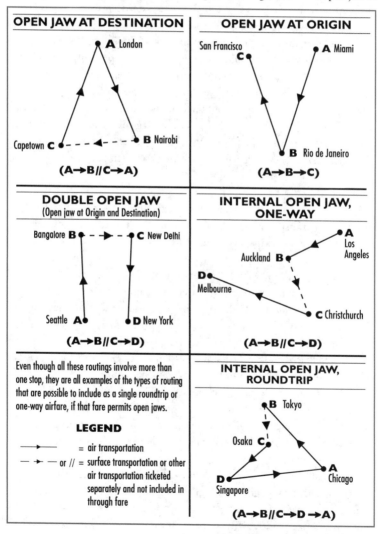

OPEN JAW AT DESTINATION

A London
Capetown C — — — ◄ — — — B Nairobi

(A→B // C→A)

OPEN JAW AT ORIGIN

San Francisco C   A Miami
B Rio de Janeiro

(A→B→C)

DOUBLE OPEN JAW
(Open jaw at Origin and Destination)

Bangalore B — — ► — — C New Delhi
Seattle A   D New York

(A→B // C→D)

INTERNAL OPEN JAW, ONE-WAY

A Los Angeles
Auckland B
D Melbourne
C Christchurch

(A→B // C→D)

Even though all these routings involve more than one stop, they are all examples of the types of routing that are possible to include as a single roundtrip or one-way airfare, if that fare permits open jaws.

LEGEND

⟶ = air transportation
— ► — or // = surface transportation or other air transportation ticketed separately and not included in through fare

INTERNAL OPEN JAW, ROUNDTRIP

B Tokyo
Osaka C
D Singapore   A Chicago

(A→B // C→D →A)

the origin, destination, or both, as long as each surface segment (gap between the points of the open jaw) is between places in the same region (the same continent is usually sufficient). Sometimes the combined flights have to be on the same general route, sometimes not, depending on the airline and fare.

Most people conceptualize their plans in terms of continuous roundtrips, without considering whether open-jaw tickets would be preferable. For all but the shortest and simplest trips, they often would be. The simplest application of open-jaw routing is for people wanting to explore a moderate-sized region within which surface transportation is available and cheaper than air travel, but within which distances and/or costs are a disincentive to backtracking: the solution is to get an open-jaw ticket arriving at one end of the region and returning from the other, and make your way in between by other means.

If open-jaw tickets would suit your needs, you'll probably have to ask to find out if they are available. Neither airlines nor discount agencies advertise open-jaw prices, even when they are available, simply because listing prices for all the possible combinations would take up too much space. Where they are available, open-jaw tickets are priced as the average of the roundtrip prices for the two different legs or, equivalently, the sum of the half-roundtrip prices. You rarely save money by getting roundtrip rather than open-jaw tickets.

AMENITIES

When you buy an airline ticket, you are paying for transportation. If all you want is transportation, all that matters are the rules governing your use of a ticket for transportation: When can you go? Where? On what conditions? At what price?

The travelers on whose business the airlines make the most money, however, are business travelers who aren't paying for their own tickets, and for whose business it would therefore be futile to compete on price. Airlines throw in a variety of what they call amenities or "ancillary services" to attract the business of the non-price-sensitive: frequent-flyer mileage credits, special meals, preferential and advance seating assignments, eligibility for upgrades if space is available in business or first class, etc.

All of these things are nice, if they don't cost anything. Don't let the sizzle distract you from the steak, though: the minute you indicate to the airlines, or an agent, that you are concerned with whether your tickets will come with these side dishes, you have told them that your priority is other than strictly price.

I've said it before, and I'll say it again: airlines set prices according to criteria intended to identify willingness to pay. If you care about frequent-flyer mileage, seat assignments, meals, upgrades, or the like, you are by definition not so price-sensitive. If you insist on these "ancillary services," you are obviously willing to pay for them, and the airline knows that it can get away with charging you more for them, or for a ticket that qualifies for them.

Some airlines restrict both consolidator tickets and/or tickets at their cheapest published fares by making them ineligible for frequent-flyer mileage credit ("NO FF MILES" or "NO MILES"), special meals ("NO SPECIAL MEAL" or "NO SPML"), and/or advance seat assignments ("NO PRERESERVED SEATS" or "NO PRS"), for which published-fare ticket holders are eligible. This is not because these amenities are expensive (except for frequent-flyer mileage credit) or because they can't afford to provide them on cheap tickets. These petty restrictions on amenities are primarily tools to identify those passengers who are willing to pay more, and to induce them to do so.

ARRANGING YOUR AIR TRANSPORTATION

The first step in arranging your air transportation—once you have chosen your initial list of desired destinations—is to decide whether, as discussed at the start of this chapter, you want to arrange your flights and tickets directly with an airline, through a travel agency, or on your own as a do-it-yourself travel agent.

If you want to try to do it yourself, or deal directly with airlines, see the *Resource Guide* for some directories of low-fare airlines, airline route maps, and other places to start. But if you want help from a travel agent, where do you turn?

Choosing a Travel Agent

There's a travel agency in every major town in the United States, and dozens in every major city. In 2010, almost 10,000 travel agencies were authorized to issue airline tickets in the United States alone. That's only about half as many as when the previous edition of this book was published in 2007, but it's still a lot. With so many choices, how can you find which agent and agency will be best for you?

CHOOSE A DISCOUNT AGENT

You may not think of yourself as being concerned primarily with discounts, but for complex multistop travel, you'll still be best served by a discounter. As I explained in the previous section of this chapter, many discount prices are available only through specialized travel agents, and not available directly from the airlines or from travel agencies that sell tickets at published fares. Published one-way fares are so much higher than discounted prices on many routes that constructing tickets around the world, or for any complex multistop itinerary, without discounts is likely to drive the price beyond the means of even the rich.

The right travel agent can be extremely helpful even if you are choosing between published fares. Without a travel agent, travelers have no independent consultant to bring new competitors, new fares, and nonintuitive routes to their attention, and airlines can get away with charging more with less competition.

Going to a discounter will help you find an agent who will side with you, not with the airlines. Travel agents have traditionally been agents of the airlines, not agents of travelers, with a legal obligation to advance the financial interests of the airlines against those of passengers. Some agents take this seriously, and consider it their duty to report you to the airline if they find out, for example, that you intend to use only half a roundtrip ticket when a one-way ticket would cost more than a roundtrip. If you come across an agent like this, take your business elsewhere.

Such agents are rare, though. Regardless of the law, most travel agencies and agents—except for the big online travel agencies like Travelocity.com, Expedia.com, Orbitz.com, Priceline.com, Opodo.com, and the like—consider themselves consultants to, and advocates for, passengers, not airlines. Airlines realize this, and dislike it, but can't do much about it. Suing travel agents who search for and advise clients of the lowest rather than the highest fares, for breach of their responsibility as the airline's agents, would be a public relations disaster, even if such an action would be entirely within the airlines' legal rights.

You want an agent who considers it their job to get you the best deal, not to get the airlines the most money. The agents on your side are the ones willing to describe themselves as discounters and publicly promote the availability of tickets at prices below the airlines' published fares. They are also the ones most likely to charge for their services, whether their fee is included in the price of tickets or quoted separately. If you want a travel agent to work for you, rather than to work for the airlines, you should expect to pay them for that service.

Airlines and the big online travel agencies will not like some of the things I say in this book. I sincerely believe, however, that the interests of the airlines as well as of travelers are best served by making air travel accessible and affordable to as many people as possible, not by jacking up the price or accentuating the exclusivity of air travel.

CHOOSE A TRAVEL CONSULTANT, NOT A TICKET BROKER

Don't get carried away looking for the ultimate in discounts. Even the most price-sensitive travelers, especially those who aren't intimately familiar with their destination, may find that it's worth paying a bit more for reliability, service, and a modicum of advice.

Shopping *solely* on price is a good way to ensure that the agency from which you eventually buy your tickets has cut its margin so thin that it can't afford to provide an acceptable standard of service. Labor costs are the largest expense for travel agencies, and the cheapest agencies can't afford to put experienced people on the phones or serving clients face to face. They discipline their employees to spend no more time with each customer than is essential to close the sale.

I can't pretend to impartiality on this issue, but my impression from working with thousands of around-the-world travelers is that their tendency is to overestimate the importance of price and underestimate the value of expertise.

Travel agents don't call themselves "travel consultants" for nothing. Most people planning a trip around the world need, and want, professional consulting and advice that they won't get from anyone but a specialized sort of travel agent. Most people simply don't know, and can't know in advance, what problems to anticipate or even what questions to ask. Travel agents who sell tickets as a commodity at the lowest possible prices, assembly-line style, simply don't, and can't, provide that expanded service. And only an independent travel consultant—who isn't beholden to any one airline—is likely to be able to find which airlines' routes will be best for you.

CHOOSE A SPECIALIST

Choosing a discounter is, in a sense, just a special case of the larger principle of choosing an agency or agent with a specialization appropriate to your travel plans. It's difficult to separate choosing an agency from choosing an agent. Both are important. The agency needs to be soundly financed and accredited, and have discount contracts with the appropriate airlines (or knowledge of, and working relationships with, their wholesale consolidators). The agent needs to have expertise in your sort of travel, and in the kinds of travel services about which you want advice, whether they are cruises, package tours, or long-haul airfares.

Some agencies specialize exclusively in travel of a particular type, or to a particular destination country or region. Other agencies have specialists in different areas.

Some travel agents claim that a competent travel agent can handle any kind of travel arrangements, anywhere in the world. However, travel and tourism is, by some accounts, the largest industry in the world. It is far too complex a topic for any one person to know everything about.

Most air tickets sold in the United States are domestic roundtrips, and most international tickets sold in the United States are the simplest roundtrips to Canada, Mexico, the Caribbean, and Western Europe. In the United States, international travel is a relatively small, specialty niche. More and more travel agencies in the United States specialize primarily in cruises and tours—on which they are paid commissions—rather than airfares. CRSs and travel agencies have cut back dramatically on the technical training they provide to frontline travel agents. The typical U.S. travel agent knows dramatically less about airfares and air ticketing than was the norm 20 years ago.

Agencies in the United States that call themselves generalists are in fact, by the nature of the U.S. travel market, specialists in domestic travel, cruises, tours, and resorts. I would no more recommend buying an international ticket from an all-purpose travel agent than buying a package tour to Disneyland from a long-haul international airfare specialist.

The situation is a bit better in some countries such as the U.K. or Australia where a higher percentage of travel is international, and where discounting is more widely known and accepted. Travel agents on the high streets of midsized provincial towns in England regularly sell both tickets on charter flights and consolidator tickets on scheduled airlines, although they still won't know what to do with inquiries about more complex routes. On the other hand, there are countries where discounting is unheard-of and regarded as though it were illegal, immoral, or beneath contempt. If you don't know the country, it's hard to know what to expect. The first questions to ask a travel agent are, "Do you specialize in international airfares?" and "Do you sell consolidator tickets?" If the answer to either question is "No," you are probably wasting your time, and that of the agent. Thank the person, politely, and find another agency or agent.

TYPES OF DISCOUNT TRAVEL AGENCIES

There is no agreed-upon terminology for the various types of discount agencies. The most important differences for travelers are between wholesale and retail discounters, and between agencies whose deals are limited to particular markets and those that handle tickets to a wide range of international destinations. Depending on your itinerary, I recommend buying your tickets either from a retail agent specializing in your specific destination or interest, or a specialist in around-the-world and multistop tickets.

Many people have heard that they should look for a consolidator or "bucket shop." I'll try to explain what I think these terms mean, but they are used inconsistently within the industry. Consolidators, bucket shops, and other sellers of discounted international tickets basically fall into three categories: wholesale consolidators, destination specialty agencies, and long-haul specialists who deal with many destinations and with multistop tickets.

Wholesale Consolidators: Consolidators are agencies that have direct agreements with the airlines to get paid more than the standard commission, and thus are able to rebate some of that commission in the form of discounts to retail and/or wholesale customers.

In many cases, especially with larger airlines, consolidators are wholesalers who sell only through retail agencies, not directly to the public. Some people in the travel industry consider the term "consolidator" to refer exclusively to wholesalers, and would say that an agency isn't really a consolidator if it sells tickets directly to travelers.

Buying from a wholesaler who also sells directly to the public may be fine if you want a straightforward roundtrip ticket. But of course many itineraries aren't like that, and most people need a retail agent's help to figure out what's the best ticket for them.

Most publicly available lists of consolidators indiscriminately mix wholesale consolidators who also sell directly to the public with retail agencies, some of which don't have any direct contracts with the airlines.

REAL LIFE

If you are ever in an immigrant or ethnic neighborhood and can't figure out where people are from—and don't want to ask directly—the easiest way to find out is to look in the window of the nearest travel agency to see what destinations are being advertised.

An annoying number of people try to get wholesale prices from consolidators by falsely claiming to be travel agents. It doesn't work, and only alienates retail and wholesale agents alike. If you aren't really a travel agent, you won't be able to pass for one. Don't try.

Destination Specialty Agencies: Destination specialists include both tour operators and agencies selling tickets to the home country to immigrants and ethnic communities.

Frequently an agency operating tours to a particular country will have a discount agreement with the airline it uses for its tours (such as the national carrier of the destination) and will also sell wholesale tickets on that route. One reason it does the air-only business, even if the markup on air tickets is very low, is to boost its volume of production (sales) with the airline, as many discount contracts are contingent on a specified sales volume and/or have bonuses based on sales thresholds. The agency may be willing to sell tickets at retail as well; the problem in getting an air ticket from such an agency is that you're apt to get quite a hard sell for a tour, and no advice or encouragement for independent travel.

Other destination specialists sell tickets primarily to immigrants and their descendants traveling to visit friends and relations, or carry on business in the "old country." They sell few tours, because most of their customers are staying with local acquaintances. Ethnic specialty agencies often offer the cheapest roundtrip tickets, but have very limited offerings and are sometimes unaccustomed to dealing with people from outside their communities.

Some of these offices sell other products or provide other services in addition to functioning as travel agencies. Airline tickets may actually be a loss leader to attract customers for their other line(s) of business. It may be worth it to such a business to sell someone a ticket home at or slightly below cost, once or twice a year, if that gets them a loyal year-round customer for their barbershop, tax preparation service, beauty salon, insurance brokerage, café, notary, paralegal, or whatever.

You can often find agencies like this through publications targeted at immigrants from the country you want to go to. Even in foreign-language ethnic publications the travel ads are generally recognizable, with at least the phone number, the destination cities (names or three-letter airport codes, which are the same regardless of the language), and the roundtrip prices in Latin letters and numbers. A quick glance at the ethnic press will give you the best idea of the absolute lower limit of possible prices for tickets bought long in advance for travel in the most unpopular season on the worst airlines with the worst connections in the most undesirable or expensive stopover points.

The lowest advertised price is usually either a loss leader and/or a bait-and-switch gambit to attract callers. The lowest advertised prices for trans-oceanic tickets from the United States, for example, generally range from wholesale cost for the cheapest ticket to about US$20 below cost, and generally exclude legally required surcharges, fees, and taxes that can add a couple of hundred dollars to the rice of a roundtrip ticket. (The U.S. Department of Transportation makes sporadic spot checks of the ads in mainstream newspapers, but largely ignores those in the ethnic press.) It is unlikely that you will actually get a ticket for your itinerary at these prices. Even in the most expensive season the lowest advertised prices are usually for travel in low season, whenever that is.

But if you want the cheapest possible roundtrip from the United States to India, Ireland, Nigeria, or any other place from which there are large numbers of immigrants, you will find the lowest prices at a no-service "bucket shop" within the appropriate ethnic community. No all-purpose agency is likely to be able to beat the lowest prices of the agencies that sell nothing else but a massive volume of roundtrip tickets to a single destination. (I don't know how the term "bucket shop" originated, though I've heard lots of stories—all of them probably apocryphal. For a time, it seemed to be acquiring a wider meaning, but its usage seems to have reverted to describe only bare-bones ticket brokers like these.)

Long-Haul, Multistop, and RTW Specialists: Long-haul and multi-stop agents subvert the airlines' conspiracy against discounting in all of the ways that I've been talking about in this chapter: negotiating discount contracts with airlines that let them sell tickets for less than the airlines' published fares, buying tickets through wholesale consolidators on routes and airlines for which they don't have their own contracts, importing and exporting tickets from countries where they are cheaper, and so forth.

Long-haul agencies, and especially RTW and multistop agencies, specialize in knowing international airline route systems, fare rules, and the full range of consolidators (every airline has many consolidators); ticketing and fare construction techniques; and an arsenal of other tricks of the trade.

Long-haul and multistop agencies serve a limited and specialized subset of the air ticket market. They are concentrated in a few world cities including San Francisco, London, and Sydney, but these days the Internet makes it possible for them to operate from a wider range of places.

It can be worth looking far afield (with email and the Web, your travel agency does not have to be physically near you) to deal with a good long-haul specialty agency. The overwhelming majority of travel agents don't even try to compete with their knowledge of the global ticket market. For that matter, most agents couldn't construct the sorts of routings the better long-haul and multistop agencies specialize in (especially customized around-the-world itineraries) at any price.

Around-the-world tickets are the epitome of the long-haul agent's art. Constructing a set of around-the-world tickets requires both deciding at what points to break the tickets into segments and getting the best price for each segment (where each ticket may actually, with stopovers, cover several legs of the journey). It also requires advising travelers on destinations and routes, as most people aren't sure when they start planning an around-the-world trip exactly what stops they want to make, or in what order. Good around-the-world agents are rare, even in specialized agencies, but your average travel agent doesn't even know where to begin.

There are sometimes advantages in terms of consumer protections to dealing with an agency in your own country (see *When Things Go Wrong* later in this chapter), but if there are no local discount specialists it may be worth buying tickets from an agency abroad. You don't have to be in, or flying from or to, a city or country to deal with an agency there, if it can give you the best value for your money in price and service. Long-haul specialists on the Internet cater to a global clientele.

Many consolidators won't deal directly with the public, and wholesale ticket price tariffs are confidential. One of the most important skills for a long-haul agent is having a feel for the wholesale ticket market. It's one thing to ask your local agent to try to buy you a consolidator ticket. It's quite another for the agent to know which consolidator, where, has the best price for what you want. Most bucket-shop tickets, if you inspect the validation, are not issued by the agencies you buy them from. If you already knew exactly where to buy your tickets, you could sometimes get a slightly better price directly. But the odds are that you couldn't and wouldn't find the best deal for yourself—the whole system is deliberately stacked against just that.

Around-the-world air ticketing is one of the smallest and most specialized of travel niches. There are probably no more than a hundred agencies and a thousand agents in the world who really specialize in these sorts of tickets. Look for someone who specifically advertises around-the-world and multistop tickets if that's what you want. Look for agencies that advertise sample around-the-world prices, but who encourage you to pick your own destinations rather than to chose from a shortlist of routes.

TELLING GOOD AGENCIES AND AGENTS FROM BAD

There is no simple or certain way to judge the qualifications or expertise of a travel agency or agent. Travel agency certification and appointment requires financing and technical competence in the mechanics of issuing tickets. In the United States, it requires no knowledge of destinations nor any evidence of competence to give travel advice. Travel agents talk about professional standards and credentials, but the travel agent community is too diverse for any likely agreement.

Different factors are appropriate to consider in choosing between travel agencies versus individual agents. What's important in an agency are adequate capitalization, sound finances, management integrity, and willingness to allow agents to spend time giving advice and not just selling. What's important in an agent are skills, appropriate specialized knowledge, an ability to relate to you and your trip, and a consulting, rather than sales, attitude. The same agency may have agents of varied expertise, with varied approaches to their work.

There is no one best agent for everyone. People are different, and travel differently. One of the most important and least-asked questions to ask a travel agent is, "How do you travel when you travel yourself?" An agent who wouldn't take the kind of trip you want, even if they had the time and money, is probably a poor choice to help you plan it. An agent's knowledge of your destination may be of little help if their knowledge is about the five-star hotels and you want to stay in local huts.

Look for an agent who views herself or himself as a consultant, advisor, and facilitator, rather than as a salesperson. Find someone who takes the time to ask questions, to listen to the answers, and to respond to your concerns. It's a very bad sign if an agent tells you a price without asking you any questions first, unless your trip is simple and your inquiry is unusually precise and complete. A good agent customizes each itinerary to best suit the wants and needs of the individual traveler; don't waste your time on an agency that sells around-the-world or multistop tickets from a limited menu or brochure. If one agency won't give you a price for what you want, go to another one that will.

As with other professional advisors and consultants, personal referrals from your acquaintances who've taken similar sorts of trips, and were happy with the service they received, are a good starting point in finding an agent. Part of being a good specialist is knowing the limits of your expertise. Agents often know which of their peers are reputable and which aren't. Good agents, if they are unable to help you, will admit ignorance and often will refer you to someone else who is reliable and more appropriate.

One thing not to rely on is favorable references provided by the agency itself. Except for complete frauds, even rip-off agencies have satisfied customers. The test is what they do when things go wrong. Most are pretty reliable, but you can't expect the best service at the lowest price. To the extent that two agencies have access to the same deals, and that the difference between their prices reflects differences in their labor costs, small variations in price have a disproportionate effect on the level of service they can afford to give.

Listings of specific travel agencies in guidebooks aren't much use either. I've worked for travel agencies that have been written up in many guidebooks, so maybe I shouldn't say this, but most lists of agencies I see in guidebooks and references about cheap tickets intermingle reputable, disreputable, and long-out-of-business agencies. That's not the guidebook writers' fault: it's mostly that agencies come and go, or go bad, too often for any publication to keep up with the changes.

Don't even consider buying tickets from an agency that is not appointed by the International Air Transport Association (IATA). Agencies in the United States usually receive their IATA appointments through either or both the International Airline Travel Agents' Network (IATAN) and/or the Airline Reporting Corporation (ARC), whose logos are frequently displayed in their offices and on their literature. "Subagents" and non-IATA/IATAN/ARC agencies cannot issue any of their own tickets, but must purchase them all from other agencies, wholesalers, or the airlines. Since the basic qualifications for IATA, IATAN, and ARC appointments are proof of financial means and ticketing experience, non-IATA/IATAN/ARC agents are, by definition, inexperienced, under-financed, or both.

If you aren't sure of an agency's status, there's a simple test: ask to see some tickets they have issued. Don't write a check to a payee whose name doesn't match what's in the "issuing agency" box on any of their tickets. It's perfectly OK if many, even most, of their tickets, or all of your particular tickets, come from airlines or other agencies, but it's a red flag if the agent you're dealing with hasn't passed the tests or posted the bonds to be able to issue any tickets themselves.

In the U.K., don't buy tickets from any agency that doesn't list an Air Travel Organiser's Licence (ATOL) number on its advertisements and receipts. (See the section *When Things Go Wrong*, later in this chapter, for more on consumer protection.) You can contact the U.K. Civil Aviation Authority at +1-44-20-7453-6424, or search the directory of ATOL numbers on the CAA website at www.caa.co.uk, to find out if an ATOL number is valid and to whom it belongs.

In the United States, look for a California Seller of Travel (CST) registration number in travel agency ads. Any agency with a national clientele has customers in California, regardless of where in the United States they are located. If they haven't bothered to register with the state, or display their required registration number, that's a bad sign.

Anywhere you encounter it, membership in the American Society of Travel Agents (ASTA) is a positive sign. But there's no reason to avoid nonmembers of ASTA; many good agencies in the United States don't choose to belong.

Except in certain other countries with their own licensing systems, most other memberships, accreditations, and endorsements are of little or no value to consumers in judging travel agencies. Some tourist boards and other trade associations issue certificates to specialists in destinations or types of travel, but there's little way for you to tell which are meaningful and which are handed out to every agent who requests a packet of literature about a destination, or attends a single marketing seminar. In any event, many of the best agents got their training through on-the-job apprenticeship and have no formal credentials.

Don't buy tickets from an agency that doesn't accept credit cards, if you can avoid it, whether or not you actually intend to pay by credit card. The fact that an agency doesn't accept credit cards is a strong indication that either it doesn't specialize in discounted tickets, and thus hasn't needed to establish a credit-card merchant account (airlines accept all major credit cards directly, on the agent's behalf, for full-fare tickets); or it has too little business experience, or too little capital or business credit, to qualify for a merchant account; or its merchant account has been revoked, which generally happens only if it has an excessive percentage of chargebacks (charges disputed by customers). If an agency accepts no credit cards, that's a red flag that its finances or business practices are suspect in the eyes of some people who should know: its bankers.

As for discount travel agency reliability, it varies. Caveat emptor. These agencies tend to be wheeler-dealers, and of necessity they cut their margins thin. Find out how long the agency has been around. Check it out with any professional or accrediting organizations to which it belongs. (See *When Things Go Wrong* later in this chapter for some suggestions.) Go to the office in person to check it out, if you can. If you don't completely trust the company to deliver, or the price is so good that you can't resist going through with a deal that seems too good to be true, pay by credit card so you can refuse the charge if you don't get your tickets. You'll probably have to pay 3–6 percent more for using a credit card, but it's simple, cheap, and effective insurance.

Before you pay for tickets, have the agent make confirmed reservations for as many of your flights as possible and give you a commitment that you'll have all or most of your tickets in hand within at most a couple of weeks if they are being sourced in-country, a month if portions of your tickets need to be issued overseas. It you don't completely trust the travel agency, it may be worth it to your peace of mind to pay somewhat more for tickets that can be issued more quickly than for tickets that might not arrive until just before your departure.

If you have any doubts about an agency or agent, check directly with the airlines immediately before paying for your tickets to make sure that you are holding confirmed reservations. This is not always possible, as some of your flights may be on airlines that have no representation in the country in which you are buying your tickets. But where possible, it's a good idea. It's all too easy, and common, for bad agents to sell tickets to people who aren't really confirmed.

For various reasons, tickets for one or two legs of your trip, even if you pay well in advance, may for legitimate reasons have to be picked up from the airlines or agents along the way, or sent to you later.

But if an agency suggests that you will have more flexibility if you don't make reservations and just get your tickets "open," or that you will be safer picking up your tickets along the way than carrying them with you, something is wrong. Most likely this means the agency won't issue your tickets until just before you start using each piece of your tickets. This is standard operating procedure for some large agencies of long standing, but I disapprove of it and think it's not in travelers' best interests. There's no excuse for holding other people's money at risk. In some jurisdictions, including California, it's illegal.

Some agencies will offer to sell you vouchers for tickets to be issued in the future, subject to your agreement to pay any fare increase in the interim. If you accept such an arrangement, you have no protection if the airline increases its fare or discontinues service on the route before your tickets are issued. Don't sign a blank credit-card authorization, or pay for vouchers, without a written guarantee of the price for the actual tickets. Even if the agency guarantees the price, you have little recourse if anything happens to the agency between when you pay them and when they pay for your tickets.

If an agency issues portions of your tickets, one at a time, as you travel, they will be holding your money for months before they spend it. If an agency says there's no limit to the duration of your travels, it's a virtual certainty they are talking about taking payment now, issuing tickets later, and using your money in the meantime to solve their cash-flow problems. Don't let them do this. The only times to accept vouchers for tickets to be picked up overseas are when you are leaving on too short notice to get tickets in hand before your departure, or when the particular fare requires that tickets be prepaid for issuance directly by the airline at the point of departure (as has been the case at times for tickets originating in the Philippines and certain other countries).

When to Buy Your Airline Tickets

There is no simple answer to the question, "When should I buy my tickets?" One of the reasons to call a travel agent long in advance of a big trip—even a year before your departure—is to get their expert advice as to when to buy your tickets, along with a ballpark estimate of how much they might cost. For those with a choice of when to buy, factors to consider are the duration of your trip, the season in which you will be traveling, how far in advance the airlines set their discount rates, whether you will need to have your tickets before you can get visas, and, of course, how far ahead you are sure of your plans.

In general, the best time to buy tickets is usually between two to four months before a low-season departure, four to six months before a high-season departure, and perhaps longer in advance for travel during December or other peak seasons such as Lunar New Year in East Asia, Hajj in Saudi Arabia, or Passover in Israel.

REASONS TO BUY TICKETS FURTHER IN ADVANCE

Unlike discounted tickets purchased directly from the airlines, most consolidator tickets have no advance-purchase requirements. I've sold tickets to people leaving the same day around the world. This does not mean that tickets will be just as cheap at the last minute. On the contrary, you will get the best price and have the most choices if you buy your tickets as far in advance as possible, unless there is a specific reason not to (discussed later in this section).

If you buy tickets at the last minute, the cheapest seats on the cheapest airlines may already be sold, and you may have to pay much more for another airline or for a more expensive reservation category ("booking class"). Some countries also require confirmed reservations or tickets before they will issue you a visa.

Worst of all, you may find at the last minute that there are no flights on the route you planned, that your itinerary will be much more costly than your budget allows, or that all seats on a flight you counted on are sold out.

Getting the best price often requires having tickets issued in different countries. Some of your tickets may still be paper tickets, and sending payments to suppliers abroad and getting tickets back by air mail can easily take three weeks. Clearing international payments, even for electronic tickets, sometimes takes a couple of weeks. If you want to have your tickets in hand at least a week before your departure, at the best possible price, you need to pay for them at least a month before your departure. On shorter notice, you may be limited to potentially more expensive locally sourced tickets.

Published RTW fares typically require 14 or 21 days advance purchase, in order to keep them from being used by business travelers. But as with consolidator tickets, the more important constraint is how far in advance the limited number of seats allocated to those fares is booked up.

Whether with consolidator tickets or a published RTW fare, finding and verifying the best fare for an itinerary, deciding between alternatives, and finalizing reservations for specific flights often takes a couple of weeks from the first call to a travel agent to when a traveler is ready to pay for tickets. So you should contact a travel agent at least six weeks before your intended departure date if you don't want to be in a rush, longer if you want the best possible price and the most choice of flights.

Published around-the-world fares typically require 14 or 21 days' advance purchase. Because the best deals for first- and business-class travel are often published fares, it is particularly difficult and expensive to arrange a first- or business-class multistop trip on short notice.

REASONS TO WAIT TO BUY TICKETS LATER

The only good reasons to delay buying tickets are to wait for airlines to set discount prices for your travel dates, to extend the validity dates of your tickets, or because you haven't yet made up your mind where you want to go or when you want to leave.

Airlines wait until they have a good idea how full their planes will be before they decide how deeply they need to discount their tickets to fill their planes. Most airlines set their consolidator prices only one or two seasons at a time, anywhere from two to six months in advance.

Some low-fare airlines set schedules and prices and accept reservations up to a year in advance, like traditional airlines. Others act more like consolidators or charter operators, and fix their schedules and prices only one or two seasons at time, when they feel they can better predict demand. As with everything else about low-fare airlines, there are no standards or rules.

Some consolidators offer discounts on flights departing many months in the future. If the airline that is likely to be cheapest has already set its prices, an agent has every reason to tell you so to close the sale early. Sometimes you can get a really good deal by buying tickets up to a year in advance, but it is often better to wait until more airlines have set their discount rates. The best time to make reservations is usually just after most airlines have fixed their discount prices for your travel season.

However, waiting to buy your tickets in the hope that some airline will set lower rates is always a gamble. It is riskiest for high-season or holiday travel; if no better deal materializes there may be no cheap seats left, or no seats at all, by the time you decide to buy your tickets. For example, international flights to virtually all places, regardless of whether you think of them as "Christmas destinations," are most heavily booked throughout December and into January. The cheapest December seats to many points in Africa are sold out in July or August.

If your trip will last more than one year from the date you buy your tickets, you will only be able to buy part of your tickets before your departure. If you tell a good agent your entire planned itinerary, and how far you are confident you will get within a year, they can advise which tickets it would be best to purchase in advance and where it will be best to buy the rest. (See *Buying Tickets En Route* later in this chapter.)

Because tickets are valid at most one year from the date of issue, and it can take a month of that year of validity for you to get the tickets, the practical limit to the duration of a trip, for which you purchase all your tickets at once, is about eleven months.

For shorter trips, it makes sense to wait to purchase your tickets until within one year of the last date you might want to return, so that you can buy your tickets all at once. If you plan to travel for more than nine or 10 months, you may be better off buying your tickets in two or more stages, especially if you aren't certain how soon you'll want to return home. It's a real drag to cut your trip short solely because your tickets are about to expire. Far more people extend their trips longer than they had planned than come home earlier than they expected, so don't risk being forced to return sooner than you want to.

If you wait to buy your tickets, you risk that flights will fill up and/or prices will increase while you are waiting. Agents don't usually get advance notice of price increases, and unticketed reservations can be canceled without notice.

The longer your trip, the more likely that your plans will change en route. Tickets bought in a single package are usually cheaper than tickets bought one flight at a time, but it's a false economy if you have to throw them away and buy other tickets when you later decide to go somewhere different. Buy tickets no further than you are certain of your desired route.

Getting a Price Estimate

Once you have chosen a tentative set of destinations, the next step is to contact airlines or a travel agency to get more precise estimates on how much air tickets will cost to include specific stops in a specific order on specific airlines.

You may want to visit a travel agency in person, at some point, to check it out, but it's often easier to make initial inquiries by phone or email. Rating an around-the-world itinerary can take an hour or two of work, for which the agent is paid nothing if you end up getting the ticket elsewhere. Most agents will give only a very rough estimate of the fare unless you make clear, by given them a nonrefundable deposit, that you are really serious about getting your tickets from that agency, and aren't just shopping around. Deposits have been standard in the U.K. and other countries for years, and are gradually becoming the norm in the United States as well.

There's little point in trying to go to an airline ticket office, even if you can find one. For tickets at RTW fares, they won't help you on the spot, but will tell you to phone their "RTW desk" of specialists.

Whether with an airline or a travel agent, a published RTW fare or a package of point-to-point tickets, don't be surprised that the price isn't in the computer and can't be provided immediately while you are on the phone. Inquiries from people who are leaving right away are likely to be worked on and answered soonest, and it's normal for a price estimate to take a couple of days.

Airtreks.com, where I used to work, had the first (and still one of the most sophisticated) online RTW price estimation tools. Its look and feel has since been imitated by all three of the major airline alliances for their published RTW fares. As of 2011, all of these and other airlines' and travel agencies' websites are only planning tools to help you explore possibilities and get estimated prices. There's still no website that lets you reserve or purchase any sort of RTW ticket online, without talking to a human agent. I think the software is getting close to the point where that will be possible, but only for a limited subset of the simplest itineraries, and only for published RTW fares.

Factors That May Affect the Price

Before you start contacting airlines or travel agencies, review the following list of factors that may affect the price of your tickets, and be sure your inquiry includes all the information an airline or travel agent will need to give you an accurate estimate and to tell which tickets will be best for you. If you don't volunteer this information, and they don't ask, they'll have to base their estimate on some standard set of assumptions about what you want, which may not be correct.

STARTING AND ENDING CITIES

The essential information most often omitted from requests for estimates is the most basic: where people want their tickets to start and end. Most people assume that their starting and ending cities are obvious, but they aren't. You may want

Factors That May Affect the Price of Your Ticket

Consider the following checklist before contacting your travel agent.

Starting and Ending Cities: A substantial proportion of long-haul tickets are one-way, or begun and completed in different places.

Lists of Destinations: Include all the places you intend to go, even if you think that they have to be ticketed as side trips or separate tickets, or that you will have to purchase tickets locally. Separate the must-see destinations from those that are optional.

Surface Transportation: Tell the agent if there are specific sections of your trip that you wish to travel by surface transportation (land or water), or would be willing to travel by surface means to save money.

Ages of Travelers: Infant, child, youth, or senior? You need to specify.

Starting and Ending Dates: If you aren't leaving for at least a month, it's usually sufficient to specify what month you intend to depart and what month, at the latest, you intend to complete your travel on these tickets. However, it is counterproductive to specify an exact departure date if you don't have to leave on exactly that day.

Direction of Travel: International fares are not the same in opposite directions. Finding the cheapest price and route each way is a separate problem.

Openness to Modifications: Are you interested in possible modifications of your proposed itinerary if they would save you money?

Personal Schedule, Sequence, or Airline Requirements: Most people are willing to make specific stops in whatever order is cheapest. If you aren't, tell your agent.

Likelihood of Future Changes: How likely is it that you will need to change your departure dates, stopover cities, or route after buying your tickets?

Budget Limitations: Given a budget, an agent can suggest whether meeting it is likely to require you to cut a few, many, or certain especially expensive destinations, or whether it will leave you money to add more destinations if you want.

Class of Service: Unless you say otherwise, agents will assume that you want prices for third-class (coach or economy) air travel.

Excess Baggage: How much and what type of luggage you have can sometimes affect which tickets are the most cost effective.

tickets starting in the same city as the agency you are contacting for an estimate, but the agent doesn't know that. You may take it for granted that you want your tickets to include a flight back from what you specify as your final destination to where you started from, but not everyone does: a substantial proportion of long-haul tickets are one-way, or start and end in different places. Agents who specialize in around-the-world and multistop tickets are especially likely to get inquiries from all over and for flights from other places. I've gotten telephone calls from customers on every continent—in this case, *including* Antarctica— and it's not unusual for around-the-world agencies to get email from Asia asking about prices of flights from Europe to the Americas, or to have customers in the United States buy tickets starting in Australia and ending in Africa.

LIST OF DESTINATIONS

Include all the places you intend to go, even if you think they have to be ticketed as side trips or separate tickets. You may be right, but if you don't tell an agent, and it is possible to include flights to those places more cheaply in some other way, you've deprived yourself of the possibility of a pleasant surprise. Give the agent a chance, and in the majority of cases they'll be able to include, at less cost as part of through tickets, at least some additional destinations you thought would have to be side trips. Don't exclude domestic flights within your own or any other country from your request for an estimate.

Don't include a place in your list of destinations just because you think you have to change planes there to get to where you really want to go. There's more than one way to get almost anywhere, and the cheapest route and connection point may not be the most obvious one. By specifying a route or connection point, you may unwittingly rule out a cheaper one you didn't know about. To get the best advantage of the agent's expertise, list the places you really want to go, and let the agent figure out the best way to get you there.

Don't specify a particular airport (rather than a city or place name) unless your plans really require you to fly in or out of that airport rather than any other airport in the city or region. Doing this unnecessarily limits your agent's search. There may be more than one airport (even if you've only heard of one) and one you haven't heard of might be cheaper. If you say, "I want to fly to Heathrow," your agent will infer that you are unwilling to fly in or out of any of the other London-area airports (Gatwick, Stansted, Luton, or London City Airport) even if one of those would be much cheaper. Airline databases are organized by city names, not by island or region names. For example, databases list "Denpasar" (town name) rather than "Bali" (island name). So sometimes even a good agent may need to ask you the name of the city associated with the airport on a particular island or in a particular region. But if price is your most important consideration, let the agent suggest the cheapest airport in the area. You can always choose to pay more for a different airport if you don't like the agent's first, cheapest proposal.

If there are some places that are essential, and some that are less important, say so. One way to prioritize your goals is to flag each place on the list you give your travel agent as mandatory, optional, or incidental. An even better way is to divide your destinations into an A-list (mandatory), a B-list (highly desirable but inessential if the incremental cost is more than some threshold amount), and perhaps a C-list (worth stopping in if it doesn't add to the cost). Once you start working on your plans with a travel agent, you'll probably add some places to the C-list when your travel agent mentions them as free or minimal-cost additions, or as possible stopovers at connection points you'll have to pass through anyway to get to A-list and B-list destinations.

If you are trying to decide whether specific options are worth it, be as precise as you can about your priorities. "I'd like to stop in Hawaii if it wouldn't add too much to the price," doesn't give an agent much to go on. Where in Hawaii? What's too much? "Honolulu, if not more than US$500 additional" is more helpful.

SURFACE TRANSPORTATION

If there are specific sections of your trip that you want to travel by surface transportation (land or water), or would be willing to travel on the surface to save money, tell the agent. It's a good idea to identify which stretches you want to travel for the sake of the journey (a train trip across North America, Eurasia, or Australia, for example), and which you are planning to travel only in the hope of saving money. That way the agent won't waste time looking into flights for sections that you wouldn't want to fly, no matter what the price, but will know to tell you if surface travel in other places will cost as much as the additional cost of including flights. If you mention what means of surface travel you plan to use, an agent familiar with the region may be able to offer suggestions about its speed, cost, comfort, or feasibility. If you plan any major side trips by surface transportation, particularly to countries not included on your air route, it's a good idea to mention them as well, as those countries may turn out to have visa, onward ticket, or other entry requirements about which an agent can warn you.

STARTING AND ENDING DATES

If you aren't leaving for at least a month, it's usually sufficient for a first-order estimate to specify what month you intend to depart and what month, at the latest, you intend to complete your travel on these tickets. Sometimes you may need to specify when in the month you will depart (e.g., if that month is divided into several fare seasons), but it is counterproductive to specify an exact departure date if you don't have to leave on exactly that day.

If for some reason you need to leave on a specific date (not before and not after), you should say so explicitly, realizing that it may increase the price substantially. It can be a very expensive mistake to make schedule commitments on the ground before verifying prices and confirming reservations for flights. If price is an object, find out the cheapest route and airlines and their schedules, make reservations, and only then make business appointments or commitments for tours or meetings.

AGES OF TRAVELERS

Airlines define children as those who are traveling before their 12th birthday and infants as those who are traveling before their second birthday. Tell an agent before working out a price estimate or itinerary if you will be traveling with children and/or infants. The cheapest airlines and routes may be different for adults versus children and infants.

Do not assume that there is any standard discount for children, or that infants fly free on international flights, as they do on domestic flights within the United States.

Child Discounts: These vary widely. Full child fares are typically between 50 and 75 percent of full adult fares. But full fares are high, and discounted prices for adults are often lower than full child fares. Discounted adult fares are not necessarily combinable with any further discounts for children, so the cheapest ticket for a child may be at a discounted adult price. The cheapest ticket for a child can cost anywhere from 50 percent to 100 percent of the cost of the cheapest adult ticket on the same flights. Children not accompanied by an adult are carried only at the discretion of the airlines and, on most airlines, only on payment of an adult fare plus a service charge for looking after the unaccompanied child.

Infant Discounts: Infants must have paid tickets for all international flights on all airlines. Infant fares are typically 10 percent of full (not discounted) adult fares, and are subject to the same taxes as adult tickets. Some airlines, at their discretion, provide bassinets or other special accommodations (if space is available) for infants on long flights. But an infant ticket does not guarantee a bassinet or a separate seat; you must be prepared to hold an infant on your lap. If you aren't willing to do that, pay for a ticket for the infant at a child fare. Infant roundtrip tickets to distant international points, such as from the United States to Africa or South Asia and back, range up to US$200–400. Infant tickets around the world, on routes that would cost adults US$2,000–3,000 at discounted prices, might cost US$400–500.

Youth and Senior Citizen Discounts: Some airlines offer special youth or student fares and discounts for senior citizens. These are only occasionally cheaper than the cheapest consolidator tickets, but are sometimes easier to change, if space is available. As with children's discounts, student and senior citizen discounts are rarely combinable with other discounts: being a student or a senior citizen won't entitle you to any reduction of the price of a consolidator ticket. Tell an agent if you and/or anyone else in your party qualifies for student fares or senior citizen discounts, but don't expect it to make any great difference to the total price of a set of multistop tickets.

DIRECTION OF TRAVEL

International fares are not the same in opposite directions. This sometimes comes as a surprise to travelers accustomed to domestic fares, which are usually the same between the same cities in either direction. Between countries, the fare from B to A can be twice the fare from A to B, or vice versa. It's quite common for an airline to offer discounts in one direction on a particular flight, and no discounts at all the other way. Rules and conditions for flights in opposite directions can be different as well.

So the prices of a package of one-ticket tickets around the world, or on any international route, in opposite directions, are entirely independent of each other. Rarely are the same set of airlines and connecting points cheapest to the same destinations in opposite directions. Finding the cheapest price and route each way is a completely separate problem.

Most around-the-world travelers, in order to be in certain regions in certain seasons or for other reasons, have a preferred overall direction of travel (although as noted earlier, your route need not go in a continuous direction). If you truly don't care, or are open to reversing your general direction for a much better fare, say so. A good agent can usually tell fairly quickly if one direction or the other is likely to be dramatically cheaper, without the need to work out precise estimates for both.

Published RTW fares are an exception. They vary greatly according to the country where you start your trip, even on the same airlines and route. But starting from the same point, they are more or less the same in opposite directions around the world on the same route, with only modest variations determined by unidirectional taxes on specific flights.

PERSONAL SCHEDULE, SEQUENCE, OR AIRLINE REQUIREMENTS

If you have to make stops in a certain sequence, have already made specific schedule commitments—a tour, a cruise, a wedding, business appointments, whatever—or need to be on specific airlines or flights, tell the agent.

Most people are willing to make specific stops in whatever order is cheapest. If you aren't, tell your agent; that way time won't be wasted trying to save you money by rearranging your list of destinations.

The dates and even the months of all flights between the first and the last are usually irrelevant to the price estimate, unless it is essential for you to leave, or arrive in, certain places on exact dates. Because the cheapest flights may not operate on the particular days you need to travel, you may have to pay considerably more to travel on some days than others.

The less time you want to spend in each city, the less likely it is that the cheapest flights will operate on the days you want. This is the main reason why tickets for quick trips around the world, especially by business-people who want to spend only a couple of days in each city, usually end up costing more than tickets for much lengthier leisure trips. If you can, make your air travel reservations for such a trip before making your business appointments. Just tell the agent what you need: "I need one business day in Bangalore, three in Shenzhen, and two in Sydney, in whatever sequence would be cheapest."

In most cases, travel funded by the U.S. government must be on U.S.-based airlines wherever possible. Large parts of the world, including almost the entire continent of Africa, aren't served by any U.S. airline, and the rules in such cases are a bit arcane. If you are constrained by these or other rules to travel on certain airlines, it's essential for an agent to know to give you a meaningful price.

Finally, if you are meeting or traveling with someone else who already has tickets, this can both simplify the agent's task and greatly increase your cost. You can't count on finding seats on the same flights as your traveling companion for the same price they paid, or at any price; if you want to travel together it's important to make your reservations as soon as possible. If one of you is getting your ticket paid for by someone else, or with frequent flyer miles, and one will have to pay, try to work out both prices before either of you buys your ticket. If you start shopping for the second ticket only after the first one has been purchased, you may find out that it's on the airline that offers the smallest discounts or on a flight that has no more seats available.

BUDGET LIMITATIONS

Don't be coy about your budget. Given an approximate budget for air tickets, an agent can suggest whether meeting it is likely to require you to cut a few, many, or certain especially expensive destinations, or whether it will leave you money to add more destinations if you want. You may save an agent hours of research into prices and save yourself a few days' wait for an estimate that would be completely beyond your means.

CLASS OF SERVICE

Unless you say otherwise, agents will usually assume that you want prices for third-class (coach or economy) travel.

Upgrading from coach to second class (business or club class) or first class is neither simple nor inexpensive. The airlines and routes that are cheapest in coach may be completely different from those that are cheapest in first or business class. Discounts on first- and business-class tickets are generally smaller than coach discounts, and many airlines offer no discounts at all in first or business class. So first- and business-class passengers are even more likely than coach passengers to have to be willing to accept less-preferred airlines and routes in return for discounts. But the people who travel in business and first class tend to be the least flexible about airlines and routes, for the same reasons that they are flying in the front cabin in the first place.

Discounted business-class tickets typically cost at least twice as much as discounted coach tickets to the same set of cities, and usually even more than that. My rule of thumb is that discounted business-class tickets typically cost at least US$100 more per flying hour than discounted coach tickets. If you wouldn't be willing to pay twice as much for business class as for coach, or even more for first class, don't waste an agent's time researching the best first- or business-class prices.

Travelers accustomed to fully refundable, easily rerouted full-fare first- and business-class tickets should also keep in mind that discounted tickets in any class will be more difficult (if not impossible) to reroute or refund. Buying complex discounted tickets with substantial cancellation and change penalties is likely to prove a false economy for business travelers who often cancel trips at the last minute or change their destinations en route.

LIKELIHOOD OF FUTURE CHANGES

How likely is it that you will need to change your departure dates, stopover cities, or route after buying your tickets? It may be worth paying more for tickets that are more flexible with respect to any of these things, especially date changes, or buying tickets for only the part of your journey for which you are sure of your destinations and route.

Tickets with flexible dates for most or all flights are available for not too much more than fixed-date tickets on many routes. Tickets on which destinations can be changed are much harder to find at a discount. If an agent says that it will be no problem to completely reroute your trip, or change destinations, probe carefully to find out if that means tickets aren't going to be issued for each of your flights until just before your departure, allowing the agent to sit on your money, at your risk, in the interim.

EXCESS BAGGAGE

How much luggage you have can affect which tickets are best. As discussed later on in the *Baggage* chapter, there's no longer any standard free baggage allowance. Every airline is different, with some charging for even carry-on luggage while others allow a carry-on bag plus two checked 23-kg (50-lb) suitcases at no extra charge. The same airline may have different baggage allowances and excess baggage charges on different routes.

I've seen demonstrations by computerized reservation systems of software that would allow them to compare charges for baggage, and to factor those "ancillary fees" into their rankings and displays of fares. These have yet to be deployed, however, because airlines have refused to provide information about baggage charges or other fees in any standardized format.

What does this mean? Tell your travel agent if you expect to have an unusually large amount of luggage, so that they can try to avoid quoting you prices for tickets that would have especially high excess baggage fees. But don't expect an agent to be able to give you any automated estimate of total baggage charges for a complex or multi-airline itinerary. The only way to figure out the free baggage allowances and excess baggage charges is for you, after you have an estimate, to consult each airline individually to find out its baggage rules for that particular portion of your route.

Travelers with especially valuable, fragile, or important items in their luggage may prefer to pay more for more direct routes or ones with fewer plane changes, to minimize the possibility of loss, damage, or delay of their luggage. If you want the most direct flights, say so and be prepared to pay for them.

OPENNESS TO MODIFICATIONS

Are you interested in possible modifications of your proposed itinerary if they would save you money? *Rigid* is a dirty word in U.S. culture, so everyone is "flexible." Be realistic: how flexible are your plans? Would you be willing to fly from New York rather than Boston, to stop in Amsterdam rather than Paris, or to take a train from Bombay to Delhi if each of those choices would save you US$50? US$500?

If you could save considerable money by some slight change in your itinerary, a good agent should point that out when asked. If you are indifferent between several choices, you can say so: "leaving from wherever on the West Coast of the U.S. or Canada would be cheapest," "returning from wherever in Western Europe would be cheapest," "stopping in either Bangkok, Kuala Lumpur, or Singapore."

If you ask for the cheapest price, a good agent will suggest whatever direction of travel and sequence of stops would be cheapest. This is not always a consistent course from east to west or west to east, nor is it always the most obvious or direct route. Flights simply don't exist on many frequently requested routes. Most around-the-world itineraries require at least some connections in places that weren't in travelers' initial lists of requested destinations.

WHEN DO YOU PLAN TO BUY YOUR TICKETS?

If you specify a departure date within 3–6 months, you'll probably get a fairly precise estimate of what your tickets will cost if reservations can be made and confirmed and you are willing to pay within a week or two.

If you ask for estimates for tickets you don't actually plan to buy until months in the future, either because you aren't yet ready to buy or because it isn't yet within a year of your intended completion of travel, you may only be able to get a rough estimate of what your tickets will cost, and what routing and airlines are likely to be cheapest.

In the early stages of planning and budgeting, many people find that getting a rough preliminary price estimate can help them figure out what set of stopovers is likely to be both feasible and affordable. A good agent can also troubleshoot your proposed itinerary and give advance warning of potential problems as well as advice on how to avoid them: "You aren't allowed to cross between India and China by land," or "You aren't allowed into Indonesia or Australia unless you already have a ticket out of the country."

An agent can't and won't spend many hours figuring out exact current prices, all of which could change tomorrow, if you don't plan to buy your tickets until months later. What you can get is a rough estimate, usually to the nearest US$500. The simpler your itinerary and the closer you are to being ready to buy tickets, the more precise the estimate.

Because changes to published RTW fares must be approved by each of the airlines participating in the fare, they change much less frequently. But changes to surcharges, taxes, which flights have seats available for the RTW fare, or which airlines are members of the alliance can all affect the total price for tickets at such a fare, even if the "base" price is unchanged.

Interpreting Price Estimates

A price estimate for airline tickets should specify the airlines, the set and sequence of stops, any special rules or restrictions, which (if any) of the dates can be changed after ticketing, and at what (if any) cost.

Be aware that a price estimate for tickets is only an estimate, not a firm quote, no matter what language is used. Fares and ticket prices are not and cannot be guaranteed until tickets are paid for in full and issued. This holds true even if you make reservations directly with an airline for tickets at a published fare, receive a written or printed itinerary, and are told that your reservations will be held until a specified time. A reservation guarantee means the airline won't cancel your reservations, not that it won't change or discontinue the fare. All honest itineraries and invoices will say, somewhere in the fine print, "Fares are not guaranteed until ticketed."

Airlines' discount contracts with agents permit the airlines to change prices and terms at any time without prior notice. All estimated prices are subject to the availability of space, unless that agent has already made confirmed reservations for you. A common mistake is to compare estimates for prices on unnamed airlines, or on airlines or fares on which no space is available, with estimates for prices for which space is actually available. An estimated price for tickets on an unnamed airline or airlines means almost nothing. Don't presume that space is actually available until you have a confirmed itinerary showing specific flights and confirmation numbers.

An agent has to base an estimate on certain assumptions. Unless you tell them otherwise, they will probably assume that you want the cheapest available coach tickets on any airline, that you will be able to fix your dates before purchasing tickets, that you will use all your tickets within one year of the date you pay for them (not the date of departure), and that you are willing to accept nonrefundable tickets valid only on certain airlines.

REAL LIFE

You never know what "surcharges" or taxes you'll have to pay in addition to an advertised fare, or what fees an airline will tack on for things you expected would be included in the base price. On the Web, the only price that provides a meaningful basis for comparison shopping is the one on the final payment screen that says, "If you click here, your credit card will now be charged this amount" including any surcharges, taxes, and fees for checked baggage, seat assignments, and so forth. Similarly, you need to look closely at an emailed estimate, or probe carefully on the phone, to find out whether the price you've been given is the all-in total you'll have to pay. If you haven't gotten that far, but only looked at the initial price displays (and not all the fine-print footnotes), you don't really know how much a ticket will cost, or how much more you'll have to pay for your luggage when you check in for your flights.

If the price the agent quotes you has other restrictions, she or he should tell you. For example, it is sometimes much cheaper to use tickets that permit travel only during certain seasons or are valid only for six months rather than a full year.

Agents shouldn't suggest airlines or flights that they wouldn't take themselves. But if you don't like an agent's suggestions or would prefer a different routing or set of airlines and connection points, make your wants known.

The cheapest prices are usually for midweek departures (Monday through Thursday, or Sunday through Thursday, depending on the airline). You can expect to pay US$20–50 more to leave on a weekend (Friday through Sunday). But in some cases it makes no difference. If exact days make a big difference, ask on which departure days an estimate applies. If you ask for the lowest possible price, most discount agencies will include a discount for payment by cash or check in the estimate they give you. Ask if they accept credit or charge cards, and how much more the tickets will cost without the cash discount.

A good estimate may give a variety of options, such as different cities in which you could arrive, depart, or stopover for the same or a similar price. If you are interested, an agent should be able to tell you which additional stopovers an estimated price would allow at little or no additional cost, which other potentially interesting stopovers could be added at significant (but potentially worthwhile) additional cost, which stopovers could be eliminated for substantial cost savings, and/or which alternative stopover points could be substituted at the same price (e.g., "any one city in Europe served by Qatar Airways"). You should also be able to get an estimate of how substantial your savings might be if your stops or dates were rearranged (e.g., "The price would be US$200 less if you left before the end of May rather than in early June"). While you are still considering options, it's more reasonable to ask questions in this sort of "How would it affect the price if . . .?" form than to expect detailed or exact price estimates for multiple itineraries.

Finalizing Your Route

Depending on the degree of certainty in your plans when you first call an airline RTW desk or a travel agent, it can take several successive revisions—first of cities and routes and then of dates and flight times—to arrive at your final itinerary. You may want to do research about possible stopovers or alternate destinations you hadn't considered, or reconsider how important certain places or a certain sequence of stops are. This is one of the best reasons to start getting ticket price estimates well in advance, before you've locked yourself into any commitments.

Feel free to ask about alternatives ("About how much more would it cost to add a stop somewhere in Africa, and where would be cheapest?" "About how much, if anything, would I save if I skipped this stop?" "Is there somewhere else in that region that would be much cheaper?" "Is it feasible to take a train from Q to R, and would we save anything if we did?"). But keep in mind that changing even one stopover point can require completely different airlines and fares and an hour of research. Telling agents more about your plans and the purpose of your trip enables them to make appropriate suggestions for the itinerary with which you'll be happiest.

If you don't like an agent's proposal, say what's wrong. It's your trip, and the agent should want you to go away—and come back—happy. If you call a discount agency, they will probably start with the cheapest airlines and routes to your destinations. But that's no reason for you not to insist on more direct flights or different airlines, if they are available and you feel they are worth it. If an agent won't give you what you want, find one who will.

Keep in mind, though, that a good agent has probably started by finding the cheapest available airlines and routing, which is probably what you asked for. So the answers to all questions of the form, "Could I do something else instead?" are likely to begin, "Yes, but it will cost more." A skilled specialist can give you the best price in significant part by finding the cheapest set of airlines and sequence of stops. You can ask for prices on specific airlines if you need them, but specifying particular airlines and flights you want to take, or rearranging the stops in other than the cheapest sequence, can easily double or triple the price of your tickets.

Making Reservations

Once you have agreed on an estimated price for a specific route and set of airlines, chosen between any stopover alternatives, and decided on your preferred dates for each flight, the next step is to try to make reservations.

DEPOSITS

Some travel agents will ask for a deposit before they will make reservations for you. Such a deposit is usually not refundable unless the agent is unable to confirm reservations for you for the estimated price. If you change your mind after making a deposit, and decide not to travel or to get your tickets from another agent, the deposit goes to pay for the agency's consulting services. Typical deposits, if required, might range from US$50 per person for a simple one-way or roundtrip consolidator ticket to US$500 or more per person for tickets around the world.

A booking deposit is a service charge for the agency's time and advice. Any deposit that isn't applied to your tickets goes to the agency, not the airline; scheduled airlines do not accept partial payments or deposits for individual tickets. A deposit does not guarantee the fare. A ticket cannot be issued and the fare cannot be guaranteed until the airline is paid in full. (Fares aren't guaranteed even after tickets are issued. Airlines almost never assert their right to collect additional money for fare changes between ticketing and travel, although Allegiant Air—a small low-fare domestic U.S. airline in the United States—floated a proposal to do so in 2011.)

It is largely a matter of local custom whether agents require deposits for individual bookings on scheduled airlines. In the U.K., most agents require deposits before they will make reservations for any discounted tickets, even simple roundtrips. In almost all countries, deposits are required before agents will work on pricing or booking around-the-world or multistop international itineraries.

In the United States, it used to be rare for agents to ask for deposits. Since 1995, elimination of base commissions paid to travel agents in the United States has forced agents to reassess their business practices. Many now require deposits before investing a lot of time in complex itineraries, or charge hourly consulting fees. It's not unreasonable: most professionals require a retainer before they'll provide anything more than a brief initial consultation, and a travel agent may have to do a couple of hours' work just to give you an initial price estimate. If a travel agency doesn't require a deposit or charge an hourly consulting fee, they can only afford to give you limited free advice. You get what you pay for.

Deposits for groups work differently than deposits or service fees for individual tickets. Reserving a block of space for a group almost always requires a deposit to protect both the agent and the airline against having the space go empty if the group doesn't materialize. In such a case most of the group deposit does go to the airline, not the agent, and the airline may be willing to give a contractual guarantee of a price in exchange for an initial deposit of 10–25 percent of the total price and a commitment to a date for full payment. Get the details in writing before you make a deposit for a group. Charter operators also sometimes guarantee prices in exchange for partial payment, on condition that the final balance be paid by a specified date.

Unless there's a nonrefundable deposit, making reservations does not place you under any obligation whatsoever. You owe nothing to the airlines if you cancel or change your reservations prior to paying for tickets. An agent who charges you for changes to reservations, prior to full payment, is simply charging you for the time to make the changes.

NAMES ON TICKETS

You must specify each passenger's full name (matching whatever ID they will use while traveling, which almost always means their passport for international travel), gender, and date of birth at the time you first make your reservations. If you aren't sure exactly how your name is shown on your passport, check before you make reservations. It can be difficult or, if space on any of the flights has filled up, impossible to change names on reservations once they are made. Online, especially when you are trying to use a website in a language in which you aren't fluent, take special care to enter the names in the right order. Do they want LAST/FIRST MIDDLE or FIRST MIDDLE LAST?

Misspelled names on reservations and tickets, while unfortunate, are common, do not usually cause any problems, and are usually better left alone once reservations have been made. However, passengers traveling on tickets with a different surname (such as a married or maiden name) or substantially different given or taken name (such as a nickname) from the names on their passport may experience considerable inconvenience or delay en route. It is important to give full, correct passport names when you make your reservations.

Because the price of your tickets may depend greatly on whether space is available in particular booking classes on particular airlines on your travel dates, it is helpful to give an agent the legal names of all those who will be traveling when you first ask for an estimate, particularly if you want to leave soon or have very specific date requirements for certain flights. If an agent has your names and there are only a few seats left, the space can be held for you for the best fare. Otherwise you risk having the last seats reserved by someone else while the agent is waiting to get the names of the travelers.

CONFIRMED DATES VS. OPEN DATES

I strongly recommend that you make confirmed reservations for each flight before you pay for any of your tickets. That way you can be sure that the tickets you are buying will permit you to fly on an acceptable schedule on which space is available. It's more work for an agent to make reservations than just to issue open tickets, but it's almost always in your interest to have confirmed reservations whenever possible.

"Open" tickets are tickets issued with no reservations at all. Open tickets have a deceptive allure of freedom. If you have an open ticket, it's tempting to think that you can fly whenever you want. But that's not what an open ticket means. An open ticket allows you to fly only when the specified airline has a flight between the specified places on which space is available. If you insist on buying open-dated, unconfirmed, or waitlisted tickets, you assume all risk that space will not be available. You are not entitled to a refund or to any waiver of refund penalties if you can't use such a ticket because there are no seats available. If you do buy open tickets, try to make reservations as soon as you decide when you will want to travel.

When you want to use open tickets, you may find that all flights are full for some time (perhaps because of a local holiday, festival, season, or special event of which you were unaware) and thus that you have to wait for some time for space on an onward flight, particularly if such a flight operates only once or twice a week. Even some daily flights can be fully booked a month or two ahead at busy times of the year.

It's easier to change the dates of confirmed reservations than to make reservations to use open tickets. Once you buy an open ticket, the airline has your money whether you ever fly or not. If flights are full, the airline can keep your money, and never have to provide any services. Some airlines would rather confirm someone who hasn't yet paid for a ticket, and will pay only if

REAL LIFE

A few summers ago, two visitors to the United States came to me for help with British Airways tickets they had bought from an agent in Switzerland for flights from Geneva to San Francisco, with an open-dated return from Orlando to Geneva via London. After several weeks in California, they were driving cross-country to Florida and wanted to make reservations for their flights home at the end of August.

I had to tell them that throughout the summer from Orlando to London all seats on British Airways that were allocated to tickets like theirs, and during August all coach seats at any price, had been sold out for more than a month. Trying to get on a waiting list would have been pointless because their preferred flights were already far overbooked. Had they tried to make reservations for specific dates prior to buying their tickets, they would have discovered the tickets were virtually useless for their plans. As it was, their only choices were to buy expensive new tickets home on another airline (which they couldn't afford), to go home after September when seats were available (which vacation schedules wouldn't permit), or to go home more than a month earlier than they had planned (which is what they decided to do).

they are confirmed, than confirm someone who already has an open ticket. A few airlines are notorious for telling people with open tickets that no seats will be available for months—even when their planes have lots of empty seats—and making them pay large sums to upgrade their tickets, or buy entirely new tickets at higher fares, unless they want to wait forever. If you have a confirmed reservation and want to change it, the airline knows it will have to provide the transportation you've paid for, one day or another, and has no reason not to allow you to make a change if space is available.

WHEN TO BUY OPEN TICKETS

I would buy open tickets without confirmed reservations only if it's impossible to obtain confirmation in advance, such as for flights farther in the future than the range of the airline's reservation system (usually 10–11 months into the future), or when the airline will only give confirmation locally at the point of departure, or on some especially remote routes flown by airlines that don't have offices in the United States or don't participate in computerized reservation systems. These are circumstances to buy open tickets by necessity, not by choice.

If a travel agent is reluctant to reserve specific flights for you, take it as a warning that the airline's schedule is such that if you found out the actual schedule, you wouldn't want those tickets (e.g., the only flights involve a three-day layover in a dangerous, expensive hellhole), and/or that space is not likely to be available on the dates you are likely to want to fly, and/or that the agency has cut its profit margin so thin that it can't afford to take the few minutes to make your reservations (which is a pretty good indication that it'll be even less willing to take time to help you if you have problems once it has your money).

Some travelers buy open tickets because they are afraid that if they buy tickets with reservations for specific dates, they might get stuck with fixed-date tickets by an agent who promises them changeable tickets. If you mistrust an agent that much, buy your tickets elsewhere. Pay a little more to someone you trust to provide the promised tickets and to make confirmed reservations.

SCHEDULES, TIMES, AND FLIGHT DURATIONS

If you make reservations in advance, you'll be forewarned as to the frequency, times, duration, and likely ease or difficulty of changing your flights. Many people overestimate the frequency of international flights and underestimate the amount of time they will spend in transit in the course of a trip around the world.

If you are going directly from one side of the planet to the other, you may be obliged to spend a night or two en route, even on the fastest and most expensive flights. Flying time for some scheduled *nonstop* flights is more than 18 hours. Even the most direct routes between many cities take two to three days of total travel time. If you are accustomed to 30–60-minute connections between domestic flights in the United States, don't be surprised to find that 4–18-hour connections between international flights are common. In parts of the Third and Fourth World, flying can be an all-day project no matter how short the flight: you go to the airport first thing in the morning and hope that by the end of the day you have gotten to your destination.

Most Long-Haul Flights Operate at Most Once a Day. Many flights, and on some significant routes the only flights, operate less often, sometimes as infrequently as once a week. If there is daily service on a route, it is likely to be at the same time each day. "What day(s) of the week does that airline fly between those cities?" is usually a more appropriate question than, "What times are their flights on such-and-such a day?"

Most people, especially independent travelers without advance hotel reservations, find morning arrivals more convenient than evening arrivals. Similarly, most people prefer late-night departures to late-night arrivals. If there is more than one flight on the day you want, most thoughtful agents will book you on a morning flight or an overnight flight that arrives in the morning, unless you tell them in advance that you prefer otherwise.

If a competent agent has booked you on a flight that arrives at 0200 (2 A.M.), it's probably because there is no alternative for the same price. Many factors other than passenger convenience influence airline schedules, such as optimum use of expensive airplanes and competition between airlines for gates and landing, takeoff, and customs slots at preferred times. The cheapest airlines sometimes get the worst time slots.

Flights between Northern and Southern countries are usually scheduled to optimize connections for passengers from the North who generate most of the revenue, resulting in less than optimal arrival and departure times in Southern cities. Indira Gandhi International Airport in New Delhi, for example, is busiest between 2400 and 0300 (midnight and 3 A.M.), and half-deserted at midday.

All Times Shown in Airline Timetables and on Itineraries Are in the Official Local Time. Some countries enforce the use of an official time at variance with local custom. Timetables in the USSR were in Moscow time across 10 time zones. China continues to decree the use of Beijing time for all official purposes, including tickets and printed timetables, throughout its possessions, which would otherwise span four time zones.

In East Turkestan, where the sun may rise at 0300 (3 A.M.) and set at 1500 (3 P.M.) Beijing time, local people use several inconsistent varieties of unofficial "Xinjiang time." There are similar situations in Tibet. "What time is it?" in these areas is a highly politicized question, and the answer may depend on your informant's ethnicity (Han Chinese, Uighur, Tibetan, or whatever) and political allegiance as well as the proximity of the secret police. It can be hard to get a straight answer; some Han Chinese, especially people in state enterprises (such as tourist offices and state-owned hotels) are reluctant to admit the existence of local time. But you should always verify which type of time (Beijing time or some other time) is meant.

Timetables and tickets in East Africa are always in official ("European" style) time, even where local people all think in the alternate numbering of the hours referred to as "African," "Swahili," or "Ethiopian" time. (See the section on time systems in the *Life on the Road* chapter.)

Standard Itineraries Don't Show Flight Duration. Flying time for a particular flight is hard to figure out without being certain of the time differences between departure and arrival cities. Ask the airline or your travel agent to give you a separate printout of actual flight durations and times and the locations of intermediate stops on multistop flights (some CRSs permit this), or have them go over this information with you.

Itineraries Will Show Whether or Not Flights Are Nonstop, but Don't Necessarily Show Whether You Have to Change Planes. Under current law in the United States and most other countries, airlines are permitted to give a single flight number to two or more connecting flights, and to advertise the set of flights thus designated as a direct or through flight, despite the change(s) of planes. One of the two connecting flights may even be operated by a different airline.

The airlines' own telephone reservation agents are the worst offenders in not telling you that you will have to change planes. "Oh, yes, we fly from A to B" from an airline agent may well mean that they fly from A to their hub at C, and from C to B, with a change of planes and a 24-hour layover, at your own expense, in C. Even if they say, "We have a flight from A to B," that flight may well involve what is euphemistically referred to as a "change of equipment" at C. Most people would describe this as a set of connecting flights by way of C, and certainly not as a direct or through flight. If you aren't sure, ask specifically whether a through or direct flight is on the same plane.

Why do the airlines do this? Airlines that don't really have direct flights between two places, but who want make the connecting flights by way of their hubs or gateways appear more attractive, give connecting flights through flight numbers to compete with airlines that really do have direct (same-plane) service. It's cheaper to add labels than to add flights. By having flights from San Francisco, Los Angeles, and Chicago to New York, and from New York to London, and by giving the New York–London flight four flight numbers (one number from New York to London, and one through flight number including each of the connecting flights from San Francisco, Los Angeles, and Chicago), an airline can pretend to offer direct service from each of the four cities while actually paying to operate only one trans-Atlantic flight.

This fits the textbook definition of fraud. Airlines label connecting flights as direct or through flights for the sole purpose of misleading people and hiding the implications of the change of planes. The worst case is a flight with a change of equipment at the point of arrival to a country, such as a flight from Europe to the West Coast of the United States with a change of equipment at an airport in the East or Midwest. You have to get off the plane, claim your luggage, go through customs and immigration, check your luggage back in, and then get on another plane to complete the flight. You might even have to transfer to a different terminal, especially if one leg is a "codeshare" operated by a different airline. Such flights should not be called direct.

Travel agents didn't come up with this scheme and can't do much about it. Airlines won't always permit travel agents to book connecting flights as two separate flight numbers. In the United States, the consumer fraud divisions of several states have sought to stop the labeling of connecting flights as direct, but regulation of the airline industry has been preempted by the federal government, which has as yet taken no action on this.

I encourage travelers to complain to the airlines, and to the federal government, whenever you find yourself on "direct" flights that aren't. The same goes for other airline scams like advertisements for "half roundtrip" or "one-way based on roundtrip" (huh?) prices, or advertised prices at which no seats are really available. These practices wouldn't be allowed in any other industry, and much of the blame rests with government regulators who have chosen to look the other way as systematic fraud has become standard operating procedure in airline marketing.

Tickets and Itineraries Won't Necessarily Show the Name of the Airline That Actually Operates the Flight. A large and increasing number of "codeshare" flights are labeled with one or more flight numbers of airlines other than the one that operates the flight. Airlines claim code sharing and alliances enable them to offer better services such as through ticketing, baggage transfers, and frequent-flyer mileage credits between alliance partners. But that's a lie. None of those services requires alliances or code sharing. The international standards that the airlines themselves established decades ago permit any airlines, not just alliance partners, to publish through fares and establish interline ticketing and baggage-transfer agreements. Any travel agency can sell tickets on any airline that participates in the industry-standard financial clearinghouse and joint agency accreditation scheme, including tickets at a single through fare for a multi-airline journey. And even alliance members often give frequent-flyer mileage credit for travel on nonalliance airlines, without code sharing.

Code sharing is unnecessary for, indeed irrelevant to, any legitimate purpose or actual service. Code sharing doesn't enable an airline to fly to any more places. It just enables the airline to mislead travelers into thinking that they fly to places they don't. As with direct flights that require a change of planes, I call that fraud, and encourage those of you who encounter it in the United States to complain to the Department of Transportation (see the *Resource Guide*).

You check in for most codeshare flights at the counter or gate of the operating airline, not the airline whose name appears on your tickets. Codeshare flight numbers aren't always posted at airports, or are only posted in the proper terminal (which you can't find without knowing which airline operates the flight). Ask what airline to check in with, at which terminal, when you call to reconfirm each flight, especially if you think it might be a codeshare or the flight number is four digits long (which is frequently a clue that it's a codeshare flight).

WAITING LISTS

If it isn't possible to confirm reservations for the price you want on the flights you want, and you aren't in any hurry to buy your tickets, the airline or a travel agent may be able to put you on a waiting list for one or more flights or give you an itinerary showing that certain flights are on request or not yet confirmed. (Or maybe not—some airlines now allow waitlisting only for their highest fares.)

If only a few reservations on each flight are allocated to the cheapest tickets, you may be waitlisted for a cheap "booking class" on a flight on which only a few people are confirmed, and which is likely to end up flying half empty. That you are on a waiting list for a particular booking class and corresponding fare does not mean that a flight is full or sold out.

Airlines won't tell you, and won't usually tell travel agents, exactly how many people are on the waiting list, or how far overbooked a flight is. The more closely agents work with particular airlines, and the more tickets they sell on a particular route, the better their ability to get you confirmed and the better their sense of your chances of confirmation.

Confirmation of requested or waitlisted flights is never a sure thing. If the airline or travel agent can't confirm you within a few days, give up and find another option, even if it's more expensive. If you can't be confirmed, it doesn't matter how low the price would be if you were confirmed. The only prices that ultimately matter are those for which reservations can be confirmed.

A common problem is to be given a low price estimate, get on a waiting list, wait for weeks without confirmation in hope of a really cheap ticket if you are confirmed, and end up not getting confirmed for that ticket and having to buy a much more expensive ticket at the last minute. Some bad agents deliberately quote prices on flights they know they have little or no chance of confirming, in order to get you hooked into a form of bait-and-switch in which they will end up selling you a much costlier ticket later on.

If a travel agent has placed you on a waiting list, you may be able to improve your chances of getting confirmed by calling the airline yourself. But you should only do so after the travel agent has put you on the list, and only if they are having trouble getting you confirmed. Do not be surprised, and do not argue, if the airline mentions that the reservation was made by an agency other than the one you dealt with. It may have been necessary or required for your agent to make the booking through a wholesaler either as a condition of the fare or to use "block" space held by another agent or wholesaler on an otherwise sold-out flight.

If you are confirmed on less-preferred but acceptable flights or dates, you can get on the waiting list for your preferred alternatives at the same time. As long as your tickets permit date or flight changes, you can stay on the waiting list up until the time of the flight, even after you have your tickets. Just keep checking with the airline at intervals. If and when the waitlist clears, you'll have to choose between the original and the newly confirmed flights. Airlines won't hold confirmed reservations on more than one option.

DON'T MAKE YOUR OWN RESERVATIONS

Don't try to make your own reservations directly with an airline and then try to shop around for the best price at which to have them ticketed. Doing this reduces your chances of getting the best price, and may result in all your reservations being entirely canceled without prior warning.

There are many booking classes, and there is no way you can tell in which class to make reservations for the cheapest fare. The cheapest published fare may be booked in one class, the cheapest discounted fare in another. And if a travel agent makes reservations for you, they may be able to use block space held by them or by a consolidator for all or part of your itinerary.

Some airlines automatically cancel all reservations, whether or not confirmed, of anyone found to be holding multiple bookings. You and your travel agent(s) may be given no warning before both sets of your duplicate reservations are canceled. If you've already made reservations directly with an airline or another travel agency, that should be the first thing you tell a new travel agent. If you don't, the new agent may make another booking for you, and both your reservations may be canceled.

IF YOU CAN'T BE CONFIRMED

Price estimates for tickets made before you have reservations are best-case estimates of what the price will be if you can be confirmed in the appropriate booking classes on flights on the specified airline(s) and route. An estimate is no guarantee that space will be available for that price. Travel agents should give realistic estimates of probable availability, but they are sometimes overly optimistic, or just guess wrong.

If you can't be confirmed for the estimated price, you will have to choose either to pay more than estimated for tickets on the same route, or revise your route or choices of airlines. An agent will probably give you a new proposed itinerary, based on whatever is closest to the original estimate in schedule, route, and price. You are under no obligation to accept it, and there are probably other possibilities. If these choices involve other stopover possibilities, you may want or need to do further destination research before you decide. In the worst case, you may have to go back and forth several times with the agent, at successively higher prices, before you find an acceptable price and routing for which you can actually be confirmed.

It's annoying to have to revise your plans just when you thought you had made your decisions and were ready to make your reservations. Just don't blame it on the agent—the most tempting target because they, not the airline, are the one you are dealing with directly—unless you suspect them of deliberately misleading you about the likely prospects for confirmation. If you suspect this, go elsewhere for your tickets. This happens often with many bad agencies; indeed, it's their standard modus operandi and the classic form of travel agency bait-and-switch. (The ongoing dilemma of legitimate agencies is whether to advertise or estimate prices they know aren't likely to be available, or whether to state prices that will appear excessive compared to bait-and-switch ads.) But don't jump to conclusions. Travel agents don't control seat allocations and only get what the airlines give them to sell. Predicting when which booking classes will be available on which airlines can be an exercise in crystal ball–gazing. You have to rely on your own judgment of the agent's and agency's integrity.

Paying for Tickets

When your reservations are confirmed, the airline or travel agency will give you an itinerary showing the flights, dates, times, airlines, price, and deadline for payment. Airlines keep shortening their time limits, but you should have at least a day to review and consider the itinerary before you have to pay. In no case, even if you are in a rush, should you authorize payment before you have seen a complete itinerary.

If full payment is not received by the deadline, the agent or the airline may cancel your reservations, although they can be rebooked if the space and the fare are still available.

You can't expect an agency to release tickets until a personal or company check has cleared, which can take 5–10 business days for out-of-state checks within the United States. For tickets needed on short notice you may have to pay by credit or charge card, cashier's check (bank check), traveler's checks, money order, electronic funds transfer, or cash.

If you pay for discounted tickets by credit or charge card, you'll probably have to pay 3–6 percent more than if you pay by cash or check. This may seem strange, because the airlines charge the same amount no matter how you pay, but it is a consequence of the nature of discount tickets.

When you buy tickets at a published fare, the actual charge to your card is made by the airline, which receives the full amount and eventually pays part of it to the agency as its commission. Because the airlines have extremely large volumes of business, they are able to negotiate very low fees, as a percentage of their charges, from the credit- and charge-card companies and banks. The fees they pay are close enough to their costs of processing check payments, and collecting on bad checks, that they choose to absorb any slight difference in total costs.

But if an airline processes the charge, they have to charge the official fare. In order to charge your card less than the published fare, a travel agency has to process the charge through its own merchant account, not through the airline. Banks regard travel agencies as prone to disputes and chargebacks by

REAL LIFE

Paper tickets have many advantages over electronic tickets. And for technical reasons, some tickets—even on major airlines—still must be issued in paper form, so you can't assume that all tickets will electronic. But you'll rarely be given a choice. If you don't already have a paper ticket (an actual ticket, not just a confirmation), choose the "print receipt" option whenever it's offered at an automated check-in station, or ask a ticket clerk or travel agency to print you a copy of the "passenger receipt coupon" for each ticket. That's the only sure way to prove you have a ticket if the airline's computers are down or they lose the electronic record of your e-ticket, as airlines do far more often than they will admit. A paper ticket (or, failing that, a printed copy of the passenger receipt coupon) will also give you a better chance of being able to use your ticket on a different airline in case of a canceled or rescheduled flight, airline strike, or other problems.

customers that are costly for them to investigate, and that may lead to losses that the banks have to absorb. In some countries it's almost impossible for a travel agency to get a credit-card merchant account. As smaller businesses, travel agencies have to pay much higher percentage fees for processing of charges than do the airlines, even when they can get their own merchant accounts. If a travel agency charges US$100 to your card, they only get US$94–97; the bank with which they have their merchant account keeps the other 3–6 percent as what it calls its "discount." The agency doesn't get the money instantly, either; it takes 2–5 business days.

Profit margins on discounted tickets aren't always enough to permit agencies to absorb the bank's credit- and charge-card discounts. In order to offer the option of credit-card payment, they have to charge what amounts to a surcharge.

Here's where the real problem comes in: credit-card companies don't want consumers to realize that paying by credit card costs more money, even if it does. Court challenges have compelled them, most reluctantly, to permit merchants to give discounts for cash or check payment, but have thus far upheld their right to prohibit surcharges for payment by credit card. What's the difference? Semantic. Travel agencies, like gas stations and other narrow-margin merchants, are required to use confusing and evasive-sounding language about cash discounts, rather than credit-card surcharges. It isn't their idea, and they don't like it. If you don't like it either, complain to the credit-card companies and urge them to allow credit-card surcharges to be honestly and plainly labeled as such.

For your own protection, never authorize credit-card charges by phone, especially for as large and complex a purchase as a set of tickets around the world. If you want to pay by credit card, mail, fax, or email (if the agency will accept a digital signature) the agency a written authorization attached to a copy of your itinerary, so you have it in writing both how much you agreed to pay and what tickets you are supposed to receive.

If you are authorizing a charge over the Internet, print the complete itinerary, terms and conditions, and charge authorization (or save complete screen captures of these Web pages, and make sure you can open the saved copies) before you push the "buy" button. More than once I have needed these printouts or copies to dispute an unauthorized or improper charge from an airline.

The agent may be able to issue some of your tickets as soon as your payment has cleared. Others may have to be issued by the airlines or by wholesalers around the world. Don't expect to get tickets on the spot, even if you pay cash, unless you've been specifically told, in advance, that this will be possible. It can take two or three weeks to get all the components of a set of around-the-world tickets issued, if portions have to be issued by consolidators abroad. If you pay a month in advance, this gives you a safety margin of about a week for unexpected delays in ticket issuance or shipping.

Regardless of whether you are dealing with a travel agent or directly with an airline, always make absolutely sure, for each flight, whether you have an electronic or paper ticket. Some airlines and some itineraries still require paper tickets. Assume your tickets are all electronic, show up for a flight without your paper ticket, and you could have to pay for a new ticket on the spot if you want to fly.

Paper tickets are preferable, but are being phased out by the airlines in favor of electronic tickets. That leaves you little recourse if, as happens regularly, you show up at the airport and the airline can find no record of your e-ticket in their database. You should get a printed confirmation with a reference number for each e-ticket. If possible, get a printout of the entire "passenger receipt" coupon showing the full details of the e-ticket: "fare basis" code, fare calculation, endorsements, etc.

It shouldn't take more than a month to get your tickets from a reliable, honest agent, barring unusual complications. The most justifiable reason for delay, especially with complex tickets or one where any portion comes from overseas, is that one of the prices has changed and a different source or fare construction has to be found. Customers find this hard to understand, but it isn't always possible to email an overseas supplier to verify every price each time an estimate is given to a potential customer. Even if it is verified at the time of the estimate, or at the time of the customer's payment to the agency, it could change by the time the agent's payment reaches the supplier, by air courier, 2–3 business days later.

Like it or not, fares and prices change constantly, and no estimate is or can be guaranteed until the tickets are actually issued. Good agencies will absorb small price fluctuations in the interest of keeping customers' business and good will, but sometimes a price change greatly exceeds what can be covered from the agency's markup. You'll be offered a choice of paying more to cover the price increase, or getting your money back.

Once the agent has your tickets, you should either pick them up in person or have them sent to you by messenger, Express Mail, FedEx, or the like. A complete set of tickets around the world will usually include at least some paper tickets. Don't trust airline tickets to regular mail.

Proofread your tickets, one flight coupon at a time. Mistakes are made by agents, airlines, in transmission of messages between computers, and in misunderstandings of what you, the customer, wanted. Minor discrepancies in flight times on tickets are nothing to worry about—times on tickets are only advisory, and over the course of a long trip are prone to change some, anyway—but differences in travelers' names, flight numbers, dates, airlines, or cities should be brought to the agent's attention immediately. Time is of the essence if some errors are to be corrected without further expense. If you don't understand anything on your tickets, ask the agent to explain it.

With paper tickets, you should also double-check your tickets after you check in for each flight, before you leave the counter. Make sure the correct flight coupon, and only the correct flight coupon, has been taken. It's surprisingly common for a harried ticket agent to tear out the wrong coupon, or for two coupons to stick together and get pulled for one flight. Once you leave the counter, such a mistake can be almost impossible to correct without buying new tickets.

Amazingly, airlines claim the right to increase fares even after tickets are issued, but I've only heard of two that ever do, and then only if tickets are issued "open," i.e., without confirmed reservations for specific dates. I assume that they are trying to prevent regular business travelers from beating fare increases by stocking up on undated tickets for future travel just before scheduled fare increases. Once you have confirmed reservations and tickets in hand, but not before, you can consider your price to be, for all intents and purposes, fixed.

In consideration of other travelers, you should tell any agent or airline with whom you have made reservations if you decide not to use them, so that they can release the space to someone else who wants it. Don't assume that your reservations will be canceled automatically. They probably will be cancelled eventually, but it's only courteous to cancel the reservations as soon as you decide.

Reconfirming Reservations

As soon as you have your tickets, you should call each airline to reconfirm your reservations—that is, to tell the airlines that you will definitely be using your reservations. They might tell you that you don't have to reconfirm reservations at all, or that you have to reconfirm again closer to the flight date, but it's never too soon. Reconfirm early and often until each flight.

You should reconfirm your reservations for each flight at least 72 hours before that flight departs. If the airline has not heard from you by then, they are entitled to (and you should assume that they will) cancel all your reservations for all the flights in your itinerary and give your seats to someone else. Your tickets will usually remain valid, but you will have to start over from scratch in making new reservations.

The most common misunderstanding of reconfirmation is to think that you are supposed to reconfirm *within* 72 hours of the scheduled departure time, and thus deliberately to wait to try to reconfirm until after your reservations have already been canceled for failure to reconfirm. You should call more than 72 hours ahead, not less than 72 hours.

If your tickets are issued less than 72 hours before your departure, you should call the airlines as soon as you get your tickets. In such cases the agent should reconfirm your reservations as soon as tickets are issued or received, but all airlines prefer (and some require) that you reconfirm directly, not merely through your travel agent.

If you will be connecting directly from one airline to another, particularly if the first airline has an office in the United States and the second does not, the first airline may be able to send a message to reconfirm your reservations on the second airline as well. Whenever possible, though, it is best to call each airline separately.

Airlines never charge for reconfirming reservations. If airline employees ask you for money to make or reconfirm reservations, they are asking for a bribe. A few bad airlines are notorious for grossly overbooking their flights and then only reconfirming passengers who pay hefty bribes.

Most airlines operating in the United States and Canada have toll-free 800, 866, 877, or 888 numbers for reconfirmation. These numbers are all listed with directory assistance at 800-555-1212. If the airline doesn't have a listing with toll-free directory assistance, and you can't find their local reconfirmation numbers on their website, ask your travel agent when you get your tickets.

It's a good idea to reconfirm all of your flights before your first departure, if the airlines have offices or representatives where you are, just to be sure that you really have reservations. Doing so does not, however, obviate the necessity to reconfirm your next onward reservations at each point where you stop over, at least 72 hours before continuing your journey. Suppose you fly from A to B, spend a week in B, and then fly on to C. At some time after arriving in B, and at least 72 hours before your flight from B to C, you must contact the airline on which you plan to fly from B to C to reconfirm your intention of using your reservations on that flight.

It is usually easiest to reconfirm your departure from a city if you do so at the airport when you first arrive, thus avoiding any problems using the local telephone system or communicating in the local language. It's sometimes a bit of a nuisance—you may have to go around from the arrival area to the departure area to find a ticket counter where you can reconfirm your onward flight, just when you are eager to get out and about in the new place—but I find it's usually worth the effort to reconfirm on arrival.

You can reconfirm your reservations either in person at the airline's counter at the airport or a city ticket office, or by phoning the airline's local phone number. Local telephone numbers for reconfirmation of reservations in each city an airline serves are usually listed on ticket jackets and airline websites, and are available at airline ticket counters and city offices. Have your tickets handy when want to reconfirm your reservations, because the airline may need to verify your ticket numbers, booking class, or other information on your tickets. If there's a language barrier, it may be helpful to know that "RR" is the status code for "reconfirmed" reservations.

It can be difficult or impossible to reconfirm your onward reservations while in remote areas. If you will be trekking in Nepal, for example, and will return to Kathmandu just in time for your onward flight, you will need to reconfirm your reservations before you leave on your trek, or arrange for the trekking company to do it for you.

If you are staying more than a few days, it's a good idea to check again to see if the time or date of your flight has been changed, and to verify when you must check in. Airlines try to notify passengers of schedule changes—that's why they always ask for a local phone number when you reconfirm. But budget travelers often don't know where they are staying and don't have a reliable fixed phone number.

Some airlines will not reconfirm you unless you give them a local phone number. If you have to, make one up, or give them the number of some big hotel (whether or not you are staying there) picked out of a guidebook. The risk of not being notified of a last-minute schedule change is preferable to the near-certainty of having your reservations canceled if you don't reconfirm. Remember that if the airline doesn't have a way to notify you of last-minute changes it's your responsibility to keep checking with them regularly, up until the day and time of the flight, for possible changes.

Insist on reconfirming your reservations, even if the airline says it isn't required. Eliminating the reconfirmation requirement is a labor-saving measure for the airline, not a service to passengers who need to know, as far in advance as possible, if their reservation has been lost or their flight has been rescheduled. And no matter what the airline tells you, they still might cancel your reservations if you don't reconfirm them. If the flight is over-booked, those who haven't reconfirmed will usually be the first to have their reservations canceled.

Airlines do not guarantee their schedules. If you are booked on a dozen flights over a period of six months, you can expect that the schedules for two or three of them will change in that six months. Schedules for international flights are rarely changed more than a few hours at a time, but you cannot rule out the possibility that the weekly Tuesday-morning flight on which you were booked could have become the weekly Friday-night flight by the time you fly.

Airlines use robots to rebook passengers when flights are canceled or changed, to save themselves the cost of rebooking people by hand. But the robots usually work one flight at a time, ignoring connections. It's routine to find that you have been automatically "protected" on flights that no longer connect. If you don't reconfirm your reservations and the exact schedule, you may not find out about problems like this in time to get them corrected.

Dates, times, and flight numbers may all change. Each time you re-confirm, verify the flight number, date, and departure time and those of any flights to which you will be connecting without an intermediate stopover of more than 72 hours. Don't just ask "Am I still confirmed?" or you may be told "Yes" without being told on what flight or when you are confirmed. Especially with a flight that might be a codeshare, or when departing from an airport with more than one terminal, verify with which airline and at which terminal you should check in, and how long before the flight you need to check in. Most airlines require you to check in at least two hours before international flights, but more time is required for special security checks on certain routes.

Reconfirming your reservations does not prevent you from later chang-ing them if you decide to move on sooner or later than you had planned. If you change your reservations, however, you must be sure to reconfirm your new reservations. If you have reservations and decide not to use them (usu-ally because you have decided to take an earlier or later flight), especially if you change your mind when you have already reconfirmed, please be con-siderate enough of others to call and cancel your reservations. Everyone on the waiting lists for that flight will thank you. No-shows (people who make reservations but don't show up for flights) force airlines either to overbook or to fly with empty seats. Overbooking inconveniences travelers when the airlines, forced to guess, guess wrong about how many people won't show up. Empty seats force airlines to raise prices to everyone to cover their costs. Don't be a no-show.

If you already have your tickets and change from one flight to another, you can reconfirm your new reservations at the same time as you make them. Reservations for flights leaving within 72 hours should be reconfirmed at the same time as they are made.

Finally, when you reconfirm your reservations it is a good idea to ask each airline for its "record locator" for your reservation. This is a string of 4–6 letters and/or numbers that identifies your reservation with that airline; you will have a different record locator for your reservations with each airline. Having your record locator will help the airline find your reservation more quickly if you need to make changes.

SPECIAL SERVICE REQUESTS

Some airlines require you to print your own boarding pass online before you go to the airport. Others require you to do just the opposite, and get your boarding pass at the airport. Ask when you call to reconfirm your flight. You can usually request specific seating when you make or reconfirm your reservations, but on no airline are seat assignments guaranteed, even if you are issued a boarding pass in advance. Airlines always reserve the right to substitute equipment—a larger or smaller plane, a different model, or one with the seats arranged differently—at any time, regardless of what is shown in timetables or on itineraries.

Even airlines that reserve most seats in advance generally assign certain seats only at check-in. Many travelers prefer the "bulkhead seats" in the front row of each section of the cabin, which have extra leg room. But these are often assigned only at the gate, and priority for them is given to passengers with special needs for extra space (e.g., with a broken leg in a cast or an infant in a bassinet).

More and more airlines charge extra for certain seats, or for the privilege of reserving any specific seat. "Ancillary fees" like these are a growing profit center for airlines around the world. With the cheapest tickets, be prepared to take whatever seats are left after frequent flyers and those who paid for "preferred" seats have taken their pick.

Some people prefer aisle seats, so they can get up to walk around, fidget, stretch, or use the toilet without having to disturb their seatmates. Others prefer window seats so they can spread out, settle in, and work or sleep uninterrupted. Some find being near the window enhances their fear of flying, and prefer to be in the middle section of a twin-aisle widebody. Others, like me, think they aren't getting their money's worth if they are missing out on the unique perspective of the view from the air. ("I believe that anyone who flies in an airplane and doesn't spend most of his time looking out the window wastes his money," wrote Marc Reisner in the introduction to *Cadillac Desert*.) It's a good thing our desires differ: if we all preferred the window, or all preferred the aisle, fewer of us could be satisfied with our seat assignments.

Frankly, I've never understood the fuss some people make about airplane seating preferences. Unless you are a business traveler on a short trip to a distant place, your time in planes is a small fraction of your time on the road. No car or bus seats, and in most places only first-class train seats, are as comfortable as third-class seating on most airlines. I've spent 18 hours in the worst seat on a Boeing 747 (the one next to the emergency door where the normal knee and leg space is occupied by the rigid housing for the inflatable escape slide/life raft that protrudes into the cabin from the inside of the door). I'd have chosen another seat if I could (I was traveling on a discounted ticket that didn't allow me to prereserve a seat) but even the worst seat on any airliner isn't that bad.

If you want special meals, you should request them when you reconfirm your reservations, as many airlines will not honor special meal requests made less than 48 or 24 hours before departure. Special meal options vary by airline. Some airlines, for example, have as many as four choices of vegetarian meals (Chinese, Hindu, Western, and ovo-lacto) while others have none.

If you will require special seating, assistance, or services for any reason, you should let the airline know your needs as early as possible, the more so the more unusual or difficult to accommodate your needs are. It's best to make any requests yourself, directly to the individual airlines, as not all interfaces between airlines' and agents' computer systems can be relied on to correctly transmit special service requests, or responses to them. Airlines automatically tell people whose requests aren't on record, "Your travel agent didn't request this properly." Usually, in my experience, the travel agent did request it, but the message wasn't received or acted on properly. If special services are important to you, it's worth calling the airline to make them directly, and to make sure they are understood.

FREQUENT-FLYER MILEAGE CREDIT

Not all discounted tickets are eligible for frequent-flyer mileage credit, but many are. If you want to receive credit in a frequent-flyer program for certain flights, you should give the airline your frequent-flyer number when you reconfirm your reservations and when you check in for each flight, and save your boarding passes and the "passenger receipt" coupons of your tickets until you see the credit for the flights on your frequent-flyer mileage statement.

If your mileage is not credited on your next statement, you can still get credit by sending your boarding passes and receipts directly to the frequent-flyer program for manual processing. This is especially important in order to receive credit in one airline's frequent-flyer program for flights on another airline, because such mileage is less likely to be credited automatically.

Canceling and Changing Reservations En Route

Once you're on the road, it varies according to the airline and the type of tickets you have whether it's easier to make changes directly with the airline (at a ticket office, by phone, or online, again depending on the airline and tickets), or through the travel agency that originally issued the tickets.

Don't make new reservations for a different flight without canceling the original ones. If you do, both sets of reservations may be canceled automatically as duplicates, even if they are for flights on different dates or at different times, or you may be charged for a second set of tickets for the new flights.

In general, it's better to make changes online, or in person at an airline ticket office, rather than by phone, so that you can get written confirmation of the new reservations and any change fees or other charges. Make changes by phone, and it's your word against theirs as to what you agreed to.

Airlines will sometimes say that they are "unable" to help you because your ticket was issued through a travel agency, and that you are "required" to go through your agent for any changes or other assistance. This is almost always both untrue and illegal. Technically, it's the airline that issues the ticket, even when it does so through an agent, and the airline that is bound by the contract. The airline just wants to shift the burden of customer service onto travel agents whenever it can. But it's usually easier to contact your travel agent in such a situation than to argue with the airline. In an emergency, though, if there's no time to contact your travel agency, insist on having the airline deal with you directly.

If the airline is unable to confirm space for you on a flight you want, you have three choices. You can ask to be put on a waiting list and check back at intervals to see if you are confirmed; it's best also to confirm space on an alternate flight in case the waitlist doesn't clear. Or you can go to the airport and stand by for space freed by last-minute cancellations, if the airline or your travel agent says that's allowed with your tickets. Or lastly, contact your travel agent for assistance in confirming the flight you want.

If you have an open ticket, and the airline is uncooperative in making reservations for you, this last alternative may be your only viable option. Airline employees have been known to demand bribes to confirm space for passengers with open tickets, in which case the agent from whom you bought your tickets may be able to help.

Changes made to your reservations after your departure, whether by you or the airline, or bookings made for "open" tickets, will not necessarily show up in the agent's computer. So you'll need to tell the agent your name(s) and the exact flight(s) on which you want to be booked.

Depending on where you are, it may be difficult for the agent to reply. If you don't get an answer, that doesn't mean that the agent hasn't made or confirmed reservations for you. Check with the airline a few days later to see if you have reservations on the flight(s) you want. If your original reservation is still not confirmed, have the airline check to see if it has new reservations for the same flight(s) on a separate record with a different record locator number.

If you decide that you won't take a flight on which you are booked, it is extremely important to cancel your reservations for that flight, whether or not you are ready to make new reservations on another date or at another time.

You don't need to cancel the rest of your reservations, just the flight(s) that you know you won't be on. But if you don't cancel your reservations, and fail to show up for the flight, the airline is entitled to cancel your reservations for all the rest of your flights, and to tell any other airlines on which you are booked to do likewise.

In order to encourage people to tell the airline if they don't plan to use their reservations, many airlines penalize no-shows. If you don't show up for a flight, and don't cancel your reservations, you often forfeit any possibility of a subsequent refund.

If you cancel your reservations for a particular flight and are considering not using that ticket at all and submitting it for a refund, it's advisable to do so in person so that you can get written confirmation of the cancellation and of any refund value or credit. It's all too easy, and too common, for an airline to claim it has no record of your e-ticket when you try to make new reservations, use a credit, or request a refund.

Buying Tickets En Route

Most people who travel around the world end up buying some air tickets along the way, either because they add side trips, left some gaps in their itinerary, decide to travel by air where they had planned to travel by land or water, or only bought tickets for part of their trip before their departure, to leave flexibility to decide the rest of their route and schedule later. The more time you spend on your trip, the more likely this is; if your trip lasts more than a year, you're sure to have to buy your tickets in stages.

If you will be buying tickets in stages (some before you depart and more along the way), make sure your initial set of tickets satisfies the following criteria:

- The tickets must end in a country you will reach within a year of buying them. (Otherwise some of them will expire unused and be wasted.)

- They must end in a country you can get into without an onward ticket.

- They should end in a location where you can buy an onward ticket for a reasonable price (or from which you can make your way by land or sea, without an onward ticket, to somewhere you can do so).

- They should end in an area where you will be staying long enough to arrange onward tickets.

Once he or she knows your entire plan, a good agent can advise you where is likely to be the best place to break your tickets, which ones you should buy before you leave, and where or how to buy the rest en route.

You don't have to buy tickets locally if you can get a better deal from a travel agency back home, or someplace else entirely. Travel industry protocols are set up to enable travel agents and airline offices anywhere in the world to issue tickets originating and terminating anywhere in the world. The country of sale is not necessarily the country of origin for the flight. There are boxes on every ticket that would never be needed if tickets could be sold only in the country of origin of the flight.

You may be able to get a good deal on onward tickets, even while you are overseas, from an agent in the United States, your home country, or somewhere else entirely. This is especially likely to be true if you find yourself needing a ticket in a country where there are no local discounters. As a travel agent I had clients in Japan, China, and several countries in Africa and South America, for example, who found that tickets, especially one-way tickets, originating in these places were cheaper bought from an agency in the United States than bought locally.

Of course the best place to find agents willing to sell tickets originating anywhere, and send them to you wherever you are, is on the Internet. Around-the-world agents, as a group, were among the first travel agents on the Internet. Any retail agent with a major business in exporting and importing tickets to a worldwide clientele is accessible by email.

That doesn't mean that buying around-the-world or multistop airline ticket can be a completely automated process, or that you have to make a choice between buying tickets from Internet robots or from a human travel agent. The best of the around-the-world and multistop specialty agents offer Internet tools to help you plan your trip, estimate prices, and evaluate preliminary alternatives; personal email, telephone, or in-person consultation to help you optimize your itinerary and answer your questions; and availability of customer service by email throughout your trip in case you have problems with your tickets.

If you plan on buying tickets from a travel agent in your home country, or anywhere else, while abroad, it's worth checking before you leave to make sure they will be willing to do this and to find out how best to work with them from wherever you'll be. Work out how you'll be able to arrange payment, and how they'll deliver any paper tickets.

Lost or Stolen Tickets

Treat paper airline tickets like cash. It can be difficult, time-consuming, and expensive, when it is possible at all, to replace them if they are lost or stolen.

You may have to pay in full on the spot for replacement tickets, and the airlines are not obligated to refund the price of the original tickets until they have expired unused, which may not be for a year. If you're traveling on an electronic ticket, original receipts may be essential to get past security checkpoints, as proof of onward passage for immigration purposes, or if the airline loses

REAL LIFE

More than once, when I've had an e-ticket for an international flight, I've had to wait for the airline to generate a paper confirmation or receipt to satisfy immigration officials and/or airport security guards before I was allowed to check in for my flight.

the record of your reservations or e-tickets, as can happen.

Travel agents cannot replace lost or stolen tickets. All claims for replacement or refund of lost or stolen tickets must be made directly to the airline on which the original ticket was validated. Before any claim can be considered, the airline will need you to provide, or will need to obtain from the issuing agent, the details of the missing tickets.

You have the best chance of obtaining timely replacement—rather than long-delayed refund—of lost or stolen tickets if you can present photocopies of each missing ticket or e-ticket passenger receipt coupon to the airline with your request for its replacement.

If you don't have copies of your tickets, the airline cannot replace or refund them without first verifying the issuing agency or office, date and place of issue, ticket numbers, routing, fare basis, validity dates, and how much you paid for the tickets.

Even in the best of circumstances, time differences may mean that you have to wait two days for the airline office where you present your refund claim to send a message to your travel agent in the United States, and get an answer back, usually by way of that airline's U.S. office. If weekends and holidays intervene, you could have to wait longer.

If the airline agrees to replace or refund your missing tickets, it will require you to pay a service charge, typically US$50–100 per ticket. It will also require you to sign a sworn declaration that you did not sell, give away, or gamble away your original tickets and that you will reimburse the airline for the value of the tickets if they have been, or are later, used for travel by someone else.

Airlines are not required to replace lost or stolen tickets. Some airlines categorically refuse to replace lost or stolen tickets under any circumstances. If you lose a ticket on such an airline, or have it stolen, you will have to pay in full for a replacement ticket, at the prevailing price (which may be much more than you originally paid).

Don't think that e-tickets eliminate the risk that tickets will be lost. Airlines can and do lose e-ticket records. But they tend to deny that this is even possible unless you can show them positive proof that you really had an e-ticket. The best evidence is a printed "passenger receipt coupon" in the same format as the receipt coupon of a paper ticket.

If the airline loses the record of your e-tickets, they'll probably try to get you to buy new full-fare tickets, with a promise that it will all be sorted out later and your money refunded. Don't do it. Buy new tickets, and you are unlikely ever to see your money again. Instead, show them the evidence of your tickets and insist politely but firmly that they transport you without additional payment, even if that means you have to wait a day or two while they verify with their head office or your travel agency that you did, in fact, have tickets. If they refuse to transport you, get a statement to that effect before you leave the check-in counter—on airline letterhead, signed by the station manager. Make sure it says that you presented yourself for check-in in a timely manner, showed your e-ticket receipt, and were refused passage. Tell them you need such a statement to submit with your refund claim. When you get home, if you have good evidence that you had a ticket, sue the airline. Airlines are reluctant to admit that they lost their record of an e-ticket, though it happens regularly. After the fact, I've known them to make up all sorts of lies, such as that the passenger simply didn't show up for the flight and thereby forfeited the value of their ticket.

Cancellations and Refunds

If you cancel all or part of your trip after you buy your tickets, you will have to submit the unused tickets or e-tickets for eventual refund, less penalties. Refunds can take up to a year.

Partially used tickets are usually completely nonrefundable. If you've used part of a ticket issued for an entire trip around the world at a single published RTW fare, the airline will subtract the full, unrestricted fare for each flight you have taken from the total you paid to calculate the residual refund value, if any. Because normal one-way fares are so high, a ticket at a published RTW fare typically has no refund value after the first few flights.

If you change your route or set and sequence of stops, you may have to buy new tickets and apply for a refund of the unused ones, less penalties. If you buy new tickets, you will have pay for them in full. Even if the old tickets are wholly or partially refundable, you will not get a refund for them until later. If tickets are reissued or exchanged for new tickets, however, the value of the old tickets can sometimes be applied directly to the value of the new tickets (less penalties, plus a reissue fee of US$50–250, and any difference between the fare for the old and new routing or destinations).

For this reason, it's best to exhaust your efforts to exchange your existing tickets for tickets closer to what you want, to have them reissued, or at least to find out how much those options will cost before you buy any new tickets. Once you have bought new tickets, it's too late to apply any of the value of the old tickets to the new ones. One of the most costly mistakes—often encouraged by airlines, who profit from it—is to buy new or replacement tickets on the assumption that the old ones will be fully, freely, and/or immediately refundable.

It is essential that you cancel your reservations, prior to the scheduled flight(s), if you wish to obtain a refund for tickets for those flights. If you don't show up for a flight for which you hold confirmed reservations, the airline is not obligated to give you any refund. If you cancel your reservations in person at an airline office, ask for written confirmation of the cancellation. If you cancel your reservations by phone, write down the name and title of the person at the airline who canceled them for you, the date, the place, and the telephone number at which you reached them. Some airlines will not give refunds without proof that reservations were canceled.

Some people think that if they cancel their reservations, or don't travel, they have "canceled their tickets" and will automatically receive a refund or credit. It's not as simple as that, or so fast. Technically speaking, you cannot cancel tickets. You need to cancel your reservations to protect your right to a refund, but that's not sufficient; you still need to submit the physical tickets or a formal request for refund of e-tickets before the airline or agent can process them for refund. No ticket, no refund. Full-fare tickets can be submitted for refund directly to the airline, but discounted tickets must be submitted for refund through the agent who sold them to you, because only that agent knows how much you actually paid.

If you have an electronic ticket, or were going to travel on a ticketless airline, refunds can be even more problematic. With physical tickets, you have an unused paper ticket to prove that you didn't travel. With an e-ticket, it can be much harder to prove that you didn't actually travel. Airlines don't send refund checks or issue credits for unused e-tickets automatically. You have to go through the same process as for a refund of a physical ticket, with the additional burden of proving that you didn't travel. You don't have to wait for physical tickets to be returned, but airlines can still take months to process e-ticket refunds.

If you don't use an e-ticket, try to get your ticket coupons printed out (to submit with your refund request) when you cancel your reservations. If that isn't possible, ask for a printout of your e-ticket receipt and a written confirmation on airline letterhead or itinerary paper that you canceled your reservations, signed and dated by an airline employee with their title and employee number. When you submit your refund request, get similar written confirmation of that as well, to prove that you made a refund claim and exactly what tickets were involved. Because of the lack of a verifiable "paper trail," problems with e-ticket refunds are common.

Each ticket, whether for one or several flights, must be processed separately. With paper tickets, you need to submit all unused flight coupons and the associated passenger receipt coupon(s). Old-style tickets are written or printed on little booklets of thin carbon paper that bind together up to four flights on one ticket. Some tickets are still issued that way, and some are still handwritten. But most remaining paper tickets use the "ATB" ("automated ticket and boarding pass") format, in which each flight coupon is a separate computer-printed card. With ATB tickets, it can be hard for those not skilled at reading tickets to tell which flights are part of the same ticket, especially where one ticket covers flights on more than one airline.

Once you return a ticket to the agent, the agent returns it to the airline with a refund claim form. If the agent bought the ticket from a wholesaler, they have to go through the wholesaler, who submits it to the airline in turn. Eventually, if the airline approves the refund claim, it calculates how much is due, after penalties, and notifies whoever issued the ticket (the wholesaler or retail agent) of a credit. The wholesaler then pays the agent, who can then pay you; both the wholesaler and the agent deduct their own penalties, fees, or service charges from the refund as they pass it along. At the end of the day, you might get a check or a credit to your credit card, or you might get airline credit or a voucher you can only use for future tickets on that airline.

Frontline agents take the brunt of travelers' complaints about fares, refunds, and penalties, but agencies are really at the airlines' and wholesalers' mercy when it comes to refund processing.

If you are submitting a ticket to an agent for a refund, you should expect the agency to charge you a cancellation fee. When a ticket is sold, and then submitted for refund, an agency has to do the same work it would have to do if you actually traveled, plus the work of processing the refund. Unless it deducts some sort of fee or service charge from the refund, it ends up having done all the work of selling and refunding the ticket for free. For a travel agency, processing a refund is invariably more time-consuming and labor-intensive than issuing the tickets was in the first place.

Airline cancellation penalties vary widely. A typical set of tickets around the world consists of 3–10 separate tickets, each of which has its own cancellation rules and penalties of anywhere from about US$50 to 100 percent. Typically, the eventual refund for an entirely unused set of around-the-world tickets is somewhere around half of the total price originally paid and takes 3–9 months. It is not always possible to know in advance the exact amount of the refund, since refunds for tickets priced in foreign currency can be affected by currency fluctuations.

If you have to cancel your trip for medical reasons, try to get a letter to that effect from a doctor. Depending on the airline and fare, some or all of the normal refund penalties may be waived for medical reasons. Many people mistakenly assume that all airlines and agents always waive all cancellation penalties in cases of cancellation for medical emergencies, but this is not correct. Even legitimate and documented medical reasons may not be cause for waiver of penalties, depending on the rules of the airline, fare, ticket, and agent. Some airlines only waive penalties if you or a traveling companion dies, and some not even then. I know of no law in any country that requires airlines to give refunds if you are unable to travel for medical reasons.

One reason the airlines are increasingly reluctant to give medical exemptions from cancellation penalties is that they have been widely abused by passengers with fraudulent or forged medical excuses. It's tempting to ask (or even pay) a friendly doctor to write a letter for you when hundreds or thousands of dollars in penalties are at stake. But some airlines spot-check medical refund documentation, so if you submit a fraudulent or forged note from a doctor, both you and the doctor risk criminal prosecution for attempting to defraud the airline. This sort of fraud only makes the airlines more suspicious and slows down legitimate refund claims. If an airline won't waive penalties for your legitimate medical claim, the people you should blame are all the people who've ripped off the airlines in the past with bogus medical excuses.

Most international airlines that still make any special allowance for medically required cancellations now require an original letter, signed and dated by a doctor, on the doctor's printed letterhead; or a certified copy of a death certificate. It's hard to tell in advance whether a doctor's note will make a difference to your refund, and it's difficult to obtain one after the fact, so it's always best to get one at the time you get sick or injured if there's any chance that it might require you to cancel or change your flights.

The most common causes for cancellation are accidents, illnesses, family emergencies, and other circumstances covered by trip cancellation and interruption insurance. This sort of insurance is advisable, as the cost is generally far less than the difference between discounted tickets with cancellation penalties and fully refundable full-fare tickets. (For more information, see *Travel Insurance* in the *Safety and Health* chapter.)

When Things Go Wrong

There's a whole closet of fears of what can happen after you give your money to a travel agent or airlines for airline tickets, or click the "buy" button on a website. What happens if the agency goes bankrupt or never gives you your tickets? What if you show up at the airport and the airline says they have no record of your e-ticket? What if the airline cancels the flight, discontinues service on the route entirely, or goes out of business? How can you reduce these risks, and what can you do if you have problems or complaints?

PROBLEMS WITH AIRLINES

Most complaints about airlines relate to secondary aspects of service, not to the basic question of whether they provide transportation from point A to point B as contracted. But even basic transportation can be an issue if the airline discontinues service on a particular route, or shuts down entirely.

Discontinued Routes: What happens if you buy a ticket to fly from A to B on Airline C, but by the time you want to use that ticket Airline C no longer flies from A to B?

Airlines are constantly adding new routes and dropping or changing old ones. Flights that are being heavily discounted because the airline has trouble filling them are sometimes those that end up being discontinued entirely. Most of the time, the airline itself is still in business, and it's only a particular route that is dropped from its schedule. Low-fare airlines are especially quick to cancel flights on routes that prove unprofitable.

As long as the airline is still flying, it wants to keep its customers' goodwill, and it will usually do much more than it legally has to. If the airline still serves A and B, it will invariably accommodate you on whatever route or connections it still flies between the ticketed points, even if your ticket was issued as nonreroutable or valid only on direct flights that no longer exist. You may end up flying a few days earlier or later than you had expected, or taking longer to get where you are going, but these sorts of things aren't usually a problem for long-term travelers. Sometimes you get a stopover you hadn't paid for, or a night in a hotel at the airline's expense in some city where you have to make connections. If you do, make the most of it. Airlines aren't required to put you up, even if you have to spend the night, but you can always ask, and in case of involuntary rerouting, they usually will.

If the airline no longer flies to A and/or B at all, it has two choices: it can endorse your ticket to another airline or it can give you a refund. Try to get it to endorse your ticket to any other airline that will get you to your destination, or an acceptable alternate destination. (Sometimes when a route is discontinued, it's because circumstances in the destination are such that you'd no longer want to go there, and you'd actually prefer an alternate destination.) If you were already flying on the cheapest airline, on a discounted ticket, a refund of what you paid for that portion of your ticket is almost certain not to be enough to buy a ticket on any other airline.

The decisive factor in whether you are provided with a refund or alternative transportation is usually whether you had confirmed reservations for a specific date, or only unconfirmed or "open" tickets. Your only right in either case is to a refund, and your only sure protection is trip cancellation and interruption insurance. In practice, if you have specific reservations you will usually be provided with alternative transportation, while if you have only an "open" ticket you will only get a refund.

Airlines look at it like this: if you hadn't made any reservations, you had no expectations of flying on any particular date. Once the airline has given you a full refund you are in exactly the same situation as if you had never bought a ticket on their airline in the first place, and you have no cause for complaint. If you have reservations for a specific date, on the other hand, it will usually honor your expectation of transportation by making some arrangement, at its expense, not yours, to get you there around that date.

REAL LIFE

When Bangladesh Biman Airways discontinued its flights from Bombay to Athens a few years ago, passengers holding open tickets on the route were given refunds equal to about half the cost of the next cheapest tickets from India to Europe. Passengers with confirmed Biman reservations had their tickets endorsed to Egypt Air, after which they were allowed to make further date changes between Egypt Air flights, if they wished. Egypt Air flew them from Bombay to Cairo, gave them a sightseeing tour to the pyramids during their layover, and flew them on to Athens. The same thing would be less likely with e-tickets than it was then with paper tickets, and would be impossible with a low-fare airline that has no interline agreements.

Airline Bankruptcies: Airline bankruptcy is a risk no matter which airline you have tickets on. Don't assume that it's a greater risk abroad. Until the 1990s, airline bankruptcy was primarily an issue with airlines in the United States. The United States is virtually unique in having no government-owned airlines and no single airline on which its national prestige depends. In the United States, the government subsidizes the airline industry as a whole but takes a minimal role in protecting individual airlines. The United States also has had far more airline bankruptcies and shutdowns than any other country, of airlines large (Pan Am) and small (USAfrica Airways, Independence Air, etc.), and the U.S. government has a proven record of letting airlines go out of business even when that will strand passengers.

Elsewhere in the world, most countries had a government-owned airline whose continued operation was considered a national priority. But increasingly, national airlines have been at least nominally privatized. Privatizing the national airline, and then allowing it to go bankrupt, can be a form of de facto repudiation of government debt. That's an attractive option for many governments, and the risk of airline bankruptcy is now worldwide.

A travel agent that sells you a ticket valid at the time it is issued is not responsible if the airline later goes bankrupt. In this circumstance, the only place for you to seek a refund is directly from the airline, through its trustees in bankruptcy. Because secured creditors take precedence, and because struggling airlines by definition have highly leveraged and precarious cash-flow positions, there is usually nothing left for ticket holders when the remaining assets of a bankrupt airline are liquidated.

In general, no law requires other airlines to honor tickets from a bankrupt airline. Why should they? If they do, they write off the costs of transporting holders of worthless tickets on a bankrupt former competitor as a marketing cost, in the hope of winning the loyalty and future business of frequent travelers on the route. Sometimes other airlines will offer a special concessionary fare, just high enough to cover their costs, to holders of tickets on the failed airline. But you can't count on such generosity.

The only way to protect yourself against losing your money if an airline goes out of business between when you buy your tickets and when you travel is to buy travel insurance that covers "supplier default." (See the section on *Travel Insurance* in the *Safety and Health* chapter.)

Other Issues with Airlines: What can you do if an airline violates its terms and conditions—fails to provide transportation when you have a valid ticket, refuses to give you a refund to which you are entitled, discriminates against you, fails to compensate you or reimburse your expenses for overbooking or delay (where, as in the European Union, that's required), or—most common—engages in false or deceptive advertising? You can sue the airline, which is usually complicated and expensive. Or you can get government regulators involved by making a complaint to the U.S. Department of Transportation or the comparable agency in the country where the airline is based, the ticket was sold, or the incident occurred. Your rights and the procedures for making a complaint vary by country. See the *Resource Guide* for contacts for complaints against airlines in the United States and the European Union.

PROBLEMS WITH TRAVEL AGENTS, TOUR OPERATORS, AND CHARTER OPERATORS

While travel agents must meet certain accreditation standards set by those airlines, the airlines try to avoid taking responsibility for travel agents' actions or getting involved in relations between travel agents and their customers.

Until you get your tickets from an agency, the matter is one of local law. Agencies must post bonds to help ensure that the airlines will get paid if the agency goes bankrupt, but tickets already issued by an agency remain valid even if the agency's bond is insufficient to pay off the airlines, as it often is if an agency goes out of business. The standard bond for agencies in the United States is US$20,000, far less than many agencies' weekly payments to the airlines.

Once you get your tickets on a scheduled airline, you are protected against the agency, even if the agency you bought the tickets from goes out of business the day after you buy the tickets, and whether or not the agency has paid the airline. Once you receive valid airline tickets, most issues are between you and the airline, and are governed by the airline's conditions of carriage and the applicable national laws.

Your rights in a dispute with a travel agency, tour operator, or operator of charter flights are limited to those available under the laws of the jurisdiction in which the other party to the dispute operates or is incorporated, or where the transaction occurred. Local rules vary. If you plan to buy tickets or a tour in another country, either check out that country's laws or assume that the rule is caveat emptor.

One of the big issues in buying tickets or other travel services online is dealing with different legal and consumer protection regimes. You may be in Country A, and buying a ticket for a flight from Country B to Country C on an airline based in Country D. But if you aren't careful, you may find that the website where you made the purchase is based in, and governed by the laws of, Country E. Quite possibly the operators of the website chose Country E for its favorable (to them) consumer-protection laws. Caveat emptor.

The U.K. Air Travel Organiser's Licence System: The world's best system of consumer protection for air travelers is in the U.K. There, all sellers of airline tickets or tours that include airfare, except in cases where a ticket on a scheduled airline is supplied immediately in exchange for payment, must have an Air Travel Organiser's Licence (ATOL), which is issued by the Civil Aviation Authority (CAA). ATOL holders must include their ATOL number in advertisements and brochures, and on confirmation invoices and receipts. "If it hasn't got an ATOL, don't book it at all," is the advice of the CAA for U.K. buyers of air tickets or any package that includes air transportation.

To obtain an ATOL, an applicant must provide the CAA with audited accounts including profit-and-loss statements for the previous three years (or a current balance sheet for a new business) as well as financial projections for the year including a cash-flow forecast and budget of income and expenses. A major reason few ATOL holders fail is that in the U.K. underfinanced companies

REAL LIFE

When the world's most customer-unfriendly airline, Ryanair, tried to charge me for a ticket issued several hours after their website told me my purchase request had been rejected because their systems were down, I got my money back through a credit card chargeback. I don't think Ryanair ever paid up, but the bank that issued my card took the loss, not me—even though it was an international charge from Ryanair's head office in Ireland.

or individuals don't get licenses to sell air travel in the first place.

ATOL applicants must also post a bond with the CAA to cover the cost of providing for their customers if they go out of business. The size of the bond is proportionate to the size and nature of the business and must be reviewed and renewed each year. If an ATOL holder fails, or is financially unable to provide the contracted tickets, air transportation, or other tour services, the CAA uses the licensee's bond money to provide those services, or refunds, to all those who have paid. If the bond is too small, any shortfall is made up from an Air Travel Trust administered by the CAA and funded by a fee of UK£2.50 (about US$4) on each booking—essentially a government-administered air travel insurance scheme.

The record of the CAA in administering this system is impressive. Claimants against failed ATOL holders do not have to sue or advance money out of their own pockets; the CAA steps in directly to arrange transportation home or pay refunds. In 1995, the first year in which the current ATOL rules were in effect, 11,000 people were flown home by the CAA when tour or charter operators failed while they were abroad. Refunds were paid to another 125,000 people who had not yet commenced their travels. Repatriation costs and refunds totaled UK£16 million (US$25 million). By 2010, the numbers were up to 43,000 repatriated to the U.K. and 133,000 given full refunds when tour operators or charter operators went bust.

The ATOL system was prompted by concerns about the reliability of travel agencies, tour operators, and charter operators, not scheduled airlines. An ATOL number can be based on an airline's guarantee that the agency is appointed by the airline, and that the airline will guarantee the validity of tickets sold or issued by the agency. If the ATOL agency goes out of business after taking your payment, the airline is still required to give you a ticket, whether or not the agency paid the airline. Once you have your ticket on a scheduled airline, however, the seller's ATOL number does not protect you against failure of the airline. There have been efforts in Parliament to close this gap, but thus far to no avail. Thus, even in the U.K. you need to take out supplier default insurance to be protected against bankruptcies of scheduled airlines.

The ATOL scheme protects travelers at minimal cost while being welcomed by legitimate travel agents and tour and charter operators as enhancing their credibility and putting their underfinanced and dishonest competitors out of business. Its exemplary success, which has improved rather than detracted from the position of the U.K. as one of the world centers of airline ticket discounting, puts the lie to any claim that effective consumer protection regulations cannot coexist with an open and vigorously competitive market. I commend it to the attention and careful study of would-be regulators, and of consumers, in other countries, especially as the model for any future national system of protection for travel consumers in the United States.

The California Seller of Travel Law: In the United States, the federal government has exclusive jurisdiction over airlines, but most transactions with travel agencies and other travel companies are governed by state and local law. Mainly in response to concerns about fraudulent sales of package tours and failures of charter operators, rather than tickets on scheduled airlines, several states have enacted licensing requirements for sellers of travel.

The most important of these is the California Seller of Travel (CST) law, which took effect in 1996. Despite significant problems, the CST law is being held up (as California laws often are) as a model for other states. For that reason, and because California is one of the world's centers of discount airline ticket sales, it warrants a closer look at what, if any, protection it provides.

The CST law was obviously inspired by the ATOL law, but differs from it in critical ways:

First, it applies only to sales by California businesses to customers in California; it provides no protection to interstate sales. These would be exclusively the province of federal law, if there were any on this issue, which there isn't. It's laughable to suggest that the sale of travel is not at least a national, if not a global, business.

Second, while the CST law requires sellers of travel to register, it requires no evidence that they have adequate working capital or realistic budgets. Registration is purely clerical: anyone, or any business, can register as a CST for a minimal fee. The contrast in this regard between the questions asked on the ATOL application and CST registration forms is striking.

Third, the Travel Consumer Restitution Corporation (TCRC) set up under the CST law does not itself do anything to arrange transportation or any other travel services in the event of bankruptcy or default of a CST registrant. The TCRC will only reimburse travelers, after the fact and after they prove their claims against a registered seller of travel, for costs of alternative arrangements, which they will first have to make and pay for out of their pockets.

Fourth, because most CST registrants need post no bond, and because the restitution fund is financed only by an assessment on registrants limited by the law to US$200 per registrant per year, with a target balance of only US$1.6 million, there is no guarantee that enough money will be available to pay the claims that could arise if a large tour or charter operator or agency goes under. (As I've noted, about US$25 million a year is spent on repatriation and refunds in the U.K., which has only about twice the population of California.)

Fifth, despite having weaker provisions, the CST law has not won the acceptance or support from the industry that the ATOL prototype has.

The bottom line is that the CST law provides even California travel consumers, buying from registered California sellers of travel, little real protection, and provides a poor model to anyone considering similar legislation.

U.S. Consumer Protection for Credit-Card Purchases: By far the strongest consumer protection provisions in the United States are those applicable to credit- or charge-card purchases. The single best way for buyers in the United States to protect themselves against an agent (or airline) taking their money but not producing tickets is to pay with a credit or charge card.

You aren't required to pay credit-card charges for goods or services you didn't receive. If you haven't received your tickets, you can contest the charge when your bill arrives. The matter is referred to the chargeback departments of the bank that issued your card and the bank with which the agency has its merchant account, both of which function as arbiters. The burden is on the agency or merchant to prove that you authorized the charge and that you got what you paid for. If it can't come up with proof (a written and signed charge authorization and copies of tickets), it's an open-and-shut case, and the charge will be removed from your bill without your ever having to pay.

Once you dispute the charge, your bank takes over as your advocate with the merchant's bank: you don't have to do the work of making demands on the merchant or trying to collect. If the agency or other merchant is out of business, or the bank can't get its money back, that's not your problem. It's the bank that advances money to the merchant, and the bank that is required to absorb any uncollectible losses from disputed charges.

If you pay by cash or check, the agency has your money. If it doesn't deliver, you may have to sue, and the burden is on you to prove that you didn't get your tickets. If the agency goes out of business before you can get a legal judgment and collect on it, you're out of luck.

These provisions only apply to purchases made in the United States with credit or charge cards issued by U.S. banks. In practice, disputes with foreign merchants by holders of U.S.-issued cards are referred to the same chargeback departments, who try to follow the same procedures as they would with a U.S. merchant. If the merchant can't document authorization for the charge, or delivery of the goods or services, and the card-issuing bank can't get the money back from the merchant's bank or the merchant, it isn't required to remove the charge from your bill or take the loss. Usually, however, it will, in the interest of keeping your account and to avoid being accused of being complicit in any fraud or illegal activity by the merchant.

How aggressively the chargeback department will pursue your dispute with a merchant, and how willing it will be to remove a disputed charge from your bill, depends to a significant degree on the status of your account and how much the card-issuing bank wants your business. A bank where you also have other accounts, especially savings, investment, or retirement accounts, may go further to keep your business than one with which you only have a credit card.

There are usually separate customer service and chargeback departments for holders of higher-fee premium (gold or platinum) credit and charge cards. In disputes with merchants, banks are more likely to give the benefit of the doubt to premium cardholders than to holders of standard cards. This is the best reason I know of to pay the extra fee for a "silver," "gold," or "platinum" card.

Don't go overboard with chargebacks. They are appropriate mainly in cases where a merchant doesn't deliver at all, or is out of business; they are not an appropriate way to deal with disputes over terms and conditions. Don't charge back an entire amount if only part of it is in dispute. Treat a chargeback as only half a step short of a lawsuit: a next-to-last resort before turning to the courts. Merchants justifiably don't like people who initiate legal action without first trying to resolve their disputes informally. Once you initiate a chargeback, you have defined the relationship with the merchant as adversarial, and can expect few concessions. If a dispute is a matter of judgment, interpretation, or misunderstanding, rather than of simple nondelivery, your best bet is to try to negotiate a settlement directly with the merchant, if you have time, before contesting the bill and initiating a chargeback.

Unjustified chargebacks against travel agents usually involve people who change their minds after authorizing a charge for tickets or other travel arrangements and before receiving their tickets or vouchers or leaving on their trip. They think that because they had not yet received the tickets, or never used the tickets, they shouldn't have to pay for them. It doesn't work like that. From the moment you authorize a charge for tickets or travel arrangements, you are morally and legally bound to pay the bill. The agent relies on your authorization to start sending payments to airlines or other suppliers as soon as your charge is approved. If you dispute the charge, you are stiffing the agent unfairly. If you change your plans, you must pay the bill, bring any tickets or vouchers you have received back to the agent, and wait—perhaps several months—for any refund, less any cancellation penalties.

Consumer Protection in Other Countries: Some countries license or regulate travel agencies, but in others there is no special system of licensing or regulation of air ticket sellers, and sales of air tickets are subject only to whatever general rules apply to any retail sales. Rules may vary within the country. Canada, like the United States, regulates travel agencies at the provincial rather than the federal level. Absent any special provision to the contrary, your only legal recourse if you don't get what you pay for is the legal system in the jurisdiction of the sale. If you buy tickets in a foreign country, that's probably no use: you aren't likely to be sticking around long enough to sue anyone. All you can do is to try to choose a reliable agent in the first place. (See the section earlier in this chapter on *Choosing a Travel Agent.*)

If you pay by credit card, you may have some recourse through your card-issuing bank, but your rights vary from country to country, and in many countries it's almost impossible to find an agency that accepts credit or charge cards in payment for discounted tickets. You can take out travel insurance to cover losses from supplier bankruptcy or default, but that too is hard or impossible to find in many countries. Read the fine print closely: most travel insurance policies will not cover purchases made directly from suppliers or agents in other countries. These are strong reasons to buy tickets through an agency in your home country, against which you can have recourse under your local procedures or through travel insurance.

Where to Complain: Complain first to the people who caused the problem. If it's a complaint about service by an airline, complain to the airline. If you don't like a hotel, complain to the hotel management. Travel agencies don't own the airlines and are limited in their ability to control airlines' behavior or obtain redress for grievances against them, especially as to the quality of service.

If you have a financial dispute, complain to whomever you gave your money to. Your money may have been passed on to someone else—it's not uncommon for there to be a chain of three or four intermediaries between a retail agency and the airline or supplier of travel services, especially if the supplier is in a different country—but it should be possible to forward your complaint and claim down the same chain.

Good businesses want to hear from dissatisfied customers, and would rather have a chance to make things right, or at least explain their side of the story, than have you denounce them for something that might not have been their fault, or for which they would have been willing to compensate you. Be realistic and fair—asking for your entire payment back because of a minor problem with your trip will only reduce your chances of a mutually agreeable settlement—but do specify exactly what you want done, or how much you want to be paid.

Many businesses in the United States belong to Better Business Bureaus.

Complaining to the Better Business Bureau (BBB) is usually a waste of time. The BBB is not a consumer organization but a business organization. Like most self-regulation schemes, its main purpose is to enable businesses to claim that the government doesn't need to protect consumers because merchants are policing themselves. It is designed by businesses to protect their images, not to be an advocate against them. The BBB has no enforcement power whatsoever. It can cancel a merchant's membership if the merchant doesn't answer your complaint at all, but as long as the business sends any response a complaint is simply logged and forgotten as unresolved. The BBB is, in my opinion, a sham; many businesses know it is and refuse to waste their money on membership. Membership in a BBB is no measure of legitimacy.

Although it is also an industry self-policing organization, the American Society of Travel Agents (ASTA) has a much better track record of pursuing consumer complaints. ASTA requires its members to adhere to certain standards of ethics and business practices, including responding to complaints, and can expel members who are found not to. In the United States, I would hesitate to do business with an agency that is not a member of ASTA, and I would not do business with one whose membership has been revoked or withdrawn. An agency that doesn't renew its ASTA membership probably does so to forestall an expected expulsion, because it doesn't want to bother to answer complaints at all, because it doesn't care about its reputation, or because it can't afford the dues. Any of these are bad signs.

ASTA's Consumer Affairs Department (see *Consumer Protection* in the *Resource Guide*) provides an informal mediation service to assist in resolving disputes with members and a complaint reference service that will give you a profile of past complaints to ASTA, if any, about travel companies. You can check with ASTA for an agency's complaint record and membership status, or for information on how to pursue a complaint against a member.

Remember that all agencies, especially large, long-established ones with lots of customers, are likely to have had at least some complaints. The red flags are many complaints, recent complaints, a high proportion of unresolved complaints, revocation of ASTA membership, or use of the ASTA logo despite not being an ASTA member.

ASTA functions as an industry networking group, so many tour operators and non-U.S. travel agencies with U.S. clients or clients visiting the United States are members. There's a fair chance that any local agent in another country that does business with people or companies in the United States belongs to ASTA. ASTA will get involved in mediating disputes with any member, even ones involving local transactions with members in countries outside the United States.

Consumer Protection on the Internet: For the most part, Internet ticket purchases are subject to the same consumer protection rules as in-person, telephone, or mail-order purchases. Your most important protection, on the Internet as anywhere else, comes from the rules for credit-card payments and disputes. The most important things to do to protect yourself are to pay by credit card, to read all the rules before you pay, and to print out or save your final confirmed itinerary, price, and all the rules and conditions before you click "Buy."

Most disputes over ticket purchases involve people who don't read, don't understand, or don't pay attention to the rules for cancellations, refunds, or changes to their tickets. Because they don't intend to cancel or change their plans, they don't notice or don't remember the cancellation or change penalties, or perhaps that the tickets can't be changed or refunded at all. Later, they complain about the penalties: they say, quite truthfully, that they don't remember being told that the tickets weren't refundable, reroutable, changeable, or whatever.

I know nobody reads the fine print, especially when it's so easy just to click on "I agree." But if you don't read the rules, you have no cause for later complaint if you don't like them. On the Internet, the only way you can later prove what you agreed to, what you were supposed to be charged, or what the rules of your ticket were supposed to be, is to print them all out, or save them (and check that you can open the saved copy) before you buy, and save them until your trip is complete.

While the basics of consumer protection are the same online as anywhere else, the Internet poses a variety of special issues of its own: security, privacy invasion, identity theft, and so forth. These are important, but beyond the scope of this book. Security, privacy, and consumer protection questions peculiar to the Internet, as well as advice on using the Internet for travel planning and purchasing and while on the road, are dealt with at length on my website and in my companion volume in this series, *The Practical Nomad: Guide to the Online Travel Marketplace.*

Travel Documents

Travel documents—passports, visas, and other government permits—are an unavoidable necessity of international travel, required for crossing international borders or for travel within particular parts of a country. Most around-the-world or multicountry travelers need visas in addition to a passport for at least some of the countries they visit. The more you travel, the less you will like passports and visas, but the best way to avoid problems with travel documents is not to leave them to the last minute.

To a government, a "travel document" is what you use as proof of your identity and nationality when crossing an international border. Usually this is a passport, although certain kinds of special documents are issued to stateless people (i.e., people who do not have citizenship in any recognized country) for purposes of international travel. In common usage, the term "travel documents" also applies to visas and other entry and travel permits.

This chapter follows the chapters on transportation because most people don't get visas until after they've arranged their long-haul air transportation. Sometimes there are good reasons to wait as long as possible (as long as you leave ample time for delays and surprises) before actually having your visas issued—reasons such as maximizing the period of visa validity. Some visas can't be issued until you have made onward airline reservations, or even have tickets in hand. But I strongly urge you not to make definite plans or buy

Key Advice About Travel Documents

- Get a passport before you try to travel anywhere across any national border, even just between the United States and Canada or Mexico.

- Verify the current visa and entry requirements of each country you want to visit directly with each country's embassy or consulate.

- Remember that governments don't think travel is a right. Maybe it should be, but in practice it isn't. Other countries don't have to let you in if they don't want to. Ask for permission politely and respectfully.

- Approach visa applications and border crossings as learning experiences and opportunities, not confrontations or ordeals.

- Play by the rules. When you are dealing with foreign governments, you are not in control. Trying to claim special privileges (especially as a citizen of the United States) or to assert your nonexistent authority will only reduce the chances that you'll be allowed to go where you want.

tickets without first carefully investigating the documentary requirements for the trip you want to take. I've known people to invest months of effort, commit themselves to a schedule, and buy expensive nonrefundable tickets, only to find out the rules have changed since the "current" guidebook they relied on was researched, and they cannot get the visas or permits their plans require.

PASSPORTS

If you are considering any international travel, one of your first steps should be to obtain a valid passport. If you already have a passport make sure it is still valid and will remain valid until at least six months, preferably a year, after you return to your home country. There are exceptions to the rule, but in general anyone wishing to cross any international border, anywhere in the world, must present a valid passport issued by the government of the country of their citizenship.

In theory, international treaties ratified by many countries, including the United States, guarantee the freedom to travel as a human right—regardless of whether you have a passport or other travel documents. In practice, as discussed in the sidebar *Freedom to Travel?*, it can be extremely difficult to exercise that right.

Passports are strongly recommended for all international travel, even in cases where they aren't strictly required. If you don't have, or can't get, a passport,

- Respect foreign laws, even if you don't like them. Violations of other countries' customs and immigration rules are no joke. They are real crimes with nasty names like "smuggling," "theft," "fraud," "subversion," and "espionage," and penalties to match.

- If you're a U.S. citizen and you want to be treated better by foreign governments, lobby our own government to treat foreign visitors and would-be visitors to the United States better.

- Never judge a country by its border guards, customs and immigrations inspectors, or police. Would you want foreign visitors to judge the United States by the conduct and attitudes of the immigration, customs, border patrol, or airport security officers of the Department of Homeland Security?

For more information on the topics in this chapter, see the *Resource Guide* in the back of the book and the links on the Practical Nomad website at www.practicalnomad.com.

or if you insist on traveling without one, you'll probably need some other official identity document with your photo on it for any air travel, including domestic air travel within the United States and most other countries.

The United States doesn't have a national ID card, and domestic air travelers within the United States used to be able to travel without identity papers. This made it relatively easy to travel on other people's tickets and thus to buy and sell partially used tickets. However, in 1995, in response to a bomb scare, several major U.S. airports and airlines implemented what were intended to be temporary checks of all passengers' ID documents. The airlines suddenly realized how much potential revenue was being lost by people traveling on other people's nontransferable tickets, and the ID checks were made nationwide and permanent. It's still not clear whether it's the U.S. government or the airlines that have actually imposed the ID requirement, but for better or worse, it seems to be here to stay.

At minimum, you'll be subjected to more intrusive searching (pat-down of your person and opening of your carry-on bags) and possibly additional questioning if you try to check in for a domestic flight within the United States without showing a government-issued ID with your photo on it. If you show up for an international flight without a passport, you will probably be refused boarding. If you don't have a driver's license, and don't want to get a passport, most U.S. state governments will issue residents a state photo ID for

Freedom to Travel?

Do passports serve more to facilitate travel, or to facilitate government control of travel? Do you have a right to a passport, a right to travel without a passport, or both?

Public debate on these questions in the United States and Western Europe has been going on for more than 200 years, since passports and demands for them first became widespread. For some of the history, see John Torpey's *The Invention of the Passport* and Mark B. Salter's *Rights of Passage*. I've been involved in this debate myself as an advocate for travelers' rights (see my website and blog at www.hasbrouck.org), and as a consultant to the Identity Project (www.papersplease.org) on travel-related civil liberties and human rights issues.

The U.S. Constitution only hints at a right to travel in the First Amendment: "Congress shall make no law…abridging…the right of the people peaceably to assemble." But freedom of travel is much more explicitly recognized in the fundamental international documents of human rights than in those of U.S. Constitutional civil liberties.

Article 12 of the International Covenant on Civil and Political Rights (ICCPR), signed by the United States in 1992 and ratified in 1997, provides that "Everyone lawfully within the territory of a State shall, within that territory, have the right to liberty of movement and freedom to choose his residence. Everyone shall be free to leave any country, including his own…. No one shall be arbitrarily deprived of the right to enter his own country." Several other treaties have similar language.

The ICCPR is interpreted and enforced by the UN Human Rights Committee, which has adopted strict standards of necessity for any rules that require special documents or government permission for either domestic or international travel. These standards are intended to prevent governments from imposing measures like Soviet restrictions on exit permits needed to leave the country, or South African passbook laws that restricted movement within the country and access to passports for travel abroad.

The U.S. Constitution provides that international treaties ratified by the United States are "the law of the land," but enforcing international law in U.S. courts is difficult. As of 2011, the U.S. Supreme Court has recognized the right of pedestrians to travel by foot on public rights-of-way without carrying identification papers, but has refused to consider whether airline passengers have a right to travel by common carrier without showing proof of their identity.

Human rights are nowhere on the agenda when the world's police convene to set standards for travel security, as I observed when I attended meetings of the International Civil Aviation Organization on passports and travel documents. Regardless of what the laws and treaties say, the people making the rules presume that any government in the world has the authority to impose whatever restrictions it pleases on any traveler who crosses its borders. To suggest otherwise would be taken as an attack on their national sovereignty.

I encourage you to assert and defend your rights, including your right to travel without having to prove to any government who you are, where you want to go, or why. But those challenges are likely to be more successful in your own country, where you have better legal "standing" and are more likely to know the procedures, than while you are abroad. I go along with a lot of bureaucratic demands when I'm a guest in another country that I would question or refuse to comply with when I'm in my homeland. And in this book, I've tried to describe the "realpolitik" of the law on travel documents, border crossings, and airport procedures as it is enforced, not as I think it ought to be.

nondrivers that's accepted for domestic U.S. flights. But a passport costs only a little more than a state ID and opens the door to the entire world. Do yourself a favor: get a passport.

Most other countries also require air travelers to carry and show photo ID. Typically, on domestic flights locals must show national ID and foreigners must show passports. In countries where prices for locals and foreigners differ, this also ensures that foreigners have paid the foreigners' price. It is sometimes possible—although illegal—for foreigners who can pass for locals to travel on local-price train tickets. However, it is almost impossible for foreigners to travel on local-price air tickets without forged local identity papers to match their tickets.

I recommend you start working on getting a passport at least 4–6 months before you plan to leave. Most people don't need that long to get the travel documents they need, so don't panic if you're leaving in a couple of months or weeks and don't yet have a passport. But if you're interested enough in international travel to read this book, and don't have a passport, do yourself a favor and start the process now. You cannot begin to apply for visas until after you receive your passport; you may need to send your passport back and forth to several embassies or consulates to obtain visas; and some visas take several weeks each to issue.

RFID Passports

If your passport has this logo on the cover, that means it's an "e-passport" with a radio-frequency identification (RFID) chip laminated into the cover or one of the pages. The same logo is used on signs to identify special lanes at immigration checkpoints, airports, and borders that you have to go through if you have one of these passports, so that the data on the chip can be read, logged, and compared with what's printed on the passport.

e-Passport symbol

The information stored on the chip includes everything printed on the main page of the passport, including a digital version of your photo. Space is also reserved on the chip to store a log of your movements accessible to anyone who subsequently reads the chip. This part of the chip isn't (yet) being used in U.S. passports, although it is in Malaysian and perhaps other countries' passports. The data on the chip is encrypted, but the code has already been cracked.

The RFID chip itself is actually a tiny radio transponder that can be read from up to at least a meter (3 feet) away, even through your pocket, purse, or luggage. I've seen this demonstrated with a reader small enough to hide in a backpack or a suitcase. With the information read from the chip in your passport, an identity thief would have everything they need to "clone" a perfect copy of your passport. And since each chip transmits a globally unique serial number, stalkers or others could use them to track you wherever you go. There's no way to show your passport at an airline check-in counter, currency exchange, or hotel desk without running the risk that the person behind you in line will read all your data off the chip without your knowledge, or that the hotel or other business will send a record of your visit, identified with the date and place and your chip number, to add to your credit record and other marketing databases.

I personally met with the head of the U.S. Passport Office to urge him not to put these chips in U.S. passports, as did many other technical experts and privacy advocates. Our objections were ignored, and the United States bgan issuing RFID passports in 2006. Many other countries have done likewise. You won't be given a choice of whether you want a chipped passport. If you have one, you can limit the extent to which it is used to track you by keeping it wrapped in aluminum foil or in a foil-lined or metalized envelope.

It may take longer than you think to track down and order an original of your birth or naturalization certificate—a prerequisite to getting a passport. And as more people need passports, such as for travel across the U.S.–Canada border, where they weren't previously required, backlogs of applications have increased passport issuance times substantially. Between 2007 and 2009, as the United States was phasing in passport requirements for travel to and from Canada and Mexico, the time required to get a passport during the peak spring application season for summer travel shot up from 4–8 weeks to 4–8 *months*. The U.S. and Canadian passport issuance offices raised their fees in order to hire more staff, and by 2011 the backlogs had been significantly reduced. But processing times for applications through normal channels remain unpredictable.

The *Passports* section of the *Resource Guide* gives information on passport issuance offices and application procedures for citizens of some of the principal English-speaking First World countries: the United States, Canada, the U.K., Ireland, Australia, and Aotearoa/New Zealand. This information, like all third-party information about government rules, should not be taken as definitive. Rules change. Verify current requirements, fees, office locations, etc., with the relevant authorities before making definite plans, submitting a passport application, or going out of your way to visit a passport office.

U.S. Passports

Given the lengths to which some people from other countries will go to acquire a U.S. passport, it may be surprising that only about 25 percent of U.S. citizens have a passport, the smallest percentage of any First World country. (The percentage has gone up sharply in recent years, but that's more as a result of immigrants and long-term permanent residents getting U.S. citizenship than of native-born U.S. citizens getting passports.)

U.S. passports are the most valuable and widely useful travel documents in the world, getting you into more countries, more easily, than any other. If you hold a

REAL LIFE

U.S. citizens can get a credit-card sized "Passport Card" instead of, or in addition to, a traditional passport booklet. The card is cheaper than the passport book, but it's only valid for travel to and from Canada and Mexico. If you think you might travel anywhere else in the world, get a passport book. Get a card, if at all, only in addition to a passport book, as secondary backup ID to facilitate getting your passport book replaced if it's lost or stolen. Passport cards have even longer-range RFID chips than those in passports, so keep your passport card in a foil sleeve if you don't want to broadcast your U.S. citizenship.

Travel Documents

U.S. passport, you are one of the world's travel elite. Consider yourself privileged, and take advantage of the opportunities it gives you.

In addition to the information below on U.S. passports and applications, the U.S. Department of State website at http://travel.state.gov/passport has current forms, fee schedules, instructions, and a searchable database of places where passport applications are accepted.

APPLYING FOR A U.S. PASSPORT

U.S. passports are issued by the Passport Agency (a branch of the State Department). If you are a citizen and resident of the United States, it is easiest to apply for or renew a passport at a post office. Postal workers will check your application and documents and forward the application to the Passport Agency with their certification that they have verified your citizenship and identity. The Passport Agency will send your passport back by mail. Many post offices and certain city and county clerks' offices accept passport applications. If your local post office doesn't, someone there can tell you the nearest office that does. You can also apply in person, by appointment only, at one of the Department of State Passport Agency offices. But the Passport Agency strongly discourages applications at its offices and subjects them all to an extra fee for expedited service (US$60 per person, as of 2011).

If you are renewing a passport, you can do so by mail. But even then you should bring the envelope to the post office unsealed, and have the postal worker verify you've completed all the paperwork properly before you send it in. If you are outside the United States, you can apply for a new passport, such as for a child born abroad of U.S. parents, or renew your existing passport—preferably well before it expires—at any embassy, consulate, or diplomatic office of the United States.

The application form for a U.S. passport asks when and where you are considering travel, which needlessly deters some people from applying until their travel plans are

REAL LIFE

Not long ago, I got a late-night phone call for advice from an acquaintance who planned to get on an international flight the next day, and had discovered he didn't have a valid passport. Why? He hadn't bothered to check his passport, and hadn't noticed that it had expired. Fortunately, he was in San Francisco, where there's a passport office. He got an appointment at the passport office downtown for 12:30 P.M., showed up with his bags packed, and made his 6 P.M. flight (4 P.M. check-in) with his new passport. That's not something you want to put yourself through if you can avoid it.

certain. The only reason for the question is to prioritize rush applications by departure date. Of those who pay for rush service, those who are leaving soonest, or who are going to places for which they will need time to get visas, will get their applications processed first. Don't perjure yourself on the form, but don't worry about whether your destinations (or travel dates) might change. You won't be penalized if you don't go, or go someplace else instead, and where you say you are thinking of going will not be recorded in your passport.

Passports can be issued the same day if necessary, but only at one of a handful of Passport Agency offices in major cities (see the list in the *Resource Guide*). Rush applications are processed in order of urgency. Most people requesting same-day service are told to come to pick up their passports a few days later, unless they are leaving that very day.

If you really need a passport right away, be prepared to spend all day, if necessary, at the passport office. It is possible, though, to get a passport and get on a plane the same day. People going abroad unexpectedly on short notice—most often for business or for family emergencies—do it every day.

Passport application forms and instructions are available at Passport Agency offices, from post offices, or on the Internet. Whether applying at a post office or Passport Agency office, be sure to bring all of the following:

- two recent passport photos (Get plenty of extra photos while you are at it, for visa and other permit applications.)
- your original birth certificate (not a photocopy)
- your driver's license or state photo ID card
- your previous passport, if any, whether or not it is still valid
- the passport fee in cash, personal check, traveler's checks, or money order (US$135 new passport fee for an adult, plus US$60 rush charge applied to all applications at passport offices)
- if you require your passport the same day, your paper tickets, e-ticket receipt, or itinerary from an airline or travel agency showing that you are scheduled to depart the United States within two weeks

Passport Agency passport offices are open for in-person applications by appointment only. You must call ahead to be assigned a specific time to show up with your application. Call or check the State Department Passport Agency website before you go to verify whether any of these requirements, especially the fees, have changed. If your documents aren't in order at the appointed hour, you'll be sent away and won't be able to come back until you've made a new appointment.

If you don't have both a birth certificate and a state photo ID card or driver's license, or any previous passport, or if you weren't born in the United States, check with the Passport Agency in advance for other acceptable forms of proof of citizenship and identity.

If you are applying for a passport for a child under age 14, both the child and at least one parent or legal guardian will have to appear in person at the post office, passport office, or other passport application acceptance office. You'll also need proof of parentage and, unless both parents show up in person, written permission from the absent parent, or proof of sole custody or guardianship. See the Passport Agency website for the permission forms and details.

Unless you request otherwise, you'll get a standard 28-page passport. That's plenty for most trips around the world, unless they involve a lot of country-hopping. If you expect to fill up more pages than that over the next 10 years, you can get a 52-page passport at no additional charge, if you ask when you first apply. Make sure your request for a 52-page passport is prominently indicated on the application form itself, especially if you applied by mail. Requests made on a separate cover letter are apt to be separated from the forms during automated processing and disregarded, as happened one of the times I renewed my passport. If you apply at a passport office, make sure you point this request out to the clerk when you hand over your application. You can get extra visa pages added to your passport or have it replaced if it fills up with entry and exit stamps and visas, but either is an expensive and time-consuming nuisance. Adding pages to a U.S. passport used to be free but now costs US$82. It's easier and cheaper to ask for a thicker passport when you first apply.

The Passport Agency says that normal passport application processing and delivery by mail within the United States takes 6–8 weeks. It's best to allow considerably longer, at least 3–4 months. For an extra fee you can speed up the process by having your passport returned by Express Mail, which is fast, secure, and traceable. Registered Mail is secure but slower than regular mail; Priority Mail is no faster than regular mail and is equally untraceable. As with any valuable item, don't send your passport by regular mail.

Though standard U.S. passports are valid for 10 years from the date of issue or renewal, you shouldn't wait until your passport has expired to renew it. Because many countries will not admit you unless your passport is valid at least six months beyond your intended date of departure from (not arrival in) the country, I recommend renewing your passport a year before it expires. If you've packed your passport away, aren't sure where it is, haven't looked at it in a while, or don't know exactly when it expires, get it out and check it now.

If you need any further impetus to get your passport (and visas) well in advance, consider what happened in 2007–2008 when the Unites States started requiring passports for travel to and from Canada and Mexico. The Passport Office was swamped with applications, and the time required to get a passport went from weeks to months. Appointments at passport offices for in-person rush applications were fully booked weeks ahead. Congressional staff found themselves spending most of their time trying to help desperate constituents who needed passports more quickly. With a flood of Canadians trying to get passports for travel to the United States, which didn't used to require a passport, there were similar backlogs at Passport Canada. Tens of thousands of U.S. and Canadian citizens had to cancel or postpone planned trips abroad. Visas are solely the responsibility of the traveler, not airlines, cruise lines, or tour operators. People who had bought nonrefundable tickets but not travel insurance were out the cost of their tickets or other prepayments. You never know what will happen. Get a passport now, while you are thinking about it.

If you are citizen of a country other than the United States—even if you are a permanent resident and have a U.S. green card or reentry permit—your passport must be issued or renewed by the government of the country of which you are a citizen. U.S. passport offices do not provide services to holders of non-U.S. passports. If your non-U.S. passport has expired, or is about to, you will have to contact the embassy or consulate of your country of citizenship to renew your passport.

PROBLEM COUNTRIES

Restrictions are imposed by the U.S. government on U.S. citizens and their use of U.S. passports for travel to an ever-changing list of countries. As of 2011 the only country to which travel by U.S. citizens was generally prohibited was Cuba, but there were restrictions on bringing back souvenirs from Iran and Sudan. The rules for Sudan may change with the independence of southern Sudan.

It's legal for U.S. citizens to visit almost anywhere except Cuba, even most of the rest of the "Axis of Evil."

North Korea is no longer subject to U.S. travel restrictions, although it's rare for U.S. citizens to be given tourist visas to North Korea. People I know who have visited North Korea have found it strange but interesting.

REAL LIFE

It may come as a surprise to some readers, but visitors from the United States to Iran since the late 1990s consistently report a warm welcome from most people they meet in Iran and other countries in the U.S. "axis of evil."

Travel to Syria is allowed, but it's against U.S. law for U.S. persons to do business with Syrian government-owned banks or the Syrian national airline, which can cause some complications if you don't check out the rules in advance. Banks and credit card companies are encouraged by the government to enforce even broader prohibitions on Syria-related financial transactions than are required by law, so it's best not to try use U.S.-issued credit, debit, or ATM cards in Syria, or to visit U.S. banks' websites from a Syrian Internet address. Just don't let that scare you away from visiting. I found Syria well worth a visit and the people overwhelmingly hospitable, though I wouldn't want to live there.

It's entirely legal to travel to Yemen, which I also found fascinating and friendly. But while I had no problems when I came back, some U.S. visitors to Yemen—especially U.S. Muslims—have been severely hassled by the U.S. government on their return to the United States.

That leaves Cuba as the only country it's a violation of U.S. law for U.S. citizens to visit as tourists. Thousands of U.S. citizens travel to Cuba as tourists every year, but it's important to be aware of the possible consequences before taking such a trip. U.S. citizens cannot legally be denied reentry to the United States, but can expect harassment, fines, and possible prosecution if their passport has been stamped in Cuba. Citizens of other countries can also be, and sometimes are, fined if they bring Cuban goods into the United States, even inadvertently.

Even after the changes in U.S. regulations announced in early 2011, tourist travel directly from the United States to Cuba is still not permitted by the U.S. government. U.S. travel agents are forbidden to arrange flights or tours to Cuba for tourists of any nationality. The only legal travel to Cuba by U.S. citizens or from the United States is for purposes other than tourism, such as for certain family visits and cultural and educational exchange programs with licenses from the Office of Foreign Assets Control of the U.S. Department of the Treasury, which administers U.S. trade embargoes. Only travelers on these licensed programs, or meeting other exceptions to the embargo regulations—and not tourists—are allowed on the few direct charter flights between the United States and Cuba. All other travelers, including all tourists, must go illegally by way of a third country. It's quite easy, and relatively low-risk if you are careful. But it is illegal.

Most travelers from the United States to Cuba go by way of Canada or Mexico, although connections are also possible through various other countries in the Caribbean and Central America. Flights from Canada or Mexico to Cuba, and any desired advance hotel or tour bookings in Cuba, must be arranged through an agent in Mexico, Canada, or elsewhere, not through an agency in the United States. If you don't speak Spanish and have only limited time, it is probably least complicated to arrange an excursion from the United States to Cuba on a package-tour basis through Canada. You can reserve flights from Canada to Cuba in advance through a Canadian agency, with or without a package tour. Going via Mexico (there are flights from Mérida, Cancún, and Mexico City) may be slightly cheaper on an air-only basis, although it's harder to arrange in advance if you don't speak Spanish. Flights to Cuba are also available from Caracas and several places in the Caribbean, as well as from Europe.

Don't try to connect directly, or to check your bags through between the United States and Cuba, in either direction. When returning to the United States, claim your bags in Canada or Mexico and remove any Cuban tags. U.S. authorities have begun watching certain airports, especially Montréal and Toronto, for passengers arriving from Cuba and going directly to flights to the United States. So it's better to leave the airport, spend a night in Canada or Mexico, and come back to the airport the next day to fly home to the United States.

The forms for reentry to the United States ask you to list *all* countries you've visited since leaving the United States. You either have to lie (itself a crime) and say only "Canada" or "Mexico," or risk lengthy questioning, search, and possible sanctions by including Cuba on your customs declaration.

Make sure you don't have any Cuban markings in your passport or on your luggage, and don't attempt to bring any detectable Cuban goods back into the United States. Search your own belongings carefully before you go to check in for your flight back to the United States. Many people have gotten in trouble because of an overlooked "Hecho en Cuba" ("Made in Cuba") label, or an obviously Cuban item such as a CD of Cuban music. And there's always a risk that the U.S. government could find out about your trip through your airline reservations, even if you fly to Cuba from another country.

The U.S. government would certainly frown on your trip to Cuba, and might consider it a crime. On the other hand, there are strong arguments that the U.S. embargo of Cuba is illegal. For decades, U.S. citizens have been engaging in campaigns of civil disobedience, openly defying the U.S. embargo and asserting the freedom to travel to Cuba. Many others have traveled quietly to Cuba, for any of the reasons they might travel anywhere else. But although only a small proportion of visitors to Cuba have been sanctioned by the United States, you shouldn't risk consequences that you wouldn't be willing to face.

For more information, check with travel agents in Canada, Mexico, or almost anywhere else outside the United States, where tours to Cuba are legal and are widely and openly advertised. Or check the websites of Cubatur, the Cuban national tourism promotion office, in Spanish at at www.cubatravel.cu or in English at www.gocuba.ca or www.travel2cuba.co.uk.

REAL LIFE

Some examples: U.S. citizens can travel freely (provided they have obtained the proper visas in advance) between India and Pakistan, even though that's almost impossible for Indians or Pakistanis. Only limited air and land routes are open, but neither the Indian nor the Pakistani visa officers or border guards seem to mind that foreigners have visited the other side of their border with their enemy. There are no flights or land border crossings between Ethiopia and Eritrea, and each country considers the other's citizens to be enemies, but as long as you fly by way of a third country (as of 2008, when I did it, the cheapest connections were via Sana'a, Yemen), foreigners can visit both of these warring neighbor countries without difficulty. Other hostile countries such as Greece and Turkey allow foreigners to cross between them but subject them to especially thorough customs inspection. On the overnight train, we were awakened and questioned, twice, once by Greek and once by Turkish border guards.

Hostile Countries

Passports can present special problems if you want to visit countries hostile to each other. Some countries will not let you in if your passport shows you have previously visited certain other countries. This is most likely to be a problem if you want to visit Islamic countries after visiting Israel. Syria and Lebanon, among other countries, will not admit anyone whose passport shows evidence of a visit to Israel. This isn't true of all Muslim-majority countries, of course: exceptions include Egypt, Jordan, and Turkey, all of which now have diplomatic relations and open borders and/or flights to and from Israel. A variety of tactics can sometimes, but not always, get around these rules and situations. And sometimes citizens of third countries can travel between countries even when that's impossible for their own citizens. Plan carefully for situations like these, and be prepared to adjust your plans if circumstances and rules change at the last minute.

LOOSE-LEAF VISAS AND ENTRY/EXIT STAMPS

In some cases it is possible to avoid having the visa or entry and exit stamps of a pariah country appear in your passport (by "pariah" I mean a country that is disapproved of internationally; I don't mean that I agree with these judgments). Russia and many other communist countries used to issue visas as separate documents, which was intended to prevent the United States or other capitalist governments from blacklisting or discriminating against visitors to the Second World during the Cold War. Cuban authorities are usually willing to put entry and exit stamps for U.S. citizens or residents on a separate paper if you make it a point to ask them, politely but clearly, each time you present your passport. Israel used to do likewise, but has become much more reluctant to do so, and won't unless you make a special request. Be sure you make this request, and that the border officials understand it, before you hand over your passport. You must be very careful to avoid any indication of your visit to the pariah country in your passport. If you get an entry stamp on a separate paper, keep that paper with your passport throughout your stay (you may have great trouble leaving the country without it), but remove it as soon as you leave and before showing your passport to officials of any other countries.

DUPLICATE PASSPORTS

It is sometimes possible to obtain two passports from the same country, with the second passport valid only for travel to a specified country. In the United States, these passports were most often issued for travel to South Africa or Israel, because almost every other country in Africa barred entry to anyone with South African visas or passport stamps, and most Islamic countries barred entry to those with indications of having been in Israel. But it's now possible to travel throughout Africa with South African visa stamps, and in more and more places with Israeli ones. Syria, Lebanon, and Saudi Arabia, however, still ban those who admit to having been to Israel. Anti-Zionist countries will search you thoroughly for a duplicate passport for Israel or a loose paper with Israeli entry and exit stamps if a discontinuity in the entry and exit points in your passport (e.g., exit by land from Egypt, followed a few weeks later by entry by land to Jordan) leads them to suspect that you've been in Israel. Given these problems, I can think of few circumstances in which a duplicate passport would be useful to a U.S. citizen and tourist, although the U.S. State Department will still consider applications for them on a case-by-case basis if you believe you need one. Check with your country's Foreign Ministry or with your country's consulate or embassy if you are abroad. If you are a U.S. citizen, check with one of the State Department's passport agency offices.

Dual Citizenship

"Dual citizens" or "multiple citizens" are entitled to citizenship of more than one country. Some of these people have more than one passport from different countries. Dual or multiple citizenship is usually acquired by unusual circumstances of birth. My mother, for example, was born of U.S.-citizen parents on the territory of what was then the British colony of India and had become, by her 21st birthday, Pakistan. When she turned 21 she kept exclusive U.S. citizenship, but had she realized her options she could have chosen multiple citizenship with the U.K. and (by the terms of partition) either India or Pakistan. In a world of increased global mobility and intermarriage, voluntary and economically compelled migration, and involuntary displacement of peoples across national borders, multiple citizenship is more common than might be imagined.

The advantage of dual citizenship is that it can get you into more countries: if you have trouble getting a visa for a country with one of your passports, there's a chance that a different country's passport will get you in, let you stay longer, and/or generate fewer hassles. You must figure this out before you apply for a visa or try to enter the country, and you have to use the same passport to enter, travel throughout, and leave that country. Even friendly countries won't like it if you apply for a visa first with one passport and then with another, or show one passport on arrival and a different one on departure; in the worst case, you could be held on suspicion of espionage or smuggling or prosecuted for immigration fraud.

If you use one passport to visit a country that is seriously hostile to a third country from which you also hold a passport (e.g., you use a U.S. passport to travel to Syria while also holding an Israeli passport, or use a U.S. passport to travel to Pakistan while also holding an Indian passport) you'll at least need to hide your other passport throughout your stay. But it's safer not to bring it with you at all. Discovery of your dual citizenship, while in a hostile country, is likely to mean, at a minimum, immediate expulsion as persona non grata and a permanent ban on reentry.

Immigrants usually lose their former citizenship (if any) when they become citizens of their adopted country. But most immigrants prefer not to give up their original citizenship, and more and more countries (including the U.S.) are changing their laws to allow dual and multiple citizenship.

The problem with dual citizenship for travelers is that it may be involuntary: a substantial minority of countries refuse to recognize voluntary renunciation of citizenship. If you were born outside the country of your parents' and your citizenship, there is a good chance you are considered a citizen of another country, whether or not you realize it or have ever had a passport from that government. If you return to the country of your birth or former citizenship, you run the risk that it will still consider you a citizen, even if you and your adopted country no longer do. This can lead to your not being allowed to leave without obtaining a new passport and exit permit from the country whose citizenship you have renounced or never knew you had. You may be subjected to such requirements of local law as taxes (including back income or excise taxes for the period when you were out of the country), military conscription, family law (your marriage, divorce, or adoption may not be recognized even if it is valid in the country of your other citizenship), and defamation or national-security law (i.e., you can be held to answer, as a local citizen, under local law, for critical or "antinational" statements or actions even if made while in another country on another passport).

These are particularly common problems because escaping conscription, war taxes or other taxes, arranged or child marriages or inequities of family law, and differences of opinion with the national government or national-security apparatus are all common reasons for people to have emigrated in the first place. Check local rules carefully before you visit any country with a conceivable claim on your citizenship. For U.S. citizens, special pitfalls affecting dual citizens and immigrants from other countries are usually covered in the country-specific information from the U.S. Department of State. A foreign government, even that of a country in which you hold dual citizenship, can offer only very limited assistance if you are prosecuted as a local citizen.

Passports and Documents for Families and Children

It used to be common to include dependents (children, spouse, historically even accompanying family servants) on the same passport with the head of the family. It's still possible in some countries, but don't do this unless you have to. Each person should have a separate passport. It's especially tempting to include an infant on its mother's passport, just to have one fewer document to carry or worry about losing. But what if there's an emergency and one has to return home while the other has to stay; e.g., if one is hospitalized and can't travel, while the other must be rushed to another country for surgery or treatment? Without a separate passport, the dependent can't travel alone, no matter what happens. It's possible, strongly recommended, and in more and more countries required, to get a separate passport for even a day-old infant.

Involuntary and illegal international transportation and trafficking in children, international flight with children in custody disputes, transborder adoption brokering, recruitment of child prostitutes, and out-and-out child slavery—all of these problems are gaining global recognition. As with sex tourism and trafficking in women, not much is really being done—too much money is at stake for that—but to make a show of addressing these problems, many countries have imposed special documentary requirements on minors crossing their borders to ensure that they have legal permission from their parent(s) or guardian(s).

A minor child accompanied by both parents is likely to get little special scrutiny if all three (child and both accompanying parents) have the same family name. If the parents have different family names, bring a copy of the child's birth certificate. If either parent's, or the child's, name on the birth certificate doesn't match the name on the passport, bring documentation of the name change.

If only one parent or guardian will be traveling with the child, your documents will—and should be—closely scrutinized every time you take an international flight or cross a border. Bring proof of parentage, adoption, or guardianship as well as notarized permissions from all parents or guardians not accompanying the child. If someone other than a parent or guardian is the child's companion, it is essential to get notarized permissions from both parents or any guardian(s) for the child to travel with the appointed companion.

Even if you plan for both parents and their child or children always to travel together, parents might want to consider getting permission letters notarized, before an extended trip, and giving them to each other, so that either parent has permission to travel with the children, without the other parent, in case of emergency. If it's needed, it might be hard to find a notary in a hurry.

This didn't used to be required, and it may seem excessive, but it's not. I hear regularly from grandparents, parents with different surnames from their children, divorced parents (even if they have sole custody but don't have proof of it), and other travelers with children who are turned back at borders or refused boarding on international flights because they don't have notarized proof of permission, from both parents, to travel internationally with the children.

Note that this permission to travel, to be carried with you, is different from the separate parental permissions required for issuance of a passport to a minor. A power of attorney authorizing the traveling companion to make health care and emergency treatment decisions for the minor child is also a good idea for any but the shortest trip, lest vital time be lost trying to contact the parents or guardians from a remote or inaccessible place.

Minors traveling by themselves, without either parent, should be prepared to present proof of permission to travel from both parents or guardians. Airlines have their own special requirements, varying by airline, for transporting unaccompanied minors, if they are willing to do so at all. Most airlines charge unaccompanied minors an adult fare to compensate for the additional cost of looking out for them. Verify the rules with each airline well in advance.

Lost or Stolen Passports

If your passport is lost or stolen, report it to the local police at the first opportunity. Get a copy of the police report, or at least all possible details about it (name and title of the officer to whom it was reported, where, when, file number, etc.) and a letter from the police confirming that you have reported the loss or theft of your passport. Take the police report to your country's nearest consulate or embassy. It will expedite matters greatly if you have a photocopy of the missing passport. Carry a photocopy of your passport somewhere separate from the passport itself. Exchange passport copies with your traveling companion. Leave another copy of your passport with someone back home. And email a scanned image of it to yourself, so you can print out a copy from a cybercafé in an emergency.

If you renew your passport, or get a new one for some other reason, save the old one even though it's no longer valid. An expired passport is perhaps the single most useful document with which to start—even better than your birth certificate, because it has a photo—if your personal documents are lost, stolen, or destroyed and you need to replace them all from scratch. I'd normally leave it in a safe deposit box (in case my house burns down) or with a contact back home while I'm travel-

> **REAL LIFE**
>
> One stateless refugee from Iran, Mr. Mehran Karimi Nasseri, lived in the transit lounge at Charles de Gaulle Airport in Paris for 11 years, from 1988 to 1999! By the time he was allowed to enter the European Union, psychologists feared that he had become so "institutionalized" to life in the airport that he would be unable to function in the world outside.

ing abroad. But some people bring an expired passport with them (especially if they've been traveling long enough to have accumulated more than one), packed separately from their current passport, as backup identification. A U.S. "passport card," if you have one, can serve the same function and is smaller and sturdier.

The United States has an embassy (or another office such as an "interests section" that fills its role and can issue replacement passports) in virtually every country to which it is legal for U.S. citizens to travel. But not all countries can afford to maintain that kind of global diplomatic presence. Citizens of other countries thus may find themselves without a passport in a country where their country does not maintain an embassy. This can be an extremely difficult situation: you may not be permitted to leave without being able to show proof of when you entered, or you may be fined on the presumption that you lost your passport to hide the fact that you overstayed your visa.

You shouldn't agree to leave without a passport until you are certain that the country to which you are departing will let you in. If it doesn't, you could be trapped in no-man's-land at the border, or in the airport, in limbo without a passport and unable to go anywhere. If you are stateless, you either have to make special arrangements, confirmed in writing, that you will be allowed to proceed to some country where you have verified that your passport can be replaced. Or you have to get, and prove that you have, permission to return directly home. This is quite a drag if you're halfway around the world, in the middle of your trip. In a real emergency, go to the embassy or consulate of whichever locally represented government has the closest and friendliest relationship with your country's government. At the very least they will probably help you contact your country's government to find out how you should proceed.

U.S. and other First World embassies overseas can be extremely suspicious of budget travelers seeking replacement of lost or stolen passports. Too many travelers who have run short of money overseas have found that passports are their most valuable and salable remaining possessions. (U.S. and Canadian passports may be the most valuable of all passports on the black market.) Expect to be questioned closely about how your passport was lost or stolen, to pay a stiff fee for its replacement, to have to execute a sworn declaration that you didn't sell it, and to have the whole replacement process drag on for several weeks. It might take only a few days, but it's likely to be that fast only if you're a well-dressed middle-aged white businessman.

Replacement passports issued outside the country of your citizenship are often valid for a shorter time than passports issued in your home country, although in the case of U.S. passports, replacements can be issued as valid for a full 10 years. Replacement passports are technically just as good as any other but are sometimes viewed with suspicion by immigration officials in subsequent countries who wonder if you destroyed your old passport to get rid of something that would have precluded entry to their country, such as a visa or entry stamp from an enemy country, or a notation that you had previously been deported, forbidden to return, or declared persona non grata. So if you get a "temporary" replacement passport issued abroad, I'd recommend renewing it (thus getting a new standard passport) as soon as it's convenient after you get back to the United States or your home country.

Once you've replaced your passport, you'll have to replace any visas that were in it, starting with your visa (and/or entry stamp or permit) to the country you are in at the time. It's harder to get visas replaced than it is to get them in the first place, and it generally involves considerable delay. It's a judgment call that you have to make before you approach each embassy or consulate. You may have an easier time if you simply say you want a visa than if you say you had one but lost it or had it stolen. But if the country's record-keeping is sufficiently systematic to indicate you already had a visa, and you didn't say that, suspicions may be aroused and you may not get a new visa at all.

I'm getting ahead of myself. Before you can replace a visa, you have to get one. Just what is a visa, anyway?

VISAS AND OTHER PERMITS

Many people are intimidated by visas. Visa rules are arbitrary and sometimes strict, and by the time you realize you've made a mistake it can be too late to do anything about it. If you plan ahead, however, visa rules will rarely prevent you from going where you want.

Visas are legal documents issued by governments, so dealing with them inevitably requires a certain familiarity with, and tolerance for, bureaucracy, legalism, and jargon. I'll try to explain as simply as possible—without sacrificing critical details—what visas are, how to find out if you need them, how to get them, and what else you need to know about entry requirements and crossing international borders.

What's a Visa?

A visa is an authorization (usually a stamp in your passport, but sometimes a separate document or a record in an electronic database) issued by the government of the country you wish to visit, as one of the preconditions of admission to the country. However, a visa is not a guarantee of admission to any country. Claiming, "I have a visa so you have to let me in," is a good way to get yourself denied admission. On arrival, you may also have to show sufficient funds to support yourself, an onward or return ticket, and/or whatever else the particular country requires. Other typical requirements are discussed later in this chapter.

U.S. citizens can visit many countries without visas and can obtain visas to some other countries on arrival. Citizens of some other First World countries have a pretty easy time as well. But you should check the current visa requirements of each and every country you will visit or pass through before you finalize your plans or purchase tickets. You may need to get a separate visa for each country, you may find that it is not possible to stay as long as you had hoped, or you may not be able to afford to meet the requirements to go to some countries at all.

Why Do I Need a Visa?

As discussed earlier in the sidebar *Freedom to Travel?*, most countries consider themselves to have complete discretion to prohibit, restrict, or impose whatever conditions they please on most visits by citizens of other countries. International law recognizes an inalienable and unrestricted right to return to one's home, but is less clear, at least in practice, on a general right to tourism or travel to other countries. Some countries entirely prohibit tourism. Others impose all sorts of restrictions, conditions, and bureaucratic procedures to be followed by would-be visitors. Some countries have predictable biases regarding who they admit; others

REAL LIFE

In 1993, an entire tour group from Malaysia was arrested on arrival in Boston by immigration officials who couldn't believe that they were really tourists on a US$6,000 per person around-the-world package tour, rather than illegal immigrants. (Yes, that was a very cheap price: it was a very fast tour, emphasizing opportunities for shopping.)

Business or Pleasure?

Visits for business or employment of all types often require a visa, even where tourists from the same country don't need visas. Business visas are often subject to more complicated, expensive, and above all time-consuming application and approval procedures. As a result, it used to be routine for business travelers not to bother to get visas or declare the business purpose of their trip, especially for brief visits for meetings or other activities for which they are not receiving a salary in the destination country. They entered other countries as tourists, without visas. Most of the time this was tolerated, with a wink and a nod, as long as you played by the implicit rules: If you are entering a country as a tourist, don't say you are coming for business.

There have always been occasional problems for people who don't realize that they are supposed to have a business visa, or that they are supposed to say they are "just a tourist" when they arrive for sales calls, negotiations, consulting, conferences, or trade shows without a visa. I was almost denied entry to the U.K. once when I momentarily forgot what I was supposed to say to the kindly seeming immigration inspector. (It's hard to distinguish "travel writing" from "tourism," and there's an element of research work in all my travels. She let me in, eventually, with a caution to keep my story straight and simple the next time.) Lately several countries, including but not limited to the

are inexplicably arbitrary. Count on nothing. Consular officials don't have to give you a visa, give you any reason why they won't, or answer to anyone except their home government. Treat them with the utmost respect and courtesy, no matter how well or badly you may feel they are treating you.

In the case of the United States, immigration inspectors are required to refuse entry to anyone they suspect of planning to work in or immigrate to the United States, even if that person has a valid tourist visa. Yet many visitors to the United States find that ordinary Americans are remarkably friendly to individual foreign tourists. And as a U.S. citizen, I've been warmly welcomed in countries like Pakistan where the first question asked of me was, "Why is the U.S. government so hostile to our country?" Don't judge any country by its government or its border guards, no matter how strong the temptation. Get a visa, if need be, go there, and experience it for yourself.

The underlying principle of most entry requirements is reciprocity. If Country L is willing to admit citizens of Country M without visas, Country M will usually do the same for citizens of Country L. If another country has

United States, have been cracking down on casual business visitors without visas. The issue got worldwide publicity in 2006 when reporters from major media outlets in the U.K. and Australia, arriving in the United States for short visits to conduct interviews without the special visas technically required for working journalists, were refused entry and detained until they could be deported on the next flights home. Anywhere in the world, a "tourist" arriving in a business suit, saying they intend to stay for six months, or discovered to have a briefcase full of résumés, or whose latest Facebook status update (yes, border guards will Google you if they get suspicious) says they are en route to a job interview, will arouse suspicion that they are really intending to take jobs away from local people — without permission.

Read the rules for entry without visa or for tourist visas carefully, in advance, to see what, if any, business activities are permitted without a special visa. If you can, get a proper business visa--the hassle is likely to be less than the hassle of denial of entry and/or deportation. If you decide the only way to get your business done is to be "just a tourist," have as simple and plausible an explanation as possible ready in case you are asked, don't have any inconsistent evidence with you (including data on your computer or in your mobile phone), and stick to your story consistently.

made it especially difficult for citizens of your country to get permission to visit, it's probably in retaliation for the special difficulties its citizens face in visiting your country. If you want visa rules relaxed, start by lobbying your own country's government to relax its rules for foreign visitors.

If you're a U.S. citizen, in particular, try to keep visa hassles in perspective: I know of no country in the world whose consular, immigration, and customs authorities consistently treat would-be foreign visitors worse than does the United States. And no country has a more rigid "onward ticket" requirement for entry than the United States, has more complicated and confusing visa forms, or is less tolerant of people who don't speak, read, or write the one official language. All applicants for tourist visas to the United States are required to appear in person at a U.S. consulate or embassy for an interview-cum-interrogation. The majority of U.S. tourist-visa applicants from some countries are turned down. For those citizens of most of the world who need visas, a tourist or transit visa to visit or even just change planes in the United States costs a *minimum* of US$140. All foreign visitors to the U.S., including tourists and travelers in transit, are fingerprinted and photographed on arrival, again on departure, and while changing planes en route between other countries via the United States (such as between Asia, Europe, or Canada and Latin America).

Under the Visa Waiver Program, citizens of certain First World countries are allowed to visit the United States without visas provided they have a return ticket and meet various other criteria. All other visitors to the United States need visas. Check with any U.S. embassy or consulate, or the U.S. State Department's website for foreign visitors to the United States at http://travel.state.gov/visa, to find out whether citizens of your country are currently included in the Visa Waiver Program and the current requirements for visa-free entry to the United States.

Fortunately for U.S. citizens, the allure of tourist dollars is such that few other countries treat U.S. citizens who want to visit half as badly as the United States treats foreign would-be tourists. U.S. citizens are the world's greatest beneficiaries of nonreciprocal visa-free entry requirements and fees.

All visa requirements are subject to change at any time without warning or notice. Don't rely on guidebooks or word-of-mouth from people who have visited a country in the past. Check the current visa requirements directly with the consulates or embassies of each country you plan to visit. Don't rely on embassy or consulate websites: many aren't kept up to date, and it's much safer to phone or, if possible, visit a consulate or embassy in person. The more countries you plan to visit, the earlier you need to get started. List every country you will pass through, no matter how briefly. Find out each country's requirements, and get answers to such questions as:

- Do I need a visa, given what country I am a citizen of (i.e. what passport I will be using)?
- Where do I need to apply? (Some countries allow you to apply at any of their embassies. Some countries require you to apply through their embassy or consulate in your country of citizenship or residence.)
- How long will I be allowed to stay?
- Will I need an onward or return ticket?
- Are there other restrictions on entry or travel that I should know about?

For each country that requires a visa, get a copy of the application form, all instructions, and the address and phone number of the nearest embassy or consulate that issues visas. Find out if visas for the country are stamped in passports, issued as separate documents, or issued electronically.

If you have a passport from a First World country and are planning a trip through many countries, typically most will let you in for a short visit without a visa, and the remainder will give you visas pretty much for the asking, provided you follow the proper procedures. You may find that a few places you want to go won't let you in at all, or will do so only if you comply with requirements that would be impractical or cost more than you would be willing to pay. A critical few will probably have entry requirements (such as stay limits or requirements for onward tickets or entry and exit only at certain points, or limitations on how soon after it is issued you have to use your visa) that, while not prohibitive, will compel you to adjust your route, schedule, or means of transport. For this reason, even if you don't actually get your visas until you have your tickets, you should verify the entry requirements of every country you plan to visit before you schedule or pay for any tickets or tours.

Where Do I Get a Visa?

Permission to enter any country's territory must be obtained from that country's government, or the representatives of that country's government abroad. In most countries the division of the national government that deals with the admission of foreigners is the Foreign Ministry or Ministry of Foreign Affairs; in the United States the relevant branch is the Department of State. In either case its offices outside its own territory are called embassies or consulates.

An embassy is a country's primary diplomatic office in another country, usually located in the other country's capital. All embassies issue visas. (Among Commonwealth countries, all of which nominally recognize the British monarchy as their common sovereign, what would otherwise be an embassy is called a "high commission," headed by a "high commissioner" rather than an ambassador.) A consulate general is a subsidiary office in another city, but one that usually performs almost all of the functions of an embassy, including issuing visas. A consulate is a lower-ranking office and may not issue visas; you may have to apply to a consulate general or embassy for a visa. An honorary consulate is the lowest level of

REAL LIFE

The most common real-world visa complications for people planning a trip around the world are (1) onward ticket requirements, when you plan to depart the country by land or haven't bought your onward air ticket yet, (2) length of stay limitations, and (3) countries that require you to apply for visas in your home country, when you're leaving home too far in advance for a visa issued before you leave to still be valid when you get to their country.

diplomatic representation. An honorary consul is usually a part-time diplomat (an honorary consulate usually shares its office with the honorary consul's business or professional office) and does not ordinarily issue visas, although some do.

It's not always obvious to first-time international travelers, or to those who simply haven't needed a visa before, that your own country's government has no role whatsoever and can offer no assistance (unless you are a government official) in obtaining permission for you to visit other countries. If you are a U.S. citizen, don't waste time asking the U.S. State Department or a U.S. embassy or consulate whether you need a visa to some other country, or appealing to them for assistance if some other country turns you away. They have no authority over such matters and will not be able to help you. Because of the frequency with which it is asked such questions, the U.S. State Department has compiled a summary of other countries' entry requirements for U.S. citizens. It is useful but not authoritative, has no official weight, is often out of date, and should not be relied on. Specialized references for travel agents and airlines (see the *Resource Guide*) are updated more often, although they are still only informational.

WHO'S IN CHARGE?

The first step in figuring out whether you need a visa is figuring out what country exercises sovereignty or actual control over the place you want to go. If you know what country you wish to visit, it's relatively easy. But if the region you want to visit is colonized, occupied, or divided, you have to figure out who's in control of the particular part you want to visit.

Some divided regions are often mistakenly thought to be unified, independent countries. Borneo and New Guinea, for example, are islands, not countries, though many people interested in visiting them assume that such large places must be sovereign. Borneo includes all of one country (Brunei) and parts of two others (the Malaysian states of Sarawak and Sabah and the four Indonesian states of West, East, South, and Central Kalimantan). New Guinea is divided about in half between Papua New Guinea (often called PNG, which also includes New Britain and some smaller islands) and the Indonesian-ruled provinces of Papua and West Papua (formerly Irian Jaya). Completely different rules apply to visitors to each part of these islands, as well as different ways of getting there and away.

Visas for possessions of the United States such as Puerto Rico, Guam, American Samoa, or the U.S. Virgin Islands must be obtained from U.S. embassies or consulates.

Visas for France's overseas territories such as French Polynesia and Kanaky (New Caledonia), and overseas departments such as French Guyana,

Réunion, Guadeloupe, and Martinique, must be obtained from the embassies or consulates of France.

Visas for Northern Ireland, Bermuda, various Caribbean islands of the British West Indies and British Virgin Islands, the Falkland (Malvinas) Islands, and Gibraltar must be obtained from the embassies or consulates of the United Kingdom of Great Britain and Northern Ireland.

Visas for East Turkestan ("Xinjiang Province") and Tibet must be obtained from China.

Visas for the Cook Islands (capital Rarotonga) must be obtained from Aotearoa/New Zealand.

Visas for Kashmir must be obtained from either Pakistan or India, depending on which side of the Indo-Pak cease-fire line you want to visit. The Kashmir Valley has been annexed by India but is presently unsuitable for tourism because of fighting between Kashmiri nationalists and the Indian Army. The Karakoram Highway to and from China goes through areas administered by Pakistan pending a plebiscite throughout Kashmir—to which plebiscite India has renounced its commitment. Ladakh and Jammu are considered part of Jammu and Kashmir State and are controlled by India.

Visas for Western Sahara (the Sahrawi Arab Democratic Republic or SADR) have to be obtained from the embassies or consulates of Morocco, which claims the right to rule the entire territory.

Visas for the different regions of Kurdistan must be obtained from the embassies or consulates of Turkey, Syria, Iran, or Iraq, none of which admit that such a place as Kurdistan exists, or want anyone to visit who might think or learn otherwise.

As of this writing, visas for even the self-ruled areas of Palestine must be obtained from Israel. This is quite likely to change, with the Palestinian authorities eventually obtaining some autonomous power to authorize visits. Check the most current rules before you head for this area.

Some sovereign microstates find it too expensive to maintain their own foreign service, and contract with some other country (usually the former colonial power) to represent them and handle their diplomatic affairs abroad. For some it was actually a condition of independence and internal autonomy that they allow their former rulers to continue to handle their foreign relations.

Monaco, for example, is independent but is represented abroad and allows entry and exit to be controlled by France. Instances of this elsewhere are declining but still surprisingly numerous, particularly in the Caribbean (represented by various European countries) and the Pacific basin (represented in different cases by the United States, France, Australia, and Aotearoa/New Zealand, depending on which sphere of influence different island groups are or were in).

UNRECOGNIZED OR UNREPRESENTED COUNTRIES

Certain countries present particular problems in finding embassies or consulates, for any of several reasons. Some countries control territory and have functional and reasonably stable internal governmental infrastructure but aren't recognized by foreign countries. Notable examples of such countries as of 2011 were Somaliland and Puntland. Some countries either don't recognize each other (usually because of hostility) or don't maintain representation in each other's countries, usually because they can't afford to maintain embassies in low-priority countries with which they have little trade or exchange of people. In such cases you will probably need to obtain visas in some intermediate country along the way, as is discussed in *Getting Visas Outside Your Home Country* later on in this chapter.

Occasionally two countries that have broken off diplomatic relations but that still have important issues to negotiate will have their interests represented by intermediary countries. It works like this: the U.S. Interests Section of the Embassy of Switzerland in Cuba is technically a part of the Embassy of Switzerland but serves to represent the interests of the U.S. government in dealings with the government of Cuba. In actuality this is often a shell game: the U.S. Interests Section is likely staffed by nationals of the United States, not Switzerland (although they carry Swiss diplomatic credentials) and is located not in the same building as the Embassy of Switzerland but in a separate building, formerly the U.S. Embassy, which now flies the flag of Switzerland. Where one exists, an interests section may or may not be able to issue visas. The Iranian Interests Section of the Embassy of Pakistan to the United States, for example, issues visas to U.S. citizens who want to visit Iran. The staff of an interests section is generally preoccupied with diplomatic business other than tourism (espionage, for example), and has an inherently tenuous status. So don't expect them to offer more than limited assistance to travelers.

Sometimes countries maintain representative offices other than embassies or consulates in each others' countries, at a level short of full diplomatic recognition. For example, a Vietnam liaison office opened in Washington, D.C., in 1995, several years before the United States and Vietnam exchanged ambassadors or established full diplomatic relations.

As a condition of the agreement to situate the headquarters of the United Nations (UN) in the United States, the United States is required to allow UN members, even those not recognized by the United States, to maintain missions to the UN. So the governments of Cuba and North Korea, which have no embassies in the United States, have offices at the UN in New York. However, these offices are allowed to remain only on condition that they confine themselves to representing their countries to and at the UN. Under pain of expulsion from the United States, they cannot issue visas, provide tourist information about their countries, or otherwise function as embassies. Don't even think of asking them to do things that would jeopardize their diplomatic status.

Direct flights between two countries require bilateral agreements that can only be negotiated and agreed to if the countries maintain diplomatic relations. So if you are flying directly from Country A to Country B, you can more or less count on finding an embassy of B in A, and vice versa, or at least mutual recognition by the two governments. If you are traveling indirectly (stopping or changing planes in some other country in between) or by other means than air, check carefully in advance to be sure there is an embassy where you will need one.

DIPLOMATIC PARIAHS

Countries considered international pariahs, for one reason or another, may be denied recognition or the exchange of ambassadors as a sign of other countries' disapproval of their existence, governments, or policies. At various times, Israel and South Africa have been major victims of such policies. Until the 1990s, both had embassies in most First World countries but few Second, Third, or Fourth World countries.

If a country doesn't recognize a government, it generally doesn't recognize passports issued by that government as valid travel documents. So Israeli and South African passports weren't valid for travel in most of the world, and citizens of those countries were only able to travel widely if they held second passports from other countries.

The situation with respect to both countries has changed markedly since the 1995 elections in South Africa and the creation of areas of limited Palestinian autonomy. Almost all countries now recognize South Africa and admit its passport holders. In addition, South Africa has opened new embassies in all the larger African capitals and many other countries. South Africans may now travel almost everywhere. Israel is still unrepresented and Israelis are barred from travel in many countries, including most OIC (Organization of the Islamic Conference) countries in Africa and Asia, but not nearly as many as before. Israelis (and foreigners) may now cross back and forth between Israel, Egypt, and Jordan. Israelis may travel to India and Thailand, although not to many other South and Southeast Asian and African countries.

DIVIDED COUNTRIES

Some divided countries with claims on each other's territory don't recognize each other and/or break off relations with any country that recognizes the enemy.

The governments of North Korea (the Democratic People's Republic of Korea, or DPRK) and South Korea (the Republic of Korea, or ROK) each claim to aspire to the reunification of Korea—on their own terms. North

Korea's two neighbors, China and Russia, and a few other socialist countries recognize both the DPRK and the ROK. Almost all other countries, including some of the non-Russian ex-Soviet states, recognize only the ROK. It is almost impossible to arrange travel to the DPRK except as a side trip from China or Russia.

China (the People's Republic of China, or PRC) claims that Taiwan Province is an integral part of its territory. Actually, Taiwan is an offshore island with a distinct people and culture that was only ruled by China for a small fraction of its long recorded history. For many years the Kuomintang Party (KMT), which ruled Taiwan after it fled the revolution in China, considered the Republic of China (ROC) to be the legitimate government of all China, including the mainland.

For now, most countries, including the United States, recognize only the PRC. Money talks, though, and the lure of Taiwanese economic aid has persuaded a number of small, mostly poor Third and Fourth World countries, of which Paraguay is the largest, to recognize Taiwan rather than the PRC as being the government of "China." More importantly, Taiwan has been able to maintain functional relations, trade ministries, and visa-granting offices—embassies or consulates in everything but name and diplomatic status—even in countries that formally recognize China's claim to sovereignty over Taiwan. In the United States, visas to Taiwan are issued by a network of offices of the Coordinating Council for North American Affairs of the Republic of China on Taiwan, or CCNAA. Similar offices, with a plethora of euphemistic names, represent Taiwan in many other countries. A full list is available from any of these offices, the Taiwan Visitors Bureau, or any of the Taiwanese airlines.

Neither the PRC nor the ROC cares whether you have visited the other or have the other's visa stamps in your passport. Taiwanese are actually major investors in, and traders with, the PRC, largely by way of Hong Kong. As of 2011, there were still no direct scheduled airline services across the Taiwan Straits, although negotiations to allow them have been underway for years.

BAD NEIGHBORS

Many neighboring countries have border disputes and poor relations. Often they accuse each other of supporting "separatist" or otherwise dissident groups or movements in each others' territories, or have conflicts over transborder migration (the U.S.–Mexico conflicts over this are by no means unique). In such cases, relations may be strained; even where borders are open, obtaining visas in a neighboring country may be harder than in some neutral country farther from the dispute.

A notable example is India and Pakistan, between which relations are as hostile as those between the United States and the USSR at the height of the

Cold War. It's actually quite easy, interesting, and worthwhile for foreigners to cross back and forth between India and Pakistan. Officials and ordinary people in both countries welcome visitors from the other side. There are usually direct flights, inexpensive ones at that, between Delhi and Lahore, and sometimes between other cities. But very few locals are allowed across the Indo-Pak border. I once had lunch with a professor at one of the leading universities in the region whose life's work was the study of regional political relations, yet who had never been permitted to visit the other side.

The two countries, barely on speaking terms with each other, allow only minimal diplomatic staff in each others' countries. Periodically they aggravate the problem by expelling each others' representatives or closing consulates for spying under cover of diplomatic immunity. As a result, there are always too few visa officers, sometimes none at all, which means long waits.

If you want to visit both India and Pakistan, try to get visas for both in other countries somewhere—anywhere—outside South Asia. The same goes for other mutually hostile countries: try to get visas to both in your home country or, if that isn't possible, at least somewhere else that is neutral.

SOURCES FOR VISA INFORMATION

While the government of the country you wish to visit is the ultimate arbiter of its visa requirements, it is best to review visa requirements and application procedures first with a good travel agent or, if you can afford it, a commercial visa-processing service. You can spoil your chances of getting a visa at all if you don't know what to tell the embassy about your profession, purposes for visiting, etc. Some countries, for example, will give visas to visitors such as students, researchers, journalists, or businesspeople with professional reasons for their visits, but not to tourists. Other countries give visas to tourists but not to researchers, journalists, or people wanting to do business. It may be essential to emphasize certain things on your application for a visa to Country A, and essential not to mention the same things at all when dealing with the officials of Country B. A travel agent or visa service familiar with the country you wish to visit can advise you what to say and not to say (within the bounds of honesty) to maximize the chances that your requests for visas will be approved.

It can be difficult to get clear information from some consulates and embassies. Visa services may provide copies of visa application forms on their websites, but they make money by submitting visa applications for you, not by giving advice on how to apply for visas on your own. Visa requirements can be imposed, removed, or changed overnight, and visa information and forms on the Internet or in guidebooks or other printed references can be out of date. If you have trouble understanding the forms or instructions, a travel agent familiar with consular lingo may be able to interpret them for you. Travel agents who can't or won't give you basic advice on visa requirements either don't specialize in international travel or have cut their profit margin too thin to allow them to take the time to give good service. Travel agents can't be expected to know all the visa rules of every country or to process your visa applications for you for free. But they should be able to tell you generally which countries require visas (as of the latest information they have been given), give you addresses and phone numbers of consulates, and warn you of the most commonly encountered onward ticket and other special requirements (such as needing a local sponsor or proof of prepaid accommodations or tours).

Do not rely on guidebooks or Internet sources as authorities on visa requirements. Consulates' and embassies' websites, especially those of small, poor countries, often aren't up to date. If possible, call or visit in person to confirm the essential details. Good guidebooks do have helpful information on unusual rules or country peculiarities, but rules change all the time. And it is imperative to verify anything in a guidebook or on a website with a consulate, embassy, or good travel agent. If a guidebook says that citizens of your country can get visas for Country P from an embassy in City Q, but the embassy of Country P in your country says this is not possible, it's much more likely because the rules have changed than because the embassy doesn't know its own rules. It would be a serious, albeit common, mistake to set off for Q, counting on getting a visa there, unless you want to go to Q regardless of whether you can get into P.

Visa–Free Entry and Visas on Arrival

Many countries admit U.S. citizens without visas, or issue visas on arrival for tourist visits of limited duration. If the embassy or consulate tells you citizens of your country don't need visas for stays of your intended duration, you can probably take what they say at face value, although you still need to find out what items—photos? Cash? Onward tickets?—you will need at the border to be admitted.

Entry without a visa almost always requires an onward ticket and/or proof of sufficient funds to buy one and to pay one's expenses for as long as one is authorized to stay. If you want to leave a country by land or water, or to buy your onward ticket in that country, it is more likely that you will need to get a visa. Visa-free entry permits and visas on arrival sometimes authorize travel only to certain parts of a country. If you want to travel to remote, politically sensitive, or specially protected regions, you are more likely to need a visa and even a special permit in addition to a visa.

Visa-free entry to the United States is limited to tourists who are citizens of certain countries that the United States allows to participate in the Visa Waiver Program and who have certain types of machine-readable passports. Check the rules, and check your passport, to see if you need a visa, before you set out for the United States.

Many people misunderstand "You *can* get a visa on arrival," or "You *can* extend your visa once you are there," as meaning, "You *should* wait to obtain your visa upon your arrival," and don't get visas in advance unless they have to. I advise exactly the reverse. It's almost always easier to get into a country if you have a visa in advance, even if visas aren't strictly required. Getting a visa in advance will save time and complications at the border, and will make you less vulnerable to demands for bribes or to changes in visa rules. It's easiest if you apply for a visa in the country where you are a citizen. If your application for a visa on arrival is, for any reason, denied, you have little

> **REAL LIFE**
>
> You can transit most countries by air without going through customs and immigration. The major exception is the United States, where all transit passengers must go through full entry and exit formalities. Allow plenty of time if you have to change planes in the Unites States, for example when traveling between Asia and Latin America. In Singapore, you can change planes at the main terminals without border formalities, but I had to go through customs and immigration (twice) and get my passport stamped for arrival and departure in order to get from the no-frills "Budget Terminal" where my Tiger Airways flight from Australia arrived to the main terminals for an onward flight on United Airlines.

recourse other than to turn back. If you apply in advance and are at first turned down, you may have time to correct the deficiency in your application and try again. Similarly, it's apt to be easier to pay a little extra for a longer-duration visa, if that's an option, than to have to waste time later, while you are traveling, to get your visa extended.

Visa Services and Travel Agents

It is generally better for you to obtain your own visas, rather than to have a visa service or travel agent obtain them for you, unless you don't have time to do it yourself or can't get to a consulate or embassy and need a visa for one of the few countries (notably China) that doesn't accept visa applications by mail. Visa services and travel agents generally charge about US$50 per visa over and above the fees charged by the consulate or embassy. For this fee, they will obtain the application forms and instructions, advise you on how to fill out the forms, and take or send your application and passport to the embassy or consulate and back again.

Your visa application is no more or less likely to be approved if it arrives through a travel agent or visa service than if it comes directly from you. Visa services and travel agents don't pay bribes and have no special influence on consular officials. If you call a visa service and ask them "Can you get me a visa for Country Q," they'll say, "Sure. No problem." What this means is if you satisfy all of the requirements for admission to Country Q, the visa service can get you the forms, show you how to fill them out, and send them to the embassy. If the embassy of Q has already told you a visa application can only be approved if accompanied by an invitation from a citizen of Q in good standing on a form endorsed by the Ministry of Foreign Affairs of Q, applying through a visa service will not obviate or change that requirement. Visa services have little control over the processing of your application once a consulate or embassy has your documents. Visa services can guarantee neither results nor processing time.

The biggest advantage of visa services is that all the good ones in the United States, regardless of where they are based, have representatives in Washington, D.C., who can "walk" your visa applications from one embassy to another in rapid succession. This saves you the two days it would take by Express Mail or Federal Express to get your passport back from each embassy, verify the visa was issued correctly, and send your passport on to the next embassy. If you ask an embassy to send your passport directly to another embassy, you have no way to know which embassy is responsible if it is lost. You can't and shouldn't trust an embassy to return your passport to anyone but yourself, your travel agent, a very trusted friend, or a visa service. If you need many visas in a hurry, you may have no choice but to use a visa service, but this is an expensive option that can usually be avoided by planning ahead.

The only countries for which you may need special help from a travel agent are those few that require special "visa support" such as an invitation or proof of a prepaid tour (notably Russia and some other former Soviet republics) or for those that don't issue visas in your country.

How to Apply for Visas

The essential thing to keep in mind is that in applying for a visa you are asking for a favor, not claiming a right.

Most of today's sovereign countries were colonies when I was born in early 1960. Eighteen new countries became independent in that year alone. In Northern countries, especially those that were (or still are) imperial powers, we take sovereignty for granted—even in the United States, whose great contribution to global political thought has been its revolutionary defense of the right to wage armed anti-imperialist guerrilla warfare against the occupation forces of a foreign ruler, as articulated in a Declaration of Independence that is used as a model for the manifestos of many a modern national liberation movement. Formerly colonized Southern countries that have more recently won their independence, frequently at great cost, cannot be expected to be so sanguine about their sovereignty.

The right to determine who comes and goes is considered an essential signifier of sovereignty. To imply to embassy or consular officials that you have a right to visit their country—as you do if you ask, "How do I get a visa?" rather than, "May I please get a visa?" or "What can I do to maximize the chances that you will choose to give me a visa and let me into your country?"—is to imply that they aren't really sovereign, and that foreigners, like the former colonialists, are exempt from the obligation to comply with their local laws. In such a situation they are likely to feel that self-respect, and their duty as diplomats to uphold the national honor and preserve the perquisites of the national government, compel them to assert their sovereignty by denying your request. You may think this sounds far-fetched, but I've seen it happen. Diplomacy is often carried out by symbolism, and these are the terms in which diplomats are trained to think.

> ## REAL LIFE
>
> While the number is growing, as of 2011 the number of countries charging U.S. citizens the same US$140 for a tourist visa that their citizens have to pay for tourist visas to the United States remained small. Most countries that do charge U.S. citizens US$140 for a visa are doing so not to deter U.S. visitors but to call attention to how much their citizens have to pay for U.S. visas. They'd be happy to agree to a mutual lowering or elimination of visa fees, if the United States would go along.

Travel Documents

On the other hand, if you approach consular officials with genuine humility and deference, as someone who likes their country and wishes to be allowed the privilege of sharing its pleasures and learning more about it by visiting, they are usually happy to oblige. Attitude and sincerity are everything. I've rarely encountered a visa officer who didn't seem to want to issue me a visa, as long as the rules of the government they worked for allowed them to do so.

Most consulates give application instructions either on the visa forms, on a sheet accompanying the forms, or less often on their websites. Failure to follow the instructions can cause your application to be summarily rejected and the fees forfeited. You do not necessarily, or even usually, get your money back if you are refused a visa. Most consulates are reasonably accommodating and helpful, but some are minefields of bureaucracy. If the instructions aren't spelled out in the materials from the consulate, call the consulate and verify each of the items in the sections below, before you take or send in your application.

In 1998, Australia became the first country to issue "electronic travel authorizations" (ETAs) instead of stamping visas in passports. The United States started its own "Electronic System for Travel Authorization" (ESTA) in 2009. Other countries are likely to follow suit once the bugs are out of these systems. The ETA and ESTA application processes are completely different than that described in this chapter. You apply for an ETA to Australia through your travel agent or the airline on which you will be flying to Australia, or (for an additional fee) through the Australian government's ETA website. You apply for an ESTA to visit the United States online at https://esta.cbp.dhs.gov. All other purported ESTA application websites for the United States are "phishing" scams operated by identity thieves and other criminals. ESTA has facilitated the creation of an entire industry of fake ESTA application websites.

A link between the Australian government computers and the computerized reservation systems (CRSs) used by airlines and travel agents permits the government to verify that you have an onward flight reserved before they issue the ETA, and permits the airline to verify that you have an ETA before they let you on their plane to Australia. Insist on getting a printout of your ETA from the travel agent or airline that obtains it for you. You'll need it if the CRS, the government's computer, or the link between them is down when you are checking in for your flight to Australia. The Australian government says printouts aren't necessary, but I've had several clients who would have been refused boarding if I hadn't given them printouts of their ETAs.

Read the rules on the Australian government ETA website before you apply, as there are restrictions on ETA eligibility that aren't mentioned on the ETA forms provided through travel agents. In particular, the ETA application doesn't warn that you are supposed to go through the full visa application process at an Australian embassy or consulate, instead of getting an ETA, if you have ever been convicted of any crime anywhere. Even what seems to you to be a minor driving or drug offense could be considered a crime, even if you paid a ticket without ever going to court. If you aren't sure, check before you leave for Australia to see if you'll need to get a visa.

BRING YOUR PASSPORT

When applying for a visa, unless told otherwise, assume you must send or bring the embassy or consulate your actual passport (not a photocopy), valid until at least six months after your proposed date of departure from the last country you intend to visit. If only a copy of your passport is required, that means the visa will be issued as a separate document, not stamped or pasted into the passport. In such cases the copy need only be of the "data page" with your name, date of birth, photograph, passport number, place of issue, and dates of issue and expiration of the passport.

Before you start getting visas for a trip, make sure you have enough blank pages for all the visas, entry stamps, and exit stamps for the entire trip. If your U.S. passport is already full of visas and stamps, you may be able to have extra blank visa pages sewn in by the passport office, for a fee of US$82. (This used to be free.) Citizens of some other countries may need to replace or renew their passports when the visa pages are filled. Allow two full pages for each country you plan to visit: one full page for each visa plus another page per country for entry and exit stamps. You probably won't need that many pages, but it can help you avoid the hassle of applying for (and paying for) a new visa because it was in a passport that filled up and had to be replaced.

The longer the trip, the more pages you will need for reentry permits, visas, visa extensions, or additional entry and exit stamps for multiple or extended visits or additional countries you hadn't included in your original plans. If it looks like you might run out of passport pages before you get home, check with one of your country's embassies or consulates at the next possible opportunity—especially if your country has few consulates or embassies in the region—to see about having pages added or getting your passport replaced.

APPLICATION FORMS

Most countries allow you to submit photocopies of their forms; however, each must be signed with an original signature in ink. A few countries accept applications only on their original forms. A faxed or photocopied signature on the form(s) is never acceptable. If you will be applying for someone else (e.g., if one of you is going to a consulate or embassy to get visas for several traveling companions), get the forms and have your traveling companion(s) sign them in advance. If you aren't sure how to fill out some parts of the form, have them sign several blank or partially completed forms (three or four copies will generally suffice) so that you will be able to submit the applications once you find out what to put in the remaining blanks. You will not be able to apply for a visa for someone else (e.g., someone out of town or in another country) without an original signature on one or more application forms.

Standard questions on visa forms include the following:

- current name
- name at birth (if different) or any other names ever used
- names of parents
- marital status
- name of spouse
- date and place of birth

- current citizenship/nationality ("Citizenship" and "nationality" are often distinct terms and can have peculiar local meanings: "nationality" is sometimes used to distinguish first- and second-class citizens under local law. Foreigners can usually get away with giving the name of the country that issued the passport in response to both questions; e.g., I always put "USA" in both places on forms, and have never had a problem.)

- citizenship/nationality at birth (same issues as above)

- passport number (You'll memorize this before long, because it's required on hotel registration forms in most countries.)

- date and place of issue of passport (You'll memorize this too.)

- home and/or business addresses (If only one is required, use whichever sounds more respectable.)

- occupation (This is sometimes a tricky question: certain occupations, varying from country to country, may be disfavored or suspect. "Journalist" and "missionary" are usually bad. "Student," "writer," and "artist" can be good or bad. "Teacher" is usually much better than "student.")

- name and address of employer (Long-term travelers don't generally have a bone fide current employer, but "unemployed" and "traveler" are unacceptable answers and "self-employed" is often suspect. Officials rarely if ever check, so if you quit your job to travel you can probably get away with giving your previous employer. If you are self-employed, give your "doing business as" name [e.g., "John Doe Consulting"], or a current or recent client. If you are or recently were a student, you can usually list the school as employer.)

- religion (If you are even nominally religious, you should be honest but no more specific than necessary; e.g., write "Christian" rather than "Protestant" or any specific sect or denomination. Individual Jews are generally welcomed in even the most Islamist and anti-Zionist countries as long as they aren't Israeli citizens and don't have Israeli stamps in their passports. Citizens of Islamic countries, whether or not they are personally Muslim, are subject to harassment throughout the Christian and Jewish First World no matter what their personal beliefs, so they might as well be honest on the forms. Atheists—regarded as infidels everywhere outside the Second World, and widely persecuted—may wish to consider remaining closeted and allow themselves to be taken for Christian, as I often do. Pagans, Wiccans, and adherents of "new religions" are likely to be misunderstood and/or regarded as heretics or would-be proselytizers, and may wish to do likewise. Missionaries—generally disfavored as agents of cultural imperialism—and religious pilgrims—sometimes given the best treatment, sometimes the worst, depending on the relationship between the government and the religion in question—should check with their religious authorities for possible special procedures before they apply.)

- whether you have previously visited the country to which you are applying
- dates of any (or the most recent) prior visit(s)
- whether you have ever previously had a visa application rejected, been denied entry, or been deported or declared persona non grata in this country (Occasionally they ask if you've been kicked out of any country, on the theory that if some other country didn't want you, they probably don't want you either.)
- names(s) of any relatives or friends you intend to visit (It's best to leave this blank unless local sponsorship is required, to avoid possible hassles for you or local contacts.)
- purpose of visit ("Tourism" is generally acceptable and sufficient. Mentioning any possibly business-related purpose will trigger a requirement for a business visa, which can be much more time-consuming, complicated, expensive, or impossible to obtain, as discussed in the sidebar *Business or Pleasure?)*
- desired duration of visit (Err on the high side.)
- desired number of entries (Err on the high side. If possible, ask for "multiple-entry" rather than a fixed number of entries.)
- intended date of arrival (Most visas don't specify an exact date, so this isn't usually critical; check in advance if you have any doubt.)
- intended place(s) of entry and exit (Find out in advance if you will be held to these; usually you won't but sometimes you will, although they can often be changed later, for a price.)
- place(s) you intend to visit (Again, find out in advance if these will actually be entered on your visa; they usually won't.)
- "sponsor" or "person or organization to be visited" (If you see this question, get professional advice from a travel agent or visa service before you submit the application.)
- whether you have ever been arrested or convicted of any crime, anywhere, and if so the full particulars of the offense(s) and disposition(s) (For many years the United States and Australia were the only major countries that asked this question of all visitors, but recently they've been joined by China and Japan. Canada doesn't always ask, but sometimes does, and has access to U.S. criminal records from the FBI. No matter how minor or long ago the offense, answering, "Yes," to this question is likely to lead to lengthy questioning and may lead to your being required to go through a more complicated visa application process or being denied entry entirely. Be prepared to give full, precise details including dates and citations to statutes. Saying you don't remember exactly what you were charged with won't be well received. Something that you think of as relatively minor and noncriminal, such as a citation for a traffic violation, drunk driving, or possession of a small quantity of drugs, may be considered a serious crime under some other countries' laws—even if you

just paid a ticket and never went to court. Don't assume that you can get away with lying about your record. Increasing data sharing among police worldwide makes it more and more likely that you'll be caught in a lie that will make your situation even worse. I expect many more countries to start asking about visitors' criminal records. I welcome readers' reports on where and when this has happened, your citizenship and offense(s), and whether or not you were admitted to that country after having committed your special crime.)

Every country has a few other unique questions of its own. I continue to be amazed at the variety of things governments consider relevant to their decisions on whom to admit.

PHOTOGRAPHS

Most countries require two or three photos of each visa applicant. Visa and passport photos are of standard size worldwide, although local identity cards in some countries use photos of other sizes. Color inkjet or laser prints are usually unacceptable unless they are of such high quality that they can be mistaken for photographic prints. (Your home printer probably isn't good enough.) Visa photos are almost always cheaper in quantity, so always order a few extra as on any extended trip you are likely to need photos for visas and other special travel permits obtained en route. All kinds of documents require visa photos, often multiple photos, from visas themselves to visa extensions, trekking permits, permits for special areas, liquor permits (for tourists in Islamic countries), scuba diving certifications, and public transit passes.

Be very careful of how you look in your visa photos, as it may determine where you are allowed to go. To maximize your chances of admission to other countries, groom yourself carefully and put on a jacket and tie or comparably respectful attire. When you get a photo you are happy with, get a copy of the digital image file. You might not be looking so respectable, and it might be harder to get a good photograph taken, when you need more photos on the road. When you are someplace prints are relatively cheap, get 10 or 20 at a time. Most countries specify that visa photos must have been taken within six months or a year, but unless your appearance has changed or the photos have a date printed on them, this requirement is difficult to enforce. Unless told otherwise, sign each photo on the back in ink and staple them to a top corner of the visa form(s) to keep them from being separated from your application.

LENGTH OF STAY AND NUMBER OF VISITS

Before you apply for a visa, you need to decide approximately how soon you will be entering the country in question, how long you want to stay, and whether you will enter the country more than once. Keep in mind that every time you so much as leave the transit area of an airport in a country—even to spend a single night en route between other countries—you will have to go through customs and immigration. If you take a side trip from one country to another country and back to the first, you will need a double-entry visa (or a second visa) to reenter the first country. Review your planned itinerary carefully, counting every entry and how long you will be in each country, to determine what visas you will need. It's surprisingly easy to overlook an extra

REAL LIFE

The one time on my last trip around the world that a longer-duration visa wasn't available, and I had to extend my visa after I entered a country, it took me almost an entire day of going back and forth to government offices and wrestling with foreign-language forms and bureaucracy. I got the visa extension, but I would happily have paid more for my initial visa to avoid that experience.

entry "in transit" or a small side trip to a neighboring country. Be sure that the visas you want are actually available for the countries you wish to visit (some countries simply don't give multiple-entry or long-stay visas) before you commit yourself to an itinerary that will require them.

If you aren't sure whether you will need a longer-than-minimum stay or multiple-entry visa, and the cost isn't absolutely prohibitive, get a visa for the longest stay and largest number of entries you might conceivably want. Contrary to what some people will tell you, it is almost always easier to get a long-stay multiple-entry visa in advance, preferably before you leave your home country, than to get separate visas for each entry or to extend your visa once you've entered on a short-stay or single-entry visa. Permits to enter without a visa, or visas issued at the border, are often issued for a shorter stay and/or with the condition that they cannot be extended or renewed. Visa extensions and renewals are a time-consuming hassle at best, aren't always possible (they are especially difficult for visitors to the United States), generally entail substantial fees (and sometimes bribes), and should be a last resort where long-stay visas can't be obtained in advance at any price, or where your plans change drastically en route.

In many countries applicants for visa extensions or renewals are presumed to be seeking illegal employment. If you are even considering the possibility of under-the-table employment or long-term residence, get the longest-duration multiple-entry tourist visa possible, preferably before you leave your home country, even if the price seems unpleasantly high. If you actually find a job, especially if as a tourist you are allowed only a few months entry at a time, and have to leave the country and come back in at regular intervals, you'll be glad you got a multiple-entry visa. You'll avoid getting quizzed each time, as you would if you had to keep applying for new visas, as to why you keep coming and going and if you are really just a tourist.

Overstaying a visa is a serious offense. You have broken the law, you want to leave, but both the government of the country you are in and the individual officials with whom you are dealing have you at their mercy. You can usually get out by paying a fine, but the fines are set high enough to be a significant deterrent and source of revenue for the government. Fines of US$50–100 per person per day that you overstay your visa are common, although much higher fines are possible. Demonstrate that you have that much money by paying the fine, and the border guards are likely to want a comparable amount in bribes for themselves as well. Overstaying a visa to the United States or technically sophisticated countries will get you entered into the computerized database of undesirables and prevented from coming back to that country for an especially long time. There's more and more sharing of immigration information between governments, so getting a black mark in your record with one country is increasingly likely to cause you problems in others as well.

It's essential to understand clearly just what the validity dates of your visa mean, so that you don't get visas too far in advance, for too short a stay, or for the wrong dates. The most common reason to have to get visas along the way is that you are traveling for a long enough time that visas issued before your departure would expire before you got through some country. Every country does it a little differently, but most visas follow one of the following two patterns. Regardless of which system is used, you will probably be asked your intended arrival and departure dates on the visa forms. You should figure out which system is used before you fill out the forms.

Fixed Dates: The most restrictive countries (including as of this writing Russia, some other former Soviet republics, and Vietnam) issue visas for a specific range of dates: your visa is valid from date X to date Y. They may have an overall stay limit (for Vietnam, it's 30 days) or they may be limited only by the range of dates for which you have booked a tour, prepaid accommodations, or been invited by your local sponsor. Unless you need every day of the maximum visa duration, give an arrival date a few days earlier than you intend and a departure date a few days, even a week, after you intend. When arranging an invitation or sponsorship, try to get one that covers at least a week on either side of your intended stay.

You can be admitted to the country later than the arrival date on your visa, and you can leave earlier than the specified departure date, but you cannot arrive any earlier or leave any later. If you show up early, you will be turned away.

Changing the dates on a fixed-date visa, once it is issued, generally requires paying a new visa fee. If the original visa required proof of reservations or sponsorship, changing the dates will require similar proof for the desired new dates. The positive aspect of fixed-date visas is that there is generally no limit to how far in advance they can be issued, as long as you know the exact dates you intend to visit.

Validity from Dates of Issue and Arrival: Most visas have two distinct ranges of validity dates: an overall validity period, beginning from the date of issue of the visa, and a stay limitation, beginning from the date of arrival. A typical Chinese visa, for example, might read, "Valid for one entry, within 90 days from [date of issue], duration of visit not to exceed 30 days."

The language is sometimes ambiguous. In this example, must you be out of the country within 90 days of getting the visa? Or might you enter the country 80 days after getting the visa, and not leave until 30 days later, 110 days after getting your visa? Different countries use the same language and mean different things. Remember, they are the ones who decide what their rules mean and enforce them. What you think your visa "ought" to mean is quite irrelevant. If you have any doubt, ask. If there's a language problem communicating with the consular officials, draw them a picture: a map of their country, stick figures of you entering and leaving, and calendars showing the dates you plan to come and go.

It can be inconvenient if a visa has to be used within a short time of issue. Brazilian tourist visas issued in the United States for U.S. citizens, for example, typically allow multiple entries of up to five years from the date of issue of the visa, with the permitted duration of each stay (up to 90 days) to be determined at the point of entry or arrival. But the first entry to Brazil must be made within 30 days of date the visa is issued, or you have to reapply and pay the US$140 (reciprocal with the U.S. tourist visa fee for Brazilian citizens) visa application fee again.

This can tempt you to wait to get your visas until the last minute, on arrival or in a neighboring country. It's usually preferable, though, to get visas in your home country (the country of your citizenship) whenever possible. Because it's more difficult to conduct a thorough investigation of a visa applicant on the spot at a border, visas issued at the border are often more restrictive than visas issued through the normal, more leisurely process in the applicants' home countries.

Many people, for example, wait until they get to Hong Kong to obtain their visas for the rest of China. However, Chinese visas are no cheaper or easier to get in Hong Kong. But it's not necessary to go through Hong Kong to get to many other places in China. Going from Europe or North America to Beijing or elsewhere in northern China via Hong Kong is particularly indirect. If you can, it will probably be easier, cheaper, and quicker to get your visa for China in your home country before you leave.

REAL LIFE

Brazilian visas require you to enter Brazil within 30 days after your visa is issued, and I was out of the United States for more than 30 days before I got to Brazil. At the Brazilian Embassy in Buenos Aires, the same US$140 that would have gotten me a five-year multiple-entry visa if I had been able to apply in San Francisco got me a only a 90-day visa, and that only because I made a special plea for a longer validity period than the 30 days they gave most applicants in BA.

FEES

Visa fees and acceptable forms of payment vary widely. Almost all embassies and consulates accept certified or cashier's checks and postal money orders. Some also accept cash (often exact change only); some accept personal checks. Some accept neither, some accept both. Most will accept traveler's checks, but only if you have checks for the exact amount due. Few embassies or consulates accept any credit or charge card. In countries with currencies that aren't freely convertible, some consulates and embassies will only accept payment in U.S. dollars or euros or other "hard" currency, not in local currency. It's not uncommon to have to pay the fee in U.S. dollars or euros, but to get change, if you don't have exact change, in nonconvertible or devalued local currency.

PROCESSING TIME

Some consulates take a month to process routine visas and charge as much as US$150 extra per visa for same-day service, if they are willing to provide it at all. Others routinely issue visas on the spot while you wait, at no additional charge. Consulates and embassies observe the holidays both of their home countries and of their host countries. Many accept visa applications only during a few hours of the day, and/or require that applications be submitted by a certain time (typically in the morning) if visas are to be picked up the same day (typically late in the afternoon). Before going to any consulate or embassy, call to verify the days and hours it will be open for the services you want.

PROOF OF ONWARD OR RETURN PASSAGE

In order to avoid having to bear the cost of deporting foreigners who run out of money, many countries (including the United States) require that tourists present proof that they have tickets out of the country before they are allowed into the country. Sometimes this proof is required before a visa will be issued, sometimes not until you arrive at the airport or the border. You may not even be allowed to board a flight bound for such a country without showing an onward ticket to the airline on which you will fly into the country.

Many countries (again including the United States) have shifted the burden of enforcing onward-ticket and other immigration rules onto the airlines.

For each passenger an airline transports to the United States who is denied entry for any reason, the airline must pay an administrative fine of US$3,000. The airline is also responsible for the costs of deportation (i.e., the airline must transport the person back or pay another airline to do so) and for the costs of detention pending deportation. A good-faith effort to verify that passengers have proper documents for admission to the United States is not sufficient grounds for waiver or reduction of the fine or responsibility for costs. Millions of dollars in fines are levied every year. With this kind of money at stake, airlines can't afford to take risks. Unless they are certain that you will be admitted, they will deny you boarding. It doesn't matter that had you gotten to the country you might have been able to persuade the immigration officer that you had enough money to pay for a ticket out, or would be leaving by a route for which tickets could only be purchased in-country.

Many people are tempted not to take onward-ticket requirements seriously because they heard from someone who got in without showing an onward ticket. But often the source entered by land or water, not by air. Or the source entered by air and didn't realize that the airline clerk at check-in looked at the next coupon—the ticket out—as well as the ticket in, and that the immigration officer didn't need to ask for or look at onward or return tickets because the airline had already done it.

Airlines have no discretion to waive onward-ticket requirements. They have no reason to anyway: if you have to buy an onward or return ticket on the spot, before you can board your flight, the airline with whom you are trying to check in is the one from which you will most likely buy it. Your plea to an airline to transport you to a country with an onward ticket requirement will fall on deaf ears.

If you do somehow get to such a country without an onward or return ticket, you will have to buy a full-fare ticket out of the country, on the spot, before you will be allowed to clear arrival customs and immigration. If you arrive at a land border where there is no ticket office, you will be turned back.

> **REAL LIFE**
>
> I've only once been denied boarding on an international flight. I had copies of papers showing that a visa to be issued on arrival had been requested by the consulate where I had applied, and verbal assurance that it was approved, but I didn't have anything in writing proving that the visa was actually waiting for me. The airline didn't want to take the risk, and I got stuck for a week in a place where I had only intended to change planes.

Travel Documents

Some countries will accept a letter or voucher from a travel agent certifying that you have paid for your tickets, even if you have not yet received them, as sufficient proof of onward or return transportation for a visa. They will still check your actual tickets on arrival; don't think that you are home free when you get a visa. Others will accept proof of sufficient funds to pay your way out, usually shown by a current bank statement or, on arrival, by a sufficient quantity of cash or traveler's checks, in lieu of an actual ticket out. Some countries enforce their "ticket out" requirements more strictly than others, but don't count on being able to break the rules. You are slightly more likely to be admitted without an onward ticket if you arrive by land or water rather than by air. A roundtrip bus, train, or ferry ticket, even if nonrefundable, is also apt to be less expensive than an air ticket out.

Fellow travelers will try to tell you lots of tricks for avoiding onward-ticket requirements. Put them out of your mind. Governments call these scams "immigration fraud," and they consider them serious crimes, even if you are "just" a tourist. The way to deal with onward-ticket requirements is to comply with them by having an onward ticket before you board a bus, train, plane, or ferry bound for a country with such a requirement.

If you can't get the ticket you actually plan to use in advance (most often because tickets for surface transportation are only available locally, or perhaps because you intend to walk, bicycle, or hitchhike), get another ticket that will satisfy the immigration requirements and that you can refund later. The easiest ticket to refund in another country is an airline ticket purchased with a credit card directly from a major airline with offices in many countries. A fully refundable ticket purchased directly from the airline is the most expensive kind: you may have to tie up hundreds of dollars, and a refund may still take months. But given time, you can get your money back. Tickets purchased from a travel agency may only be refundable through that agency—no good once you are in another country; and tickets purchased by cash or check may be refundable only in the local currency of the country of purchase—no good if it's not freely convertible. If you intend to refund a ticket, get a printed copy of the "passenger receipt" coupon and inspect it before you leave the counter where you purchase it. Refuse to accept a ticket with any "endorsements" on it restricting refunds, especially restrictions on the place or currency of refund.

PROOF OF SUFFICIENT FUNDS

Occasionally you'll be required to provide proof that you have enough money to support yourself during your stay. If you're a First Worlder planning to spend as much in a month in a Southern country as the average annual income of its citizens, it may seem absurd that its government is worried that you might become a burden on its economy, or take jobs away from locals who are paid US$5 a day or less. It's not as far-fetched or unreasonable as you may think. For one thing, far too many thoughtless people from rich countries actually do run out of money, impose themselves on the hospitality of their hosts, and expect someone else to bail them out and/or pay their way home. Poor countries can't afford to subsidize rich but imprudent travelers who take their First World privilege so much for granted that they expect not to have to suffer the consequences if they run out of money. Their attitude is deeply offensive to locals

REAL LIFE

Some of my U.S.-citizen friends have gotten married in other countries because they couldn't get visas for family members from Third World countries to attend a wedding in the United States. One or two family members at a time could get visas to visit their U.S. relatives, as long as they left other close family members behind. But when the whole family applied at once to come to a wedding, they were refused visas as presumptively intending to immigrate together.

Travel Documents

and is reminiscent of the arrogance, assumption of privilege, and appropriation of local resources of the former colonial masters. Let me put it more bluntly: if you expect local people to take care of you if you run out of money, you have the attitude of an imperialist and can expect to be treated like one.

In addition, there is an element of reciprocity in many immigration requirements. Southerners who seek to visit the North, no matter how rich they are and how secure their jobs at home, are invariably suspected of intending to immigrate permanently, to work illegally (taking jobs away from locals, even if the only jobs open to undocumented immigrants are ones most locals don't want or wouldn't take for the low pay), and/or to impose themselves on the local welfare system. Southerners seeking to spend even one night in Western Europe in transit between, say, Africa and the Americas are often required to have proof of fully prepaid hotel reservations and onward tickets before they can get the required transit visa. The same goes for people from Latin America who need to change planes in the United States to get to Asia. One of the few ways Southern governments have to educate Northerners about how they treat would-be visitors is to give them a small taste of these rules when they visit the South.

Proof of sufficient funds is sometimes an alternative to proof of onward tickets, and where possible is usually preferable, enabling you to get your visa before you actually have your tickets and giving you more flexibility in your onward route. For visa applications, sufficient funds are usually demonstrated by a bank statement. On arrival, as discussed later on under *Border Formalities,* you'll need hard cash or traveler's checks.

INVITATIONS, SPONSORSHIP, AND TOUR REQUIREMENTS

An invitation to a particular country or proof you have reserved or paid for tours or accommodations are uncommon requirements, but are by no means unheard-of. In most cases it is possible to arrange for an invitation or for pre-paid tours or accommodations, but the cost may be beyond your budget. This is especially likely to be true for countries such as Bhutan, where all tourist services must be reserved through a single (monopolistic and overpriced) government tourist agency, or where the government allows only a limited quota of tourists and auctions the visa allotments to the highest-bidding tour operators. Once you find out about such rules, you may decide not to go to these countries at all, or to spend much less time in them than you had hoped. This is one of the most important reasons to check all visa requirements well before you buy your tickets or commit yourself to travel in particular places, and to advise your travel agent of every country you plan to visit (whether or not it is included in your air itinerary).

Countries such as these are among the few places where guidebooks (at least those for independent travelers) can really be helpful in getting visas. Guides for independent travelers often give advice on loopholes in sponsorship requirements, which are the cheapest tours and accommodations that satisfy prepayment requirements, and leads for finding sponsorships or invitations for sale. Just be sure to verify anything in a guidebook with a travel agent experienced with the country or with the country's embassy or consulate.

Travel agents and tour companies can sometimes arrange invitations or sponsorship without your having to actually book a tour, or for a longer period of time than that of a tour. Some companies, occasionally even the official government tour operators, sell invitations to travelers who aren't on tours. Booking a two-day tour or a couple of nights in a sufficiently expensive hotel, in some cases, will suffice to get you an invitation for a week or two. Just because a country doesn't give visas to "tourists" doesn't mean tourists can't get visas. In several countries the norm is for hotels or tour companies to invite their guests and clients for "business" visits, their business being, I suppose, spending money on travel. Most independent travelers in Russia have business visas obtained in this way; even guests of the hostels in Moscow and St. Petersburg are considered business, not tourist, visitors. Similarly, government-approved hotels in some of the Gulf Cooperation Council (GCC) countries like the UAE and Kuwait can "sponsor" visitors who need tourist visas.

IMMUNIZATION, HEALTH, OR MEDICAL CERTIFICATES

Very few immunizations are required by governments anymore for short tourist visits. Health, not the law, is the main factor in deciding which immunizations you need. A sizable number of countries, however, require some sort of certification of acceptable health from applicants for long-stay visas, especially those seeking residency or employment visas.

The most problematic of medical requirements is that visa applicants present proof of a recent negative AIDS test. Only a few countries require AIDS tests of all foreign visitors. But many countries require testing of all long-term visitors and bar even short-term visitors who volunteer that they are HIV-positive. You should ask the consulate or embassy of any place you plan to spend a long time or seek work or residency whether it requires AIDS testing, and if so, who has to perform the test, when, and what form of certification of the result is required. Be realistic: You can't expect to get away with lying about your HIV status if you have HIV medications in your luggage.

SPENDING OR MONEY-CHANGING REQUIREMENTS

Another way of keeping out the riffraff and boosting the contribution tourists make to the national economy is to require that tourists change a certain amount of money into local currency upon arrival. In some countries this is a flat amount per person; in others it's a per diem amount for each day one's visa or entry permit is to be valid. Either way, the exchange is likely to be at an artificially low rate, and one is forbidden to exchange the local currency back into any other currency.

About all you can do is to change the excess local currency on the black market, but it may be worth so little (because of the rate at which you were forced to buy it) that it's not worth the risk of getting caught (or entrapped) by black marketeers. When you have to change money on entry to a country like this, don't count on getting any of it back. This sort of requirement is almost never mentioned on visa forms. If you don't ask, and it wasn't in effect when your guidebook was researched, you won't find out about it until you get to the border or have already gotten off the plane. If you don't have or don't want to spend that much money, you'll be stuck. So make it a point to ask when you apply for a visa if there are any currency-exchange requirements upon entry.

ENTRY POINTS, EXIT POINTS, AND ROUTES

The mere existence of a land border between two countries is no guarantee of the existence of a border crossing. There are no permitted crossing points, for example, anywhere on the land borders between India and China, India and Myanmar/Burma, or Ethiopia and Eritrea. Moreover, many border crossings are open to locals but not to foreigners or tourists. Tourist visas to many countries frequently require entry and/or exit only by air, sometimes only at a single airport. Do not assume just because there is a border, or even because a map shows a road or railroad across it or a customs and immigration post at it, that you as a foreign tourist will necessarily be able to cross the border at that point.

Sometimes you must specify your intended points of entry and exit on your visa application. Sometimes you can change them later, sometimes not.

INTERNAL TRAVEL RESTRICTIONS OR PERMITS

Parts of some countries are entirely closed to tourists. In most cases, permits for visits to restricted areas, if they are obtainable at all, can be obtained only after you arrive in the country. Issuance and denial of these permits is highly arbitrary and often at the discretion of local officials. As of 2011, some noteworthy countries with restricted areas other than border regions that are entirely off-limits to tourists, or that require special permits, are China (Tibet and parts of East Turkestan), India (parts of Kashmir, the northeast, the Andaman and Nicobar Islands, and other border areas), Pakistan (parts of Kashmir, the Northwest Frontier Province, the Northern Areas, and other border regions), Indonesia (parts of Papua and West Papua), Malaysia (parts of Borneo), Nepal (most trekking areas), and Eritrea (anywhere outside Asmara, even outlying villages just outside the city limits).

A visa or entry permit is generally valid throughout the country, but there are a few exceptions. Military reservations, war zones, and areas near borders with hostile neighbors are usually off-limits to civilians and foreign tourists. "Politically sensitive" or "minority" areas of the country are often closed to tourists, even those with visas to visit the country at large. These terms are usually euphemisms for areas where the authority, jurisdiction, or legitimacy of the central government is not accepted by the local population, and/or where dissent is being repressed. Frequently the "protection" of minority, indigenous, or tribal peoples is used by central governments with less-than-benign motives as an excuse to prevent contact with foreigners.

In a few countries, your visa lists, and is only valid in, specific cities, districts, or provinces. Most but not all countries such as this are countries requiring prearranged tours or sponsorship, and the city list on such a visa is limited to those cities specified both on your invitation and your visa application. This makes it essential to discover any such requirements before you request an invitation, much less apply for a visa. If an invitation is required, check whether it must specify a list of places to be visited and if so, whether your visa will only be valid for those places.

REAL LIFE

I have yet to have a request for a permit to visit a specific place within a country turned down, but it's sometimes required days of waiting and uncertainty. Your mileage may vary. And there are places I didn't even ask for permission to go, even though I would have liked to.

Getting Internal Travel Permits: There is no standardization in where or how to get permits for restricted areas once you are in a country. Sometimes you have to get them in the national capital, even if the region you want to visit is thousands of kilometers away. Sometimes you have to get them in the provincial or district capital or in the nearest village. Access to restricted areas is usually controlled by police, soldiers, or some sort of ministry of internal affairs. By and large, these are not the friendliest people to deal with. At a personal level, they may want to help friendly tourists who are genuinely interested in their country and have no ulterior motives. But if you turn out to be a journalist, human rights worker, or other "troublemaker," the person who approved your permit could lose their job. You are at the mercy of their discretion, and they know it. The worst case is that they are supposed to turn you down, and you can only go where you want by persuading them to break the rules. They can test your humility, patience, and knowledge of how to adapt and get things done in the local culture.

Guidebooks often have useful information on where and how to apply for permits to restricted areas. They can be helpful, but offices move, rules change, and even a new guidebook may already be out of date. Try to check with other travelers who have recently gotten the permit you want before trying to get one yourself, or before setting off for some place where you hope to be able get one. It may help to do some other business in the area first to learn how to conduct yourself properly. Plan your approach carefully, and be on your best behavior. Remember, they are in charge, and will not recognize that you, a foreigner, have a legal right to travel anywhere. Demands will get you nowhere. Have a good reason to offer for your request: idle curiosity is not likely to suffice, nor is simply "tourism." Your best chances lie in establishing a genuine human rapport with the permit-issuers, on their terms. Offering bribes, unless they are requested as "fees," is more likely to harm than help.

If restrictions are attached to a permit, don't jeopardize the chances for future travelers to get permits by breaking the rules of yours. If a special permit is required, you can take it for granted you'll be the object of special scrutiny while in the restricted area. Some permits require you to hire an approved guide or military escort or to travel in a certain manner. Our permit to visit the Khyber Pass, between Afghanistan and Pakistan, required us to hire a private car at our own expense, but which came with our personal soldier to ride shotgun, gratis. We were the only ones to receive permits on a day when a long line of other tourists, who hadn't observed the local dress code or proprieties, were being turned down. On the drive, there wasn't any real danger, and the soldier had only a carbine while the tribesmen, who materialized from the rocky surroundings when the car overheated, all had Kalashnikov assault rifles. But his presence was a signal to people in the tribal areas around the pass that we were under the protection of the central government, and his bayonet came in handy to unjam the sticky hood latch when the radiator overheated. We were advised when we got the permit to tip both soldier and driver at the end of the day, which we did, happily.

SENDING VISA APPLICATIONS

The only safe ways to send a passport or to have it returned are by personal or messenger delivery, Express Mail, FedEx, or similar traceable delivery services. It is not safe to send your passport by regular or certified U.S. Mail. Certified Mail is not expedited and can neither be insured nor be traced if lost. Registered Mail is handled separately and must be signed for by each postal employee who handles it; it's extremely secure but extremely slow. Registered mail between California and Washington, D.C., can take three weeks or more each way.

If you can, apply in person. Get a receipt for your passport when you drop it off, and bring the receipt with you when you pick up your visa. If you can't apply in person, I recommend sending your visa application by Express Mail or FedEx and enclosing a prepaid Express Mail or FedEx return envelope and completed airbill. You can put an Express Mail stamp on the return envelope or have the return FedEx shipping charged to your credit card. Keep a record of both the shipping and return air bill numbers so you can have the shipment traced if the embassy or consulate doesn't receive your passport, or if you don't receive it back when you expected.

Call the embassy or consulate the day it should have received your application (the next business day if you sent it by overnight express) to confirm receipt and to verify what day to expect it back. If someone says it wasn't received, have it traced. If it was delivered, tracing will give you the name of the person at the consulate who signed for it, and you can call back and ask for the person by name. If you don't receive your visa and passport the day you expected, call again to confirm they were sent back to you. If the embassy or consulate says they were sent, have the return airbill number traced. If, after tracing, the embassy or consulate and the Postal Service or FedEx disagree as to whether your passport was received or sent back, trust the Postal Service or FedEx. Most embassies and consulates are reliable, but passports can still get lost. Don't let your passport out of your hands if you are leaving so soon that you won't have time to replace it if it is lost. Embassies and consulates do occasionally lose passports, some more often than others. Finally, proofread each visa carefully as soon as you receive it, as mistakes (including misreading applicants' handwriting on the visa forms) are surprisingly common. If the visa isn't in a language you can read, try to find someone who can read and check it for you, such as someone else waiting in line at the consulate or embassy when you pick it up.

All this may sound intimidating, but it shouldn't be. I have yet to see a foreign visa application as confusing as a U.S. tax return, and most are much simpler. Most U.S. travelers have never had a visa application turned down, or been turned back at a border. Plan ahead, fill out the forms, follow the rules, be patient, and soon you'll be on your way.

Visas for Citizens of Different Countries

Any or all of the visa rules may be different for citizens of different countries. Always inform your travel agent and any visa services, embassies, or consulates you speak with of your citizenship, or they are likely to give you the wrong information about visa requirements, fees, and rules. In general, they will assume you are a citizen of whatever country you are in, but you can't count on that any more than you can count on them to guess correctly what passport you hold if you don't tell them.

Make sure you know what passport each of your intended traveling companions is holding. Longtime well-assimilated residents of one country may still be citizens of another country. You may have to adjust your plans to accommodate the restrictions placed on your traveling companions.

Rumors, reports from other travelers, or even printed advisories about visa and entry requirements are worse than useless unless they specify the citizenship of those to whom they apply. (It's especially unfortunate, given the global reach of the Internet, how often Internet inquiries or postings about visa requirements fail to mention travelers' nationalities.) Your friend, or your friend's friend, who had no trouble getting a visa to such-and-such a place, may not have had the same passport as you. One of the most common reasons for visa problems is relying on advice from people who turn out to be citizens of a country that is subject to different rules of admission.

In general, citizens of First World countries are able to visit many countries without visas and get tourist visas to all but a few of the rest without undue difficulty. Citizens of Southern countries—Central and South Americans, Asians except Japanese, and especially Africans—need visas to almost everywhere, and are likely to require prepaid accommodations to visit most Northern countries. You may be a doctor, banker, engineer, U.S. resident and

> ### REAL LIFE
>
> Most countries are reluctant to admit people who are or may become stateless or who don't have passports. Stateless people (mainly refugees) have great difficulty traveling, and you should let your travel agent know as early as possible, or consult an immigration lawyer, if you or someone traveling with you is stateless (e.g., traveling with a refugee reentry permit or any travel document other than a passport).

Travel Documents

Travel Documents

green-card holder, or the spouse of a U.S. citizen, but if you're from the global South, most Northern visa officers are still likely to assume by your passport (and perhaps your skin color) that you are just another would-be illegal immigrant. That was true even before 11 September 2001. Since then, Southerners visiting the North are likely to be treated as suspected terrorists. Citizens of Second World countries are often treated as badly as Southerners as well when they try to visit the First World.

Note particularly that your residency in a country or your relationship to a citizen of that country is relevant only to your entry into that country and no other. Given the difficulty of obtaining a U.S. green card (permanent residency certificate and work permit), many green-card holders think their travel difficulties to other countries are over. Not so at all. A U.S. green card, in conjunction with your passport, will help you return to the United States. It is of no value whatsoever in seeking to enter or leave any other country, and exempts you from none of the visa or other requirements normally applicable to people who hold whatever passport you hold.

Getting Visas Outside Your Home Country

If you will be traveling for only a few months, you may be able to get all the visas you'll need before leaving your home country. Do so if you can. You won't save money or time by getting your visas outside your home country. Visa fees are generally set by nationality, so you will have to pay the same amount for a visa to a given country no matter where in the world you apply. Better to spend a little time and a few dollars on postage and phone calls in your home country, where you know how things are done and foreign consular staff speak your language, than to spend days of your vacation trying to find consulates and figure out procedures in a foreign city where the instructions may all be printed for local citizens in their national language, where no one may speak your language, and where you may have to leave your passport at each consulate or embassy for several days. Embassy and consular officials are selected for their language ability in the (or a) local language; in another country, you have no right to expect them to speak or

REAL LIFE

Unable to get an Eritrean visa before I left the United States that would still be valid when I got there more than nine months later, I went to Eritrean embassies in four countries on three continents before getting a visa. In the end, my application was approved only because of some extraordinarily good luck and the consistent friendliness of Eritrean people, including government officials.

print forms in your language and have no cause to complain if you can't speak or read the language of whatever country you are in. Document checks are routine in most of the world: are you prepared to explain to the police who stop you, in a language they will understand, that you have no identity papers this week because you left your passport with your visa application at the embassy of Country X? Hotels in most countries check passports when you check in, so you may not even be able to change hotels, much less leave the city, while you wait for your visa. The only visas to get abroad are those you *can't* get before you leave home.

Visas for a growing number of countries can only be issued by the embassy in the country of which you are a citizen. U.S. citizens are only supposed to be able to obtain visas for these countries from their embassies in the United States, although exceptions are sometimes possible if you have enough money and/or patience. (If you are turned down for a visa in the United States, it can't hurt to try wherever else you have a chance. Just don't count on having better luck anywhere else). It's easy to get the wrong idea about this from reading guidebooks. Guidebooks to a country usually list neighboring countries in which you can get visas, and what they cost according to current information when the book was researched. This is useful information to those who arrive in the region without the necessary visas, and only then decide that they want to visit the country. But don't think that because you *can* get a visa in the next country, or because visas were cheaper when the book was researched, it will be easier or cheaper to get visas in a neighboring country than in your home country. Getting visas in neighboring countries—like doing anything else at the last minute—should be treated as a last resort.

The embassy where you apply may also have to check with officials in its home country, and perhaps with the embassy in your home country, to see if there is any reason not to give you a visa. (Every country, including the United States, maintains a blacklist of people who have been declared personae non grata.) If the communications infrastructure in the country where you apply is poor, getting approval from the home office can take days and sometimes weeks, especially because the home office may have little motivation to reply. It's often easier for a bureaucrat not to answer than to say, "No."

The country for which this is most often a problem for U.S. citizens is India. The lists of U.S. citizens who have offended the government of India are maintained by the embassy and consulates of India in the United States. If a U.S. citizen applies for a visa to India anywhere outside the United States, they have to wait—often for weeks—for approval from the Indian consulate in the part of the United States where they live before their visa to India can be issued. In the United States, on the other hand, U.S. citizens can get visas to India issued the same day.

The longer your trip, the more likely it is you will have to get some visas along the way. Plan this carefully. For each country for which you will need to get a visa en route, find out where that country has a diplomatic office that issues visas, and be sure you will be staying in that area long enough to get a visa. Give yourself a generous time allowance for delays.

If you plan on getting a visa for Country Q in City R, call the embassy of Country Q in your home country, well before you buy your tickets (much less leave your home country), to verify that Country Q still has an office in City R that will issue visas to citizens of your nationality.

BORDER FORMALITIES

At first, borders may seem intimidating and strange. After you've been traveling for a while, they will seem mostly bureaucratic and boring, and it will take an effort to continue to see them as an exciting first glimpse of a country and its ways. For those who haven't experienced this already, here are a few tips, with the caveat that procedures often change, and every country does things just a little bit differently.

Airport and Airline Security

If you are crossing an international border by air—as you probably will much of the time—you'll have to deal with airport and airline security inspections even before you get to the government border inspections.

Americans are sometimes worried about whether foreign airlines and airports have adequate security, and the U.S. government feeds these fears by its periodic complaints about foreign airport security. In practice, aviation security is as good or better in other parts of the world—many of which have been dealing with terrorism for much longer—than in the United States. Where the United States leads the world is in government surveillance of travelers, rather than security, as I've reported extensively on my website and in my blog. Fundamentally, terrorism is rare because few people are terrorists.

Of course, airport and airline procedures have changed since 11 September 2001. It's arguable whether these changes are actually related to safety or security, and it's equally arguable whether safety or security changes were really needed. Many of the changes appear to be intended to reassure travelers, and make us feel less afraid, rather than to make us safer. (See the sidebar *Travel Safety and Civil Liberties: Fear vs. Danger*.)

It used to be that travelers who were used to domestic U.S. flight procedures had to learn a whole new set of rules for international flights, and vice versa. Since 11 September 2001, there has come to be much less difference between procedures for domestic U.S. flights and those for international flights. No one who has gotten accustomed to the procedures for domestic flights in the United States (time-consuming and elaborate baggage inspections, intrusive pat-down searches and scanners, demands for and scrutiny of identity documents, more varieties of more heavily armed security personnel in airports, etc.) should be greatly surprised by anything that happens on a typical international flight or in an airport elsewhere in the world.

MILITARY PRESENCE

Airports are considered to be of great military importance. Many airports routinely handle both civilian and military flights. The success or failure of coups, revolts, and invasions has hinged on military control of airports. Consequently, airport guards almost everywhere but in the United States (where TSA checkpoint staff aren't law enforcement officers at all, despite the way they act) are typically an elite class of national police, soldiers, or both.

In the United States, National Guardsmen in camouflage clothing with M-16s appeared in airports only briefly after 11 September 2001. Elsewhere in the United States, police are rarely seen outside ghetto areas carrying more than pistols, and soldiers rarely function as police. In most other countries, the nuances of the distinction, if any, between soldiers and police are likely to be invisible to foreigners without military training. It is perfectly normal, and no indication of any special reason for alarm, to see military fortifications encircling an airport, or to have your papers checked by soldiers in full battle dress carrying rifles or machine guns. This isn't a response to the events of 11 September 2001: soldiers have been part of standard operating procedure at airports around the world for years. I don't mean to condone governmental paranoia, and I certainly don't want to encourage complacency in the face of the militarization of civil society. But if you haven't seen this before, you do need to get used to a more naked assertion of the violence that underlies governmental power, so that you are prepared and don't misinterpret or overreact to its manifestations at airports and elsewhere.

LUGGAGE

When you check in for your flight, international or domestic, your identification papers will be checked, and your luggage, including both checked and carry-on items, is subject to inspection. Airlines are entitled to require you to open your luggage for inspection for prohibited items. I've had my bags opened by airport security more often than by customs.

Many items that are permitted in checked baggage are prohibited in carry-on luggage. Each country and airline makes its own judgments about what to permit on its flights, so it's useless to argue, "But some other airline or country let me carry this on."

Travel Safety and Civil Liberties: Fear vs. Danger

Fear has profoundly affected travel ever since 11 September 2001. It's understandable that travelers are afraid. But what are we afraid of? And how should we deal with our fears?

Fear is nothing to be ashamed of. Fear is instinctive, whether it be fear of flying, fear of terrorism, or fear of the unknown. Fear serves a purpose in the human animal: it warns us of danger. And our most irrational fears ("phobias") are, almost by definition, those least subject to conscious control.

Because fear is perceived as a sign of danger, our instinct is to assume that whatever is scary is dangerous, and that the degree of danger we're in, is proportional to the fear we feel.

Most people are aware that the correlation between fear and danger isn't perfect. But as I discuss in the chapter on safety and health, there's a far greater difference between fear and real danger than most travelers imagine. Before you go to a place you haven't been before, read a good guidebook to find out about the dangers you don't know to be afraid of, and to learn what are the scary-seeming things that are really harmless and nothing you need to worry about.

Serious problems tend to arise, however, when we attack the sources of our fears while mistaking them for sources of danger.

We're afraid of flying, for example, so we avoid flying, even though the alternative, surface travel, is actually much more dangerous. Similarly, we avoid the unknown, the "foreign," because it raises our instinctive fear of the unknown — not because "strange" places are actually more dangerous than our daily lives at home.

Looked at in terms of danger, it's hard to understand the decisions made by so many Americans in the aftermath of the attacks of 11 September 2001. Many people from the United States chose to confine their travel to the United States — the place where the attacks took place — rather than going to safer places abroad. But looked at in terms of instinctive fear of the unknown, it makes perfect sense: when you're afraid, you avoid the scary — and anything strange is scary.

Similarly, "profiling" of airline passengers was in effect on September 11, but proved a failure in terms of safety. But because the profile matches the profile of most people's fears, selectively searching those who fit the profile is highly effective in allaying those fears (except, of course, if we're in the class of people, mainly those of South Asian or Arab ancestry, being selected for special scrutiny) even if it doesn't make us any safer.

Many people understand, intellectually if not emotionally, that making travel safer won't necessarily make it less scary. What's less obvious, but at least equally important, is that making travel less scary won't necessarily make it any safer. Current events can tempt us to attack people and things who pose no real danger. In doing so, we'll attack our own freedom and security, ultimately making ourselves less safe. The consequence would be the sacrifice of our freedom to our fears, without gaining any safety or security. That would be tragic for travelers and civil liberties alike.

If an electronic device can't be opened for inspection without damaging it, the usual test is to require you to turn it on and demonstrate it at the security checkpoint. If it doesn't operate, it might be a case hollowed out to hold a weapon, and it won't be allowed through. This is no joke: if your laptop computer or camera's batteries are dead when you get to security, and you've already checked your power cord or adapter, you risk having your expensive appliance confiscated and destroyed. If it isn't working, the batteries are low, or you have the least doubt whether it will function on demand at security checkpoints, put it in your checked luggage.

Some airlines bring the luggage carts out on the runway alongside the plane and make each passenger identify their luggage again just before boarding the plane. If a bag hasn't been personally identified by a passenger who has been seen to board the plane, it will be turned over to the bomb squad for destruction. Unattended baggage in waiting areas is similarly presumed to be dangerous, and is removed and destroyed. In some countries with ongoing civil wars waged in part by bombings in public places, such as the U.K. and Israel, it can be difficult to persuade a stranger to watch your bag while you go to the toilet.

All baggage, checked or carry-on, will be scanned at some point, whether in your sight or not. Magnetometers (metal detectors) and other scanners can damage magnetic storage media as well as photographic film. Whenever possible, don't bring your only copies of data with you on a plane on magnetic media (i.e. the hard drive of a computer or music player). If you have important electronic data such as digital photos on your hard disk, consider copying them to flash memory (much less likely to be damaged than a

REAL LIFE

Flying from Paris to New York I once got a lesson in the importance airlines attach to unaccompanied baggage when I was delayed at immigration after checking my bag. As I became convinced that I would miss my flight, two security guards came running up, calling out, "Mr. Abouk? Mr. Abouk?" I recognized this as a semblance of my name, Hasbrouck. They pulled me out of line, whisked me through passport control, and hustled me off to the gate at a run. My traveling companion, already on board, was startled to see me arrive as though under arrest, with a guard on either arm! The door was immediately closed and the plane left, a few minutes late. I was lucky they found it easier to delay the flight and find me than to search for my luggage and remove it before the flight could depart.

Airlines have reason for these concerns. In 1985, an Air India flight from Toronto was blown up over the Atlantic Ocean, killing all 329 people on board. The bomb was in the luggage of a terrorist who checked it through from a connecting flight from Vancouver but who never boarded the Air India plane. Today, baggage is matched with passengers, and unaccompanied bags removed and destroyed, even on domestic flights in the United States—not just on international flights or flights within other countries.

hard disk) or CDs or DVDs (optical devices immune to magnetometer or X-ray damage).

Airport Taxes

To get out of most countries you have to pay some sort of "departure tax," "airport fee," or "security fee," which can be anything from US$5 to more than US$100 per person. Some countries arrange to have these taxes and fees collected by the airlines at the time of ticketing or check-in, while others collect them directly from travelers at the point of departure. Some departure taxes apply only to air travelers, while others apply equally to those departing by other means. Be prepared for possible departure taxes when buying international train, bus, or ferry tickets; at stations and docks; and at land border-crossing points. Usually you pay more on departure than on arrival, but the United States charges more to get into the country (as of 2011 a total of US$28.50 in arrival tax and three separate "user fees" for the "services" of customs, immigration, and agricultural inspectors) than to get out (US$17.90 in departure tax and security fee), paid when you buy your tickets.

The departure tax can be a larger problem if it isn't collected at the time of ticketing and you don't have the appropriate currency to pay it at check-in or the payment point. One of the first things you should do when you get to the airport is figure out how much the departure tax is and where and in what currency you need to pay it. Sometimes the tax must be paid in local currency, sometimes in foreign "hard" currency. Find out which before you exchange your local currency, as there may be no more money changers beyond the point where you have to pay the tax. If you don't see any signs indicating where to pay the tax, ask fellow travelers. Local businesspeople have probably been through this particular airport before and are most likely to know its procedures.

Two common systems are to collect the tax at a counter or kiosk near the international departure check-in area, or to have it collected by airline staff at the check-in counter. If you try to check in and your tickets are in order, but the airline clerk indicates that something is missing, it probably means you need to go back and pay the tax. If you get a tax sticker or stamp on or in your ticket, boarding pass, or passport, or a chit or receipt for the tax, hold onto it until you are out of the country. You never know at what point(s) it will be checked again, maybe even as you are walking down the jetway or across the tarmac to your plane.

Immigration

Customs and immigration are often spoken of together. They are actually distinct functions, usually performed by different officials. Immigration is concerned with the passage of people across international borders, customs with the passage of luggage, cargo, money, and goods. The norm is to go through immigration or passport control first, then customs, both on arrival and on departure, although occasionally both functions are performed by the same person or at the same desk.

Immigration officers can ask you anything they feel is relevant to their determination of whether to let you in, and if so for how long. You have no other choice but to answer their questions: international law construes your attempting to cross a border as consenting to as thorough and intrusive an interrogation and search as that country deems necessary. As a practical matter, it's hard for your country not to let you come home (although in recent years the United States has tried to prevent some U.S. citizens from returning from trips overseas, effectively exiling or banishing them), but you can't do much to force any other country to let you in if they don't want to.

MAINTAIN A GOOD ATTITUDE

I don't mean to imply that you'll get the third degree. Most immigration inspectors are underpaid and bored, but nonetheless courteous and friendly. If they ask you personal questions, they are probably genuinely curious, just trying to make conversation, or practicing their language skills. Your best bet is to approach them with the attitude of a guest: "I'm interested in your country, and I'm grateful to you for being so hospitable as to allow me to visit." Begin to learn how local people do things. Start practicing your greetings in the local language. This may be difficult when a guard has an Uzi or Kalashnikov machine gun pointed at you, but that's just standard operating procedure at many borders and throughout many countries. It bears repeating that though a visa may be necessary, it is never a sufficient condition for entry. Flourishing your visa as though it gives you the right of entry or deprives the immigration officers or border guards of discretion to turn you away will only alienate them and invite them to reject you. If your visa says, "Good for one visit, for up to 60 days," the immigration inspector at the border has discretion to admit you for 60 days, two weeks, 24 hours, or not at all. The way to maximize your chances of a longer stay is (surprise!) to treat the officials as human beings, be "nice," and above all don't be demanding.

BRIBES

Do not offer bribes. If a bribe is really essential it will be described as a "fee," "fine," or "tax," and should be paid as such. You'll do yourself far more damage by offering a bribe when it isn't called for than by waiting for the rare official to make it explicit by demanding a "fee." Bribes are much less common than most guidebooks would have you believe. I've only had to bribe a border guard once (it was described as a fee but I knew it was a bribe because, in a receipt and red-tape-crazed country, I got no receipt), and I know people who've traveled around the world two or three times and never paid a bribe.

IMMIGRATION REQUIREMENTS

Immigration inspectors may check that you have onward or return tickets, or sufficient funds to pay for onward transportation and to support yourself for the duration of your permitted stay. You can expect both to be checked again on arrival even if you had to show them earlier to get a visa.

Practically speaking, long-term travelers, even those on a budget, should have a sufficient reserve for emergencies, in cash or traveler's checks, to satisfy most countries' requirements. At most borders you should be prepared to show at least US$500 in the South, US$1,000 in the North, in hard-currency cash or traveler's checks. Up to US$2,000 can improve your chances anywhere. You can probably get in with less, but you risk being limited to a shorter stay. Traveler's checks are less likely to be confiscated or demanded as bribes, since they are harder for a corrupt border guard or inspector to spend than is cash.

Credit cards are sometimes helpful and may be considered sufficient proof of adequate financial means. You can't count on it, though. Proof of the means to buy an onward ticket may be accepted in lieu of the ticket itself, especially if you enter the country by land or water rather than by air. If you don't have an onward ticket, find out in advance how much one costs, and be prepared to show that much money. Credit cards are more likely to be accepted as evidence of your ability to pay for a ticket out than as evidence of the ability to support yourself in the country. This is entirely justified, since in many countries airline tickets are almost the only things you can pay for with credit cards. ATM cards are next to useless for this purpose, since there's no way for the border inspectors to verify your bank balance.

PAPERWORK

It's perfectly normal for visitors, even those who already have visas, to have to complete a variety of paperwork on arrival. Airlines frequently give out some or all of the forms for entry to the plane's destination for you to complete during the flight. Take advantage of the opportunity to do so, and to consult with fellow passengers and/or the flight attendants if you aren't sure how. The form for entry to the United States by non-U.S. citizens is by far the most complicated I've seen. Most airlines seem to agree, and the in-flight magazines of international airlines serving the United States usually contain lengthy multilingual explanations of what to put in the many inscrutable English-only boxes.

A common system is to give you a form on arrival that must be completed and turned in on departure. This may be one or more of the copies of your visa application, entry application, or visa; a stub or portion of your entry permit; or an "entry/exit form," "immigration permit," "tourist card," or some other document. You may have to produce this form each time you register at a hotel; have it stamped or notated by the hotel each night; or have it stamped by the police in each city you pass through or stay in.

If the border officials hand back any official documents with your passport, including copies of any of the documents you gave them, check before you move on to see if you will need them when you leave. If you aren't sure, or don't understand the answer (most likely because of a language problem), assume that you will.

You can take it for granted that anything clipped or stapled into your passport on arrival, or an obviously two-part or half-completed form, is some sort of entry/exit document that you will be required to show to get out of the country. Guard it as carefully as your passport. If you lose it, you will be presumed to have thrown it away to hide having exceeded your authorized stay or because you entered illegally, and will at a minimum be fined. If you have a chance, especially if you are going to be spending a long time in the country or traveling extensively to remote areas, make a few photocopies of your entry/exit form(s), and secrete them with the copies of your passport.

Travel Documents

Customs

Many people find customs and its terminology and procedures even more intimidating than immigration. It's really just bureaucracy: most travelers have nothing to declare and have no serious problems with customs.

CUSTOMS DECLARATIONS

The first steps when going through customs are to fill out a customs declaration form, sometimes also a currency declaration, and to decide whether you have anything or nothing to "declare." To "declare" something means exactly what it implies: to tell the government of the country into which you are bringing it that you have it. Declarable items are not necessarily illegal.

Governments have all sorts of reasons for making you declare certain kinds of things. They may restrict the quantities of an item that can be imported, or subject them to "duty" (see the following) in order to protect, and thus promote, local production of similar items. They may want to know about certain categories of goods that might contain forbidden materials (most often this applies to books, other printed materials, recordings, objets d'art, antiques, archaeological artifacts, high-value portable electronics, and any sort of vehicle), so as to subject them or the people carrying them to special scrutiny. They may just want to keep records of the import and export of certain goods. Whatever the case may be, they don't have to give you a reason.

Traditionally, you stepped up to a counter where you were asked, "Do you have anything to declare?" and you answered either "No" or "Yes, I have such-and-such quantities of such-and-such items." Nowadays declarations are usually made in writing on a form completed and signed on arrival (or distributed on the airplane and completed in flight) or by choosing to go through a "red channel" or "green channel" at the exit from the immigration hall. Going through the green lane (usually indicated by a green traffic light, a green sign, or "Nothing to Declare") is the equivalent of saying, "I have nothing to declare." Going through the red lane (red traffic light, red sign, or "Items to Declare") means, "I *might* have something to declare."

> ### REAL LIFE
>
> When I requested a copy of my permanent file from U.S. Customs and Border Protection, I found that it included a two-page incident report on my having asked, on arrival at Logan Airport in Boston, if I could bring in an apple and a couple of slices of bread I had left over from breakfast in London. "PAX VERBALLY DECLARED FOOD. 1 APPLE WAS SEIZED. BREAD WAS INSPECTED AND RELEASED. NO PENALTY." (See my website for how to request your own travel records.)

No matter how many times you've been through the process, read the customs declaration form before you sign it. Different countries require you to declare different things. Requirements change, and they are often stated in peculiar (or peculiarly translated, if translated at all) terminology. Occasionally you'll run across border officials who make a habit of entrapping travelers in some obscure declaration requirement (failing to declare that they have a cell phone, for example) and shaking them down for fines or bribes in exchange for allowing them to proceed. The best way to avoid such problems is to make sure that your declaration is scrupulously complete.

If you aren't sure which exit to use, use the red channel. If you aren't sure whether to declare something, then go through the red channel and ask. When you get to the front, before you hand in your declaration, say, "I have [quantity] of [type of item]. Should I declare it?" If you don't understand the answer, or still aren't sure, list the item(s) on your declaration.

DUTIES AND TAXES

Duties and taxes on imports and exports cause much unnecessary confusion. Unless you are a professional importer or exporter, you don't need to worry about them any more than you worry about paying sales or value-added tax on the things you buy at home. For the curious, here's a summary of the terminology and rules.

A duty or tariff (as in the "General Agreement on Tariffs and Trade," or GATT) is a tax a country imposes on imported goods of a certain type. Almost anything you can think of is subject to duty somewhere. A duty is usually assessed either per quantity (so much per liter of distilled alcohol or per meter of silk cloth, for example) or as a percentage of the value of the imported goods (200 percent of the assessed valuation of imported automobiles, for example). In general, the baggage and possessions of a traveler are considered to be "imports" subject to the usual duties of the country into which they are brought.

Two standard exceptions to the duty rules combine to create the phenomenon of the "duty-free" shop. First, most countries exempt certain quantities of particular goods from the usual duties if they are brought in by travelers for their personal use. Second, most countries do not charge a duty or impose local sales taxes on goods that are exported or imported solely for reexport to another country. Goods sold by duty-free shops are free of local taxes and duties on condition that the goods are only for export and cannot be used or consumed in the country of purchase. To enforce this requirement, duty-free shops are usually located beyond the immigration checkpoints in the departure or transit areas of airports. The world's largest are in Dubai, where the transit terminal resembles a cacophonous shopping mall with everything from jewelry stores to luxury-car showrooms. Not the place for peace or quiet between flights!

As long as your purchases from the duty-free shop are within the amounts exempt from duty in the country of your destination, they are taxed in neither country. Naturally, this exemption is most useful if they are (1) small (so that you can easily carry them with you), (2) heavily taxed, and (3) expensive (to make the savings worthwhile). The merchandise for sale in duty-free shops is just what one would expect: small, expensive items subject to high "luxury" and "sin" taxes, especially the most expensive brands of hard liquor, perfumes, tobacco products, watches, and designer jewelry. If you regularly buy these items, and if you are on the last leg of your trip home (so that you don't have to schlep them around through a bunch of other places), it makes sense to buy them at a duty-free shop. If you're not in the habit of buying products like these, and somewhat lower prices aren't enough to make you take a sudden interest in them, or if you've got a lot of other stops before you get home, don't waste your time in duty-free shops. Anything not subject to special taxes will be cheaper at ordinary shops and markets elsewhere than it will be in the airport. This tends to be particularly true of local folk arts, handicrafts, clothing, souvenirs, and the like.

Some people, and some books, will advise you to try to make a little money by buying the maximum amount of whiskey and cigarettes you can bring into the next country duty-free, and then trying to sell it on the black market on arrival. This is always illegal, often dangerous, and rarely even profitable. It's axiomatic that black-market prices and potential profits are highest where prohibitions are most strictly enforced. Where there's money in it, there's danger. Where it's no problem, there's no money in it. Some countries look on alcohol the way others look on cocaine, and vice versa. Even in a country where it's legal to bring in whiskey for your own use but not for sale, merely having it may identify you as decadent and disrespectful of local mores to the border guards who are deciding whether to admit you, turn you away, or shake you down.

The only time I buy anything in a duty-free shop is on my last leg home or if I'm stuck with local currency that I can't exchange and that isn't worth anything outside the country. Better to spend it on overpriced souvenirs than to throw it away, although sometimes the money is sufficiently interesting-looking to make a better souvenir than the overpriced trinkets one could buy with it in a duty-free shop.

REGISTERING DECLARED ITEMS

Some items must not only be declared (e.g., "two cameras, one cell phone, and one laptop computer") but must be itemized by make, model, and serial number on your entry/exit papers or in your passport itself on the page with your visa or entry stamp to the country. When this is required, it means that the items in question are heavily dutied and/ or taxed. Many countries deem importing foreign-made luxury goods—cameras, automobiles, etc.—to be a less appropriate use of scarce foreign exchange reserves than importing of capital goods (machine tools, manufacturing machinery, textbooks) that will increase the country's production capacity. Luxury consumer goods are often subject to higher duties and taxes than any other class of imports.

> ## REAL LIFE
>
> The only thing I had stolen from me on my last trip around the world was a cell phone snatched from my breast pocket by a pair of pickpockets on a street in downtown Dar es Salaam, Tanzania. I was lucky I hadn't had to register it on entry, and didn't have to pay what would have been substantial import duty on it, even though its value in Hong Kong, where I had bought it, was fairly small.

Tourists and short-term business visitors—whose money the country wants, and whom it doesn't want to alienate unduly—tend to carry just such goods, such as cameras, portable audio equipment, and laptop computers. The usual solution is to exempt certain quantities of common impedimenta of tourism from the normal duties, provided that visitors bring them solely for their own use while in the country and (most importantly) agree to take them away again when they leave. The quantity limits, which vary by country (typically one or two still cameras, one video camera/recorder, one audio player and/or recorder, one portable computer, and so forth) are imposed with the assumption that anyone bringing in larger quantities of goods intends to sell or give them away in the country.

Some people think that having the serial number of their camera or computer noted in their passport on entry is for their protection or will make it easier to take it out of the country. It's not and it won't. Items like these are recorded in your passport for the sole purpose of making it harder for you to leave the country without them, so that you won't evade duties and taxes by bringing them in as a tourist, duty-free and tax-free, and give them away (to a friend or relative) or sell them while in the country. Customs officials are after people who try to finance their trip by bringing in heavily dutied or taxed items like laptop computers and selling them on the black market.

I wouldn't try to smuggle these things; declare them if they are listed on the forms. However, I would never go out of my way to declare them on arrival where it wasn't required or ask that they be noted in my passport. If some item is noted in your passport and is lost or stolen, you will have great difficulty leaving without paying the duties and taxes required to import the item. Duties can be as much as five times the value of luxury goods like these, so the cost may be prohibitive.

It is imperative to report such a loss or theft to the police immediately. At a minimum, you will need proof that you have reported the loss or theft and that the police have been unable to find or recover the item. Getting this proof can take days. Because the police know you can't leave without the documentation only they can provide, they are likely to take the opportunity to ask for bribes for expediting the process. But if you offer a bribe without prompting, they can make your situation worse by arresting you for attempted bribery or demand a larger bribe not to do so. All in all, it can be a big hassle.

On the other hand, registering an item with the customs service (in the United States, it's U.S. Customs and Border Protection, www.cbp.gov) can be useful in avoiding duty when you return home. If you plan on taking something with you on your trip that you bought in the United States, that was made in another country, and that's expensive enough to be subject to duty if you were bringing it into the United States for the first time, you can register it with the CBP before your departure. Take the item to the nearest CBP office, complete CBP Form 4457, and they will give you a certificate to show on your return to prove that you bought it in the United States before your trip, and thus that it isn't subject to duty when you "reimport" it to the United States with you when you come home. The United States has relatively few import duties, however, so this is unlikely to be an issue.

ART, ARTIFACTS, AND ANTIQUITIES

One reason people travel is to see monuments and artifacts of the history and culture of the places they visit. Too often, they find that the finest examples of local artistic, cultural, and even architectural traditions were long ago looted by imperialist collectors and archaeologists. Even the finest murals from inner rooms of rock-cut tombs and temples were sawed out in sections, hauled away, and reassembled as the prized exhibits of museums in London, Paris, Vienna, New York, Boston, Chicago, and elsewhere, leaving gaping holes in the walls of the sanctuaries for those who visit these sites today.

To stem the ongoing theft of what they have left of their cultural heritage, and to preserve the attractions of their country for citizens and future visitors alike, most formerly colonized countries have special restrictions on the export of artworks, antiquities, and archaeological artifacts. Typically, these things are defined as national treasures, and their export is categorically prohibited. Exactly what constitutes an antique or an artifact isn't always clearly defined, but common sense is usually a sufficient guide. Here's a rule of thumb: If you can afford it without having to think about the price, it's probably a legal fake.

Real antiques cost real money. Good modern reproductions of museum pieces, or modern works in classical styles, can be harder to get out of the country than obviously fake "antiques" or works in modern styles or media. This is unfortunate, because it reduces the export market that might support continued work in traditional artistic styles. High-quality modern art in a classical medium or style is really one of the best souvenirs, if you can afford it. But bringing it out of the country is likely to require at least a purchase receipt, the more official-looking the better. In some countries, you'll need certification from a government agency or appointed specialist (art historian or curator) that the work is not an antique or national treasure.

In creating a demand for antiques, buyers and collectors are also to blame for creating a financial opportunity for impoverished local people who can earn the equivalent of a year's wages in a day by working in the jungle digging up burial mounds instead of plowing fields. The damage will only stop when those who can afford to buy these treasures choose not to.

Don't buy antiques or archaeological artifacts. Don't buy anything else from people who sell these things, and tell them why. Encourage other travelers to boycott them. If someone shows you a piece of pre-Columbian pottery, don't say, "What a find!" Say, "Doesn't that belong in a museum, where everyone could see it?" If each visitor takes away a tangible piece of the past, nothing of the past will be left for the future.

Buying or smuggling forbidden antiquities or artifacts is considered not merely theft but theft from the collective cultural heritage of a people. You aren't just stealing: you are stealing from a nation. In many countries all antiquities, in whomever's possession, are officially deemed the property of the state. Even if the objects you buy or take have no ritual or religious value (which they often do), you aren't just taking souvenirs: you are stealing icons of the identity of a people. You are stealing the national soul and will be treated accordingly. You can expect little sympathy from your own country's government if you are caught and fined or imprisoned for trafficking antiquities or archaeological artifacts.

SMUGGLING

Forbidden items, quantities of items that should have been declared and weren't, and quantities of items in excess of those declared are all considered contraband. Carrying contraband across borders is smuggling. Failure to declare an item that should have been declared is considered smuggling even if the item could have been declared without penalty, as is going through the "green" channel when you have anything, even something legal, that should have been declared. This is a crime, often a fairly serious one.

You will probably only have to make a declaration of goods, and perhaps pay duty, if you have accumulated souvenirs or gifts worth more than the duty-free allowance. Luggage weight limits, and the impracticality of carrying large quantities of stuff very far, make this most likely on the last leg of your trip, when you may have bought a bunch of gifts for friends back home and several bottles (more than the duty-free limit) of foreign liquor that you can't get at home.

Don't bother to try to smuggle this sort of stuff in. To have to "pay duty" isn't a fate worse than death, and it's not worth risking serious fines to avoid the modest duties on a moderate excess of gifts and souvenirs or a few extra bottles of alcohol. If it's worth bothering to carry it home, it's worth paying the duty on it. The best souvenirs and gifts are things that aren't available at home at any price, not things bought solely because they are slightly cheaper than they would be at home.

If they are caught, some people think they can get away with saying they "forgot" to declare something, and they will at worst have to pay the duty. At worst, you will have to pay the duty, pay a fine, and go to jail. If you declare it in the first place, all you have to do is pay the duty.

Because foreign tourists are less likely to be suspected of smuggling than locals at some borders, smugglers often try to hire them as freelance couriers for all sorts of contraband. Professional smuggling for profit is too risky for amateurs. Leave it to the pros. Smugglers (or their agents) hang out in places frequented by travelers, especially places frequented by budget backpackers. If your money is running out, the fast and easy-seeming money may be tempting. Don't do it.

Smuggling wouldn't pay well if it weren't dangerous. The contraband may be a commodity that seems innocuous to you, or that you've never heard of, but no one would be smuggling it if there weren't serious sanctions against it, or such high duties on it, or such scarcity of it that people were willing to kill for it. If someone wants you to smuggle something, and won't tell you or show you what it is, assume the worst: that its possession could be a capital offense.

Foreigners and tourists aren't above the law. Foreign tourists have been executed for possession of drugs in Singapore and Malaysia, and foreigners caught smuggling alcoholic beverages into Saudi Arabia can be beheaded. It doesn't happen often: knowledge of the possible penalties scares most people away. Capital punishment doesn't deter crimes of passion such as murder, but it does deter purely economic crimes, such as smuggling, by all but the most economically desperate people (or those ignorant of the risk).

Foreigners convicted of smuggling or other crimes, whether in the United States or any other country, are not deported immediately. They must "serve" their sentence in a local prison, and pay off any fine, before being deported.

If you choose to carry contraband, you have a moral obligation to tell everyone traveling with you. If you are in a taxi or minibus, and carrying drugs, there's a good chance that everyone in the vehicle will at least be arrested, and quite possibly imprisoned for some time, if you are caught. The local driver may be more severely punished than you or any of the other foreign travelers, especially if you've hidden the contraband anywhere in the vehicle other than on your person. You have no right to risk other people's lives or liberty without their knowledge or consent.

SEARCHES

You are subject to as complete a search as the border authorities choose to conduct. If nobody who went through the green channel was searched, nobody would declare anything or go through the red channel, and the system wouldn't work. Spot checks and searches are made at random and on the basis of hunches, profiles, watch lists, and informers' tips. Don't be surprised if, from time to time, you are approached after you've gone through the green channel, just as you are about to leave, and are asked to "step over here" or "into this room" for further questioning and/or search.

They can ask you anything they want, whether or not you deem it relevant to your entry to the country. You don't have to answer, but they don't have to let you in. Honesty is, I think, the best policy for most travelers. They can open your luggage and examine everything inside it. They'll usually give you a chance to open it for them, but they'll cut or break it open if you won't.

They can pat you down, feel all over you, or strip you naked and examine your body cavities. Women entering most countries are entitled to insist that body searches be conducted in private by female officers, but at remote border crossings this may not be honored, or might entail being detained for hours waiting for a female officer to arrive. People entering the United States who are suspected of having swallowed condoms or balloons full of drugs can be, and are, confined in a "dry cell" without a toilet for several days, and made to defecate in a bucket until the entire contents of their intestines have been excreted and examined for drugs.

REAL LIFE

My traveling companion and I were terrified when, as we were leaving one country with strict currency controls, we realized that I had forgotten about one of our stashes of emergency money when we were filling out our currency declaration on arrival. They searched us and our luggage carefully enough to find it on our departure. It was a police state where arrestees are known to disappear without a trace, so we were lucky they believed it was an honest mistake, and eventually let us go with a lecture.

The people who search your belongings aren't required to repack your bags or put things back where they found them. You can ask them, politely, and they may give you minimal help, maybe let you use some of their tools, if you obviously won't be able to proceed without it and are holding up the line. But they are entitled to dismantle your suitcases or vehicle looking for drugs, if they feel like it, and then stand around laughing at you and at your most intimate possessions while you try to put them back together and repack them. You can't count on any compensation for damage done in the course of a search, even if no contraband is found.

MONEY

Currency declarations are a special kind of customs declaration. Sometimes they are made on the same form as the rest of your customs declaration, sometimes on a separate form. As with other immigration and customs forms, you should retain your currency declaration (if it is given back to you) on the assumption that you will have to turn it back in when you leave the country. Know how much money you have, in which currencies and forms (cash or traveler's checks), before you get to customs. You don't want to attract attention by digging it all out of your luggage and counting it in plain view.

Some countries don't care how much money you bring in or out, or in what form. The United States allows the import and export of any amount of any currency except currencies of blacklisted countries like Cuba, and only requires you to declare amounts over US$10,000 in cash or "negotiable instruments" such as traveler's checks.

Other countries have a range of currency declaration requirements and restrictions. Typically, First World countries care mainly that you have enough money to pay your way during your stay. If the local currency is "hard" or freely convertible on the open market, they don't much care whether you

REAL LIFE

A friend arrived by land at the border of the Democratic Republic of the Congo as part of a group on a package tour. Because everything was prepaid, none of them had much cash, although they all had credit cards. As the one most fluent in French, it fell to my friend to explain the concept "credit card" to the border officials, and to convince them that these pieces of plastic were (in some places, although none for hundreds of kilometers) considered the functional equivalent of money. Finally getting their grudging assent, he turned to his fellow tourists and had them all wave their cards in the air for the inspectors to see, like extras in an AmEx advertisement.

have your money in dollars, pounds, euros, yen, or whatever—as long as you have enough, but not so much as to look suspicious.

Some poorer countries make you exchange a certain amount of money on arrival, either a fixed amount per visitor or a per diem for the duration of your intended stay. In such cases, you'll either have to change your money into nonconvertible currency (with which you can't do anything except spend it in the country) or at an artificially low exchange rate (which makes it more akin to a head tax on tourists). These requirements are annoying but straightforward, and there is nothing you can do about them. Don't waste your time trying to argue: insisting that you can't afford to change that much money will only convince them not to admit you to their country.

Second World countries all used to have controlled currencies that were worthless anywhere else. This has changed. The huge discrepancies between "official" and "market" exchange rates have been greatly reduced and private money-changing legalized in most places. Currency declarations are still required, but where there's no big black market, not much attention is paid to them. (See *Changing Money* in the *Bottom Line* chapter.)

These days the strictest currency controls are found in certain Third and Fourth World countries, often ones suffering from hyperinflation and excessive national debt, where the official exchange rate (at least for tourists) is grossly disproportionate to the exchange value of the local currency on the black market. Currency controls are used to prevent visitors from cutting costs by buying local currency at the more favorable black-market rate. By forbidding you from importing local currency, or limiting the amount you can bring in to a nominal amount, they prevent you from buying it cheaply on the black market outside the country. And by keeping track of how much foreign currency you bring in and out, they try to stop you from changing money on the black market within the country.

This latter task is difficult and requires constant vigilance. It works like this: when you arrive, you declare how much money you have. Whenever you exchange money legally, you get an official receipt. When you leave, you turn in your arrival declaration and all your receipts, and declare how much money you have left. If the sum of all the receipts and your remaining foreign currency adds up to less than the amount you declared on arrival, you are assumed to have exchanged the difference illegally on the black market. Unfortunately, the same result can be produced by miscounting your money on arrival, or by losing any one of your receipts during your stay. Be extremely careful not to lose your exchange receipts unless you are absolutely sure that you won't need them when you leave.

Visitors can get around the system by hiding and not declaring on arrival the money they intend to exchange on the black market. This leaves customs officers little choice, if they are actually to enforce the law, but to conduct aggressive searches and interrogations of arriving visitors to ferret out hidden money. These searches can be humiliating, but consider how little space it takes to hide a US$100 bill or a €500 note (500 euros are worth about US$650), and how thorough a search it would take to find one hidden in someone's underwear, the lining of their luggage, or the insole of their shoe.

As with other kinds of smuggling, the only places where there are real savings in black-market money-changing are those where it carries at least some risk. Don't change money on the black market until you've been in the country long enough to be reasonably sure that it's both worthwhile and safe. Expatriate foreign residents are probably the best sources of information about where, how, and at what price to change your money. Be discreet and polite in asking anyone—expats, locals, or fellow travelers—about black marketeering. Everyone may be doing it, but it's still a crime.

Health Inspections

There are two possible types of health inspections and immunization requirements at international borders: those because of conditions within the country you are entering (extremely rare), and those related to conditions in a country you are leaving, or which you have recently visited (a possibility in cases of yellow fever or unusual disease outbreaks).

Most people expect health requirements on entry to be related to health hazards in the country in which you are arriving, but that's not the way it works. Rules at borders are designed to protect the country against external threats, in health as in other matters. If yellow fever is already endemic, a country doesn't care if people who arrive are infected with, or immunized against, it. But if you arrive *from* a country with an endemic contagious disease like yellow fever, or an outbreak of mad cow disease, countries where those diseases *aren't* prevalent will want to be sure that you have been tested or immunized before they let you in, or may quarantine you until they can tell if you are infected. So health requirements on entry are mainly about what diseases are uncommon where you are arriving, but common where you have previously been.

The key to sorting this out is the sequence of countries you will visit, and the amount of time you will spend in each. That's what a competent travel health professional will need to know before they can provide you with immunization recommendations or warnings about possible quarantines. In general, health inspectors at borders are interested in where you have been for the 30 days before arriving in that country.

The primary reason for immunizations is health, not government requirements, as is discussed in more detail in the *Safety and Health* chapter. You should, however, have your International Certificates of Vaccination (yellow book) handy at borders, because it may be ritualistically examined even where no immunizations are required.

Countries that require AIDS tests for entry generally require them before they will even issue visas, so you are unlikely to be confronted with a border AIDS-testing requirement. Many countries don't require tests but do ask if you have AIDS or any other communicable disease. In most cases, if you say you are HIV-positive, they won't let you in. If you say you are HIV-negative, they are extremely unlikely to check your word.

Agricultural Inspections

Some countries, particularly geographically isolated ones such as island nations, have special inspections or "disinfecting" procedures in an attempt to prevent visitors from bringing in exotic (nonnative) strains of plant or animal diseases, parasites, blights, pests, or vermin.

Sometimes an inspector walks through the cabin of the plane, before passengers disembark, spraying pesticide or disinfectant in the air and over the passengers. It's ineffectual and annoying, but there is nothing much you can do about it.

Spraying aside, agricultural inspections should be taken seriously. A foreign disease or blight, to which local strains of crops or livestock are not resistant, or a pest that has no local predators, can devastate agriculture. There are many historical examples of ruinous results from inadvertent import of vermin, pests, and diseases.

It's easy for even dead animal or vegetable material to harbor microscopic eggs or seeds. Once introduced, pests can be impossible to eliminate. If you bring in an agricultural pest—lurking in some harmless-looking fruit or flowers you can't resist bringing home—people whose crops are ruined will curse you for generations to come.

The United States, Australia, and Aotearoa/New Zealand have particularly stringent agricultural inspections. In general, you are forbidden to bring meat or fresh fruits, vegetables, or plants into these countries. Canned or

REAL LIFE

The United States doesn't spray arriving visitors with disinfectant, but U.S. Customs and Border Protection will insist on washing all your shoes for you on arrival, while you wait, for free, if you check the box on the entry form that says you've been near animals. One incident report in my CBP travel history file reads, "PAX ARRIVED FROM ARGENTINA...IN A LIVESTOCK SHOW. HIS SHOES WERE CLEANED AND DISINFECTED FOR POSSIBLE CONTAMINATION."

preserved foods may be allowed, but you can't always count on it. All agricultural products must, and should, be declared.

California, the center of fruit and vegetable growing in the United States, has its own agricultural inspection stations at borders with other U.S. states as well as at airports and international borders. Driving into California from another state, you have to stop at a checkpoint and declare your fruits and vegetables. Any agricultural products suspected of harboring pests or blights are subject to confiscation and destruction, without compensation. Hawaii has similar state agricultural inspections of passengers and cargo arriving from the U.S. mainland, as does Western Australia for arrivals from other Australian states.

Dress for Success

When dealing with border guards, customs and immigration officers, and the officials who decide whether or not to issue special travel permits, it's most important to conform to local norms of dress, appearance, and behavior.

That doesn't mean you should try to pass for a local. Unsuccessful attempts to "go native" are often resented and interpreted as condescending. It's all too easy to misunderstand the symbolic meaning of an article of apparel or ornamentation, and inadvertently wear something you've seen beautiful local people wearing on the streets that actually identifies you as, say, a prostitute. It's safer to appear to be what I (and the officials with whom you are dealing) hope you are: a friendly, respectful foreigner. If you are obviously a foreigner, especially one visibly of a different race or ethnicity, the question to ask is "How would this official consider it respectful for a foreigner like me to dress and behave?" rather than, "How can I make myself look like a local?"

I'm not saying you have to respect the bureaucrats, or pretend you do if you don't, but neither do you have to go out of your way to tell them what you do think. You

REAL LIFE

For most of my life, my appearance fit the profile of a hippie. Until it started to thin with middle age, and I cut it shorter, my hair was in a long ponytail and I had a full beard 15 cm (six inches) long. In the tropics I wear sandals, even to business meetings. Nonetheless I routinely get into places where most tourists aren't allowed, and I've never been turned down for a visa or official permit. I've never been treated like a hippie, been searched for drugs, or had my bag opened (except once when it broke open on the baggage conveyor). Even in notoriously anti-hippie Singapore they didn't cut my beard or hair but only asked me, with friendly curiosity, if such a long beard itched!

may think they are thugs working for a government that rounds up the local people at gunpoint to put them in slave labor camps. However, you won't get to talk to those local people at all if you voice those opinions to the permit-granting or denying officials.

In your own country, you know the nuances of expressions of disrespect or disagreement, and what you risk by showing them. In a foreign culture, you risk making a much more hostile or personal statement than you intended by voicing criticisms or flouting local norms. Besides, like many officials, they may have their own personal criticisms of the government and its policies.

Never present yourself at a government office in shorts, T-shirts, or jeans; in clothes that aren't clean; or without having recently bathed and groomed yourself. Why take the chance, even in Australia, where certain styles of shorts are considered respectable attire for men in many settings, or in the United States and Canada, where jeans are acceptable almost everywhere? At land border crossings in the bush in the Third or Fourth World it may be difficult, but you'd still be amazed at the extent to which local travelers in such a place manage to spruce themselves up on arrival. After all, an intercity bus ride may be the trip of their lifetime.

I know some people who carry an entirely separate outfit just for border crossings. But if you feel that you need a whole new wardrobe to look acceptable at the border, maybe you should think again about whether your day-to-day attire is giving more offense, or closing more doors, than you have realized or want.

Attitude and Behavior

Some visitors tend to focus exclusively on dress and external appearance to improve their success rate with local bureaucrats. These things are important, but less so than attitude and behavior.

In most places I'm taken for an expatriate foreign resident rather than a tourist. Part of making a good impression is certainly dress: my customary traveling clothes are long pants (not jeans) and long-sleeved shirts with collars, and I carry a tie to put on at borders and official offices. But the biggest factors, I think, are attitude and behavior. My delight at getting to another country is always genuine, and I anticipate with pleasure my first opportunity—border formalities—to experience its ways. I approach each encounter with official-dom as an adventure and a learning opportunity. Try to cultivate these attitudes, even if they aren't easy or instinctive.

Behavioral norms vary greatly from place to place. While waiting in line, watch how local people in front of you act (do you sit? Stand? Bow? Shake hands?). If a particular permit or bit of official business is especially critical to your plans, don't apply for it on your first day in the country. Go to some

REAL LIFE

I was scared the first time a soldier pointed his gun at me while I was trying to ask that my photographic film not be put through the X-ray machine. I kept my hands in the air and kept talking. I was on the verge of giving up—better to lose my photographs than my life—when a higher-ranking officer noticed what was happening, recognized my lead-lined film bag, and told the soldier to lower his gun and hand-inspect it. Fortunately, digital cameras have eliminated the need for most travelers to worry about having photographic film x-rayed.

other offices, do some other business, and get a feel for local ways. If you've merely omitted one step or document, you may be able to come back once it's completed, but once an application has been denied, you don't usually get a second chance.

Above all else, accept that you are not in control. You may not like it, but you cannot do anything about it. Many people, particularly from privileged Northern backgrounds, who are accustomed to getting their way, are deeply threatened by having to place themselves at someone else's mercy. People from the United States and Australia, with our ideologies of self-sufficiency as the measure of self-worth, can be among those most uncomfortable in situations of dependence on others' judgments and decisions. Even those without conscious racism may find that subconscious racism enhances their discomfort if they are in the hands of people of another race whom their culture has taught them to fear. This is especially true at borders and in police and guarded government offices where those people of the race they associate with danger are, in the normal conduct of their jobs, pointing guns at them.

These people tend to react in exactly the worst way due to their (correct) perception of a loss of control. Because this threatens their sense of self, they try to take control of the situation, which is bound to come across to local officials as an assertion of superior status. This is most counterproductive of all when those making this assertion are from a country with an imperialist history (the United States, U.K., France, Russia, Japan, etc.) or from a race with a history of illegitimately claiming superiority over the race of the official. This pushes all the wrong buttons of the postcolonial psyche.

The usual result is an escalation by both parties of their claims to being in charge. "No, you listen to me," "I have a right . . .," "You must . . .," "I need . . .," "Who do you think you are?" In such a war of status, authority, and obligation, the traveler will always lose. Better to accept from the start what you will eventually be compelled to accept anyway: they are in charge. That you perceive that you need something does not imply that someone else perceives an obligation to give it to you. Do you feel obligated to give your money to every beggar? Poor people know better than the rich how little anyone really needs.

Situations of dependence, inferior status, and lack of privilege may be, for Northerners, among the most important learning experiences of world travel. Most people never have the degree

> ### REAL LIFE
>
> Try to keep your cool and be polite, whatever happens with officials. Don't raise your voice, and don't make any sudden movements or threatening gestures. Train yourself to relax and slow down when you are tempted to panic.

of privilege that Northerners take for granted. To come to terms with what it is like to be in such situations is to come to terms with what life is like for most people in the world. Some people confront this shortly after they are inducted into the military, or when jail or prison doors close behind them, and they realize that they have to take what's coming whether they like it or not. Some people experience it, even in the North, by being on the bottom of the hierarchies of class, wealth, age, race, ethnicity, or gender-based privilege. Some people experience lack of privilege for the first time when they travel abroad.

Remember, your self-worth comes from self-respect, not from anyone else's judgment of you. There is no shame in doing things under duress, or being judged falsely. Don't let it get you down or make you panic or lose your temper. One of the central lessons of the Gandhian analysis of power is that submission need not mean disempowerment. The most effective way to resist the impositions of illegitimate authority is simply to retain your pride while doing what you have to do.

I won't pretend it's always fun, but awareness and anticipation of these situational dynamics can help you keep your reactions under control and avoid making bad situations worse.

Travel Documents

Safety and Health

"Sound Body and Mind"

TRAVEL SAFETY AND HEALTH RISKS

Most people think of the risks of travel in terms of exotic illnesses, flight safety, and terrorism. Typically, travelers' concerns for a safe trip manifest themselves in three questions: "Is this a safe airline?," "What shots are required for this country?," and "Is there a government advisory about terrorism in this country?"

Statistically speaking, however, these questions say more about travelers' fears than about the actual dangers of travel. Travel by land or water is far more dangerous than travel by air; serious injury—most often from road accidents—is much more likely than serious illness; most violent crime against travelers is economic, with no obvious political content and no relation to terrorism; hygiene and behavior have more effect on travel health than do inoculations; and government advisories are a poorer indication of the risk of violence than daily newspapers.

The real hazards aren't what most people are afraid of, and just listing the factors that make for a safe trip fails to address some of the things most travelers fear. (See the sidebar *Fear vs. Danger* in the previous chapter.) This chapter is therefore, of necessity, as much about fear and its causes as about actual travel risks, safety, or health.

I realize, of course, that fear is not a rational phenomenon. Nothing I could say, and no amount of evidence I could produce, would allay some

Key Advice About Safety and Health

- Don't be afraid to travel.
- Take trains, where possible, rather than buses, cars, or trucks. Don't ride motorized two-wheelers. Outside the First World, don't travel by road at night. If there is no train and the roads seem unsafe, consider flying.
- Bring a water purifier. Don't drink the water outside the First World without first boiling, treating, or purifying it.
- See a doctor or health professional at least a month before any trip outside the First World, and follow his or her advice about immunizations and other preparations. Get a prescription for sterile disposable hypodermic needles, and bring them with you. Talk to your doctor about nonsystemic intestinal antibiotics for traveler's diarrhea.
- Don't have unsafe sex, or at least have safer sex.
- Read the local newspapers and pay attention to what's happening around you. Talk to local people, not just other travelers.
- Buy trip cancellation and interruption insurance, or be sure you have another way to pay, to cover the cost of cutting your trip short and coming straight home in an emergency.
- Verify that your medical insurance covers you when you are abroad. If it doesn't, consider changing insurers or getting supplemental travel health insurance. Find out in advance what forms or documentation you'll need to submit with an insurance claim for medical expenses abroad.

For more information on the topics in this chapter, see the *Resource Guide* in the back of the book and the links on the Practical Nomad website at www.practicalnomad.com.

people's fear of flying or fear of terrorism. But choosing an airline they think of as safer is unlikely to allay their fears either. Driving rather than flying will only increase the risk of injury or death. And you're in no greater danger of terrorism while traveling than you are if you stay home.

Be honest with yourself about your fears. If you know you'll be too frightened to have a good time or a productive trip, it doesn't really matter whether your fears are well founded. You may want to try to change your fears, or learn to deal with them differently. But that may not be quick or easy, or possible at all. If you can't overcome your fear, you should change your plans, and do something less scary that you can enjoy.

If you *want* to travel, and fear is getting in the way, knowing that your fears are unsupported by risk statistics is unlikely to make you unafraid. But that knowledge and understanding may free you to deal with, and overcome, your fear as a phenomenon in itself.

I am neither a health professional, a psychologist, or an actuary (a specialist in the statistical analysis of risk), and this chapter is not intended as a replacement for professional health advice. Rather, it is intended as an overview of common concerns about travel safety and health, and an introduction to some risks you may not have thought about.

Transportation Safety
SURFACE TRANSPORTATION

Road travel and, to the extent that you use it, water travel outside the First World are likely to be the most dangerous parts of your trip. Road accidents are the principal cause of injury and death to travelers abroad. "An estimated quarter of a million people worldwide die in automobile accidents each year," according to the Worldwatch Institute. The United States accounts for only about 10 percent of that number, despite the fact that a much larger proportion of the world's cars are driven in the United States, over greater distances.

For example, both the U.S. military and the Peace Corps consistently report that the most frequent causes of death and injury for their personnel abroad are motor vehicle accidents. Military personnel are most often hurt or killed in cars and trucks. Peace Corps workers, with less money, are more likely to be hurt or killed on the more cheaply obtained two-wheelers: motorcycles, scooters, and mopeds.

Motor vehicles are the leading cause of accidental death even in the United States, where we have some of the world's best roads and safest and slowest highway drivers. Road travel is significantly more dangerous in most other First World countries than in the United States or Canada, largely because of higher speeds. Americans are often surprised and frightened to find that Europeans routinely drive and pass other vehicles at 110 km/h (70 mph) on narrow two-lane roads between hedgerows with blind corners and no shoulder ("verge" in British usage). Europeans are equally shocked to find that the maximum permitted speed in North America, even on a straight, flat, limited-access multilane divided highway (dual carriageway)—the fabled American open road—is at most 120 km/h (75 mph) even in the rural West, and that most American drivers don't go much faster than the speed limit.

A passing note to those tempted to speed or break other traffic laws while traveling: don't. Traffic violations that would entail minor fines in your home country may land you in jail in another, because traffic police often don't trust that a foreigner given a ticket will pay it, or that a foreigner cited and released will show up later in court.

Bus and car crashes are frighteningly common in the Second, Third, and Fourth Worlds, where roads and vehicles alike are in much poorer condition than in the First World. Even in places with very few motor vehicles, they are always running into each other, and/or off the roads. The Worldwatch Institute reports that "developing" countries have fatality rates per vehicle mile up to 20 times higher than industrialized countries. One newspaper editor in the United States told me that he got in the habit of using stories of Third World road crashes for filler at the bottom of columns, just because they were so common on the wire-service feed. On any given day, he could count on finding a current story about a lot of people getting killed in a crash. "Didn't a bus just run off the road somewhere?" became shorthand in the newsroom for, "I need a one-paragraph story to complete this page."

Trains are everywhere significantly safer than any road vehicle. I haven't been able to find comprehensive world statistics on train and bus safety, but in the United States the automobile accident rate per passenger-kilometer (or passenger-mile) is almost 10 times that of Amtrak trains.

Boats, especially smaller ferries, are at least as dangerous, per passenger-kilometer, as are cars and buses. Ships and ferries are a smaller factor in overall travel safety only because most people take them only for short distances, where there is no alternative. Most ferries and ships that sink or capsize either were overloaded or were traveling in flood or storm conditions for which they were unfit or unprepared. Use common sense. Take a critical look at the ship or boat, and the conditions, before you board. If you are chartering a boat, try to get a sense of the captain's competence. Don't take it for granted that ships or their captains are licensed, regulated, or inspected by the government, or that any of these things proves they are safe.

It may not reassure you about safety in the air, but as nearly as I can determine, you are more likely to be killed driving to or from the airport (even on the safest roads) than on any given flight, even on the least safe airline. If you want to play it safe, fly. If you don't fly, take a train if there is one. Locals, and even many guidebooks, often recommend buses as faster, more frequent, and more direct than trains. Rarely do they mention how much safer trains are than buses, which only becomes more true the poorer the country.

Road accidents are the most common reason for long-term travelers to cut their trips short and come home early. During my 15 years as a travel agent, I never heard of one of my clients having been in a plane crash. A couple of times a year, I heard of one who had been seriously hurt in a road crash. And this in spite of the fact that most of my clients traveled at least 10 times as far by air as they did by land.

Given that most of the danger of travel is in surface transportation, and that most independent travelers choose to travel mainly by bus or train, flying more and choosing trains rather than buses may be the two simple choices you can make that will most increase your chances of surviving your trip.

I don't necessarily recommend that you fly whenever possible. Traveling around the world involves, of necessity, taking some risks. And there are many other factors than safety to consider. If the price is the same as flying, and I have the time, I almost always take a train: I see more, meet more diverse people, and eat better food. Trains are generally more comfortable and, in much of the world, more reliable. Given the need for early check-in and the likelihood of delays and cancellations of flights, fast trains are often as fast as planes for distance up to at least 1,000 km (600 miles): an all-day journey whether by air or rail. Changes in airline and airport procedures that increase the total time required for a trip by air have substantially increased the distance over which trains are competitive with planes.

AIR TRAVEL SAFETY

I can only repeat what I've said already: air travel is safe. Air travel safety is, or should be, a nonissue, except to the extent that it influences you to fly rather than to use other means of transportation.

There are differences between the safety of different airlines. But all airlines are so safe, compared to surface travel, that the choice between the most and least dangerous airline in the world will have a negligible effect on your chances of surviving your trip. Your time in the air is the safest part of your trip, and the part you should worry about least. Relax and enjoy it. Anywhere in the world, how you get to the airport has more effect on your safety than which airline you fly on. On scheduled jet flights, it makes no sense to worry, on grounds of safety, about which airline or type of airplane you take, where you sit, or other similar issues.

Perhaps the least rational thing to do about airline safety is

REAL LIFE

U.S. citizens can register their itinerary (countries to be visited, dates, and any known local contact info) with the State Department "Smart Traveler Enrollment Program" (STEP) at https://travelregistration.state.gov. If you register, the State Department will email you with notices of any changes to its advice for travelers in those countries, and will have you on their list in the event of an emergency or evacuation of U.S. citizens. What I like best about this system is that it eliminates the need to visit a U.S. embassy or consulate—often the most conspicuous terrorist target in town—in person to register.

Should We Travel?

Should we still travel around the world, after what happened on 11 September 2001?

Yes, absolutely. A decade later, there is time for perspective. The events of September 11th carried, I think, a clear message that isolationism is impossible in an interconnected and interdependent world. Now more than ever before, we need international awareness and understanding. We need to recognize our common humanity — and the suffering that unites us — with people everywhere of all races and cultures. And we need to understand the ways in which, for better or worse, our decisions affect others (and vice versa) around the world. What greater victory could we hand any terrorists than to allow them to deprive us of our humanity, and to drive us to emulate them in isolating ourselves from world opinion?

But is it safe to travel? And to travel overseas?

Yes, absolutely. Now more than ever. The September 11th attacks disabused us, I presume, of any notion that staying home can keep us out of harm's way. Bad things can happen anywhere. And travel abroad is no more risky than travel in the United States — in fact, statistically speaking, it's often safer. Not that this means people from other countries should stay away from the United States! We have our share of crazies, as does every country, but you'll find that the United States is still a wonderful place to visit, and on the whole most

to choose to travel by land or water instead of flying. Certainly the stupidest advice I've ever seen in a government travel advisory was the U.S. State Department's recommendation that U.S. government employees in Russia travel by land rather than by air. It's difficult to believe that the people who issued this advisory had ever been on a Russian road. Aeroflot is far from the world's most dangerous airline, and even the worst of the other Russian domestic airlines are so much safer than Russian roads or rails that safety is one of the strongest reasons to fly, not drive, when in Russia, as anywhere else.

FEAR OF FLYING

If air travel safety is (or should be) a nonissue, fear of flying is, unfortunately, an all-too-real issue for many people. I can offer only limited advice, but I'll try to offer a few observations about the fears that many travelers have described to me, in the hope that this will help some of you come to terms with your fear of flying.

Americans remain (knock wood) very welcoming to foreigners. Most of the risks of travel, as I'm constantly reminding other travelers (and reminding myself), are the commonplace risks of our everyday lives at home: car accidents, slips and falls, etc. Most of travel safety at home or abroad is simple common sense, like not forgetting to watch where we're putting our feet when we're distracted by looking at the sights and scenery.

Is it safe to fly?

Yes, absolutely. Now more than ever. Per mile, air travel is a hundred to a thousand times safer than any alternative means of transportation. Your time in the air is unquestionably the safest part of your trip. One of the saddest consequences of the September 11th hijackings is that they scared large numbers of people into driving rather than flying, increasing the numbers of people — tens of thousands — killed on the roads in the United States each year. Fear of flying is real. It's common. And it's understandable. But fear is a very different issue from safety. If you're afraid, deal with your fear — even if that isn't easy. But don't assume that airplanes are dangerous just because they are, for you, scary. At the end of the day, our safety and security depend on understanding between people around the world — understanding that is the result, above all else, of the direct personal contact, experience, and learning that result from international travel.

The first step in dealing with fear of flying is recognizing that the issue is your fear, not actual safety. Fear is real, as is the pain and anxiety it causes. You may feel you need to do certain things when you fly, such as choosing certain airlines or airplanes, in order to feel comfortable before or during the flight. But in the long run, pandering to your fear will not eliminate it. Only confronting your fear itself will enable you to understand, overcome, or cure yourself of it.

Most people in First World jet-age societies realize that people who are too afraid ever to get on an airplane have a problem, and that their problem lies in their fear and not in airplanes. Many people who have only a mild or moderate fear of flying may be experiencing a rational response to a societal myth (albeit a false myth) more than a consciously irrational phobia.

Unfortunately, the news media—supposed guardians of truth—reinforce the myth that flying is unusually dangerous, and that the alternatives are less so. If 10 or 100 people are killed in an airplane crash, anywhere in the world, it is front-page world news. For that matter, even one death in an air crash, or an unscheduled landing in which no one is hurt, is often major news in the United States. There is never a front-page headline, much less one every day, to remind us that 100 people died on roads in the United States and 1,000 on roads around the world yesterday, and the day before, and the day before that.

Whatever the reasons, it seems clear that our society manifests not so much an individual as a collective social phobia about flight. Perhaps it is a mechanism to mask our even more extreme collective social denial of the risks of the road. Too much would have to change in the infrastructure of our society, or we'd have to go about our daily affairs in too much fear, if we were to acknowledge how dangerous the cars that we depend on are.

For some people, simply learning how little factual basis there is for fear of flying may be sufficient to reduce or eliminate their fear. For people who want assistance, particularly those with extreme fear (especially those who are unable to bring themselves to fly at all), several airlines and other organizations (see the *Resource Guide*) offer classes in overcoming fear of flying. These courses typically include counseling, group discussions, exercises in relaxation and preparation, flight simulations, and finally a short graduation flight on a chartered plane so that course participants don't have to worry about being embarrassed by their fear in front of experienced and unafraid people. The groups that run these claim a high success rate, and I've heard several accounts of people who were able to fly for the first time after completing such a class.

HEALTHY FLYING

Airplanes feel more uncomfortable and unhealthy than they are in any physical sense, because of the psychological discomfort produced by feeling out of control and by having other people intrude into what mainstream culture in the United States teaches us to regard as the "personal space" surrounding us. (In some other cultures, it's not considered at all invasive to find yourself pushed against other people's bodies in a public setting.) The health effects of flying come primarily from the cabin atmosphere, and secondarily from sitting still for so long. What else is there to affect your health when all you really do on a plane is sit in an armchair for a few hours?

Low Air Pressure: Virtually all airplanes used by scheduled passenger airlines have pressurized cabins, including most turboprops. The only exceptions are some of the smallest piston-engine planes (air taxis, bush planes, or flightseeing planes) that carry only a handful of passengers and fly at such low altitudes that no pressurization is needed.

Aircraft cabins are not, however, maintained at sea-level pressure. At cruising altitude, cabin pressure is typically equivalent to the normal air pressure at an altitude of about 2,500 meters (8,200 feet) above sea level. A lower pressure would place the passengers in danger of altitude sickness; a higher pressure would place more stress than necessary on the cabin walls and fuselage, which have to contain the pressure.

People who have difficulty breathing at sea level have progressively more difficulty at higher altitudes. When people are advised by a doctor not to fly, it's usually because of the lower air pressure. Such people are usually also advised to avoid spending time on the ground at high altitudes.

Low Humidity: At cruising altitude, aircraft cabin air is drier than the air in the driest desert. It would be possible to humidify the cabin air, but if this were done, pressure fluctuations would cause condensation, which could short out electrical equipment. Few airline passengers realize that they are in the driest environment they will ever experience. Nor do they deal with it appropriately. It's easy to get dehydrated in any desert, and far easier if you don't realize that you're in a desert. In air as dry as that on an airplane, it's almost impossible to avoid some degree of dehydration.

Most of the discomfort experienced by airplane passengers is actually unrecognized dehydration. If you get headaches or feel light-headed during or after long flights, for example, it's probably because you are dehydrated. The low air pressure, which requires you to breathe a larger volume of air (which carries away more moisture) to get the same amount of oxygen, accentuates the dehydrating effect of the low humidity. Some travelers who don't like using airplane toilets make things worse for themselves by deliberately reducing their fluid intake so they won't have to urinate in flight. Not having to urinate regularly is a sure sign of dehydration.

The only way to avoid dehydration is to drink lots of fluids before, during, and after each flight, especially a long flight. It's almost impossible to drink enough to keep yourself properly hydrated on a long flight. Worse, many of the drinks you are offered in flight are apt to be alcoholic or caffeinated, both of which make you urinate more and enhance dehydration.

I drink as much water as I can (a liter or quart or more) just before boarding any long flight. I bring at least a liter water bottle on any flight, and drink a total of two or three liters or quarts of fluids on a transoceanic flight. If that sounds excessive, consider how much you would drink during a comparable amount of time sitting in the shade in the desert, and then allow for the fact that the air on an airplane is much drier.

This still isn't enough to avoid arriving moderately dehydrated. I keep drinking as much as I can for several hours after I arrive. To rehumidify my throat and nasal passages, I try to get out into humid air, and/or take a shower or steam bath, as soon as possible after a flight.

Sitting Still: As more people take longer nonstop flights on longer-range planes, concern has increased about "deep vein thrombosis" (DVT): potentially

The Political Economics of Airline Safety

Aeroflot, the leading Second World airline, did some things very differently than First World airlines. The United States and the USSR, the world's two greatest technological rivals (especially in aerospace), pursued parallel but often quite different technological paths, each with its own technical standards, norms, and expectations about how things are done. One of the most interesting things about visiting the former USSR is seeing the areas — small and large — where Soviet engineers found different but equally valid solutions to similar technical problems. Separate doesn't mean equal, but neither does different mean inferior.

Many foreigners, accustomed to pristine cabins and (at least on long-haul flights) restaurant-quality food, confuse "service" with safety. They assume that if an airline doesn't wash or paint the interiors of its aircraft cabins as often as other airlines, it doesn't overhaul the engines as often either. They have it backwards: with limited resources, it's better to spend them on safety-related mechanical and aeronautic essentials than on cleanliness or esthetics.

As long as Aeroflot didn't publish statistics on its safety record, there was at least some excuse for the persistence of the myth that Aeroflot was unsafe (even if the myth's primary cause was anticommunist, anti-Soviet bigotry). But Aeroflot's publication for the last 20 years of better safety statistics than many of the world's international airlines should by now have dispelled that myth. Aeroflot's international safety record looks even better now that Aeroflot Russian International Airlines has divested itself almost entirely of domestic flight operations within Russia.

Other than its budget and service philosophy (transportation for proletarians, at proletarian prices, decades before airlines like Southwest or EasyJet adopted that concept), Aeroflot's big advantage was that as long as it used Russian-made planes, its expenses for aircraft construction and maintenance, pilot training, and fuel, not to mention labor, were all in local currency — even on international routes where most revenue was in hard currency. This gave Aeroflot an enormous edge over airlines everywhere in the world except North America and Western Europe (the only other regions, with minor exceptions, that build their own large passenger jets). And, given the continued undervaluation of the ruble, Aeroflot may have an edge over North America and Western Europe too. Most countries have to buy their planes, spare parts, and pilot training from the United States, Western Europe, or Russia. The poorer ones — those least able to afford it — also have to pay for maintenance services that they aren't equipped to provide in their own countries. Those airlines that still use Soviet or Russian-made planes are able to afford (in rubles) standards of equipment maintenance and staff training that most Second, Third, and Fourth World airlines can't hope to match if they have to send their planes back to factories abroad if they want them inspected or overhauled.

The most unsafe *international* airlines, according to statistics I've seen, are mostly in Africa. That's an indictment not of Africa, but of the impoverishment and marginalization of Africa by the international financial system. Worse still, I suspect, are *domestic* airlines in poor countries, which are often wholly or largely unregulated and report few if any statistics. The worst are probably those in countries that have devalued currencies, that have few tourists or wealthy foreign travelers (who can afford to demand a higher standard of safety), but that are large enough in area and population, and where surface transportation is bad enough, to create sizable domestic airline markets despite their poverty. Domestic flights in, for example, Nigeria or the Democratic Republic of the Congo come immediately to mind.

In 1992 I traveled entirely around the world on Aeroflot (one of two airlines at that time on which that could be done — there are none in 2011), flying more than 30,000 km (20,000 miles) on international, domestic, and interrepublican flights within and between four of the former Soviet republics. The service on international flights was good, and I never doubted that I was safer flying than I would have been driving. I would definitely choose Aeroflot again, all else including price being equal, over some airlines based in the United States.

Safety and Health

deadly blood clots that can form when you sit upright for hours without exercising, and blood pools in your legs. Physician Edward O'Neil Jr. has a review of the ongoing medial research on DVT in *A Practical Guide to Global Health Service,* listed in the *Resource Guide.* Assuming you're going to fly, you can minimize the risk by standing up and moving your legs as often as possible, and by wearing knee-high (over-the-calf) compression socks on long flights. Ordinary "support socks" don't squeeze your legs firmly enough to stimulate blood circulation or keep down the swelling of feet and legs—get medical-grade "graduated compression" ones from a pharmacy, uniform store (they are worn by many nurses, food service workers, and teachers who spend all day on their feet), or Internet sock store. I'm not a doctor, and I don't know if they really reduce the risk of blood clots on long flights or bus rides, but they greatly increase my comfort.

JET LAG

"Jet lag" is the disruption of the body's normal daily rhythms that results from traveling across time zones more rapidly than your body can adjust, and trying to function on a cycle out of sync with your body's internal clock. Jet lag has nothing per se to do with flight or jets, of course, although only airplanes cross time zones quickly enough to produce its symptoms.

If you travel from one time zone to another, your body takes time to readjust. In the extreme case, if you fly across the pole of the earth to a place on the opposite side of the planet, so that it is noon at your destination when it is midnight at your departure point, it's normal for it to take as much as one to two weeks for your body to fully adjust to the new time zone. There aren't many flights this close to either pole, though I was once on one with a 12-hour time difference. Lesser time changes will require less adjustment time. Until your body synchronizes itself with the time zone where you have arrived, your natural cycles will make you sleepy in the daytime and awake and alert at night, according to the patterns in the place you left.

There is no way to prevent or eliminate jet lag. The body's clock is autonomous and self-regulating, not under any conscious control. "Scientists are working on it," as they say, but don't appear close to finding a rapid way to reset the body's internal clock. Jet lag pills, diets, and miracle cures are either pure quackery or at most tools that can somewhat reduce, not eliminate, the time it takes your body to adjust to rapid changes of time zone. Some people naturally take more time to adjust to time changes than others, but with sufficiently large and rapid time changes everyone experiences some degree of jet lag.

The only things that have been proven to reduce the time it takes to adjust to a new time zone are exposure to as much sunlight as possible on arrival (ordinary artificial light is not bright enough to make a difference) and shifting your daily cycle before departure (by waking up and going to sleep earlier or later) in the direction you wish your body to adapt for your destination. The latter works only if you are free to keep strange hours for several days before you leave, and if you plan carefully and have a good understanding of your body's cycles.

If jet lag is unavoidable, why should you worry about it? Developing an awareness of jet lag and your body's rhythms can help you better cope with and be prepared for its effects. For several days after you take a long east–west or west–east flight, keep track of what time your body thinks it is, based on what time it is in the place you left, and your body's normal rate of adjustment, and take that into account in your activities. Awareness of your biological rhythms is the key to coping: anticipating, recognizing, and allowing for jet lag.

Don't try to drive when your body thinks it is the middle of the night, is least alert, and wants to sleep. Don't waste your time lying awake trying to sleep when your body thinks it is midmorning and is keeping you fully alert. If you think about your body's cycles in advance, you can plan accordingly so you don't schedule an important business meeting on your first day in a new time zone at a time when you can predict that your body will be trying to put your mind to sleep. Instead, schedule a late night out, when your body will think it is daytime and wouldn't let you sleep anyway.

I carry a watch that shows the time in two time zones, and I keep conscious track of what time my body thinks it is. With practice, you can often feel the physical and mental manifestations of your daily cycles. Body temperature, for example, varies daily by more than one degree C (two degrees F). When I feel myself unusually cold and want an extra sweater on my first day in a new time zone, I know that it is because my body, in the night phase of its cycle, is reducing my temperature, and I am reminded to make allowances for the fact that my mind is probably at its nighttime low ebb of alertness and function. Similarly, when I wake up hot in the middle of the night, I know that my body, thinking it is morning, is warming me to wake me up, and that it is probably pointless to keep trying to sleep or stay in bed. I might as well get up and make what I can of the night. I actually find dawn walks in new cities, usually prompted by jet lag, to be a particularly educational and enjoyable way to get a feel for places. I have vivid, pleasant memories of the first mornings after most of my long westbound flights.

Travel Illnesses
TRAVELER'S DIARRHEA

The most common travel ailment is traveler's diarrhea. You're likely to get diarrhea from time to time no matter how careful you are. It's unpleasant but temporary and rarely life-threatening.

The best way to reduce your risk of diarrhea is to boil or treat (with iodine or a filter that includes iodine) the water you drink, and not to eat uncooked, unpeeled fruits or vegetables.

> **REAL LIFE**
>
> When one of my clients had to cancel or cut short a trip because of illness, it was almost always because of an illness unrelated to travel.

The major danger of diarrhea is dehydration; if you keep drinking adequate amounts of fluids, diarrhea often goes away on its own, without the need for drugs. Drugs should be a last, not a first, resort.

If it's possible, stop and rest until you recover; it's not worth trying to travel or keep up a schedule with diarrhea. The likelihood that you will get diarrhea and be unable to travel for a few days every few months in the South is one of the reasons not to plan a fixed itinerary that doesn't leave you free to take a few unplanned days to rest and recover wherever you might get sick.

SEXUALLY TRANSMITTED DISEASES

The most common serious diseases of travelers, and those for which travelers most often need professional medical treatment, are AIDS and other sexually transmitted diseases (STDs).

This should come as no surprise. Travel is romantic—that's part of its attraction and joy. There's always been a special genre of romance and fantasy about travel and travelers. Some people travel in search of love and/or sex, and some find either or both unexpectedly. When someone called me from halfway around the world to try to change the route of the rest of their trip, the most common reason for the change was having fallen in love with another traveler with a different itinerary.

Some travelers are celibate or monogamously coupled, but lots of travelers aren't, and they may have sex with other travelers and/or with local people they meet along the way. Travelers have always been, and remain, among the major transmission vectors of all communicable diseases, but especially of sexually transmitted diseases.

It's tempting to wish that your vacation travels could be a vacation from concerns about safe sex. But that would be a serious mistake. Rates of HIV infection among sex workers in Bangkok, or among the general population in some African countries, are higher than they are among sexually active gay men in San Francisco, or intravenous drug users in New York City. Other STDs are equally prevalent, or more so. Increasingly many strains are resistant to antibiotics, and some—like herpes—are incurable.

It's also common, largely as a result of unconscious race and class bias, to assume falsely that sex with fellow travelers, especially those from backgrounds like yours, is automatically safer than sex with prostitutes or other local people.

A very high percentage of sexually active travelers get one or another (or several) STD at some point in their travels. A sizable percentage of your fellow travelers are carrying one or more STDs. Avoid unsafe sexual practices, and be as safe as you can, no matter who your partners are. Be prepared for the possibility of sex even if you don't expect it; people have been known to change their minds.

Unfortunately, some of the places where the risk of STDs is highest are places where prostitution and sex tourism are pillars of the economy, and where little is being done to promote safer sex or awareness of STDs, lest fear of AIDS or other STDs detract from the profits of the sex industry. You won't be reminded of AIDS or other STDs, or of the dangers of unsafe sex, in the places where it matters most. Try to remember this at appropriate moments as you travel.

Condoms and other aids to safer sex are among the health and hygiene supplies you should bring with you. Condoms and other contraceptives aren't always available, and they are often of unreliable quality. Bring plenty: if you end up with extras, you'll have no difficulty giving them away. Sexual lubricants are also hard or impossible to find in many places: one person I know was asked to bring sexual lubricant to some people abroad, as one of a handful of the most-coveted things from the United States that they couldn't get locally.

Venereal disease clinics are a fixture of travelers' ghettoes around the world. Long-term or follow-up treatment (which you are especially likely to need if you get infected with a disease strain that is resistant to common antibiotics) can pose more of a problem.

In regions with strong sexual taboos, considerate treatment of sexual or reproductive health issues may not be forthcoming even from medical professionals, especially for women and gay men.

EXOTIC AND TROPICAL DISEASES

Horror movies notwithstanding, rare and exotic diseases are just that: rare. The common tropical diseases are the ones you will find described in standard health guidebooks and health advisories; the more serious common ones are those for which the greatest efforts have been made to develop vaccinations and treatments. New contagious diseases, such as SARS in 2003, or the intermittent outbreaks of diseases like Ebola fever, are by their nature unpredictable, impossible to plan for—and infrequent.

There is a certain "Heart of Darkness" fear of the unknown behind travelers' fears that strange (to them) places may harbor strange plagues. Without meaning to belittle the risks of diseases, I think most travelers worry about them more than is warranted.

You should, of course, get any immunizations or other shots recommended for the places you are going, take any recommended prophylactic drugs against common diseases (principally malaria) for which there are no vaccines, and take appropriate preventive measures (such as long clothing and insect repellent) against local parasites and vectors of disease. Beyond that, worrying will get you nowhere.

OTHER MEDICAL ISSUES

Travelers actually have more problems abroad from conditions that predated their travels, and from illnesses and injuries that they would have been just as likely to have at home, as from illnesses peculiar to travel to the places they are visiting.

Safety and Health

The travelers who most often require medical evacuation, for example, are elderly passengers who have heart attacks on cruise ships (which, presumably, they would have been just as likely to have at home), followed in frequency by people injured in road crashes, divers, climbers, and other travelers engaging in activities that are intrinsically dangerous anywhere in the world.

Get a thorough general physical examination, and a dental examination and cleaning, before any long trip abroad, especially if you'll be in very poor, remote, and/or dangerous places. More than one of my clients learned from a predeparture checkup of an illness or condition that precluded taking their planned trip. If there are medical procedures or dental work that might need to be done while traveling, but that could be taken care of before you leave, elect to have them done at home, before your trip. Planning to go abroad for elective procedures that are cheaper elsewhere than in your home country is one thing ("medical tourism"), but you don't want to have to have *unplanned* medical or dental treatment abroad if you don't have to.

If you wear glasses or contact lenses, get an eye exam as well. Make sure you have both a written copy of your current optical prescription (you can get an eyeglass prescription filled in many cheap-labor countries for much less than it would cost for new glasses in the First World) and a spare pair of glasses in the sturdiest, most crush-proof case you can find.

I recommend strongly against contact lenses for travel outside the First World, particularly in dry, smoky, polluted, or dusty areas. Contact lens supplies are heavy and bulky to carry and hard to find or expensive in many areas. Sterile conditions are hard to obtain, and eye infections are a serious risk. If you insist on wearing contact lenses, it's essential to carry medication for eye infections and to know how to use it. Eye infections can cause permanent vision damage unless treated immediately.

Travelers who have worn contact lenses for years, grown accustomed to them, and prefer them to eyeglasses may be tempted to disregard this advice. Lots of travelers set out with contact lenses. Most of them soon switch to glasses, as I do whenever I leave the First World. I'm not sure I've met anyone who has kept on wearing contact lenses after more than a month or two of continuous travel outside the First World.

If you have any preexisting illnesses or medical conditions that might require treatment, bring an ample supply of any appropriate medications and supplies. Know what to do if your condition flares up, and carry documentation of your condition so a traveling companion or health worker will know what to do if you are unable to tell them.

If you do get sick, medical care almost anywhere else in the world is cheaper than it is in the United States, sometimes even free. Visiting foreigners are covered under reciprocal agreements between many countries' national health plans. Most physicians in Third and Fourth World cities were trained in the First World and speak at least some English, although if you get really sick or badly injured, you'll probably want to come home for treatment by your regular health care provider. You may be afraid to seek medical treatment abroad, but more and more people who don't have medical insurance are choosing to have major nonemergency surgery or other medical procedures done in countries where they are cheaper than in the United States.

DISABILITIES AND PHYSICAL LIMITATIONS

People with preexisting physical conditions that affect their ability to travel, such as blindness, paraplegia, or mobility limitations, tend to write off the possibility of travel outside the First World. Guidebooks for travelers with disabilities focus on First World destinations where the most money has been invested in the technological infrastructure for travel by people with disabilities, such as wheelchair ramps, lift-equipped buses and taxis, and braille signage.

Outside the First World, guidebooks for disabled travelers focus on a small number of specialized operators of group tours for people with disabilities. (See the *Resource Guide* for some sources of information on accessible travel.) The possibility of independent Third World travel is scarcely ever mentioned.

Depending on your condition, the Third World may not be as inaccessible as you think. While it is certainly true that there are few, if any, special facilities for disabled people, that doesn't mean that there aren't other ways to provide for your needs. Care and assistance for disabled people are among many areas where labor-intensive low-tech methods are used in the South to solve problems that we in the North are accustomed to seeing addressed through capital-intensive higher-tech means. These are often just as effective, if different, solutions to these problems. Where labor is cheap, they may be more appropriate.

People with disabilities will probably have to give up, temporarily, much of their self-sufficiency if they want to travel in the South. But if you are prepared to pay people to help you, you may find that you can get to far more places, and do far more, than you had imagined. Where there are no wheelchair ramps, you can hire people to carry you. Where there are no Braille signs, you can hire a personal guide and interpreter of the sights. Hiring a full-time personal attendant or two to carry you on and off trains and help you around may be no more expensive, in a Southern country, than hiring a self-drive car or van with hand controls would be in a Northern one.

In the South, where labor is cheap, it's perfectly normal to have personal servants, and in hiring attendants, guides, porters, or escorts you are only doing what a local person with your disability, and as much money as you have, might do. The greatest difficulty may simply be finding reliable people to hire, or lining them up in advance.

For those with disabilities who find this concept intriguing, and are excited at the possibility of finding ways to travel in places they thought would be off-limits or unmanageable, John Hockenberry's *Moving Violations,* the memoirs of an international diplomatic and war correspondent who uses a wheelchair, provides some excellent examples and food for thought.

Violence and Crime

Many people are worried about crime, terrorism, war, and political violence as factors in travel. These worries are understandable, but largely unfounded. Whatever we once thought, we've all learned that the United States is not exempt from terrorism. Most victims of terrorism, in the United States and around the world, are people in their own homes, workplaces, and communities, not travelers.

Despite the widespread hostility toward various policies of the U.S. government, individual American tourists are in serious danger of terrorism or political violence in very few places. (See the sidebar *Should We Travel?*)

Americans have tended to identify very strongly with the U.S. government, and thus to identify foreign peoples with "their" governments. Not so in most other countries. Most of the world's people don't live in democracies and don't expect governments or their policies to be indicative of the desires of the people. Some of the places I've been most warmly welcomed were ones where the U.S. government was widely hated. Many experienced travelers report similar experiences of being invited into homes where the first question asked was, "Why is the U.S. government doing X, Y, or Z to our country? Why does your government hate us?" People in the most "anti-American" places are, on the whole, remarkably friendly to American people.

You are unlikely to end up in a war zone inadvertently if you pay the least attention to local current

REAL LIFE

The only two countries commonly visited by U.S. tourists where, as tourists, they are in greater danger of violent crime than they are at home in the United States are Brazil and South Africa—both of which have many similarities to the United States in the social conditions that give rise to violent crime. Teresa P. R. Caldeira's *City of Walls: Crime, Segregation, and Citizenship in São Paulo* is a brilliant exploration of those dynamics of fear, crime, and violence, and how they shape urban geography in Brazil and elsewhere.

events. It's certainly a good reason to read the local newspaper(s) and watch local or regional TV news, or at least Al Jazeera in English, when you get a chance—not just *USA Today* or CNN, which will tell you about events in the United States but much less about what's going on where you are.

Past wars pose more serious and less obvious dangers for tourists than current wars. Large areas of the world, including several entire countries, should be avoided due to land mines. Most heavily mined countries were poor even before the wars that generated the minefields and have little money even to mark known minefields. Local people in these areas take it for granted that everyone knows not to wander around anywhere they don't have to, or pick up or touch anything on or in the ground.

Modern warfare does not confine land mines to well-defined minefields. There are perhaps 100 million unexploded mines scattered in dozens of countries around the world, and 5–10 million more mines are produced each year. These mines, some from as long ago as World War II, kill thousands of civilians a year in areas no longer at war.

Any list of war zones would be rapidly out of date. But the pace of mine clearing is so inherently slow that travel to the countries presently heavily mined will remain dangerous for decades or centuries.

Many of these countries have never been of major tourist interest. But the lure of Angkor Wat still draws many tourists to Cambodia in spite of the hazards. I'm not out to scare people unduly. I want to encourage travel wherever it's possible. But anyone who is tempted to go to Cambodia should know that field research by Physicians for Human Rights estimates that "In Cambodia...one out of every 236 people has lost at least one limb to an exploding mine." Do you really want to risk being next?

If you don't want even more of the world to be rendered off-limits by land mines, I encourage you to support the International Campaign to Ban Landmines (www.icbl.org). The ICBL was little known when I mentioned it in the first edition of this book but gained prominence when it won the 1997 Nobel Peace Prize. The "Ottawa Treaty" banning landmines came into effect in 1999, but as of 2011 the United States remained one of the most important countries not to have ratified it, and one of the world's major advocates of continued manufacture and deployment of land mines.

Terrorism aside, few countries have as much violent crime as the United States, and in few countries are criminals as apt to be armed, especially with guns, as they are in the United States. At the same time, foreigners afraid of U.S. crime may be reassured to hear that most lifelong U.S. residents have never been the victim of a violent crime. Travelers anywhere in the world are far more likely to have their belongings stolen than to be violently attacked.

Violence against women and children is a problem throughout the world. But most of this violence is within families, not against travelers or other strangers. American women traveling abroad, whether in Europe or in the South, in groups or couples or alone, generally report much higher levels of sexual harassment than in the United States, but a lower level of perceived danger of sexual assault or violence. Much of the danger of sexual assault or rape, from the anecdotal evidence I've heard, is the danger of date rape by fellow travelers in guesthouses and hostels, not of rape by locals. (See the *Resource Guide* for sources of advice and mutual support for women travelers.)

Americans and other travelers from countries where significant sectors of society are coming to disapprove of excessive family violence may find it hard to get used to seeing women and children "put in their places" in public or private by elders and male family members. If you complain, realize that you risk having the violence redirected at you. Some visitors to the United States, on the other hand, may find it equally hard to accept that some strangers in the United States will feel entitled to criticize them if they hit their wives or children, while others will even call the police to try to have them arrested.

HEALTH PREPARATIONS

Preparing yourself for travel is as much or more about getting yourself in shape as about seeing a doctor. But you should do both.

Physical Fitness

Do you need to be young, strong, and physically fit to travel around the world?

The short answer is "No." But it does raise some issues: How strong and fit do you have to be to travel around the world? And what are the most challenging real-world physical tasks that travelers need to be prepared for?

STRENGTH AND FITNESS

Brute strength is rarely needed for travel. We may think of the Third World as the land of "hard traveling," but the places where the physical infrastructure of travel is worse tend to be those where the service infrastructure of people to help you (carrying your luggage, for example, where the path is unpaved and there is no motorized transport available) is better and cheaper.

Lots of people with limited physical ability—small, frail, sedentary, very old, very young, out of shape—travel around the world every year, many of them on their own. I know women who've gone around the world, alone, in their 80s, and come back eager to do it again. Even for people with significant physical disabilities, more is possible than you might imagine, if you are willing to put up with having to pay people to help you over the rough places in the road rather than being able to get by on your own with more technically sophisticated aids to personal mobility. (See the sections on travel with disabilities and physical limitations earlier in this chapter and in the *Resource Guide*.)

There are places where travel is genuinely and unavoidably hard work, mainly because of the rigors of long-distance ground transport in roadless areas, and/or a lack of accommodations at any price that satisfy First World standards of minimal comfort. But those are almost all either in parts of the Fourth World where there are few tourists, not even healthy young back-packers, or involve particular types of travel like trekking that are inherently physical anywhere in the world. There are lifetimes of other parts of the world to explore.

If you live a sedentary life, particularly if you drive everywhere, it makes sense to get in as good shape as possible for walking before you set out on an extended journey on which you won't always have a car. In general, however, physical and mental stamina is more likely to determine the limits of where you can comfortably travel than the maximum weight you can lift or how fast you can sprint.

PHYSICAL CHALLENGES

What are the real-world physical challenges that ordinary travelers should be prepared for?

Walk: Even very leisurely sightseeing on foot and by public transit is likely to involve at least 10 km (6 miles) a day of walking. You don't have to spend all day, every day, sightseeing. The more slowly you travel, and the more time you spend in each place, the less likely you are to come up against your physical limits trying to see too much in too little time. But if you plan a busy travel agenda, be sure you're in good shape for the amount of pavement-pounding it will require.

Lift: Unless you're on an escorted tour with baggage handlers every-where, it can be difficult if you can't lift your luggage up a high step onto a bus, truck, or streetcar, or into a luggage rack above your head. There will usually be someone nearby willing to help, but occasionally there won't be, or there won't be anyone you are prepared to trust with your luggage at first glance.

Climb Stairs: The kinds of infrastructure adaptations we've gotten used to in the United States since the passage of the Americans with Disabilities Act—in particular, elevators and ramps in public facilities—are not (yet) the norm even in the rest of the First World. Often there's only one elevator, escalator, or fu-nicular. If it's out of service, the alternative is to take the stairs. Museums, in my experience, are generally pretty good about providing for visitors with limited strength and/or mobility. But it's routine to have to go up or down a couple of flights of stairs to get on or off a train or subway. In some steep towns and cit-ies, streets and footpaths become flights of public steps. (Complicating matters, some of the steepest cities in the world are also those at the highest altitudes.) Hotels with elevators can be scarce or nonexistent, depending on where you are. It's reasonable to expect, and to negotiate, a lower price for a room that requires climbing more than two flights of steps. But you should expect to have to climb up and down at least a couple of flights of steps several times a day. For many travelers with limited strength, the most difficult thing they routinely have to do is to get their wheeled luggage up or down stairs at entrances and exits from train stations and at pedestrian over- and under-crossings.

Carry or Drag: If you can't carry or wheel your own bag(s), you can usually take a taxi or rickshaw, or pay someone to carry your luggage to and from the place you are staying. Most of the time, wheeled luggage will ease the way. If you've arranged your schedule (or lack of a schedule) so that you don't need to be in a hurry, you can go slowly and stop and rest as often as you like, maybe even sit on your wheeled luggage to rest if it's sturdy enough. But if distances are short enough for almost everyone to walk—in a small but touristic town, for example—and/or if none of the porters seem trustworthy, there will be occasional times when you have to make your way to your hotel or hostel, with your luggage, on your own. If the distance is much more than a mile, and there's lots of traffic, there's probably some sort of motorized transport available. But the places where there is no motorized transport are likely to be those where the roads or paths are unpaved. Half a dozen times in my last year-long trip around the world, I had to cover more than half a mile of rough stone paving blocks, rounded cobblestones, or coarse gravel—the worst possible surfaces for wheeled luggage. If you aren't prepared at least occasionally either to put your pack on your back and carry it if it has straps, or to drag it over such a surface, that will put some significant limits on where you can go.

Stand: You won't always find a convenient seat if you get tired and need to rest. Even if you'd be willing to sit on the floor or the sidewalk in a pinch at home, you probably won't feel like doing that in places where there are no sidewalks and the streets are covered with animal (and perhaps human) excrement. You might have an unexpectedly long wait for a bus on a street corner, or you might board a crowded bus, not find a seat, and get stuck in a traffic jam for an hour or two. If you look ill or faint, people are likely to give up any available seat for you. People in most of the rest of the world are considerably more deferential to elderly, pregnant, or disabled people, in such situations, than is the norm in the United States. But traveling on your own can be difficult if you can't stay on your feet for a couple of hours at a time.

Endure: Especially in transit—on vehicles of all sorts, or while waiting for transport—you can find yourself in physically uncomfortable circumstances for hours at a time. How long are you prepared to wait around the bus yard for a vehicle to fill up with passengers before it leaves? For how long can you tolerate a cramped seat on a bouncing bus on an unpaved road, with other passengers pressing against you on all sides, perhaps with too much smoke and too little ventilation, or perhaps with a frigid draft? Many buses in other countries are more comfortable than Greyhound, but sometimes the conditions turn out to be worse and the journey longer than you expected. You can usually (not always) carry some snacks with you, but keeping to a regular meal schedule is sometimes impossible. When you're judging whether the ride will be bearable, be realistic about your tolerance for sustained discomfort and your confidence (or lack thereof) in what the trip will be like and how long it will take. Consider both your physical and mental stamina. After how long a journey, at the end of the road, in a strange place (perhaps in the middle of the night if you are delayed, even if you were scheduled to arrive in the daytime), will you be too tired or feeling too debilitated to find your way to a place to stay, managing simultaneously to stay sufficiently open to the experience and not to take your tiredness and discomfort out on your traveling companion(s) or the people you meet, yet sufficiently alert and wary not to set yourself up to get ripped off by pickpockets, muggers, or con artists?

Listen to Your Body: Most people who overexert themselves while traveling do so not because it was necessary to get where they wanted to go, do what they wanted to do, or see what they wanted to see, but because they were too distracted by the sensory overload of being in a strange place—whose sensations, after all, they had come for the purpose of experiencing—to remember to pay attention to the pain, tiredness, or other sensations of their own body signaling that it's time to rest. Before you put yourself in such a deliberately and profoundly distracted state, practice paying attention to your body's early warning signs. The excitement of travel is a powerful drug that, like adrenaline, can keep us from noticing our pain, tiredness, hunger, or thirst until it's too late for a quick recovery. On the road, remind yourself to stop periodically and ask yourself, "Do I need to slow down? Do I need to stop and rest for a bit? Drink? Eat? Sleep?"

There are things I didn't do on my last trip around the world, in my late 40s, that I might have done had I gone to those places on my first such trip in my 20s. But there are also things I noticed and learned on my last trip, seeing things with more experienced eyes, that I might not have appreciated if I had seen them earlier in my life. Travel while you are younger and more fit, if you can, but travel when you are older too, even if you are less fit.

Immunizations
WHAT SHOTS DO YOU NEED?

Current international and U.S. government inoculation and antimalarial requirements and recommendations for all countries are available from the

World Health Organization (WHO) and the U.S. Centers for Disease Control and Prevention (see the *Resource Guide*).

In addition to country listings of vaccination requirements, WHO and the CDC produce advisories intended for both health professionals and lay readers on the health hazards of each world region and what to do about them. Included are preventive and treatment strategies for particular diseases, such as malaria, and information about current disease outbreaks, epidemics, and emerging diseases and health hazards. CDC advisories are much less politically biased than U.S. State Department travel advisories. Most of the inoculations WHO and/or the CDC recommend are not required by any government—they are matters of health and safety, not law.

Some immunizations require a series of injections several weeks apart, and you shouldn't get too many shots at once. You generally need to start taking most antimalarial drugs two weeks before you expect to arrive in a malarial area. So you should start getting immunizations and prescriptions at least a month, better six weeks, before your departure. Most people expect injections, but some immunizations are actually oral vaccines.

In order to know what vaccinations and prescriptions to recommend, a doctor or clinic will need a complete list, in sequence, of all the countries you plan to visit. The sequence is important because some countries require immunizations against certain diseases only if you have previously visited other countries where those diseases are found.

If you don't have one already, get a passport-sized yellow "International Certificates of Vaccination" booklet when you get your first immunizations. Most travel doctors and immunization clinics provide them. Make sure each immunization is entered in your yellow booklet with the doctor's signature, date, and stamp. Keep your yellow booklet with your passport; it can be essential when crossing borders and impossible to replace if lost. If you lose it and can't prove that you have had the required immunizations, you may have to be immunized on the spot at a border, by whom and with whatever equipment happens to be available, whether it is sterile, unsterile, or reused.

WHERE SHOULD YOU GET YOUR SHOTS?

If you're going on a long or arduous trip, the first place to go should be your regular doctor, health maintenance organization (HMO), or health service. You should get a general health checkup before an extended trip, and you might as well get your immunizations, antimalarial prescriptions, etc. at the same time and place. Some HMOs and public health services have in-house travel clinics or travel health specialists on staff.

If you don't have a regular health care provider, your doctor is unfamiliar with travel health issues, or you are certain you are in good general health and are only taking a short trip, there are specialized travel clinics in some major international gateway cities. Some are downtown, to serve business travelers. Others are located at or near airports or seaports. Still others are at major teaching hospitals. Travel clinics generally keep the usual vaccines in stock and provide prescriptions for antimalarials, antibiotics, and/or syringes or other prescription travel health supplies. You may have to go to a travel clinic or city or county public health department for some of the less-common immunizations, as some vaccines are expensive and have such short shelf lives that most doctors don't keep them in stock.

Some travel clinics are strictly immunization centers, offering minimal advice or other services. The most efficient have drop-in hours when no appointments are needed for standard services, and charge only per immunization. These are usually the cheapest and easiest places to go if that's all you need. Others, especially those that are part of teaching hospitals, offer more comprehensive travel health counseling and advice. They tend to require advance appointments and to charge much more, including per-visit fees in addition to fees for immunizations. But their personnel are willing to spend more time answering your questions or explaining recommendations for special cases.

Health and Hygiene Supplies

The book *Staying Healthy in Asia, Africa, and Latin America* has detailed health, hygiene, and first-aid packing lists for travel to more and less remote areas.

Staying Healthy is the first thing you should buy for your travel first-aid and medical kit. Read it before you leave, and bring it with you. Long before I began to write this series for Avalon Travel and before *Staying Healthy* was published by Avalon Travel, I carried a copy on each of my trips abroad and I recommended it to all of my clients. I'll give only a few additional health, hygiene, and medical-kit packing notes.

Toilet paper (even American-style toilet paper) is available most places there are foreign tourists, even in places where most local people don't use it. I try to pack several rolls anyway: if I start out with half a dozen rolls of toilet paper in my luggage, I know I'll have room for the books I'll acquire along the way. You may tend to accumulate souvenirs or other things to bring home, rather than books—my usual traveling companion accumulates textiles—but the principle is the same.

Condoms, other contraceptives, and sexual lubricants aren't reliably obtainable outside the largest cities in many regions, and sometimes uncommon and expensive (or of poor quality) even there. Bring enough to last a long while, and stock up when you can. Women should consider bringing medication for vaginal yeast infections. Yeast infections are common side effects of travel stress and antibiotics, and the medication can be hard to find.

Tampons are hard to find and expensive in much of the world. If you have a strong preference for a particular type, you may have to carry enough for many months at a time. Sanitary napkins are more widely available, though again of erratic quality. Some women travelers switch to menstrual pads or sponges that can be washed and reused, such as those that are used by most women in the world. Some find they prefer them and never switch back, even after they return home to the First World. However, when traveling in areas with questionable water quality, make sure to use only potable water for washing the pads or sponges.

Some sort of antidiarrheal medicine, whether prescription or over-the-counter, is essential in an emergency on a long bus or train ride. Many travelers also carry a course of prescription antibiotics to treat the causes of serious or persistent travelers' diarrhea. The traditional systemic antibiotics can have significant side effects such as extreme sun sensitivity, so be sure to ask your doctor about the newer nonsystemic intestinal antibiotics. They've worked well for me on recent trips.

If you can, bring a few sealed disposable sterile needles and syringes. These are available over the counter in most of the world, but not necessarily just when you need them. Get a supply when you have a chance. If you ask your doctor while you are getting your immunizations, they might write you a prescription for needles and syringes, or they might just give you some from their own stock. If you need an injection (such as of antibiotics for severe infection), you may need to supply your own needle and syringe. This is actually the normal practice for those who can afford new needles in many countries.

Needles and syringes are routinely reused, often without sterilization or cleaning with bleach, in much of the world. Dirty used needles are sometimes repackaged and resold as new and sterile in some countries. Injections and blood transfusions in many countries carry a serious risk of AIDS or other blood-borne diseases.

Many people are afraid to carry needles and syringes, lest they be suspected of being drug addicts. If it came to that, I'd rather come under suspicion of drug use than get HIV/AIDS from a contaminated needle. In practice, I've never had a problem carrying needles and syringes in my medical kit, with or without a prescription, and I've never heard of anyone else having a problem either, unless they were also carrying illegal drugs.

A discussion of this topic on the Internet prompted people to write in from all over the world, all reporting that they had carried syringes across all sorts of borders without incident or difficulty, even when their packs had been searched, their medical kits opened, and the needles scrutinized. The only place I worry about it at all any more is coming back into the United States, where I make sure I have the prescription with my needles, or just throw them away before my final flight back to the States. And of course I never carry illegal drugs across borders.

To avoid problems at borders or elsewhere, carry prescription drugs only in their original labeled prescription containers. If you normally buy them in large quantities, resist any temptation to transfer them yourself to small, unlabeled containers. Instead, the next time you have your prescription refilled, have your pharmacist package and label a suitably small quantity of each drug separately in a travel-sized container. It's a nuisance for the pharmacist, but they should do this if you ask.

TRAVEL INSURANCE

"Travel insurance" is a confusing term, as it is used to refer to insurance against many different types of risks: travel medical insurance, medical evacuation (medevac) insurance, trip cancellation and interruption insurance, supplier default insurance, baggage insurance, etc. Many "travel insurance" policies offer a bundle of different coverages and options. Travel insurance policies may exclude certain countries, certain activities, certain airlines or other travel companies, or certain types of events (riots, civil unrest, natural disasters, etc.) that may be exactly what you want coverage against. Read the fine print to be sure you understand what you are paying for and what is (and isn't) covered.

Some travel agents and tour companies provide information on travel insurance, but you should never buy travel insurance directly from a travel agent or tour company. Your payment should be made directly to the insurance company or an independent insurance agent. If you pay travel agents or tour companies for insurance, and they go bankrupt, you are likely to find that they had failed to pass on your insurance premium to the insurance company and that you are not insured.

Some tour companies allow you to pay an additional fee, up front, in exchange for a waiver of their usual penalties if you have to cancel your trip. In effect, this means that you are paying a higher price for a less-restricted ticket or package. This is not really insurance, though it's quite legitimate. It may or may not be a good deal, depending on the relative sizes of the waiver fee and cancellation penalties, but you should at least look at the numbers and consider it.

Some regular insurance agents handle travel insurance, especially long-term comprehensive travel medical insurance. If you're traveling for six months or more, or if you plan to travel regularly throughout the year, it may be cheaper to include travel coverage with your regular health coverage than to buy a separate policy targeted at travelers. Check with your insurance agent to see what they can offer. Liability insurance is another type of coverage that may be cheaper and easier to arrange as a "rider" on your homeowner's or renter's insurance than as a separate policy.

You can also get travel insurance from specialists in the field. These include travel insurance companies, direct providers of medevac and travel emergency services, and independent travel insurance brokers and agencies that can help you compare the offerings of different insurers. Some such companies are listed in the *Resource Guide* to help you get started on your research.

I recommend trip cancellation and interruption insurance and, if available, supplier default insurance for all long-term travelers who can't afford to self-insure. Travel medical insurance, medical evacuation insurance, and liability insurance are appropriate for some but not all travelers, depending on your situation, overall health, activities you plan on your trip, and what (if any) other insurance you have.

COMPREHENSIVE TRAVEL MEDICAL INSURANCE

Comprehensive travel medical insurance is for people who don't have any other medical insurance, even at home. Since most people who can afford it have health care coverage in their home country, often through their employer or a national health insurance scheme, comprehensive travel medical insurance is mainly of interest to long-term travelers who've left their jobs and lost their insurance coverage at home, or to those living and working outside their country of citizenship or permanent residence. The best policies for long-term travelers are often those marketed to expatriates rather than to travelers. Check publications and websites targeted at expats and international students and volunteers for advice and recommendations on this sort of insurance.

Since comprehensive health insurance covers most medical expenses while you are traveling, even routine care, premiums are high: US$5–10 a day or more, which many long-term budget travelers consider to be prohibitively costly. Travel health insurance won't usually (except in the case of special plans for foreign visitors to the United States) pay overseas bills directly; it will only reimburse you after the fact. It is generally secondary insurance; that is, it will only reimburse whatever your primary insurance (if you have any) won't pay. If you already have health insurance, it may already provide better coverage than you realize for expenses for emergency treatment abroad. Such medical care as is available in many places is often inexpensive or free anyway. And if you get really sick or badly injured, you'll probably want to come home rather than having major surgery or long-term treatment abroad.

For all these reasons, you may not want this sort of insurance unless you don't have any other health insurance, are in especially poor health, are especially cautious, or are taking a relatively short trip to an expensive place.

A common alternative strategy is to keep up your regular health plan at home while you are traveling, self-insure for the risk that you will have to pay out of your own pocket for any health expenses not covered by your insurance, and buy trip cancellation and interruption insurance (see below) to cover the cost of getting home—where your regular insurance will pay for follow-up treatment—if you should become badly hurt or seriously ill.

EMERGENCY TRAVEL MEDICAL INSURANCE

Emergency travel medical insurance is for people who have medical coverage at home but whose health plan at home doesn't cover them while they are traveling. Emergency travel medical insurance only covers emergency services abroad; once you get home, you're on your own (or presumably, back under your regular home coverage) for any necessary follow-up treatment or continuing care. Most health insurance plans and health maintenance organizations in the United States include their own provisions for emergency care while abroad, at least for trips of less than 30 days. Check with your current insurer or HMO before you waste money on an emergency travel medical plan that might duplicate your existing coverage.

Supplemental or emergency medical insurance is essential for all foreign visitors to the United States. Because the United States has no national health program, it also has no reciprocal agreements to provide care for visitors whose health care at home is provided by their countries' national health systems. Health care in the United States, for those without insurance, is almost entirely on a cash basis. Only the most limited emergency medical services are available to those without insurance or the means to pay. Medical treatment in the United States is several times more expensive than in most other First World countries, and many U.S. doctors and medical facilities will not provide services, except in life-or-death situations, without advance payment or proof of insurance. A single day in a hospital as a result of a car crash in the United States could easily cost more than US$10,000.

Don't even think of visiting the United States without a supplemental medical insurance policy, preferably from a company with its own U.S. office that can make payments directly to U.S. health care providers, rather than requiring you to pay and reimbursing you later. Most travel agents specializing in travel to the United States can provide information on insurance plans of this sort.

Carry proof of insurance at all times while in the United States. Most insurance companies will issue you an insurance card with a contact number that a doctor or hospital can call, before providing medical services, to verify that you are insured and that payment will be made. Keep this card in your money belt with your other essential documents.

Safety and Health

MEDICAL EVACUATION INSURANCE

Medical evacuation (medevac) insurance covers the cost of an air ambulance and related services if you are so badly injured, or become so ill, that you can't come home (or get to a suitable medical facility) on a scheduled commercial passenger flight.

Emergency medical evacuation by chartered air ambulance can be prohibitively expensive. Cost aside, arranging for an air ambulance, attending physician and nurse, customs and immigration clearance for the onboard equipment, life-support facilities at each refueling stop, etc., is more than most people could or would know how to do on their own. But medical evacuations are less common than people think. Even very badly injured travelers usually can come home on regular flights after no more than a couple of weeks of emergency treatment and stabilization abroad.

> **REAL LIFE**
>
> When my father was evacuated from Brazil to Boston by air ambulance in 1991 for emergency brain surgery, the bill for the evacuation, not including the surgery or treatment, was over US$20,000. Fortunately it was paid for by his insurance, because he was abroad on business and had comprehensive travel health coverage through his employer.

Most places with airports have scheduled service that can get one to a city with a sophisticated modern hospital more quickly than an air ambulance could arrive. The kinds of risky sports and activities that are most likely to lead to the need for evacuation, such as scuba diving, mountain climbing, and motor sports, are often specifically excluded from insurance coverage as uninsurable risks.

Medical evacuation insurance is most appropriate if you will be taking an especially dangerous trip (but not one involving an activity excluded in the fine print of the policy) or one through regions inaccessible by, or with especially infrequent, commercial air service. If you aren't insured and can't afford an air ambulance, you may have to wait longer to recover, and endure considerably greater discomfort or pain, to fly home on a scheduled airline. If you can afford it, it's probably a good idea in any case, and if you ever need it you certainly won't regret the expense of insurance. But if you can't afford it, I probably wouldn't let that alone stand in the way of your trip.

TRIP CANCELLATION AND INTERRUPTION INSURANCE

Trip cancellation and interruption insurance covers the cancellation or refund penalties and the cost of getting home if you have to cancel your trip, or cut it short, for specified reasons. The covered reasons vary (read the fine print), but

Safety and Health

typically include injury or illness to you, a traveling companion, or a member of your immediate family. (Definitions of "family member" vary. Again, read the fine print.) Itinerary changes due to the outbreak of war or a terrorist incident in an intended destination may or may not be included, or may be covered only at additional charge.

Trip cancellation and interruption insurance used to be available even to people who didn't buy any other form of travel insurance. But underwriters of this sort of insurance suffered a wave of losses for canceled trips after 11 September 2001, and since then have been reluctant to provide it except as part of a bundled package that insures against other, more predictable risks. Companies that sell travel insurance are frustrated, since the underwriters pulled out of this niche just when demand for this type of coverage spiked up. Given the demand, I expect this sort of insurance gradually to reappear on the market, although at higher prices than before and with exclusions for many of the contingencies that travelers actually want to insure themselves against.

Although most tickets around the world will allow you to change the dates of each flight at little or no charge, they will not permit you to change the airlines or sequence of connections. So getting home on the original routing, even if space is available on the next flight on each leg of the trip, could easily take you two or three weeks if you have many stopovers scheduled. The alternative, of course, is full-fare, fully reroutable and refundable tickets. But the cost of trip cancellation and interruption insurance, if you can find it unbundled, is a tiny fraction of the difference in cost between fully refundable, reroutable tickets and discounted nonrefundable, nonreroutable tickets. It's cheaper to get tickets with penalties and get trip cancellation and interruption insurance than to get fully refundable tickets.

Trip cancellation and interruption insurance won't cover you if you simply change your mind, or if the reasons for a business trip change. Some but not all plans cover you if you are denied a visa or denied entry. Most won't cover you for preexisting medical conditions. Other than these, the reasons for canceling or cutting short a trip that they do cover are the most frequent reasons for people with nonrefundable tickets to have to change their plans.

Family emergencies are an especially common reason to need trip cancellation and interruption insurance. Most people are uncomfortable with acknowledging that a parent or other immediate family member is in sufficiently poor health that cutting short a trip in case of hospitalization or death might be necessary. But this is actually a common reason to come home early, and if you bought insurance, at least your choice of whether to come home if someone gets sick or dies won't have to be influenced by concerns of cost.

Road accidents—which can leave you in no condition to continue your trip and in need of lengthy rehabilitation and follow-up treatment that you would prefer to undergo at home—are the other most common reason for needing and using trip cancellation and interruption insurance.

Because the likelihood of a claim is directly related to the length of your trip, but the premium is typically the same percentage of the insured trip cost whether you will be leaving tomorrow and home in a week or leaving in six months and home in a year, the longer your trip and the further in advance you buy your tickets, the better the buy this sort of insurance is likely to be. I highly recommend trip cancellation and interruption insurance—if you can get it without having to buy an expensive bundle that includes lots of other coverage you don't need—for all long-term travelers.

SUPPLIER DEFAULT INSURANCE

Supplier default insurance covers any money you lose because of the bankruptcy of an airline, cruise line, tour operator, or other provider of travel services. Most trip cancellation and interruption policies used to include supplier default coverage, but supplier default coverage has been drastically cut back since 11 September 2001. Some travel insurance companies no longer offer it at all, while others pick and choose which travel suppliers they will insure. Read the fine print. (For more advice on airline bankruptcies, see the *Air Transportation* chapter.)

LIABILITY INSURANCE

Insurance provided by your credit card issuer as a no-added-cost "perk" to cardholders might cover damage to rental cars. If you think you might rent a car in a foreign country, check with your card issuer before you leave to find out exactly what they cover, and whether that coverage applies abroad or only in your home country. Your own automobile insurance may also provide some coverage when you are driving a rental car, again with the possibility of geographic limitations.

> ## REAL LIFE
>
> On my last trip around the word, the availability of an optional third-party liability add-on was the deciding factor in my choice of a travel insurance plan.

But what if you don't own a car, or are canceling your car insurance while you are abroad? At most, your credit card company will reimburse damage to the car you have rented. You might be able to self-insure for damage you might do to another vehicle in a collision. But what if you are driving a rental car, and someone else is injured or killed in an crash for which you are held responsible? No credit card covers this sort of liability to third parties.

An accident like this is a real possibility that could leave you liable for hundreds of thousands of dollars if someone dies or is permanently disabled. If you don't have third-party liability coverage that applies while you are driving a rental car abroad, you need it. Ask your insurance agent about the cost of adding a liability or "umbrella" rider to your homeowner's or renter's insurance policy—that's likely to be much, much cheaper than a separate policy.

Few travelers think about their potential liability to third parties for injuries or deaths on the road, or realize that they need liability insurance. As a result, it's rarely part of a standard "travel insurance" package. It's likely to be an added-cost option if it's offered at all, and more likely to be available with plans marketed to expatriates than those designed for tourists, including business people, NGO staff and volunteers, students abroad, and/or missionaries. That's too bad, because when it is available—as a rider to a travel, homeowner's, or renter's insurance policy—it's quite inexpensive. You can get probably get US$100,000 of coverage for less than US$100 per year. US$500,000–1 million would be a safer amount of liability cover, especially if you have substantial assets or savings (a house and/or retirement accounts) that you could lose in case of a judgment against you for lost wages, lifetime care, etc. for someone injured or killed in a car crash or other accident.

Safety and Health

Baggage

"When in Doubt, Leave it Out."

AIRLINE BAGGAGE LIMITS

How much baggage you could take with you on airplane flights without extra charge used to be fairly standardized, with almost every international airline in the world enforcing one of two baggage rules. Depending on the airline, route, and fare, you were allowed a total of 20 kg (44 lb) of free baggage per person (*including* carry-on items as well as any checked bags), or you were allowed two checked bags of up to a specified size each. Under the piece rule, the maximum weight of each bag used to be 27 or 32 kg (60 or 70 pounds), but in recent years most airlines have lowered it to 23 kg (50 pounds).

In the last few years these baggage standards have completely broken down. Some "low-fare airlines" have started charging extra for all checked or carry-on items, regardless of size or quantity. Few traditional airlines have gone quite that far, but they have been emboldened to lower their free baggage limits, and to do so in increasingly idiosyncratic ways.

There's still a fundamental difference between whether free baggage limits and excess baggage charges are determined by the number of items or by weight. But under a piece rule, you might be allowed two free checked bags, one, or none. Under a weight rule, you might be allowed 20 kg without extra charge, 15 kg, 10 kg, 5 kg, or none. The same airline may apply different rules on different routes or for different fares. And different rules may be applied to

Key Advice About Baggage

When in doubt, leave it out.

- Keep your luggage within the standard international airline baggage limit: 20 kg (44 lb) total per person including all carry-on items. Anything more than 20 kg puts you at much greater risk of having to pay excess baggage charges.

- Check with each airline for the baggage rules applicable to your flight and fare. There is no longer any universal or guaranteed free baggage allowance, and some airlines now charge extra for *all* checked or carry-on luggage.

- Always get to the airport prepared to check all your luggage. Never count on being allowed to carry it on, regardless of its size or weight.

- Don't cut corners on key items of your gear like your pack and water purifier. For prolonged hard traveling, the best quality you can afford is worth the price.

- Carry your passport, tickets, and other vital documents in a money belt or otherwise hidden inside your clothes. Carry backup copies, and leave another set of copies of all of these documents behind with a trusted friend.

- Make sure you back up electronic as well as paper data, in case your cell phone, etc. gets lost, stolen, or broken. Have a backup plan in case the password to your email or other online accounts is stolen or hacked.

- Don't feel dependent on any of your things, or worry too much about what you forget, lose, or break. You can find almost anything you really need along the way, or find some local substitute to serve the same purpose. Be prepared to improvise.

- Don't count on care packages. Mailing things home is usually more or less affordable and reliable, but slow. Having things sent to you while you are traveling is often difficult and/or expensive.

For more information on the topics in this chapter, see the *Resource Guide* in the back of the book and the links on the Practical Nomad website at www.practicalnomad.com.

Baggage

passengers on the same plane, depending on whether their tickets show a flight number of a "codeshare" airline, what fare they paid, or other factors.

As of 2011, airlines in the United States and elsewhere were embroiled in bitter disputes with consumer protection authorities, travel agencies, and reservation systems over whether or how they disclose these baggage rules and fees, both on ticket sales websites and in e-ticket confirmations.

On paper tickets, the "BAGS" box on each flight coupon showed whether your baggage allotment would be determined by weight ("20K" for coach), or if you would be allowed the greater 2-piece free baggage limit ("PC"). Paper tickets, however, have largely if not entirely disappeared. U.S. regulations require airlines to provide each passenger with an actual "ticket," but that rule is almost universally violated, and e-ticket confirmations typically omit most of the information about fares and rules that used to be printed on paper tickets.

For now, the only way to tell how much luggage you will be allowed to bring is to call each airline or go to their ticket counter, after you have bought your tickets. Ask the airline to look at your electronic ticket record (which you can't usually see), and tell you what the free baggage allowance will be for you, using those tickets, on those specific flights. If you can't do so any earlier (e.g., because the airline in question doesn't have an office in your country), check the baggage limits when you reconfirm each flight. Excess baggage charges can be prohibitive, so you really don't want any surprises at the airport when you've already packed your bags and are ready to check in. It used to be uncommon, if not rare, to see people having to repack their bags and throw things away at the check-in counter to satisfy baggage limits. Now at many airports it's a common sight.

Many Americans find all this hard to believe. They say, "I travel all the time, and I've never been limited to 44 pounds." They infer from this, erroneously, that they will never actually be limited to 20 kg or charged for excess baggage. But excess baggage fees are a growing revenue and profit center for struggling airlines around the world. Free baggage allotments are being reduced, and the rules—already stricter in most other countries than in the United States—are being more and more strictly enforced everywhere.

Not all airlines strictly enforce luggage limitations. But it's possible to get a strict check-in clerk on any given airline and flight, so you can't count on checking or carrying on more than the rules allow. To see if you're within your free baggage allowance, do as the airline will do: pile everything you aren't actually wearing on a scale, including your purse, shoulder bag, camera or computer bag, and anything else you plan to carry on or check.

Baggage limits on flights within the United States used to be exceptionally loosely enforced. Airlines would routinely waive excess baggage charges. However, the integration of baggage record-keeping with passenger reservations (through systems in which baggage tags are printed directly by, and logged in, computerized reservation systems), has largely eliminated the discretion of counter and gate agents to check excess bags without charging for them.

Whether you are allowed to carry your luggage on is a separate question from whether you are charged for it. Even if all you have is a single bag small enough to fit under the seat and weighing less than 20 kg, the airline is not obligated to let you carry it on. Airlines typically reserve the right to make you check any bag weighing more than five kg (11 pounds).

If there isn't room on the plane, the airline is entitled to send your free baggage separately (usually on the next flight, whenever that may be). Don't argue if the airline wants to do this. Better to do without your luggage for a week, if that's how long it is until the next flight, than to overload and endanger the whole plane and everyone on it. Travelers commonly encounter small planes and small baggage limits like these on flights to safari camps in Africa, to short mountain airstrips in Nepal, to small islands anywhere, and to small jungle clearings in Indonesia and Papua New Guinea.

What Are You Allowed to Carry On?

Don't rely on this or any book or website to tell you which specific items you will or won't be allowed to carry on. There is no way to know for sure until you try. The "rules" can change at any time, and much is left to the discretion of the people searching you and your bags. In the United States, the TSA refused to show me the rules when I asked for them under the Freedom of Information Act, and told me that it would "create public confusion" for people to rely on TSA press releases or their website. If you aren't sure about something, try to ask the checkpoint staff about it before you check in, so that you can move it to your checked baggage if they say you can't carry it on.

Excess Baggage

Excess baggage is very expensive. The default charge for excess baggage on international flights, in the absence of a different rule published by the specific airline, is 1.5 percent of the full unrestricted fare per excess kilogram (even if you are traveling on a discounted ticket), payable separately for each flight. If you must take excess baggage on some portion of your trip, shop around: some airlines charge a flat rate per piece of luggage, up to some specified size and weight, that is substantially lower than the per-kilogram charges would be.

Airlines are not required to accept excess baggage at all. On some small planes that service remote areas such as African safari camps, they simply don't have room for it and won't carry it at any price. Nor will excess baggage necessarily be put on the same flight with you, even if paid for as accompanied baggage.

Unaccompanied baggage is considered air freight and charged at cargo rates. Air cargo rates are higher per kilogram per kilometer (or per pound per mile) than most coach rates for passenger transportation, and airlines have higher profit margins on cargo than on passenger operations. Shipping excess baggage separately by air will be substantially more expensive in almost all cases than paying excess baggage charges. It is also much easier to get goods through customs as accompanied luggage—even in excess, dutiable amounts—than as unaccompanied freight. Barring special problems, you can walk all your accompanied luggage through customs as soon as you arrive. If you ship something separately it can take weeks to clear customs, or cost substantial "expediting fees" or bribes to get it sooner.

These differences in the price, speed, and ease of customs clearance of accompanied baggage vis-à-vis air freight are the reason express shipping companies subsidize air tickets for couriers to accompany their most urgent consignments. The amount the courier company contributes toward the cost of the courier's ticket is offset by the savings on shipping charges and customs clearance time.

Oversize Items

Size limits vary from airline to airline. It is irrelevant to Airline J whether Airline K accepted something or charged extra for it on some other flight. If you have or expect to have anything larger than an ordinary suitcase, or weighing more than 20 kg (44 lbs), call each and every airline on which you plan to travel, in advance, to find out whether it will accept it and, if so, how much it will charge for an item of its weight and dimensions.

Rules for oversize baggage (e.g., surfboards, bicycles, skis, and scuba gear) vary greatly from airline to airline. Most airlines have set fees for specific items of this sort. Check with each airline on which you are booked for its fees (some carry surfboards for free, some charge US$150 per board per flight) and regulations. Does it require bicycles to be dismantled and/or boxed? Does it provide the boxes, or must you have your own? Does it require oversize baggage to be checked in early? How early? If you will be changing planes, find out if you will be charged additionally for each flight, or only once for the entire through journey—which may depend on the fare(s).

Animals and Plants

Transporting pet animals is even more complicated and expensive. Tickets for pet transportation are generally closer in price to tickets for people than to the charges for an amount of excess baggage similar in size and weight to that of the pet. If you want to bring a pet, tell your travel agent or airline as early as possible. Check with the airline(s) and any country to or through which you'll be taking an animal to verify their procedures for cages, check-in and pickup times, vaccinations, quarantine, etc.

Many countries require arriving animals, or those of certain species or categories, to be quarantined (isolated) under observation for a period of time in order to tell if they have any diseases not found in the country. This is to ensure that arriving animals won't bring in exotic diseases or parasites to which

Baggage

Check It or Carry It On?

Travelers can be divided into those who always try to carry everything on, and those who try to avoid carrying on any more than essentials. I suspect I'm in the minority in the latter category, but here are some of my reasons:

- When changing planes, I'd rather have the airline be responsible for transferring luggage and guarding it during the transfer and layover. That way I don't have to watch it, carry it into the airport toilet or restaurant, etc. This is most important if I have a long enough layover to want to go into the city or outside the airport, or if the change involves a change of terminals and/or airports. If the airlines are willing to handle the transfer, I'll happily let them.

- I've been in many places where I had to check bags anyway. Because you have to be prepared at the check-in point for the possibility that you may have to check your main pack (and thus have to have your essentials separated out so that you can carry them on if necessary), why not just check the things you are already prepared to check? If you expect always to carry everything on, you may be unprepared and ill-equipped if you have to check some things, or you may rashly check everything and be really out of luck if your bag is lost or delayed.

- You may have to check your bag because the plane is full and the overhead bins are full; or because the type of plane has no, or less than usual, space for carry-on bags; or because you have something in your bag that isn't allowed in your carry-on luggage for "security" or other reasons; or because your bag weighs more than five kg (the carry-on limit in some places); or simply because the airline feels like it (they can make you check anything). As more items are prohibited from carry-on luggage, the less likely it is that you'll be able to carry everything on, and the more it makes sense to plan to check as much as possible. Rules change at any time, so you can never tell with certainty, in advance, what you will and won't be allowed to carry on.

- It is often faster, sometimes substantially so, to check your bag and then breeze through the security inspection to the gate than to wait for your entire pack to be searched as carry-on at the checkpoint. It's a toss-up whether fragile items are more likely to be damaged by baggage handlers, if well packed, than by hurried cops or soldiers trying to probe unfamiliar objects or pry them open to see if they contain bombs when they are searching carry-on items. (I recall some very nervous moments when I had a fragile souvenir in my carry-on, and wasn't sure how easy it would be to rewrap it safely, on the spot, once it had been opened. If you have to go through this, bring repacking materials with you.) You can leave the airport more quickly on arrival if you don't check your bags, if all goes well, but you can often arrive at the airport later if you plan to check your bags. I more often find myself arriving at the departure airport late and in a hurry than needing the maximum time advantage in leaving the airport at my destination.

- Even if I have time for my bag or pack to be searched as a carry-on, I may not wish to call attention to every little item in my luggage. I often carry legal items that I would just as soon not have waved about, passed from hand to hand, be asked to explain, or have brought to the attention of the governments of the countries to or from which I am traveling or in which I change planes. Yes, all luggage is subject to search by customs and border guards, but in practice departing checked airline luggage is much less likely to be opened than is carry-on luggage. For example, I've often seen guards pulling tampons and other such personal items out of carry-on baggage, waving them about, and demanding that the people carrying them explain what they are (through a language barrier). I'd rather leave such things in the bag I check.

local animal populations, especially commercial livestock, are not resistant. You will have to pay the cost of keeping your pet in quarantine for this time. Find out in advance how long your pet will have to be quarantined, and how much it will cost.

No doubt some readers are wondering why anyone would take a pet with them around the world. Some people buy tickets around the world when they are relocating overseas for most of a year and want to visit other places on the way there and/or the way back. Sometimes they want to bring their pets with them for the year abroad, particularly if they have children. I don't think the cost and hassle is likely to be worth it, but some people do.

Imports of living plants are subject to even more stringent controls. Inadvertently imported weeds that interfere with agriculture, plants that crowd out indigenous species, and plants harboring blights, pests, or diseases have caused immense damage to agriculture and natural ecosystems in many countries. The decision to introduce a new plant species into a bioregion where it isn't already found is not one to be made lightly, nor one to be made by amateurs. Once a new plant or pest is introduced it can be impossible to eradicate (many pests and blights have stages in which they are invisible). Moral: Do not take animals, plants, or seeds—including meats

Baggage

(even cooked sausages), fruits, vegetables, or flowers—across international borders, no matter how innocuous (and attractive) they may seem.

Lost Luggage

If your luggage doesn't arrive on your flight, file a report and description with the airline for tracing. Most "lost" luggage either got left behind or put on the wrong plane. The airline will usually notify you and deliver your luggage to you once it finds it. Airlines won't volunteer to pay to replace things in delayed luggage, but if you ask, can present receipts, and don't appear to be trying to inflate your expenses or take advantage of the airlines, they're usually willing to reimburse reasonable expenses.

Attach labels, with at least your name, securely to both the outside and the inside of each piece of your luggage. If your luggage is mangled in a conveyor, outside tags are likely to be torn off. Keep enough clothes and other essentials such as required medications in your carry-on luggage to tide you over for a few days if your checked luggage is misplaced or delayed.

CHOOSING YOUR LUGGAGE

Many factors go into your choice of luggage: sturdiness, security, comfort, capacity, personal preference. Whatever you do, choose carefully and don't scrimp. Living out of a suitcase for months, you'll become acutely aware of its every shortcoming. It's worth spending twice as much to get exactly what you want.

Types of Primary Luggage

Most long-term travelers settle on a single soft-sided "travel pack" made out of the heaviest possible nylon fabric, with either backpack straps, wheels and a handle, or both.

ON YOUR BACK OR ON TWO WHEELS?

It's a matter of personal taste. On my most recent big trips I've used a pack with both wheels and backpack straps. Wheels are great on hard, smooth surfaces, but there are plenty of rough roads and unpaved streets without sidewalks in the world. Dragging wheeled luggage for any distance on cobblestones, through sand or gravel, over piles of rubble, or up and down steps can be quite a chore. Taxis or porters aren't always an option. These aren't just Third World issues: You'll find streets of steps and roads and paths paved with coarse stone "Belgian block" in plenty of European cities and towns, not to mention long flights of steps to and from pedestrian under- and overpasses and transit stations. On the other hand, there's no point in having heavy padded straps on your luggage if you are never going to use them. Think about what you will actually do in a variety of conditions, and choose your luggage accordingly. I put my pack on my back only rarely, but dragging my pack in the few places where it couldn't roll would be such unpleasant work that I still feel the straps are worth their weight. My partner, on the other hand, prefers dragging her pack if necessary to having the extra weight of backpack straps.

PROPER FIT

The fit of a pack is very personal, depending on your height, build, and posture. Don't buy your pack by mail order, over the Internet, or anywhere you can't try it on. Test a pack on your back with weight in it, adjusted to the best fit possible, for as long as your patience and that of the store will permit. Good travel gear stores such as REI have sandbags or other weights handy

REAL LIFE

Twice in my travels my luggage has missed a connection and ended up in the wrong city. In each case, my bag was delivered to the place I was staying, undamaged, three or four days later. When it happened on a domestic flight in the United States, when I checked in for my next flight with the same airline, I was reimbursed against receipts for up to US$100 in clothes, toiletries, maps, and film bought while my luggage was missing. When it happened on an international trip to the Third World, with an Asian airline very conscious of lost face, both my traveling companion and I were upgraded to business class on our return flight by way of apology for the airline having misplaced our luggage.

and expect you to wander around the store with a pack on your back. It may take half an hour before you can begin to tell whether a backpack will be comfortable after months of constant use. Make sure wheeled luggage rolls smoothly, turns easily, and has a handle that extends to the right height and at the right angle for maneuverability and comfortable balance for your body.

GOOD WORKMANSHIP

Whatever sort of bag you choose, check the design, construction, materials, and workmanship closely. Look for a bag without entangling external straps but with sturdily attached rings or loops by which to tie or lock it to luggage racks and bus roofs. Look for double-stitched seams sealed with waterproofing and bound against fraying, and the largest, best possible quality wheels, zippers, and fittings. Most soft luggage fails first in the wheels, frame, handles, zippers, seams, or points of stress where straps are attached. Unless you plan to put your pack on your back, you'll sometimes be dragging the wheels through sand and gravel. Make sure it has wheels and bearings that will stand up to

Baggage

that sort of abuse. Long-term independent Third or Fourth World travel is the torture test of luggage. It's possible to get a bag with a lifetime guarantee of the wheels, handles, frame, zippers, and stitching. It may be worth it (it certainly has been for me), and it's a good indication of sturdy construction, but you are unlikely to be able to have warranty repairs made until you get home.

MENDING

I use heavy-gauge nylon thread for mending, but fine fishing line and dental floss have both been recommended to me for use in sewing up torn luggage. If you can, seal the seam and stitching after any mending. On a long trip, I carry a small tube of seam sealant and some patching fabric.

WATERPROOFING

Waterproof all the stitching in your bags with seam sealant from a camping-supply store before you use it, even if it's brand-new and supposedly water-proof. While you're at it, seal the seams in your waterproof raincoat, jacket, or poncho. When your bus is caught in a downpour with your bag on the roof, or your bag is thrown in a mud puddle or left out in the rain on a cart at an airport for an hour or two while waiting to being loaded on your plane, you'll be glad you waterproofed it. Waterproofing won't ensure everything stays dry, but not waterproofing will ensure that everything gets wet.

STRAPS

If you want to bring a pack that has straps so you can carry it on your back, ei-ther get a "travel pack" with removable straps, or one that has a zippered panel to cover the straps, or bring a sturdy bag large enough to entirely enclose the pack. The straps of ordinary backpacks are prone to snag in airport baggage conveyors, causing the bags to be torn apart. Some airlines won't accept ordi-nary backpacks as checked luggage, or refuse to accept any liability if they are damaged. Some people mistakenly think that the point of convertible travel packs is to look like a "suitcase," and thus appear more respectable. But outside the First World, a convertible travel pack is a symbol of (foreign) wealth. The real point of the cover over the straps on a convertible pack is to enable you to check it as airline luggage without having to sign a liability waiver.

BAG COVERS

Whichever type of luggage you choose, a cover bag adds weight but protects your luggage against water, dust, mud, and scrapes and renders it much more nondescript. It's especially useful protection when you have to tie your bag on top of a bus. If you can't find a ready-made cover bag, consider having one custom-sewn. Travelers in many parts of the world routinely encase their luggage in cloth bags (usually sewn of muslin, canvas, or burlap sacking or nylon sailcloth), and doing likewise is the best way to keep yours from standing out as that of a (potentially rich) foreigner.

APPEARANCE

Cover bag or not, choose luggage that's generally nondescript in appearance, not something in flamboyant colors that scream "high-tech and expensive" and will cause it to be singled out by every potential thief. Use some form of cheap but distinctive marking (diagonal strips of colored tape or marker on the sides, for example, or distinctive bits of ribbon or straps) to enable you quickly to distinguish your bag from other similar bags when you're trying to spot it on a baggage carousel or verify at a glance that it's still on the roof of the bus after a meal stop or still in the luggage rack at the end of the car on a train.

LOCKS

Make certain it will be possible to lock each and every external compartment on your bag. In the United States, the Transportation Security Administration claims the right to break into locked bags unless you use special "TSA-approved" locks for which the TSA has a master key. (Of course, since all TSA-approved locks are opened by the same skeleton keys, many thieves have these master keys too.) Outside the United States, many airlines refuse to accept checked bags unless they are locked. Locks are even more important on buses and trains, and when you are walking or standing in a crowd with the zippers to pack out of your sight on your back behind you.

Get a small combination lock (you don't really want to

REAL LIFE

Since 2003 the Transportation Security Administration has asked air travelers in the United States to leave their bags unlocked. If you lock your bags, the TSA might break the locks to search your bags. But many airlines' "conditions of carriage" provide that the airlines aren't liable for damage to checked luggage unless it is locked. There's a clear contradiction between the demands of the TSA and of airline contracts. To make matters worse, there have been repeated scandals involving theft from luggage by organized groups of TSA screeners. It's likely to take the courts years to decide who is responsible for damage done to locks and luggage by the TSA, or for items missing from bags broken open by the TSA. Internationally, at least, I still recommend that you always lock your bags. If your bags or locks arrive damaged, file a claim with the airline to whom you consigned them, and let the airline sort it out with the TSA.

Baggage

carry around and keep track of keys, do you?) for each compartment, and don't forget to lock your day pack. Make sure the lock for the main compartment is large enough to use as the lock on your hotel room door. The size commonly used for gym lockers should be just right. Cheap hotels don't always provide locks, or don't provide secure ones. Instead, they have hasps on the doors; guests are expected to provide their own padlocks. A combination lock, rather than a lock with a single key, is especially useful for this purpose if you will be sharing rooms with your traveling companion. If there won't be any other way to secure the bag to luggage racks, consider bringing a short (perhaps 12–18-inch, 30–45 cm) length of chain or braided metal cable to use with your main lock for this purpose, especially while sleeping in open-compartment railroad cars.

Secondary Bags

Resist any temptation to carry multiple small bags rather than one large one. At times it will be all you can manage to keep a safe eye and hold on one bag while jostling through a crowd or on or off a bus or train. If you bring a small day pack as well as a larger pack, make sure you can stow it entirely inside, or attach it securely to your main pack. A zip-off day pack that attaches to the outside of a backpack is all too easily unzipped by thieves when it's behind your back and out of your sight, even while you are walking. Despite their drawbacks, it can be hard to find a travel pack without a zip-off day pack, but I recommend it. If you're stuck with a bag with a zip-off day pack, at least make sure its construction is such that you can lock the day pack securely onto the pack so it can't be unzipped or cut free, and that you always remember to lock the day pack onto the main bag.

> ### REAL LIFE
>
> As a member of the REI cooperative, I've given travel planning clinics at REI stores across the United States. At every store the staff report that they regularly get customers who have had their zip-off day packs stolen and are trying to buy replacements.

THEFT

Fanny packs, belt pouches, shoulder bags, and knapsacks are all vulnerable to slashers. You defeat the security value of a sturdy main pack if you carry your valuables in a thinner bag. Make sure that even the thinnest parts of the fabric and straps are thick enough to resist a good-sized knife, and that the straps can't readily be opened or released from behind. Even a belt pouch worn in front of your body is easy to snatch if the strap can first be cut or opened in back.

DAY PACK CONTENTS

Identify exactly what you will need for a day's sightseeing or exploring (sunglasses, water bottle, guidebook, map, camera, spare batteries and memory chips, cell phone if you will be carrying one, rain jacket or sweater, etc.) and how it will fit in your secondary bag. Even if you don't do a full-blown travel test with your primary bag, at least try out your secondary bag (most likely a shoulder bag, belt pack, or day pack) for a few days to make sure it's comfortable and holds what you want without tempting you to carry around too much. You'll be carrying it almost all the time, so make sure it's just right.

If you check your main pack on a flight, bring whatever essentials you would need for the next week, and couldn't easily buy, in whatever you carry on. Airlines rarely lose luggage, but even good airlines misplace a bag or two on each flight. Sooner or later, you'll arrive somewhere without your checked luggage. Your bag will almost always turn up, usually in a few days, but if it's sent on the next weekly flight, you might have to do without it for that week. Be prepared.

Carrying Valuables

Carry your passport, tickets, address list, contact numbers and addresses for reporting your credit cards lost or stolen (remember, toll-free numbers won't be accessible outside North America), and other critical documents in a money belt or some other sort of pouch hidden entirely inside your clothes.

Never carry anything valuable in a belt or pouch outside your clothes: an external belt pouch is the obvious place for your valuables

REAL LIFE

One of my most versatile travel garments is a vest I designed for myself with four zippered pockets in the lining large enough for my airline tickets, passport, and other valuables. It's especially good for airports: tailored like the vest of a suit and worn with a tie, it makes me look much more respectable and businesslike to customs and immigration inspectors, at a small fraction of the weight and bulk in my luggage of a suit jacket. Because it fits closely, it would be almost impossible for a pickpocket to get into the inside zippered pockets while I'm wearing it. It also enables me to keep my passport and tickets secure but accessible for the inevitable succession of inspections and checkpoints, without my having to get in and out of my money belt in public. I've had several vests like this over the years: when one gets worn, or my size or shape changes as I age, I have a new one made the next time I'm someplace tailoring is cheap. The most recent one cost the equivalent of about US$20, custom tailored in Qatar in 48 hours.

Baggage

and will be the first thing any thief demands if you are robbed. Don't trust a money pouch around your neck, even inside your clothes: if the strap is strong enough not to break if snatched, it's strong enough to strangle you if snatched. It's especially dangerous to reinforce a fragile-looking cloth neck strap with wire strong enough to become a garrote. Your life is worth more than your money.

BACKUP YOUR DOCUMENTS AND DATA

Before you leave, and after you've completely packed, empty your money belt onto a photocopy machine and make three or four copies of everything in it except the cash. Everything. If it's important enough to be worth carrying in your money belt, you'll want the copies if your money belt is lost or stolen. Don't forget to include copies of any essential data that you keep in electronic form, such as the contacts stored in your cell phone or PDA and the email addresses or other information you've stored online. An identity thief who gets hold of your email password might alter or delete any of your stored data.

> ## REAL LIFE
>
> Organized criminal gangs hack or bribe their way into cybercafés (or open their own!) and monitor visits to banking websites to capture logins and passwords they can use to empty your accounts.

If you can find it, use waterproof paper for copies of critical documents and information. Some map and travel stores sell waterproof paper for use in making waterproof printouts from digital map databases. Look for it near the map CDs or the print-on-demand topographic map kiosk. If you are writing things like your contact list to carry in your money belt, use pencil or waterproof, nonbleeding ink. Test it. Anything in your money belt will be subjected to prolonged damp, sweaty heat.

While you are making photocopies, scan the same vital documents. Email them to yourself, and to a trusted friend. But don't rely on the scans alone—have backups on paper. It's common for email and files to be lost in a server crash, or inadvertently deleted. Don't keep vital data in your regular email account, or it will be accessible to any thief who gets your email password (an increasingly common form of crime against travelers, especially those who use cybercafés or other public Internet terminals). Keep it in a separate backup email account you use only for emergencies or, better, leave it with someone you trust who can send it to you if you need it.

PACK DUPLICATE DOCUMENTS AND COPIES OF DATA

Pack a set or two of copies of your documents in your luggage, separately from your money belt, in a waterproof pouch or ziplock bag. (I bury one copy in my main pack and another in my day pack or shoulder bag.) Leave a set with a trusted contact whose phone number you have memorized and who could email or fax copies to you (or to a secure trusted third party, like the consulate or embassy where you are getting your passport replaced) in an emergency. Ticket or passport numbers and issue and validity dates are helpful, but the numbers alone are no substitute for photocopies, faxes, or scanned images if you need

> ## REAL LIFE
>
> If you want to keep in touch with people you meet while traveling, don't just put their contact information in your cell phone or write it in an address book. Make multiple copies, and periodically mail and/or email updates to a trusted friend who has agreed to hold them for you. Cell phones and address books are easy to break, lose, or have water-damaged or stolen.

lost or stolen documents replaced. If you are traveling with a trusted companion, exchange copies of each others' documents.

I carry a copy of my most critical data, including my address book and scanned images of my passport and other documents, in password-protected encrypted form on an extra-rugged waterproof USB flash drive. Learn to use a program like Truecrypt to encrypt your data, and considering getting something like a Corsair "Flash Survivor" USB flash drive. It has a cylindrical aluminum case with O-ring seals that—unlike typical flash drives—is likely to survive common hazards such as dropping it in the street (even if it gets run over before you can retrieve it) or leaving it in your pocket when you wash your clothes.

MONEY

Carry the current day's supply of local currency separately from your passport, main supply of U.S. dollars or other hard currency cash, or other essential documents, so you don't expose the real valuables every time you buy something. Put enough official-seeming but inessential stuff in your wallet, along with a day's supply of local currency, so that a thief who takes it will believe he's gotten everything.

If you are going to need something from your money belt, get it out in advance, while you are someplace private. *Never* go into your money belt in public, or give any indication that you have one. Restrain the impulse to check it in public if you think you might have been robbed. A favorite tactic of pickpockets is to feign an obvious attempt to snatch something from you. Their hope is that you will instinctively check your pockets or hiding places, thereby pointing out to them where you have your valuables. If you fall for

REAL LIFE

A trick to protect against pickpockets or simply losing things out of your pockets (such as when sleeping on a jolting train) is to sew strips of Velcro inside the openings of your pockets. You can get sew-on Velcro tape by the yard at some camping-supply and sewing-notions stores. Bring extra to alter the pockets of clothes acquired on your journey. Leave a gap in the Velcro at one edge of the pocket just large enough to get one finger in to pull the Velcro open. It sounds odd and takes some getting used to, but pulling open the Velcro requires a hard enough pull and makes enough of a tearing noise to get your attention and scare off a pickpocket. Try it! There's more and less heavy-duty and more and less scratchy Velcro, marketed for different purposes. Try to find the heavy-duty but less scratchy kind of sew-on Velcro for this use.

this trick, an accomplice will follow up with a more subtle and precisely targeted second grab, either almost immediately while you're still startled, or just after you've relaxed your guard again.

POCKETS

Never carry anything of any value in a rear pants pocket or outer shirt or coat pocket. Any outside pocket can be picked. For a price, you can get travel garments that come with hidden or interior pockets. Or, if you have clothes made or altered, you can have secure zippered or Velcro hidden pockets put in wherever you find convenient. This sort of tailoring can be very cheap in the South, so I wouldn't spend too much extra money getting special travel clothes before your departure. If you want pockets to hold a particular type of object, such as an airline ticket jacket, leave a sample with the tailor as a guide for the size and shape of pocket to make.

PACKING SUGGESTIONS
Weight

Whatever luggage you bring, make sure it weighs under 20 kg (44 lb) and has space and weight to spare (for the things you'll inevitably acquire along the way) when packed with everything you want to bring. You'll sometimes have to walk considerable distances, and some of your sightseeing will probably be done with all your luggage with you.

The more experienced the traveler, the less she or he tends to bring. Airline rules impose an upper limit on how much luggage you can bring without paying prohibitive excess baggage charges (see the beginning of this chapter), but you probably shouldn't bring even that much unless you are comfortable carrying it all on a lengthy walk.

Don't try to carry the maximum the airlines allow—20 kg (44 lbs) is too much for most people to carry comfortably on a long trip, and you'll pick up things along the way. After a shakedown period, most long-term travelers find their luggage weighs between 10 and 15 kg (22 and 33 lb), depending on personal style and the climate. Hot, dry climates require the least amount of clothing and the most

room for extra water. Cold weather requires heavier clothing; humid weather requires more frequent changes of clothing. In more remote areas you may have to do more walking, encouraging you to lighten your load, but you may also need to carry things you don't need in cities, such as a sleeping bag or tent and perhaps a heavier first-aid kit.

I won't presume to tell you what to bring, and this isn't a comprehensive packing checklist. Rather, the following sections will give some limited advice on specific items about which travelers, especially novice travelers, often have questions, or that you might not think to bring.

Eyeshades and Earplugs

Eyeshades and earplugs are essential if you want to be able to sleep on video buses, in waiting rooms, or in hotels with inadequate sound insulation or where you need to keep the lights on to keep the cockroaches at bay. You can always find *something* locally to cover your eyes and plug your ears. But if you want comfort or are picky about fit, find what type works best for you, and bring them with you. You can't really tell without actually trying to sleep with them in a brightly lit, noisy environment. I find that padded Bucky brand eyeshades, for example, are worth their high price for their better fit on my face, while my stepfather can't tolerate most earplugs except Doc's Proplugs, which come in finely graduated sizes to fit different ears.

Sleeping Bag or Sleep Sack

One of the most difficult decisions can be whether to bring a sleeping bag. They are big, heavy, expensive, and hard to sell for a good price or to send home from overseas.

Bringing a sleeping bag is a matter of personal preference. I've carried a lightweight sleeping bag on some trips even to generally hot places and haven't

Baggage

regretted it. Sometimes the only clean hotel or the only available space on a train is overly air-conditioned. Sometimes bed linen is filthy or nonexistent. Sometimes it's simply cold at night, even in midsummer in hot climates, especially in the desert and at high altitudes where the temperature can drop by 25 degrees C (45 degrees F) from day to night.

A lighter alternative to a sleeping bag is a "sleep sack": basically a pair of thin sheets (or one larger sheet folded in half) sewn together along three sides and open at the top, like an uninsulated sleeping bag. Ready-made sleep sacks—cheaper cotton or more expensive lighter-weight silk or synthetic—are available from some hostels, hostelling organizations, RickSteves.com, REI, and other travel stores (search for "sleep sack" or "sleeping bag liner"). A sleep sack provides cleanliness but little warmth; it rolls up much smaller than a sleeping bag but isn't much lighter than the lightest bag. It comes down to your priorities of space in your pack versus warmth.

Camping and Trekking Gear

If you will be camping or trekking for only a small part of your trip, it's probably easier to rent or buy tents, boots, parkas, etc. locally than to lug them through lots of places where they aren't needed. Don't count on beating the weight limits on luggage by wearing your boots or parka onto the plane, unless you're prepared to wear them on every flight throughout your trip.

TENTS

Camping is the cheapest form of accommodation in much of the United States, Canada, and Australia, but you can't get to most campsites in those countries without a car. And if you have a car, you needn't be concerned with how heavy your tent is. Big, heavy, old tents suitable for car camping but too heavy for backpackers are very cheap at military surplus and similar stores. You might as well buy one locally if you want it for a camping road trip in one of these countries if it is the only place you'll use it, rather than pay a lot of money for a lightweight backpacker's tent and haul it around the world. Accommodations are sufficiently cheap in most Third and Fourth World cities and towns that few travelers want a

REAL LIFE

We bought a picnic cooler ("esky"), plates, bowls, cups, utensils, etc. for a road trip across Australia at a Salvation Army second-hand shop in Melbourne, and donated them to another "Salvos" in Darwin just before returning our rental car several weeks later. You could do the same for a tent or other camping equipment in the United States or Canada.

tent unless they are really backpacking in the wilderness. Even small towns in remote areas have some sort of hotel.

One region where you might want a tent is Africa, especially for extended or overland travel away from big cities. The safari tradition and style of travel has created a better infrastructure of developed campsites in East and Southern Africa than in most of the Third World, and there are places in Fourth World Africa where there are no hotels, or no cheap ones. A tent is particularly useful if a bus or truck stops for the night, or gets stuck for a week, in the middle of nowhere or in a place where the only beds are bug-ridden.

CAMPING STOVES

Try not to bring a camping stove, even if you plan on backpacking. Airlines are legitimately concerned that stoves or fuel containers could leak, burst, catch fire, or explode. Don't try to sneak a stove or fuel bottle onto a plane. For safety's sake, be honest about what's in your luggage; if the airline won't accept it, leave it behind. Pressurized butane, propane cartridges, and gasoline are obviously explosive and unacceptable. You could bring a stove that uses fuel cartridges and try to buy cartridges on arrival. But you have to accept the risk that you might not find them and might have brought the stove for naught. You could bring a gasoline (petrol) stove with a totally empty and clean fuel tank, and buy fuel locally. But you might have to leave the fuel tank or the whole stove behind if you can't clean out all trace of flammable residue before you go home or go on. Airline staff can and will check camp stoves carefully, and refuse to accept them as luggage if there's any smell of fuel or any evidence that they've ever been used. At some airports frequented by campers, "Do you have any camping equipment?" is a standard question at check-in. What they are really looking for, and will keep off the plane, is your camp stove.

Your best chance of getting on the plane with a stove is with one that burns what is called, in U.S. usage, "kerosene." (The same liquid fuel—the primary constituent of the fuel for jet airplanes—is called "paraffin" in British usage. Paraffin in U.S. usage means a petroleum-derived wax used for candles, not a liquid fuel. You can't predict which term will be used where in the world, and lots of confusion ensues.) Unlike gasoline, which is highly volatile and explosive, kerosene is merely flammable. It's also more widely available than gasoline, especially in lightly populated areas. You are unlikely to be allowed to check a can of kerosene or a kerosene stove with a full tank on a plane, but you have some chance of checking a kerosene stove with a clean, empty tank. Kerosene stoves are more expensive and harder to use than gasoline or propane stoves, but reliable lightweight backpacking ones are available.

Clothes

In my opinion, clothes are one of the least important things to worry about when packing, especially because most will wear out in a few months of hard traveling. Before long, most of your clothes will be ones you've acquired along the way.

SIZES

If you are an unusual, hard-to-fit size or shape, you'll have to choose carefully so that what you bring will see you back home (unless you are going someplace where clothes can cheaply be made to measure, in which case bring some particularly well-fitting items for a tailor to use as patterns). Europeans and Americans of average size may find that they are unusually large by the standards of most countries, and that most clothes made for locals are too small in parts of Asia and Latin America (although your weight may vary widely while you're traveling).

LOCALLY BOUGHT CLOTHES

If you find some specific items are essential to your comfort—a particular sort of lightweight long underwear or a particular style of bra—by all means bring some. (Proper fit is more important with underwear than outerwear, high-quality underwear has a higher warmth-to-weight ratio than any outerwear, and high-tech underwear can be hard to find in many places.) But with a few other exceptions the best clothes to wear are locally bought clothes. I have yet to find a place where whatever sort of clothing was locally appropriate wasn't locally available. If you don't bring enough of the right clothes, or need different clothes for different places, you can get them where you need them. If it's hot, buy lightweight clothes in local styles. If it's cold, buy a locally knit sweater or two. You'll be comfortable, you'll fit in better with the locals, and you'll come home with wearable souvenirs. When someone asks you, "Where did you get that great shirt?" there's a certain cachet to being able to answer, "I bought it in a street market in a slum in Maputo, Mozambique."

The one obvious exception is if you're going to a cold, expensive place, such as Japan or Switzerland in winter, in which case it would be best to get

> ## REAL LIFE
>
> My current wardrobe includes an Uruguayan sweater, a French scarf, a Bolivian felt hat, Turkish cotton underwear, boot socks from Aotearoa/New Zealand, and a beret made in China and sold to me by a Senegalese street vendor in New York—all purchased locally whenever and wherever I needed them.

Baggage

your warm clothes someplace cheaper. I recall buying an extra Kashmiri sweater and European-style long pants and shirts in the heat of New Delhi in November in preparation for my next stop, Paris.

SHOES

Bring good shoes. Comfortable, durable shoes are a distinctively First World luxury. American athletic shoes are status symbols throughout the Second, Third, and Fourth Worlds, and with good reason. Most Fourth World people wear no shoes at all. Most Third World people wear simple rubber or plastic flip-flop sandals. And Second World people long had to wear shoddy, uncomfortable shoes that were often held up as the epitome of ill-made communist consumer goods. When available locally, good shoes are usually expensive. If you don't want to wear cheap sandals, choose your traveling shoes with care.

I know one experienced, very self-sufficient traveler who arranges to have a new pair of his favorite walking shoes sent to him every six months or so, wherever he is. I bring a pair of lightweight walking shoes or boots and a pair of good sandals or dress shoes, depending on the climate.

For both comfort and reduced risk of blood clots in your legs on long flights and bus rides, consider getting a couple of pairs of medical-grade "graduated compression" socks. (See the section on air travel safety in the *Safety and Health* chapter.) You can find them at some pharmacies, uniform stores, medical equipment outlets, and by online mail order.

Water Purification

Many parts of the world lack sewage treatment systems, and you should assume that tap water anywhere is undrinkable unless and until you can assure yourself otherwise. For the most part, only people from the United States expect to drink tap water while traveling.

BOTTLED WATER

More and more travelers are relying on buying bottled water, but sooner or later you'll find yourself somewhere bottled water isn't available. If you don't have some way to purify or treat contaminated water, you'll drink whatever water is available, and you'll get sick. Or you'll drink no water at all, and soon get dangerously dehydrated. You can't trust bottled water from street vendors: in places where a bottle of purified water sells for a significant fraction of a day's wages, local entrepreneurs will go to great lengths to make used bottles refilled with impure water look new and freshly sealed. You'll probably be able to tell you've been conned as soon as you take your first drink, but by then it's too late.

Boiling water is an effective way to render almost any water drinkable, but that isn't always practical when you are traveling. If you do plan on boiling your drinking water, make sure you have suitable water bottles. The type of plastic used for most bottles in which water is sold will shrink, crumple, and leak if filled with boiling water. Nalgene bottles will hold boiling water without leakage or damage, but aren't always easy to find while you are traveling. Bring boilable water bottles with you, preferably with at least 2 liters (2 quarts) capacity per person.

IODINE TABLETS OR WATER PURIFIER?

You should bring either iodine water purification tablets (light and cheap, but give water a foul taste, and are not recommended for long-term use due to the possible adverse health affects of iodine accumulation in your body) or a backpacker's water purification system (heavier, cumbersome, and expensive, but doesn't flavor or taint the water with chemicals). The cost of a purifier (US$75–150) may seem steep, but it's a small part of what you could easily spend on bottled water if you're traveling for months. Purifiers are designed for varying degrees of treatment, which is why some medical authorities are reluctant to endorse them. "Purifiers" that use either a second-stage ultra-filter or a trace of iodine (much less than if iodine were used alone) to kill viruses are more effective than simple "filters," and are more convenient than either boiling or iodine tablets.

For the last several years, I've been using a "mixed oxidant" water purifier from REI. It's expensive, a bit complicated to use, and requires special though long-lasting batteries. But it's a fraction of the size and weight of a filter/purifier like the ones I used to use, seems sturdy and reliable (it was originally designed for military field use in Afghanistan and Iraq), yet can easily treat even large containers of water. When you're not traveling, you can keep it with your home emergency supplies.

Cameras and Photographs

Whether to bring a camera is one of the things to think about most carefully. Having photographs of your trip can be nice when you get home, and for many people photography is itself a major reason to travel. But having a camera sets up a barrier between you and everyone you meet. Having traveled both with and without a camera, I'd generally recommend against bringing one, or at least against carrying it all the time. If you're unsure, try sightseeing for a day in an unfamiliar town, trying to meet and talk to people, once with and once without a camera around your neck all day.

If you bring a camera, bring the smallest and cheapest camera that will serve your needs, so that you won't feel you need to carry it with you all the time for safekeeping, can easily keep it out of sight when you aren't using it, and won't be heartbroken if it gets lost, stolen, or broken. Consider resistance to dust, humidity, and physical shock, as well as power requirements. If your camera requires anything other than standard AA or AAA batteries, bring spares. If the batteries are rechargeable, make sure you have suitable power adapters for the charger (see *Electrical Power Adapters* later in this chapter for information about batteries, chargers, and power supplies).

TYPES OF DIGITAL CAMERA MEMORY

Digital cameras use a bewildering variety of similar, but incompatible, removable memory chips: memory sticks, multimedia cards (MMC), smart media cards, and three different sizes of secure digital (SD) cards: standard, mini, and micro. All of these work basically the same way, but they are different sizes and shapes and have different connectors. Which is best? All else being equal, the one that's cheapest per image, easiest to find, and most likely to be compatible with whatever computer you find in a cybercafé or at a friend's home or office. As of 2011, this was secure digital (SD or SDHC, depending on the capacity) memory. SD cards are the de facto standard for the majority of digital cameras as well as a large variety of other portable electronic devices such as palmtop computers and PDAs. In a pinch, you stand a better chance of being able to borrow an SD card from someone else until you can download your photos, or of buying one locally (even at kiosks or small local shops in tourist destinations) than any other kind of memory chip. And far more cybercafés have SD card readers (sparing you the need to install any special drivers for your camera's cable connection) than have readers for other types of cards. Mini- and micro-SD cards can fit in, and often come with, adapters that allow them to be used in standard SD-card devices, so they are a good option as well.

As an alternative to solid-state memory cards, you can get portable storage devices with miniature disk drives like those in an iPod, or store your photos on the hard disk of a laptop computer. Except as a stopgap measure in an emergency, I don't recommend either option. Microdrives have tiny moving parts and are extremely fragile. As with any computer hard disk, they eventually "crash" and fail catastrophically, without warning. Friends of mine have lost large photo collections when their microdrives crashed. Memory cards, on the other hand, have no moving parts and are harder (though not impossible) to break. Hard disks are cheaper than the largest flash memory chips, but the difference isn't worth the lower reliability.

BUYING MORE MEMORY

Bring as much digital storage media (cards, disks, or whatever) as you might possibly need, especially if you might be shooting video. The more memory you have, the more pictures you can take before you have to transfer your

Baggage

photos to a computer and burn them onto CDs or DVDs. It's worth shopping around for memory cards: some camera shops charge five times as much for the same cards as Internet or storefront discounters. Prices on the road will be higher still. Generic memory cards are produced in the same chip factories as the brand-name ones, and seem to work just as well. Check with local electronics discount stores or Internet price-comparison websites like Pricewatch. com. Memory cards are expensive and small enough to be easily lost or stolen. Beyond a certain size you may be better off with more smaller cards, so you don't lose so many photos if something happens to one of your memory cards. That can happen easily and in many ways, such as if the connectors on the card get bent or twisted.

BATTERIES AND CHARGERS

A few digital cameras use standard AA or AAA batteries, which are available anywhere in the world. But single-use batteries are expensive and produce extremely toxic waste, so even with such a camera you might want to get a couple of sets of rechargeable batteries and a compact battery charger. Third World batteries are often expensive and of extremely poor quality. They won't last as long, and they are more likely to leak or corrode and ruin your equipment. If you aren't using your camera for a while, remove the batteries.

If you are bringing several electronic devices—a digital camera, a cell phone, an MP3 player, etc.—try to get ones that can share the same batteries or at least the same charger. Most likely that will mean either AA or AAA batteries, or devices that can all be charged (if you have the right adapters) from a single USB charger.

Most digital cameras use proprietary batteries that are expensive, hard to replace while you are traveling, and can only be recharged either in the camera or in a special charger. A separate charger with a spare battery is much better than a charger built into the camera: you can leave one battery in your hotel room charging while you are using the other in the camera. And only the charger and battery, not the entire camera, is at risk of being stolen while it's charging.

Hong Kong-based aftermarket vendors like Dealextreme.com sell made-in-China spare batteries and other accessories (chargers, cables, adapters, etc.) for cameras and other electronic devices for a fraction of the cost, even including shipping, of name-brand "original equipment" camera batteries and accessories. The quality isn't always as good (although it's sometimes as good or better), but the prices are so much lower than those of U.S.-based importers that I've come out well ahead despite the occasional dud battery that wouldn't hold a charge even when brand new. Mail delivery from Hong Kong is reliable although sometimes unexpectedly delayed. So if you want things to bring with you on a trip, order them at least a couple of months before you plan to leave.

Finding a safe place to leave a camera, cell phone, or other electronic device plugged in and charging can be a particular problem for travelers staying in hostels or other dormitory accommodations. Hostels are very aware of the problem, but there's no simple fix. Proprietary batteries and chargers are less likely to be stolen, since they are unlikely to fit anyone else's devices.

If you're going to be trekking or traveling "off the grid," you can get solar battery chargers for AA or AAA batteries. But solar chargers are only available for standard batteries or for batteries that can be charged from a USB port, not (yet) for most proprietary camera batteries. If you think you'll need to rely on a solar charger, get a camera that uses standard AA or AAA batteries.

TRANSFERRING PHOTOS TO A COMPUTER

You can delete photos you don't want, to make room for more, directly on your digital camera or camera-phone. To do anything else with your pictures—edit them, crop them, email them, or upload them to a website—you first need to get them onto a computer. (Yes, you could upload or send photos directly from a smartphone, but that's the sort of phone usage that will quickly rack up a huge international roaming data bill.) Different cameras have different kinds of connections, but in general you can either connect the camera directly to the computer with a camera-specific cable, connect a memory card reader to the computer, or use a cybercafé's memory card reader, if they have one for your type of memory card (SD card, memory stick, or whatever). Connecting the camera may require installing driver software on the computer. A better choice is a USB card reader that doesn't require any special drivers. These can be tiny (barely larger than the memory card) and cheap (less than US$10), so it's worth bringing one with you to fit whatever sort of memory cards your camera uses. Some laptop computers have built-in memory card slots, usually for SD/SDHC cards, which will also fit mini-SD or micro-SD cards with the proper adaptors.

It's one thing to use a digital camera with your own computer, once you've installed the software and gotten it all set up. It's another thing to use it with a strange computer in a cybercafé. Before you leave home, take your travel kit to a friend's computer or a cybercafé and test your ability to get your photos off your camera and onto a CD or DVD. Otherwise you're likely to discover too late that you didn't bring an essential connector or the necessary drivers or other software.

EDITING PHOTOS

Most digital cameras come with image editing software you can install on your PC. On the road, you'll also find basic (and sometimes advanced) image editing software at most cybercafés. Especially if all you want to do is select, organize, and crop your photos, and you don't use a specific high-end image

Baggage

editing program, it's probably counterproductive to bring a laptop computer with you solely or primarily to deal with your digital photos. You can probably do it in a cybercafé, without the expense, risk of theft, and fragility of a laptop with a hard disk. (See below for more on choosing and using laptop, netbook, tablet, and smaller computers for travel.)

STORING PHOTOS, SENDING THEM HOME, AND POSTING THEM ONLINE

In theory, you could email all your photos home. But the slow connections to the Internet available from many parts of the world could make this prohibitively time-consuming. From time to time, you'll find a cybercafé with a truly high-speed Internet connection. But many people I know who've set out intending to maintain a photo blog while they travel around the world have abandoned their plans as soon as they hit their first Third World country and discovered how much time it takes. Be prepared to go for substantial stretches between fast Internet connections. I either carry a netbook and a portable DVD burner or use cybercafés to burn my photos to DVDs periodically.

Make copies regularly of any photos you want to keep. It's common to lose a memory card, break off or damage the connector, leave it in your pocket when you wash your clothes, or accidentally erase it. The larger the memory card, the greater the chance that you could lose weeks or months of photos with a single mistake.

Most cybercafés will burn a DVD for you for US$5–10 or so, once you've transferred your photos to their computer. CDs and DVDs are fairly durable, and they are immune to airport X-rays and metal detectors. But they can get dropped, broken, or scratched, so I'd burn at least 2 (preferably 3) copies of any photos I wouldn't want to lose. If you are traveling with a companion, you can each carry a set, and you can mail another set home or to a trusted family member or friend.

CAMERAS AND OTHER ELECTRONIC DEVICES ON AIRPLANES

If you want to carry your camera on, you may have to open it and/or remove the batteries at the airport security checkpoint. So make sure it's charged if you're going to try to carry it on. A few airlines categorically forbid batteries in carry-on luggage, and will confiscate any they find. If that's the case, they will *usually* warn you in time for you to pack your camera and any other battery-powered devices in your checked luggage.

Music Players

Audio devices are among the more problematic of common travel devices, relatively fragile and a magnet for thieves.

Many travelers like portable stereos for listening to music in waiting rooms and on long bus and train rides. I prefer conversation to music, and I don't think people who isolate themselves in their headphones even realize how much they are missing out on conversations with other travelers. I know, though, that it's partly just a matter of taste, and that some people get more impatient than others at delays or long trips without music, or feel lost outside their accustomed musical environment.

Personal music players are security blankets for a lot of travelers. Put on your headphones and a familiar piece of music, close your eyes, and you can escape from strange, perhaps threatening or overwhelming stimuli into a comfortingly familiar inner world. The danger is that you'll become so dependent on your iPod as a psychological crutch against culture shock that you won't know what to do if it's stolen or breaks down. The barriers it helps maintain will keep you from getting past your fear to the point where you can fully experience your surroundings.

If you bring a portable music player, bring a cheap one you won't miss if it's lost, stolen, or broken. (Once again Dealextreme.com has some of the cheapest.) Judging from the anecdotes I've heard, MP3 players are the items most often stolen from travelers by other travelers, even though most travelers carry cameras worth more than their music players. Be especially watchful of your music player inside dormitories, hostels, and guesthouses. MP3 players with flash memory and no moving parts are more likely to survive rough traveling than those with tiny internal hard disks. A player that uses a standard removable memory card, rather than a soldered-in internal memory chip, will let you move the card and your stored music to another device, even if the player itself fails, as long as the chip is still good. But any device can suffer mechanical failures that render your music or other data unrecoverable, or get lost or stolen. Back up your music collection before you leave home!

E-Book Readers

There are paperback book exchanges in most hostels and guesthouses. But the selection may be limited and not to your taste. In some countries such as India, best-selling English-language novels are widely available in locally printed editions for a fraction of their price in the United States. In others such as Australia and South Africa, the same books are twice as expensive as in the United States, regardless of whether they are locally published or imported. In other countries there may be few books available in English, at any price, other than textbooks or fairly specialized works.

One way to always have an adequate supply of reading material is to bring a Kindle or other dedicated e-book reader. You can read e-books on a smartphone, but most people find the screen too small to read a whole book that way. You can also read e-books on a netbook, but you probably don't want to have your computer out and open in many of the places like waiting rooms and stations where you might want to pass the time with a book.

Most of the competing models of e-book readers use similar display technology that's easier to read and has vastly longer battery life than a typical computer display. Depending on the device and where in the world you are, you can download more books either wirelessly over a built-in cellular modem, or with a cable connection to your laptop or a computer in a cybercafé.

A dedicated e-book reader is one more electronic device, charger, etc., to carry, but it's a solution for those who worry about not being able to carry enough books, especially in places where they are hard to find or expensive.

Internet Access Devices

You can find cybercafés in very remote locations. I've gotten connected to the world electronically from a hut walled with mud and dung in an African town that wasn't physically connected to the world by any paved road. (Four users were sharing a 56Kbs dial-up connection, so it was *slow*.) There's public Internet access, for a price, at Everest Base Camp. If I just want to browse the Web, I find it easier to rent a desktop computer in a cybercafé with a full-sized keyboard and display than to use my laptop.

> **REAL LIFE**
>
> My recommendation for a long trip is to bring the smallest Internet access device you are comfortable using that will enable you to access financial websites securely, without having to do so from insecure cybercafé computers. Test it with your bank's website(s) before you leave.

Wanting to stay in touch by email, browse the Web, or edit digital photos doesn't mean you need to carry your own computer around the world. There are, however, other good reasons to carry your own computer or other Internet access device: if you need to be able to connect securely and privately (especially to manage your finances online); if you need to use specific programs or access data that won't be available or accessible from a cybercafé; or if you want to be able to use your computer in places other than cybercafés (planes, trains, hotel rooms, etc.).

All cybercafés and public Internet terminals are inherently insecure. (See the sidebar *Risks of Internet Money Management* in the chapter on finances, *The Bottom Line*.) All of them. Always. No matter how secure the website, your browser, or your email encryption. On a public terminal, you can never be sure that your keystrokes and the display aren't being remotely monitored and/or recorded by the operator of the cybercafé or a remote hacker—before they can be encrypted (encoded) or secured for sending across the Internet. With your own laptop or other device, you can (if you are sufficiently careful and skilled) make sure that everything sensitive is encrypted before it leaves your machine. The primary reason I carry my own computer on longer tourist trips is to be able to manage my money online. I carry the smallest device that will serve that purpose.

What sort of device should you bring? There's a more finely graduated range of sizes of Internet access devices than you probably realize exists, particularly in between the smallest netbooks and the largest smartphones.

LAPTOP, NETBOOK, TABLET, AND SMALLER COMPUTERS

As a portable Internet access device, a full-sized laptop is overweight, overpriced, and overkill. Unfortunately, there has been relatively little effort put into development of good handheld Internet terminals. Most laptop computers have been designed primarily as stand-alone portable PCs, not Internet devices. Because most people in the United States travel by car, not by bus or train or on foot, they are more concerned with performance than with small size or weight. Laptop computers for the U.S. market are designed accordingly.

As of this writing, iPads and other "tablet" devices are still relatively fragile and expensive, and many of the first generation of tablets lack connectivity options and functionality that travelers might want. Especially if you want a keyboard and the option of wired Ethernet connectivity, the best handheld email and Web terminal devices have been from companies few people in the United States have heard of.

Most of the smaller Internet access devices have been developed for European and Asian markets. I've been using various smaller "netbook" computers made in Japan, Korea, Taiwan, and Malaysia since the mid-1990s, even before the introduction of the Psion net-Book (still one of the best ever) in 1998. But netbooks didn't become widely available in the United States until around 2008, when Asus introduced the first Linux "Eee PC." Unfortunately, by 2011

REAL LIFE

When Dell's netbook product development team invited me to a focus group to discuss their products for travelers, I was amazed at how little concept they had of travelers' needs. They assumed that everyone travels with a car, and would want to use their computer primarily while driving. I suggested they visit one of the local San Francisco hostels that evening to see how real globetrotters were using their netbooks, but I doubt they took me up on it.

Baggage

the small Linux flash-memory netbook craze had come and gone: Most of the netbook makers shifted their U.S. product lines to emphasize larger and more expensive models, and it has become difficult to find a netbook with Linux preinstalled (it's a much more stable, efficient, reliable, and contrary to myth, easier to use operating system than Windows, especially for netbooks or smaller devices) or without a hard disk (which makes it much more fragile than one with all solid-state memory). The larger netbooks are still cheaper and smaller than full-sized laptops, but no longer as ideal for travelers.

It has once again become necessary to seek out more obscure sources if you want anything smaller than a 10-inch netbook (nominal diagonal screen measurement), but larger than an iPhone or more capable than an iPad. And if you want Linux on your laptop, you may have to install it yourself, which defeats much of the ease-of-use of having any operating system preinstalled by an expert and configured optimally for your hardware.

Don't be discouraged if most laptop salespeople show you things that are way too big to lug around all the time. There are smaller alternatives, if you are prepared to seek them out from specialty vendors like Dynamism.com who import them from Asia and convert their user interfaces to English. Lilliput-ing.com has reviews of current devices in this class. (See the *Resource Guide*).

Because most laptop computers are bought or leased by businesses that trade them in regularly for newer models, there's a glut of high-end second-hand "off-lease" and trade-in laptops a year or two old. A laptop you take traveling won't look new for long, anyway. If you want a full-sized laptop, and don't insist on the latest model, you can find adequate but bulkier used ones for as little as US$200 from mail-order surplus dealers like SurplusComputers.com, where I've bought several of my own and my family's computers.

If had to bring a computer, what sort would I recommend? There are three main variables in the choice of an Internet access device for travel: size, performance, and price. You can have any two, but not all three. Here are some possibilities, as of 2011, depending on which are your priorities:

Size and Price: A US$100 low-end seven-inch netbook made for the domestic Chinese market, running Windows CE or Linux. I saw the first prototypes of these from Shenzhen manufacturers at an electronics trade show in Hong Kong in 2008, just months after the Taiwanese Asus Eee PC netbooks began to take off. Two years later a variety of models were available at this price from Dealextreme.com or other exporters. Drawbacks: Slow processor, limited memory, won't run full Windows applications. You're on your own for support.

Price and Performance: A US$200–300 surplus full-sized laptop (probably off-lease and a couple of years old) from SurplusComputers.com or a similar surplus dealer. Drawbacks: Big and heavy. Relatively short battery life compared to a netbook or smaller device, especially since the battery won't be new and may have lost some of its ability to hold a charge.

Size and Performance: One of the cutting-edge Asian-import devices from Dynamism.com, such as a viliv N5 (the cheapest of the lot, and the one I'd buy), Fujitsu U/G90, or Sony Vaio P. Each of these runs a full version of Windows (or Linux) with performance comparable to a full-sized netbook, but is about half the size of a seven-inch or nine-inch netbook. Prices range from a little less than US$1,000 to almost US$2,000. You pay a lot for the miniaturization. Drawbacks: Expensive to buy, or to get replacement parts for. Essentially unavailable in stores in the United States, so you'll have to buy online, sight unseen. The keyboard and screen may be just big enough, or just a little too small for you to use comfortably.

The Middle Ground: The Linux version of the Asus Eee PC 901 is the most powerful, rugged, and best suited for travel use of the earlier, smaller netbooks. This is what I'm using for business trips as of 2011. Asus Eee PCs are the most common netbooks worldwide, and thus the easiest to get help with, find parts for, or get repaired. Drawbacks: No longer in production, so you'll need to look for a used one on eBay or Craigslist. Prices are highly variable, but currently run US$100–300 for one in good condition.

Everything I've said about particular models is likely to be obsolete before you read this, but if you search for those I've mentioned, you should still be able to find descriptions, photos, and reviews that give you an idea of what I'm talking about.

You may think I'm obsessed with size and weight, but you may be too after a few months on the road. After having used larger, more powerful laptops, many of my friends have become jealous of my much smaller and lighter machines, even though they lack some feature of heavier models. If I had to buy a new computer today, for limited but essential use on an extended non-business trip outside the First World, I'd buy a seven-inch or nine-inch netbook or an even smaller "ultramobile" clamshell device with a keyboard but without a hard disk. Not a full-sized laptop, and maybe not even a full-sized netbook, but still something larger than an iPhone and able to do more than a keyboardless "tablet" device. Your needs may be different, and your mileage may vary.

SMARTPHONES AND PDAS

The easiest way to connect to the Internet wherever you are is through your cell phone, iPad, or PDA, or a cellular data modem attached to your laptop or netbook. But the charges for data usage while traveling can be a nasty surprise. Your iPhone or iPad service plan may include unlimited data usage in your home country for a flat monthly rate, but I know of no cell phone plan from any operator anywhere in the world that includes unmetered global roaming for a flat monthly rate. Outside your home country, and maybe a couple of specific others if you have a special plan that includes them, all data usage will be charged by the megabyte. Those charges are high: It could cost you US$1 to download a single Web page. I know people who've come home to a US$10,000 international roaming bill (that's not a typo!) for a month of routine use of an iPhone or Blackberry.

You may be using the Internet (and running up your bill) without even knowing it. Your device may check for new email automatically, generating data charges even if you have no new mail. iPhone apps may perform their functions by "phoning home" in ways or at times that you aren't aware of. Do you really know which data are stored in your device, and which are stored on, and accessed as needed from, a server somewhere on the Internet?

If you are carrying an iPhone or other data-capable device, make sure you learn how to turn off cellular data sending and receiving *completely* when you are abroad. And if the cost of international data roaming is going to keep you from using the features of your device, consider whether you might be better off not bringing your smartphone, or bringing a simpler and cheaper phone and/or PDA (and/or a paper address book!) instead.

If you do plan to use your smartphone or PDA for critical Internet access, such as online banking, test it before you leave to make sure it has a Web browser that can access all the key features of your bank's website. I had to try three different and progressively harder-to-install and slow-to-use browsers on one of my PDAs before I found one that was fully compatible with my bank's website, and I had to switch from one of my netbooks when my bank started refusing connections to its website from any of the browsers available for it. If you are using a smartphone "app" rather than a Web browser, it can be impossible to tell how whether the app encrypts your data. Unless you are sure that an app encrypts your data, it's safer to use the secure version of a website (with a URL that starts with "https://" instead of "http://"), rather than an app, for financial or other sensitive information.

BUYING COMPUTERS OR ELECTRONIC DEVICES ABROAD

Is it worth waiting to buy a new computer someplace it will be cheaper? If you are coming from the United States, probably not unless what you want isn't available here at all. The United States is actually one of the cheapest places in the world to buy consumer electronics. There are no taxes or duties on most electronics imported into the United States from Asia. Many people from Latin America or Europe take advantage of trips to the United States to buy big-ticket portable electronic devices, almost all of them made in East Asia, for less than they would have to pay in their home countries. Countries like Brazil and India charge high duties on imported electronics in an effort (thus far completely unsuccessful) to encourage the development of domestic electronic hardware industries to accompany their successful software industries. Foreign visitors such as Brazilians are a prominent presence among shoppers at stores like B & H Photo Video (highly recommended) and its counterparts in New York and elsewhere in the United States.

The only places where computers and electronics tend to be cheaper are those where they are actually made: China, Taiwan, Japan, Korea, Singapore, and Malaysia. If you don't speak Chinese, Japanese, or Korean, the best place to buy Chinese, Japanese, or Korean electronics is probably Hong Kong or maybe Singapore or Malaysia (or online). There's a lot of stuff made for the Chinese domestic market that isn't readily available any further afield than Hong Kong. It's usually so cheap that you would assume from the price that it would have to be shoddy junk. Sometimes it is, but sometimes it's of surprisingly good quality and unbeatable value.

Many cool Japanese and Korean electronic gadgets aren't distributed in the United States. Unfortunately, most of them have user interfaces and documentation exclusively in Japanese, Korean, and/or Chinese, not English. Very little English is spoken in the shops in Akihabara and even less in electronics stores elsewhere in Japan. You're pretty much on your own to figure out what things you see in Japanese stores do and how to operate them.

Some of the best-designed small travel computers are no longer made. Nothing in production in 2011 matches the build quality of a Psion 5mx, Psion netBook, or some discontinued HP and NEC Pocket PC/Windows CE devices. You can still find these, quite cheaply, on eBay or through resellers like UsedHandhelds.com, but don't get one unless (1) you are certain that it has Wi-Fi, supports both WEP and WPA Wi-Fi encryption, and preferably also has Ethernet (wired Internet) connectivity, and (2) you are prepared to deal with any software, configuration, or usage problems on your own. (If you don't know what these terms mean, or why they might matter, you probably shouldn't be buying a device like this.)

Import duties and taxes can make East Asian electronics—even simple-seeming "commodity" components like memory chips—50 percent more

Baggage

expensive in the European Union or Australia than in the United States, and two or three times more expensive in India or the Mercosur countries of South America. In a foreign country, it's harder to comparison shop or find the lowest prices. Order things by mail from abroad when you're in such a country, or have them sent from home, and you could have to pay taxes and duties on them when they arrive. So get any spare batteries, accessories, adapters, chargers, etc. you might need before you leave home, or they could cost you much more later on. You can always mail them home or sell them to fellow travelers or locals if you find you never use them.

REPAIRS ON THE ROAD

Lower labor costs in most of the world make it worth repairing things that would be thrown away in the Unites States, Japan, or Western Europe. There are actually business models in collecting discarded items like cell phones in the United States, shipping them in bulk to China for repair, and selling them back into the Unites States by mail order on eBay as "refurbished" items.

Cell phone repair has become a basic service available even in small towns in most of the world. It helps if the repair person speaks or reads some English, but not much is typically necessary if you can demonstrate, point to, or pantomime the failure mode.

The problem is that critical replacement parts may not be in stock (if you have a locally uncommon and nonstandard device) or may be heavily dutied and/or taxed, as discussed above. The best places to get electronic gadgets are thus ones with low-cost skilled labor, some English, and a ready supply of parts. Since the manufacturing of small electronic components worldwide is centered in Shenzhen (the Silicon Valley of China) and the surrounding Pearl River Delta region, that puts Hong Kong at the top of the list of best places to get broken or malfunctioning gadgets repaired, followed by major cities in the Philippines (nearby, with slightly higher parts prices but almost equally cheap labor and much more English) and Dubai (a duty-free port and transshipment point for Chinese goods, with lots of skilled immigrant "guest workers" from poor countries) or similar places in the Gulf.

Of course, you don't have a choice of where your gear will break down, Murphy's Law says it will happen in the most inconvenient place, where labor (e.g. Switzerland) or parts (e.g. Brazil) are expensive. Plan accordingly.

CARRYING A COMPUTER

Avoid carrying a computer or camera in a fancy case or one with a brand name or logo that might as well say, "Steal me." Use a nondescript case, preferably one with no labels or logos, that doesn't look like a computer or camera case at all. The same goes for other expensive devices, but laptop computer and SLR camera cases are the most easily recognized because of their greater size and, for cameras, distinctive shape. One of the overlooked advantages of computers smaller than standard laptops, and of smaller cameras, is that they are less conspicuous. Most people think that the case for my netbook is an odd-shaped purse or a Filofax organizer, not a computer, and I have a smaller device with a Web browser and email client that fits in my pants pocket.

Computers, cameras, and electronic devices are especially vulnerable to theft, shock (dropping or falls), vibration, crushing (as in piles of luggage), dust (seal them in plastic bags on dusty bus or train rides; salty dust is worst), damp (again, salty damp is worst), and smoke (yes, including ordinary levels of cigarette smoke). Try to protect them against these hazards, and not to use them more than necessary in situations where any of these will be likely.

If you bring any computer, PDA, or smartphone with you, have a backup plan in case it is lost, stolen, or broken, and all your data is lost. Laptop computers aren't designed to withstand many of the bumps and shocks they get in routine First World use, much less world travel. One fall from a desk or table is often enough to crash a laptop's hard disk or break the screen. With a smaller screen, no hard disk drive, and no moving parts except the keyboard, netbook and smaller computers are much more rugged than larger ones, but not immune to sudden catastrophic failure. There's always the possibility that your computer could be stolen, as every year several hundred thousand laptops are in the United States alone. You can get insurance from Safeware.com to cover the monetary loss (see the *Resource Guide*) but money won't help much if you've lost irreplaceable data. To add insult to injury, even if something is insured or under warranty, you could be charged import duty and taxes on the full price of a replacement item shipped to you abroad.

Electrical Power Adapters

Using electrical or electronic equipment with foreign power supplies can be more difficult than most people think.

There are two standard voltages (110–120 volts and 220–240 volts), two standard AC frequencies (50 and 60 Hz), and about a dozen common types of wall outlets and corresponding plugs in use in different parts of the world. The United States uses 110–120 volts, 60 Hz AC, and three types of partially compatible plugs and outlets: two-prong unpolarized, two-prong polarized (one prong slightly wider than the other), and three-prong. Not all countries have a single national standard; I've found three incompatible plugs and two different voltages and frequencies in different parts of the same country.

There is no easy, simple, or cheap device that will enable you to use electronic devices with power systems other than those for which they were designed. Voltage and frequency converters are relatively heavy and expensive.

Plug adapters are deceptively cheap and simple: using an adapter to plug something into the wrong voltage can ruin the equipment or cause it to overheat, catch fire, or explode. The danger is greatest if you inadvertently plug 110–120 volt devices (such as those made for use in the United States) into 220–240 volt power supplies (such as those throughout most of Europe). Japan uses 100 volts (half the country including Osaka at 60 Hz, the other half including Tokyo at 50 Hz), which is just enough of an undervoltage to damage much equipment made for the United States.

Most electrical and electronic equipment will not work on the wrong voltage. Many manufacturers produce different models for different countries (for most types of equipment only two basic models are required, for 100–120 and 220–240 volts) rather than trying to build a single universal or dual-power model. If you want to use something in a particular place, you have to find out what kind of power (voltage and frequency) is used there and buy a model designed for it. Only after you are sure that it has the proper type of power supply should you get a plug adapter, if necessary, to plug it in. Don't worry too much about finding plug adapters—no matter how unusual the local electrical outlets are, you can always find adapters to plug in devices with U.S., U.K., and continental-European standard plugs.

Many digital cameras, portable stereos, laptop computers, and cell phones—the electronic devices most often carried by travelers—are available with multiple-voltage power supplies capable of operating from all standard power types with only plug adapters and no need for external voltage or frequency converters. The key words to look for or ask about are an "autoswitching" or "universal" power supply, rated to accept an input range of at least 100–240 volts, 50–60 Hz. (110–240 volts will work everywhere except 100-volt Japan). The charger for my digital camera is rated for 100–240 volts, 50–60 Hz, while the one on my computer is rated 90–264 volts, giving it an additional margin of tolerance for brownouts (even in Japan) and surges. There's rarely any difference in price between the same product with a single-voltage power supply or with a "universal" adapter, but you have to check carefully to be sure of what you are buying.

The same device may be distributed with different AC adapters, depending on where it's sold. The manufacturer can save a few cents per item by supplying a 110–120 volt power supply with the U.S. model, on the assumption that most U.S. buyers will never travel overseas. Product specifications don't always distinguish whether the AC adapter is available in two alternate models, one for 100–120 volts and one for 220–240 volts, or whether there is a single model capable of operating on either voltage. Sometimes the only way to tell for sure is to open the box and read the label on the adapter before you buy.

Third World electrical systems pose additional problems, even if you have the proper plug adapters and equipment with a universal power supply. Power supplies in much of the world are intermittent. That a country or city has a central electrical power supply does not imply that power is available 24 hours a day, every day. Power may be supplied only for certain hours each day, or at unpredictable hours if the generators or their fuel supply are unreliable. Power lines may go down or short out, and distribution problems may make power outages common even where there's no problem with generation. In some places there is no city power, and hotels or other buildings have electricity only while they run their own generators, which they don't usually do around the clock.

If generating capacity is inadequate to meet city or countrywide demand, the most common load-management strategy is that of "rolling blackouts" or "load shedding," when power is deliberately shut off to some areas to keep the overloaded system from shutting down entirely. (Californians experienced these, briefly, in the summer of 2001.) Depending on the extent of the capacity shortfall, your hotel's neighborhood may have power for 20 hours a day or two hours a day. Sometimes there is a predictable daily or weekly schedule or rotation, sometimes not. This is a problem if you are using equipment that can be damaged by a power failure while it is plugged in and in use, especially a computer. If the power is unreliable, it's safer to use your computer on the batteries, unplugged, and shut it down while it's plugged in to recharge.

Most battery chargers and rechargeable devices are such that if the power supply from the wall plug ("mains" in British usage) fails while the charger is plugged in, the batteries will gradually discharge through the charger until they are completely dead. So you can't count on waking up or coming back to a recharged set of batteries if you leave them plugged in to charge overnight or while you go out for the day. Some equipment could lose data or settings this way. Try to find equipment designed so the batteries can be removed from the equipment while charging; if you can't, unplug your devices when you aren't actually using or charging them.

Odds and Ends

One small item you might not think to bring is a pocket compass. I use mine constantly, mainly to orient myself when using city maps. You get off the bus or come out of the subway and know from your map that you want to walk north. Or you get on the bus, knowing you want to go north but are unsure if this bus will go the right way. The sun isn't visible, and you don't speak the language. Which way is north? Especially if you're good at reading maps, you'll find a compass—even the tiniest one—more useful than you could ever imagine.

As a general-purpose tool, I recommend a Leatherman tool or similar good-quality multitool with pliers—it's expensive, but worth it. The pliers in a multitool make it useful in many more situations and for many more tasks than a Swiss Army knife or other tool without pliers.

If you don't have one already, get a small waterproof LED flashlight (torch) or headlamp.

Snapshots of your home, neighborhood, family, friends, and workplace, or postcards of your home city or region, are handy when people ask about your life and where you are from. You might even want to bring extras so you can give them to people who befriend you or help you out.

Consider having some business cards ("name cards") printed up with your permanent contact information. They'll save you copying your address out over and over to exchange with people you meet. When you're dealing with businesses or bureaucrats, having "business" cards (even ones that don't mention a business or title) can often enhance your perceived status and legitimacy. You can buy pages of blank card stock preformatted for business cards from any office supply store, and print yourself up a few cards on your computer. Or you can get a few hundred cards in a standard design for US$30 or so from any print shop. If you run out, you can get more printed abroad for even less.

Don't bring anything of sentimental value, or anything valuable that isn't essential. But a number of other items can be hard to find when you want them, and are apt to come in handy. Here are a few I haven't already mentioned and that you might want to consider adding to your kit, in no particular order:

- large ziplock plastic bags for separating things in your pack, and for keeping them dry when your pack gets soaked (No pack is really waterproof.)
- a few large Tyvek envelopes—sturdier and lighter than manila folders for keeping papers, folded maps, etc. clean, dry, and sorted
- a flat rubber universal sink stopper (so you can wash out your clothes in sinks that don't have stoppers)
- safety pins (They double as clothespins that can't blow off the line.)
- a small roll of tape (Some people favor duct tape; I prefer package sealing tape.)
- a few rubber bands and paper clips
- a small sewing kit (needles, thread, thimble, buttons, etc.)
- a small first aid kit to carry with you all or most of the time (Even small cuts and scrapes can get infected quickly in dirty, tropical conditions.)

- ten meters (yards) of the strongest lightweight waterproof braided cord you can find—"parachute cord" or something thinner (to use as a clothesline, for tying together gear, and a thousand other odd jobs)

- a meter (yard) or two of picture wire (very strong and versatile for diverse jury-rigging and mending tasks)

- a couple of self-adhesive nylon patches or, if you can find it, a small roll of nylon cloth tape of the sort designed for repairing camping tears or punctures in packs, raincoats, etc.

- Velcro strips to have sewn into the pockets of clothes you buy or have made (10 cm or 4 inches is enough for a typical pocket.)

- a rigid cardboard or plastic tube just long enough to fit in your pack (Without a tube, it's almost impossible to get prints, maps, posters, or artwork home undamaged.)

- an electrical cube tap (so that you can plug several chargers or devices into a single plug adapter, without having to buy three plug adapters)

- A multicountry electrical plug adapter (Some countries have unique electrical plugs, but the four sets of prongs on one of these adapters will enable you to plug in to about 90 percent of the world's electrical outlets. Some also include a USB charging port. The most elegant but expensive of these is the "Swiss World Adapter." Dealextreme.com and others have cheaper knockoffs that are slightly less convenient to use).

- a "Sharpie" or similar medium-point permanent marker for labeling packages you mail and CDs or DVDs you burn

- Small Post-it notes for marking pages in guidebooks

SENDING THINGS FROM HOME

Don't count on being able to have things sent to you while you are traveling abroad. If you forget something, run out of something, or discover you need or want something you hadn't thought of before you left, you'll probably have to find it locally, do without, or pay a prohibitive amount for shipping from home. If there are things you'll want for only part of your trip, it's generally much easier to bring those things with you and send them home when you're done with them, rather than to schedule the part of the trip using those things at the end and have to have them sent to you midway, while you are traveling.

International package shipping, whether by post or through private shipping companies, is either very slow or very expensive, and it can be hard to find an address to which you can have things sent. American Express offices will accept only mail—letters and small packets of papers or documents—for

Baggage

REAL LIFE

A friend ran out of mefloquine after six months in South America and asked me to send him more in Bolivia. Mefloquine is a prescription antimalarial drug that is hard to find outside the First World, but which is effective against some malarial strains that are resistant to more commonly available drugs. Local strains of bacteria, parasites, and viruses are most likely resistant to whatever antibiotics or other drugs are most readily available and used locally.

Despite the unlikelihood that I would be trying to send illegal drugs *into* a major drug *exporting* country, it took an entire day of negotiations with several levels of supervisors at the local DHL courier office and pages of paperwork—original signed prescription forms and sealed pharmacy packaging, customs declarations, and waivers—before I was allowed to pay almost as much in shipping as the price of the medication to have them sent to La Paz. It probably wouldn't have been possible if I weren't already known to the DHL office as a legitimate travel agent and shipper of documents to the Third World (not a stranger or potential drug dealer).

American Express clients. American Express offices will not accept or hold parcels, packages, deliveries from any sort of private delivery service (FedEx, DHL, etc.), or anything that has to be signed for. General delivery or "poste restante" (postal services for sending mail or packages to be held for pickup at a specified post office) are generally adequate for noncritical letters (which could as easily have been sent as email), but insufficiently reliable for urgent or valuable shipments. Private air shipping services have dramatically improved their service to the Third and Fourth Worlds—you can FedEx things to Mongolia, for a price—but they can be very expensive, and someone has to be there to sign for them when they arrive.

Any international shipment is potentially subject to customs duty (see the chapter on travel documents). Small, valuable items— the sort of thing you might be tempted to have shipped to you— are often subject to duty. A friend accidentally left her camera with an acquaintance she visited in another country. She could have had it shipped back to her, but the duty to bring it into the country where she was would have exceeded the value of the camera.

If you need something to continue your trip, you need to know when it will be available for pickup. (If you send things home from abroad, on the other hand, you usually aren't too concerned with how long it takes them to arrive or clear customs.) Shipping times are unpredictable, and mail sent for general delivery will only be held for a limited time before being returned, destroyed, or sold as unclaimed. Postal parcels can take weeks or months to clear customs. So even if you know your own schedule precisely in advance (which you may not) there is no way to send a parcel, especially by the cheapest means (surface or boat mail) with any assurance that it will be available for pickup at the time you will be in the place where you are sending it.

Some travelers try to save weight by shipping heavy items they will need for only part of their trip to somewhere they can pick them up along the way. This makes sense only if you have a reliable contact who lives there, to whom you can ship your items and who can hold them until your arrival. That works if you have lots of lead time for delays in shipping and customs, and if the items are heavy or important, but not truly essential. A certain percentage of mail does get lost even within or between First World countries, and international parcel insurance is expensive.

People are commonly tempted to ship ahead trekking, camping, and sports equipment (a reasonable idea if you have a reliable local contact to whom to ship them); warm clothing for cold climates (ditto, if you are going first to the tropics or to places where it is summer, and then to an expensive cold country); guidebooks (worthwhile only if they can't be bought along the way); and maps (a judgment call, as they are often unavailable locally but are usually both lightweight and important enough to carry with you).

Resupplying prescription drugs, if you run out and can't find them locally, is the most difficult thing. Try to bring enough to last through your trip if at all possible. Shipping and courier companies are extremely wary of being used by shippers of illegal drugs, making it extremely difficult to get them to accept shipments of any drugs, even legally prescribed pharmaceuticals. Some drugs that are legal in the Unites States are illegal even with prescriptions other countries, and vice versa. Try to find out the rules before you try to ship or carry any drugs across international borders.

SENDING THINGS HOME

It's possible to send things home from most major cities. Most parcels will, eventually, reach their destinations. But the process of mailing is, in many cases, neither simple nor quick, and unless you pay a small fortune, your things may take months to arrive by surface mail. Don't plan on mailing things home if you can help it. If you must, send the things you would least mind losing, even if they are expensive, and do not send things with great sentimental value. If you have to mail a package home, budget a full day for the process. If it doesn't take that long, consider yourself lucky.

Unless you want to pay a fortune for air shipping by FedEx, DHL, or their ilk, try to find a post office that regularly deals with foreigners. Sometimes there's a special office for international mailings. Wrap everything you

Baggage

REAL LIFE

Everything I've ever mailed home from my trips around the world has eventually arrived in good order, although it sometimes took months. On my last trip, I mailed packages home from eight countries on five continents. Prices varied greatly from country to country, but the average postage to send a two-kilo (4.5-pound) package to the United States was about US$20.

want to send carefully and tightly. Pad fragile items well, and make sure they don't have room to shift. Don't seal your parcel before going to the post office, as postal workers may need to inspect the contents before they will accept your package for mailing. In some areas of the world, you may find that parcels have to be sewn up in cloth or otherwise specially packed, in which case there will probably be someone providing this service outside or near the post office.

Local mailing procedures vary, but you should always be sure that all stamps on your letters and parcels are canceled in your sight. If they aren't, the stamps may be stolen and resold or reused, leaving your mail with insufficient postage. International parcel post rates vary too widely for any useful generalizations. Because postal rates are based on the official, often artificial, exchange rate, mailing can be either insanely cheap or insanely expensive, depending on the relationship between the real and official value of the local currency.

For information on sending and receiving letters as a means of communications, see the section *Postal Mail* in the following chapter under *Keeping in Touch*.

Life on the Road

TRAVELING COMPANIONS

Your choice of who to travel with is really inseparable from, and should be made simultaneously with, your choice of where to go. You may want to change your destinations to accommodate the wishes of a desired companion, or you may want to choose a different companion or set out by yourself if you find that your would-be partner wants to go to different places than you. Few choices will affect the nature and quality of your travel experience more than your choice of traveling companion(s), or your choice to travel alone.

My impression is that too few people think carefully enough about their choice of traveling companions. Whatever the reason, it's certainly the case that more people are dissatisfied, after the fact, with their choices of companions (including, for some, the choice of whether to travel alone) than are dissatisfied with their choices of destinations.

REAL LIFE

Sometimes I travel for adventure, excitement, education, and immersion in the place I'm going and its sensory stimuli. Sometimes I travel for vacation, rest, relaxation, contemplation, and an escape from sensory stimuli. One of the worst trips I've ever had—with some of my best friends—was when I wanted the latter, and my companions wanted the former.

Before you commit yourself to a long or complicated trip together, try to take a short "shakedown" trip, at least a weekend getaway, to get a feel for each other and how you will travel together. It'll be well worth the expense if it spares you a disastrous long trip with someone incompatible—or a lost friendship.

Make sure you agree not just on where you want to go but on what you want to do there, and why. One of the most common mistakes in travel planning is to get together with a group of people who want to go to "the same place," and not to realize until you get off the plane that one of you wants to spend time on the beach, one in the shops, one in the temples, one in the museums, one in the cafés, one in the villages, one in the mountains, and one in the brothels. That may be possible, but if the are going to split up immediately on arrival, there isn't much point in going out of your way to travel together in the first place.

Make a list of where you want to go, what you want to see or do there, and what your goals and priorities are for the trip. Do this separately, without consulting each other, and then compare your lists.

Because reasons for going places or seeing things vary so much, and because it's often the small details of daily traveling life that cause the most friction, it's especially important not just to list destinations or sights of interest. Get together with everyone with whom you are considering traveling, and have each one of you describe to the others, in as much detail as possible, what they envision a typical day or two on the road would be like: what you will do, where you will stay, where you will eat, how you will get around, how you will make decisions, etc. As you listen to your prospective traveling companion(s), try to actually visualize the trip described, and to compare it with your own vision of the trip you expect to take.

These predeparture exercises are no less necessary if you plan to travel with a spouse or lover. Travel can place severe stress on a relationship, in ways different than love, marriage, or living together. Don't take for granted that someone you love and/or can live with happily is someone with whom you'll want to travel, or that someone you fall in love with on the road, and with whom you love traveling, is someone you'll love to settle down with or live with at home. People who set out in couples should leave themselves open to

Key Advice About Life on the Road

- Choose your traveling companion(s) at least as carefully as your destinations. Consider how you want to travel, not just where, in choosing your companion(s).

- Travel responsibly and sustainably. Consider the impact of where and how you travel on both the physical and cultural ecology of the places you visit.

- Travel in as local a way as you can. You'll spend less, learn more, and do less ecological damage.

- Don't worry. Things will work out. Most pretrip nightmares don't materialize. The necessities of travel are the necessities of daily life; everywhere in the world you'll find that people have ways of dealing with them.

- Expect more severe culture shock when you return home than while you are traveling. "Home" may not have changed, but you will have, and your home will seem different to your changed self.

For more information on the topics in this chapter, see the *Resource Guide* in the back of the book and the links on the Practical Nomad website at www.practicalnomad.com.

the possibility that they might split up along the way, and that even if they do, they might want to be together again once they get back home. Travel can bring out behavioral traits and aspects of people's personalities that aren't visible, or don't cause problems, at other times. Don't take for granted that you know your lover's tastes in travel if you haven't traveled together before.

I've made long international trips both alone and with my partner. I know that the issues that cause the most problems in our relationship, and to which we have to pay the most attention when we are traveling, are, at least on the surface, quite different from those that dominate our disputes at home.

There are a variety of travel matchmaking services: travel clubs, "traveling companion wanted" ads in travel magazines, and Internet travel mailing lists, bulletin boards, and chat rooms. These may be helpful ways to make initial contact with potential traveling companions, if you want them and can't find them any other way, but I wouldn't commit to an extended trip without meeting all my companions face-to-face. As when answering any personal advertisements, make sure any sexual hopes or expectations are made explicit in advance.

Regardless of who your traveling companion is, don't think you have to spend all your time together as a single unit. Many travelers spend more of their time with their travel partner than they would ever otherwise spend with anyone, including a spouse or lover. You might even want to plan to take breaks from each other's company, whether for an hour, a day, or a week at a time. Some travel experiences are only available to solo travelers. It's a recipe for resentment for neither of you to feel able to cope on your own, and even worse if only one of you feels dependent on the other. Be alert to particular disparities in power and dependence if one of you is better at communicating with local people (either because of better knowledge of a language or better skill at nonverbal communication), is much more familiar with the place, or is much more experienced at travel.

Women are much more likely than men to take on a traveling companion primarily because they don't feel confident that they will be able or comfortable enough to travel alone. At the risk of presuming to give advice to women about a problem men don't usually share, allow me to suggest that mere fear of solo travel may be the worst reason to take on a traveling companion, unless you can find someone with whom you have a great deal more in common than your fear. *A Journey of One's Own: Uncommon Advice for the Independent Woman Traveler* by Thalia Zepatos (see the *Resource Guide*) has more thoughts for women on the choice of whether to travel alone or with a partner.

That you both want to visit the same place or region says little about whether you have common interests, goals, desires, or travel styles. If the main thing you have in common is your fear of traveling alone, you aren't likely to get along well on the road. You'll tend to reinforce each other's fears, not empower each other to embrace and experience local cultures and ways. Interacting mainly with each other out of fear of the unknown, you'll rapidly get as tired of each other, lovers or not, as people can in any marriage of convenience, unless you are lucky enough to discover that you have many shared interests other than wanting to travel and not wanting to do so alone.

Many such traveling partnerships break up mid-trip, often in ways that leave resentment on both sides. Typically, one or the other partner grows out of the fear faster than the other. The one who is ready to travel more adventurously and get off the beaten track, or is no longer afraid of solo travel and wants to go off alone, resents being held back by the other. And the other one resents being pushed to change, or feels "abandoned," or accuses the partner of "betraying" their agreement to support each other, the raison d'être of their partnership.

If at first, or in particular places, you aren't comfortable traveling alone, rest assured that there will be other travelers who feel likewise, and with whom you can join up. It's common for pairs, trios, or larger impromptu groups to come together for anything from a day's sightseeing excursion to a month's trek or overland journey through a country or region. Some travelers who leave home and return alone spend most of their days in the company of other travelers, whether for safety or conversation or to save on hotel costs. Even people who prefer to travel alone often team up to share chartered vehicles in places where public transportation is expensive, impractical, or doesn't go where they want, such as for a camping trip across the United States or Australia or for drives through African wildlife preserves.

You have to try hard to find a place where there are so few travelers that ad hoc companionship isn't available to those who want it. I generally avoid travelers' ghettoes and hangouts, but they are excellent places to find partners for onward travel or excursions. Hostels, guesthouses, and cafés everywhere have bulletin boards for "companion(s) wanted" and "rides to share" notices. When you both are already on the road and can meet face to face, it's a lot easier to figure out whether you and a prospective fellow traveler have similar styles and will get along than if you try to choose a travel partner before your departure or over the Internet.

TOURS AND GUIDES

Escorted tours around the world are few, especially compared to the incredible diversity of itineraries followed by independent travelers. Tours are usually very expensive relative to independent travel, and limited in time relative to the duration of most independent trips around the world. The longer the duration of your trip, the more the greater cost of travel by tour becomes a factor. And there are also significant ecological and other reasons to prefer independent travel even if you could afford a tour. Most around-the-world and other long-term travelers, both of necessity and by choice, end up traveling unescorted, independently (i.e., not with an organized group), and arranging their own accommodations and other travel services as they go.

Ecotourism and the Ecology of Independent Travel

Ecotourism and "responsible travel" are growing trends, reflecting rising public awareness of the ill effects and irresponsibility of much tourism, and a desire on the part of increasing numbers of travelers genuinely to immerse themselves in the places they visit.

But what is "ecotourism?" How should a concern for the environment influence the way you travel? And is it really more "green" or "responsible" to take an ecotour than to travel on your own?

All travel, and especially long-haul air travel, has adverse ecological consequences. Unlike trains, which if electrified can get power from a variety of renewable sources, airplanes all fly on fossil fuel ("jet fuel" is kerosene). The present window of opportunity for transoceanic air travel—affordable to large numbers of people—is likely to be, in historical terms, a brief one before the world runs out of oil. There are no electric or hybrid airplanes, and there is no such thing as "sustainable" or "low-impact" large-scale air travel. Nor, even according to the aviation industry's own experts, is anything like that on the horizon in the foreseeable future.

More of the effects of travel on the physical environment are related to transportation, such as petroleum extraction, refining, distribution, and burning, or the cutting of trees and paving of land for roads, than anything about what you do when you get where you are going. It makes no sense to label a trip as "ecotourism" if it involves flying 20,000 km (12,500 miles) from one continent to another and back for only a few weeks.

If what you are seeking is an environment relatively uncrowded and undamaged by people, a more ecological choice for North Americans may be to stay closer to home. As the most geographically (if not culturally) diverse country on earth (only China and maybe India can compare), the United States has become a major ecotourism destination for travelers from overseas, especially from crowded parts of Europe and East Asia that lack American-sized open spaces, parks, wildlife preserves, and wilderness areas. I'm hoping that my next "big" trip will be by bicycle across North America.

Given that getting there by air is an unavoidable ecological cost of long-distance travel, ecological responsibility in travel means both minimizing the avoidable environmental costs and trying to make a positive contribution in some other way to offset them. That's what ecotourism is supposed to be about.

There are serious problems, though, in realizing those goals in any prearranged tour, largely stemming from the high costs of these tours. Tour operators in the First World spend more on marketing, support, and other costs in their country (where wages, after all, are at First World levels) than on tour services in destination countries in the Third or Fourth World. This is another way of saying that tourist services purchased locally in a Third World destination country would typically cost no more than half what they would cost as part of a tour prearranged through a First World operator. Tour travel itself, moreover, is skewed toward more expensive, usually meaning higher-impact, travel.

Few people would knowingly pay twice as much to arrange a tour through an operator in their own country if they believed themselves capable of arranging it locally, or doing it themselves independently. So tour operators have a vested interest in promoting fear, disempowerment, and ignorance on the part of would-be travelers, and in keeping people from learning how to travel on their own, as part of persuading them that they can't or wouldn't want to travel on their own and that it's worth paying the price to book a tour in advance.

To compound the problem, most self-styled ecotourism publications and websites are financed primarily by advertising from tour operators, and thus can ill afford to criticize or to provide information that would reduce the market for the products of the industry on whom their existence depends.

There is an obvious contradiction between persuading people that they need a tour operator as an intermediary between themselves and the local people and environment, and persuading people to immerse themselves in and learn about the local environment by interacting with local people.

Prearranged tours add foreign agents, middlemen, and communications and money-transfer costs to the costs of services provided in the destination country, thus greatly inflating the price of travel. And those agents and middlemen all have an incentive to push tourists to more expensive tours to maximize their commissions. Because travel on a tour basis is more expensive, people on tours are, on average, richer people (or at least people traveling more expensively) than independent travelers. And there's the rub, or at least part of it.

Wealth is power. The more expensively tourists are traveling, the more power they wield to have the local environment altered to suit their needs and desires. And, quite frankly, richer people are more accustomed than poorer people to having their desires accommodated regardless of the consequences for others. They frequently have higher expectations of Western norms of luxury and service, and are less culturally diverse than a more economically diverse range of tourists would be. The result is that these tourists create greater material and cultural pressures to reshape the local environment in a Western mold than would an equal number of tourists traveling more cheaply.

The poorest tourists simply don't have the economic clout to transform their destinations. They have to learn the local culture and language, even perhaps studying them before they arrive, to survive and get around. Of necessity, they stay in the places local people stay, eat the local food, and use the local mass transportation. Having more time than money, and being more dependent on local goodwill, they are compelled to be both more patient and more tolerant. They can't afford to change things much, and they leave them pretty much as they found them.

People traveling more expensively are also likely to have less time, and, being more rushed, are both more able and more willing to make ecological (and other) compromises to fulfill their travel agendas in their limited time: flying rather than taking trains, driving rather than walking, and in general supporting infrastructure changes (with their collateral environmental damage) to make the "marquee attractions" more "accessible." They also have less time to develop an awareness of what this sort of tourism "development," and the effect of their own visit, leaves behind.

Anthropologist and travel scholar Klaus Westerhausen makes all these points strongly in his study of the most independent, lowest-budget, longest-term backpackers, and the changes in the places they visit, *Beyond the Beach: An Ethnography of Modern Travellers in Asia* (see the *Resource Guide*).

People traveling on their own who can't afford to charter private transportation are less likely to get into the most environmentally fragile areas, because these are likely to be without regular public transport. There is a strong argument, in fact, for city tourism as having less impact on either the physical or the cultural environment than the tours to less densely populated (or even unpopulated) areas that are more often thought of, and promoted, as ecotours.

Even the more sensitive travelers on prearranged tours are limited in their opportunities either to become aware of the ecological implications of their visits or to adapt their styles of travel to minimize those effects. Distributing the costs of prearrangement over many people makes group travel more affordable than individualized prearranged travel, so travelers who prearrange their itineraries are more likely to be in groups than ones or twos. Participants in escorted groups inevitably do much of their socializing within their groups, making them less aware of the local culture and their own effects on it than independent travelers immersed in and interacting constantly with the culture. Tour groups are further insulated from such interaction and awareness by their escort, who inevitably has a vested financial interest in making them feel good about their experience.

Equally important is the fact that even those who want to adapt can't, because everything on the tour has been committed to before the tour began. Unfortunately, what the traveler has committed to is more the image of the tour than the experience of the tour, because the tourist has to buy and pay for the tour before experiencing it. No matter how wonderful the tour is, it won't sell if it doesn't promise (in advance) what people think (in advance) they want, or think will be appropriate. What they find they want or decide would be appropriate when they get there matters much less.

Even some tour operators admit, in confidence, to arranging trips in a way that they themselves would never choose, but that "the customers want." If prepaid tourists discover on arrival that what they thought they wanted, and have already bought, is culturally or ecologically inappropriate, they are stuck. Travelers who make their arrangements locally are more likely to notice, and at least have a chance to consider before committing themselves, the implications of the style of travel they are contemplating.

I don't want to seem too critical. I strongly support ecotourism. I do want to encourage travelers to acknowledge responsibility for their effects on the physical and cultural ecology of the places they visit, and to use the lessons they learn from travel to live more responsibly when they return home.

Ecotourism operators run the gamut from politically committed, money-losing environmental organizations to utterly unprincipled hucksters looking for new marketing angles to sell the same old tours in new "green" packaging. But nothing about ecotourism or responsible travel, or their values, requires a tour, and even the best tours have several strikes against them, as I've tried to explain.

Independent travelers, of course, run the gamut too. It's all too easy to fall into a rut of going from one place listed in a guidebook for foreigners, or recommended by other foreigners, to another; to stay and eat only in places catering to, and patronized exclusively by, other foreigners like you; to spend most of your time in ghettoes of foreigners; to socialize mostly with other foreigners; and to interact with local people only as service providers. Some people argue that, to the extent that they succeed in getting "off the beaten path" or into newly touristed areas, independent backpackers are the vanguard of cultural imperialism and the destructive effects of mass tourism.

But I would argue strongly against letting yourself be talked into an "ecotour" as necessarily being a "more ecological" or "more responsible" way to travel than traveling on your own. (For both sides of this debate, see the "Backpackers" and "Guidebooks" special issues of Tourism Concern's journal, *Tourism in Focus,* listed in the *Resource Guide.*) To me, the key thing is that if you make your own arrangements, you have to take personal responsibility for the ecological implications (physical and cultural) of the way you travel. Traveling independently means not having a tour operator to rely on for ecological awareness or decision-making. It's past time, however—at least in my opinion—for independent travel to be recognized as offering more diverse possibilities for ecotourism, and greater opportunity for responsible tourism, than any tour.

Local Tours and Guides

If you can't or don't want to do something on your own, it's often better to arrange for a tour, guide, or helper locally than to try to book one in advance from abroad.

Some people are afraid to wait until they arrive to book a tour, lest it be too difficult to arrange on the spot. Rest assured that it is just the opposite: unless money is truly no object, it is usually easier and safer to arrange a tour locally. You will have more choices; it will be much easier to get firsthand references, check out the tour operator, and make an informed choice; and the prices, even for tours with operators with agents abroad, are typically only half what the same tours would cost if booked from abroad. Typically only a fraction of the higher-priced local operators have agents abroad.

Booking online directly with a local operator abroad isn't usually quite as expensive as going through a foreign agent. But you are likely to find when you arrive that people on the same tour who booked locally were charged less. And you're likely to have to pay all or a substantial part of the tour price up front, with essentially no recourse if it turns out not to be as advertised. I'll prepay online for a night in a hotel on arrival in a new country, sight unseen. But I wouldn't think of booking an entire tour that way.

The main exceptions are things that are rationed in some way, or which only a limited number of people can do, and for which the quota is likely to be filled, or all the permits taken, by the time you arrive at the destination or the jumping-off point. Permits for raft trips through the Grand Canyon, for example, are allocated months in advance, based on a waiting list several years long. But there are fewer exceptions like this than most travelers fear.

Locally operated tours run the gamut from half-day or full-day guided sightseeing trips around a city by bus or van to two-week package excursions by air to neighboring countries. You can hire a guide, translator, porter, or car and driver by the hour, day, week, or month—whatever you want and can afford.

The best way to learn about and choose between local tour operators and guides is personal investigation and firsthand references from fellow travelers. Visit the office (if it's a big enough operation to have one). Look at the vehicles. Talk to the people yourself. Whether you are hiring a freelance guide or booking a two-week package tour from a large local company, talk to at least one, preferably two, different fellow travelers who have used its services before. When you are on the spot, there's no need to settle for anything less than such direct and detailed information.

It's not hard to find references and recommendations of the good guides and companies, and warnings about the bad. The pros and cons of guides, porters, and local tour companies are a standard topic of conversation in every travelers' hangout. Mention that you are considering a tour operated by Company C to Place D, or are negotiating with head Sherpa E to arrange a trek, and you are apt to be inundated with advice about their pros and cons. As with recommendations farther afield, remember that not everyone likes the same thing, or the same sort of tour. Some companies are unequivocally bad, but few are unequivocally good for all tastes. Listen to what everyone has to say, but choose what you think will be right for you, even if it's not what everyone else is doing or would want to do. Among the advantages to booking locally are that a greater degree of customization of your itinerary is usually possible—and that you are more likely to know how you want the tour customized once you get to the jumping-off place and talk to people just back from similar trips.

Where tourists have come from different countries and speak different languages, English is the most common "link" language for tour narration, even if it's nobody's first language. City tours may be available in other languages as well, but in big cities they are always available in English. The same is largely true for at least the more common longer tours.

You can sometimes trade your services as a language tutor and practice conversationalist for the services of a guide and translator. There are even language exchange websites like Tourboarding.com that will match you up with local people who will provide a place for you to stay in exchange for a certain number of hours a day of English conversation practice. Don't agree to this unless you are willing to keep your end of the bargain. If you want your guide or host to do their best, do the best job of teaching that you can in return.

Overland Expeditions

Almost the only affordable *long-term* tours other than cruises are a variety of so-called "overland expeditions," primarily in Africa and Eurasia. These trips are distinguished by their distinctive mode of transportation and accommodations: short-wheelbase high-clearance trucks (or occasionally vans or buses) outfitted with seats that convert to sleeping berths for 10–30 passengers.

Depending on the operator, weather, and terrain, you either sleep in bunks installed in the truck or in small tents you set up each night. Occasionally you may stay in a hotel in a town. Meals are usually prepared and eaten collectively in a camp kitchen from ingredients bought in local markets, supplemented with a limited supply of food provided by the expedition outfitter.

The quoted prices for expedition tours are very cheap considering their duration but are rarely all-inclusive. Typically, the tour price paid to the operator in advance covers only a seat/berth in the truck, any furnished gear (you may have to bring your own tent and/or sleeping bag, or pay extra to rent one), and the salaries of the driver/guides (usually two or three per truck). Contributions to a shared fund ("kitty") for food and other joint costs along the way, as well as all restaurant meals, hotel stays, fees or tips to local guides, museum and park entrance fees (especially high at some African wildlife preserves), and personal expenses, are usually additional.

Typical routes for expedition tours are between East Africa and Southern Africa or Europe and West Africa (via the Sahara). Typical trips are anywhere from 3 to 12 weeks in duration, sometimes longer if you combine several sequential trips.

Imagine spending all day, every day for weeks, riding in a truck with a group of people you didn't choose as companions and who start out as strangers, and camping every night with the same group of people. Sometimes the group coalesces and most of the people get along with each other; sometimes not.

When you stop, you all get out of the truck together. You do get some time for individual sightseeing, if you so choose, in cities. But most days you are on the road, in or near the truck, all day. Most of your opportunities to see local things and talk to local people are constrained and shaped, for the worse, by the simultaneous presence of your 10 or 20 traveling companions, all trying to join the conversation or take pictures of the same sight.

I can't recommend overland expeditions as "tours" because of the limited opportunities they give their passengers to actually experience and interact with the people and places they drive through, because the group dynamics are so unpredictable (notwithstanding the best efforts of the driver/guides), and because such a high proportion of people who set out on these trips don't complete them. I should note, however, that most of those who drop out continue traveling on their own, and that some of them feel that the overland expedition experience helped empower them to travel on their own in places they wouldn't otherwise have felt comfortable starting out alone.

Because of the high dropout rate, expedition trucks frequently have spaces available on an ad hoc basis for people who meet them along the way and are willing to pay a prorated price (often quite negotiable) to join them for part of a trip. You can't count on finding an expedition operator with spare seats on a specific route at a specific time. But if you happen to meet one, joining on temporarily may be the best away across a stretch where there's little or no public transit such as the Sahara, and for a limited stint the price may be excellent value for the transportation alone.

ACCOMMODATIONS

Even experienced travelers planning their first independent trip to a new part of the world sometimes fear that they won't find a place to stay. There are a variety of ways, most of them easier than you might think, to have a bed waiting for you, or find one as you arrive. Experienced travelers rarely worry about finding a place to sleep, not because they've learned any special room-finding skills but because they've learned that's it's not really that hard to find rooms on arrival.

I should note, however, that choices of accommodations ("Is this place really worth US$5 a night more than the other?" "Should we agree to take this room for this price, or keep looking for a better or cheaper hotel?") figure prominently in the rankings of things about which traveling companions argue. This is definitely one of the things to talk through with prospective companions before you agree to travel together.

HOSTELS

Hostelling International is one of the world's largest accommodation providers. Most "youth" hostels accept reservations. Almost none have age limits.

Procedures vary. Check with the local affiliate of Hostelling International for details. (See *Accommodations* in the *Resource Guide* for worldwide HI contacts.)

HI operates its own computerized reservation system for hostels in international gateway cities. Most other hostels accept reservations by phone and/or mail, and increasingly many (but by no means all) take reservations over the Internet. Book as far in advance as you are sure of your plans. Hostelling organizations have trouble affording large enough facilities in popular cities.

Hostels as such are few outside the First World. But hostels offer the cheapest reservations in (otherwise expensive) major cities in the United States, Canada, Western Europe, Japan, Australia, and Aotearoa/New Zealand.

As long as they don't claim to be affiliated with Hostelling International, any place that wants to do so can call itself a hostel. Standards and services of private and unaffiliated hostels vary. Overall, in my experience, private hostels tend to have a younger, more party-oriented clientele. Guests at HI hostels tend to be quieter, with less alcohol and more of a mix of ages including both seniors and younger children. The *Resource Guide* lists several directories of private hostels.

HOME EXCHANGES

You go on vacation from Point A to Point B. You leave your home empty in A, and rent a place to stay in B. Meanwhile, there's probably somebody else traveling from B to A, leaving their home vacant in B and renting a place to stay in A. Wouldn't it be nice if you could connect with each other, and arrange to each stay in the other's home? In a nutshell, that's a home exchange.

When it works, a home exchange is almost miraculous: You each get the use of an entire fully furnished and equipped home—probably much larger and more comfortable than any vacation home you could afford—and *neither of you pays a penny!* Nothing else comes close for value in long-term vacation (or other travel) accommodations.

Why doesn't everybody do this? The catch has always been the difficulty of identifying someone compatible and trustworthy, with the mirror image of your itinerary, wanting to travel between the same places, on the same dates, in opposite directions. That, however, is exactly the sort of matching task for which the Internet is perfect.

Arranging a home exchange is usually a three-step process. First, you sign up with a home exchange matching service and complete a profile of your home, when you want to travel, and where you want to go. Then, the service posts your listing in their directory of available homes for exchange, and gives you access to other members' listings. When you find a potential match, you can contact them by email and/or phone to get to know each other, see if you think an exchange will work, and negotiate the details.

You can take as much time, and ask as many questions, as you like, before you decide whether you're willing to let someone live in your home while you're not there. Of course, you'll be living in their house at the same time, so you both probably have the same concern for having your homes be well cared for. Mutual trust and advance planning are essential.

How easy it will be to arrange an exchange for your home depends largely on the attractiveness and location of your home, and your own willingness to trust a stranger. Home exchanges are most attractive for families and longer stays. If you own a home, and if you want to settle down somewhere abroad for a month or two, a home exchange may be the way to afford it.

HOSPITALITY EXCHANGES

Hospitality exchanges are similar to home exchanges, except that they involve hosting people in your home while you are there, and staying with other people in their homes, rather than exchanging the use of your home for theirs.

As with home exchanges, hospitality exchanges are generally based on directories of members of a matching service. Also as with home exchange networks, most hospitality exchanges now operate on the Internet. You sign up as being willing to consider requests for hospitality by visitors. When a fellow member of the service wants to visit the place where you live, they can contact you and ask if you're willing to put them up on certain dates. You can always say no, without any obligation to give a reason, although of course the system works on mutual generosity and willingness to play host as often as you play guest. When you want to go somewhere, you can contact fellow members in that location to see if one of them might be willing to put you up.

Hospitality exchanges are not a substitute for other sorts of travel accommodations, and visits are generally limited to a few days. Guests are often expected to help with household tasks, although the norms of the relationship vary from one hospitality exchange service to another. Hospitality exchanges are mainly a way to meet people in a different place, and get experience of what their lives are like, rather than a way to cut the cost of travel. Many hospitality exchange networks are organized around "affinity groups" of people who share certain values or interests. It's not for everyone, but at its best a stay in a local person's home can be the highlight of your trip.

HOMESTAYS

Whether or not you've arranged it in advance, try to stay with local people whenever you get a chance: friends, relatives, friends of friends, people you meet along the way, people whose "guesthouses" or "hostels" are no more than spare rooms in their houses. You'll often be more crowded and less comfortable than in a hotel—one of the greatest luxuries of life in the United States, relative to even other wealthy countries, is how much living space most of us have—but you'll learn more and have more fun. Family homestays (the most informal sort of "bed-and-breakfast") were for some years the standard form of budget accommodation in much of the Second World, where budget hotels are only gradually appearing.

Some people, especially women, worry about whether to accept offers of hospitality, especially from strangers. Use the same caution you would in the United States. Many things that would be considered sexual harassment in the United States are considered flattery elsewhere, but violation of a woman's honor is a much more serious offense in many other countries than in the United States. I've heard more anecdotal stories of sexual harassment and date rape between foreigners at backpackers' guesthouses than between foreign travelers and local hosts.

Sooner or later some of the people you've stayed with—perhaps those you least expect—will make their way to your country, and your home, expecting you to put them up. Do so. Graciously.

If you're uncomfortable with this idea, don't let people you meet take you into their homes. It's unfair and improper, to say the least, to accept offers of hospitality you wouldn't be willing to reciprocate. If they offer you the best room in their house, realize that they would probably expect you to do likewise.

RENTAL HOUSES AND APARTMENTS

In some places renting a house or apartment can offer better value than a hotel, even for stays as short as a week. A furnished house or apartment is an especially good deal for families or groups and/or if you want to be able to cook for yourself.

Apartments are less standardized than hotel rooms, so its usually best to wait until you arrive and check them out in person before you commit yourself. Make sure you understand exactly what is, and isn't, included in the price—local norms may be very different from those where you're from.

Real estate, residency, and/or visa rules often make it technically illegal for a foreign tourist to sublet an apartment by the week or month. In New York, hotels that don't like the competition from private sublets got a law passed in 2010 outlawing short-term rentals in any building not licensed as a hotel. In many countries you have to register with the police or another government agency when you move, and it's technically against the law to establish "residence" unless you hold a residency permit or visa.

This shouldn't alarm you, but it does mean that: (1) you shouldn't be surprised if there's a certain slightly black-market feel to private apartment rental negotiations and arrangements, (2) you shouldn't rent from someone you don't

REAL LIFE

In 2007, we spent two months in a one-bedroom top-floor apartment in a high-rise sliver building with a doorman, a block from a "Subte" station in one of the best neighborhoods in Buenos Aires. It currently rents for US$285 a week (equivalent to US$41 per night), fully furnished, including all utilities (cable TV, high-speed Internet, etc.) and weekly maid service. By the month, it's even cheaper. That's a price in line with the local market: there's a glut of condos for rent to foreigners by local people who took out mortgages denominated in U.S. dollars before the Argentine Peso collapsed in 2001–2002, and who are desperate to get enough rent (in U.S. dollars) to keep up their payments. Meanwhile, with tourism to Argentina booming but little local capital available for new hotel construction (and foreigners scared to invest), a good hotel room in such a great location would be likely to cost more than twice that much, for much less comfort.

trust, since you may have little recourse from the law if things go wrong, and (3) you should expect to be asked to pay in cash.

U.S.-based vacation rental websites have relatively few listings in the Third and Fourth Worlds, most of them in upscale destination resorts. In foreign cities, you may have more luck with local websites that list apartments and houses available for short-term rentals. (We found our apartments on several visits to Buenos Aires through Bytargentina.com.) In other places, you can find them through storefront agencies or bulletin boards in tourist or expat neighborhoods. Craigslist.com, Franglo.com, and similar websites often have ads for short-term sublets from expats who are going away on vacation or home leave. In general, expats are the best source of information about what sorts of short-term rentals are available at roughly what prices, and how to find them.

HOTEL RESERVATIONS

It's possible to reserve a hotel room in advance in most large cities, even most Third World capitals, but often only at the most expensive hotels. Sometimes there is no middle ground. The only hotels set up to handle advance reservations from overseas may be the Intercontinentals and their ilk. In many Third and Fourth World cities there are few if any midrange hotels between, say, US$20 and US$150 a night; in some the spread is even wider: there are local-style hotels at local prices and five-star international hotels at five-star prices.

A common request to a travel agent is, "Can you reserve a midrange hotel—say, US$50 a night—for my first night in City X?" In many cases, it's not possible, and I wouldn't always recommend it even when it is.

Cheap hotels don't participate in computerized reservation systems. Few midrange hotels listed in Moon or similar guides to regions outside the First World, or that I would recommend, can be reserved by travel agents by computer.

The cheaper the hotel, the less likely it is to pay a commission, the less likely it is to cover the cost of faxes or phone calls, and thus the more likely that a travel agent will have to charge you a fee for faxing or phoning to make reservations you could as easily make for yourself.

REAL LIFE

More than once I've asked at the front desk how much a room would cost, made reservations for half that price online from a cybercafé around the corner or using the Wi-Fi in the hotel's own lobby, and come back to the counter five minutes or half an hour later (it sometimes takes a little while for online reservations to be sent to the hotel from the website) to check in. Hotels don't like it, but they are the ones who set their prices that way, and it's perfectly legal.

Cheap hotels are cheap in part because they haven't invested in participation in travel agents' computerized reservations systems. You may be able to make reservations directly with them by email, phone, or fax, but unless you have a reference from a reliable fellow traveler, you'll have to commit yourself to a place sight unseen, which is generally an unnecessary risk. Question people who recommend a hotel as to how recently they stayed there, what it was like, and their tastes in travel.

The cheapest hotels that can be booked from abroad are often an otherwise poor value, because they rely on one-time transient business, not the loyalty of repeat guests, and their competitive advantage is the very fact that they can be booked from abroad, not anything to do with their facilities or service.

Hotels that you reserve directly on the Internet are even more of a risk, since you don't have a local travel agent through whom to seek recourse if there's a problem. Frequently the hotels popular on the Internet with first-time foreign visitors are those that have invested in their website rather than their service. It's common to show up at such a place, hoping for a "local" experience, to find that all the other guests are from the United States and booked it online through the same website that attracted you to it.

Which online travel agencies typically have the best hotel deals varies substantially from region to region. See the *Resource Guide* for listings of some of those I recommend and use in different parts of the world.

Hotel Discounts

Why do hotels sometimes offer lower prices through travel agencies and tour operators than if you contact the hotel directly?

Airlines, hotels, and other suppliers of travel services often give travel agencies and tour operators lower prices for services on condition that those prices be used only for constructing packages or bundles of services sold for an inclusive price, and not sold for separate one-off sale.

As long as the prices of components aren't itemized, packaging keeps both consumers and competitors from knowing just how deeply any given travel service provider is discounting. Bundling of services from multiple suppliers serves the suppliers' goal of price opacity. Equally important, it serves the agency's goal of opacity: packaging makes it impossible for either customers or suppliers to know how much the agency has marked up the total price of the package.

Instead of selling products or services at prices set by suppliers, and having their margin limited to either a publicly disclosed transaction fee (typically limited by competition to an unprofitable minimum) or a commission fixed by the supplier, packaging and its inherent price opacity permits a travel agency or tour operator to set its own selling price and thus to set its own markup.

This system of pricing and sales based on an opaque markup set by the agency, rather than a commission set by the supplier or a fixed agency fee, is called the "merchant model," because in this type of sale the agency is the "merchant of record" who processes the sale, and thus whose name appears on the credit-card charge receipt and statement. As the merchant, the agent collects the full payment from the customer, pays a contracted wholesale net price to the supplier(s) of travel and other services, and keeps

Regardless of where you find what seems to be a good deal on a hotel, try to check directly with the hotel, to see if they'll match the price, before you make your reservations through an agency, third-party website, or other intermediary. And vice versa: If you ask about prices at the front desk, and they tell you, "Our lowest prices are online," the hotel doesn't seem like it's about to sell out, and you have time, you might as well check prices on the websites most likely to have discounts before you agree to pay the walk-up price.

The price isn't always the same, as I've just said. But if it is, all else being equal, it's better to make your reservations directly with the hotel, for two reasons:

the balance of the markup as its profit, rather than having the supplier collect the full payment and remit a commission or fee to the agency, as had traditionally been the system. This is essential the same as the way "consolidator" airline tickets are priced.

The typical merchant-model hotel markup is an amount that consumers would find outrageous if it were disclosed. After 9/11, when hotels were desperate, online travel agencies were keeping an average of 25–40 percent of what they charged travelers for merchant-model hotel bookings! Hotels have fought back for a larger share, but billions of dollars a year in margins on merchant-model hotel bookings, not commissions or fees for bookings at prices set by suppliers, are still the backbone of online travel agency profits.

Among the important but little-noticed implications of the "merchant model" are that (1) it subjects the agency to many state consumer protection regulations governing tour operators (most of which don't apply to entities that function solely as suppliers' agents), and (2) it makes the agency liable, as merchant, for the actions of travel suppliers, instead of the agency being merely an agent for the supplier. In the merchant model, hotels, airlines, and other providers of travel services are subcontractors of the merchant, for whose fulfillment of the contract the merchant (i.e. the agency) is responsible. Online travel agencies may try to evade or disclaim their responsibility, but the bottom line is this: the company against whom to request a credit card chargeback, or to make a claim against in small claims court if your chargeback is denied, is the company whose name appears on your credit card statement as the merchant. In the "merchant model," that's the travel agency or packager.

First, there is much less risk of showing up to find that the hotel has no record of your reservation, which is always a risk when you book through any intermediary. Even if you make your reservations online, that doesn't mean they're instantly or automatically transmitted to the hotel or entered into its own room inventory management system. Frequently, bookings made through online travel agencies are transmitted to the hotel by individual faxes, which can easily be misplaced or overlooked by front desk or reservations staff. Whenever possible, print out your reservation confirmation to show to the hotel when you check in. If that's not possible, be prepared to show the front desk your confirmation on the screen of your laptop, or in a pinch to use their computer, or go to a cybercafé, to show them or print out an email confirmation.

If you made your reservation through an agent or intermediary, and the hotel has no record (or an erroneous record) of your booking, your ultimate recourse is with the company with whom you have a contract (and in whose name your credit card was charged, if you paid in advance). In most cases, especially with discounted or merchant model hotels, that's the company behind the website, not the hotel. If you can't tell before you confirm your reservation who to call, at what phone number, if you show up late at night at the hotel and they say they've never heard of you, that's not a website you should be using to make your booking. Always write that phone number down, and be sure you have it handy when you try to check in.

Second, making your booking directly with the hotel means that the hotel gets 100 percent of your payment, rather than as little as 50 percent of your payment if you book through some discounters or packagers. If you already know what price is currently being offered online, they will often agree to match the online price in order to keep a larger share of your payment.

Hotels don't necessarily treat you differently depending on how much you've paid, but those that do are guided by the amount of revenue they receive (the wholesale net price paid by the discounter, packager, or tour operator), regardless of how much it's been marked up for retail sale to you. Some hotels will give you the best room available after they've accommodated higher-paying customers, while others will assign you to the worst remaining room, no matter how many rooms they have empty, in the hope of getting high-paying last-minute walk-in customers for their better rooms. In my experience, this is the sort of decision in which front desk staff tend to have a lot of discretion. So if you booked a room at a deep discount, it's especially important to be on your best behavior when you check in. If you have a confirmed reservation, you are entitled to a room. Anything else, or any better than the worst room in the house, is at the hotel's discretion unless it was explicitly specified and confirmed. Demands or argument will be entirely counterproductive.

HAGGLING WITH HOTELS

In some shops, priced are fixed. In others, everything is negotiable. In some places you can tell by the type of shop, or simply by whether there are price tags. Sometimes there are fixed-price stores right next to shops where you have to haggle. How can you tell? Ask, "Are these prices fixed?" Perhaps surprisingly, you'll almost always get a straight answer. If the posted prices are merely a starting point for bargaining, a shopkeeper will tell you, so as not to lose potential business by discouraging you from making a lower offer.

Unlike shops, hotels won't usually give you a straight answer. But no matter what the hotel says, all hotel asking prices are negotiable, whenever (1) the hotel knows they are going to have empty rooms that night, (2) there are other comparable hotels nearby that also have empty rooms, and (3) you are genuinely prepared to go elsewhere, or not to stay as many nights, if they don't lower their price.

In circumstances like this, someone on the premises—yes, even at the Ritz-Carlton—is empowered to give you a discount. That doesn't mean they have to

> **REAL LIFE**
>
> In a Turkish bazaar, you have to bargain for everything. When I asked the proprietor of a cybercafé in Istanbul, "How much will it cost to print this document?," the answer was, "How much do you want to pay?"

give you a discount, but they can if they want to put "heads in beds." If the person at the front desk says they can't help you, either they expect the hotel to be full that night, they don't believe you are really ready to walk or will find anywhere else to stay, you are talking to the wrong person, or you've worded your request wrong. When I show up without reservations, I routinely haggle successfully with hotels in the United States, even upscale and chain hotels where most guests assume that the walk-up asking price is "take it or leave it."

Better hotels don't like to damage their reputation by admitting that they can't fill their rooms without offering discounts, especially if there's anyone else in the lobby who might overhear and ask for a deal too. So it's more polite to ask, "Do you have any rooms available at a lower rate that I might qualify for?" than to ask directly, "Can you give me a lower price?" Front-line staff might not have the authority to make up a price, but they almost always have the authority to give you the "corporate," "tour group," or some other discounted rate, regardless of whether you actually qualify.

If nothing else is said, the first price you are quoted will be the price for a one-night stand. If you plan to stay longer, even just two or three nights, that's a reason to ask for a lower nightly rate. Rates by the week can be anywhere from 25 to 50 percent less than nightly rates. The real issue, of course, is whether they expect to have empty rooms, and think they will lose your business to a competitor if they don't offer you a lower price.

It's less obvious that a hotel is giving discounts if they take the form of amenities rather than prices. So you'll often get more by asking for an upgrade to a better room, early check-in, late checkout, or breakfast included in the rate, if you want any of those things, than by asking for a lower base rate. If you haven't tried it, you'd be amazed at how often you can get breakfast included just for the asking, although there's no guarantee that you'll get anything as substantial as a full English or American breakfast.

Taxes aren't usually included in quoted hotel rates. 15–25 percent is common. To avoid surprises, always ask about taxes and any other fees you'll have to pay before you agree to a price. As with anything else, if you didn't ask first, you can't complain later if it isn't to your liking.

The time to bargain is before you book. Once you've made reservations, you are committed. Don't count on any amenities that weren't specifically promised before you made your booking, and don't waste your time or the hotel's by asking for a lower price, free breakfast, etc. just because you find out after you arrive that someone else is paying less than you are, or that comparable hotels nearby have lower rates. If you want to be able to haggle, you have to be willing to take the risk of showing up without reservations.

GUIDEBOOKS AND WEBSITES

Good guidebooks will give you an idea of the sort of accommodations—guesthouses, hostels, homestays, etc.—that you are likely to find in a particular place, and perhaps even in what neighborhood of the city you are likely to find the cheap ones concentrated. Look for books written by people who travel the way you do, on your sort of budget.

It's easy to choose your lodgings entirely from those listed in a guidebook or on some website, but it's neither necessary nor recommended. Places listed in books or that have the highest rating on a popular website are guaranteed a steady stream of customers, books or printouts from the Web in hand. If a guidebook lists two places in a neighborhood, odds are that there's a third across the street or around the corner that's not in the book and that has to, and does, try harder to provide better service. I find the general information in guidebooks or online information sites about types of lodging and ways of doing things in particular countries more useful than specific places to stay. Types and styles of accommodations vary greatly from country to country, and it helps a lot to know what to look for, and in what part of town. My own preference is to try to stay at places that aren't in guidebooks, that I didn't find on international websites, and that have few foreign guests.

"Current" editions of guidebooks are typically based on research at least one, more often two, years old. Check the date of any guidebook, and allow for changes and inflate your price expectations accordingly.

Hotel review websites are plagued by "shills": People who post reviews without revealing that they are really associated in some way with the hotel they are praising, or with the competition for the hotel they are criticizing. Sometimes they are posted by the owner or manager of the hotel, their family, or their friends. At other times they are paid shills.

What can you do about this? Don't believe everything you read. A few glowing reviews by shills (or negative reviews of the competition) can make the difference between profit and loss for a small hotel, guesthouse, or bed-and-breakfast. If there are only a few reviews of a place, assume that there is a good chance they've been planted by friends or foes. If there are many reviews, act like a statistician, and start by dropping the outliers. And always remember that there's no accounting for taste: Even impartial reviewers may have a completely different reaction than you to the same conditions or situation. Every review reflects the reviewer as well the thing reviewed—and on the Web (except perhaps in the blog of someone you know personally), you only know how reviewers describe themselves, not what you would think of them if you met. At the end of the day, the best defense against all manner of hotel hucksterism is not to commit yourself to any hotel until you get there and can see it yourself.

(See the *Internet Information Sources* section in the *Choosing Destinations* chapter for more on how to find and evaluate online travel information and advice.)

LOCAL RECOMMENDATIONS

Talk to people on the plane, train, etc., especially people who are from the place you are going to, and on their way home. Most people are proud of their home and happy to talk about it to foreigners. If you already have specific lodging in mind, ask a local if they've heard of it, or of the address. They may never have heard of the hotel, but they may be able to warn you off if it has a bad local reputation or is in an undesirable or unsafe neighborhood.

Even if you don't get specific hotel recommendations, you're likely to get good advice about local transportation and sightseeing. I always ask, "Where should I go that most tourists don't go?" If you hit it off with locals and they are going your way, they may offer you a ride, or even invite you to stay in their home.

TOUTS

People who worry that they will be unable to find anywhere to stay probably have yet to encounter "touts," people who are paid to find customers for shops, services, and especially hotels. They may be on the staff of a hotel, or more often the hotel simply puts out the word that anyone bringing a customer in the door gets a certain cut of the first night's rent. Touts are essentially a labor-intensive form of advertising. It is more appropriate technology for most of the world, I'd say, than a computerized reservation system.

In a poor country, the hotel's cut is enough to motivate large numbers of otherwise unemployed or underemployed people, often children or teenagers (who are also likely to be the ones studying English or other foreign languages at school) to hang out at airports, bus and train stations, and ferry docks propositioning likely looking people (i.e., any foreigner, especially with a backpack). Many taxi drivers also work as touts.

You don't pay the tout's cut directly; it will automatically (and inescapably) be included in the price the hotel quotes you if you come in with a tout. It's not uncommon to be followed by more than one tout, even if you've picked out or been referred to a hotel already, and then to have them both argue with the hotelier about which one brought you in and should get paid.

A tout may not take you to the best or cheapest hotel, but you don't have to accept the first place, or any place, you are taken to. And if you just want to get to sleep, you can always take a room for just one night and look for somewhere better, at your leisure and without your luggage, the next morning. You'll find it easier to find places, and get better prices, in the morning without your luggage. The later it is, and the more burdened you appear to be, the more desperate and willing to pay you will be assumed to be.

Anywhere you need one, you'll find a tout (or one will find you). Touts only get paid if they succeed. You can count on them to find you the last vacant room in the city. At times you may think of touts as just a nuisance. I'll always remember the sight of police beating a crowd of touts back with sticks to make way for our bus to get into the station in one tourist town. But when it's late, you have no reservations, and you just need to find somewhere to sleep, let the touts help you. Their cut is a small price to pay for expert assistance.

WAIT UNTIL MORNING

If you arrive too late at night, you may be better off spending what's left of the night in the airport. A few hours in a waiting room until it gets light and the city wakes up may be better and safer than searching for a room at 0300 (3 A.M.).

At more than one airport, I've found that the staff have assumed that anyone arriving late would stay the night. They led me straight to a quiet, dark lounge or courtyard full of other foreigners dozing on couches, chairs, and the floor. Waiting rooms and trains are among the places that even noncampers find a sleeping bag handy.

It's rare not to find a hotel (more often many of them) within walking distance of any major train station. But if you don't, or they are too seedy for your taste, or you don't want to go out until dawn, there are hotel rooms inside or adjacent to some train stations and airports that are rented by the hour to arriving, departing, and transit passengers. In South Asia, where they have a long tradition, they are called "retiring rooms." In Japan there are "capsule hotels" near train stations with tiny sleeping compartments that were first developed to serve "salarymen" who missed the last train home.

STYLES OF ACCOMMODATIONS

You typically have two main choices in a Third World country, particularly one on a "standard" backpacker tourist route, or with a well-developed infrastructure for independent budget travel. On one hand, there are dormitory or hostel-like "guesthouses" catering almost exclusively to, and providing many special services for, foreigners. Services at such places may include ride sharing and notice boards, equipment rental, local sightseeing recommendations and tours, and directions to the next major stop on the standard tourist route in each direction. On the other hand, there are more expensive low- to midrange local hotels, usually catering to middle-class local travelers.

Most foreign backpackers stay in the foreign-backpacker hostels and guesthouses. Because these are usually the only places that rent beds in dorms, rather than private rooms, they are usually significantly cheaper for a solo traveler than the cheapest local hotels that are clean and comfortable enough to be acceptable to most foreigners. And they are usually the most obvious and easiest places to find, the ones most guidebooks and fellow travelers will recommend, the ones most touts will take you to first if you look like the sort of person who stays at them, and the ones at whose door some backpacker buses for tourists will drop you off instead of stopping at the regular city bus terminals.

I'd like to encourage you, if you can afford it, to spend the extra money to stay at local hotels, or at least to try them from time to time. (For a couple, a room in a local hotel may actually cost no more than two dorm beds in a hostel.) The advantages, to my mind, are many. In a local hotel, you get to spend time with locals and learn about their lives, something that won't happen in a guesthouse for foreigners. Local travelers can be one of the best sources of advice, tips, and recommendations that other foreigners don't know about and you won't find in guidebooks.

The staff is less likely to be tired of answering the same ignorant questions from every foreigner and more likely to be willing to help you. If foreigners don't often stay at a hotel, or eat at a restaurant or street stall, the proprietor is likely to feel that your patronage enhances the status of the establishment and to make an extra effort to please you.

It's all too easy to get stuck on a standard tourist route, seeing, staying, and eating with the same fellow travelers in guesthouses and cafés in town after town, night after night. Hanging out mainly with other foreigners, as is to a degree inevitable if they are the people you stay with, slows down the process of cultural assimilation and can blind you to the local culture and values.

If you get in the habit of only staying in places where you see other foreign faces, you become less likely to consider going off the beaten track to a place where you know, or suspect, that you won't find such a hostelry because there aren't enough foreign visitors to support one, and local travelers prefer private rooms. But visits to places with fewer foreign visitors are, as a rule, much more rewarding than time in tourist centers.

Wherever you stay, never agree to pay for a room without inspecting it carefully. Americans, who are used to standardized chains that can be counted on by brand name alone to provide a predictable set of features and level of comfort and cleanliness, are known worldwide for their willingness to rent rooms sight unseen. You don't have to take the first room you are shown, either. Feel free to ask for a better or a cheaper room, or one that's different in some way.

Sooner or later, you'll end up in a bad hotel. Whatever happens, remember that, "You can take anything…for a little while," as my friend Kay Burns quotes her friend Mary O'Shaughnessy. Even if you've reserved a room, you're only committed for one night. All hotels raise their rates for those who arrive late, tired, and desperate. You can stay one night and look for somewhere better or cheaper in the morning, at your leisure and without your luggage.

A FEW WORDS ABOUT TOILETS

Some people are afraid of foreign toilets and look down on unfamiliar designs of toilet as primitive and unsanitary. This is really a cultural issue more than anything else, but because it often becomes an issue in the choice of hotel rooms, I'll discuss it here.

There are two basic types of toilet in the world, for those who have toilets—at least one billion people, possibly two, have no toilets and use the fields, woods, or roads. "Westerners" sit on toilets that are essentially chairs with holes in the seats. "Easterners" squat over holes at floor or ground level. A well-made squat toilet slopes down slightly toward the hole to drain spills and has raised blocks or footpads 2–5 cm (1–2 inches) high, a little larger than foot-size, on either side of the hole to keep your feet clean and dry. "Westerners" wipe themselves with sheets of soft paper after using the toilet. Other people wash themselves with water after using the toilet, usually using their left hand to wash with.

There is nothing more or less modern, per se, about the European or "Western" sitting toilet versus the Asian and African or "Eastern" squatting toilet. Either type may be clean or dirty, may be dry or water-flushed, and constructed of porcelain, metal, wood, or other materials. There is no reason to think that people should or would want to learn to use sitting instead of squatting toilets, or that those who squat are primitive. Many people accustomed to squat toilets (or to using a bidet) find the thought of putting their bodies directly on a toilet seat that hasn't been washed since someone else sat on it, or of wiping themselves with a piece of paper instead of washing properly with water, to be appallingly unhygienic.

Another option, the bidet—you sit on the toilet, then wash yourself at the bidet rather than wiping with paper—is common in parts of Europe and Latin America.

There is a strong anatomical argument that squatting is a more natural position in which the body functions better and more comfortably. A large number of "Westerners" find that they prefer squat toilets once they try them.

Where toilets aren't clean, the argument in favor of Asian ones over European ones is compelling. Far better to squat over a dirty hole than to sit on a dirty seat. In most of the world, sitting toilets are rare. Local people can't imagine that one could be expected to sit directly on the seats, so when confronted with a European toilet they squat on the rim of the bowl, or on the seat, leaving them filthy. (Don't be surprised to see footprints or shoe marks on the seat of a Western toilet.) A squat toilet is more likely than a sit-up toilet to flush properly even if the drain is partially blocked and the water pressure low.

Where you have a choice of a hotel room with a Western toilet and one with an Eastern toilet, the room with the Western toilet will typically be more expensive, and the toilet dirtier. Most of the time preference will not be an issue, however: when you need to go, you'll use whatever is available by way of a toilet, or the local equivalent thereof. If squatting doesn't come naturally to you, or is hard, practice your deep-knee bends before you leave.

FOOD

Sometimes, as at a roadhouse in the Australian outback, the only place in town to stay may also have the only place to eat, unless you have facilities to cook for yourself. Generally, though, you have more choices of places to eat than of places to sleep. How do you choose, especially if you want to get off the tourist track by avoiding restaurants listed in guidebooks?

In pedestrian districts, I ask people coming out of a restaurant how their meal was and whether they eat there often. If locals eat there regularly, when there are many other options nearby, that's a good sign.

If no one is leaving a restaurant when I arrive, and I can't just ask people as they are eating (as one often can at a street stall), I rely on whether it passes what my partner and I have christened "The Happy Eater Test":

- Are there people in the restaurant? (If not, it might be because you have arrived at the wrong time of day for locals to eat. The restaurant might be OK, but it's a bad sign. And if nobody's eating, you can't tell if the food will be any good.)

- Are there people eating? (It doesn't matter whether the people drinking, talking, writing, or smoking hookahs look happy. People go to bars, clubs, and even places labeled as "restaurants" for lots of reasons other than the food. Make sure that some people have come for the food rather than anything else, and focus on the faces of the people with plates of food in front of them.)

- Do the people eating look happy? (A restaurant crowded with unhappy eaters might have gone downhill since getting written up in a guidebook, might rely on one-time transient customers and not care if they don't come back, or might simply have the only available food in that area at that time. If the eaters look unhappy, and there's a choice, look elsewhere for your meal.)

If there are certain things you can't eat, get someone to write them down for you in the local language(s)—ideally, in pencil or waterproof pen or on a sturdy card you can keep handy in your pocket whenever you go out to eat. Make it a priority to do this the first time you get a chance: before you leave home, while you are in the boarding area waiting for a flight to a destination with a different language, or on the train, bus, or ferry to a place with a new language. Without having them in writing, it can be almost impossible to explain allergies or other dietary restrictions across a language barrier. Don't try to go into the reasons why you do or don't eat certain things, as that will only lead cooks and servers to try to guess at what will or won't be OK. Keep it simple: "I can't eat milk, butter, or cheese." "I can't eat meat, fish, or fowl." If you say or write that you can eat something ("I can eat fish" or "I can eat eggs"), there's a chance that will be taken as a request, and you may be served nothing else.

GUIDEBOOKS FOR INDEPENDENT TRAVELERS

Guidebooks vary greatly in their intended purposes and audiences. Look for ones written by people who travel the way you do, on your sort of budget, with your sorts of interests. Don't be surprised if you don't find many: most guidebooks are written for people with less time, more money, more limited interests, and more fixed advance plans than most long-term budget travelers.

The more difficult a place is for independent travelers, the less likely most guidebooks are to say anything about practicalities. This is because if a place is difficult to travel in independently, most people who go there will go in escorted groups. Most guidebooks are, for maximum sales potential, written for the largest possible audience.

If most people who visit a place are in escorted groups, there will be little market for a guidebook that emphasizes how to go it alone. Instead, guidebooks to such regions tend to focus on the meaning and interpretation of the sights included on the standard tour itineraries, or perhaps on how to choose a package tour. Such books may make interesting reading before or after your trip—"practical" guidebooks often give short shrift to social, cultural, political, ethnic, religious, and artistic background and interpretation—but if they don't answer your basic "how-to" questions, they might not warrant space in your luggage. Lines like, "You will probably be taken to see the . . ." and "You will probably stay at the…Hotel," or simply the absence of any information about how one gets to the places described, should alert you that a particular guidebook is not intended to meet the needs of independent travelers, and that independent travel in the region it covers may not be easy or common.

The bottom line is that independent budget travelers are, especially in the United States, a very small niche market served by only a small number of highly specialized guidebook publishers. There are a few independent guidebooks to particular places. But most English-language guides to independent budget travel are part of one or another series of guidebooks from the name brands of the field, such as Avalon Travel's Moon and Rick Steves' guides, Lonely Planet's Travel Survival Kits and On a Shoestring guides, Footprint Handbooks, Rough Guides, Bradt Guides, the Let's Go series, and so forth. (See the *Resource Guide* for reviews of the major guidebook series for independent travelers.)

None of these series covers the entire world, but together they come close, with substantial overlap (and competition) between them. Each has a standard format, but the volumes in each series vary greatly depending on the knowledge, skills, and perspectives of the individual authors. I've found good and bad titles in each of the series I've used. Some of the same authors have written guidebooks about different places for more than one of these series. But don't buy any book just because it's part of a series. Try to talk to people who've used a recent edition of that particular volume. Keep an open mind. The best guides for some places aren't part of any series. Some are self-published by their authors, as the first titles from both Moon and Lonely Planet once were.

Don't take any guidebook or website as gospel. Each person experiences the same place differently, even if it hasn't changed—which, after all, is one of the main reasons to want to see things for yourself in the first place. You may be older or younger, richer or poorer, more or less adventurous, or simply interested in different things than the author(s) of any given book or website. Leave yourself room to form your own impressions as you travel.

Some destination guidebooks, like the Rick Steves and Let's Go guides, are updated (albeit sometimes cursorily) every year. You can usually identify these by a prominent identification of the issue year or designation of the annual edition on the cover. Such a guidebook can be expected to have been updated in the year preceding the issue date, i.e., the 2013 edition should give information accurate as of 2012.

Most Moon, Lonely Planet, and competing guidebooks to areas outside the First World are updated every two to four years. They should, but rarely do, have a prominent identification of the press date or the range of time during which the research and writing was done. Check any guidebook carefully for a line such as, "Prices given in this book are those that were in effect as of [date]," or "Research for this book was conducted during the period from [date] to [date]." Typically, you have to look closely at the copyright, publication, and edition notices to figure out when a guidebook was written and revised. Remember that a new printing does not necessarily mean any change to the text. Figure that research for a new book or edition was probably done one to two years before its publication date. Adjust your expectations of prices for inflation, exchange-rate changes, and the inevitable price increases at those establishments listed in guidebooks.

Updated does not mean fully researched or written from scratch. Hotels may be visited, or they may simply be telephoned to verify that they still exist and to get their new prices. Most general and descriptive copy—the sorts of things you read to decide where to go, as opposed to where exactly to stay once you get there—stays the same from one edition to the next.

The thicker and weightier the book, the harder it is for an updater to check every detail for each new edition. A provincial town may be added to a guidebook because a writer happened to visit it on one research trip. If it's days off the usual travel routes, and not especially recommended or interesting, it may not be visited again for two or three editions. It's quite possible to find that the isolated beach was ruined by an oil spill, or the cheap hotel was demolished to make room for a soot-belching factory, five years before the current edition of your guidebook was printed.

Some publishers and authors keep descriptions of war zones and otherwise off-limits areas as they were when it was last possible for foreigners to visit them, even when these descriptions are long out of date. Such information is better than nothing, but only if its nature is clearly identified, which it isn't always.

Locally produced guidebooks, unlike local language texts, are rarely of much practical use to independent budget travelers (although they may be of considerable educational value for what they reveal of how local people see foreigners). Local writers, even when they try to write for foreigners, tend to have too little perspective to realize which aspects of their ways of doing things will need explaining, or how to explain them in terms that will be familiar to audiences in the United States or Europe.

Those people in most Second, Third, and Fourth World countries who write well enough in English and who are sufficiently conversant with U.S. or European ways to be capable of writing a practical guide for foreign visitors are precisely those who have the sorts of skills and privileges that enable them to leave their homeland to make more money elsewhere. The dearth of good locally published guidebooks is a symptom of the "brain drain."

Locally produced cultural and artistic guidebooks are often more helpful, particularly in regions whose art and culture are little noticed in the United

States. Where they can be found in English or another language I can read, I find newspapers, magazines, popular novels, and even textbooks intended for local audiences to be, on the whole, better guides to the local culture, issues, mindset, and worldview than anything written for, much less by, foreigners.

MAPS

Finding maps locally is hit or miss, with little rhyme or reason to how useful or easy to find they will be. Online maps are useful only when you can get online (Internet access from your cell phone or PDA is apt to be prohibitively expensive outside your home country) and have access to a high-quality printer (you can't always predict in advance what portion of an online map, or at what scale, you will need) or have your device out and on (and at risk of snatch theft and/or breakage) when you need to consult a map.

I recommend bringing with you whatever (printed) maps you think are essential, particularly large-scale maps of countries and regions and any specialized maps you'll need for trekking or the like. I bring the best maps I can find, regardless of expense, and I've never regretted it. I've often been the envy of other travelers for having better maps than anything in their guidebooks or available locally. If I don't have enough space in my luggage for both, I'll usually bring a set of good maps in preference to a guidebook.

Within cities, you can probably get by on the maps included in a Moon Handbook or Lonely Planet guidebook, with some help, especially on transit routes, from whatever city map you can find locally. Government and transit maps are usually better than so-called "Tourist Maps." The former can be superb (e.g., in China and

REAL LIFE

Coming back through the desert from a day at the beach to the city of Doha, Qatar, we got lost at dusk in a sandstorm in a maze of half-built highways through a seemingly endless construction zone with nobody else in sight. (All of Doha is a construction zone, and is likely to remain so at least until Qatar hosts the 2022 soccer World Cup in an array of new stadiums, training grounds, team housing, hotels, and other facilities, none of which existed when the venue was chosen in 2010.) Grateful to have a vehicle with a GPS, our host switched it on, and it told us what to do: "Go one kilometer. Make a U-turn. Go one kilometer. Make a U-turn. Go one kilometer. . . ." We'd still be driving in endless circles if we'd relied on the GPS. Instead, after a couple of laps we turned at right angles and drove a compass course in a random direction until we crossed a road we recognized.

in many major Latin American cities). The latter tend to have pictures of tourist attractions rather than any useful detail, and to be carefully designed to limit their coverage to the areas most visited by tourists. Good maps of larger regions are usually harder to find locally than good city maps.

If you want to get off the standard tourist track, you need to go to places that aren't mentioned in guidebooks. For that you'll want a good map—one that's not designed for tourists, and not limited to tourist districts or destinations. Practice comparing what you see on maps with what you see "on the ground." Learn to read maps like a geographer, sociologist, or intelligence analyst, and a good map will indicate not just how to get to a known place, but what you are likely to find in a neighborhood or region that you don't know anything about except what is shown on the map.

Maps of most of the world are substantially harder to find in the United States than are guidebooks to the same places. If you can't find the maps you want locally, check the *Logistics* section of the *Resource Guide* for listings of specialized map stores in the United States and the U.K. with comprehensive catalogs and worldwide mail-order services.

COMMUNICATION
Languages

Most people traveling around the world, or to any large number of places, don't stay in one region long enough to learn very much of any language they didn't already know. You can probably get around most big cities with only English. You'll probably need at least some French in parts of Africa, some Spanish in Central and South America (or Portuguese in Brazil), and some Russian anywhere in the former USSR, but even that isn't essential.

Even a few words of another language, however, will not only make life much easier but open a remarkable number of doors that you would otherwise never even have known existed. Even the slightest knowledge of the local language (or even of another foreign language) can be surprisingly useful and sometimes essential. (See the sidebar *Most Useful Languages for World Travel.*) And you're far more likely to inadvertently patronize or offend those with whom you have no common language. If you learn nothing else, learn how to say, "Hello," "Thank you," "Please," and "I'm sorry." Once you get those key words and phrases down, try to learn your first complete sentences in the local language: "I'm sorry, but I don't speak _____. Do you speak English, please?" Don't expect people to speak English to you automatically, just because you're a foreigner.

DOESN'T EVERYONE SPEAK ENGLISH?

It's a common axiom that, "These days, everyone speaks English," and there's a certain truth to it. No language is as widely studied as English, and no one

Going Out of the Way to Help

You don't have to have a language in common for someone to help you.

We were studying our map in Urumchi, East Turkestan, trying to figure out the way back to our hotel, when a smiling Chinese soldier (in a uniform accessorized with a pearly necklace and a lace-frilled blouse) came up to us, obviously offering to help. She spoke no English, and we spoke no Chinese. She gestured to the map. We pointed to our hotel on the map. She led us to the bus stop, waited with us for the proper bus, led us on, bought us tickets, rode with us, led us off the bus at the proper stop, and marched us up to the entrance of the department store next to our hotel!

It took us a moment to realize that she must have thought we were pointing at the store on the map. A finger is an imprecise pointer, and it was a very precise Chinese map. Now she was waiting for us to let her know what we wanted to buy. She may have been part of a foreign army of occupation, but she had gone out of her way to "Serve the People" by helping us, and we couldn't just walk off to our hotel. She would think us ungrateful and probably never help a lost tourist again. We hastily thought of something we could buy (fabric and thread to sew up a package we were about to send home), and communicated it to her (with pantomime of sewing). She led us to the sewing notions counter, bowed, turned, and went away beaming at her good deed. Having preserved her face, we bought our sewing things and continued on to our hotel.

monolingual in any other language would have nearly as easy a time traveling around the world as a monolingual English speaker.

But most people in the world—even in places where English is the official "national" language—don't speak English. India, for example, is commonly, and correctly, cited as a country where it's easy to get around with only English. But only a few percent of Indians speak English. Fewer are actually fluent, though there are still more English speakers and a larger English-language publishing industry in India than in, say, Canada. South Asian English is as distinct and as "legitimate" a dialect of English as is, say, Kiwi or Australian.

Most Useful Languages in World Travel

Certainly the most useful language to know, if you want to travel to a wide variety of countries around the world, is English. There are few large cities or heavily touristed places anywhere in the world where you can't find some people who speak at least a little basic tourist English.

There are places where no one speaks any language except the local one(s), but it's possible to communicate basic travel needs ("food," "toilet," "place to sleep," "transport to the place I'm pointing to on this map") with no mutual language at all. A well-designed set of pictographs helps; the best are the laminated Kwikpoint cards (see the *Resource Guide*). You'll get more out of a visit if you know a language understood by at least some of the locals, but not knowing any locally understood language shouldn't stand in the way of going wherever you really want to go.

That said, the most useful languages for world travelers who are already fluent and literate in English are those that are used by at least a significant subset of the people throughout a large area where English isn't widely used.

Depending on the region of the world in which you are most interested (and leaving aside the varying difficulty of learning different languages), that would include:

- Spanish (useful throughout Latin America — even in Brazil, spoken Spanish is widely understood, and knowledge of written Spanish is adequate for understanding much written Portuguese.)

English is not an easy language to learn as a second language. It has an unusually large vocabulary in common usage, unusually many irregularities, words and pronunciations borrowed and derived from an unusually wide range of other source languages, and almost no standards of spelling whatsoever. We who are native speakers are lucky. Be considerate of those who are not. Use plain, simple language and common, unambiguous words. Don't use slang, unobvious idioms, or (except in a technical context) jargon. For some basic tips and pitfalls to avoid when you are trying to communicate in English with nonnative speakers or use foreign-language websites, see the sidebars *The Web Really Is Worldwide* and *Using Foreign Websites*.

SEPARATED BY A COMMON LANGUAGE

Americans should know that, despite the increasing use of American English as the standard language of international business (and an increasing effort by students of English as a foreign language to learn American pronunciation

- Mandarin Chinese (useful throughout East Asia, and to a lesser degree in many other places)

- Arabic (used as a second language by the literate classes throughout the Islamic world, even where Arabic isn't the primary language)

- French (mainly useful in North, West, and Central Africa, but losing ground to English; a good complement to English because English is especially disfavored in the Francophonie, and few speakers of French as a second language also speak English — people usually learn one or the other but not both.)

- Russian (English is not widely spoken in the former USSR, and some people speak Russian in surprisingly many other places.)

Other less widely useful possibilities (either languages that are less widely spoken, or spoken in places where English is more common, so another language is less necessary) would include:

- Hindi or Urdu (useful in a large region of South Asia, but in most of that region it's relatively easy to get around in English.)

- Swahili (East and Central Africa)

- German (the lingua franca and a common second language in much of Central Europe, and continuing to displace Russian in that role; also the most widely spoken foreign language, rivaling English, in Turkey and some other countries)

and slang), British English is the international standard of written and spoken English, and that which you are most likely to encounter anywhere outside the Americas. If American travelers encounter English words or phrases that seem strange (such as "WC," "paraffin lamp," or "torch"), they should consider the possible British meanings for those words (such as "toilet," "kerosene lamp," "flashlight" for the examples above). Try to avoid using expressions whose meaning depends on whether they are interpreted as British or American—or are specific to any other English dialect, for that matter, such as those discussed by Braj Kachru in *The Other Tongue: English Across Cultures.*

MAKE AN EFFORT

Even if you don't learn more than a few words, it's worth making whatever effort you can to learn the rudiments of any language widely spoken anywhere that you'll be for more than a few weeks. Don't be afraid to fail, to mispronounce, or to mangle the language. You are certain to be better received even if you try and

REAL LIFE

In Bolivia, we spent three days on a jeep tour through the Atacama Desert. Our driver was a native speaker of Aymara. Our cook, his wife, was a native speaker of Quechua. They spoke to each other in their mutual second language, Spanish. Neither of them spoke a third language. The other tourists in the group were two couples from Brazil, only one of whom spoke English well and one of whom spoke no English at all. Our only common language was Spanish, which we all spoke at least a little, although it was none of our native languages.

fail to communicate in a locally used language, than if you make no attempt at all to communicate in any language other than English. Perhaps surprisingly, even your crudest efforts will be especially appreciated by those who are proudest of their language.

The key elements in learning a new language, communicating with limited common language, and communicating nonverbally are a lack of inhibitions and a willingness to try, to make mistakes, and at times to fail completely. You have to accept that you will sometimes make a fool of yourself or come across as a churl, even when you get your message across. People who restrict themselves to saying what they are confident they can say properly say much less and learn languages more slowly.

In a pinch, try any and every language you know. You'll be surprised how often you'll find someone who knows the same foreign language as you, in a place you would never have expected and where it's no one's native language. A common language need not be anyone's first language and often isn't.

LANGUAGE LEARNING MATERIALS

Other than online, it can be difficult to find classes or textbooks in the United States for some major regional languages such as Arabic or Swahili. Fortunately for English speakers, textbooks, dictionaries, and phrasebooks for students of English are produced in virtually every country and language of the world.

These materials are intended for people who already know the local language(s) and are trying to learn English, not vice versa, and are often of poor quality. But they are usually cheap, readily available, and far better than no dictionary or phrasebook at all. The choices of words, phrases, and expressions for translation can also be a good introduction to the concepts that are considered important in the local culture.

In some multilingual countries and regions where English is used as a link language, one can even find textbooks for locals intended to teach local and regional languages through the medium of English. This is especially true in India, where no one language is spoken by a majority of the people and

English is the second language of most university-educated people. Rather than separate texts for learning, say, Hindi, for speakers of Tamil or Telugu, one is likely to find "Learn Hindi through English" texts for use by people from throughout the country.

If you can't read or pronounce the local language, you can still point to the group of characters alongside the English word or phrase you want to communicate in a phrasebook or bilingual dictionary. Someone who can't speak or read any English can reply by looking up an answer in the other half of the book (assuming it's a bidirectional dictionary or phrase book—some aren't), then pointing at the English alongside it. In a country like China with widespread literacy, you can carry on a surprisingly complex, if slow, exchange this way.

If you have time to study a language before you leave, the best way to develop or improve your conversational ability is through practice. People all over the world want to learn English. Through language exchange websites, you can find an Internet "pen-pal" who speaks the language you want to learn and who will trade email correspondence or instant-messaging and conversation practice in their language for the same with you in English. Everything is negotiable, but the most common pattern is to arrange a weekly schedule of Skype or other VoIP calls, divided equally (once you both have at least minimal ability to communicate in the other's language) between the languages each of you is trying to learn.

If you both have webcams and adequate bandwidth for video calls, you can explain your words with gestures and "show and tell," which are especially helpful for beginners. If all goes well, language exchange partners often end up meeting in person when one of them travels to the other's country.

NONVERBAL COMMUNICATION

Sign language, gestures, and onomatopoetic sounds have limited utility in the *total* absence of common spoken or written language. They can, however, enormously extend the communicative value of even a few words of a common language. Play "Charades" with your traveling companions before you leave, or in waiting rooms or

REAL LIFE

Hotel reservation websites are most useful in places where the language is written in a completely different writing system like Chinese or Arabic, so you can't even recognize names on signs. If you book a hotel through the English-language version of a Chinese website like Ctrip.com or eLong.net, you get a bilingual confirmation that includes the name and address of the hotel in Chinese to show to taxi drivers or passers-by, so they can take you there or point you in the right direction even if they speak no English and you no Chinese.

on boring journeys, to improve your ability to get across essential travel concepts ("Where is the toilet?" and the like) nonverbally. Several companies (see the *Resource Guide*) make laminated pocket cards with "vocabularies" of simple pictograms to illustrate common travel concepts (train station, toilet, doctor, etc.). These can be surprisingly useful as aids to nonverbal communication.

Some things need no words: anyone walking into a hotel with luggage is presumed to want a room; anyone walking into a restaurant is presumed to want a meal; anyone walking into a depot is presumed to want to buy a ticket or board a bus or train to somewhere; anyone studying a map is presumed to be trying to get to the place they point to on the map; and nothing more need be said for most people to make an effort to help you.

LANGUAGE ETIQUETTE

Be considerate of the effort people are making to understand and assist you. If you don't speak a word of their language, it's your fault, not theirs, if they understand your language imperfectly. If you walk into a restaurant, can't read the menu, and are brought a meal, you are obligated to pay for it (and to make at least a show of eating it) even if you find it inedible. Never mind that it wasn't what you thought you were signing that you wanted and that you think it overpriced. They are more likely to have tried to accommodate a distinguished guest by serving you a local delicacy (albeit perhaps one that is expensive and an "acquired taste") rather than to have intended to turn your stomach or overcharge you.

It's sometimes rude to accept a pro forma ritual offer of hospitality, but in general it's safer to take offers of assistance at face value and to assume that to refuse them will be taken as a sign of hostility. Saying "No" can make the one offering lose face and should be done as tactfully as possible.

REAL LIFE

I've done better in some other alphabets. I can mostly sound out Cyrillic or Greek, for example. But on multiple visits to different regions of China over the course of 20 years, I've only learned to distinguish two characters: the ones for "Men" and Women" on the doors to toilets.

Alphabets

If you'll be spending much time in a place with a different alphabet, it's worth learning the letters of the local alphabet to sound out signs, place-names, etc., written in Cyrillic, Greek, or whatever, even if you don't learn to read or speak the language (see the *Alphabet Table*). Aside from the virtue of being able to use a map in the local language, once you can sound them out, many common words in Russian

The Web Really is Worldwide

They don't call it the "World Wide Web" for nothing. Most Internet users are in countries outside the United States, and the percentage of all Internet users who are in the United States continues to decline as more of the rest of the world gets online. Here are some tips for interpreting information from other countries and making your messages and postings comprehensible to people in other countries.

- Never assume anything about where a person or website is located, unless they tell you explicitly. Most email addresses and URLs are ".com" addresses that could be anywhere in the world. Even in national top-level domains, it's common to have an email address or URL associated with a different country than where a person or business is actually located. When in doubt, ask.

- Respect nonnative speakers of English. If they've learned your language better than you've learned theirs, or you haven't learned theirs at all, they've come more than halfway to meet you. Make every effort to try to be understood and to understand. Be tolerant of their mistakes.

- Avoid abbreviations and acronyms. You'd be surprised how often an abbreviation or acronym has more than one usage.

- Avoid using words that have different meanings in different variants of English (U.S. English, British English, South Asian English, etc.). Avoid sports or other metaphors specific to particular cultures. Avoid slang. Use simple, unambiguous language.

- Identify jokes and attempts at humor with "<joke>" or some similar, explicit label. Humor is hard to translate, and a misunderstood joke may offend or confuse the reader.

- Specify times of the day in military time ("09:00–17:00", not "9–5", "9 A.M.– 5 P.M."). Outside the United States, all timetables are in 24-hour time. "A.M." and "P.M." are rarely used, and the abbreviations for them vary. If you have any doubt whatsoever whether someone is using 12 or 24-hour time, ask.

- Specify time zones (important if you are trying to arrange a voice phone call) by the name of the largest or best-known city in that time zone, not by time zone name or abbreviation. Locally-used time zone abbreviations like "ET," "EST," or "PDT" are not internationally standardized nor recognized. Does "Central Time" mean Central North American Time, Central European Time, or Central Australian Time? "Chicago time" leaves no ambiguity.

(continues on next page)

The Web Really is Worldwide *(continued)*

- Never write a date in numbers only. Always spell out the name of the month. In most of the world, "8/6/2015" means "8 June 2015." In the United States, it usually means "August 6, 2015". If you write a date in numbers, no one can tell which you mean.

- Whenever possible, specify precise dates (month, day, and year). Usages like "this week," "Tuesday next," "the third week in November," or "this coming July" can often be misunderstood (especially by nonnative speakers of English) as meaning the day, week, or month before or after what you intended. In different places and cultures the week is considered to begin on Friday, Saturday, Sunday, or Monday. Instead, say, "July 2013," "the week of 16–22 November 2014," etc.

- Always specify all units of measurement. If you're comfortable with them, use metric units whenever possible. Everyone in the world outside the United States uses metric units except when dealing with people from the United States who don't understand the metric system. If you must use U.S. units (feet, miles, gallons, degrees Fahrenheit, etc.), it's imperative always to specify what units you're using. Confusion is especially likely to result when you're talking about temperature, since the temperature units in both Celsius and Fahrenheit are called "degrees" and have the same abbreviation, even though they are completely different.

- Always specify the currency you are using whenever you mention any prices. Using "dollar" or "$" without specifying which country's dollar you are referring to, or assuming that "dollar" always means "U.S. Dollar," is perhaps the most common "ugly Americanism" of Internet usage. It leaves everyone uncertain of your meaning, confuses most readers, and annoys even those who guess correctly what you mean — especially people from countries whose currencies are also called "dollars." Similarly, "rupees" can mean Indian Rupees, Pakistani Rupees, Nepalese Rupees, Sri Lankan Rupees, Mauritian Rupees, and so forth. If prices are listed in "dollars" or with merely a dollar sign, double-check what currency they mean, to avoid unpleasant surprises when you get the bill.

  If you know them, and can use them correctly, the three-letter International Standards Organization currency codes such as "USD," "CAD," "GBP," "INR," "JPY," and so forth are the best choice. These are specified in ISO

Standard 4217, and can be found on most currency-exchange websites. If you don't know the ISO 4217 currency code, spell out both the country and currency name. The only acceptable, widely recognized non-ISO currency abbreviations are "US$," "C$," "A$," "NZ$," and "S$," but even for these the ISO abbreviations are preferred in global usage.

- Write telephone and fax numbers, including those in the United States, in the complete international "plus" format, including the country code as well as the area code or city code. Be prepared to do some detective work to figure out how to call numbers in other countries. Phone numbers on websites are likely to be specified as dialed from within the country, not as dialed from abroad. Worse, they may be "toll-free" numbers (like 800 numbers in the United States) that can't readily be dialed from other countries, forcing you to dig through the website to find another phone number you can call from abroad.

- Specify the country whenever you are talking about a place. Don't assume people will deduce correctly from the context whether you mean San Jose, California, United States, or San Jose, Costa Rica. Just because you've only heard of one city or town with that name doesn't mean there isn't another in the same or a different country. Careless people have been known to buy a cheap ticket to "Sydney" only to find themselves on a plane to Sydney, Nova Scotia, Canada, rather than Sydney, NSW, Australia!

- Never underestimate the potential for misunderstanding, either by yourself or by others. Don't guess what someone means, or what they think you mean. If you have the least doubt, ask.

and Greek are obviously recognizable cognates of their English equivalents. At first glance, this may look like a formidable task, but it actually takes only a few days for most people to be able to recognize Greek or Cyrillic. Hindi or Hebrew is harder; more difficult still are scripts like Arabic (and related scripts used for Persian, Urdu, etc.), in which the ligatures make it harder for novices to distinguish the individual letters and there are fewer cognates with English.

You need different coping and navigation strategies in a place where you can't recognize what the signs say than in a place where, even if you don't know what they mean, you can still recognize what the words are and maybe even how they are pronounced. I can pick out the name of my destination from those written in Turkish (in the Latin alphabet) on a departure board or on signs on a row of buses, but not if the place-names are written in Arabic, Urdu, or Chinese. In

Alphabet Table

Hebrew		
א	aleph	'
ב	beth	b, bh
ג	gimel	g, gh
ד	daleth	d, dh
ה	he	h
ו	waw	w
ז	zayin	z
ח	heth	ḥ
ט	teth	ṭ
י	yodh	y
כ	kaph	k, kh
ל	lamedh	l
מ	mem	m
נ	nun	n
ס	samekh	s
ע	ayin	'
פ	pe	p, ph
צ	sadhe	ṣ
ק	qoph	q
ר	resh	r
שׂ	sin	ś
שׁ	shin	sh
ת	taw	t, th

Greek		
Α α	alpha	a
Β β	beta	b
Γ γ	gamma	g, n
Δ δ	delta	d
Ε ε	epsilon	a
Ζ ζ	zeta	z
Η η	eta	ē
Θ θ	theta	th
Ι ι	iota	i
Κ κ	kappa	k
Λ λ	lambda	l
Μ μ	mu	m
Ν ν	nu	n
Ξ ξ	xi	x
Ο ο	omicron	o
Π π	pi	p
Ρ ρ	rho	r, rh
Σ σ	sigma	s
Τ τ	tau	t
Υ υ	upsilon	y, u
Φ φ	phi	ph
Χ χ	chi	ch
Ψ ψ	psi	ps
Ω ω	omega	ō

Cyrillic		
А а		a
Б б		b
В в		v
Г г		g
Д д		d
Е е		e
Ж ж		zh
З з		z
И и, Й й		i, ī
К к		k
Л л		l
М м		m
Н н		n
О о		o
П п		p
Р р		r
С с		s
Т т		t
У у		u
Ф ф		f
Х х		kh
Ц ц		ts
Ч ч		ch
Ш ш		sh
Щ щ		shch
Ъ ъ	hard sign, silent	
Ы ы		y
Ь ь	soft sign, silent	
Э э		e
Ю ю		yu
Я я		ya

The letters in the right-hand columns are approximate English phonetic equivalents of the foreign letters in the left column. The alternate forms of various letters are dependent on where the letter falls in a given word.

places where I'm completely illiterate, I always carry a pad and pencil, and I try to find someone bilingual to write down the address or name of the place I want to go to (and maybe a description of what I want there) in the local language. If I'm going to the bus station to buy a ticket to Aleppo, I'll ask someone at the hotel or in the bazaar who speaks a little English to write the address or name of the long-distance bus station on one sheet to show a taxi driver or passer-by to get me there, and "I want a one-way ticket to Aleppo on 12 November" on another to show the clerk at the ticket window when I get there. And I always carry a card (well hidden, since I'll need it if I'm robbed or pickpocketed) with the name, address, and telephone number of the place I'm staying, written in the local language, to get me back there if I get lost.

Units of Measurement

Every country except the United States (and some colonies and "possessions" of the United States) uses the metric system of units. Americans who want to travel abroad must learn to deal with metric units. You can get tables of equivalents and calculators with conversion programs, but in the long run it's better to learn to think and make mental estimates of quantities directly in metric units, without having to convert them to U.S. units. That way it's more likely that it will be intuitively obvious in what units signs or prices are posted, and you'll be more likely to recognize if you're being short-weighed or otherwise cheated.

Outside the United States, all signage can be presumed to be in metric units. Which metric unit may not be posted, or may be in a language you don't understand, but if you can think in metric you should be able to tell from the approximate magnitude whether, for example, the distance on a road sign is in meters or kilometers, or a price is per gram or kilogram. It seems to be particularly difficult to learn to think in a different temperature scale, and Americans abroad may need to remind themselves repeatedly that temperatures everywhere else are given in degrees Celsius (also called Centigrade), not Fahrenheit.

Nonstandard units are sometimes used, particularly for foodstuffs and other commodities in local markets. Good guidebooks will sometimes tip you off to this. Prices in such cases are usually negotiable, anyway, and if you are in doubt you can usually get the quantity you are haggling over measured out for inspection before you agree on a price. Sometimes not, and every practiced traveler has been known to buy more than they could possibly use of something, and on some other occasion to get only a tenth of what they expected for the price, as a result of confusion of units. Take it in stride; consider it part of the price of your education in local customs.

People in other countries, especially those who have visited the United States and had to deal with U.S. units, sometimes remember to do visitors the favor of reminding them that they are using metric units. Foreigners in the United States can expect no such consideration. Most native-born U.S. citizens have never traveled abroad, are barely aware that the internationally standard metric system exists, or regard the metric system as an exotic foreign curiosity. They certainly won't call your attention to the fact that they are using nonstandard units, because in their minds they are using the only standard units they know. In the United States, "How much is that in kilos?," "How far is that in kilometers?," or "How hot or cold is that in Celsius?" will get you either blank looks or completely wrong guesses.

Visitors to the United States may chafe at having to learn an absurdly complex set of units that they will need to know nowhere else, but there is no real alternative. See the *Conversions Tables* at the back of the book for a guide to the meaning of U.S. units of measure in standard (metric) terms.

Don't trust people who try to do conversions for you, because they frequently get them wrong. ("Let's see: is a pound about 450 grams, or is it 4.5 kilos?") U.S. units are far too confusing for most people who didn't grow up with them to keep straight. Ask people to state quantities and measurements in units to which *they* are accustomed, and either learn to think in those units yourself or do your own conversions.

In the United States, quantities of many foods used in cooking are specified by volume. This is true even of dry solid foods that are sold by weight, not by volume! However, many U.S. kitchens have no scale. In the rest of the world, cooks measure most such foods by weight, and every kitchen has a cooking scale (metric, of course). It can be difficult to figure out volumetric equivalents for weights of foods. So if you bring a cookbook back to the United States from abroad, it will have instructions like, "start with 200 g of flour." You'll need to get a digital scale that can be switched to metric units to use a foreign cookbook in the United States. The same is true in reverse. If you want to be able to use U.S. recipes anywhere else, you'll need a set of volumetric measures (measuring cups and spoons) and, if they aren't graduated in U.S. units, appropriate volumetric conversion tables for tablespoons to cubic centimeters and the like.

Times and Dates

TIME

Everywhere except the United States, all tickets, timetables, public notices, and signage are in 24-hour time. There is no ambiguity. If your ticket reads "0600," you are scheduled to leave at 6 A.M. If it reads "1800," you are scheduled to leave at 6 P.M. If you see "10:00–16:00," "1000–1600," or simply "10–16" as the only numbers on a sign in a language you don't understand in front of a museum, it's a safe bet that it's open 10 A.M.–4 P.M.

In the United States, 24-hour time is used only in the military and is popularly referred to as "military time." Official notices, posted hours of open-ing and closing, and even transportation tickets, schedules, and timetables are invariably in 12-hour time. Sometimes "A.M." or "P.M." are spelled out, but in common usage they are often left implicit. Only by knowing the context, and the cultural norms, can you tell if "Open 8–3" means 20:00–03:00 (as it might for a nightclub) or 08:00–15:00 (as it might for a shop). For a restaurant, it might mean either, depending on the clientele.

On tickets and in timetables "A.M." is sometimes shortened to "A" and "P.M." to "P." Often a less obvious, more ambiguous code is used, such as printing "A.M." times in medium-weight roman type and "P.M." times in italic or boldface type, or vice versa, or printing one or the other in parentheses or in a different color. There is no standard. In the United States, it is imperative always to ask whether times are A.M. or P.M. In U.S. usage, "7 o'clock" is just as likely to mean 7 P.M. (19:00) as 7 A.M. Many visitors miss planes, trains, buses, and appointments, or show up 12 hours early for them, by erroneously assum-ing that hours less than 12 are before noon (A.M.), or by confusing or failing to recognize the codes used in a particular timetable for "A.M." and "P.M."

If you have a flight, train, bus, or ferry to catch after midnight, do your-self a favor and write it in your calendar for the previous day: "Be at the airport at 2300 (11 P.M.) on June 17th," rather than "Flight leaves at 0200 (2 A.M.) on June 18th." It won't do any good to get up in the morning, look at your itiner-ary, and realize that your plane left without you several hours before.

Official schedules everywhere use the same clock. But local people may spec-ify times in other ways. Is an invitation for an "evening" meal for 1800 (as it might be in the U.S. Midwest) or for 2200 (as it might be in Spain or Argentina)? Until you've been in a place long enough to figure out its customs, you have to ask.

Other than U.S. 12-hour A.M.–P.M. time, the time system that causes the most confusion for visitors is used in much of East Africa, and is variously re-ferred to as "Swahili Time," "Ethiopian Time," or "East African Time." This sys-tem divides the day and night into 24 hours, but starts from "zero hour" at sun-rise and sunset at what we would call 0600 (6 A.M.) and 1800 (6 A.M.). "2 o'clock in the morning" in Zanzibar is what we would call 0800 (8 A.M.). "9 o'clock in the afternoon" in Addis Ababa is what we would call 1500 (3 P.M.). And if the long-distance bus leaves for Nairobi at "11 o'clock at night," that means it leaves before dawn at 0500 (5 A.M.). East Africans think in this system. You can't tell when they are converting into "your" time, and when they do they often make mistakes. So you always have to ask, "African time or European time?"

CALENDARS AND DATES

The Christian calendar is used for schedules and most business purposes every-where in the world, even in non-Christian regions where a different calendar is used for religious purposes. Aside from knowing when holidays will be, it's rarely necessary to know what year, month, or day it is in any but the Christian calendar. The largest exception is the month of Ramadan, during which observant Muslims fast from dawn to dusk. Exceptions are made for travelers, but travel anywhere in the Islamic world is different—and usually more difficult—during Ramadan.

In the United States, the month is usually given first, followed by the date: "August 2nd," "August 2nd, 2009," or "8/2/09." In most of the rest of the world, and invariably in international usage, the date precedes the month: "2 August," "2 August 2009," "2/8/09," or "2-VIII-09." To further complicate matters, many foreigners convert their dates to the U.S. format when communicating with people in or from the United States. So there is no way to be sure whether "11/6/08" means November 6, 2008 (the most likely meaning in the Unites States) or 11 June 2008 (the likely, but not certain, meaning in the rest of the world). Because of the inherent ambiguity of such usage, months should never be written or abbreviated in numbers. Always write out, or abbreviate, the name of the month in letters.

Because all international airline tickets are written in English, any travel agent or airline employee must know how to recognize the date format used on tickets, in which the name of the month in English is truncated after the first three letters: "02AUG09," "06NOV08," "11JUN10." This is a good form to use when, for example, you are sending an email message to request a reservation at a hotel where you aren't sure whether, or how well, anyone speaks English, or when writing down a reservation request to give to a booking clerk at a train station with whom you have no common language.

Most printed representations of the Christian calendar in any language follow a common format, with each week as a horizontal row, starting with Sundays (most English-speaking countries) or Mondays (France and the Francophonie) as the left-hand column and the days of the month arranged from left to right and then top to bottom. The exception is in the former USSR and some other places formerly in the Soviet "bloc" or sphere of influence. On Russian calendars, each week is a vertical column, starting with Mondays as the top row, and the days are ordered first from top to bottom and then left to right. The difference sounds simple, but it's harder to get used to than you might think.

Weekly schedules are largely determined by the dominant religion. In Christian countries most offices and some shops are closed on Sundays, sometimes also on Saturdays. In Islamic countries most offices and shops, depending on the orthodoxy of the country and the proprietor, are closed on Fridays, sometimes also on Thursday afternoons. Orthodox Jews in all countries close their businesses from well before sunset Friday to sunset Saturday. Some businesses in Israel are required to close during those hours; Israel's national airline, El Al, grounds its entire fleet of aircraft during those hours, considerably complicating its scheduling and raising its costs. The hegemony of Christianity is such that most countries that are neither Christian, Muslim, nor Jewish not only use the Christian calendar but, for those who get a day of rest, some version of the Christian workweek.

> ## REAL LIFE
>
> You can tell which way to enter the date on a website, even if the months are named in an unknown language, by which field has 12 choices in the drop-down menu (month) and which has 28–31 choices (day of the month).

Daily business, office, shop, and restaurant hours vary more from establishment to establishment than from country to country. Government offices may have standard hours nationwide, and it can be helpful to know whether most people take a nap after lunch or eat dinner especially early or late by the norm of your own country. But you can't assume too much about any particular business's hours of operation just because a guidebook tells you that "Most businesses are open 09:00–17:00." If you are planning to be in a city for only a few days and will need to deal with a particular business or office, call ahead (or have someone, such as the hotel concierge, call ahead for you if you don't speak the language) to verify its days and hours, even if you have a guidebook that lists the hours of the specific office, as these things do change from time to time.

Numbers

Except for nonmetric U.S. units of measurement, only one number system (the base 10 place-value system) is in common use everywhere, and there is a tendency to think of numbers as universal and invariant. Forms of written and other symbolic representations of numbers, however, vary more widely than most people realize. In different places numbers may be communicated by at least two distinct sets of finger signs, calculator displays, two important forms of written numerals, and three major types of abacus.

FINGER SIGNS

Whole numbers up to 10 are often indicated with the fingers. This is the normal way of indicating how many items you want to buy if you don't speak a common language. For larger numbers or negotiating prices, which usually involves numbers of more than one digit, you'll need something more sophisticated.

Europeans and Americans raise a number of fingers, on one or both hands, corresponding to the number they want to indicate. Many gestures with upraised fingers are obscene in one place or another, and pointing at people is often thought of as rude and/or insulting. Be alert to how people react, and stop using a gesture immediately if it appears to give offense. Consult a local person if some gesture keeps being misunderstood or taken unkindly.

There are standard one-handed Chinese signs corresponding to each digit up through 10. These are so taken for granted in China (representing up to a sixth of the world's population, after all) that it is hard for many Chinese people to believe that foreigners don't understand them. It is as difficult for many people in China to recognize that a foreigner holding up fingers on both hands might mean "seven" as it is for most foreigners to recognize that a Chinese gesture with the fingers of one hand might mean "seven." Pointing or beckoning with raised fingers is especially rude in China, and it is best to avoid indicating numbers with your fingers unless you have learned the one-handed Chinese signs.

Russians use yet a third system: they count by curling fingers into their palm, rather than by extending fingers. If some fingers are curled in, and some extended, it's the number of curled fingers that is being indicated. It's a small conceptual shift, but surprisingly difficult to adjust to.

ELECTRONIC CALCULATORS

Electronic calculators are ubiquitous even in the Third World, and money changers and businesses that cater to foreigners around the world have calculators on which to show prices to customers who can't speak the language or read the price tags. All calculators use "European" numerals, as discussed below. The problem with relying on calculators is that if you have to be shown a price on a calculator, you will be known not to be able to read the price tags and will generally be charged more for your ignorance. To merchants, "calculator dependent" means "dupe." The ability to use any other means of communicating numbers will enable you to negotiate better prices.

WRITTEN NUMERALS

Numbers spelled out in words, or included with text, are written in as many forms of letters, numerals, characters, and scripts as are written languages. Only two forms of numerals, however, are in general use in signage, pricing, accounting, and the like.

Nomenclature poses a problem. I choose to call these two sets of digits, as represented in the adjacent chart, "European" and "Arabic" numerals, respectively, while recognizing that neither of these labels is standard. There are no standard labels.

What I refer to as "European" numerals are used in most of the world, including all of the Americas, Europe, Turkey, Oceania, and most of East Asia. These are often referred to as "Arabic" numerals, because these evolved from Indian numerals by way of Arabian numerals, and to distinguish them

Numbers Table

Printed European	Handwritten European	Arabic
0 or Ø	*0* or *ø*	•
1	*1* or *1*	١
2	*2*	٢
3	*3*	٣
4	*4*	٤
5	*5*	٥ or ٥
6	*6*	٦
7	*7* or *7*	٧
9	*8*	٨
9	*9*	٩

from "Roman" numerals. But Roman numerals are obsolete, and today the principal alternative to European numerals is a set of numerals used in Arabic. So calling the numerals used in modern European languages "Arabic" would only confuse matters.

What I refer to as "Arabic" numerals are used in some (not all) countries that write their languages, such as Persian and Urdu, in Arabic script. One scholar labels these "Eastern Arabic" numerals, while noting that Arabs refer to them as "Indian" numerals because they are closer to the original Indian forms than the alternative European forms that evolved from them. In Pakistan, Iran, and most (but not all) Arab and North African countries, the use of Arabic numerals is almost universal except on specialized signs and publications intended strictly for foreigners.

India and Israel are the principal countries in which both systems of numerals are widely used. Arabic numerals are used by Muslims and Urdu speakers in India and by Arabs in Israel. European numerals are used by Hindi speakers and most other non-Muslims in India, and by Israeli Jews. (There's another set of Hebrew numerals, but they are rarely used in commerce even in Israel.) In either country, it's a clue to the shopkeeper's religion and identity.

Several of the Arabic digits are prone to be mistaken for different

European digits. The Arabic five looks like a European zero, and the Arabic six like a European seven or one (as discussed below). If you'll be spending much time any place where Arabic script is in common use, take a little time to learn the Arabic numerals so you can read posted prices and check the addition on bills. There are minor variations in how Arabic numerals are written, but except in fancy calligraphy they are all recognizable once you've learned the basic forms.

Numbers are written the same way with either type of numerals, in base 10, place-value notation, with the least significant (smallest) digit farthest to the right. Numbers in either system are aligned vertically and added in columns.

Three of the European digits have variant forms, two of which sometimes cause confusion.

Zero is sometimes crossed, especially on computer printouts, or when it is necessary to distinguish the numeral zero from the letter O. Some people don't know what to make of a crossed zero, but no one is likely to mistake it for any other digit.

Seven and one cause problems. Europeans cross their sevens and write their ones with a bold upstroke, or exaggerated serif, to the left of the top of the main stroke. Americans don't cross their sevens and often write their ones as a single, unadorned vertical line. Americans often mistake a European one for an uncrossed seven; Europeans often mistake an American one for an uppercase letter I, or can't make anything of it at all. It's safest to cross your sevens and write your ones with a minimal but visible upstroke.

In American and British usage, a comma is used to separate each group of three digits (e.g., millions from thousands) when writing numbers larger than 1,000, and a period ("decimal point") is used to separate digits greater than one from those less than one. In Continental European usage, these are reversed: a comma is used in place of a "decimal point" and a period is used as a thousands separator. What is written in the United States as "12,345.67" would be written in France as "12.345,67."

Outside of Europe and North America, it's difficult to predict which of these styles of writing and punctuating numbers will be used. As with most such things, it depends largely on colonial history and spheres of influence. Be alert to the possibility that either style may be in use.

In South Asia, large numbers are expressed, even in English usage, in "lakhs" (hundreds of thousands) and "crore" (tens of millions), rather than in millions and billions. Commas are accordingly used to separate lakhs and crore, rather than millions and billions. What would be written elsewhere as "100,700,000" and read as "one hundred million, seven hundred thousand" would be written in South Asia as "10,07,00,000" and read as "ten crore, seven lakhs." When no units are specified, quantities expressed in lakhs and crore can be presumed to refer either to rupees (the national units of currency in India, Pakistan, Sri Lanka, and Nepal, each with a somewhat different value) or to numbers of people. The population of India, for example, is about 120 crore.

THE ABACUS

For addition and subtraction, an abacus in the hands of a skilled user is faster than any electronic calculator. The abacus remains in use, especially by older people, in China, Japan, and the former USSR and by people from these regions in other places.

It's not hard to learn how to use an abacus, and it's easier still to learn just

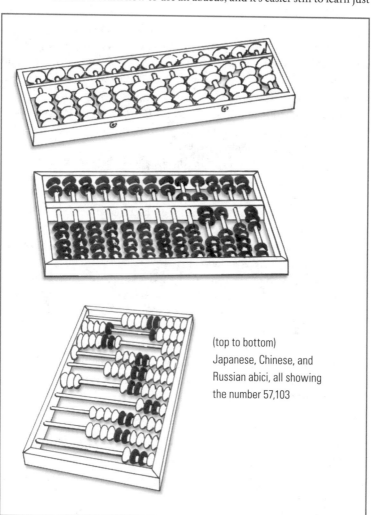

(top to bottom) Japanese, Chinese, and Russian abici, all showing the number 57,103

enough to read numbers displayed on an abacus. If you can read an abacus, you can tell how much other customers are paying even when their money changes hands too quickly for you to count it. An abacus is an ideal tool for negotiating prices, because you don't have to reenter an entire number but need only slide back and forth those of the beads that correspond to the difference between the asked and offered amounts, moving fewer and fewer beads as you approach agreement. And because, despite its ease, few foreigners learn how to read an abacus, someone who is abacus-literate will be presumed to be have some knowledge about local prices and will probably be offered a price closer to the local norm in the first place.

The Chinese and Japanese styles of abacus are fundamentally the same and are read exactly the same way. Each consists of a frame holding a row of vertical rods (most often of bamboo) divided by a horizontal bar toward the top of each rod. On each rod are sliding beads, usually of wood. The beads on each rod are used to represent one digit. The number of rods, and thus the maximum number of digits that can be represented, varies from abacus to abacus. As in writing, the least significant (smallest) digit is by convention represented on the right-hand rod, with progressively larger digits (tens, hundreds, etc.) on successive rods to the left.

On a Japanese abacus (*soroban*) there are four beads on each rod below the separator bar and one bead above it. On a Chinese abacus, there are five beads on each rod below the bar and two above it. The significant beads are those that are slid against the separator bar. Each upper bead that is moved down to the bar counts five, and each lower bead that is moved up to the bar counts one. So the digit eight is represented by sliding one bead down from the top and three up from the bottom.

The extra beads on the Chinese abacus enable one to represent numbers as high as 15 in a single column, which is useful in borrowing and carrying between columns, at intermediate stages of calculations, without having to do so in your head.

The Russian abacus (*stchety* or *schoty*, literally "counter") is oriented at right angles to the Chinese or Japanese, with the beads on horizontal rods or more often wires, usually arched upward slightly from the frame so that the beads have to be lifted over the crest of the bow to move them from one side to the other.

There is no separator bar, and there are 10 beads on each wire. Each bead that is moved to the left side of the frame counts one. The beads are usually colored in black and white, with the two center beads on each wire the opposite color from the four outer beads on either side (4–2–4), but that is just to facilitate telling, at a glance, how many beads have been moved from one side to the other. The black and white beads count the same.

The least significant (smallest) digit on a Russian abacus is represented on the lowest wire, with successively larger digits above it. Toward the bottom of the frame is a wire with only four beads (colored 1–2–1). This is not considered a digit. It acts like a comma or decimal point and is most often used in shops to separate kilos (above) from grams (below).

ORDERS OF MAGNITUDE

No matter how numbers are communicated, be aware that the units and the position of the decimal point are rarely explicit. In the United States, the same price may be written as "$15.00," "15.00," "$15," "15-," or simply "15." On a display of fabric, this would be understood to be a price per yard (of whatever width); on coffee, per pound (or perhaps per half-pound, in a specialty shop); on beer, for 6 bottles, or 12, or 24, depending on the packaging. Only someone familiar with the cultural norms of the country could tell which is implied, and even then would sometimes have to read the fine print on the price tags or ask.

If, through inflation, the fundamental unit of currency has become so small that little can be purchased for less than hundreds or thousands of currency units—as a rule of thumb, any time currency is denominated in units worth less than one U.S. cent (1¢, or US$0.01)—you can count on one or more zeros being dropped from prices in common usage. The trick is in figuring out whether a marked price of "1" means 10, 100, 1,000, or 1,000,000 currency units, something you can only learn by asking and by watching what others pay.

If you are shown a price and aren't sure how many zeroes to add or where to put the decimal point, offer the smallest amount you think it could possibly mean. If you are wrong, they'll let you know, and no real harm is done even if they act insulted. Of course, if you offer 10 times too much (not as absurd as it sounds in a new place where prices may be much less than those to which you are accustomed), they will simply nod and accept the windfall, leaving you poorer and no wiser.

REAL LIFE

The former mint in Ouro Preto, Brazil, now a museum, includes an exhibit of successively devalued coins and notes showing the stages by which, over 50 years, the unit of national currency was replaced by one 18 orders of magnitude larger, but once again having the same name. One "real" today is worth the equivalent of more than 1 followed by 18 zeros of the original "reals." At times in that process, notes were issued worth as many as 10 million of the then-current currency units.

CURRENCY UNITS

Abbreviations for currency units are not standard and are often omitted in common usage. To make matters worse, many countries have currencies with the same name, and prices for foreigners are often stated in foreign currencies. With dozens of different "dollars" in use in different parts of the world, but the U.S. dollar the most universally recognized currency, it can sometimes be very hard to tell if a quoted price is in U.S. dollars or local dollars (which may be worth only a fraction of a U.S. dollar).

An unambiguous set of internationally recognized two-letter country codes and three-letter currency codes has been adopted by the International Standards Organization (ISO) and should be used whenever possible. The ISO code for each country's currency consists of the two-letter code for the country followed by a third letter, usually the first letter of the name of the unit of local currency. So, for example, the United States of America is "US," and the local currency is in dollars, thus the ISO abbreviation for US dollars becomes USD. Similarly, the United Kingdom is abbreviated as "GB," and the currency is the British pound, abbreviated as "P," which yields the currency code of "GBP." Some are less obvious than others, and people who make up what they think to be the ISO code for a currency often get it wrong.

ISO country and currency codes are recognized by most travel agents and airline staff. The two-letter ISO country codes are becoming more widely known as a result of their adoption as geographic suffixes to Internet domain names everywhere except in the United States. (If someone's email address is janedoe@something.com.au, her host computer is in Australia; marysmith@something.edu.ca is an address in Canada.) Oddly, the ISO country codes are not used or recognized in postal addressing. The three-letter ISO currency codes are in common use in some places and recognized by virtually all banks and money changers. It's becoming increasingly common for banks and money changers to post exchange rates in ISO codes rather than abbreviations or symbols like "$," "£," or "¥," a trend I applaud.

Much (but not all!) of Europe uses the same unit of currency, the euro, ISO code "EUR." There are coins for euro cents (€0.01) and for amounts up to €2. Euro notes are the same throughout the region. Euro coins issued in different countries have different images on the back side, but you can use any euro coins or notes anywhere throughout the eurozone. As of 2011, major Western European countries not (yet) in the eurozone include the U.K., Switzerland, Norway, Sweden, and Denmark. (For more on which currency to carry cash in, and other questions about money, see the next chapter, *The Bottom Line*.)

KEEPING IN TOUCH

It's nice to get messages from home, and from time to time it's essential for travelers to contact people back home, or vice versa: to take care of business, deal with the unexpected, or pass on important news. Communicating on the road is getting easier all the time, but it still has its pitfalls. Here are some suggestions for using the Internet, phone, fax, and postal mail to stay in touch and take care of business without breaking the bank.

Internet Access

The Internet is the primary means of communication for international travelers. Email is cheap, fast, allows both parties to ignore time differences, and is available almost anywhere there are power and phone lines. In places with adequate bandwidth, voice-over-Internet (VoIP) phone services like Skype are usually the cheapest way to phone home.

WAYS TO GET ONLINE

Regardless of whether you want to get online to browse the Web, send and receive email, or make VoIP phone calls, there are basically three ways to do it while you are traveling:

Use Rented or Public Computers in Cybercafés, Libraries, Etc. Advantages: you don't have to bring a computer with you. The cybercafé or whatever has already

REAL LIFE

There's always a possibility that your email message might not reach its intended recipient because their system thinks the message is spam and filters it out. Resend your message, and the same thing is likely to be repeated. If you don't get an answer to an email message that calls for a response, assume that it wasn't received, and follow up with a fax or a phone call.

REAL LIFE

The Internet isn't everywhere. Almost, but not quite. Once you leave the First World, be prepared for the possibility that you might be unexpectedly offline for days or weeks. On my last trip around the world, I was in countries where Internet access was available nowhere outside the capital city, where it was so slow even in the capital that I couldn't send an email message before it timed out, where it was available only via cell phone data connection (slow and prohibitively expensive), where an entire region had lost its connection to the Internet when a fishing trawler broke a major undersea cable, and where repressive governments had shut down Internet access or set up national firewalls that blocked the websites or services I needed to use.

REAL LIFE

I've heard multiple sticker-shock horror stories from travelers who used their Blackberry or iPhone only for email and limited Web browsing, not voice calls, and ran up bills of US$10,000 or more per month in per-megabyte international data roaming charges. I know of no provider who offers unlimited worldwide voice or data roaming for a flat monthly fee. There have been some such plans in the past, but they have been terminated with little warning, leaving travelers who were relying on them in the lurch.

taken care of the Internet connection. Disadvantages: you have to find a public computer. You can only use it in that location. You might have to pay by the hour (e.g. in a cybercafé) and/or wait your turn (e.g. in a library). Public terminals are inherently insecure, and most of them are infected with viruses and malware that might also infect any flash drives, camera memory cards, etc. that you use at a public terminal.

Bring Your Own Computer, and Connect at Wi-Fi Hot Spots. Advantages: it can be secure (if you know what you are doing). You can do your reading and writing (of email messages, blog posts, etc.) offline, and only need to find a hotspot or pay to connect for long enough to send and receive. Disadvantages: you have to carry a computer, charger, cables, adapters, etc. Your computer might get lost, stolen, or broken.

Connect from a Cell Phone or Smartphone, or Use One as a Modem Tethered to Your Computer. Advantages: easy (once you get it set up and debugged). Can be secure. Available almost anywhere. Disadvantages: prohibitively expensive. Per-byte data charges, especially for international roaming, typically rule out accessing the Internet from or via a cell phone, except in emergencies. Slow connection in most places. You have to carry your own computer or be restricted to a very small screen and limited Web browser. Any cell phone, but especially a smartphone, is a magnet for pickpockets and snatch thieves. Initial setup for mobile data or tethering, either with a new device or with a new SIM card, can be difficult (more so, of course, if you are trying to activate and configure data service with a new SIM card bought in a place where you don't understand the language). Some prepaid SIM cards don't include data service at all, and it's not always easy to tell before you buy.

CYBERCAFÉS, WI-FI HOTSPOTS, AND PUBLIC INTERNET ACCESS POINTS

Cybercafés aren't just for travelers. In much of the world, cybercafés or "Internet shops" by some other name (*locutorio,* "LAN house", etc.) are the standard mode of Internet access and most people's introduction to Internet use. Why not? Most of the world's people can't afford a "personal" computer. And even for those with their own computers, Internet access from a cybercafé can be less expensive than from home, where data connections may be charged by the byte. Only in the United States is unmetered "all you can download for a fixed monthly rate" Internet access the norm.

REAL LIFE

At a coffee shop in the United States, you pay for food and drinks, and the Wi-Fi is "free." At many Internet shops in the Middle East, you pay by the hour for Internet access, and the refreshments—tea, coffee, and sweets, served at your workstation—are complementary.

Typical prices for Internet usage range from US$1 per hour in the Third World to US$5–10 per hour in the First World. Where the rates are higher, the minimum time increment usually is smaller, so even at more expensive places you can often get online for 10 minutes to check your email quickly for no more than a couple of U.S. dollars or euros.

FINDING INTERNET TERMINALS AND WI-FI HOTSPOTS

It's usually easy to find a cybercafé or Internet access point or hotspot once you arrive somewhere. Whatever they are called, they'll probably use the word "Internet" in their ads and on their signs. "Internet" seems to be the same in every language, or at least to be recognized: a foreigner saying "Internet?" and looking lost will usually be pointed in the right direction pretty quickly.

Many but not all places that have public Internet terminals also have Wi-Fi available to connect your own computer, and vice versa. A hotel that has Wi-Fi in the lobby (common) or also in the rooms (less common) probably also has one or more "courtesy" Internet terminals for guests, perhaps with a 15-minute or 30-minute time limit per user. Regardless of any official limits, don't hog the Internet if others are waiting.

Except in public facilities like libraries, or unless Wi-Fi is "free" to all customers (i.e. built into the price of food, drinks, lodging, etc.), you can expect to pay about the same amount per hour to use the Internet from your own computer over Wi-Fi as to use one of the cybercafé's computers.

In wealthier places where more people can afford their own computers, Wi-Fi hotspots are more common than public Internet terminals. In poorer places where a private computer is a greater luxury, cybercafés are more common. Within a wealthy country, the best area in which to find a cybercafé is a poor and/or transient neighborhood, such as one populated by "guest workers" who use Internet shops to keep in touch with friends and family back

REAL LIFE

Ads in the airport in Cebu, in the central Philipines, market high-speed Internet connections to Filipina mothers working abroad. Pay for broadband Internet at home for the children you are leaving behind, and with Internet video chat you can "Keep in Touch While You're on the Other Side."

home. Searches for cybercafés have led me to the Turkish quarter of Vienna, Indonesian and Filipino neighborhoods in Hong Kong, and other urban adventures.

Can't find a cybercafé? Look for a youth hostel or backpacker guesthouse, even if that's not where you want to stay. Hostelers and backpackers are a core market for cybercafés. Even if a hostel doesn't provide Internet access, they'll know where to find it (and will probably have that information posted on the hostel bulletin board). Failing that, find a library—they'll know where to find the Internet, even if they don't have their own public terminals or Wi-Fi hotspot—or ask poorer immigrant "guest workers" who seem likely to have family abroad. If you have a common language, the cleaners, maids, or security guards at a hotel, especially an upscale one in a country where wealthy people have Internet access at home and don't use cybercafés, may be more likely than the concierge to know where to find a cybercafé.

Public Internet access terminals have different roles in different places, especially where most local people don't have their own computers or don't have high-speed Internet connections. I've been in places where most local use of cybercafés is for phone calls over the Internet, and cybercafés advertise themselves primarily as call shops. In other countries, cybercafés are mostly centers for multiplayer network games, and are located and advertised as gaming parlors. (Not the quietest or calmest places to work on your journal or correspondence!)

Hotels that cater to foreign business travelers often have "business centers": miniature all-purpose service bureaus that provide faxing, photocopying, printing, Internet access, and sometimes other services such as rush business-card production, secretarial services, and/or foreign language translation. In the most poorly connected country, the hotel where the international businesspeople and journalists stay may be the only place with a reliable Internet connection, even if it relies on a satellite dish on the roof (to bypass the dysfunctional local phone system) and costs US$5 a minute.

In an emergency, ask expats or local computer users, very politely, if they know anyone who could send an email message for you. Be as quick as you can, unless they tell you they have unmetered Internet access. Per-minute

Places to Look for Internet Access

Where do you find a public Internet-access terminal or hot spot? Here are some places to start:

- cybercafés
- hostels
- hotels
- libraries
- telephone calling shops (*locutorio* in Spanish)
- computer gaming centers ("LAN house" in Brazil, "PC bang" in Korea)
- transient and immigrant "guest-worker" neighborhoods
- airports
- bus and train stations
- business service centers
- computer stores
- photocopy shops
- convention and trade-show centers and venues
- colleges and universities
- friends and hosts

access costs and per-message or per-byte charges for both sending and receiving email might be many times higher for them than you may be accustomed to in, for example, the United States.

PREPARATION AND PRACTICE

However you plan to connect, the keys to making successful use of the Internet while traveling are preparation and practice.

You can't predict what hardware or software you'll find available in a cybercafé, library, or wherever. Be prepared for a Windows PC or a Macintosh, Microsoft Internet Explorer or Mozilla Firefox, or maybe even something different like the Linux operating system or the Opera browser. The more different systems and programs you're familiar with, the better your chances of being able to do what you need to do on a strange computer.

Try doing whatever it is you'll want to do on the road from a cybercafé or public Internet terminal in your hometown. Try to check your email or send a digital photo from a friend's computer you haven't used before, with a

REAL LIFE

Silicon Valley may love the idea of "pervasive" computing, but the ubiquity of the Internet isn't always a good thing for travelers.

In 1989, when I took my first trip around the world, long-term travelers took for granted that we would be almost completely out of touch except for occasional pickups of weeks- or months-old mail at prescheduled AmEx or poste restante (general delivery) post offices. When we read in the newspaper that there had been a major earthquake in San Francisco, it took us almost a week to get through by phone to find out what had happened to our apartment. Day to day and week to week, our only contact was with the people and places we were visiting. It was scary sometimes, but it was life-changing.

Today, ease of access to email everywhere makes that seem like ancient history. Travelers are no longer cut off from home, and no longer have to live our lives in the places we visit: we can travel anywhere, but keep our sense of who and where we are planted firmly in our circle of email buddies, instead of the places and people physically nearby. All too often, the result is to heighten the detachment of travelers from our destinations and hosts, and reduce the amount we learn from cultural immersion.

It's nice to know that your friends are available by email if you need support. But if you can, try to disengage yourself, at least some of the time, from your virtual community, and engage yourself fully in where you are in the *real* world.

different browser and operating system than you are used to. Or take your portable computer to a cybercafé and try to connect it to the Internet.

Maybe everything will work right the first time. If so, you're lucky. More likely, you'll find that there's some missing piece of hardware or some software compatibility or configuration glitch that limits what you can do or prevents you from accomplishing some task you'd counted on. In that case, you're even luckier that you found the problem before leaving home, while you still have a chance to solve it before your trip. Problems discovered only after you're on the road often can't be solved until you get back home again.

When you're home and checking your email every day, you're unlikely to fill up your email box. But when you are traveling, you may only check your mail once a week or less. Try to get an email account with as large a size limit as possible. Before you leave, try forwarding all your email to the account you'll be using while traveling, and letting it accumulate for a week or two to see if you exceed your quota. It's common for mail to travelers to be returned with a "mailbox is full" message, or to be deleted without notice to the sender.

BACKUPS AND PRECAUTIONS

Don't count on uninterrupted Internet access to vital data like your address book, itinerary, or financial data. Back them up, and bring backups with you. The server or connection might temporarily be down when you need it; your ISP, email provider, or other service provider might go out of business or increase its fees; or you might need it when you're in the odd place with no Internet access.

Don't rely on a hard disk or flash drive either, unless you have it backed up in some other format. Hard drives crash. If something goes wrong or you pull a flash drive out of the USB socket while it is writing, you can lose your data.

You can probably fit your contact list and address book, URLs of favorite Internet sites, any documents you might want to consult, and scanned images of the documents in your money belt on a single encrypted CD you can use

REAL LIFE

At least four of my acquaintances have lost their electronic address books and/or stored email when they were forced to change ISPs or email providers suddenly and unexpectedly, without having backed up all their data. For each of them, it was a disaster. For two of them, this happened during extended stays overseas. These were good friends and former housemates of mine, but we didn't find each other again until almost 10 years later, long after they had returned to the United States.

in any computer. Bring a couple of copies, carefully packed. CDs are fairly sturdy, but can get scratched or broken if they are dropped or stepped on.

While you are at it, make copies—perhaps on the same CDs—of your paper address book, the data on your electronic organizer or PDA, and the phone numbers stored on your cell phone. Any of these can be difficult or impossible to reconstruct if you lose them while traveling.

You'll undoubtedly add addresses of people you meet along the way, so be sure to make regular backups of your updated info, and/or email copies of your updated info to your home address or a friend periodically. You can eventually replace a passport, but the truly heartbreaking loss for most travelers whose luggage goes missing is the loss of their address book and the contact information for the people they've met on their trip.

Email and attachments often aren't received usably. If you send digital photos or critical data by email, don't delete the originals until you get confirmation that the email has been received and that the photos or data are viewable. If you keep a journal you want to preserve, send copies of each entry to a couple of different email addresses, and don't delete the original you carry with you until you have confirmed that someone has received it and backed it up.

Using Foreign Websites

Online, you don't have to shop locally, and you won't necessarily get a better deal that way. Some hotels in Europe dump their "distressed inventory" through U.S.-based websites for half the prices they offer even through discounters within Europe. My European friends have been shocked at some of the off-season rates I've gotten that way. In Africa, South America, and Australia, I've gotten dramatically lower prices renting cars through websites in the United States than through the same international companies' local websites in those countries. The same is often true for car rentals in Europe. (Although in two out of three of these cases it also led to double billing that took me months to straighten out with my credit card issuer and the car rental company.)

Still, there are times when you will find yourself trying to make reservations, pay for something — a hotel room; a rental car; tickets on a local airline, train, bus, or ferry — or simply get information on a website that's "foreign" to you in some way, or from a computer in a cybercafé, library, bed-and-breakfast, etc. that's set up for another language.

Here are some the potential problems to be prepared for in such circumstances:

The language of the website. If the page is all Greek to you (or some other alphabet or writing system), look for the word "English" somewhere on the home page (if the page is really complex, use the "find in page" feature of your browser to search the page), an icon of the Stars and Stripes or the Union Jack, or a pull-down menu with flags and/or names of countries or languages. The entire site may not be translated, but even a summary English-language version of the home page or site map may give you enough clues to enable you to accomplish a specific task. Reservation sites have a fairly standard format, and with a little practice you can usually recognize basic things like departure and arrival time, flight (bus, train, ferry) number, and so forth. As long as the place names are written in the Latin alphabet, they'll probably be recognizable even if spelled and alphabetized in a slightly different sequence from the standard anglicizations (e.g. München instead of Munich). If there's some key word or phrase that you can't figure out, try feeding it through a machine translator like Babelfish.yahoo.com, Freetranslations.com, or Google Translate. Any of these services can translate either a snippet of text you cut and paste into the translation box, or (less reliably) an entire Web page if you paste in the URL. These translation sites cover different languages, so check the other translation sites if the first one you try can't handle the language you want to translate from or to. You can navigate most websites through these translators, but they rarely work to actually make purchases through secure ("https://") websites.

The language of the operating system. Microsoft and Apple are multinational companies, and distribute their software in many languages. In a cybercafé, expect all the menus and commands like "file," "print," and "settings" to be in the local language. You may need to ask for help just to find and launch a Web browser. The good thing is that English is the global language of computing, and the resident geek at a cybercafé almost anywhere in the world usually can read and write basic computer instructions in English, and will usually understand, "English, please?" from a puzzled foreigner in front of a computer as meaning, "How do I switch the keyboard and menus to English?"

The Web browser and other software. Don't count on finding the same software you are used to. Maybe you'll find Safari on a Macintosh, when you are used to Windows. Or maybe the OS will be Windows, but the browser will be Opera or Firefox rather than Microsoft's Internet Explorer. All these browsers are basically similar, but it's easier if you familiarize yourself with them in English before you try to deal with them in another language.

The language of the keyboard. If you haven't encountered this before, try to imagine typing on a keyboard on which some of the letters have been rearranged, and/or replaced with special characters that don't occur in English, accent marks, etc. They may or may not be labeled: People who type regularly in a particular language get used to the standard keyboard layout for that language, touch typists don't care at all about the keycap labels, and English-language keyboards may be cheaper than ones labeled in an obscure character set. There's usually a command (not usually intuitive) to switch between the other language and English. Especially if you are a touch-typist on the English QWERTY keyboard, the French AZERTY keyboard will drive you nuts. It doesn't just have extra diacriticals (accent marks) but has a different arrangement of the 26 basic letters! Of course, it's even harder for AZERTY French typists to use a QWERTY keyboard that doesn't have any diacriticals. I've sent and

(continues on next page)

Using Foreign Websites *(continued)*

received lots of email messages from cybercafés that were full of character transpositions and unwanted diacriticals, and which began, "I can't figure out how to switch this keyboard to English."

The country where the ticketed journey originates. Many websites (especially those in the United States, but in other countries as well), are designed to serve customers in a specific country or countries, and won't allow you to make reservations or purchase tickets for a journey originating anywhere else. It's not that they aren't allowed to sell such tickets (international airline ticketing systems are designed specifically to enable any airline office or travel agent to issue tickets for travel originating anywhere in the world), but they don't choose to do so for their own business reasons.

The country of the credit card billing address. Many websites (again, especially in the United States), won't accept a credit card for payment unless the billing address for the card is in their country. Some credit cards are only valid in a specific country, but usually it's just a business decision that foreign credit cards are more likely to be stolen or fraudulent. The most annoying thing is that few such websites bother to warn away foreign customers. You only find out they won't accept your business after you have completed a booking and entered your credit card details to try to pay.

The country of the ticket delivery or confirmation address. Some websites refuse to sell a ticket or make a booking if you specify a delivery address in another country. Sometimes that's because of potential difficulty, delay, or additional cost in shipping tickets internationally, especially for paper tickets. In other cases it's just a business decision, or merely bad Web design that assumes a certain address format such as a six-character postal code when your zip code is either five or nine digits long. As with the credit card billing address, you probably won't find out until your nearly complete purchase is rejected.

Never store any of your passwords or log-ins on a disk, flash drive, cell phone, or PDA unless you've encrypted them with a strong password. Learn and discipline yourself *always* to delete the cookies and cache when you are finished using any public terminal. Identity thieves are the new virtual pickpockets. They target travelers, and you probably won't figure out that your data has been stolen until it's already been used to rip you off.

VIRUSES, MALWARE, AND PUBLIC COMPUTERS

The majority of cybercafés and other public computers are infected with viruses and malware. These might seem like just a nuisance, but they might also monitor your keystrokes, looking for passwords to email or banking websites.

Many of these viruses propagate through flash drives and memory cards. Upload some photos at a cybercafé, then use that memory card in your laptop, and the odds are your laptop will be infected as well as the card. Promiscuous sharing of flash drives and memory cards between a Windows laptop and public terminals is virtually certain to leave your laptop badly infected with multiple viruses—the sort of problem that's hard to eliminate without reformatting the whole computer and reinstalling the operating system. Always scan memory cards and flash drives for viruses after using them in a cybercafé or other unknown computer, such as when you've put your thumb drive or card in a friend's computer to share some photos.

Essentially all viruses and malware found in the wild are specific to Windows. The best way to avoid these problems is not to use Windows on a laptop or netbook you take traveling, even if you use Windows at home. A Linux laptop, netbook, or other portable device is immune to Windows viruses and malware, and can safely remove them from flash drives and memory cards.

Telephones

Telephone systems and calling procedures vary greatly from country to country, and are undergoing great change. Fifteen years ago, when the first edition of this book was published, you might have had to go to a special international calling office in the central telephone building or the main post office to make an international call. Today, that system is rare, and calling is potentially cheaper but also more complex than ever.

Good guidebooks to a country should explain how to use the phones, where to find public phones, and which calling and payment system is cheapest. But phone systems are changing fast, so be prepared for things to be different than when the guidebook was researched. If you think you'll be making calls locally, and aren't sure what the system is, ask someone on the plane before you arrive, or in the airport, where you are likely to find English speakers.

DIFFERENT PHONES FOR DIFFERENT FOLKS

The best way to make, receive, and pay for phone calls depends on how you travel and on how many and what type of calls you make and/or receive. Obviously, it may be hard to predict before your trip exactly what sort of phoning you'll do. But the most expensive way to make calls is to use the same calling card number associated with your home phone that you use when you are traveling in your own country, or to use your cell phone with the same phone number that you use at home. If your calling card or phone works abroad at all, international "roaming" charges from landline or wireless phone companies in the United States can run US$5 per minute and up.

Here are some recommendations for better options, based on different phone usage patterns and travel styles:

Occasional International Calls Home: Ask around when you need to make a call. Depending on the country, it will probably be cheapest either to buy a prepaid phone card locally (phone cards that can be used in multiple countries are typically more expensive) and use it from some sort of public phone, to go to a call shop (where you pay by the minute), or to go to a cybercafé that has Internet phone software preinstalled and charges for its use by the minute or hour.

Occasional Incoming International Calls: If all you really need is to get messages, get a voicemail account, preferably one that will let you check your messages online. Make sure your account comes with adequate storage capacity, in case you don't check your messages for a couple of weeks. And remember that a toll-free 800 access number to check your voicemail will only be accessible in the United States and Canada, not further abroad.

In an emergency, if it is essential for someone to be able to call you back, consider buying a secondhand cell phone and a prepaid SIM card with a local number (see the sidebar *Wireless Phones*).

Occasional Outgoing Calls within the Country Where You Are Traveling: If automated public phones are common, you usually need to buy some sort of prepaid phone card for local calls from public phones, since card-only phones have replaced coin phones in most countries. If you don't have a cell phone, and plan to use public phones, it's generally a good idea to get a telephone card as soon as possible after you arrive. Depending on the country, they're sold from vending machines, at post and telecommunications offices, and/or in convenience stores, newsstands, tobacconists, and the like. Prices typically start at US$2–5. Sometimes you throw telephone cards away when you've used up the stored value, but more often you can "recharge" a card, at the same places you buy them, for less than the price of a new card. For long-distance domestic calls, it's usually cheaper to go to some sort of call shop, or a cybercafé. Keep in mind, though, that if you rely on any of these calling modes, people will have no way to call you back. And while phone booths aren't disappearing quite as fast in some other countries as in the United States, they are getting harder to find as they are displaced by cell phones.

More Frequent Outgoing and Incoming Local Calls: If you'll be making a lot of local calls, or want people to be able to call you back, set yourself up with a cell phone and local number. (See the sidebar *Wireless Phones* for how that works and the jargon you need to know.) Bring a multiband GSM cell phone with you or buy one the first place you need it, and buy a prepaid SIM with a local number in each country where you will be staying a while.

The price of prepaid SIMs has gotten so low that once you have the phone it can be worth getting a SIM and local number in any country where you are using a phone for more than a week. Often a SIM costs no more than US$5–10, especially in poor countries where few locals could afford more than that as the price of entry to the telephone world.

Obviously, if you are in a place where you don't speak a local language, and few people speak your language, you aren't likely to have much use for a phone for local calls. As a backup for countries where you will be staying for too little time, and/or making too few calls to justify the cost of a local

REAL LIFE

On my last trip to the U.K., I was accosted by SIM card vendors before I'd gotten off the platform at St. Pancras Station where my train from Paris had arrived. For £10 (about US$15), I got two prepaid "Lebara" SIM cards for my traveling companion and myself, each with a local U.K. phone number good for the next six months and each with £5 of initial calling credit. Calls between the two Lebara SIMs were free, which would have made the deal worthwhile even if we had just used them as walkie-talkies between each other for our week's stay. Credit could be added in £5 or greater increments with vouchers sold at newsstands and other shops. Online top-ups were advertised, but wouldn't work without a credit card with a billing address in the U.K. Outgoing calls to landlines anywhere in the U.K. were 5p (US$0.08) per minute. Calls to U.K. cell phones on other networks were 10p (US$0.15) per minute. Incoming calls from anywhere in the world were free as long as I was in the U.K., so I could give out my local number freely if people needed to call me back. When I got back to the United States, all I had to do was swap the SIM back to my original one, and I was connected again at my U.S. number, without having to carry two phones (as long as my phone was multiband, GSM, and unlocked).

Wireless Phones

What's called a "cell phone" or simply a "cell" in the United States and a few other countries is called a "mobile phone" or just a "mobile" in most of the rest of the world. There's no clear pattern to which word is used where in the world. If one term isn't understood, try the other.

You may have heard that American cell phones can't be used abroad, but that's only half true. Most cell phones in the United States and Canada operate on incompatible, nonstandard systems and won't work anywhere else. But service on the "Global System for Mobile" (GSM) standard — in operation essentially everywhere in the inhabited world except South Korea and Japan — is available in the United States and Canada, with coverage extending to the majority of the population. As of 2011, GSM service is available in the United States from T-Mobile and AT&T, and in Canada from Rogers, among other companies. The frequencies used for GSM services in North America aren't used in many places outside the Americas, but GSM phones are available that cover multiple bands, so the same phone can be used both in North America and elsewhere in the world.

One of the advantages of GSM is that the phone number and account details are on a removable, interchangeable, thumbnail-sized smart card ("SIM card," or simply "SIM"), separate from the phone handset. Once you've got a suitable multi-band GSM phone, you can swap your SIM card for a new one — it takes less than a minute — and you've got a new, local phone number in a new country.

Some cell phone companies "lock" their handsets so they can only be used with their own SIMs. But the codes were broken years ago, and it doesn't normally cost more than US$20 to have a phone unlocked on the spot by a cell phone repair shop, kiosk, or freelancer. Phone unlocking is a gray-market business in some countries, but it's legal in the United States under a special exemption to the copyright "anticircumvention" law first granted in 2006, and renewed and expanded to iPhone "jailbreaking" in 2010. Some GSM operators in the United states recognize that international roaming is a selling point for their phones, and will give you the unlocking code for the asking, after you've had your phone for a couple of months, as long as you've paid your bills on time. Or you can buy an unlocked phone from someone other than your phone service provider — the whole point of the GSM standard is that the phones are interchangeable, unless they are locked.

The key point is to make sure that you have a phone that is GSM, unlocked, and works on the frequency band(s) in use in the countries where you will be traveling.

GSM World (www.gsmworld.com), the GSM trade association, has a directory by country of GSM operators and which bands they use. If you aren't sure where you might want to use the phone, get one that works on as many frequency bands as possible. If you have specific countries in mind, see which frequencies have service in those countries before you buy a phone.

The 1,900 and 850 MHz bands are used in the United States, Canada, and some countries in Latin America and the Caribbean. (To confuse matters, the same band is sometimes referred to as 800 and sometimes as 850.) In the rest of the world, 900 and 1,800 MHz are used. If you can, get a quad-band phone. As of 2011, the cheapest and most widely-available quad-band phone (and thus the easiest to get repaired anywhere in the world) is the Motorola Razr V3, available used or "refurbished" and unlocked on eBay or elsewhere for US$50 or less. For the same price you can get any of various new unlocked quad-band phones made for the Chinese domestic market and exported by resellers like DealExtreme.com. As with any electronic equipment, try to find a phone with a dual-voltage or "universal" AC adapter/charger. If you can, pick up a USB charging cable as well.

Compared to the cost of calling from your hotel, or even from phone booths, prepaid SIMs for a GSM phone can be cheap enough to pay for the phone in a week or two of travel, tops — less if you're traveling on business and using the phone a lot. Regardless of whether you use the phone for outgoing calls or not, you've got a fixed local number where people can call you back, at no further cost to you, even if you're moving from city to city, in airports and train stations, or staying in hostels and budget hotels without phones in the rooms. The system in the United States, where you have to pay to receive calls on your cell phone, is quite unusual internationally. Most prepaid SIM cards allow unlimited incoming calls at no charge.

Most prepaid SIMs only work in one country. If you are going to be in many different countries for too little time to get a separate SIM for each, there are a few special SIM cards for travelers that can be used worldwide. The per-minute calling rates are much higher than for single-country SIMs, and they don't have free incoming calls, but it can be useful to have one as a backup. Specialty companies like Telestial.com sell both single-country and global roaming SIMs, or you can buy single-country prepaid SIMs once you arrive in each country where you want one.

(continues on next page)

Wireless Phones (continued)

Phone numbers can be stored either or both in the phone or on the SIM. If you are going to be using different SIMs in different countries, make sure you set up your phone to store contacts on the phone, so you don't lose them when you switch SIMs.

It's worth paying extra to buy your SIM from someone who will set it up and activate it for you, switch the voicemail and top-up menus to English (if that's an option), and show you how to add credit, check your balance, and check voicemail. Especially if the prompts can't be switched to English or a language you understand, it's likely to be easier to add credit by SMS (text message) rather than by voice menu. If the seller doesn't speak enough English to show you how to do this, see if you can get a fellow traveler to help. Don't leave the SIM card shop until you've tested making and receiving a call, and know what your new phone number is!

SIM, consider getting a global roaming SIM (as discussed in the sidebar) before you leave, to use throughout your trip.

Frequent International Calls to and from Your Home Country: If you're going to be living abroad in one place for more than a month or two, and will have high-speed Internet access, get a "voice over Internet protocol" (VoIP) account with a phone number in your home country. You can even "port" your existing landline or cell phone number to a VoIP service, although the switchover can take a couple of months. The VoIP service will provide an adapter the size of a deck of cards that you can bring with you to a high-speed Internet service, with unlimited calling back to the United States and Canada for a flat rate of about US$20 per month at current prices (plus whatever you have to pay for the Internet connection). Friends and family back home can call you at the same U.S. or Canadian number they are used to, for the price of a domestic call, and your phone will ring wherever you and your VoIP adapter are connected. If you don't have the adapter and phone hooked up to a high-speed connection (or, of course, if you don't answer), they can leave a voicemail message, which you'll get the next time you connect your VoIP adapter and phone, or check for voicemail from a cybercafé.

VoIP phones are great for expatriates, especially those who want to stay in touch by phone with their families and existing circles of friends. If you are taking your children abroad, it lets them talk to their playmates back home as much as they like. VoIP providers to consider include Skype, Vonage.com (one of the best reputations for quality of service, but some of the highest prices), and Diamondcard.us (excellent service—I use them for my international calls from home—but oriented toward more technically sophisticated users).

You can, of course, make Skype or other VoIP calls from your computer without an adapter, but you don't necessarily want to leave your computer plugged in and connected all the time. If you are going to be living some-place with a high-speed Internet connection for a month or more, it's probably worth getting a dedicated VoIP adapter.

If you aren't staying in a place with high-speed Internet access, it's pos-sible to use a VoIP account from some, but not all, cybercafés and some public Wi-Fi access points. Skype and Vonage use proprietary protocols, so you have to use either a computer running their software or their own special adapters. Diamondcard.us and most others use the SIP standard, so you can use any SIP software (such as PhonerLite.de for Windows) or adapter. Most cybercafés that allow VoIP calling already have Skype installed. If they don't already have Vonage or SIP client software installed, they will usually let you download and install it.

The main issue for VoIP at cybercafés is bandwidth. In many places there just isn't enough for VoIP calls. In other cases the cybercafé won't allow them because they can make more money from a dozen people paying to surf the Web than from one person using the same bandwidth for a VoIP call.

TELEPHONE STRATEGIES

Phoning home is a hit-or-miss affair, especially if you're trying to reach a busi-ness (or someone you don't want to wake up) in a different time zone. It's usu-ally possible to call home and leave a message, but much harder to get a reply. It may not be possible for people to call you back unless you are staying at an expensive hotel, have a voicemail service, or have a working cell phone.

A common strategy if you get an answering machine (as is, of course, likely) is to leave a message saying, "I need you to do X, or to answer question Y. I'll call you back tomorrow to find out your answer." This rarely works. For one thing, there is often ambiguity or confusion on the part of one party or the other as to what time or date (remember the International Date Line), in what time zone, is meant. In the second place, the person you are calling may be out of town for a few days, may not get the message, or may not be able to make themselves available at the time you have said that you will call back. In the third place, given the vagaries of both travel and telephone systems, you can never be sure that you will be able to call, and get through, at any precise time.

Voice-response systems often require you to enter names, passwords, or other information on a touch-tone keypad using number equivalents for the letters (ABC = 1, DEF = 2, etc.). Phone keypads in other countries may have

REAL LIFE

While we were living in Argentina, we "ported" our San Francisco phone number to a VoIP provider. It rang on a regular phone plugged into a VoIP adapter plugged into the cable modem in our rented apartment. Friends, family, and business associates could reach us at the same number they were used to, with no international charges and without even having to know that we were abroad. We paid about US$20 per month for unlimited calls to or from the United States. We kept the number as a voicemail number with the VoIP provider, at a reduced monthly fee, for the rest of our trip around the world. When we got home, we ported the number back to a U.S. phone company.

no letters, or may have them in another alphabet. The same goes for ATM and credit/debit card keypads, which can be a problem if you remember your PIN by an alphabetic mnemonic. If you haven't memorized the arrangement of the telephone keypad and the mapping of letters to numbers, bring a printed copy with you.

Faxes

Not everyone has email, and faxes are more effective than phone calls across a language barrier. Some hotels have fax machines but don't yet accept reservation requests by email. Faxes, rather than email, are more heavily used in places where the writing system uses characters or a script that makes typing more complicated than it is with the Latin alphabet.

Fax transmission protocols aren't fail-safe. Do not rely on a "transmission confirmation" printed out by a fax machine or from a computer's fax program as proof of whether or not the message was received. It is surprisingly common to get both "false positive" confirmations of faxes that weren't received and "false negative" error messages when faxes actually were received in good order. There just isn't any certain way to tell whether or not a fax was received.

As with voice telephone calls, it's easier to send faxes than to receive faxes while on the road. Don't count on getting a reply fax at a public telephone office or fax service bureau. You can only send or receive faxes when the telephone system and the electrical power are working at the same time. If both telephones and power are subject to frequent outages, the windows of opportunity for faxing may be quite limited. You can send faxes out from such a place during those windows. But someone trying to reply, and who has no way to know when the power and phones are on at the receiving end (or whether the real problem is something else, such as that they have been given the wrong number), may have poor odds of getting through. If they have to try many times, the odds increase that they will get a false confirmation, and think their reply has gone through, before it actually has. If business hours don't correspond, and the power or the fax machine are shut off at night, it may be impossible for them to reply unless they do so in the middle of the night at their end.

International Telephone and Fax Numbers

Perhaps the most common reason for people not to succeed in calling or faxing you is that they are dialing the wrong numbers. People who don't make many international calls are often intimidated by strange-looking phone or fax numbers, and have no idea how to interpret them. And the same number is likely to be written in many ways. If you get a message from someone in another country, saying to call or fax them at a certain number, the likelihood is that you don't need to dial some of the digits they have given you, but do need to dial some that they didn't give you.

It doesn't have to be like this. The number of digits in phone numbers varies, but they are actually more standardized than are the ways that they are written. And there is an unambiguous international format, supported by almost all new cell phones, in which any phone number can be completely specified.

PLUS FORMAT

The essential elements of a phone number are a country code, a city or area code (if there is one), and a local number. To write a number in international format, start with a plus sign (+), followed by the country code, followed by the city or area code, followed by the local number. My phone number, for example, is +1-415-824-0214 in this so-called "plus" format.

If you are within the same country and city or area code, you typically dial only the local number. In this instance, if you are calling from within area code 415, you would dial simply 824-0214. (From many offices or hotels with multiple lines or extensions, you would precede this with the code to get to get an initial connection to an outside line, typically 9 in the United States.)

If you are in the same country, but in a different city or area code, you dial the long-distance access code, followed by the city or area code, followed by the local number. In the United States and Canada, the long-distance access code is "1." So if you are in Chicago, you could call me by dialing 1-415-824-0214. So far, so good.

If you are in a different country, you dial the international access code, followed by the country code, followed by the city or area code, followed by the local number. In other words, you dial the international access code, plus exactly the numbers that follow the "plus" sign when the number is written in the "plus" format. The plus sign itself, like any hyphens or parentheses, is simply punctuation, and is not dialed.

The "plus" format has been adopted by all major wireless phone manufacturers as the standard for global roaming. If you enter phone numbers into your cell phone in "plus" format, your calls will be completed correctly wherever you are able to roam—without you having to know, or enter, what country you are in or the outbound international access code.

INTERNATIONAL ACCESS CODES

Note that the international access code varies from country to country, the most common code being "00." From the United States and Canada it is "011." The international access code needed for all outbound international calls from a country is something completely different from the country code needed for all inbound international calls to a country. Many people confuse these, and if you ask someone for one, you are as likely as not to be told the other. Many people assume that the international access code is the same from all countries. There's no reason for it not to be, but it isn't.

If you have the number, correctly written, in the plus format, all you need to know to call it from anywhere in the world is the international access code wherever you are. You don't need to ask, "Which of these numbers do I need to dial, or not to dial?" All you need to ask is, "What is the international access code to make a call from here?"

In the U.K., for example, the international access code is "00." So to call me from London you would dial 00+1-415-824-0214.

It is an unfortunate coincidence, causing vast amounts of confusion, that the long-distance access code within the United States and Canada is "1," and that the country code for calls to these places from other countries is also "1." The "1" in these two cases serves completely different purposes. Within most other countries, the long-distance access code is something other than "1" (most often "0," though there is no rule or standard). And, of course, every other country (except those included in country code "1") has a different country code.

In domestic usage, many people omit their country code. In a counterproductive effort to be helpful, people are wont to precede their phone number with their international access code (useful only when dialing out of their country, not into it), or their long-distance access code (useful only when dialing within the country, not internationally). The outbound international access code or the domestic long-distance access code is no more part of the number proper, and should no more be included when writing it, even if you need to dial them, than is the 9 or other number you may need to dial to get an outside line from the phone on your desk in an office or hotel.

People in the United States who write all international numbers with "011" (the international access code for calls from the United States) at the start are doing no one in any other country code a favor. The same number in New Delhi that I reach from the United States by dialing 011-91-11-123-4567 would be reached from London by dialing 00-91-11-123-4567 and from Australia by dialing 0011-91-11-123-4567. The clearest way for people everywhere to write this number is +91-11-123-4567.

CONVERTING NUMBERS TO PLUS FORMAT

Converting a number you are given by someone abroad to the "plus" format typically involves removing some extraneous leading digits (international or long-distance access codes) and adding the country code (and sometimes city or area code), if it wasn't specified. A good pocket guide to city and country codes is invaluable in figuring out how to interpret numbers given to you in nonstandard formats other than the "plus" format. There are several on the Internet, but you aren't likely to be on the Internet when you need them. See if you can get a printed one from your long-distance telephone company.

For example, the city code for London is 20. A business in central London with the local number 7123-4567 might print its number on its letterhead or fax header as "020-7123-4567" or "(020) 7123-4567," which is how you would dial it from elsewhere (outside London) in the U.K. The country code for the U.K. is 44, so in the "plus" format this would be written as +44-20-7123-4567. In the United States, the international access code is "011." So to call this number from the United States, I would dial 011+44-20-7123-4567.

AREA/CITY CODES

Phone numbers and prefixes are constantly changing. In London, for example, city codes were changed in 1995 and again in 2000. The "207" area is what used to be "171" and before that "71." It took years for books and references to be updated. A person with the number in the preceding example might well still be using old stationary showing their number as "0171-123-4567," or perhaps even "071-123-4567."

In the United States, a great many new area codes (city codes) have been added in recent years, and more codes are added each year, to accommodate demand for more phone lines, pagers, cell phones, fax lines, and modem lines. If you are trying to call a number in the United States, and get a different party or are told that no such number exists, it may be that it is in a region that has been assigned a new area code. Call the operator (outside country code 1, have your operator call an operator in the United States) to check whether there is a new area code for that city or town.

If you are given a number beginning with a zero, the leading zero is probably the long-distance access code used within the country and should not be used when calling from outside the country. Area codes for some cities in Russia used to begin with zero, but they caused so much confusion that the leading zero in these codes was finally changed to "4" in 2005. The old Moscow area code, 095, for example, became what is now 495.

COUNTRY CODES

Most country codes identify a single country. The major exception is country code 1, which includes the United States, Canada, various "possessions" of the United States (Puerto Rico, Guam, American Samoa), and several independent Caribbean countries (Jamaica, Dominican Republic) and Caribbean "dependencies" of other countries (Bermuda, British Virgin Islands). The codes for regions within countries are called "area codes" in country code 1, and "city codes" in the rest of the world. Some countries do not use city codes, usually because they don't have enough phones to need them but occasionally because they have lengthened local numbers to include the city code, making all numbers "national numbers." When calling such countries, follow the country code directly with the local number. Country codes, city codes, and local numbers vary in length, as does the punctuation (such as parentheses or hyphens), if any, within and between parts of numbers. Fortunately, if you have a number correctly written in the "plus" format, and are calling from another country, you don't need to worry about which part of the number is the country code, which the city code, and which the local number. Just dial the international access code, plus all the numbers after the plus sign, in the order they are written. The punctuation (commas, hyphens, or periods), is optional and arbitrary, is never dialed, and can be ignored.

TOLL-FREE NUMBERS

Many businesses have special numbers that can be called at no charge to the caller, even from outside the local area. These are most popular in the United States and Canada, where all numbers in country code 1 with area codes (city codes) 800, 866, 877, and 888 are reserved for these so-called "toll-free" numbers. Various sorts of "freephone" schemes, with various formats, are used in other countries. They aren't really free, of course; this just means that calls to these numbers are paid for by the recipients rather than the callers.

Unless the holder of the number has agreed to pay for incoming international calls, you can't normally call a "toll-free" number from another country. Some 800, 866, 877, and 888 numbers can be called only from the United States, some only from Canada, some from either country. Most businesses in the United States don't think the business they would get from customers abroad would justify the cost of accepting the charges for phone calls from all over the world. Because they won't agree to accept the charges, virtually no 800, 866, 877, or 888 numbers can be reached from normal phones anywhere outside country code 1. Most freephone numbers in other countries are likewise valid only within those countries.

The problem this causes for would-be visitors to the United States and Canada is that toll-free numbers are often the only phone numbers advertised or listed in literature from businesses in the travel industry such as airlines, railroads, bus lines, car rental companies, and hotel chains. If you are trying to reach such a business from abroad, and have only a toll-free number that doesn't work from your phone, try using a U.S.-based VoIP service such as Skype.com, either from your computer or from a cybercafé, that will route all calls via the United States.

RESOURCES

Merriam-Webster's Guide to International Business Communication (see the *Resource Guide*) contains a clear and concise chapter of advice on "How to Get Phone Calls and Faxes Through" as well as a great deal of useful information on telephone number and postal address formats for selected countries. Unfortunately, it focuses mainly on the First World, but travelers anywhere will find the general introductory chapters worth reading to give themselves a sense of what sorts of variations they can expect, and for general communications procedures, even if none of the country chapters pertain to specific places they are going.

Postal Mail

You can send mail from almost anywhere. Regular mail can be slow, and sometimes gets stolen, but most of it will eventually arrive. Just don't rely on it for anything urgent, essential, or valuable. (The following section gives general advice on postal procedures, addressing, and letter mail. For more on the pitfalls of sending and receiving parcels, see the *Baggage* chapter.)

ADDRESSING AND STAMPING ENVELOPES

Even in places where the local language is written in a different alphabet, you can address outgoing international mail in the Roman alphabet. For maximum comprehensibility, write the delivery address in plain block capital (uppercase) letters. Take your mail directly to a post office (international mail is sometimes handled at a separate office or counter) and insist on seeing all the stamps canceled in your sight. Uncanceled stamps are liable to be removed and resold, leaving your mail undeliverable for want of proper postage.

DELIVERY TIMES

International air mail generally takes from less than a week to a month (in the worst case) to arrive. International surface mail can take several months, and the cost savings on letters or post cards is rarely worth it. Nowhere is the sobriquet "snail mail" so appropriate as with intercontinental surface mail.

RECEIVING MAIL

There's little need for postal mail while you are traveling. Messages can be sent by email, and mail drops won't usually accept packages. But sometimes it's nice to get a postcard or an envelope from home. You can have mail (letters only, no packages) sent to American Express offices if you have an AmEx card. You can also receive mail, including packages, at major post offices by "general delivery" (often known by its French name, "poste restante").

The main problem with getting mail either care of AmEx or general delivery is that they only hold envelopes for a limited amount of time, after which they are either thrown away (more common) or returned to sender. So you have to keep your schedule. And your correspondents have to time the sending of mail to you so that it arrives before you do, but not so far in advance that it is returned before you arrive and check for it.

AmEx no longer publishes a printed directory of its offices, and the list of AmEx offices and agents on their website doesn't identify which ones accept mail for AmEx cardholders (not all do) or how long they will hold it (generally no more than 30 days, sometimes less). So the only way to find out where your friends or family can send you mail is to call AmEx, or go to an AmEx office in person, and have them check for you. But AmEx is substantially more reliable, and vastly easier to deal with, than general delivery in most places.

Formats for addressing mail for general delivery vary somewhat from country to country. The general idea is that you send a letter addressed something like this:

    DOE, Jane
    General Delivery (Poste Restante)
    Main Post Office (GPO)
    Street Address
    City, Postal Code
    COUNTRY

The letter is held at the "general delivery" department of the specified post office—in effect a sort of "will call" department—for a certain amount of time during which, if Jane comes in and asks for her mail, she will be given it. Not all post offices handle general delivery. Sometimes all general delivery mail to a city is sent to one office, which is just as well. The worst case is when you have to specify at which post office a letter is to be held. If none is specified (for example, if you don't know that there is more than one) your letter can be waiting at one office while your correspondent checks for mail at a different office across town, and is told they have none. All in all, general delivery should be a last resort, or a way to receive notes and greetings that won't be missed if they aren't received, and require no reply.

CULTURE SHOCK

"Culture shock" is the inability to adapt to, or feel comfortable with or in, the cultural setting in which you find yourself. The term "culture shock" is unfortunate, as it implies a sudden and jarring experience and suggests that culture shock will hit you hardest at the start of your trip or when you first arrive in a different culture. Very few people actually experience a rapid onset of disorientation on their first sight, sound, smell, touch, or encirclement by strange people in a strange place. At first, most people find it exciting and fun. Only as time goes on does the constant sensory overload become overwhelming. This results from not being assimilated enough to automatically filter out those stimuli to which one need not pay attention, and thus having to pay attention to everything.

Having taken, and enjoyed, short trips to exotic and diverse places is little indication of how much you will be affected by, or how well you will cope with, culture shock on a long trip. Culture shock is a long-term phenomenon, and by the time you realize that you are suffering from it, it has probably been sneaking up on you for weeks. After 4–6 months of travel, when culture shock typically reaches its peak, it is also apt to be mixed with a fair amount of simple homesickness, from which it is not always easily distinguished.

For any but the most manic, it's impossible to sustain the level of alertness and awareness of one's self and one's surroundings that is required to keep adapting to new cultures for more than a few weeks or a month at a time. The hardest work of travel is the work of cultural adaptation and learning. Plan to take periodic breaks or "vacations within your vacation," or to settle down periodically in places where you can stay long enough to acclimate to the area and relax your hyperalertness and hyperself-consciousness.

Avoiding Culture Shock Through Preparation

Preparing for travel in a way that minimizes the likelihood of an unpleasant degree of culture shock is not primarily a matter of learning specific facts about the cultures, peoples, customs, or mores of your destinations. Paradoxically, learning more facts about "the way it is" can serve to give you more fixed expectations that make it hard for you to cope when you encounter things that are unfamiliar, unexpected, and confusing—as you inevitably will, no matter how much you know. People who set out without a clue, and who know and accept that they haven't a clue, sometimes do much better, because they realize from the start that they have much to learn to get anywhere. It's important to cultivate enough patience and trust to be able to go along with things, up to a point, without being too bothered by the fact that you haven't yet figured out what's going on, or what it means.

I am not an advocate of ignorance: most travelers spend too little time studying the places they are going, before they leave, to maximize the educational value they could get out of their trips. That's OK; I also realize that education isn't everyone's primary purpose. But it's important to understand that the kind of learning that will help you avoid culture shock is the kind of learning that enhances your humility, your open-mindedness, your awareness of the extent of your ignorance, and your desire to learn more. You won't avoid culture shock with the kind of learning that enhances your sense of "being in command of the situation" or convinces you that you know all you need to know about where you are going.

Some of the people who experience the most extreme culture shock are academic experts, with the utmost book-learning of a place, who fail to allow for their ignorance of its reality. People who have been in a place in the past, and whose expectations don't allow sufficiently for the extent to which it has changed, can also be shocked, culturally and otherwise. This includes immigrants returning home after even as few as a couple of years abroad. A common theme in the writings of Southerners who move to the North, such as for education or employment, is the culture shock of their first return from school to their homeland and their village.

Culture shock is, fundamentally, a symptom of unsuccessful or incomplete cultural adaptation, assimilation, and acceptance. Preparation for avoiding cultural shock is thus primarily attitudinal: learning how to adapt to, assimilate into, and accept cultural diversity. A diverse, multicultural outlook and awareness is the best immunization against culture shock. Recognize that people elsewhere do things differently. Don't presume that different means inferior, or ascribe unfamiliar attitudes or actions to barbarism or backwardness. Instead, start with the assumption that there is a reason for a behavior that is functional in its context, and try to figure out what that is.

CULTURAL ADAPTATION

Several manuals for foreign living listed in the *Resource Guide* (intended variously for foreign students, businesspeople, missionaries, and volunteers) contain exercises and activities you can do before you leave. These activities help you to prepare yourself and developing your skills at cultural adaptation and coping.

The kinds of exercises and lessons used by trainers in cross-cultural communication, cultural adaptation, and cultural awareness are familiar to far more people today than they were a decade or two ago. As First World countries such as the United States, Canada, Australia, and, to a lesser extent, the U.K., have begun to acknowledge their multicultural, if not multinational, character, large numbers of students, especially in public (government) schools, have begun to receive at least a rudimentary consciousness-raising in cultural sensitivity and awareness of diversity. CNN and the Internet have given people a more diverse (albeit distorted by editorial selection and voice-over interpretations) range of images than were previously available, making written descriptions of other worlds seem more real.

> **REAL LIFE**
>
> Sixty percent of U.S. college students polled in 2002 believed "developing a better understanding of the values and history of other cultures and nations that dislike us" is a better approach to preventing terrorism than "investing in strong military and defense capabilities at home and abroad."

MAKE IT A LEARNING EXPERIENCE

Whoever you are and whatever you do, you are less likely to get frustrated by the differences between local ways and those to which you are accustomed at home if you treat "doing things" as a learning experience rather than as ancillary to the "real" travel goals of sightseeing or whatever. If you regard buying a ticket (or whatever bit of business) as no more than an unavoidable necessity, and the ticket-seller as no more than an obstacle on the way to the thing you have set out to see that day, you close yourself off to the chance that you might be able to learn from the transaction or the accompanying conversation. Approach these encounters as part of the travel experience, not as things getting in the way of it, and you'll stand a better chance of finding the educational silver lining in the bureaucratic clouds.

NONTOURIST OPPORTUNITIES

Some experienced travelers, myself included, seek out opportunities to do things from which they can learn about everyday nontourist life. I go into schools of English and volunteer myself as a guest native speaker for conversation practice. I go into local department stores away from tourist districts even when I have nothing to buy, to see what is on the shelves. I enjoy it when I can find excuses to go into business and government offices in different countries to see what the offices look like, how people are dressed, and how business is done.

An often-rewarding exercise is to seek out someone in your trade, career, profession, or hobby, the office of a relevant trade union or professional association, or any group with whom you have something in common. People are remarkably receptive to being approached on this basis, either in advance by email (such as through a professional association, union, or other international networking group), or on the spot: "Hello! I work as a...in America. I see that you are a...May I look at your (shop, office, etc.)? What is it like to be a...here?" At the least, you'll get a tour of the workplace. If you hit it off, you might be invited home for a family meal, the sort of thing that can be the highlight of a trip.

Poverty and Beggars

Travelers from the North on their first visit to the South often expect to be shocked by their encounters with poverty and begging. It's an extremely difficult issue, and there's certainly an argument that people who are, in global terms, rich, should be troubled by the economic differences between themselves and most of the people in the places they visit. Why are we so much wealthier than they are? Is it fair? Is it inevitable? Can we do anything about it? Should we? Must we? Beggars confront us with these questions in the most direct and personal terms, and sometimes in so many words: "You are rich. I am poor. A dollar means little to you, and much to me."

However you respond, there is no reason to let these issues deter you from travel. Travel doesn't cause the problems, or create the moral issues; travel just makes them harder to ignore. Beggars and poverty are as real when they are 10,000 km away and out of sight as they are when a beggar is standing in front of you on the street, wizened arm and empty hand extended. A permanent change in consciousness often brought about by world travel is an enduring awareness of the reality of poverty, suffering, and inequity.

At one time, people from the United States were relatively unlikely to see people sleeping in the streets or begging unless they traveled abroad in the South. Now, homelessness and begging are no longer novelties for people who've spent time in any big U.S. city.

Today, people from other First World countries, or even poorer countries that nonetheless have stronger socioeconomic safety nets, often have their first contact with homelessness and begging during foreign travel. Often, that first contact comes—unexpectedly—in the United States. Many visitors are unprepared to see so much conspicuous poverty and suffering in such a rich country as the United States.

Tourists tend to notice homeless people more than the locals, who have come to take them for granted. I've seen many a foreigner, but never once a local in any country, including the United States, photographing or filming beggars and street-sleepers. Foreigners, less inured to begging, are also more likely than locals to give to beggars, leading beggars to congregate in districts frequented by foreign tourists. This is true in the United States, and it's true around the world. As a traveler, you will be asked for all sorts of gifts and favors, from money to sponsorship for immigration to your country.

It's up to you to decide how you want to respond. Travel, and learning more about the world, can only give you a better basis for making judgments and choices about your actions and role in an interconnected world.

Philip Briggs' *Ethiopia: The Bradt Travel Guide,* listed in the *Resource Guide,* has a chapter on "Bridging the Cultural Gap" that I highly recommend. It's really more about bridging the economic gap between (rich) travelers and (poor) locals, and applicable to almost any Third World or especially Fourth World destination.

Sexual and Gender Mores

Some of the cultural norms that vary most from culture to culture are those related to sexual and gender relationships and behavioral expectations. There are many societies in which it is considered offensive, and either an invitation to rape or a sign of prostitution or perversion, for a woman to expose any skin except her face, hands, and feet in public; for a woman to go out without a male relative as an escort; for an unmarried couple to appear together in public, much less share a room in a hotel; or for even a married couple to engage in such public displays of affection as holding hands, much less hugging or kissing.

Prevailing social norms may vary greatly within a country, just as they do in the United States. What's acceptable behavior or attire in the capital city, or its more cosmopolitan neighborhoods, may be looked upon differently in blue-collar neighborhoods, suburbia, or the provinces.

Local people may not be able to afford to refuse money from rich foreigners who do such things, even while they talk behind the foreigners' backs about their bad manners or perversion. You can't assume that because "everyone" (i.e., all the foreigners, or those who adopt their manners to wait on them) does something, it

REAL LIFE

Local women are excluded from the public (male) side of life in many countries. But men who aren't part of the family are even more rigidly excluded from the private (female) side of life in those same places. Women travelers sometimes envy their male companions' ability to go out in public without harassment. On the other hand, I'm often jealous of my female companions' ability to get invited into homes and to share local women's lives. Each of us gets to see some things that are off-limits to the other.

is OK or doesn't offend the locals. I've been in many places—especially, but not limited to, romantic or beach resorts in Third World countries—where virtually all the foreign tourists dress or act in ways that the locals consider grossly offensive, but where the locals put on fake smiles and pretend not to mind because the foreigners are the source of most local money.

ISSUES FOR GAYS AND LESBIANS

Lesbians and gay men are rarely able to be entirely out of the closet, even in relatively tolerant countries such as the United States. Most gays and lesbians have some experience of having to hide the nature of their personal relationships, represent their relationships with companions as being of a different nature than is actually the case, or refrain from public displays of affection lest they offend other people around them. Constant awareness of how other people might judge and react—perhaps with violence—to expressions of sexuality or displays of affection is a matter of survival for gays and lesbians everywhere.

Pairs of men or women often travel together as platonic friends (in the case of women, often for protection against sexual harassment), rather than love. In some cultures it's common for two women, or two men, to walk hand in hand together, or embrace each other when meeting or parting, and nothing sexual is inferred from such behavior. Except when asking for a double bed rather than two single beds, it's rarely necessary for lesbian and gay couples to call attention to their sexual orientation, and most of their problems traveling are the same ones they have with homophobes at home.

ISSUES FOR STRAIGHT PEOPLE

For straight people, travel in other cultural regions is often their first encounter with these issues. If you are accustomed to being able to walk hand in hand or share a hotel room with someone of the opposite gender; to speak publicly of sex; to wear shorts, short (i.e., shorter than ankle length) skirts, short-sleeved shirts, or shirts with low necklines; or to travel alone as a woman, you will find that there are places where you either have to make adjustments to suit local mores (such as by pretending to be married to your traveling companion, or pretending to have a husband or male relative "back at the hotel"), or offend some people. I won't tell you to pander to other people's prejudices, if you have decided that they are illegitimate, but I do suggest that you give careful consideration, in advance, to actions that will alienate you from the people from and about whom you are trying to learn.

RELATIVE VALUES

Before you dismiss other cultures' sexual and gender values as "backward" or inferior, consider that some of the attitudes and practices most degrading, repressive, and exploitative of women and children are engaged in by First Worlders at the expense of Third World people. It's hard for me to see how it is fundamentally worse to keep women in purdah, or to mutilate the genitals of women at puberty, than it is for sex tourists to create the demand for prostitutes that leads to the kidnapping of women and children into sex slavery in the brothels of Bangkok or Manila; to pay starving parents to sell their babies for international adoption (some adoption agents are, in essence, modern-day slavers); or to give so many Second, Third, and Fourth World women no economic hope but to sell themselves into mail-order marriage with a First World man—usually through a facilitator or intermediary who profits from promoting the image of Asian or Russian women as more submissive than Americans or Western Europeans.

The international traffic in women and children has become such a serious problem that several countries have taken legal steps to try to reduce it, largely without success. We may not approve of these activities, but we share responsibility for them if we know about them but do nothing to stop them. I figure we have at least as much responsibility to clean up our own society's act (the "demand side" of these activities and abuses) as to complain about other societies on the "supply side." I do my own small part by refusing to knowingly deal with sex tourists or traffickers in women or children.

Immigrants Returning "Home"
U.S. IMMIGRATION POLICIES

Virtually no Asians or Africans were allowed to immigrate to the United States between 1917 and 1965. Asians were categorically barred from immigration, on explicitly racial grounds, from 1917 to 1952. The immigration quotas by national origin, for Africans and Asians alike, remained vanishingly small until the first of several reforms, starting in 1965, loosened the restrictions. There ensued a continuing small (relative to continued immigration of white people from Europe to the United States) but significant wave of immigrants of a new type. Educational, professional, credential, and job-skill preferences have meant that legal immigration from Asia and Africa remained for several decades largely confined to doctors, engineers, academics, and other holders of advanced degrees, many of whom came to the United States first as foreign students.

BRAIN DRAIN

Some of the results of these criteria may surprise you, although they shouldn't. Indian Americans have the highest average educational levels and incomes of any national-origin group in the United States. African-born Americans have the highest average educational levels and incomes of any group by continent of birth, including native-born North Americans.

There were similar increases in immigration from the South, also primarily by the most highly educated technical specialists, to various other First World countries during the same period. While Southerners also went to the Second World for education and training, often on scholarships, they were more likely than those who went to the First World to be sent home on completion of their schooling. The overall phenomenon came to be called the "brain drain," as Southern countries protested that their best and brightest young professionals were being lured away by the former colonial powers just in their postindependence hour of greatest need for skilled personnel.

THE SECOND AND THIRD GENERATIONS

As the children of the brain drain—second- and third-generation Asian Americans, African Americans, Asian Canadians, and African Europeans, for example—come of age, many of them are seeking an understanding of their parents' cultures and homelands through study and travel.

Second- and third-generation immigrants, or first-generation immigrants who left the land of their birth as infants, face special problems of cultural adjustment and understanding in "returning" to their parents' or grandparents' homelands. They may have higher expectations for themselves, and more of an emotional investment in whether they fit into the culture and society, or how they react to it. They may have to confront the realization that they aren't totally at home, or accepted as part of the dominant or normative culture, in the place their family is "from" any more than in the place they grew up. If they are returning to a place where they look like the locals, and perhaps speak the language, they may be held to a higher standard of cultural conformity. Travelers whose race and/or speech

REAL LIFE

In 1978, the students in my introductory class in South Asian civilization at the University of Chicago were almost all white. Most were would-be "orientalists" and "classicists." My interest in *contemporary* South Asia was considered strange. Today, the majority of students in similar classes at U.S. universities are second-generation South Asian American children of immigrants. At the University of California at Berkeley, where the tenured faculty of the Center for South Asian Studies was formerly entirely white, several endowed chairs has been funded by the South Asian American community. Similar changes have been occurring in other "area studies" programs that, in the United States, used to be dominated by a mix of racist "classicists" and CIA contractors.

makes them stand out as foreigners, on the other hand, are usually tolerated in violating many local norms, on the generous assumption that as ignorant foreigners they don't know any better.

Coming Home

The common assumption is that it will be most difficult to deal with the first "foreign" place you visit, and that it is easiest to work your way gradually through places more like home to those that are more different. Few people expect coming home to be difficult at all, or expect a problem in coming more or less straight home from the most exotic and remote place on their itinerary. *After that, I'll be ready to come home,* they think.

It's partly a matter of taste. Some people, like me, jump in, headfirst, all at once. Some prefer to wade in slowly, one step at a time, so that they have the reassurance of knowing they can decide to back out before they get in over their heads.

But the reality is that, for a variety of reasons, coming home can be the most culturally difficult leg of your journey. Giving yourself a chance to readjust gradually may be at least as important at the end of your trip as at the beginning.

I've often talked with people in the first days, weeks, or months

REAL LIFE

On my first trip around the world (which was also my first trip abroad), I started by flying nonstop from San Francisco to Shanghai and headed immediately for East Turkestan. I know of few places more strange to European American eyes. I returned from the Third World gradually, by way of Western Europe. I'm very glad I scheduled the trip this way, and I think it minimized my culture shock when I got back home.

after they have returned from lengthy trips. Almost without exception they report significant symptoms of culture shock. No matter where they went, the majority say that adjusting to being back in the United States was more difficult, psychologically, than dealing with anything that happened along the way.

There isn't a magic cure for this "reentry shock," although there are suggestions in some of the books in the *Resource Guide.* I recommend both a gradual return, as just described, and allowing yourself time to adjust to being back before you have to resume your "normal" routine. Plan on wanting time to reflect and absorb the lessons of the trip. You'll recover from the jet lag in a week, but you may not get over the changes that a trip has brought about in yourself for months or years, if ever. Don't rule out the possibility that your life may be completely transformed by a trip around the world, or that you won't want or be able to "come home" in a mental, any more than a physical, sense.

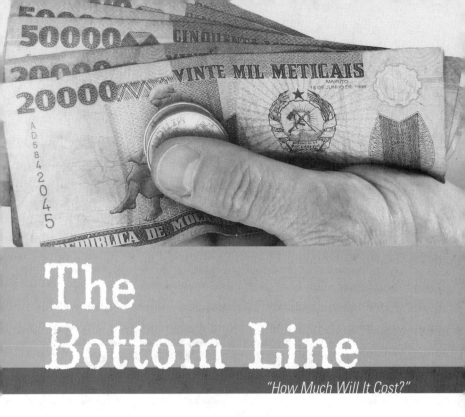

The Bottom Line

"How Much Will It Cost?"

YOUR TRAVEL BUDGET

It's paradoxical: Before they decide to take a big trip, most people overestimate how much it will cost. (See the sidebar, *How Can I Afford to Travel?* and the section on *How Much Does a Trip Like This Cost?* in the introduction.) But once they've decided to go, most people underbudget.

It's both more common and more problematic to budget too little, or not to budget at all, than to budget too much. Be realistic, and give yourself a margin for error proportional to your unfamiliarity with the nitty-gritty of travel in places you are going, the uncertainty in your plans, the flexibility that you want to leave yourself, and the degree to which you can afford to exceed your budget.

Take all prices from guidebooks, friends, and acquaintances with a grain of salt. Many budget travelers make a sport of how cheaply they can travel—or, more often, of how cheaply they can claim to travel. Those who talk most loudly and often about prices are usually those who are most boastful about their thrift.

Guidebook writers are usually honest, but the figures they give are still misleading. Guidebook writers are experienced travelers, familiar with the country and how to travel in it, and speaking at least some of a local language. As soon as they write a place up in a guidebook, the place has a guaranteed

Key Advice About Money Matters

- Budget conservatively. Most people underbudget. It's better to have money left over than to run out.

- Include everything in your budget. Often overlooked or underbudgeted major expense categories include immunizations and health supplies, luggage and gear, communications costs, land transportation such as a Eurail Pass, and additional air tickets purchased en route.

- Don't try to set a single per-diem expense figure for every country. Break your trip down by how long you plan to spend in each region or country, and budget separately for each. Don't rely on one of my sample budgets. Make your own budget.

- Expect to spend significantly more than the prices in guidebooks. Guidebooks are written by expert travelers. If you need to consult a guidebook to predict your expenses, budget at or above the high end of any range it gives. Inflation and the effect of being listed in a guidebook will result in increased prices from those in current editions of guidebooks.

stream of business from readers of that guidebook, so it can (and usually will) raise its prices. You can't realistically hope, and shouldn't expect, to travel as cheaply as the author of a guidebook, especially if you patronize the specific businesses recommended in the book.

Before using any prices in a guidebook, check to see what exchange rate was in effect at the time the book was compiled. (If the book doesn't say, throw it away, or ignore the prices.) Convert prices to your currency at that rate, even if the local currency in which the book gives prices is worth much less in your currency today. Several of the exchange rate websites listed in the *Resource Guide* provide historical as well as current rates.

As a rule, the more rapidly a country's currency is declining in value against First World currencies such as the U.S. dollar, the higher inflation is likely to be and the more likely prices are to be fixed in hard currency, usually U.S. dollars or euros. In many countries tourists are required to pay for certain services either in hard currency or in local currency purchased at an artificially high "official" or "tourist" exchange rate. This is often true of air tickets, but sometimes also of train tickets and/or hotels.

Hard-currency price equivalents are more stable over time in most countries than local-currency prices, and a better guide to what your costs will be. You can sometimes get windfall bargains in the brief period between

- Compare the cost of travel to other things you spend money on. How does the value of a trip around the world compare to the value of a new car, for example? Most world travelers live far more comfortably on the road than they could have done for the same cost at home in the United States. Long-term, independent world travel is an extraordinarily good value.
- Bring a mix of cash, traveler's checks, and ATM and/or credit cards. Don't rely exclusively on any one way of getting money.
- Don't use Internet banking unless you bring your own computer. Try to find a reliable friend or relative who is willing to help you deal with financial issues in an emergency. You can do most things online, but not everything. A trusted contact at home is crucial when the unexpected happens.

For more information on the topics in this chapter, see the *Resource Guide* in the back of the book and the links on the Practical Nomad website at www.practicalnomad.com.

the devaluation of a currency and the adjustment of prices, but such opportunities are fleeting.

Even hard-currency price equivalents are subject to world inflation. When I travel, I figure that a typical current edition of a guidebook is based on research done a year before the copyright date, and that inflation in most of the world is at least 10 percent a year.

In places where there are no hotels comparable to those in the United States or elsewhere in the First World, it's difficult to predict how much you will need or want to spend. Most people find their personal comfort level fairly quickly, but it's hard to anticipate such things as whether you'll want air-conditioning in the tropics (where the cheapest air-conditioned rooms can cost twice as much as otherwise-nicer ones with ceiling fans), or how often you'll feel the need for running water, hot water, or a private toilet and/or bath.

Around-the-world travelers have a wide range of incomes and budgets. You'd be surprised how often you see Banglamphu backpackers in tie-dye climbing into cabs from Khao San Road to Bangkok airport with garment bags full of custom-tailored suits they've had made to wear at their office jobs back home.

Given these factors, I can't give a single answer to the question, "How much will it cost?" Instead, I'll try to give an outline of items to include, and some wide ranges of possible costs for you to use in projecting your personal budget.

REAL LIFE

U.S. citizens and residents may be able to get some tax benefits from having a lower income during a year when you take time off to travel. At least through 2012, there's no tax on long-term capital gains if you are in the 0–15 percent tax brackets. If your earned income is above that threshold (about US$40,000 for a single person), the capital gains tax jumps from zero to 15 percent. The capital gains tax rates are scheduled to increase in 2013, but they will still be higher for people in higher income tax brackets. If you are going to sell assets such as a house or stocks that have gone up in value since you bought them, and your income is normally high enough that the appreciation would be taxed, or taxed at a higher rate, it might be better to sell them during a year when travel has reduced your earned income enough to put you below the capital gains threshold or in a lower capital gains tax bracket. In some circumstances, if you have a large enough amount of unrealized capital gains, the capital gains tax benefits could more than offset the lost income. If you think any of this might be relevant to your situation, consult a tax advisor.

Advance Expenses

Most people spend more before their departure—not including their airline tickets—than they ever imagined. You may find this figure shocking, but first-time international travelers equipping and preparing themselves to set off for a couple of months or more outside the First World can expect to spend, and should budget, at least US$1,000 per person, perhaps US$2,000, on equipment, supplies, and expenses other than tickets. Where does all this money go?

TRAVEL DOCUMENTS

A new U.S. passport costs US$135, US$60 more for rush service. Two or three visas (visas for countries that practice "reciprocity" cost US$135 each for U.S. citizens, the same amount their citizens have to pay for tourist visas to visit the United States), roundtrip Express Mail or FedEx for sending visa applications to any consulates or embassies you can't get to in person, and half a dozen photos for a passport and visas typically bring the total cost of travel documents to US$300 or more for a multicountry trip that includes several countries that require visas, if you don't already have a passport. If you will need visas for certain countries but can't or don't choose to get them before you leave, at least check with the embassies for the current visa fees and include them in your budget, because you'll have to pay them sooner or later, wherever you get your visas.

IMMUNIZATIONS AND HEALTH SUPPLIES

Even at a clinic that charges only per inoculation, a course of recommended immunizations for tropical Third World travel and filling the prescriptions for antibiotics and assorted other medical supplies will cost you US$200 or more in the United States. Adding the cost of stocking a reasonable first-aid kit (including adequate supplies of any medication you regularly need) is likely to bring the cost of health and hygiene preparations closer to at least US$300 (a bit less if you are sharing some of these supplies with a traveling companion; more if you are traveling alone). The prices of even nonprescription first-aid supplies and toiletries add up remarkably quickly.

Up the ante further if you haven't had a recent general physical examination (a must before a multimonth Third World trip), if you regularly use any expensive or prescription medications, or if you feel it necessary to use specific types of toiletries or cosmetics that you can't count on finding along the way. If you wear glasses or contacts, get your eyeglass prescription checked and get prescription sunglasses and a spare pair of regular glasses, unless you plan to buy these early in your trip in a country where they will be cheaper (in which case you should still budget for the cost).

I strongly recommend a water purifier for long-term travel outside the First World. Most of those worth bothering to carry cost US$75–150.

LUGGAGE

A good travel bag generally costs US$200–300. You might find one for less on sale or from a discounter or outlet like SierraTradingPost.com, but don't compromise on quality, features, or durability for a small price savings. Most other sorts of luggage you may already have won't work nearly as well. It may seem like a lot, but a really good travel bag will be hard to find along the way if you set out with one that proves inadequate or uncomfortable. If you're going to be living out of it for the duration of your trip, it's worth paying the price to get durable, well-fitting luggage exactly suiting your needs.

SHOES AND CLOTHING

As I explained earlier in the packing section, I don't recommend major advance investments in clothing. But I would recommend a set of lightweight silk or synthetic long underwear (US$40–75), if you don't have some already, and new shoes or sandals, unless yours have very little wear (say one very durable pair of shoes at US$150 and one of sandals at US$75). Buy new shoes just far enough before your departure to get them well broken in and be sure that they'll be comfortable; don't try to break them in on the road.

GUIDEBOOKS AND MAPS

You need to budget for guidebooks and maps whether you buy them in advance or as you go. Moon or comparable guidebooks are typically US$20–30 each for large countries or regions. Good maps of countries or regions the size of large U.S. states or Western European countries run US$10–20, potentially much more if you need specialized or detailed maps such as for trekking or bicycling, or are traveling to places where maps are hard to find.

Traveling at a typical pace, budget a minimum of US$25 a month on guidebooks and maps, twice that or more if you are traveling through more places quickly or a map aficionado like me, a bit less if you're the sort who never looks at a map or guidebook—though you may regret it and will never know what you miss.

OTHER ADVANCE EXPENSES

Other big-ticket items to budget for if you will be bringing them are a lightweight sleeping bag or sleep sack and any camera, computer, or other electronic equipment you plan to bring. (See the chapter on *Baggage* for some guidance on possibilities and prices.) If you bring a camera, bring as much digital memory as you think you might conceivably want, and then some. It's likely to be more expensive to buy more along the way.

Long-Distance Transportation

As I've already tried to explain, the cost of air tickets depends entirely on the specifics of your itinerary. What's easy to overlook is that your transportation costs don't end with the air tickets you buy before you leave.

You can currently fly around the world, starting and ending in the United States, for less than US$2,500 per person including taxes on certain routes. But, as I said in the *Air Transportation* chapter, scrimping on the initial price of tickets is, for most people, a false economy. If you are definitely going to some other places along the way, and will have to fly there, it will usually work out cheaper in the long run to include those flights in your initial package of air tickets, rather than to buy them later as separate side trips.

Similarly, some of the money you save on air tickets by leaving gaps in your air itinerary to be traveled by land or water must be budgeted for the cost of using land travel. Third World trains are an excellent value, as are trains in the United States for those budget travelers with plenty of time, but the costs are nontrivial.

It's easy to be misled by the seeming affordability of third-class train tickets and local bus rides in guidebooks. A high proportion of travelers from the First World, even budget backpackers, find themselves choosing first class on Third World trains and taking so-called "luxury" buses for any but the shortest journeys, finding the greater comfort well worth the extra cost.

So you may save US$150 or so by not including flights between Bangkok and Singapore, or between Delhi and Bombay, but you'll need to set aside close to US$100 of that for first-class train tickets between either of these pairs of cities. Both these train trips are worthwhile for the experience, and for the places you can see and stop off in along the way, but the bottom-line savings are minimal if you are interested neither in the train journeys for their own sake nor in visiting any of the places along the way.

Include in your budget your best estimate of the cost of traversing any gaps in your air itinerary, or of any intended side trips by land or water. If you have any doubt about the level of comfort you will require, budget for the highest available category of land transportation ("foreigners class"). Don't commit yourself to traveling in, say, "hard seat" class on a Chinese train for 24 hours unless you know you can take it. It's better than it used to be, at least between major cities, but it's still not for everyone.

Long-haul land or water transportation in the Fourth World, where it is possible at all, is usually very cheap, very slow, and very uncomfortable. Train travel in the Second World is changing but, at present, typically somewhere between the First World and the Third World in both comfort and price.

Land and water transportation in the First World, on the other hand, is apt to be a major expense. Rail or bus passes can be good values, especially compared to the cost of air tickets within Western Europe or other wealthy regions. However, they can still be a significant part of your total transportation costs, as a quick look at the following list shows:

- A one-month second-class youth (under age 26) Eurail "Global" Pass costs US$759. A similar second-class youth "flexi" pass good for 15 days of travel in an overall two-month period is US$739. A similar but first-class adult "flexi" pass is US$1,139, or US$969 each for two people traveling together.

- A 21-day "ordinary-class" (second-class) Japan Rail Pass costs ¥57,700 (currently US$675).

- A 30-day, 10,000-km (6,200-mile) Greyhound Australia bus pass costs A$957 (currently US$860) at the discounted rate for Hostelling International members. (The discount is more than the cost of HI membership.)

- A 30-day Amtrak USA Rail Pass costs US$579; a 45-day pass costs US$749.

Even if you don't make any definite commitments to a specific route, it's best to plan your route through such expensive regions in advance, both so as to estimate what it will cost and to know whether individual point-to-point tickets, a pass, or even some flights (especially if they can be included with your through tickets or if your route matches that of a local low-fare airline) will be best for your specific destinations.

Planning how you will close the gaps in your air itinerary will also give you a chance to assess the distances you plan to cover and the time it will take. When you start looking at train and ferry schedules, what seemed like "places" on the map resolve themselves into regions, countries, and subcontinents that extend over considerable distances.

Indonesia, for example, extends farther than the lower 48 states of the United States. Within the two months' maximum that tourists are allowed to stay, it's difficult to get from one end of the archipelago to the other without flying. Bangkok, Thailand, is *relatively* close to Bali, Indonesia, in comparison with the whole of Asia. But "close" in this case is 2,400 air km (1,500 miles), or a minimum of a week of travel time by buses, trains, ships, and ferries, if you don't fly.

Unless you plan ahead, you can wind up like the foreigners on their first visit to the United States who get off a plane in New York City, rent a car, and only then ask "How far to the Grand Canyon?" You can get anywhere in the continental United States by car, just like the guidebooks say, but it takes time and might cost you a lot.

To give you a sense of relative scale, it takes 3–4 days and nights by train to cross Europe, Australia, North America, or China, or 7 days and nights across Russia. Even from north to south (the shorter direction across China), Hong Kong is 1,900 km (1,200 miles) from Beijing. Africa is 8,000 km (5,000 miles) north–south and 6,500 km (4,000 miles) east–west. It's almost 1,400 km (900 miles) from one end of South Africa to the other, and that's just one country at the tip of the continent. Even in smaller Third World countries, two-day train and bus journeys are not uncommon, and at the slow pace of the Fourth World, they are routine.

A six-month to two-year trip around the world routinely includes at least US$500–1,500 worth of First World land travel (typically bus or train travel in the United States, Canada, Western Europe, Australia, and/or Japan), US$500 of long-distance train tickets outside the First World, and another US$500–1,000 for air tickets bought along the way (such as for side trips; places where, for unanticipated reasons, buses proved slower or more uncomfortable than expected; or places where there turns out to be no alternative to flying). Renting or leasing a car may be cheaper than bus or train fare for a family or other small group, but it's still expensive. And don't forget the price of gas.

There is no "typical" trip, so don't stick these numbers in your budget blindly: try to estimate your likely costs. It's especially important to get prices in advance, and to include them in your budget, for any likely side trips by air or other air tickets to be bought en route. It's not uncommon for people who rely on obsolete guidebooks to budget US$200 for a side trip that will cost US$1,000, and that they end up being unable to afford.

Daily Living Expenses

Perhaps the most obvious and also the most difficult task in estimating how much your trip will cost is estimating your daily living expenses: lodging, food, local transportation, and incidentals. How can you tell how much you'll spend in a country or region you've never been to before, or if you've never traveled abroad independently, or for as lengthy a period of time? The single budgetary question I'm asked most often is, "How much can I expect to spend per day on a trip around the world?"

There is no easy answer, but here is some general advice and a few rules of thumb:

First, don't try to estimate an overall per diem average to cover travel in different countries or regions. Break down your trip according to how long you plan to spend in each place. Budget separately for each country, or at least for each region of similar price levels and styles of travel. There is no average that will make sense in both the United States and Mexico, Singapore and Indonesia, or Western and Eastern Europe. At a minimum, estimate how much of your trip will be in each of the First, Second, Third, and Fourth Worlds, and draw up a separate budget for the time in each of those worlds.

Second, budget at the high end of the range of your uncertainty. Any of your sources are more likely to give you estimates that are lower than what you actually spend than higher. No matter how recently your sources were there, prices are likely to have increased. And in cultures that take pride in thrift, most people exaggerate how little they spent. People who were on tours or stayed in Intercontinental-type hotels should be ignored as sources of budget advice for independent travelers. Inexperienced travelers are likely to make occasional costly mistakes or be overcharged. Most long-term travelers splurge occasionally on a dose of luxury, such as a night in a fancy hotel. Budget for all of these things. It's much better to have money left over than to run out.

ACCOMMODATIONS

Costs of places to sleep are the most difficult costs to predict, in part because travelers' choices can vary so much, even in the same city. If there is nothing available between a noisy, windowless US$10 cubicle with a sagging, vermin-infested mattress, a filthy toilet and cold shower down the hall, in a hotel that rents most of its rooms by the hour to prostitutes and their clients, and a US$200 air-conditioned room with a telephone, television, and private bath with running hot water at the Intercontinental Hotel, which will you choose?

The example is extreme, but the situation is not unknown. More routinely, in the Third World, you'll face choices such as how much it's worth to you to have air-conditioning versus ceiling fans, a private room versus a bed in a dormitory, a private toilet and shower versus shared ones, a "Western" style (sitting) toilet versus a squat toilet, or reliable electricity (even if that means having a gasoline-powered generator running in the hotel's backyard).

Any one of these choices could double the price of your bed or room; together, this set of choices could make a 10-fold difference in your costs, as could the general level of cleanliness and sanitation you feel is worth paying for.

One tends to learn from travel in the poorer parts of the world that many of our perceived material needs, no matter how strongly desired, are far from essential. Most First World people are capable of making do, often quite happily, with less. One of the main determinants of one's travel costs is the extent to which one can adapt one's desires to what is locally available and affordable. A realistic self-assessment on this score should be your first step in deciding whether your spending will be at the high or low end of the range of travel costs in the regions you will travel.

FOOD

Food is the greatest bargain of travel in the Third and Fourth Worlds and the great bugaboo of travel in the First World. While you can find beds in hostels in Western Europe for little more than the price of a hotel room in China (although with less comfort in Europe than what you'd get at the same price in China, currently the world's greatest hotel bargain), many travelers find that eating in Western Europe is the most unavoidably expensive part of an around-the-world trip. Restaurant meals are labor-intensive, and it's labor that determines expense in high-wage First World countries.

REAL LIFE

The extravagant and multicultural breakfast buffets at hotels in Malaysia have to be seen—and tasted—to be believed!

Cooking for yourself is difficult to arrange and frowned on, even forbidden, by most hotels. You can manage on bread and cheese in Western Europe, but you'll get tired of it after a while, and you'll have a hard time finding a place other than a hostel where you can cook yourself a hot meal. You have a good chance of finding "apartment-hotels" or motels with cooking facilities ("self catering" in British usage) in, among other places, the United States, Canada, Australia, Aotearoa/New Zealand, and South Africa. It's no coincidence that these are countries where travel by car is especially common, because a car makes it easier to carry one's own food and even cooking utensils.

If you're eating in restaurants, you can save a lot by eating your main meal at lunch, when the same menu is typically cheaper that at dinner. Some cultures don't really go in for a substantial breakfast, but a fixed-price all-you-can-eat breakfast buffet included in the room price can be one of the best deals of all.

Many people and guidebooks will advise you not to eat food from street vendors, or that the only safe food is that in hotel restaurants. These guidebooks probably aren't for you. Following this advice for months on end would be intolerably boring and excruciatingly expensive, and not possible in much of the Third and Fourth Worlds outside the biggest cities with their international hotel chains. Prices of food, like everything else, at five-star hotels in poor countries are generally higher than at similar hotels in the United States. There's little evidence that the kitchens of five-star hotels are any cleaner than those of street vendors—you just don't see them to be able to judge. I know people who got sick even when they ate only at five-star hotels.

Most around-the-world travelers end up avoiding pricey hotel food, except where breakfast is included in the room rates, or an occasional splurge at a good hotel buffet.

You'll probably eat most of your meals at small local restaurants and street stalls. You'll probably get sick occasionally, but that's a risk I'm prepared to take. See your doctor before you go, and pay attention to sanitation and hygiene. Is the food being prepared and cooked in front of you so that you can judge, for example? The alternative is to pay 10 times more for all your food—and to miss the best and most interesting local cuisine.

LOCAL TRANSPORTATION AND SUNDRIES

Costs of local transportation, museum admissions, and other sundries are mostly negligible except in the First World, where they can cost as much as hostel accommodations.

Sightseeing by public mass transit in New York, Paris, London, or Tokyo, it's not hard to spend US$10 or more per person per day on subway and bus fares. Local transportation will cost much more if you ever take taxis in First World cities, as most travelers do at least occasionally, either because there is no bus going their way or because they can't find the bus stop or figure out the bus routes.

Museum admissions in the First World are typically US$10–20 each. (Museums in the United States are typically cheap compared to those in Western Europe.) Seeing the highlights of several museums in one day can be a pricey proposition. Admissions to theme parks such as Disneyland can be US$75–100 per person per day, not including food, drink, or souvenirs. The only Third or Fourth World admission fees approaching this cost are the entrance fees to African wildlife preserves (which offset the income lost to agriculture by preventing farming in the parks and funding efforts to suppress poaching), the fees for some World Heritage Sites, or the fees for some mountain climbing or trekking permits.

Clothing

As mentioned in the *Baggage* chapter, I have yet to find a place where locally appropriate clothes weren't also those that were most readily available locally. Plan on buying most of your clothes as you travel, and budget accordingly.

Third World clothes are cheap, but—given that most of the clothes available for sale in the First World are made with Third World labor—we are already accustomed to paying little more than Third World prices for clothes. What you can get more cheaply in poor countries is custom-made clothing. In some countries, ready-made clothes convey higher status ("She's so rich she doesn't sew her own dresses; she buys them at a store"), and made-to-measure clothing is actually cheaper than ready-to-wear.

You'll need to get new clothes as you pass from one climate to another, sometimes when you pass from one cultural region to another, and when your clothes wear out. Even the sturdiest fabrics and construction wear rapidly when they are hand-washed by hand-pounding on rocks (standard operating procedure for the South Asian *dhobi* and other Third World launderers and laundresses), and the dyes that are sometimes used in poor countries can fade relatively quickly in the tropical sun, or run if machine washed.

Gifts to Your Hosts and People You Meet

If you plan to stay with a friend or their family, you'll probably be expected to act as a courier and perhaps to bring substantial gifts. In many countries remittances from those working outside the country are the largest source of foreign exchange, and those who return (or send emissaries) from abroad are expected to send back everything from appliances to food for those left behind.

Try to sound out your contacts in your own country, before you leave, as to what is expected or appropriate. In some countries it may be a terribly insulting faux pas to offer money to defray the costs of putting you up. If your hosts are among the local elite, even in a Third or Fourth World country, they may even be so much richer than you that nothing you could contribute would even make a difference, and/or have servants so that the labor burden of houseguests for the hosts themselves is minimal. In other cases, it would be more insulting not to offer to reimburse your hosts. If you're in doubt, you can always offer nonmonetary gifts. Try to give gifts of real practical value.

You'll have to make your own judgments, in accordance with the local mores, of what to do if your hosts decline your gifts but seem to you to be genuinely in need. Norms of hospitality in much of the world are very strong. Don't be surprised if you are offered the only milk, meat, sugar, or eggs in the house, or if the whole family sleeps on the ground outside so that you can have the only bed. Just remember that you would be expected to do likewise, should the opportunity ever arise for them to visit you.

Souvenirs

The sky's the limit. Just don't get carried away and forget that you have to get them home. Knickknacks tend to seem less worth buying after you've hauled them around in your pack for a few months.

If you plan to spend serious money on specific souvenirs—a hand-knotted carpet in Pakistan, say—price similar items before you leave home. You may be surprised to find that, in a global economy built on cheap bulk shipping, the price difference at the source is so little that it doesn't offset the nuisance of dragging things home.

I prefer souvenirs that aren't available at all at home. Despite the fact that books in English, especially nonfiction, are published in even the most obscure corners of the world, almost none of them are distributed in the United States. Even books from major centers of English-language scholarship, like India, are extremely hard to find in the United States. So I always come home with as many books as I can manage. Reading the thoughts of the people in places I've visited is, for me, a way to extend my intellectual journey long after my physical return.

SAMPLE BUDGETS

I hesitate to give sample budgets at all, for fear that too many readers will look only at the trip durations and the bottom lines, adopting them wholesale. I also fear some readers will reject any realistic high-side budgets for first-time travelers as excessively upscale, or be convinced by them that world travel isn't really as feasible or affordable as I've made it out to be thus far.

These budgets are intended for relative novice travelers: more experienced travelers already know their spending rates in a particular type of country. Many people travel significantly more cheaply than these budgets, but I strongly discourage you from counting on it unless and until you have enough travel experience to be certain that you'll want to and be comfortable doing so. Per diem costs tend to be less for long-term travelers, both because the longer they spend in a place the more they learn about the local style of bargaining and ways to do things cheaply, and because they can amortize fixed costs over a longer time period.

In that spirit, here are a few estimated sample budgets. I include them to give you an idea of what a budget might look like, not to be relied on in estimating how much you will spend. Adjust these sample budgets according to your own situation. Better still, use them as a guide to the things to include in calculating your own projected budget. Remember that all prices given in this book are likely to increase with inflation.

None of these sample budgets include the inherent expenses of traveling, such as maintaining the rent or the mortgage on a house, apartment, or storage locker in your home country; paying your health or other insurance; or payments on student loans, car loans, credit cards, or other debts. These are expenses you would have whether traveling or not, but it's obviously essential to include them in financial planning for your trip. The more you can cut back on these expenses (or turn them into revenue streams, such as by subletting your house or apartment), the more money you'll have available to spend on the direct costs of travel. Obviously, these budgets don't include the value of your time, or lost income, which are actually the largest costs of long-term travel.

Nor do these examples include any allowance for tours or guides. The occasional guide for the day, day-long sightseeing tour of a city, or excursion by hired car can probably be accommodated within these budgets. But if somewhere you plan to take a multiday guided tour, adjust your budget accordingly. A few days rafting a wilderness river; a weeklong camping safari in East African wildlife preserves; a guided climb of Mount Kilimanjaro; a 10-day trek in the Himalayas; a weeklong excursion by jeep from Kathmandu, Nepal, into Tibet; or the minimum tour required to get a visa to a country that will only give visas to those on tours—any of these could set you back US$500–1,000 or more, even on a budget tour.

I don't generally like tours, but there are some things, including all of those I've just listed, that you simply can't do on your own. A high percentage of even budget travelers decide to splurge when they are in a place where they have a once-in-a-lifetime opportunity. Some expensive things really are worth it. If you know you plan a safari, trek, tour, or bungee jump, add the expected cost to your budget. Even if you don't, try to leave yourself an allowance for occasional unexpected opportunities for guided adventures and for unexpected restrictions that force you to do things on a tour basis that you had hoped to accomplish more cheaply on your own.

Note that these examples don't include any projection for earnings along the way. Unless you have a firm job commitment in advance, very unusual skills or credentials that you have verified are in extraordinary demand in some specific place, or a well-established "remote" work assignment that you are confident you can keep up on the road (even with potentially slower and less reliable Internet access), don't count on traveling for any longer than you can afford with the money you have in hand when you leave. If you want to, you may be able to find work along the way. But pickup jobs are unlikely to pay more than enough to live on. The best chances for income are if you already have a job you can do while traveling, as a freelancer telecommuting from wherever you are around the world. Some occupations permit that, especially if you'll be staying mostly in one place rather than constantly moving around. But only a fraction of people who try this succeed.

It's easiest to find work in the First World, but the jobs that are available to travelers in the First World are generally menial ones that pay menial wages—washing dishes, waiting on tables, picking fruit—not jobs on which you can save money toward further travels.

In the South, in a country where the average wage is US$1 a day, there are apt to be very few jobs that pay enough to support a First Worlder at even a backpacker's standard of living. In most Southern countries, you'll be competing for those elite jobs with a host of unemployed or underemployed local university graduates who are apt to have far more impressive credentials and more advanced training than you.

It's possible for native speakers of English with university degrees and/or credentials in teaching English as a foreign language to support themselves as English teachers, at a backpacker's living standard, in many countries. But it's hard work that not everyone is capable of or enjoys, and in those few countries where it pays enough to allow you to save money, employers are quite selective about who they hire. Don't count on it unless you have a definite job lined up in advance.

None of these budgets include alcohol or entertainment. Not because I think you're a teetotaler who doesn't go to concerts, clubs, or performances, but because individual spending on these things varies so much. If you are coming from the United States, budget whatever you spend on this at home, when you aren't working and have time to do the things you most enjoy. Nor do these budgets include health or any other insurance, since some people already have adequate insurance.

All of these examples do include a substantial allowance for contingencies. If you're lucky, you won't need it, but you can't count on being lucky. Give yourself plenty of margin for error.

Here's how one solo backpacker's budget might look for a three-month trip, including 10 weeks in good local hotels in Third World parts of Asia (China, India, etc.) and three weeks in budget hotels in First World Asia (Japan, Taiwan, South Korea, Singapore). Substituting Western Europe for Japan would increase this budget, although a similar budget might be applicable to a trip mixing more and less expensive parts of South America. I would consider this a budget for ample comfort (reasonably clean private rooms, first-class trains and buses) but not an American standard of luxury.

ADVANCE EXPENSES: US$1,000

AIR TICKETS: US$2,500

LONG-DISTANCE BUS AND TRAIN TICKETS: US$950

> Third World (first class) US$400
>
> Japan Rail Pass (14 days) US$550

DAILY EXPENSES (TOTAL 90 DAYS):

- **First World (20 days @ US$90/day): $1,800**

> Accommodations: US$50/day
>
> Food: US$30/day
>
> Local transport and sundries: US$10/day

- **Third World (70 days @ US$30/day): $2,100**

> Accommodations: US$20/day
>
> Food: US$8/day
>
> Local transport and sundries: US$2/day

- Internet (cybercafés, 2 hours weekly): US$100
- Clothing: US$150
- Books and maps: US$100
- Gifts to local people: US$100
- Souvenirs to bring home: US$200
- Contingency fund for emergencies or splurges: US$1,000

TOTAL: US$10,000

For someone trying to stretch money out over a longer time, here's how a couple's per-person budget might look for a yearlong trip, sharing double rooms and other expenses, with one month camping and/or staying in hostels in the First World (e.g. Australia), one month in bed-and-breakfasts or homestays in the Second World (Eastern and Central Europe), six months in budget guesthouses or local hotels in the Third World (e.g. Asia), and four months in the Fourth World (e.g. in Africa). This is a budget for patient, physically fit travelers willing to accept significant discomfort at times, to adapt to local ways of doing things, and to abandon any expectation of doing things the same way they would at home in the United States or Western Europe.

ADVANCE EXPENSES: US$1,500

AIR TICKETS: US$4,000

LONG-DISTANCE BUS AND TRAIN TICKETS: US$1,800

>First World: US$600
>Second World: US$300
>Third World (second-class trains, first-class buses): US$500
>Fourth World: US$400

DAILY EXPENSES (TOTAL 360 DAYS): US$8,700

- **First World (30 days @ US$70/day): $2,100**
  >Accommodations: US$35/day
  >Food: US$25/day
  >Local transport and sundries: US$10/day
- **Second World (30 days @ US$46/day): $1,380**
  >Accommodations: US$25/day
  >Food: US$15/day
  >Local transport and sundries: US$6/day
- **Third World (180 days @ US$21/day): $3,780**
  >Accommodations: US$10/day
  >Food: US$8/day
  >Local transport and sundries: US$3/day
- **Fourth World (120 days @ US$12/day): $1,440**
  >Accommodations: US$5/day
  >Food: US$5/day
  >Local transport and sundries: US$2/day

- Communications: US$700
  >Internet (cybercafés, 2 hours weekly): US$400
  >Unlocked quad-band GSM cell phone: US$50
  >Cell phone SIMs and airtime for local calls: US$250
- Clothing: US$400
- Books and maps: US$300
- Gifts to local hosts: US$300
- Souvenirs to bring home: US$300
- Contingency fund for emergencies or splurges: US$2,000

TOTAL: US$20,000

Some people are surprised that the bottom lines on these budgets are as large as they are. These budgets are, however, all-inclusive. Ask people how much they spent on a trip, and most of them will overlook some of these costs.

What sort of trip might be possible for much less money? Here's a budget for a frugal traveler spending three months exclusively in the Third and Fourth Worlds, flying to several places on one continent, staying exclusively in dormitory-style guesthouses or hostels or sharing a room with a companion in the cheapest local hotels, getting around by rented bicycle or local bus (never taxi), and traveling most long distances within the region by second-class train. This budget should make clear that the largest factor in the cost of your trip is in which world(s) you travel, and that neither airfare nor food and lodging, by themselves, make up the majority of a cost of a typical trip.

The Bottom Line

ADVANCE EXPENSES: US$1,000
AIR TICKETS: US$1,800
LONG-DISTANCE BUS AND TRAIN TICKETS (SECOND CLASS): US$500

DAILY EXPENSES (90 DAYS @ US$20/DAY): US$1,800
Accommodations: US$10/day
Food: US$8/day
Local transport and sundries: US$2/day

- Cybercafés (2 hours weekly): US$100
- Clothing: US$100
- Books and maps: US$100
- Gifts to local hosts: US$100
- Souvenirs to bring home: US$200
- Contingency fund for emergencies or splurges: US$1,000

TOTAL: US$6,700

One of the drawbacks of traveling on a low-end budget such as this is that dormitory-style accommodations are usually found only in towns and cities with substantial numbers of tourists. Unless you are willing to put up with exceptionally "rustic" accommodations, getting off the beaten track often requires staying in local hotels that, while excellent value for the price, are significantly more expensive than dorm beds in hostels in travelers' ghettoes. This budget also leaves little room for occasional short airplane flights or rides by chartered car or taxi to places that can't be reached by train or bus. A little bit more money can buy you a great deal more freedom to go where you want.

These are merely three examples, none of which may correspond to your style of travel or level of comfort, or the division of your time between more and less expensive places. They are intended to give you an idea of the kinds of things to include in your budget, not to be relied on for the bottom line.

My first trip around the world, in 1989, lasted three months and cost a total of today's equivalent of US$5,000 per person, including airfare and a Eurail Pass. That was a fairly low-budget trip. I was sharing rooms with a companion, and we were entirely in the Third World except for two weeks in Western Europe, where we stayed with friends and relatives.

My most recent trip around the world—20 years older, with both more time and more money and, yes, traveling in more comfort—was a 13-month sabbatical that cost a grand total of between US$25,000 and US$30,000 per person. We spent almost a third of our time in the First World, including six weeks in Western Europe, five weeks in Australia, and six weeks in the United States and Canada. We could have done it for substantially less, but we both had income while we were traveling: We had rented out our house, my partner had a partially paid sabbatical, and I had some income from writing and consulting work even while I was on the road (although it required me to spend more time in cybercafés than I otherwise would have). With that income and no debt, we didn't have to compromise our "wish list" much on account of cost. We didn't do things in a needlessly expensive way, and we took almost no guided tours, but we went where we wanted to go and did what we wanted to do. In some places we stayed in hostels, while in others, where we felt it was necessary for adequate comfort, we stayed in lodgings only one step below the best available. Our air tickets were more expensive than most around-the-world tickets (multiple stops on each of six continents and a convoluted route necessitated by the dates of meetings with friends and other events along the way), and we could afford major splurges like more than a month of car rental.

As these sample budgets and examples show, it's not just, or even primarily, about "traveling cheaply" versus "traveling luxuriously." Luxury is cheaper in some places than others, and there are *many* variables—how much time you spend in which regions, whether you travel solo or share a room with a companion or a car with a family, whether you cook for yourself or eat in restaurants, how much you spend on alcohol, whether you travel on your own or take guided tours, and so on—that determine the total cost of your trip.

Once again, the most important thing is to break down your trip according to the amounts of time you plan to spend in more and less expensive countries, as I've done here, and to estimate per diem expenses separately for each. Whether you spend two weeks or a month in Western Europe before continuing to South and Southeast Asia for the balance of a trip can make a US$1,000 difference to your total budget. Plan accordingly. All else being equal, I would organize the overall direction of my trip with the most expensive places at the end, so that my stay there could be cut short if my budget was running low.

HOW TO BRING MONEY

Financial systems are varied and unpredictable. ATM withdrawals are generally the easiest and cheapest way to get money while traveling, but you can't count on them always being available. Bring both traveler's checks and cash (U.S. dollars and/or euros) for times and places ATMs aren't available, aren't working, or have excessive fees.

ATM Cards

Where you can find an ATM in working order that accepts your card, ATM cards are generally the cheapest way to get money while traveling. Because ATMs dispense money in local currency, an ATM withdrawal transfers money to you from your bank account back home, and converts it to local currency, in a single transaction.

You can leave most of the money you'll need for a long trip safely in your bank (or in a money-management, investment, or brokerage account with check-writing and ATM card privileges) at home, even earning interest. If you don't want to leave that much in a checking account, you can probably arrange overdraft protection to automatically transfer money from your savings account to your checking account as needed to cover your checks.

Many ATMs have multilingual user interfaces. If there's nothing on the screen in a language you understand, look for the word "English," or the stars and stripes (United States) or Union Jack (U.K.), as the symbol for "click here for instructions in English." The major ATM networks all have directories of locations of linked ATMs on their websites (see the *Resource Guide*). You aren't likely to be online when you are looking for an ATM, but these directories can help give you an idea of how easy it will be to find ATMs linked to your bank in the places you are going. Are they only in the capital city, or are they in smaller places as well?

The Bottom Line

REAL LIFE

On our last trip around the world we were in at least two countries where we found no ATMs, and a third where U.S.-issued cards couldn't legally be used because of U.S. sanctions against the national bank (even though it was entirely legal for us to travel and spend money there).

If the ATM displays one or more of the same logos of banking networks (Star, Plus, etc.) as on your card, it will *probably* work. But it might work anyway—more and more banks are networked, and affiliations change more often than signs on ATMs are updated or cards are reissued. The only way to tell if an ATM will work with your card is to try it. If it doesn't work the first time, go to another bank rather than trying the same one over and over. Repeated failed attempts to use the same ATM will be flagged as a sign of potential fraud, and the ATM might swallow your card and not give it back!

Check your bank's rules for foreign-currency ATM withdrawals carefully before you leave. Most banks impose a per-transaction surcharge for foreign withdrawals, as well as a percentage surcharge above the interbank (wholesale) exchange rate. (See the discussion of exchange rates and fees in the section below on *Changing Money*.)

Charges and withdrawal limits can be imposed both by your bank and by the one that owns the ATM where you withdraw the money. With some cards—especially those issued by Internet banks, stock broker-

REAL LIFE

What's the best bank for long-term travelers? It depends on how much money you have. The best deals for international travelers and expats from U.S. financial institutions are offered as part of integrated "asset management" accounts with brokerages and money management companies like Schwab and Fidelity. They offer features like ATM cards with no fees for foreign transactions, and reimbursement of any fees charges by foreign banks where you use your card. Some banks offer similar asset management accounts, with varying benefits and minimum balances. To qualify for any of these accounts, however, you have to have substantial assets in a retirement account or other investments with the same institution. Similar asset management services are offered by "offshore" banks in the Channel Islands, Isle of Man, and Jersey. These are mainly marketed to expatriate U.K. citizens, but they are available to anyone who meets similar minimum investment thresholds, and you can open an account by mail or online from overseas—you need never set foot in the Channel Islands (not that there's any reason not to if you want).

ages, or other entities that don't have their own ATMs—the card issuer will reimburse the fees charged by other banks to use their ATMs. Given the prevalence of extra fees for international ATM withdrawals, this can be a significant benefit.

The Bottom Line

All else being equal, it's generally cheaper to make one larger withdrawal than several smaller ones, since there are almost always per-transaction fees from one or both of the banks involved (the card issuer and the ATM owner). Get as much money at a time as you are allowed, you are comfortable carrying in cash, and you are confident you will use before having to exchange it for another currency (you lose a percentage on every currency conversion). But if your withdrawal doesn't go through, try a smaller amount—it may be that the ATM operator has a smaller withdrawal limit than your card issuer. I've been in places where the limit at the only working ATM was as little as US$50 per day.

Don't get sanguine about the prospects for finding ATMs in the provinces just because there's an ATM around the corner from your hotel or hostel in the capital. Stock up on cash and/or ask other travelers who've just been there about ATM availability before you head for remote or rural areas.

If you plan to use your card overseas, or at any ATMs other than those of your own bank, change your PIN (access code) to one no more than four digits long. Some ATMs only transmit the first four digits of the PIN. If your PIN is longer, you might not be able to withdraw money. In the worst case, this too could result in the machine seizing your card on suspicion of fraud—a huge hassle if you're halfway around the world.

ATM and debit cards have different, worse, rules for unauthorized or fraudulent usage than do credit cards. Make sure you know what your maximum loss is if your card and/or PIN are stolen. For cards issued in the United States, your loss is usually limited to US$50, but only if you report any loss, theft, or suspicion of fraud to your card issuer within 48 hours. Check each of your statements carefully and immediately when you receive them. Report any discrepancy or suspicious charge immediately, by phone and by follow-up letter by express mail. If you don't report an unauthorized charge in time, you could lose the entire contents of your account, and/or your entire credit limit.

As at home, use caution when you choose an ATM. Whenever possible, use an ATM inside a bank. Robberies at ATMs are common, and thieves have been known to install fake ATMs as freestanding kiosks, against the outside walls of banks or other buildings, or as shells that fit over all or part (such as the card slot) of a real ATM. The fake ATM scans the magnetic strip on your card, asks you to enter your PIN, and then displays a polite message saying that it's out of cash. The thieves operating the fake ATM use this information to make a "cloned" copy of your card, and then withdraw money from your account at a real ATM.

ATM cards can't be relied on to the exclusion of other ways of accessing your money. I've seen many a traveler stranded for lack of money because they counted on being able to use a card that didn't happen to be accepted locally, or was accepted only by a bank or ATM that was closed, out of service, out of cash, or embargoed by the U.S. Treasury's Office of Foreign Assets Control (OFAC) under one or another of its sanctions programs. Have a backup.

Debit Cards

Cash withdrawals on some debit cards carrying credit card logos (e.g. Visa or MasterCard) are treated as ATM withdrawals. On other similar-looking cards from different issuers, cash withdrawals are treated as "cash advances" and subject to a minimum one month's interest, which can add another 1.5 percent or more to your costs. Check with the bank that issued your card, before you go, to see whether your debit card is really an ATM card (good) or a credit card (bad) for purposes of cash withdrawals. You can get stored-value debit cards ("traveler's cheque cards") from American Express, but unlike traveler's checks they are subject to the same fees and limitations as any ATM withdrawal. If you want a backup to your regular ATM card, traveler's checks—paper ones—are still the way to go.

Credit and Charge Cards

It's easy to imagine, in this era of electronic commerce, that you

REAL LIFE

In response to lawsuits and legislation targeting hidden fees for foreign-currency card use, many U.S. card issuers are switching from added fees for foreign-currency card transactions (ATM, debit, or credit) to added per-transaction or percentage fees for all "foreign transactions" regardless of currency. That means that even if the charge is billed in U.S. dollars, the card issuer will charge the cardholder the fee whenever the merchant's address of record is outside the United States. Some cardholders have tacked on these fees, for example, on tickets for flights originating in the United States and billed in U.S. dollars, if the airline is based in another country. These fees are entirely unjustified, as the card issuer's costs for clearing a U.S.-dollar transaction are identical regardless of where the merchant is located. The rip-off is especially egregious with airline tickets, since almost all foreign-flag airlines that do business in the United States clear payments for their U.S. ticket sales through the same U.S. financial clearinghouse that is used by U.S.-based airlines, the Airlines Reporting Corporation (ARC). Shop around, and avoid cards that charge "foreign transaction" fees.

could set off on a trip around the world with only plastic to pay for it all. Bank-card companies are fond of telling us in how many places, "worldwide," their cards are accepted. But outside the First World, credit and charge cards

"Chip and PIN" or "Swipe and Sign"?

Credit and debit cards in the United States have the card data stored on a magnetic stripe, and use your signature (matched against the signature on the back of the card) to authenticate that you are the authorized cardholder.

Credit cards in most of the rest of the world have been switching to a different system that stores the card data on a computer chip embedded in the card, and requires a four-digit PIN code instead of a signature each time they are used. You can recognize a chip and pin card by the thumbnail-sized array of metal contacts on the face of the card through which the reader — into which you insert the card — communicates with the chip.

Switching to chip-and-PIN cards requires replacing not just the cards but all the card readers in every shop, credit-card operated vending machine, and so forth. The credit card industry in the United States has been divided on whether to make the change. Card issuers' current fee schedules give them a larger cut of signature transactions than of PIN transactions, so most U.S. banks have opposed the change. Merchants support a switch to chip-and-PIN, but only if, as it was in the U.K., it's combined with anticonsumer changes in the law to make cardholders, instead of merchants, liable for fraudulent charges. The logjam doesn't seem likely to be broken without U.S. Congressional action.

For now, here's the situation: Businesses anywhere in the world that accept VISA and/or MasterCard are required by their merchant agreements to accept both chip-and-PIN and swipe-and-sign cards. But they aren't required to have automated devices capable of handling both types, and almost nobody does.

With a U.S.-issued swipe-and-sign card in Europe, or with a chip-and-PIN card without a mag stripe in the United States, you won't be able to use most credit-card operated vending machines or payment kiosks. You have to allow extra time to find and stand in line for a teller (if there is one) and have your purchase processed manually if you want to pick up a prepaid ticket at a train station, check in for a flight paid for by credit card, buy a subway ticket or pay for parking with a card, and so forth. Clerks in some places with lots of U.S. customers may be familiar with the process, but off the tourist track and in smaller establishments that don't see U.S.-issued cards often, they may have to consult a supervisor or telephone their bank for instructions on how to process a signature-authorized charge.

The biggest problems come when there's no human teller or ticket clerk available and no option for cash payment, as is common at secondary and suburban train stations and at subway, streetcar, and other transit stops. Even downtown big-city transit stations may be unattended at night and on weekends and holidays. Try to pick up your tickets during business hours at a main big-city station (even if that's not where you will be leaving from), and buy transit tickets (or a stored-value transit card) at the airport or a major terminus with an attended ticket window the first chance you get when you arrive in a new city, rather than counting on being able to do so later.

It's possible to make dual-mode cards, usable worldwide, with a chip, PIN and mag stripe, but few banks issue them. The first U.S. financial institution to start issuing dual-mode cards for its customers who want to be able to use them abroad was the State Employees Credit Union of North Carolina in early 2011. It remains to be seen whether or when larger U.S. banks will follow suit.

are of limited use for independent or budget travelers, except for large luxury splurges or emergency expenses like a hospital bill or a ticket home.

Contrary to credit-card companies' propaganda, credit cards are not widely accepted for purchases outside the First World, and sometimes only at the most expensive establishments. In a Third World country, if you have only a credit card to pay for a hotel or a meal, you may be able to eat and sleep only at the most expensive hotel in town. You can get cash advances with credit cards, but those are more expensive than ATM withdrawals.

Most credit-card issuers charge per-transaction fees for foreign purchases. These fees are a small percentage of a large purchase, but can add up quickly if you use a credit card for a large number of small purchases.

You can never predict which type of card will be accepted in a given place. It's a tradeoff: if you carry more types of cards (assuming you have them), you have a slightly better chance of being able to get cash advances, or charge things on your cards, in more places. But you have more cards to carry, more cards to lose, more statements to access and audit for fraudulent charges each month, and more financial risk if your cards are lost or stolen, especially if they are stolen in a remote or inaccessible place where it's a long time before you are able to report them stolen or check your statements.

Lost or Stolen Cards

Whatever card(s) you carry, keep copies of the cards and instructions for reporting lost or stolen cards with the copies of your other vital documents, separate from the cards themselves. If your card and/or PIN are lost or stolen, report it immediately, both by phone and by follow-up letter by express mail. (Email isn't usually sufficient to protect your legal rights.)

Remember that you can't call a U.S. or Canadian 800, 866, 877, or 888 number, or most other national "freephone" numbers, from other countries. If the card itself only gives a "toll-free" number for reporting lost or stolen cards, check your most recent statement or call the card issuer, before you leave, to get a number that you can call from overseas.

Stolen credit cards make their way rapidly into the hands of large-scale professional criminal gangs that will run up thousands of dollars of charges within days or even hours. The sooner you report a loss or theft of your card and/or PIN, the lower your liability for unauthorized use.

Some card issuers can arrange to have a replacement card issued overseas, or will send you a replacement card within a few days, anywhere in the world that FedEx serves. Other issuers, even with the same brand of card, may not be willing to send a replacement to anywhere except your billing address, by regular mail, and may take several weeks to do so. Check before you go, but be aware that these policies can change—one more reason to have a backup means of access to your funds back home, and an emergency supply with you of cash and traveler's checks.

Tell Your Bank Your Travel Plans

Banks and credit card issuers routinely monitor ATM, credit, and debit card usage to detect fraudulent usage or violations of economic sanctions. In general, that's a good thing: if your card is stolen, your bank will probably cancel it as soon as the thieves start running up a sudden flurry of charges, before you even realize or report that your card is missing.

If you aren't careful, however, these antifraud and other automated monitoring and blocking systems can keep you from legitimately using your own card. Whatever the reason your card has been blocked for suspicion of fraud or improper usage, you'll probably learn about it only when your card is mysteriously declined, and you then call your bank to find out what's up.

Some banks completely blacklist charges from certain countries. I wouldn't recommend using a credit card in Nigeria—but if you try, your bank is unlikely to approve the charge, at least without hearing from you to verify that it's legit. You're especially likely to have problems like this in Africa.

Other problems result from banks that go overboard in their avoidance of any possible violation of government embargoes, sanctions, or money-laundering rules—even if that blocks their customers from making perfectly legal use of their cards.

The Bottom Line

For example, Charles Schwab Bank—which generally offers among the best services for international travelers of any U.S. bank—froze my account without warning or notice when I tried to check my balance from a Syrian IP address. Rather then making any attempt to figure out which Syria-related transactions are with the handful of embargoed Syrians, they freeze all transactions (including deposits and preauthorized bill payments!) from any account linked in any way to Syria. It took me hours on the phone after I left Syria, and hundreds of dollars in expenses, to sort out the ensuing mess of my finances. I was never able to entirely undo the damage to my credit rating. Schwab hadn't bothered to warn me when I told them I was going to Syria, but I later learned that they will allow their cards to be used in Syria (or, I suspect, Iran) only if you give them a signed statement, in advance, attesting that you know U.S. citizens aren't allowed to do business with the Syrian government or a list of other "specially-designated nationals."

Schwab Bank's actions in freezing my account were almost certainly illegal, I was later advised by experts, but I suspect that they are standard operating procedure for U.S. banks. They'd rather violate their customers' rights than risk running afoul of OFAC. And there wasn't much I could do about it, especially while I was traveling and relying on access to that account.

Other banks will only approve charges outside your home country if you have notified them in advance of the specific countries in which you will be traveling or in which you will be making charges or cash withdrawals, and the dates you will be doing so.

If you call your card issuer to advise them of a planned trip, they will ask you what dates you will be traveling, and where. Banks in the U.S. still don't seem to have figured out that people charge things over the Internet with merchants in other countries. What really matters, and what you need to tell them and have entered in their records, are where and when you might make charges, regardless of where and when you might be yourself. I've had charges declined by my bank when I tried to buy a ticket from an airline based in Ireland for a flight from the U.K. to Germany ("You didn't tell us you would be traveling in Ireland," and indeed I wasn't, but that's where the charge from the airline showed up as being from), when I tried to make a deposit for a hotel room for my first night in Sydney while I was still in Singapore ("You didn't tell us you would be in Australia until next week"), when I tried to top up a U.K.-issued global roaming SIM for my cell phone while I was in Brazil, and when charges from a hotel were put through by its head office in another country.

To avoid surprises or problems like these, contact each of your card issuers, preferably by certified mail (keeping a copy for yourself for reference in case of later difficulties), to tell them the complete list of countries where you will be traveling or where any company with which you might authorize charges is located, and the dates when you might be making such charges (including dates before or after your actual stay in each country).

Redundancy and Backup Plans

ATM, credit, or charge cards can be lost, stolen, damaged, or left in your pocket in the wash. (Yes, this has happened to me. Commercial dryers are often hot enough to ruin the plastic.) Bank, brokerage, or credit accounts can be frozen without warning, for your own protection, if your bank suspects that fraudulent charges or withdrawals have been made. You might need to have your own account frozen if you suspect that someone was eavesdropping on you while you checked your account in a cybercafé or at a public Wi-Fi hotspot, if someone steals your email password, or if your computer is lost or stolen. And if a bank freezes one of your accounts, it might well freeze them all.

To minimize the hassles in any of these circumstances, carry more than one card issued by different financial institutions. Only get one card at a time out of your hidden stash, to minimize the risk that all your cards will be stolen at once. Keep an emergency reserve of money accessible from an account with a different bank.

Cash

Unfortunately, there is really no way to avoid carrying a significant amount of cash. U.S. dollars are the world's most widely accepted and easily negotiable medium of exchange, followed by euros. (Followed, although as an increasingly distant third, by American Express traveler's checks, which are, in effect, an unregulated private paper currency.)

Small denomination notes (outside the United States, pieces of paper money are referred to as "notes," not "bills") in local currencies are usually more useful and harder to find than larger notes, except in countries with collapsing currencies, where you may need a sack to carry US$20 worth of local bank notes. Money changers and banks usually give you your money in as few notes and coins as possible. That's fine for them, but rarely what's most useful to you. A rule of thumb for dealing with money changers: unless they hand you a large pile of notes, hand back some of the notes they offer you and ask for smaller notes and more coins.

Money changers usually give the best rates for large bills (US$100 and €100 or €500 notes). But for paying for things directly, smaller bills can be more useful. In a country where per capita income averages US$2 a day or less, changing a US$20 bill, or a local note of equivalent value, is like trying to change a US$100 bill at a corner store in the United States. It's usually possible, but the storekeeper may not like it.

I'd start a lengthy around-the-world trip with at least US$100 in US$1 bills, plus another US$500 in US$5s, US$10s, and US$20s. In a pinch, you can pay for almost anything, anywhere in the world, in exact change in U.S. dollars. You can't count on change in dollars, though. So if all you have is larger bills, you may have to overpay grossly. If you arrive when the banks at the airport are closed, do you want to have pay US$20 for a cab ride from the airport to the city that should cost US$2?

REAL LIFE

In Ethiopia and Eritrea, there were no ATMs and no banks that would cash a traveler's check. Money changers scrutinized each bill for small tears, marks, dirt, or other flaws. Only about half of the US$100 bills we'd been carrying in our money belts for the previous several months passed muster.

Depending on my destinations, I'd bring perhaps another US$1,000–2,000 in US$100 bills for places where there are no ATMs and it's difficult or impossible to cash traveler's checks, or where dollars are used in parallel or in preference to a collapsed local currency.

Since 1996, the designs of U.S. paper money have been changing, with larger, off-center portraits and other changes to make notes harder to counterfeit. Further changes, including different colors for different denominations (the norm in other countries), are contemplated in coming years. All older designs of U.S.-dollar notes remain in circulation and are equally valid, but in some countries banks and money changers may be reluctant to accept them. There's a reason for their fears: in most countries old currency is "demonetized" and taken out of circulation, or declared worthless, when new currency designs are introduced. Try to bring only new notes in the latest design.

Wherever you are, and whatever currency you are using, insist on getting the cleanest, newest-looking notes you can. In some countries no one will accept old, torn, or dirty notes, and everyone will try to pass them off on foreigners.

It may feel strange at first to carry so much money. "I felt like a drug dealer when I first got here, walking around with all this money in my belt," the newly appointed chargé d'affaires at the U.S. embassy in Kazakhstan once told me. Obviously, you can't put 100 singles in a money belt. Wrap them well and disperse them through your luggage in several packets. Keep your money belt or other document stash small enough not to be visible inside your clothes, and never open it in public if you can avoid doing so.

Reserve the limited space in your money belt or other hidden stash for the real essentials that would be most difficult to replace: your passport, your immunization record ("yellow book"), your airline tickets (and any expensive rail or bus tickets), your ATM and credit card(s), key emergency contacts (if you are robbed, your cell phone will be taken and you might be forced to turn over your email password) and enough emergency cash (some in U.S. dollars and some in local currency) to tide you over if you are robbed of everything but your money belt.

I fold a US$100 bill up in each set of copies of my documents. After all, you should only need the copies of your documents if your money belt is stolen, in which case you will need money for at least a few days until you can get your documents replaced. For what it's worth, more people lose money belts—leaving them in hotel rooms or showers, for example—than have them stolen from under their clothes, or by robbers who strip them naked. I've never lost any of my tickets or essential documents, although I've had my pocket picked of a wallet with nothing in it but a small amount of local currency. A fair number of people have their pockets picked or have their wallets, cell phones, cameras, belt packs, shoulder bags, luggage, or visible valuables stolen.

If it's hard to get hold of cash U.S. dollars, euros will do. You can change euro notes, or pay a hotel bill with them, almost anywhere. And by far the most compact way to carry a really large amount of cash is in €500 notes. But there are relatively few countries outside the eurozone where euro cash gets a better exchange rate than U.S.-dollar bills. Even in countries like Turkey where prices for hotels and other tourist services are often quoted in euros, I've almost always found merchants happy to take U.S. dollars. I often carry a modest stash of euros, but have never really needed it.

Any money changer in the world knows what U.S. dollars are worth in local currency, and can figure out what euros are worth. You can't count on any other currency as a reliable backup in the places where you have to rely on cash. The power of the euro as a global rival to the U.S. dollar has made other currencies like the British pound much less widely accepted than they were a decade ago.

Traveler's Checks

If you can afford to do so, bring a reserve of traveler's checks in U.S. dollars, to show as proof of sufficient funds for visas and at borders and in case your ATM card is lost or stolen and can't be replaced for a while.

You can get checks in major First World currencies, such as euros or Japanese yen, but not in Third World currencies. As with cash, U.S. dollar–denominated traveler's checks are the easiest to cash, followed by euro checks.

Bring primarily US$100 or US$500 checks. Cashing a check can be a tedious process that you won't want to do more often than necessary (it's not uncommon for it to take hours), and many banks and money changers charge per-check encashment fees or give better exchange rates for larger-denomination checks. Thus US$20 or US$50 checks are useful only if you will be in a country so briefly that you won't be spending close to US$100 before you would leave the country, which is really quite rare. In such cases it's usually easier just to change a US$20 bill than to bother with traveler's checks at all.

In recent years I've rarely spent traveler's checks, but I've still been glad to have them an emergency reserve. I've mostly used them as proof of sufficient funds. A pile of traveler's checks lets you prove to visa officers or border guards that you have enough money to support yourself in their country, without tempting them to take some of it for themselves the way a similar wad of cash would. An ATM or credit card won't suffice for that purpose without bank statements to back it up, which you really don't want to carry with you or make available to potential identity thieves.

MONEY TRANSFERS FROM HOME

If you have an ATM card or a credit card that can be used for a cash advance, it's easier than you may realize to have someone send you money from home. Anyone can deposit money into your bank account, and anyone can pay your credit card bill. It's withdrawals from your account, not deposits or payments to your account, that require your signature.

It helps for the person making the deposit or payment to have a deposit slip or statement with the address and account details, but preprinted deposit slips and payment coupons aren't essential. In a pinch, someone can get all the necessary information by phone or email, and they can make a deposit or payment by mail or by electronic transfer from their bank. As soon as a deposit is cleared by your bank, you can withdraw it from any ATM worldwide with which your bank is linked. It's the cheapest (only the normal foreign-currency ATM charges) and fastest (as fast as your bank clears the deposit) way to have money transferred to yourself anywhere in the world.

Don't even think of trying to have money wired to your while you are traveling. Contrary to popular belief, wiring money is neither cheap nor fast nor reliable. Procedures vary enormously from place to place and bank to bank, too much so to give general advice other than not to attempt it. I've seen too many stranded travelers whose money ran out or was stolen, trying to eke out an existence in some travelers' ghetto while they wait for money to be wired from home.

If you don't have an ATM, credit, or charge card, it is often faster and more reliable to have someone send you a bank check by air express (FedEx, DHL, or the like, or international postal Express Mail) than to try to have money wired. If your contact goes to a major bank or a foreign exchange broker, it's possible to get a check drawn on a bank in the country where you are, which you can cash with relative ease once you receive it. If not, the next best thing is a bank check (cashier's check) in U.S. dollars, drawn on a major international bank whose name is likely to be recognized by banks in the country where you are. But this is a last resort, not a first one, and is still likely to take a week or more and cost a total of at least US$50 in courier charges and fees from the banks at both ends.

CHANGING MONEY

Unless you've gotten local currency directly from an ATM, or have traveler's checks in local currency, you'll need to exchange your U.S. dollars or other foreign currency for local currency. Usually this is necessary each time you cross an international border, although in a few "monetary unions" or "financial communities" the same currency is used in several neighboring countries. (Examples of multinational currencies like this are the euro and the two regional CFA francs of Central and West Africa.)

Places to change money range from legal or illegal freelancers who approach you on the street brandishing calculators and whispering their only two words of English, "Change money?" to government and private banks and independent currency exchange offices or kiosks. Even in most English-speaking countries, signs for currency exchanges are more likely to use the French, Spanish, or Italian terms "Bureau de Change" or "Cambio" than the English "Money Exchange" or "Currency Exchange."

Don't waste too much time worrying about where and how to get the best exchange rate. While rates and fees will vary between banks, legal private money changers, and government agencies (I've been in at least one country where the best exchange rate was at the post office!), legal rates of exchange rarely vary by more than a few percent. Shop around a little if you don't like the first rate you are quoted, but don't get carried away. In my opinion, the differences in exchange rates are usually less important than the differences in convenience and reliability. Try to keep in mind how much money is really at stake. Is it really worth an hour's bus ride across town, standing in line for an extra hour, or risking getting ripped off in a backstreet deal, to save a dollar or two, or even 10?

The exchange rate published in the newspaper is usually the "interbank" rate used for electronic transactions involving hundreds of thousands or millions of dollars. You'll never get this rate for cash, traveler's check, credit or debit card, or ATM transactions. You can expect to pay 2–3 percent more than the interbank rate for credit, debit, or ATM transactions (plus any per-transaction fees from your bank for foreign charges or withdrawals), and a minimum of about 4–5 percent above the interbank rate for cash or traveler's check conversions. Worst-case retail rates for cash or traveler's checks, especially with captive markets (e.g., when there is only one money changer at the airport or the border when you arrive) can be up to 10 percent above the interbank rate.

The difference between the interbank buying and selling rates is very small—the small percentage margin is made up for by the huge size of the transactions for which the interbank rate is used. But the retail "spread" is much higher.

An easy way to figure out the margin being charged for cash or traveler's check conversion is to divide the spread between the buying and selling rates in half. If the sign in the Cambio lists the "buying" rate for dollars at £1 = USD1.90, and the "selling" rate at £1 = USD2.10, you can assume that the interbank rate is halfway in between at 2.00. Thus the Cambio is making a reasonable 5 percent margin on both buying and selling transactions.

On the other hand, suppose the buying rate for dollars (USD) is USD1 = 1,650 Tanzanian shillings (TZS), and the selling rate is 1,000 shillings = USD0.74. If you don't know the interbank rate, how can you tell if this is a good deal? The selling rate, TZS1,000 = USD0.74, is equivalent to USD1 = TZS1,350. So the interbank rate is presumably about USD1 = TZS(1,650 + 1,350) / 2 = TZS1,500. That means the spread (1,650 - 1,350) / 1,500 = 20 percent, and the money changer's margin on either buying or selling transactions is an unpleasant 10 percent. Buy or sell your shillings elsewhere, if you can.

Simply put, the smaller the difference between the buying and selling rates (converted into the same terms), the smaller the money changer's margin and the better the deal. If the math seems confusing, practice until it becomes second nature, as this technique enables you to evaluate exchange-rate offers without knowing anything about the "official" or interbank rate.

The "black market," where one exists, is by definition illegal. The difference between the legal and black-market exchange rates is directly proportional to the risks of black marketeering. The more money you stand to gain by changing money illegally, the more dangerous it is bound to be.

If the black-market rate is only slightly better than the bank rate, that probably means that the black market is only nominally illegal, and fairly safe, although you can never complain to the police if you are shortchanged or defrauded by a black marketeer. In such cases the main issue is probably convenience or availability, rather than the small difference in rates. It isn't necessarily any easier to change money, much less cash a traveler's check, on the street than at a bank. I don't usually bother with the black market in places like this.

Where there's an extreme difference between the legal and black-market rates, you can take it for granted that black marketeering is severely punished. In some countries you can get 10 times more local currency units for a dollar on the black market than at a bank, but it's a capital offense, for both the customer and the trader. On the other hand, such countries are frequently too expensive for budget travelers unless they change money on the black market. Police know this, of course, and foreign backpackers in such countries are under constant suspicion and scrutiny for black marketeering. Unscrupulous locals can also make good money in rewards from the police by informing on foreigners, even setting them up or framing them, for changing money illegally. Informing or entrapment may be more profitable and less risky than actual black marketeering. You have to be extremely careful and discreet, and if possible, avoid dealing with strangers.

Most countries fall at one or the other extreme. Least common is the situation where the black-market rate is substantially but not inordinately higher than the legal rate, and black marketeering is only moderately risky (punishable only by a moderate fine, for example, rather than by imprisonment or flogging). Make your own decision, but at least be selective about who you deal with, and where, and be conscious of the risks and benefits at stake.

Expatriate foreigners who live in a country are often the best people to consult about whether to change money on the black market, how risky it is, or how to do it most safely. At least you can ask them about the black market with little risk that they will turn you in or set you up to be arrested or ripped off. If it is worth dealing with the black market, expats may be able to refer you to reliable contacts of theirs, such as local businesspeople, with whom you can change money much more safely than with strangers on the street. Failing any contacts with expats, ask at your hotel, or at a restaurant or shop where you have established a relationship, for advice on where and with whom to change money.

Banks and money changers generally only change paper notes (bills), not coins. Try not to have any coins left over when you leave a country, or you could be stuck with a pocket full of expensive souvenirs. The United States is extremely unusual in using paper money instead of coins for denominations as small as US$1. In the U.K., for example, notes smaller than £10 (about US$16) are rarely seen, and £1 (US$1.60) and £2 (US$3.20) coins are common. Even many Third World countries have coins worth more than any coin in common use in the United States, and your pocket change can easily be worth US$20.

If you have coins or small amounts of paper currency left at the end of your stay in the country that you don't want to save for souvenirs or future visits, and that the money changers won't take, you can sometimes exchange them with travelers headed in the opposite direction. On the other hand, if you arrive in a country when all the money changers are closed, you can often find a departing traveler, or a returning local, to sell you enough local currency to tide you over until you get to a bank or currency exchange.

MANAGING YOUR FINANCES WHILE YOU ARE ON THE ROAD

While you might wish to ignore what's happening back home, life, death, and taxes will all go on. If you are going away for more than a month, you'll do well to find someone to handle the essentials of your affairs while you're gone. Most long-term travelers find someone to do these sorts of things for them—most often a parent, child, sibling, or other close friend—or try to manage them all on the Internet.

The Internet has limitations and risks. Sometimes you really need to talk to someone, and international phone tag can be complicated. Sometimes an unexpected notice arrives by mail and needs to be dealt with. The biggest drawback to routine reliance on the Internet to manage your affairs is the risk that one of your user names and passwords can be stolen when you use them to log in at a cybercafé. If you've set up your affairs so that they can all be managed online, that means they are all at risk if your identity is stolen. If you can't find any alternative to managing your money online, try to set aside a limited amount of money in a separate account for the trip, so even if it's compromised, you won't lose your life's savings. Consider carrying a miniature Internet access device—a netbook or smaller—to access money management websites. The risk of eavesdropping is much less, although it still exists, if you use your own computer rather than one provided by a cybercafé. Finally, use a bank that will give you a hardware token for more secure online access to your account. (See the sidebar *Risks of Internet Money Management.*)

It's relatively easy to pay bills online, but what about creditors who don't send you their bills electronically? Whether it's real estate taxes, professional dues, or other one-off expenses, in the course of a year there are probably some bills you will need to pay that will arrive by postal mail. One way to deal with this is to have someone check your mail, sort out the potentially important items from the junk mail—a tedious task and time commitment that shouldn't be underestimated—and scan and email you anything that looks like it might require action. The other approach is to have your bills sent to a service that will scan them for you and email them to you or let you view and pay them online. Paytrust.com (a service of the financial software company Intuit), will give you your own post office box number, and will scan and forward to you all documents that arrive at that box, for US$10 per month. We used Paytrust on our most recent and longest trip. It's not 100 percent reliable—check regularly and be alert for bills you should have gotten that don't show up in Paytrust—but it's a workable option if you don't have someone you trust who is able and willing to deal with your mail and finances while you're away.

There is no real substitute for a friend at home you can call on from time to time, or in an emergency—someone who can hold your mail for you, pay an

Risks of Internet Money Management

Internet banking, bill payment, and investment management sites offer a deceptively attractive alternative to personal assistance with your finances from a trusted friend or family member back home, but only at the price of bringing a computer with you or taking a serious risk by using public computers for money management.

All cybercafés and public terminals are inherently insecure, even when you're accessing a highly secure website. Everything you type, every mouse click, and everything you see on the screen can be, and often is, monitored and logged by the cybercafé proprietor or network administrator. Ignore anything the Web service or the cybercafé says about their security procedures. Because the data can be captured before it is encrypted for sending to the public Internet, local logging or remote monitoring over a LAN renders any website or browser security irrelevant. The capture of the data can be completely undetectable even to a computer security expert. Network administrators or hackers can install software to monitor other users on the LAN without the knowledge of the cybercafé owner.

You are equally vulnerable to local network eavesdropping, even if you use your own computer, if you connect to the Internet through an unencrypted Wi-Fi hotspot like most of those in hotels, airports, and other public places.

Cybercafés, libraries, and the like install monitoring and logging software for a variety of reasons: to keep track of time online for billing; to log sites visited for market research or "data mining"; to assist in providing technical support to people who are having trouble using the computers; to prevent children from accessing adult sites; to prevent their workstations from being used for hacking, crime, or terrorism; to enforce government censorship or surveillance orders; or because they're bored and curious about what people are doing and want to snoop on their email. Or because they are crooks. Suppose you were making US$1 an hour as a locally well-paid cybercafé system administrator, and noticed a traveler reviewing the US$10,000 balance in their online brokerage account. Would you be able to resist the temptation to take some of it for yourself?

If you sign in to an online banking, bill paying, or investment management site from a cybercafé, and someone later uses your password to transfer your life's savings to their account in Lithuania or Liberia, don't say I didn't warn you. Even if your password can only be used to pay a prearranged list of bills, a thief can charge things on your credit card, then use your password to pay your credit card bill before you have a chance to contest the unauthorized charges. (You lose most of your rights to contest a charge once you've paid the bill.)

It isn't easy to protect even your own computer against such "Trojan Horse" programs for remote monitoring of your online activity, but it is possible if you put the effort into it. Don't forget to guard against the risk that your computer it-self will be stolen. If the thief is stupid, your computer will be fenced to someone who wants a cheap computer. If the thief is more knowledgeable, your computer will be fenced to someone who will try to use the data on it for "identity theft." Never store any financial passwords on your computer unless they are encrypted with a strong password.

If all this scares you, or you aren't confident of your computer security skills, consider finding (and fairly compensating, of course) a trustworthy real person to handle your essential financial affairs while you are gone.

You can reduce but not eliminate these risks if your bank offers the option of a "hardware token" in addition to a password to secure online access to your account. A security token is an electronic gizmo a little smaller than a keyless car-door remote, with one button and a display for a numeric code. Push the but-ton, and it generates a one-time passcode that you have to enter along with your regular password to sign in to your account online.

The password changes every minute, so an eavesdropper who captures your sign-in information won't be able to sign in later without knowing the new code. (The token contains a digital clock, and the code is generated from the current time using a secret programmed into the token and known only to the bank.) If you lose the token, or it's stolen, contact the bank as soon as possible to have it invalidated and, if possible, have a replacement sent to you.

Many financial institutions offer hardware security tokens to their custom-ers on request, but few advertise them. Ask your bank.

The Bottom Line

occasional bill, send in a request for an extension of time to file your tax return (completed and signed in advance), or pass on messages in an emergency.

If there is anything this person might need to pay for on your behalf (there usually is), you'll need either to leave some blank signed checks, open a joint bank account, give them your online bill-paying password, or give them some sort of power of attorney. Signed blank checks are the most common method for trips of a couple of months; joint bank accounts are most often shared with an immediate family member and are most common for longer trips. You might also want to rent and give access to a safe deposit box holding important documents that might be needed in an emergency.

Try to make things as easy as possible for your contact and agent back home, and don't ask for any more than is really essential. Go over what you want done, and make sure you both understand clearly what is expected. Leave simple, clear, written instructions and lists. ("If such-and-such arrives in the mail, do this with it.") Make sure the contact knows where to find any papers or documents that might be necessary, such as your will or insurance policy. Leave a complete set of copies of your documents: tickets, passport, any visas, vaccination certificates, credit or charge cards, driver's license, international driver's license, traveler's check receipts, eyeglass prescription, and any pharmaceutical prescriptions. Leave complete information on anyone you might want contacted in an emergency. Leave as complete an itinerary and information on how you can be contacted as is possible.

If you rely primarily on email, you may want to get an extra email address for emergency use only, known only to your emergency contact. A burst of spam, an out-of-control mailing list loop or vacation-message error, a message with an oversized attachment, or a thief trying to delay your efforts to report the theft could fill up your regular email box and prevent you from getting urgent new messages.

Most people who travel for six months or more do have to get someone to do something for them "on the ground" back home at some point. Most people underestimate the importance of a contact back home—I know I did on my first trip—and the pressure put on the contact in an emergency. Something always happens that you forgot to plan for or didn't anticipate. It might be small, but it's still essential. Be appreciative. Reward your contact. Ask before you leave what they might like brought back, and bring it. A dinner out— the best you can afford—before you go and when you get home is an excellent demonstration of gratitude. If you had to call on your friend's help, consider giving a weekend getaway as compensation. Without someone willing to help you out, you'll have a much harder time traveling for long periods of time.

Some Parting Advice

"Bon Voyage!"

This book may seem like an encyclopedia of potential pitfalls. To some extent it is. But it isn't meant to discourage, dissuade, or scare you. If I talk about travel problems, it's to show you that they have solutions, whether you adopt my ways of dealing with them or find your own, equally valid, approaches to them. If I haven't written much about the fun components of this sort of travel, it's because they are the easy aspects, and come naturally.

No one needs to read a how-to book on the appropriate use of a US$5-a-day bungalow on a beautiful tropical beach, a US$10-a-night cabin in a secluded village at the foot of a 7,500-meter (25,000-foot) mountain, or a US$20-a-night suite in a grand old colonial hotel in the center of one of the world's biggest and most cosmopolitan cities.

Travel itself is the easy part. On the whole, most people find travel easier than they had expected. Most of the things they worry about don't turn out to be problems. The difficult part of many trips is the preparation for travel, rather than anything that happens once you hit the road. For a lot of people, including me, the most difficult step toward taking a big trip is deciding to do it in the first place. Everything else is easy by comparison. You'll make mistakes, but so what? Every traveler does. Don't worry.

The biggest travel mistake you could make, in my opinion, would be not to travel around the world, at least once in your life, if you have a chance.

600 The Practical Nomad

The price of long-distance travel is near its all-time low. Fifty years ago, air travel was only for the ultrarich. The cheapest plane ticket across the Atlantic cost the equivalent of more than what a first-class ticket now costs. Today, for a month's wages, an ordinary First World worker can fly roundtrip to almost anywhere in the world and back. There's never been a better time to travel than now.

But the window of opportunity may not last. Do it now, while you can.

Long-haul airfares, which hit bottom some time after 11 September 2001, have already started to rise in response to rising fuel prices. What will travel be like 50 or 100 years in the future? Has air travel already passed its peak? Do oil depletion and global warming mean that our ability to travel the world is at its all-time high? There are many types of airplanes, but all of them are powered by petroleum. When the fossil fuel runs out, the era of mass air travel will end, at least for a while. What will that mean for the future of travel?

On land, there are alternatives like electric trains. But what about travel between continents? Will ships once again be the only way to cross the oceans? Will we return to a world of isolated island continents, between which only a few people travel, slowly and/or much more expensively? How will our lives, or our children's lives, be different in a world like that?

For most of history, only a few people could afford to travel. Everyone else had to rely on what those few members of the travel elite—the explorers, the "jet set"—chose to tell us, when they came back, about what they had seen. For many of the world's people today, travel is still slow, expensive, and a luxury. How soon will it be that way again for us as well?

Our generation is probably one of only two or three generations in all of human history—past, present, or future—who have the chance to see the world, meet its people, and learn about it through our own direct experience, rather than having to rely on what a few other people choose to tell us about what they have seen and done. What will we make of this opportunity?

If I've talked a lot about learning, that's because learning while traveling is so much easier than learning from afar, not because it's hard work. I learned more in my first three months of world travel than in three years of college at the University of Chicago. College was also more work and less fun, even for someone like me who liked school.

You'll learn the most, and have the best time, if you travel with an open mind. As I mentioned at the start, my goal for my first trip around the world was to learn the meaning of my ignorance. I wanted to find out just how much I could trust my own world view, how much was "truth" and how much the product of my perspective as an American.

It's better to think about questions to ask than to think about what answers you expect. You'll find out what's there when you get there; if you already knew what you'd find, you wouldn't need to travel to find it. There'll be time enough for evaluation and conclusions when you get home.

Those who neither ask questions nor listen to the answers preordain themselves to learn nothing. I'm amazed by people who travel seeing only an image of the destination they formed well before their arrival, oblivious to anything inconsistent with their preconceptions.

I've sent thousands of people around the world, and met many more through my writing and in-person seminars. A few had to cut short their planned trips because of injuries from car or bus crashes, family emergencies, or (more rarely) illness. But I can count on one hand those of my clients who came home early because they weren't having fun, or because they were overwhelmed by Third World travel. It's different—that's part of its interest—and it's impossible to know what it's like until you've experienced it. But most people who travel far afield find the process among the most enjoyable and rewarding experiences of their lives.

Finally, don't forget the obvious: travel is fun. Big fun. Travel to distant and different places is an enjoyable fantasy for almost everyone. If there's one thing that I hope you've learned from this book, it's that travel doesn't have to remain a fantasy. A trip around the world is not just a dream but one that becomes a reality for tens of thousands of people every year. Whether your dream is a trip around the world, a first trip abroad, or any big trip, I hope reading this book will not be just an armchair journey but a step toward making your travel dreams come true.

Bon voyage.

A Resource Guide
for Travel Planning
and Preparation

"Where Do I Go From Here?"

This is a selective and highly idiosyncratic list. I've gone further out of my way to include things I think you won't find mentioned elsewhere than to include the things you'll probably have thought of, or heard of, already. Some of the suggested background reading may seem heavy and academic, but I've tried to pick resources accessible to general readers.

I've tried to list mainly websites, publications, and writers from the regions described, rather than by outside observers. Lest there be any doubt, the editorial content of all of the publications listed below is in the English language, except in rare cases as noted; all addresses not otherwise identified by country are in the United States.

All books listed here, even those that are out of print, should be available through your local public library. If they don't have them, they can request them for you on interlibrary loan. Independent bookstores can and will special-order any book in print, usually with no obligation. To buy out-of-print books, check with local independent used bookstores, or the Advanced Book Exchange catalog of used books available from independent dealers worldwide at www.abe-books.com. (ABE has been bought by Amazon.com, but still operates somewhat separately, and not all of the ABE catalog is listed on Amazon.com.)

In 2007, International Standard Book Numbers (ISBNs) were expanded from 10 to 13 digits. To avoid confusion, older books are listed here with the original 10-digit ISBNs, as printed in the books themselves. If you need the new 13-digit ISBN for any of these books, there's an online converter at www.isbn.org/converterpub.asp.

Check the Practical Nomad website at www.practicalnomad.com, and my website and blog at www.hasbrouck.org/blog, for updates and additional resources. Your feedback on this list and your suggestions for additions, deletions, and changes for the next edition are always welcomed.

Getting Time to Travel

Redefining Corporate Sabbaticals for the 1990s by Helen Axel
ISBN 0-8237-0453-X; 1992, 44 pp; The Conference Board, New York

Based on a survey of employers in the United States on their sabbatical and related employment-leave policies. Outlines a variety of types of formal and informal sabbatical programs, with examples. Also discusses the benefits to businesses of sabbatical programs. Usual ammunition to help persuade your employer to let you take a sabbatical.

Escape 101: Sabbaticals Made Simple by Dan Clements and Tara Gignac
ISBN 978-0-9739782-2-3; 2007, 170 pp; Brainranch Publishing; www.escape-101.com

Concise and empowering, with an emphasis on how to psych yourself up to ask for, or take, a sabbatical, and how to answer your doubts and fears.

Six Months Off: How to Plan, Negotiate, and Take the Break You Need without Burning Bridges or Going Broke
by Hope Dlugozima, James Scott, and David Sharp
ISBN 0-8050-3745-4; 1996, 252 pp; Henry Holt, New York

Equal parts empowerment, examples, and practical advice for sabbatical-takers. Especially good chapters on "Overcoming the Big Buts," "Negotiating for a Sabbatical," and "How to Use a Break to Jump-Start Your Career."

Take Back Your Time: Fighting Overwork and Time Poverty in America
edited by John de Graaf
ISBN 1-57675-254-3; 2003, 258 pp; Berrett-Koehler Publishers, San Francisco; www.timeday.org

A wide-ranging anthology on what's wrong with our lack of vacation and rest, and what we can do about it. Contributors range from labor activists like Joe Robinson (see *Work to Live* later in this section) to environmentalists, psychologists, and exponents of voluntary simplicity. The emphasis is on collective political organizing to reclaim our time, and the demand for minimum guaranteed vacation. But there are also lots of suggestions for individual action as well as arguments and evidence to persuade your boss that workers who get enough time off—including longer vacations and sabbaticals—will be more productive.

Time Off from Work: Using Sabbaticals to Enhance Your Life While Keeping Your Career on Track by Lisa Angowski Rogak

ISBN 0-471-31067-0; 1994, 209 pp; John Wiley & Sons, New York

Includes lots of good stories and case studies from sabbatical-takers.

Work to Live: The Guide to Getting a Life by Joe Robinson

ISBN 0-399-52850-4; 2003, 318 pp; Perigee Books/Penguin Putnam, New York; www.worktolive.info

Concrete advice on how to understand and overcome the fear and guilt that keep us from asking for, or simply taking, more time to do the things we really want to do—including travel. Insightful and empowering.

Background Reading

WORLD ATLASES

No single atlas is best for every purpose. Here are my recommendations for large format, one-volume atlases, for use in world travel planning. If you don't want to pay the price of the current edition, consider getting a heavily discounted copy of the previous edition from a used book store or library discard sale: a good two-year-old large-format atlas can be more useful, and cheaper, than the current edition of a lesser atlas or than one less suitable for travel planning. Note that each of the publishers of the atlases listed below also publishes other atlases, usually in smaller formats, with confusingly similar titles.

The Great World Atlas

ISBN 978-0756639846 (hardcover); 5th ed. 2008, 528 pp (46 cm x 30 cm, 18" x 12"); DK Publishing, New York

A strong alternative to the Oxford atlas for travel planning—more expensive list price, but with larger pages. Unlike most atlases, this one covers the Third World in the same detail as the First World. Easy to read, with excellent computer-generated depiction of landforms to help you visualize where you'll be going. Possibly the best one-volume topographic atlas. Much weaker on place-names, many of which appear to be taken from air navigation charts: often they are inconsistent with local or standard usage and spelling.

National Geographic Atlas of the World

ISBN 978-1426206344; 9th ed. 2010, 424 pp (47cm x 32cm, 18.5" x 12.5"); National Geographic Society, Washington, D.C.; www.nationalgeographic.com/atlas

Extremely detailed, with the best gazetteer and largest pages of any affordable one-volume English-language atlas. But covers North America and Western Europe in much more detail than the rest of the world, and emphasizes political borders over physical geography. Probably better for reference than for travel planning. Available in both soft-cover and hardcover editions. Discounts are often available to subscribers to *National Geographic* magazine.

Oxford Atlas of the World

ISBN 978-0199751280 (hardcover); 17th ed. 2010, 448 pp (38cm x 29cm, 15" x 11.5"); Oxford University Press, Oxford, U.K.

Possibly the best value for the money of any currently published one-volume English-language atlas. Eurocentric in coverage, but not inordinately so.

(See also the map suppliers listed later in the *Resource Guide* under *Maps, Guide-books, and Gear* in the *Logistics* section.)

GLOBAL SURVEYS AND REFERENCES

CIA World Factbook

Central Intelligence Agency (United States); https://www.cia.gov/library/publications/the-world-factbook/

A few pages of factoids about each country of the world, as seen by the U.S. Central Intelligence Agency. You'll find lots of pointers to this on the Internet, but it's really too limited to be much use for developing understanding or making travel decisions. I guess any *real* intelligence is kept classified.

Country Studies and Area Handbooks

Federal Research Division, Library of Congress (United States); http://memory.loc.gov/frd/cs/

Book-length *Country Studies* for individual countries and *Area Handbooks* for regions of smaller countries were prepared and updated through 1998 by the Federal Research Division of the Library of Congress. Some money for ongoing updates was appropriated in 2004. Although future updates will depend on Congressional funding, these still are, for many regions, the most detailed unclassified references available from any U.S. government agency. Written by multidisciplinary teams of academics on government contracts, these books provide an introduction to the people and the society (from the perspective, of course, of the government and military of the United States) that is often conspicuously absent from most literature intended for tourists. Current academic texts on the country or region, though sometimes harder to find, are usually more informative and acknowledge more diverse points of view.

Human Rights Watch
United States
> 350 5th Ave., 34th Floor, New York, NY 10118-3299; tel. +1-212-290-4700,
> fax +1-212-736-1300; hrwatchnyc@hrw.org; www.hrw.org

Canada
> 55 Eglinton Ave. E., Suite 702, Toronto, ON M4P 1J5; tel. +1-416-322-8448,
> fax +1-416-322-32461; toronto@hrw.org

U.K.
> 2nd Floor, 2–12 Pentonville Rd., London N1 9HF, UK; tel. +44-20-7713-1995,
> fax +44-20-7713-1800; hrwatchuk@hrw.org

HRW publishes intermittent country and issue reports on human rights crises around the world, as well as an annual *World Report* summarizing general trends and issues and surveying countries with particular human rights problems. Politically biased, to be sure, but less so than, say, the U.S. government's annual *Country Reports on Human Rights*. A good starting point for information about human rights in countries you plan to visit. (Additional offices elsewhere in the United States and around the world.)

International Affairs Resources from the World Wide Web Virtual Library
www.vlib.org/InternationalAffairs.html; www.etown.edu/vl/

The WWW Virtual Library is a nonprofit volunteer project that exemplifies the cooperative knowledge sharing of the Internet. The "International Affairs Resources" section provides links to academic sites about world regions, countries, and issues, many of them maintained as labors of love and/or teaching resources by academic experts on the respective places.

Material World: A Global Family Portrait
by Peter Menzel
ISBN 0-87156-437-8 (hardcover), ISBN 0-87156-430-0 (paperback); 1994, 255 pp; Sierra Club Books, San Francisco

In each of 30 countries, an "average" family is photographed in front of their living space, with all of their material possessions spread out in view. Each of these "big pictures" is reproduced as a large, glossy color spread, accompanied by half a dozen pages of background notes, statistics, stories, and smaller photos of the family, their country, and the activities of their daily lives.

Minority Rights Group International
54 Commercial St., London E1 6LT, UK; tel. +44-20-7422-4200, fax +44-20-7422-4201; minority.rights@mrgmail.org; www.minorityrights.org

An international human rights organization based in the U.K., Minority Rights Group International is primarily a publisher of topical books and reports on ethnic, linguistic, religious, and social minorities and on thematic issues such as refugees and indigenous peoples. What the tourist board won't tell you about whatever population subgroup the government of a country you are going to doesn't like.

Planet of Slums by Mike Davis
ISBN 1-84467-022-8 (hardcover, 2006), ISBN 978-1844671601 (paperback, 2007); 228 pp; Verso, New York and London

"Sometime in the next year or two…for the first time, the urban population of the earth will outnumber the rural…. Cities will account for virtually all future world population growth." And most of those city dwellers live in the poorer parts of cities in the poorer parts of the world. Explicitly inspired by Jeremy Seabrook's *In the Cities of the South* (listed later in this section), Davis's book provides a statistical and analytic counterpoint to Seabrook's personal stories of how the world's new urban majority lives. For critiques of a wider range of contemporary patterns of human settlement and urban geography, see *Evil Paradises: Dreamworld's of Neoliberalism,* edited by Davis and Daniel Bertrand Monk.

State of the World by the Worldwatch Institute
ISBN 0-393-32666-7; 23rd ed. 2006, 237 pp; W. W. Norton, New York; Worldwatch Institute, 1776 Massachusetts Ave. NW, Washington, DC 20036-1904; tel. 877-539-9946 (publication orders from the United States only) or +1-202-452-1999, fax +1-202-296-7365; wwpub@worldwatch.org (publication orders) or worldwatch@worldwatch.org (general inquiries and correspondence); www.worldwatch.org

Annual book-length collections of essays and research reports on regions and issues in "progress toward a sustainable society." Different topics or regions are covered each year. See the website for a catalog of topics and of articles available as separate pamphlets.

The State of the World Atlas by Dan Smith
ISBN 978-0143114529; 8th ed. 2008, 144 pp; Penguin, New York

World statistics, presented in easily read map form, on everything from population, language, and other demographics to economic resource flows and patterns of human rights abuses. Cheaper and easier to find than *The World Guide,* but not nearly as comprehensive or detailed. Check for the most recent edition.

The Statesman's Yearbook: The Politics, Cultures, and Economies of the World
ISBN 978-0-230-20603-8; 147th ed. 2011, 1,600 pp; Palgrave Macmillan, New York; www.statesmansyearbook.com

The standard, and best, Northern reference work on the countries of the world. Authoritative-seeming but hopelessly Eurocentric and Northern in perspective and selection of details, despite some interesting statistics. Expensive, unless you find a used copy at a library book sale. Some excerpts are available online for free; full text is available online only for paid subscribers. Not recommended except as a secondary reference to complement *The World Guide* (listed later in this section), but it will tell you—if you don't know already—what, if any, significance a particular part of the South holds for the North and the global economy.

Tourism Offices Worldwide Directory
www.towd.com

Not comprehensive, but a useful aid to finding government tourist information offices. The emphasis is on those located in the United States, and/or that have a presence on the Internet, but some others are listed as well. Just don't assume it doesn't exist if you don't find it here.

The World Guide
ISBN 978-1-904456-56-8; 11th English-language print ed. 2007, 624 pp; English/Spanish CD-ROM ed., 2007, ISBN 978-1-904456-58-2; Instituto del Tercer Mundo, Montevideo, Uruguay; www. guiadelmundo.org.uy; English-language ed. distributed by New Internationalist Publications, London, U.K.; ni@newint.org; www.newint.org

The single best one-volume reference about the world. Early editions were titled *The World: A Third World Guide*; the revised title reflects the reality that this is not just a guide to the South but a guide to the North as well, but as seen from the South. Compiled by a consortium of Third World journalists, this encyclopedia/almanac is the first place I turn for information about a country or place in the news with which I'm not familiar. The CD-ROM includes the complete text of the book, Amnesty International country reports on human rights, and a graphical and cartographic interface for searching, analyzing, and displaying current and historical statistical data on the countries of the world. It's an invaluable learning tool, and belongs in every school, but the printed book is more appropriate for most home users. If you buy one expensive book, sight unseen, on the strength of my recommendation, make it this one.

SOUTHERN PERSPECTIVES ON THE WORLD
Al Jazeera English
http://english.aljazeera.net

Overwhelmingly the largest, most watched, and most influential news organization not based in the First World. Live video stream and archived video and print stories available free online, even if your local cable-TV company doesn't carry Al Jazeera. Anywhere you go outside the First World, people are watching Al Jazeera and relying on it as the default international perspective on the news, so you need to know what it says even if you don't agree with it. Not just a 24-7 English-language news channel, Al Jazeera also carries news analysis, newsmaker interviews, talk shows (with viewers phoning and texting in from around the world), and documentaries about places that rarely feature in U.S. news. Based in Qatar on the Arabian Peninsula, but its English service isn't limited in coverage or influence to the Arab world. Unrivaled network of correspondents throughout Africa and West Asia; weakest in Latin America.

Apex Press

Council on International and Public Affairs; 777 United Nations Plaza, Suite 3C, New York, NY 10017; tel. +1-212-972-9877, fax +1-212-972-9878; apex@apexpress.org; www.cipa-apex.org

A nonprofit publisher, importer, and distributor of books on global issues from predominantly Southern perspectives, including the World Cultures Series of anthologies "that present world cultures to readers through the eyes of its own peoples" (*Through Middle Eastern Eyes, Through Chinese Eyes,* etc.).

Asia and Western Dominance: A History of the Vasco da Gama Epoch of Asian History, 1498–1945 by K. M. Panikkar

Originally published in 1953 in London and reissued many times, including in 1969 in the United States, in 1993 in Malaysia, and in 1999 in India. A classic history, by an Indian scholar and diplomat, of the role of Europeans in Asia. The best starting point for Europeans traveling to Asia who want to understand how—in the context of the Europeans who have gone before them—they are likely to be viewed by the Asians they meet.

Dark Victory: The United States, Structural Adjustment, and Global Poverty by Walden Bello, with Shea Cunningham and Bill Rau

ISBN 0-9350-2861-7; 2nd ed. 1999, 176 pp; Institute for Food and Development Policy ("Food First"), Oakland, CA/The Transnational Institute, Amsterdam; www.foodfirst.org; www.tni.org

An overview of neocolonialism in the "post–Cold War" world. One of the first and most important books to articulate the critique of "globalization" that now dominates North-South discourse. Dr. Bello is a Philippine American sociologist, activist, and journalist, and executive director of Food First, a research institute on hunger, democracy, and sustainable development. A concise introduction, though somewhat academic. Those interested in more recent and detailed explorations of related themes may want to browse the rest of the Food First book catalog on their website.

Development Bookshop

www.developmentbookshop.com; Practical Action Publishing, Schumacher Centre for Technology and Development, Bourton-on-Dunsmore, Rugby, Warwickshire CV23 9QZ, U.K.; tel. +44-1926-634-501, fax +44-1926-634-502

Originally founded by E. F. Schumacher (author of *Small is Beautiful*). Wide selection of books on cultural, educational, environmental, economic, and political development—not just technology. Online ordering, worldwide shipping; no retail storefront.

Resource Guide

Glimpses of World History by Jawaharlal Nehru

ISBN 19-561323-6; first published 1934–1935, Kitabistan, Allahabad, India; numerous later editions worldwide; latest ed. 2004, 1,192 pp, Penguin India; ISBN 0670058181 (hardcover), ISBN 0143031058 (paperback)

"Being further letters to his daughter, written in prison, and containing a rambling account of history for young people." Quite literally the text for a home-schooling course in world history (for Nehru's daughter, Indira Gandhi), and eminently suitable as such even today. Written from memory (and thus emphasizing themes, trends, and ideas rather than dates and details) by the greatest statesman of the 20th century, a Renaissance man and exceptional writer, and the person who, in founding the Non-Aligned Movement, first articulated the entitlement of the majority of the world's people to the dominant voice in world affairs. I couldn't imagine a better window into the Southern perspective on classical history. Best read in conjunction with Nehru's *The Discovery of India* and *The Unity of India* (a classic of anti-imperialism and antifascism) and his autobiography, *Toward Freedom*.

Global Voices

www.globalvoicesonline.org

Blogs and citizen media from around the world. A nonprofit project inspired by an international bloggers conference in 2004, "Global Voices is a community of more than 300 bloggers and translators around the world who work together to bring you reports from blogs and citizen media everywhere, with emphasis on voices that are not ordinarily heard in international mainstream media."

Imperialism, the Highest Stage of Capitalism by V. I. Lenin

Foreign Languages Publishing House, Moscow, Russia (and many other editions); free e-book editions in several formats available online

The failure of Stalinist government in Russia notwithstanding, Lenin's 1933 analysis of imperialism remains prevalent in most formerly colonized countries—which is to say, most of the world and its people. This may still be the single book by a Northerner that most influences Southern thought on North-South issues.

Neo-Colonialism, the Last Stage of Imperialism by Kwame Nkrumah

1st ed. 1966, 280 pp; most recent edition by International Publishers, New York/Panaf Books, London, 1974

By the leader of the independence movement and first prime minister of independent Ghana, and one of the founders of Pan-Africanism and the Non-Aligned Movement. A widely read analysis of how the former colonial powers maintained their economic control even after the nominal political independence of their former colonies—a key issue still throughout the South, and especially in Africa.

Non-Violent Resistance (Satyagraha) and Sarvodaya (The Welfare of All)
by M. K. Gandhi

1951 and 1954; Navajivan Trust, Ahmedabad, India (and other editions); U.S. ed. of *Non-Violent Resistance* (Satyagraha) published by Schocken Books, New York, 1961

Gandhi and Mao were the two great mass leaders of the world's two most populous countries. India's government today is no more "Gandhian" than China's is "Maoist," but Maoism and Gandhism remain the poles in relation to which other organizational theories of mass action and power are still considered. More Northerners have heard of Satyagraha, but Gandhi considered the "constructive program" of Sarvodaya at least equally important. Gandhi's advocacy of environmentalism (what would come to be known, decades after his assassination, as "deep ecology"), appropriate technology, and sustainability, long overlooked, has in recent years come to be seen as prescient by more and more Northerners and Southerners alike. Essential to an understanding of the dynamics of power and the theory of "development" in the world today. For some of the ways Gandhian tactics are being used in contemporary popular democratic movements for change around the world, see Gene Sharp's trilogy, *The Politics of Nonviolent Action*.

The West and the Rest of Us: White Predators, Black Slavers, and the African Elite by Chinweizu

ISBN 039-4480-51-1, 1st ed. 1975, 520 pp, Random House, New York; ISBN 978-2651-00-1 (hardcover), ISBN 978-2651-01-X (paperback), revised ed. 1987, Pero Press, Lagos, Nigeria

One of the most thought-provoking treatises on North-South relations and neocolonialism from a Southern point of view. Chinweizu is a Nigerian journalist, poet, critic, and occidentalist. This is not a book about Africa, or the South generally, but about the self-described "West," from the perspective of what it has meant to the rest of the world. European, including European-American, readers may feel maligned and/or threatened by Chinweizu's blunt criticism, but his are views they will encounter often if they travel in the South. One of those books that's more widely talked about than actually read; a hard book to find, but one worth searching out. Polemical, and focuses on the historical roots of current problems.

THE ECOLOGY OF TRAVEL AND TOURISM

Travelers are not alone: we are part of the culture of tourism. We travel in isolation neither from each other nor from the places and peoples we visit. Understanding the patterns of tourism and its impacts on both physical and cultural ecologies requires an essentially anthropological approach, especially if we want our travels to be responsible and sustainable. Yet for the world's largest industry, and one that involves hundreds of millions of people, tourism is remarkably little studied as a sociological or anthropological phenomenon.

Aviation Environment Federation

Broken Wharf House, 2 Broken Wharf, London EC4V 3DT, U.K.; tel. +44-20-7248-2223, fax +44-20-7329-8160; info@aef.org.uk; www.aef.org.uk

A nonprofit educational and activist organization focused on the environmental impacts of air transportation including land use, noise, and the contribution of airline emissions to climate change.

Beyond the Beach: An Ethnography of Modern Travellers in Asia

by Klaus Westerhausen

ISBN 974-4800-09-7; 2002, 272 pp; White Lotus Press, GPO Box 1141, Bangkok 10501, Thailand; ande@loxinfo.co.th; www.whitelotuspress.com

A field study by a long-term traveler turned anthropologist. Focuses on the longest-term and lowest-budget of travelers, so not representative of all independent travelers. But remarkably successfully in depicting long-term travelers as a subculture with geographically scattered enclaves and ghettoes, and in putting forward the case for independent travel as potentially more sustainable and responsible than mass package tourism. Excellent bibliography of the limited academic literature on backpacker travel.

Earthscan Publications

Dunstan House, 14a St. Cross Street, London EC1N 8XA, U.K.; tel. +44-20-7841-1930, fax +44-20-7242-1474; earthinfo@earthscan.co.uk, www.earthscan.co.uk

Publishers of perhaps the most extensive and diverse catalog of work on the impact of tourism on the physical and cultural environments. Books priced high, for academics, but it's worth searching the "Tourism" category of their website for books worth requesting from your library, including the *Earthscan Reader in Sustainable Tourism* and the widely applicable case study, *A Trip Too Far: Ecotourism, Politics, and Exploitation.* Note that the London address is a publishing office only, with no books to browse or on-site retail sales.

Ecumenical Coalition on Tourism

9/1 Ratanakosin Road, T. Watget, A. Muang, Chiang Mai 50000, Thailand; tel/fax: +66-53-240-026; contours@ecotonline.org; www.ecotonline.org

A leading voice on behalf of people in Third World destinations that are visited by First World tourists. See their website for the online version of their magazine, *Contours,* and other publications.

Errant Journeys: Adventure Travel in a Modern Age by David Zurick

ISBN 0-292-79806-7; 1995, 206 pp; University of Texas Press, Austin, TX

A low-key, contemplative, anecdote-laced reflection on the evolution of the "hippie trail" overland from Europe to Asia into today's phenomena of independent backpackers, adventure travel, and ecotourism.

Ethical Traveler

www.ethicaltraveler.org

Based in the United States but international in focus. "Ethical Traveler is dedicated to educating travelers about the social and environmental impact of their decisions, showing how travel can be a potent form of diplomacy, and giving travelers a forum through which their united voices can serve the world community."

GreenAir Online

www.greenaironline.org

An online trade journal for the aviation industry about the environmental impacts of aviation, especially on climate change. Lots of uncritical reprints of press releases, but nonetheless a useful resource.

International Coalition for Sustainable Aviation

www.icsa-aviation.org

A network of environmental organizations active on issues related to aviation. Accredited as an observer representing environmental NGOs at the UN-affiliated International Civil Aviation Organization (ICAO) and ICAO's Group on International Aviation and Climate Change. ICSA has no office or staff of its own, but works through participating member organizations.

The International Ecotourism Society

PO Box 96503 #34145, Washington, DC 20090-6503; tel. +1-202-506-5033, fax +1-202-789-7279; www.ecotourism.org

Founded in 1990 "to foster a true sense of synergy between outdoor travel entrepreneurs, researchers, and conservationists," TIES has become more and more a trade association for the ecotourism "industry."

International Institute for Peace Through Tourism

685 Cottage Club Rd., Unit 13, Stowe, VT 05672, tel. +1-802-253-2658, fax +1-802-253-2645; info@iipt.org; www.iipt.org

"IIPT is a not-for-profit organization dedicated to fostering and facilitating tourism initiatives which contribute to international understanding and cooperation, an improved quality of environment, the preservation of heritage, and through these initiatives, helping to bring about a peaceful and sustainable world, [and] to mobilize the travel and tourism industry as a leading force for poverty reduction." Dominated more by governments and the travel industry than by grassroots activists.

Making the World Safe for Tourism by Patricia Goldstone
ISBN 0-300-08763-2; 2001, 272 pp; Yale University Press, New Haven, CT

A critical (some would say cynical) journalist's history of the political economics of tourism, with a focus on the tourism industry and its relationships with governments. Particularly interesting in its exploration of the financing and marketing of tourism.

Native Tours: The Anthropology of Travel and Tourism by Erve Chambers
ISBN 978-1-57766-626-4; 2nd ed. 2010, 140 pp; Waveland Press, Prospect Heights, IL;
www.waveland.com

A concise introduction to the range of issues raised by viewing travel and tourism through the lens of anthropology.

Tourism and Sustainability: Development, Globalisation and New Tourism in the Third World by Martin Mowforth and Ian Munt
ISBN 978-0415414036; 3rd ed. 2008, 448 pp; Routledge, London and New York

Not light reading—heavy and academic—but the single best survey available of the political, economic, cultural, and physical impacts of tourism. Lots of interesting case studies and references; outstanding bibliography.

Rethinking Tourism and Ecotravel by Deborah Mclaren
ISBN 978-1-56549-169-4; 2nd ed. 2003, 244 pp; Kumerian Press (an imprint of Stylus Publishing), Bloomfield, CT; www.styluspub.com

Most studies of tourism as economic development fail to question the commodification of tourism. This "rethinking" provides a critical perspective that's unusual for getting outside the conceptualization of tourism as an "industry." Yes, there's an industry devoted to producing and selling products and services relates to travel. But travel itself is something we do, not something we buy. Exceptionally useful and wide-ranging bibliography of general resources on the topic, not limited to works cited in the text.

Tourism Concern

Stapleton House, 277-281 Holloway Road (tube: Holloway Road), London N7 8HN, UK;
tel. +44-20-7133-3800, fax +44-20-7133-3985; www.tourismconcern.org.uk; annual membership UK£24 (U.K. and Europe), UK£28 (rest of the world)

Tucked into some back rooms in a nondescript classroom building at London Metropolitan University, Tourism Concern is the world's foremost advocacy and research organization for ethics in tourism. "A membership network, information resource, and catalyst for change, promoting awareness of the impact of tourism on people and their environments." As an independent, nonprofit registered charity, it differs markedly from ecotourism organizations formed from within the travel industry, and has no direct counterpart in most other countries.

The Tourist City edited by Dennis R. Judd and Susan S. Fainstein
ISBN 978-0300078466; 1999, 340 pp; Yale University Press, New Haven, CT

Independent travelers often spend more of their time in urban than rural areas, and tourism has become many cities' raison d'être. But ecotourism and sustainable tourism are often thought of in terms of wilderness and wildlife, overlooking urban issues. Includes sections on "The Political Economy of Tourism," "Constructing Cities as Theme Parks," "Converting Cities into Tourist Sites," etc. An excellent survey of the impact of tourism on cities.

Tourists and Tourism: A Reader edited by Sharon Bohn Gmelch
ISBN 978-1-57766-636-3; 2nd ed. 2010, 506 pp; Waveland Press, Prospect Heights, IL; www.waveland.com

An extraordinarily well-selected and wide-ranging collection of case studies and essays on different aspects of the anthropology and sociology of tourism.

Tourists: How Our Fastest Growing Industry Is Changing the World
by Larry Krotz
ISBN 0-571-19893-7; 1996, 264 pp; Faber and Faber, Winchester, MA, and London, U.K.

Extremely thoughtful, well-written, and honestly ambivalent exploration of such topics as, "Can tourism save the elephants?," "The problem with tourists," "Can tourism be made responsible?," and "Can tourism save the world?"

Travel That Can Change Your Life: How to Create a Transformative Experience
by Jeffrey A. Kottler, PhD
ISBN 0-7879-0941-6; 1997, 180 pp; Jossey-Bass, San Francisco

Written by a clinical psychologist and therapist, this book is above all an introduction to the psychological phenomena of travel and how they change the traveler. The focus is on what you can do to learn more and grow more through your travel experiences, without being taken by surprise by the changes in yourself.

TRAVEL STORIES, PHOTOS, AND BLOGS
STORIES AND ADVICE FROM FELLOW TRAVELERS

One way to get an idea of what a place will be like for you is to read what other visitors say it was like for them. More and more travelers are posting their stories on the Internet, on these and other sites. Just remember that these are archives of unverified anecdotes and opinions, written by amateurs who often lack perspective on how different things may look to others. Your mileage may vary. Don't take anything you read in these places as authoritative, or rely on it alone. This section lists a few online forums, but most of the best travel blogs are one-of-a-kind, and not part of or linked from any central directory. Don't overlook blogs by locals and expatriates who live in a place in your search for "travel" blogs by visitors passing through.

BootsnAll.com
www.bootsnall.com

A large "community" site for independent, hostel-style travelers. The discussion forums are the best feature of this site—the topical and destination guides are of erratic quality.

The Practical Nomad: Edward Hasbrouck's Blog
www.hasbrouck.org/blog

Like this book, my blog is more a place for general "how-to" advice, tips, and answers to frequently-asked questions than for information about specific destinations. At the request of my readers, though, I've begun to blog more about the places I visit on my own travels.

RealTravel.com
www.realtravel.com

At first glance, this looks like it's just another hotel review site. But click on "Things to Do" or "Trips," and then on the name of the author of any entry, and you can see all of that person's journal entries—not just those about hotels. Useful for finding out what other people did, what they liked, and what they didn't like about a place you are thinking of visiting.

Round-The-World Travel Guide by Marc Brosius
www.perpetualtravel.com/rtw/

Especially valuable for giving a sense of how different travelers' experiences vary. Includes quotes from a variety of other travelers, including ones who give contradictory advice on the same issues. Very useful for finding out how other people have dealt with some of the logistical, practical, and other issues of long-term multicountry travel.

The Thorn Tree
www.lonelyplanet.com/thorntree

Lonely Planet's website has the largest, best, and worst of travel bulletin boards: more true and more false information, more contradictory or obsolete advice, more touts, more myths and rumors. Plagued by posters with undisclosed commercial interests in the places they recommend.

PUBLISHED TRAVELOGUES

I enjoy reading travel tales (and tall tales) for entertainment, but I think they have limited value in preparing for travel or learning about possible destinations. Seeing how a place appears through the biases of travelers who have gone before you won't necessarily make travel easier, and may compromise your ability to see it on its own terms. Most travelogues emphasize the experience of the traveler rather than the lives of locals, focusing on the sensational and exotic. Frequently, the most widely read travelogues are out of date, reinforcing the tendency of travelers to look for the past and neither see nor be prepared for the present. On the whole, you'll be better off with contemporary newspapers, magazines, novels, websites, or blogs from the places you plan to visit than with books or travelogues by foreigners. If you can't find books by locals, you may be better off with textbooks for classes in regional studies, or other works by foreign academics, than with travelogues by foreign travelers. I include here only a few examples of travelogues that transcend the usual limitations of this most common genre of travel literature.

An Amateur's Guide to the Planet by Jeannette Belliveau
ISBN 0-9652344-4-4; 1996, 266 pp; Beau Monde Press, P.O. Box 6149, Baltimore, MD 21231-6149; www.beaumonde.net

Like me, Jeannette Belliveau travels the world as an amateur anthropologist. This book seamlessly combines stories of her travels with the questions they prompt her to ask—both about the places she visits and about her homeland—and the lessons she draws from them about "what Classroom Earth has to teach the United States." Comparisons and generalizations are hard and sometimes dangerous for travelers, but Belliveau manages them with humor, insight, self-awareness, and respect for everyone she meets along the way.

A Continent for the Taking: The Tragedy and Hope of Africa
by Howard W. French
ISBN 0-375-41461-4; 2004, 282 pp; Alfred A Knopf, New York

As a bilingual (English and French) American-born African American, who lived and traveled throughout West and Central Africa for nearly a decade in the 1980s and 1990s, first with his family, then as a university teacher, and later as a reporter for the *New York Times,* and whose wife was born in Africa, Howard French bridges the gulf of explanation between American imaginings and African realities as well as anyone. Just don't take his stories of war-zone and political reporting as representative of normal tourist experiences in Africa.

In the Cities of the South: Scenes from a Developing World
by Jeremy Seabrook
ISBN 1-85984-081-7; 1996, 303 pp; Verso, London and New York

Jeremy Seabrook is one of the few Northern writers who chooses to write mainly for Southern publications, and he stands out for his empathy with the people he describes. This may be the single best depiction of daily life for the majority of the world's urban peoples.

The Kindness of Strangers edited by Don George
ISBN 1-74059-590-4; 2003, 272 pp; Lonely Planet, Footscray, Victoria, Australia

There are lots of books about what can go wrong when we travel. This wonderful anthology reminds us of what can go right, and how much more common the good is than the bad. "Wandering the world, I have learned two things: the first is that when you travel, at some point you will find yourself in a dire predicament.... The second is that someone will miraculously emerge to take care of you—to lend you money, feed you, put you up for the night, lead you to where you want to go. Whatever the situation, dramatic or mundane, some stranger will save you." An excellent antidote to fear and mistrust of strangers and of the unknown.

A Life Inspired: Tales of Peace Corps Service
ISBN 0964447266; 2006, 177 pp; Peace Corps, 1111 20th St. NW, Washington, DC 20526; tel. 800-424-8580 (United States only) or +1-202-692-1040, fax +1-202-692-1065; www.peacecorps.gov

The latest in a series of anthologies by returned Peace Corps Volunteers, produced and distributed by the Peace Corps as a recruiting tool. Excerpts (and many useful Peace Corps training materials) are also available on the Peace Corps website.

A Malaysian Journey by Rehman Rashid
ISBN 978-983-9981919; 6th ed. 2006 (1st ed. 1993), 287 pp; latest edition self-published and distributed by Silverfish Books, www.silverfishbooks.com

The most enlightening travel book about an individual country I have yet read. Malaysia epitomizes multiculturalism and the world *problematique* of nationalism, ethnicity, and identity, in microcosm. Rashid—a journalist and newspaper columnist with experience in Malaysia and several other countries—combines his own multiethnic autobiography with his travels in a journey of personal and national self-exploration and self-discovery. Unflinchingly honest and independent in voice, which is why it's self-published. "My book's longevity is pretty much proven," the author told me by email, and it remains in print, but new copies are almost unobtainable except in or by mail order from Malaysia and neighboring countries. Elsewhere, look for it in a library, or secondhand.

Red Odyssey: A Journey Through the Soviet Republics by Marat Akchurin
ISBN 0-06018-335-7; 1992, 406 pp; HarperCollins, New York

By some miracle this narrative of a Tashkent-born Tatar's exploration of Central Asia and the trans-Caucasus—mostly by private car, uncommon as that was in what was then still the USSR—came to be published in English by a major U.S. publisher. A disconcerting but wonderful combination of the sensibilities of the American "road trip" with a distinctly Soviet pessimism and humor. Things in the former USSR have changed, but this is still a great story.

The River's Tale: A Year on the Mekong by Edward A. Gargan
ISBN 0375705595 (paperback, 2003), ISBN 0375405844 (hardcover, 2002); 352 pp; Vintage Books, New York

Journalists often use the books they write after completing an overseas assignment to tell the longer, more complex stories that didn't fit into newspaper articles written on daily deadlines. Gargan did something a bit different: he took leave of his job with the *New York Times* to spend a year traveling more slowly, so as to give himself time to see more deeply. A thoughtful case study of how long-term, slow-moving journeys differ from shorter, faster trips.

The Size of the World by Jeff Greenwald
ISBN 034540551X; 1997, 421 pp; Ballantine Books, New York

The true story of a trip around the world without leaving the surface, as originally told in dispatches for the earliest of Internet travel sites in 1993–1994 that constituted perhaps the first online travel blog.

South from the Limpopo: Travels Through South Africa by Dervla Murphy
ISBN 0719557895; 1997, 432 pp; John Murray, London, U.K.

What the title and subtitle don't reveal is that Murphy's travels were undertaken solo, on her newest bicycle—a 60th-birthday gift to herself—and were the continuation not merely of a journey begun the previous year in Nairobi but of a lifetime of solo cycling journeys around the world chronicled in her opus of travel books. Off the beaten path (she avoids pavement, to avoid the trucks and heavy motorized traffic), she captures a straightforward yet eloquent portrait of South Africa during a time that included the first free elections and the inauguration of the first majority-rule government.

Spokesongs: Bicycle Adventures on Three Continents by Willie Weir
ISBN 1-891369-17-2; 2nd enlarged ed. 2000, 240 pp; Breakaway Books, www.breakawaybooks.com; www.willieweir.com

India, South Africa, and the Balkans—by bicycle, and without reservations, support, or "sag wagon." Neither bicycling nor travel could have a more effective, enthusiastic, or sincere evangelist than Willie Weir. Read his book and, if you get a chance, try to see one of his presentations in person. What's best about this book, and Willie Weir's pitch for bicycle travel, is how clearly he communicates the effectiveness of bicycling in humbling travelers, immersing them in the lives of the places they pass through, and breaking through the barriers between travelers and hosts.

Stranger in the Forest: On Foot Across Borneo by Eric Hansen
ISBN 0375724958; 1st ed. 1988; reprinted 2000, 288 pp; Vintage Departures, New York

Hansen truly immerses himself in the local way of life and is quite matter-of-fact about the privations and dangers that are entailed in places where the people are so poor. A good reality check on your expectations if you think you will truly live or travel "just like a local."

Take Me With You: A Round-the-World Journey to Invite a Stranger Home by Brad Newsham
ISBN 0345449126; paperback ed. with postscript 2002, 368 pp; Ballantine Books, New York (1st ed. 2000, Travelers' Tales, San Francisco)

A fascinating exploration of the differences in wealth and power between travelers and locals in the Third World. It was many years after the trip described in this book, and after the hardcover edition was published, before Newsham was able to follow through on his goal of inviting one of the people he met to visit him in the United States. The paperback edition contains a brief but worthwhile postscript on what happened when he did so.

Magazines and Websites for World Travelers

GENERAL MAGAZINES AND WEBSITES WITH GLOBAL PERSPECTIVES
Cultural Survival Quarterly
215 Prospect St., Cambridge, MA 02139-1217; tel. +1-617-441-5400, fax +1-617-441-5417; culturalsurvival@cs.org; www.cs.org; annual membership (includes subscription) US$25

The best source of information in the United States on indigenous, endangered, and minority cultures, peoples, identities, and ways of life. *Cultural Survival Quarterly* covers issues you will never hear about anywhere else, or will hear about elsewhere only years later. Anthropological in perspective. *Cultural Survival Quarterly* has published several special issues and articles on the cultural impact of tourism and on the possibility of culturally responsible tourism and tourist development, including a good mix of pro- and antitourism views.

InterPress Service

www.ipsnews.net (free); www.globalinfo.org (individual subscriptions US$30 per year)

What the Associated Press and Reuters are to world news from First World perspectives, the InterPress Service news agency is to news from the rest of the world. Global, regional, and topical news feeds in English from local journalists in more than 100 countries. Current headline stories are available free on the IPS website; archives and regional news wires are available only by subscription through Globalinfo.org or other IPS subscriber publications.

New Internationalist

ni@newint.org; www.newint.org; see website for worldwide subscription addresses, or to subscribe online; annual subscriptions UK£36.85 (U.K.), US$44 (United States), C$44 plus GST (Canada), A$88 (Australia), NZ$72 (Aotearoa/New Zealand), €47 (Republic of Ireland), UK£41.85 (rest of the world, airmail)

Edited from the U.K. and Canada, with contributors worldwide, the *New Internationalist* monthly is one of the most South-centric publications in the North. It has a strong focus on human development, North-South relations, and the reality of life for the people of the South. Publishes an unusual diversity of contributions from both Northern and Southern writers, with a healthy leavening of self-awareness that neither the editorial collective nor anyone else has complete information or the one right answer to any question.

Third World Resurgence

Third World Network; 131 Jalan Macalister, 10400 Penang, Malaysia; tel. +60-4-226-6728 or 226-6159, fax +60-4-226-4505; twnet@po.jaring.my; www.twnside.org.sg; annual subscriptions for individuals in developed countries: US$30 surface mail, US$45 airmail (lower rates for Third World subscribers; higher rates for libraries and institutions)

Third World Resurgence isn't everyone's cup of tea. It's usually dry, sometimes repetitious, plainly laid out and heavy on text, with a strong emphasis on international political economics. But it brings to my doorstep the perspectives of leading thinkers and grassroots activists from around the world. A truly global vehicle for South-South exchange, with contributing editors in Ghana and Uruguay and articles from every continent in every issue.

WorldPress.org
"News and Views from Around the World"

www.worldpress.org; www.worldpress.org/blogs.htm (world blog directory by country)

Online successor to *World Press Review* magazine, WorldPress.org is an English-language website of excerpts, translations, and links to local newspapers and magazines throughout the world. Especially useful for news in translation from countries where there are few English-language publications.

WorldView

National Peace Corps Association; 1900 L St. NW, Ste. 404, Washington, DC 20036-5002; tel. +1-202-293-7728, fax +1-202-293-7554; npca@peacecorpsconnect.org; www.worldviewmagazine.com (magazine), www.peacecorpsconnect.org (organization); 1 year membership (includes subscription) US$35

WorldView is published quarterly by the principal independent association of returned Peace Corps Volunteers. Little of the magazine is about the Peace Corps per se. But most of the writing is by Peace Corps veterans, and reflects the interests and sensibilities of past and present members of the Peace Corps: people who learn the language and live for long periods among the people, often in isolated and rural areas of the Second, Third, and Fourth Worlds. Thoughtful, sensitive, often deeply perceptive.

TRAVEL MAGAZINES AND WEBSITES FOR INDEPENDENT TRAVELERS

Each of these magazines has its own target audience and definition of independent travel. For some it means customized tours or "bespoke holidays." For others it means extreme-sports expeditions feasible only for experts willing to risk their lives. Sadly, independent international travelers are a small niche in the United States, and some of the best of these magazines have been the shortest-lived.

AFAR

394 Pacific Ave., 2nd Floor, San Francisco, CA 94111; tel. 888-403-9001 (United States only) or +1-415-814-1401, fax +1-415-391-1566; www.afar.com; annual subscription (6 issues) US$20

Bucking the trend away from print toward online-only publishing, *AFAR* launched in 2009 as a glossy print-only magazine dedicated to "experiential" travel. The founders explain that, "[Other] travel...magazines look at travel as escapist, or they often look at travel as the sightseeing—you're behind the camera and checking off the boxes of where you've been. Not about going out and touching and feeling and making connections.... Our mission is to inspire and guide those who travel the world seeking to connect with its people, experience their culture, and understand their perspectives." The focus is on independent (albeit often high-end) international travel. I only hope that *AFAR* continues to have sufficiently deep pockets to realize these worthy goals.

Matador Network

www.matadornetwork.com

One of the largest travel "magazines" on the Web, with an emphasis on international and cultural travel. Matador Network's scale and diversity can make it seem more like a collection of blogs and participatory forums, some better and more reliable than others, rather than a single tightly edited publication. But there's a lot of good material on the site. As this edition went to press, Matador network was planning to launch a print travel magazine, *BETA: The Topography of Living* in 2011. See www.matadornetwork.com/betamag for details.

Meet, Plan, Go!
www.meetplango.com

Organizers of (commercial, fee-based) forums and events for people contemplating extended travel.

Perceptive Travel
www.perceptivetravel.com

An online magazine, more or less a labor of love, that provides a place for authors of travel books to publish less commercial, shorter, and often more contemplative articles that don't fit within the constraints of the guidebook format.

Transitions Abroad
"Work-Study-Travel-Living"
www.transitionsabroad.com

A useful source of ideas for people planning long-term travel, especially those planning to live or work abroad. Emphasis on immersion and education; lots of links and directories of additional resources

Wanderlust
"The Magazine for People with a Passion for Travel"
P.O. Box 1832, Windsor, Berkshire SL4 1YT, UK; tel. +44-1753-620-426, fax +44-1753-620-474; subs@wanderlust.co.uk; www.wanderlust.co.uk; 1 year (8 issues) UK£24 (U.K.), UK£32 (rest of Europe, airmail), UK£32 (rest of the world, surface mail), UK£42 (rest of the world, airmail); UK£18 (e-book version)

The largest and most established of U.K. magazines for independent travelers, with subscribers around the world. Excerpts available on the website.

World Hum
www.worldhum.com

Perhaps the first travel magazine to be taken seriously as competition by glossy printed magazines—but without print magazines' costs and consequent need to pander to upscale advertisers. "We don't see travel only as a way to spend a couple weeks' vacation every year.... World Hum is dedicated to exploring travel in all its facets: how it changes us, how it changes the way we see the world, and finally, how travel itself is changing the world."

Resources for Specific Groups of Travelers

TRAVELERS WITH CHILDREN

The biggest issue for many parents is whether taking children out of school to travel will interfere with their education. That's unfortunate, because travel—especially independent, international travel outside the First World—is one of the most valuable educational experiences a child (or anyone else) can have. Here are some resources that, while not all of them are specifically about travel, address the value of experiential learning. (You can also find travelogues by families including children who have traveled around the world on the websites listed under Travel Stories, Photos, and Blogs.)

Consent Letter for Child to Travel

www.voyage.gc.ca/preparation_information/consent-letter_lettre-consentement-eng.asp

Any child under age 18 traveling across international borders without both parents will need a letter like this from the absent parent(s), or proof of sole custody by the accompanying parent or guardian. If the surnames of both parents and the child aren't all the same, they'll also need proof of parentage, such as a birth certificate, in addition to a passport. The point is to prevent international parental child abduction in custody disputes. The United States doesn't provide a standard consent form for international travel by minors, but this sample form from the Canadian government can be downloaded in text, MS-Word, or PDF format and edited for U.S. or any other citizenship. Note that this permission form to carry with you is different from, and in addition to, the special permission form (in the United States, Department of State form DS-3053) required when you apply for a passport for a minor.

The Family Sabbatical Handbook by Elisa Bernick

ISBN 978-1-887140-69-0; 2007, 298 pp; The Intrepid Traveler, Branford, CT;
www.familysabbatical.com

A practical guide to living abroad with your family. Different from most guides to expatriate living in being oriented toward deliberately temporary six-month to two-year trips, intended as a "sabbatical" for parents and an educational experience for the whole family, rather than longer-term expatriate life.

The New Global Student by Maya Frost

ISBN 978-0307450623; 2009, 336 pp; Three Rivers Press (Crown Publishing), New York;
www.newglobalstudent.com

More of an emphasis on settling in and living abroad than simply traveling, and underestimates the difficulty for parents of earning an income while abroad. Otherwise, this is a book I've wished existed for this section of previous editions of this Resource

Guide. Especially directed to parents who are afraid that travel, living, or study abroad as a teenager will interfere with their children's educational progress or college admission. Includes useful information about high school study abroad programs (such as the excellent Rotary Club exchanges) and a comparison of independent study abroad with foreign study programs organized from home.

Take the Kids Travelling: Survive and Enjoy! by Helen Truszkoska
ISBN 186011-950-6; 2000, 224 pp; Cadogan Guides, London, U.K.; www.cadoganguides.com

Includes advice for a wide range of travel styles and children from toddlers to teens.

The Teenage Liberation Handbook: How to Quit School and Get a Real Life and Education by Grace Llewellyn
ISBN 0-9629591-7-0; 2nd ed. 1998, 351 pp; Lowry House Publishers, Eugene, OR

Includes a chapter on "Worldschooling" that introduces the idea of travel as an "unschooling" educational activity. "Why to travel: It's cheaper than private school and far more educational. If you choose your destination carefully...it can be no more expensive than public school plus the food and electricity you consume at home.... International traveling is an especially timely thing to do as we shift into a more global economy and awareness.... We need to learn from and about the rest of the world." Good inspiration, advice, and examples. Llewellyn also founded the annual "Not Back to School Camp" gatherings for unschoolers, www.nbtsc.org.

Third Culture Kids: Growing Up Among Worlds
by David C. Pollock and Ruth E. Van Reken
ISBN 978-1857885255; 2nd ed. 2009, 320 pp; Nicholas Brealey Publishing/Intercultural Press, Boston and London; www.nicholasbrealey.com

This is a pioneering reference on international and cross-cultural childhood living. Mainly oriented toward those who spend a significant part of childhood living abroad, but notes that as little as a year abroad as a child can have lifelong effects. On first glance, the book may seem to focus unduly on the problems of third culture kids, but that's not the authors' intent: if you aren't sure you *want* to travel around the world with your children, start with the chapter on "Why a Cross-Cultural Childhood Matters." Getting a childhood head start is crucial to cross-cultural learning, as it is for language learning. So it should be no surprise that "third culture kids" (TCKs) or "global nomads"—including children of missionaries, military families, and other expatriates—have an influence on all aspects of international affairs—business, diplomacy, international organizations, etc.—far out of proportion to their numbers. Includes an excellent bibliography of further reading, resources, and support groups.

Travel with Children
ISBN 978-1740595025; 5th ed. 2009, 288 pp; Lonely Planet, Footscray, Victoria, Australia

The first edition of *Travel with Children* was written by Lonely Planet cofounder Maureen Wheeler, and the current edition remains one of the best books in their catalog. Most useful for the logistics of travel with infants and young children. Emphasis on Third and Fourth World travel.

The Unschooling Handbook: How to Use the Whole World as Your Child's Classroom by Mary Griffith
ISBN 0-7615-1276-4; 1998, 230 pp; Prima Publishing; www.marygriffith.net

This is not a book about travel, and not primarily about learning through travel. But it is about learning through experience as an alternative to classroom schooling or more structured "home schooling." As such, it might help give people planning to travel with children ideas about how to work with children and maximize the educational value of daily experience on the road. Also addresses issues in explaining the choice of experiential learning to others, and dealing with schools.

OLDER TRAVELERS
International Travel News
ITN, 2114 28th St., Sacramento, CA 95818; tel. 800-486-4968 (United States only) or +1-916-457-3643, fax +1-916-451-1118; subscriptions@intltravelnews.com; www.intltravelnews.com; 1 year (12 issues) US$44 (United States), US$63 (Mexico), US$108 (rest of the world, airmail)

The bulk of each issue of *ITN* is devoted to tips, advice, trip reports, reviews, queries, and replies from and by *ITN* readers. Zine-like format and lack of structure make it something of a grab bag, although each issue has some good stuff. A good place to get suggestions and exchange ideas with fellow travelers, if you prefer to do so in print rather than online. Just remember to make allowances for the diversity of the readership, and double-check advice and information before you rely on it. Best published source for reviews of tour operators by people who have been on their tours; less good for independent travelers. Nowhere explicitly labeled as being for older travelers, but most of the readership is over age 60.

WOMEN TRAVELERS
Go Girl! The Black Woman's Book of Travel Adventure edited by Elaine Lee
ISBN 0933377428; 1997, 288 pp; Eighth Mountain Press, Portland, OR; laneybugg@aol.com; www.ugogurl.com; US$15 postpaid from Ugogurl Productions, P.O. Box 2603, Berkeley, CA 94702

Equal parts inspiration, entertainment, and advice. *Go Girl!* includes travel stories by Maya Angelou, Alice Walker, and dozens of less well-known but equally interesting black women, as well as Elaine Lee's travel evangelism and advice. Includes lists of further resources for black women travelers, including those traveling alone (as Elaine herself did on her trip around the world).

A Journey of One's Own: Uncommon Advice for the Independent Woman Traveler by Thalia Zepatos
ISBN 0-933377-52-5; 3rd ed. 2003, 288 pp; Eighth Mountain Press, Portland, OR

Combines the author's advice with stories from other women travelers. Includes a particularly good discussion of the pros and cons of traveling solo or with a partner.

Journeywoman
www.journeywoman.com

A leading website for women travelers of all types, from vacationers to businesswomen on the go.

Romance On the Road by Jeannette Belliveau
ISBN 0-9652344-1-X; 2006, 410 pp; Beau Monde Press, P.O. Box 6149, Baltimore, MD 21231-6149; www.beaumonde.net

Everyone knows that men travel for sex and love, and that there's a "service industry" of international (male) sex tourism involving both women and men. Less talked about is that women travel for sex and love too, and sometimes find romance with foreigners even when they aren't looking for it. This is a serious introduction to what that means, from the geography of international romance to journalistic and academic reporting, personal anecdotes, and the growth of female sex tourism. Statistics, anthropological analysis, steamy stories, power, and ethics. Thought-provoking information for women for whom romance is part of the potential allure of travel.

GAY AND LESBIAN TRAVELERS
International Gay & Lesbian Travel Association
www.iglta.org

IGLTA is a trade association of travel professionals. See the website for a directory of gay, lesbian, and community-friendly tour operators, accommodations, travel agents, etc.

Out Traveler
www.outtraveler.com

Online magazine and travel resource guide for gay and lesbian travelers, from the publishers of the *Advocate* and Out.com.

Passport Magazine

www.passportmagazine.com; 1 year (12 issues) US$19.95 (United States), US$55.60 (Canada and Mexico), US$110.50 (rest of the world)

Highly international color glossy magazine for gay and lesbian travelers.

TRAVELERS OF COLOR

Go Girl! The Black Woman's Book of Travel Adventure

See entry above under *Women Travelers*.

Pathfinders Travel
"The Travel Magazine for People of Color"

P.O. Box 29783, Elkins Park, PA 19027; tel. +1-215-438-2140, fax +1-215-438-2144; www.pathfinderstravel.com; 1 year (4 issues) US$18 (United States), US$36 (rest of the world, airmail)

A glossy magazine published since 1997 in association with a black-owned travel agency, Pathfinders Travel Group. Heavy emphasis on travel within the United States, but some coverage of international travel.

TRAVELERS WITH DISABILITIES OR SPECIAL NEEDS

Able to Travel (U.S. title)
Nothing Ventured (U.K. title)
"True Stories By and For People with Disabilities"

ISBN 1-74710-208-2; 1996, 560 pp; Rough Guides/Real Guides, London, U.K.

A wide-ranging anthology of personal narratives of world travel by people with disabilities. Not really a "how-to" book, but a book that may suggest possibilities you haven't thought of.

Barrier-Free Travel: A Nuts and Bolts Guide for Wheelers and Slow Walkers

by Candy Harrington

ISBN 978-1932603835; 3rd ed. 2009, 200 pp; Demos Medical Publishing, New York; www.barrierfreetravel.net

Practical advice from the founder of *Emerging Horizons* magazine.

Emerging Horizons
"Accessible Travel News"

C & C Creative Concepts, P.O. Box 278, Ripon, CA 95366; tel. +1-209-599-9409, horizons@emerginghorizons.com; www.emerginghorizons.com; 1 year (5 issues) US$16.95

A consumer-oriented online magazine about accessible travel, primarily for slow walkers, wheelchair users, and other people with mobility limitations. Features unbiased information on foreign and domestic destinations, lodgings, travel tips, news, and resources. Accepts no advertising and no paid listings.

Moving Violations: War Zones, Wheelchairs, and Declarations of Independence by John Hockenberry

ISBN 0-78686-078-2; 1995, 371 pp; Hyperion Books, New York; www.johnhockenberry.com

Longtime National Public Radio foreign correspondent John Hockenberry details the personal, political, and technical issues of his Third World wheelchair travels. Not written specifically as a travel "how-to" book, but valuable as one, and worth reading even if you don't plan to visit any war zones and don't use a wheelchair. Highly recommended.

Destination Guidebooks for Independent Travelers

AVALON TRAVEL
"Because Travel Matters"

1700 4th St., Berkeley, CA 94710; tel. +1-510-595-3664, fax +1-510-595-4228; www.avalontravelbooks.com

Avalon Travel is the largest specialty publisher in the United States of guidebooks for independent and active travelers. Originally a self-publisher, then an independent small publisher, and now a division of the Perseus Books Group. Bigger isn't necessarily better, of course, but Avalon Travel was my first choice of publishers when I wrote my first book, and I'm proud to be part of the Avalon Travel family. The focus on independent and active travel clearly distinguishes Avalon Travel from publishers whose guidebooks emphasize packages, guided tours, cruises, and resorts. Some of the Avalon Travel books and series most relevant to international travelers are listed below; see the website for the full catalog.

Moon Travel Guides

www.moon.com

The Moon series started in 1973 with Bill Dalton's self-published *Indonesia Handbook*, which at one time was banned in Indonesia for saying too much, too truthfully, about Indonesian politics. Not surprisingly, Moon continues, in general, to have more emphasis on politics and culture than does Lonely Planet or any other major competitor. Moon's booklist began with guides to Asia and the Pacific, but is now especially strong on guides to the Americas, with guides to individual states, provinces, and regions of the United States, Canada, and Mexico, and growing coverage of Central America, South America, and the Caribbean (and scattered other places around the world). The Moon family also includes the *Moon Living Abroad* series of cultural and logistical country guides for long-term stay and/or permanent relocation, whether for work, study, volunteering, or retirement, "passionately written by authors who have taken the plunge themselves." See the website for excerpts, links to author blogs, and other resources.

The People's Guide to Mexico
by Carl Franz; edited by Lorena Havens and Steve Rogers
ISBN 1566917115; 13th ed. 2006, 560 pp; www.peoplesguide.com

Some of the best guidebooks, like this one, aren't part of any series. What's especially noteworthy about this, the best guide for independent travelers in Mexico, is that it has no lists whatsoever of specific hotels, restaurants, sites, or routes. The entire book is devoted to general advice about how to travel, including how to find destinations, places to stay, etc., on your own. I wish there were equally good books of this type for other countries or regions.

Rick Steves Guides
www.ricksteves.com

"Most guide books only tell you where to travel. Rick Steves teaches you how to travel." Deservedly the best-known guidebooks to Europe for Americans of all ages and budgets who don't want to be led around on tours. Just remember to take Rick's advice to heart: explore on your own, and don't limit yourself to considering only the places he mentions in his books.

Road Trip USA
www.roadtripusa.com

The great American road trip isn't the only way to see America, but it is one of the best, and one of the most attractive for foreign visitors to the United States. Most American guidebooks emphasize the Interstate highways (multilane divided motorways or "dual carriageways"). *Road Trip USA* is about travel on the smaller roads that are much more interesting for anyone who isn't in quite so much of a hurry. Includes routes to follow things to see and do along the way, and background reading for the drive.

OTHER GUIDEBOOK PUBLISHERS
Bradt Travel Guides
23 High St., Chalfont St. Peter, Bucks SL9 9QE, U.K.; tel. +1-44-1753-893-444, fax +44-1753-892-333; info@bradtguides.com; www.bradtguides.com

Individualistic guidebooks for "the adventurous traveller who seeks out off-beat places and the dreamer who would like to travel there but perhaps never will." Catalog emphasizes less-touristed destinations more mainstream guidebooks gloss over or ignore: an entire book on Eastern Turkey, for example, rather than the more commonly visited western part of the country. Especially detailed country-by-country coverage of Africa, West and Central Asia, and Eastern Europe. Worthwhile cultural and interpretative background reading, even if not always sufficiently attentive to the needs of inexperienced do-it-yourself travelers who don't know the local language(s).

Cadogan Travel Guides

New Holland Publishers (UK) Ltd., Garfield House, 86-88 Edgware Rd., London W2 2EA, U.K., tel. +44-20-7724-7773, fax +44-20-7724-6184; enquiries@nhpub.co.uk; www.newhollandpublishers.com/cadogan-guides.asp

An eclectic series of guidebooks, including some excellent ones.

Footprint Travel Guides

6 Riverside Court, Lower Bristol Rd., Bath BA2 3DZ, U.K.; tel. +44-1225-469-141; www.footprinttravelguides.com/

The 2011 *South American Handbook* is the 87th annual edition, and was the start of a series that has grown into a strong rival worldwide to Avalon Travel (Moon Handbooks), Rough Guides, and Lonely Planet. Written primarily for Europeans, who have much longer vacations than Americans. With less time pressure, Europeans are less likely to feel the need of a tour to ensure that they see what they came to see quickly, and are more likely to travel independently. Europeans are also more likely to have international travel experience than Americans, though, and the biggest shortcoming of the Footprint Handbooks vis-à-vis Moon or Lonely Planet is a relative dearth of hand-holding and general information for first-time travelers. Many experienced travelers wanting up-to-date hotel and attraction listings and the like (and less interested in cultural or interpretive detail) swear by them, and I've found some of their guides to be the best available at particular times for particular places.

Let's Go Publications Inc.

67 Mount Auburn St., Cambridge, MA 02138; tel. +1-617-495-9659; www.letsgo.com

A series of guidebooks written and revised annually by teams of Harvard University students. Intended for students, and often dismissed by older nonstudents. But while they may skimp on cultural background and overemphasize student ghettos and hangouts, the annual updating makes these some of the most up-to-date guides around when it comes to addresses, phone numbers, schedules, and prices. They also offer more detailed hand-holding and advice for first-time travelers than some competing guidebooks, although as first-time travelers themselves the writers have to reinvent the wheel every year, and don't always know enough to give accurate or well-founded advice.

Lonely Planet Publications

www.lonelyplanet.com

Lonely Planet Publications started with Tony and Maureen Wheeler's "how to" guide to crossing Asia by land. Now a division of the BBC (yes, the "Beeb"!) although still edited primarily from Australia, LP publishes guides to more places than anyone else, with an emphasis on the nitty-gritty details of how to get around, and a correspondingly lesser emphasis on culture, politics, and interpretation of what you'll see when you get there than many competing books from other publishers. LP writers are paid a flat one-time fee for their work, so they get no royalties and don't necessarily have a long-term commitment to keeping their books up to date. Frequently, successive editions are updated by different writers, and sections are written by different writers, making it hard to discern who is making a particular recommendation or whether you share their tastes. LP quality is erratic, especially in the guides to places where there is no other guidebook, so they are under no competitive pressure. Some LP guides are superb, but I've seen others that were worse than useless.

Rough Guides

80 Strand, London WC2R 0RL, U.K.; www.roughguides.com

My guidebooks of choice in many places. Like the Footprint Handbooks, Rough Guides cover a wider range of budgets for their European primary market, as well as a range of travel styles from backpacking to fairly upscale. One of the special strengths of the Rough Guides is their attention to contemporary popular culture in the countries they cover. Check out the *Rough Guide to World Music,* for example, for a global survey of musical genres and artists that might help prepare you for some of what you'll hear on boom boxes and buses as you travel. Rough Guides give less nitty-gritty advice on logistics than some competitors, and often fail to note which of their advice is specifically intended for European citizens, even where visa requirements or optimal routes to a destination may be very different for North Americans.

Vacation Work

Crimson Publishing, Westminster House, Kew Rd., Richmond, Surrey TW9 2ND, U.K.; tel +44-20-8334-1600, fax +44-20-8334-1601; info@crimsonpublishing.co.uk; www.crimsonpublishing.co.uk/imprint/vacation-work

From Susan Griffith's flagship *Work Your Way Around the World,* Vacation Work has expanded its line to include a wide range of specialized titles on different occupations and types of work abroad and on working in specific countries. U.S. and other readers with different passports should keep in mind that these books are written primarily by and for U.K. citizens, and that their advice on visas and work permits may not apply to those who are citizens of neither the European Union nor the British Commonwealth.

Whereabouts Press

1111 8th St., Ste. D, Berkeley, CA 94710-1455; tel./fax +1-510-527-8780; info@whereaboutspress.com; www.whereaboutspress.com

Most literary guides for travelers emphasize travelogues by foreigners, often those from long in the past. Not these. The "Traveler's Literary Companions" from Whereabouts Press consist of contemporary writing—-fiction and nonfiction, from stories and poetry to essays—about the countries by people in those countries. Most of the editors are from the subject countries, and many of the works included are by leading local writers. Some material originally in English; other pieces appear in these books for the first time anywhere in English translation. These are exactly what literary anthologies for travelers should be. The series is slowly but steadily expanding to cover more of the world.

Regional and Country-Specific Resources

Most prospective travelers read mainly travel-specific books and literature. But many of the resources I find most useful in preparing myself for travel to a country or region aren't intended primarily for travelers.

AFRICA
Africa: A Biography of the Continent by John Reader
ISBN 067973869X (paperback); 1997, 802 pp; Hamish Hamilton, London, U.K. (1997); Alfred A. Knopf, New York (1998); Vintage, New York (paperback, 1999)

A sweeping popular historical survey, anthropological in tone, with a perceptive emphasis on the relationship of physical and human ecologies. Well-documented but not academic, and highly readable.

Africa Book Centre
Preston Park Business Centre, 36 Robertson Road, Brighton BN1 5NL, U.K.; tel. +44-1273-560-474, fax +44-1273-500-650; info@africabookcentre.com; www.africabookcentre.com

Possibly the best selection outside Africa of publications from Africa. The periodical and pamphlet collections are especially interesting. Fiction and nonfiction including books from Africa and books from elsewhere about Africa. Mostly in English but some in French. Mail order only; in-person browsing by appointment only. At the time this edition went to press, the central London retail store in the African Cultural Centre (38 King St., Covent Garden) was closed during an ongoing reconstruction of the Centre.

The Africans: A Triple Heritage by Ali A. Mazrui
ISBN 0-316-55200-3; 1986, 336 pp; Little, Brown and Co., Boston

As the companion volume to a PBS/BBC television series, this could easily be mistaken for no more than a coffee-table book. But this remains one of the best introductions to the relationship of Africa's past, present, and future available in English from an African perspective, with particular emphasis on culture and identity. Influential within Africa as well as in the African diaspora.

The Africa Report
Groupe Jeune Afrique, 57 bis, rue d'Auteuil, 75016 Paris, France; tel. +33-1-44-30-19-60, fax +33-

1-44-30-19-55; sales@theafricareport.com; www.theafricareport.com; 1 year (10 issues) €39

English-language pan-African monthly from the publishers of the venerable French-language newsweekly *Jeune Afrique*. Correspondents in the key "anglophone" African countries of Ghana, Kenya, Nigeria, and South Africa and additional reporting from throughout the continent.

Africa World Press and the Red Sea Press

541 West Ingham Ave., Suite B, Trenton, NJ 08638; tel. +1-609-695-3200, fax +1-609-695-6466; customerservice@africaworldpressbooks.com; www.africaworldpressbooks.com

The largest publisher in the United States of books from Africa and the African diaspora, fiction and nonfiction, including some hard-to-find textbooks and study aids for learning selected African languages. Wide-ranging catalog of books in English (including English translations of African works), as well as a few books in African languages.

AllAfrica.com

http://allafrica.com

A one-stop Web portal for news from and about Africa in both English and French, AllAfrica.com distributes news from more than 100 African regional and national newspapers and news service. Headlines and many current news stories free; full feeds and archives available only to subscribers (US$95 per year).

Books from Africa (MEA Books)

34 Chemin Du Boise, Lac-Beauport, QC G0A 2C0, Canada; tel. +1-418-841-3237, fax +1-208-620-2136; info@meabooks.com; www.meabooks.com

Imported books published in dozens of countries throughout Africa—possibly the largest selection from any retailer in North America. Most in English or French, but some in other languages; heavy emphasis on academic, government, and some NGO publications.

Arthur Probsthain and the SOAS Bookshop

www.apandtea.co.uk

Arthur Probsthain: 41 Great Russell St. (tube: Tottenham Court Road), London WC1B 3PE, U.K..; tel. +44-20-7636-1096; arthurprobsthain@hotmail.com

SOAS Bookshop: in the Brunei Gallery at the School of Oriental and African Studies, Thornhaugh St. (tube: Russell Square), London WC1H 0XG, U.K., tel. +44-20-7898-4470; bookshop@soas.ac.uk

Two bookshops under common ownership a few blocks apart. Arthur Probsthain, across the street from the entrance to the British Museum, focuses on art, music, film, religion, languages, literature, and culture from China, Japan, Southeast Asia, the Middle East, Africa, India, and South Asia. The SOAS Bookshop specializes in the politics, history, and economics of the same areas.

Ethiopia: The Bradt Travel Guide by Philip Briggs

ISBN 978-1-84162-284-2; 5th ed. 2009, 624 pp; Bradt Travel Guides, Chalfont St. Peter, Bucks, U.K.

Includes a remarkably sensitive chapter on "Bridging the Cultural Gap" that's really about bridging the gap of wealth between rich Northern travelers and poor Southern locals. Worth reading if you are going anywhere in the Third or especially the Fourth World, not just Africa. Covers issues such as guilt and begging, tipping, overcharging of foreigners by locals, and meanness by budget travelers. The best treatment of these topics I've seen anywhere.

I Didn't Do It For You: How the World Betrayed a Small African Nation
by Michela Wrong

ISBN 0060780924 (hardcover, 2005); ISBN 0060780932(paperback, 2006), 480 pp; HarperCollins, New York and London; www.michelawrong.com

A history of 20th-century Eritrea, leading up to its independence in 1993, by a sympathetic European journalist. Eritrea may be the least typical country in Africa, as is instantly apparent to any visitor. But in another respect its story typifies the dynamic in which decisions that determine the fate of African countries (and Third and Fourth World countries elsewhere) have been made by outsiders and on the basis of global great-power politics in which the small, poor countries actually impacted were at best pawns, at worst "collateral damage."

Jeune Afrique

57 bis, rue d'Auteuil, 75016 Paris, France; tel. +33-1-44-30-19-60, fax +33-1-44-30-19-55; ventes@jeuneafrique.com; www.jeuneafrique.com; 3 months (13 issues) Đ39, 6 months (26 issues) Đ69

Nowhere is French more important as a "link" language between native speakers of other languages than in Africa, where there are probably more French speakers than in Europe. Ever since independent postcolonial Africa really was, and thought of itself as, *jeune* (young), *Jeune Afrique* has been Africa's preeminent Francophone international news magazine. Extensive free content online, including news archives by country, in French only.

New African

IC Publications Ltd., 7 Coldbath Square, London EC1R 4LQ, U.K.; tel. +44-20-7841-3210, fax +44-20-7841-3211; www.africasia.com/newafrican; annual subscription (11 issues) UK£40 (U.K.), €80 (rest of Europe), US$90 (rest of the world), UK£18 (online edition)

A monthly publication since 1966; correspondents throughout Africa; one of the few publications to cover both anglophone and francophone Africa. IC Publications also publishes *The Middle East* (listed below under *The Islamic World and the "Middle East"*).

THE AMERICAS

Américas

1889 F St. NW, Washington, DC 20006; tel. +1-202-458-3000, fax +1-202-458-6217; americasmagazine@oas.org; www.oas.org/americas; published in both English- and Spanish-language editions; 1 year (6 issues) subscription to either edition US$25 (United States and other OAS member countries), US$31 (rest of the world); see website for additional charges by country for airmail delivery

Published by the Organization of American States (OAS)—"a regional international organization of the Western Hemisphere"—*Américas* is boosterish but errs more by omission (no bad news, pessimism, controversy, or criticism of OAS member governments) than by commission. What it does choose to print gives an accurate, if relentlessly upbeat, picture of aspects of contemporary American life and culture that guidebooks focusing on the "traditional" often overlook. Particularly interesting for its depiction of the urban middle classes and of contemporary Central and South American art and culture, and for its placement of the United States in its regional context as part of "the Americas." Beautiful photos. Just keep in mind that it's a magazine of government propaganda.

Born in Blood and Fire: a Concise History of Latin America
by John Charles Chasteen
ISBN 0-393-97613-0; 2001, 352 pp; W. W. Norton, New York

A highly readable overview of the broad patterns of continental history, from the first encounters with foreign invaders to contemporary neoliberalism.

Brazzil

www.brazzil.com

Online news and opinion from and about Brazil. Among the most intellectually sophisticated, yet accessible, of readily available English-language immigrant publications based in the United States. Many articles are of interest to travelers. Noteworthy for its no-holds-barred commentary on Brazilian current affairs, culture, and politics, *Brazzil* is unusually successful in addressing itself to the interests both of immigrants from Brazil to the United States and of visitors from the United States to Brazil.

The Latin America Readers
"History, Culture, Politics"

Duke University Press; www.dukeupress.edu

A series of anthologies of stories, essays, articles, and other works from and about each country, mainly by local writers, translated into English. The series includes *The Argentina Reader*, *The Brazil Reader*, *The Costa Rica Reader*, *The Cuba Reader*, *The Ecuador Reader*, *The Mexico Reader*, and *The Peru Reader*, with more titles in preparation.

Resource Guide

Memory of Fire by Eduardo Galeano
English translation by Cedric Belfrage; 3-volume series: ISBN 978-1568584447 (vol. 1, *Genesis*), ISBN 978-1568584454 (vol. 2, *Faces and Masks*), ISBN 978-1568584461 (vol. 3, *Century of the Wind*); first published 1985; latest ed. 2010, Nation Books, New York

Open Veins of Latin America: Five Centuries of the Pillage of a Continent
by Eduardo Galeano
English translation by Cedric Belfrage; ISBN 0-85345-9916; first published 1973, 25th anniversary ed. 1998, 360 pp; Monthly Review Press, New York

Chronicles of Central and South American history by a renowned Uruguayan journalist, novelist, and poet. The *Memory of Fire* trilogy is a history of the Americas written in literary form, combining storytelling, fiction, poetry, autobiographies, and historical documents to present the points of view of the indigenous peoples of the Americas and the underclasses through the centuries. Some people find it too literary and fragmented; others find it far more moving than conventional historical writing. *Open Veins of Latin America* is more concise, analytical, and conventional polemically, though still an eloquent treatment of many of the same issues. Readers who like the style of one may not like the other, and vice versa. But try to read one or the other: these are narratives with which all travelers in Central and South America should be familiar. When Venezuelan President Hugo Chávez first met U.S. President Barack Obama, Chávez's state gift to Obama was a copy of *Open Veins of Latin America*. Also worth reading is Galeano's vivid memoir of his own life in exile and under a succession of South American dictatorships, *Days and Nights of Love and War.*

NACLA Report on the Americas
North American Congress on Latin America, 38 Greene St., 4th Floor, New York, NY 10013; tel. +1-646-613-1440, fax +1-646-613-1443; nacla@nacla.org; www.nacla.org/naclareport; annual subscription (6 issues) US$36 (United States), US$46 (rest of the world), US$28 (online edition)

An independent, nonprofit English-language source of news and analysis of Central and South America since 1966.

Santa Fe Book Corp.
18911 Collins Ave., Ste. 3301, Sunny Isles Beach, FL 33160; tel. +1-786-208-9787, fax +1-305-692-1797; info@santafebooks.com; www.santafebooks.com

Distributor in the United States for Librería Santa Fe, one of the largest bookstore chains in Argentina. Contemporary fiction and nonfiction in Spanish (and a few books in English or Portuguese) from Argentina and other Latin American countries.

South American Explorers Club
126 Indian Creek Rd., Ithaca, NY 14850; tel. 800-274-0568 (United States only) or +1-607-277-0488, fax +1-607-277-6122; explorer@saexplorers.org; www.saexplorers.org;

US$60/year individual, US$90/year couple (United States)

Despite the impossibly antiquated-sounding name, this is actually an association of backpackers. Since the 1970s, the South American Explorers Club has provided a networking center, information exchange, and facilities for independent travelers, primarily along the main north–south Andean backpacker trail. Membership gets you access to a monthly online magazine and other resources; use of the "clubhouses" and libraries of other travelers' trip reports in Quito, Cusco (Cuzco), Lima, and Buenos Aires; and the assistance of club staff and volunteer "experts" in planning your trips and answering your questions.

ASIA

The Asian Age

www.asianage.com

Edited from India and published simultaneously as *The Asian Age* in London, Delhi, Mumbai (Bombay), and Kolkata (Calcutta) and as the *Deccan Chronicle* in Bangalore, as well as online. The U.K. edition makes this one of the few newspapers from South Asia that's available in print outside the region without paying high air-shipping charges. The website includes interesting local and regional content from the editions for each Indian city.

The Asia Society and Museum

725 Park Ave. (at 70th St.), New York, NY 10021; tel. +1-212-288-6400, fax +1-212-517-8315; info@asiasociety.org; www.asiasociety.org

A long-established think tank and resource center for the study of Asia and the promotion of understanding of Asia in the United States. The bookstore includes both the Asia Society's own publications and a variety of other hard-to-find books about Asia.

Asia Times Online

www.atimes.com

An online newspaper produced in Hong Kong and Bangkok, with news and views about East, Southeast, South, and Central Asia. "We look at these issues from an Asian perspective; this distinguishes us from the mainstream English-language media, whose reporting on Asian matters is generally by Westerners, for Westerners." Especially valuable for the editorials and news analysis and the reporting on less-known regions of Asia.

AsiaViews

www.asiaviews.org

An online regional magazine featuring news and commentaries from around Southeast Asia and beyond, jointly produced by news organizations from throughout the region.

Books N Bits

11806 186th St., Artesia, CA 90701; tel. +1-562-809-9110; booksnbits@earthlink.net or bksnbts@aol.com; www.booksandbits.com

Very small but promising importer and distributor of books and periodicals from South Asia. Noteworthy for having books from and about both India and Pakistan. The only bookstore in the largest "Little India" on the west coast of the United States. Worth the 15-km (10-mile) detour if you are interested in South Asia and you're at Disneyland, or flying JetBlue Airways to or from its West Coast hub at Long Beach Airport.

China Books and Periodicals

360 Swift Ave. #48, South San Francisco, CA 94080; tel. 800-818-2017 (United States only) or +1-650-872-7076, fax +1-650-872-7808; info@chinabooks.com; www.chinabooks.com

China Books is the leading U.S. importer and distributor of books, periodicals, audio tapes, and films in English from the People's Republic of China, including everything from newspapers and magazines to reference books, travel guides, maps, and a comprehensive line of English-Chinese language-learning aids. China Books also distributes books about China from other countries, and has itself become a publisher of books about China in English.

East-West Center

1601 East-West Rd., Honolulu, HI 96848-1601; tel. +1-808-944-7111, fax +1-808-944-7376; www.eastwestcenter.org

The East-West Center is a think tank dedicated to promoting understanding between the United States and the peoples and nations of Asia and the Pacific. Largely funded by the United States and other Asia-Pacific governments, but nonetheless widely respected throughout the region. Especially noteworthy for its monographs on often-overlooked public issues and parts of the region, such as the Asian parts of Russia and the former USSR and the smaller Pacific nations and colonies. Well-researched but intended to be accessible to lay readers. Check out their bookstore on the University of Hawai'i's Manoa Campus, just across the freeway *mauka* (inland) from Waikiki.

Hollym International Corp.

18 Donald Place, Elizabeth, NJ 07208; tel. +1-908-353-1655, fax +1-908-353-0255; contact@hollym.com; www.hollym.com or www.hollym.co.kr

The leading publisher and distributor of books in English on Korea-related topics, including Korean-language textbooks and dictionaries; Korean culture and history; and living, working, and traveling in Korea. Editorial and distribution offices in both Korea and the United States.

Resource Guide

The Idea of India by Sunil Khilnani

ISBN 0-374-525919; revised paperback ed. 1999, 208 pp; Farrar, Straus, and Giroux, New York

The best book to come out of the wave of national self-examination that marked the 50th anniversary of India's independence. Beautifully written, with a superb annotated bibliography. Essential reading if you want to understand the background to contemporary India.

India-West

933 MacArthur Blvd., San Leandro, CA 94577; tel. +1-510-383-1140, fax +1-510-383-1155; www.indiawest.com; annual subscription (51 issues) US$30

More than 100 pages weekly of news and views from, for, and about South Asia (not just India) and the South Asian community in the United States, especially the western United States. Particularly interesting for its general world news and commentaries (from its own correspondents in the United States and the subcontinent, as well as reprinted by arrangement with Indian journals) on world affairs as seen from India and by Indians. Headlines and selected full stories available on the website.

Indo-US Books

37–46 74th St., Jackson Heights, Queens, NY 11372; tel. +1-718-899-5590, fax +1-718-899-7889; www.indousplaza.com

Books, magazines, and newspapers from India. In the heart of New York's best-known "Little India," only a block from the 74th St.–Broadway and Roosevelt Ave.–Jackson Heights subway stops, a short train ride from Manhattan or Kennedy Airport and a mile from La Guardia Airport. Worth a detour if you're in New York. Especially good stock of current magazines: news, Bollywood, and more.

Night Market: Sexual Cultures and the Thai Economic Miracle
by Ryan Bishop and Lillian S. Robinson

ISBN 0-415-91429-9; 1998, 278 pp; Routledge, New York and London

Combines perspectives from anthropology, cultural studies, political economics, and feminism. Much of what can be learned from this book about tourism marketing, and about tourists' and "hosts'" images of each other, is applicable to more than sex tourism and in more places than Thailand.

Other India Bookstore

Above Mapusa Clinic, Mapusa 403 507 Goa, India; tel. +91-832-263306, fax +91-832-263305; admin@otherindiabookstore.com; www.otherindiabookstore.com

Publishers and mail order distributors of books that you won't find elsewhere: "The other India generates its own literature, celebrates its own wisdom and practice, documents its own insights, and has its own marketplace. The Other India Bookstore does not keep any title from Europe or America! More than 1,000 titles can be found here, all published from either Asia, Africa, or Latin America. The Other India Press, the publishing arm of the Other India Bookstore, is the only Indian publishing house that is wholly devoted to propagating alternatives to conventional ways of perceiving and doing things."

Patpong Sisters: An American Woman's View of the Bangkok Sex World
by Cleo Odzer
ISBN 1-55970-3725; first published 1994, paperback ed. 1997, Arcade Publishing/
Blue Moon Books, New York

Field notes from an American woman's immersion in Thailand's culture and industry of sex tourism while researching her doctoral dissertation in anthropology. Anthropologists are expected to maintain an impossible double standard of observational immersion with objectivity; this book is exceptional for the writer's openness and honesty about contradictions and moral dilemmas she and many other tourists face, but which most aren't willing to acknowledge. Many of her observations about the dynamics of power between First and Third World people apply to nonsexual relationships as well. Very readable; not strident, academic, or preachy. Times have changed; sadly, much about the sex trade has not.

Philippine American Literary House (PALH)
P.O. Box 5099, Santa Monica, CA 90409; tel./fax +1-310-452-1195; palhbooks@gmail.com; www.palhbooks.com

Publisher and distributor of Philippine and Philippine-American books, mainly in English.

Rediff.com
www.rediff.com

The leading India-based Web portal (imagine an Indian Yahoo!), and one of the largest English-language news sites in the Third World. Rediff.com also owns the oldest and largest print publication for "Non-Resident Indians" (i.e., those not residing in India), the weekly tabloid *India Abroad*. But you can get much more, for free, in the "News" section of the website.

South Asia Books
P.O. Box 502, Columbia, MO 65205; tel. 866-513-4700 (United States only) or +1-573-474-0116, fax +1-573-474-8124; sabooks@southasiabooks.com; www.southasiabooks.com

Primarily a distributor to libraries and universities, but offers substantial discounts from list price to retail customers, even on single-copy orders. Huge selection, including books on all topics from India (mostly), Pakistan, and a few from other South Asian countries. They can special-order virtually anything in *Indian Books in Print*. No storefront; mail-order only.

Star Books

55 Warren St. (tube: Warren Street), London W1T 5NW, U.K., tel. +44-20-7380-0622, fax +44-20-7419-9169; sv@starbooksuk.com; www.starbooksuk.com

Books from India and other countries in Asia and Africa, including language learning materials for an unusually wide range of regional languages.

ThingsAsian.com

www.thingsasian.com

An online magazine about East, South, and Southeast Asia. Targeted toward independent travelers, with articles like a backpacker's "Honeymoon in Vietnam" (an excellent recommendation, in my opinion; my partner and I spent our 20th anniversary in Hanoi) and photographs that capture the scenery and the romance of Asia while giving a realistic picture of travel and daily life.

Travels in the Skin Trade: Tourism and the Sex Industry by Jeremy Seabrook

ISBN 0745317561; 2nd ed. 2001, 192 pp; Pluto Press, London and Chicago; www.plutobooks.com

Interviews with male visitors to Bangkok focusing on the "demand side" of the sex industry. Also includes interviews with male and female sex workers. If you want to know who supports and perpetuates the sex-tourism industry, read this book.

See also Arthur Probsthain Books and the SOAS Bookshop, listed above under *Africa.*

EUROPE

European Book Co.

925 Larkin St. (between Geary St. and Post St.), San Francisco, CA 94109; tel. 877-746-3666 (United States only) or +1-415-474-0626, fax +1-415-474-0630; info@europeanbook.com; www.europeanbook.com

The U.S. West Coast's largest importer of contemporary books and periodicals in European languages other than English. Emphasis on publications in French, German, and Spanish, but also carries some books and language-learning materials in other European languages. Will special order from European publishers.

Rick Steves' Europe Through the Back Door

120 4th Ave. N., P.O. Box 2009, Edmonds, WA 98020-2009; tel. +1-425-771-8303, fax +1-425-771-0833; rick@ricksteves.com; www.ricksteves.com

Rick Steves now hosts a public television show about travel and organizes and leads group tours, but his company and website still offer the advice for independent, do-it-yourself travelers that made him and his guidebooks famous in the first place. Includes a comprehensive set of answers to frequently asked questions, detailed information and advice for choosing Eurail Passes, and overall the single best collection of resources for planning travel from the United States to Europe.

See also Schoenhof's Foreign Books (Cambridge, MA, and Chicago), listed below under *Languages and Communication.*

THE ISLAMIC WORLD AND THE "MIDDLE EAST"

Al Hoda Books

55 Banner St. (tube: Old Street), London EC1Y 8PX, U.K., tel. +44-20-7171-1999, fax +44-20-7497-0180; www.alhoda.co.uk

Importers, publishers, and distributors of books in English about Islam and Muslims as well as from and about the Islamic world. Especially good for secular, English-language works about non-Arab parts of the Islamic world that are usually overlooked by non-Muslim sources. I always find something interesting if I take the time to browse past the theological tracts. Call to confirm opening hours before you visit.

Arabia Without Sultans by Fred Halliday

ISBN 0140218181 (1st ed. 1974, Penguin Books); ISBN 9780863563812 (2nd ed. with an updated preface, 2001, Saqi Books, London), 540 pp

We are taught to see all events in Arabia and the Middle East through the lens of religion. Halliday, in marked contrast to this dominant narrative, provides a *materialist* interpretation of the history, economics, and politics of the Arabian Peninsula. A long-time professor at the London School of Economics, fluent in Arabic and Persian among many other languages and well-traveled throughout the region, Halliday died in 2010. But his legacy of writing, *Arabia Without Sultans* in particular, may be the best basis for understanding the roots of the popular movements and changes that swept the region in 2011. His *Islam and the Myth of Confrontation: Religion and Politics in the Middle East* is also especially worth reading.

Islamic Publications International

5 Sicomac Rd. #302, North Haledon, NJ 07508; tel./fax 866-297-2307 (United States only) or +1-201-326-5602; ipi@onebox.com; www.islampub.com

No storefront; worldwide mail-order only. Much of the catalog, unsurprisingly, is on explicitly religious subjects and of limited interest to those who are neither believers nor students of Islam. But IPI also distributes secular works, mainly in English, on the peoples, politics, history, societies, and current events of the Islamic world, including places that are often overlooked.

IsraelBooks.com

Israel: Gefen Publishing House Ltd.; 6 Hatzvi St., Jerusalem, 94386, Israel; tel. +972-2-538-0247, fax +972-2-538-8423; info@gefenpublishing.com

United States: Gefen Books; 600 Broadway, Lynbrook, NY 11563; tel. 800-477-5257 (United States only), +1-516-593-1234, fax +1-516-295-2739

English-language publisher and distributor of books from Israel. Can special-order any book in print in Israel. Catalog emphasizes religious books but also includes secular fiction and nonfiction including travel guides.

The Middle East

IC Publications Ltd., 7 Coldbath Square, London EC1R 4LQ, U.K.; tel. +44-20-7841-3210, fax +44-20-7841-3211; www.africasia.com/themiddleeast; annual subscription (11 issues) UK£40 (U.K.), €80 (rest of Europe), US$90 (rest of the world), UK£18 (online edition)

Monthly since 1974, covering current events, business, and culture. IC Publications also publishes *New African,* described earlier under *Africa.*

Middle East Report

Middle East Research and Information Project (MERIP); 1500 Massachusetts Ave. NW, Suite 119, Washington, DC 20005; tel. +1-202-223-3677, fax +1-202-223-3604; www.merip.org; annual subscription (4 issues) US$42 (United States), US$46 (Canada), US$60 (rest of the world), US$42 (online edition)

Published since 1971, *Middle East Report* is a truly independent forum for all viewpoints—national, religious, secular, and otherwise—on one of the world's most factionalized regions. Also publishes special reports on countries, topics, and issues; see the website for recommended books and links for further information about the region.

See also Al Jazeera English, listed above under *Southern Perspectives on the World.* Al Jazeera is a worldwide news service, but it's based in Arabia and covers nearby regions in the greatest detail. Perhaps counterintuitively, though, Al Jazeera's English service is actually somewhat less influential in places where most people speak Arabic, and watch Al Jazeera's Arabic channel, than in places where few people speak Arabic and Al Jazeera English is the dominant international television news service.

OCEANIA

From a Native Daughter: Colonialism and Sovereignty in Hawai'i

by Haunani-Kay Trask

ISBN 0824820592; 2nd revised ed. 1999, 240 pp; University of Hawai'i Press, Honolulu, HI; 1st ed. 1993, Common Courage Press, Monroe, ME

Of all the areas incorporated into the United States, Hawai'i is the one most shaped by, and economically dependent on, tourism. Much debated and enormously influential (throughout Oceania, not just in Hawai'i), this collection of speeches and essays is still the definitive statement of the argument for Hawaiian sovereignty and the critique of contemporary colonialism in the islands. Particularly trenchant on the relationship between tourism, cultural imperialism, indigenous peoples, and national identity. See especially the introduction and the chapter on "Corporate Tourism and the Prostitution of Hawaiian Culture." A must-read for any visitor to Hawai'i, and with many lessons for travelers elsewhere in the region and the world.

A Secret Country by John Pilger
ISBN 0099152312; first published 1989, updated ed. 1992, 240 pp; Vintage Books, London; www. johnpilger.com

A controversial and critical but highly influential revisionist account of "the often invisible past" behind contemporary Australia. Written by an award-winning Australian journalist and documentary filmmaker. Some Australians may take offense at my mentioning this book at all, but it was a best-seller when first published and is still in print more than 20 years later. See Pilger's website for his other books and more recent articles and commentary on Australian and world affairs.

South Pacific Organizer
www.southpacific.org

Pacific island travel directory by David Stanley, author of the definitive *Moon Handbooks South Pacific*. Includes an exceptionally comprehensive directory of books, films, music, and links to Web resources from and about even the smallest and most obscure islands of the Pacific.

Accommodations

HOME EXCHANGES

Home exchange services have proliferated in recent years. Most let you preview their listings on their websites before you pay to join. Check to see that they have listings for the types of homes, in the types of places, that you'd like (and be able) to exchange for your own home. Keep in mind that these are only listing services: you're responsible for making your own arrangements once you find someone who's interested in an exchange. Some services allow only paid members to see or respond to listings. Others have "open listings" of members' homes available for exchange, with a mechanism to contact them through the website, even if you aren't a member, without revealing their email address to you unless they choose to respond to your offer.

Digsville
www.digsville.com

Digsville.com was one of the first Internet-only home exchange services, and one of the most technically sophisticated. You can have them email you automatically, for example, whenever someone lists a home available for exchange that matches your criteria of location, date, etc. Listings include ratings of each host by the people they've previously exchanged with. A higher percentage of members are in the United States than for some other services. Open listings. US$45/year to join and list your own.

ExchangeHomes.com
www.exchangehomes.com

Open listings. US$50 or €39 to list your own home.

First Home Exchange Alliance (FHEA)
United States: Green Theme International; www.gti-home-exchange.com; UK£25/year
United States: Invented City; www.invented-city.com; US$60/year
U.K.: Homebase Holidays; www.homebase-hols.com; UK£29/year

FHEA is a consortium of home exchange services based in the United States, U.K., and France (each of which has members in many other countries). Participants in any one of the FHEA services have access to the combined listings for all of the services, so there's no need to join more than one.

@Home Around the World
www.homearoundtheworld.com

Gay-owned and operated international lesbian and gay home and hospitality exchange service. Listings can only be viewed by members, and anonymous message forwarding is available for those who prefer not to list their contact information. UK£39 for a 2-year membership.

HomeExchange.com
www.homeexchange.com

Open listings. US$37.85 for a 3-month membership.

Homelink International
www.homelink.org

Local representatives in 30 countries and listings in more—see the website for contacts by country. Closed listings viewable only by paid members. Membership prices vary by country.

International Home Exchange Network (IHEN)
118 Flamingo Ave., Daytona Beach, FL 32118; tel. +1-386-238-3633, fax +1-386-254-3425; www.ihen.com

Possibly the first, but one of the smaller, of the Internet-based home exchange services. Open listings. US$39.95/year to list your own home.

Intervac

www.intervac.com

One of the oldest and largest home exchange networks, with local organizers and listings in 50-plus countries. See the website for local contacts by country.

Sabbatical Homes

www.sabbaticalhomes.com

Web-based service intended primarily for academics, but potentially of interest to others interested in finding academic tenants (visiting professors, traveling researchers, etc.), house-sitters, or home exchangers, especially if you want a longer-term arrangement than typical holiday home exchanges, or your dates correspond to a semester or academic year. Lists homes wanted as well as homes available, either for rent or exchange. Open listings. US$35 (academics), US$55 (others) to post a listing.

HOSPITALITY EXCHANGES

Note that many of the home exchange services listed above also list hospitality exchanges. I welcome feedback from readers on any of these or other services that you have used, and how your exchange worked out.

CouchSurfing.com

www.couchsurfing.com

A free nonprofit membership community, and one of the largest hospitality exchange networks. Generally younger demographic and a higher percentage of "crash pads."

GlobalFreeloaders.com

www.globalfreeloaders.com

Free.

Hospitality Club

www.hospitalityclub.org

Free. Claims to be "the world's largest hospitality exchange organization." More emphasis than some on international cultural exchange, not just free accommodations.

Hospitality Exchange

www.hospex.net

US$20 annual fee for listing in printed directory as well as online. Generally older (although diverse) membership.

Servas International

www.servas.org; helpdesk@servas.org (or national contacts by country as listed on the website)

Not intended primarily as a way to arrange free places to stay, "Servas is an international, nongovernmental, interracial peace association run in over 100 countries by volunteers. Founded in 1949 as a peace movement, Servas International is working to build understanding, tolerance, and world peace. Servas encourages travellers to experience other societies more deeply and with more understanding than they would be likely to do as 'just plain tourists.' Through Servas, travellers have opportunities to meet hosts, their families and friends and join in their everyday life. Where convenient, hosts may offer two nights' accommodation and invite travellers to share a meal."

Stay4Free

www.stay4free.com; info@stay4free.com

Free. Founded by a musician looking for places to stay while touring, so the members include a lot of musicians and artists.

Tourboarding.com

www.tourboarding.com

A hospitality exchange with a twist: Tourboarding matches English-speaking travelers in China with Chinese people who are willing to trade accommodations in their homes, or their services as amateur tour guides and escorts, for the chance to practice their English conversation with a native speaker for a couple of hours a day. It's still too early to tell how well this will work in practice, but it's a great idea that could work in other countries as well. Just don't sign up unless you are willing to commit the time to English conversation with your host, no matter how limited their English, and to make a sincere effort to be the best volunteer English teacher you can be.

Women Welcome Women Wordwide

88 Easton St., High Wycombe, Bucks HP11 1LT, U.K.; tel./fax +44-1494-465-441; www.women-welcomewomen.org.uk

Operated by a nonprofit trust with an international board of trustees. "There are few rules, the most important being the confidentiality of the list" of members. Membership fee (donation) UK£35 is optional, to facilitate participation by women from poorer countries.

HOSTELS AND BACKPACKER ACCOMMODATIONS

Australia Accommodation Directory

www.australia.com; click on "Accommodations", then choose "Backpackers and Hostels" under "Accommodation Type" in the search box.

Many government tourism offices and directories rate only upscale hotels, but the Australian Tourist Commission inspects, rates, and lists even hostels and backpacker dormitory accommodations. Searchable by category (even by number of rating stars within the hostel/backpacker listings!) and location. Includes ratings, facilities and services, locator maps, email addresses, and links to websites. The model of what government tourist offices ought to do to attract backpackers and facilitate their visits.

The Hostel Handbook for the U.S. and Canada by Jim Williams

722 St. Nicholas Ave., Dept. HHB, New York, NY 10031; tel. +1-212-926-7030, fax +1-212-283-0108; editor@hostelhandbook.com; www.hostelhandbook.com; single copy US$6 (United States and Canada, postpaid); US$10 (rest of the world, postpaid); payment by check or online by PayPal or credit card

This small but invaluable pamphlet and the associated website list some Hostelling International hostels and, more importantly, a large number of private and unaffiliated hostels, mainly catering to foreign backpackers. Most of these places are a bit more expensive than HI hostels and don't necessarily meet HI standards. But many of them are in places popular with hostelers where HI hostels are short of space and most hotel prices are prohibitive. Most of these places aren't listed anywhere else in print; you'd have to find them by word of mouth or on the website, which may not be available when you're walking the streets looking for a bed.

Hostelling International (HI)

International Youth Hostel Federation (IYHF), 2nd Floor, Gate House, Fretherne Rd., Welwyn Garden City, Herts. AL8 6RD, U.K.; tel. +44-1707-324-170, fax +44-1707-323-980; www.hihostels.com

Hostelling International is the brand name of IYHF, an international nonprofit organization celebrating its 100th birthday as this edition goes to press. HI offers the cheapest reliable accommodations for solo travelers in many expensive world cities. (Couples can often, although not always, find a cheap hotel room elsewhere for not much more than the price of two hostel beds.) The complete worldwide directory of IYHF affiliates and hostels is available on the IYHF website, along with links to many national IYHF affiliates. IYHF also coordinates online booking for immediate confirmation of advance reservations (usually guaranteed by credit card) at certain hostels, mainly in international gateway cities. Other HI hostels take reservations by phone, email, and/or post. For information on IYHF memberships, or for hostel reservations, contact the nearest HI national affiliate. Many HI national affiliates (including HI-USA, formerly known as "American Youth Hostels") operate storefront travel stores and information centers—check their websites for details. Note that there are lots of other private, commercial, and/or unaffiliated dormitories, hotels, and guesthouses calling themselves "hostels." Unlike the "Hostelling International" name and logo, the name "hostel" is no guarantee of anything. HI hostels aren't generally staid, but they tend to be a bit quieter, with less of a party atmosphere, and to be more comfortable for older people and families with children than the typical private or independent hostel.

Hostels.com
www.hostels.com

This U.S.-based website lists more hostels worldwide than any other, including some (not all) Hostelling International hostels and many private and independent hostels. Consider this site a complement to, not a substitute for, the HI website.

Hostelworld.com
www.hostelworld.com

An Ireland-based worldwide Web booking service for private hostels. Lists fewer hostels than Hostels.com, but lists a wider range of budget accommodations, from campsites to cheap hotels, including some in places where there are no hostels.

Russian Youth Hostel Association (RYHA)
www.hostelling-russia.ru
Youth Hostels Association of Russia (YHAR)
www.russia-hostelling.ru

There are two rival groups of hostels in Russia, both using the Hostelling International logo. Whatever their affiliation, "hostels" in Russia are more expensive but more hotel-like than hostels in many countries, with most offering private rooms as well as dormitory accommodations. Hostels are the primary source of "sponsorship" for visas to Russia for independent travelers who aren't sponsored by a tour company; some can also assist with sponsorship for other former Soviet republics. (If your hostel or host in Russia can't provide "visa support," try GoToRussia.com.) Hostels can also help with train tickets and other travel logistics. Reservations should be made well in advance (several months if at all possible), specifying all cities in Russia to be visited and the total range of dates in Russia (which must be listed on the invitation), in order to have time to obtain invitations and visas.

OTHER HOTEL RESERVATION SERVICES
All of the services listed below are ones that I've used myself in different parts of the world. No one site has the best coverage or prices worldwide, and this is not an exhaustive list.

Booking.com (a division of Priceline)

www.booking.com

Venere.com (a division of Expedia)

www.venere.com

Despite having been acquired by online travel agencies in the United States, these two European hotel booking agencies remain largely separate from their parent companies' U.S. websites. The prices on these sites aren't always less than what you can get directly from the hotels, but they list many quite adequate 2-star (and sometimes below) hotels, including traditional European budget hotels with shared bathroom and toilet facilities, that you won't find on U.S.-based hotel booking sites. And of course they let you book hotels throughout Europe in English, even at places where not everyone who answers the phone speaks good English. If possible, language permitting, try to call the hotel to reconfirm at least a day before your expected arrival, as I've experienced some glitches between the reservation services and the hotels, or with check-in procedures (where and how do I pick up my key if the front desk is closed when I arrive?) that would have been hard to sort out on arrival.

BYTArgentina.com

www.bytargentina.com

Peculiarly named but well-established locally owned bilingual English-Spanish housing reservation service for expatriates and foreign visitors in Argentina, mainly furnished apartments in Buenos Aires for rent by the week or month. There are short-term rental agencies like this in many cities and countries, typically with many more listings and better customer service in-country than international websites. The difficulty is in finding them, and figuring out which are reliable (and, if you don't speak the local language, which are able to provide services in English).

Ctrip

http://english.ctrip.com

eLong (a division of Expedia)

www.elong.net

Ctrip.com and eLong.net are online booking services for hotels in China, with minimal but adequate English-language Web interfaces (and, according to one of my readers, adequate English-language telephone customer service, which didn't used to be the case). They include many comfortable inexpensive local hotels, some no more expensive for a couple than two hostel beds, that are otherwise impossible to reserve from abroad without speaking Chinese. These websites are intended mainly for Chinese domestic travelers, so by booking through them you can lock in the local price and avoid paying a higher "foreigners' price." You can use the confirmation printout with the address in

Chinese to help people point you to the place you've reserved, and to check in even if the desk clerk speaks no English. You can make reservations as little as a day in advance, from abroad or from a cybercafé. Unlike online hotel booking services in other countries, you don't have to provide a credit card number to confirm a reservation, and you can pay cash for your room when you arrive. Be aware, though, that these sites list many hotels where few of the staff—sometimes none at all, or sometimes only one or two members of the staff who aren't always on duty—speak English. You shouldn't have any trouble checking in if you show your passport and a printout of your confirmation, but don't expect an English-speaking concierge or an easy time explaining complex service requests if you can't make yourself understood in Chinese.

Expedia

www.expedia.com

Expedia's standalone hotel or standalone airfare prices are generally poor compared to what you can find elsewhere (although generally better than those on Travelocity or Orbitz), but Expedia's prices for "packages" in the United States are often quite good, if you need a car or flight in addition to a hotel anyway. Expedia has integrated the hotel listings and prices from its Hotels.com division (but *not* those from Hotwire) into Expedia, along with Expedia's package prices, so it's generally a waste of time to check prices on Hotels.com if you've already done so on Expedia. Not much use for anywhere outside the Unites States—yes, it has some listings, but usually not many and not at preferred prices.

Hotwire (a division of Expedia)

www.hotwire.com

The first place I usually look for hotels in the United States, or business hotels in major cities in Western Europe, especially when I'm travelling on business and/or with a car, and thus don't care as much about the exact location of the hotel as when I'm on vacation and/or on public transit. Not much use in the rest of the world. Like Priceline, Hotwire gets lower wholesale rates from hotels because they hide the name of the hotel until after you've paid. Often you can make a good guess at which hotel is being offered from the list of amenities in the hotel description and by using BetterBidding.com to see which hotels other customers have gotten recently in that category and location. But don't book on Hotwire unless you are genuinely willing to accept any hotel in that area and approximate category. Usually the cheapest hotel is cheapest for a reason: maybe it's under renovation, or maybe it's just changed its affiliation from one hotel chain to another. Hotwire is a division of Expedia, but its hotel listings and prices are completely different from those on Expedia.

International Tourism Center of Japan (ITCJ)

www.itcj.jp

International Tourism Center of Japan (ITCJ), also known as the Welcome Inn Reservation Center (WIRC), operates both an online English-language booking service for accommodations throughout Japan, and hotel booking counters at Narita (Tokyo) and Kansai (Osaka) airports and a few other locations. It was established on the instigation of the government's Japan National Tourist Organization (JNTO), "to help individual overseas travelers who have difficulty in finding reasonable accommodations in Japan because of the language barrier." It's a way for Japanese hotels to fill their empty rooms without undercutting the higher prices they offer domestic Japanese customers, since the service is only offered in English and only to travelers with non-Japanese passports. Listings include a wide range of Western and Japanese style hotels, B&Bs, and hostels, in all price ranges. As with Ctrip and eLong in China, many (but not all) of these are places where few of the staff speak English, so be sure to bring a printout of your confirmation to show when you check in. Unless you book in person at their airport assistance counters, reservations must be made at least 24 hours in advance to get their special prices. Before you decide you can't afford lodgings in Japan, check out the prices on this website.

LateRooms.com

www.laterooms.com

One of the largest online agencies for discounted U.K. hotel bookings, both in London and throughout the country. Hotels in the U.K. that participate in Hotwire or Priceline, especially those affiliated with U.S.-based chains, may offer better deals through those U.S.-based agencies than through this or other U.K. agencies. But LateRooms.com has a much wider selection, including fully-furnished "serviced apartments" that you can rent for as little as a two or three-day stay, and 2-star and below hotels and B&B's that aren't listed on most U.S.-based websites. Prices vary widely, from deep discounts when rooms are still unsold at the last minute to well above "rack" rate during peak travel periods or special events.

LastMinute.com (a division of Travelocity)

www.lastminute.com

The LastMinute U.K. site offers "top secret hotels" (like the offerings from Hotwire, with which you should always compare them) and other discounted hotels in the U.K. and elsewhere in Europe. The quite different and less useful LastMinute U.S. site ("US.LastMinute.com", formerly "Site59.com"), offers mainly packages in the United States. Travelocity is adding some "top secret hotels" sourced from Lastminute.com to its offerings on the main Travelocity.com website. As of now, it's still in the early stages with too few "top secret" hotel offerings on Travelocity.com to tell how they will compare with those from Hotwire and Priceline. If you want Travelocity's real hotel deals, look on LastMinute.com.

Priceline

www.priceline.com

For the hotels in the United States and Western Europe on which it has discounted prices, Priceline typically has the lowest price through it's "name your own price" scheme—but only if you don't bid too much. Because Priceline makes you make the first offer—the worst possible negotiating system for the consumer—it's easy to offer more than necessary, giving Priceline a windfall profit. Never make an offer on Priceline without first checking the lowest prices for hotels in the same category and location on Hotwire, and checking BetterBidding.com's bulletin boards of other travelers' Priceline bids and which hotels they got. If you have time to make several bids—you can make a new one each day, if your initial bid is too low—start about 20 percent below the lowest price on Hotwire or the lowest bid shown as previously accepted for that location and category on BetterBidding.com, and work up gradually if your initial bid is rejected. It's harder to guess in advance which hotel you'll get with Priceline than with Hotwire. I've often guessed correctly with both, but you shouldn't count on any specific hotel with either. Only the "name your own price" hotels on Priceline are worth bothering with— the other hotel listings you get if you start with the search form instead of clicking first on "name your own price" are at the same prices you can get directly from the hotels. I haven't found much use for Priceline outside North America and Western Europe.

Wotif

www.wotif.com

Wotif has more than 80 percent market share in Australia and New Zealand as an online hotel booking agency. If a hotel in Oz says their lowest prices are "online," that almost invariably means that they are on the hotel's own website and/or on Wotif. com—you rarely need to look anywhere else. Several times in Australia I walked into a hotel, was quoted a price, then sat down in the lobby or went around the corner to a cybercafé and booked the same hotel for that same night for less on Wotif.com. Of course, that only works on dates and in places when there are plenty of empty rooms. You can't book ahead for busy dates, as Wotif.com won't accept reservations more than a month in advance.

Transportation

BY AIR

AirlineRouteMaps.com

www.airlineRoutemaps.com

I don't know who is behind this website, but it has been around for years, and seems reasonably well maintained. Note, however, that it includes charter airlines—on which it may be difficult or impossible to buy a one-way ticket, or a flight ticket without a tour or holiday package—as well as scheduled airlines. Maps of individual airlines' route are compiled from each airline, and thus vary in format and design. It's not obvious, but flights are listed by the geographic location of the airline that operates the flight.

Airtreks.com

7 Spring St., San Francisco, CA 94104; tel. 877-AIR-TREKS (877-247-8735, United States and Canada only) or +1-415-977-7100, fax +1-415-977-7150; www.airtreks.com

From 1998 to 2006, I was on the staff of Airtreks.com (in addition to my writing, speaking, and consulting). Founded in 1987 as High Adventure Travel, Airtreks.com is the oldest and largest travel agency in the Americas specializing in around-the-world, circle-the-Pacific, and other multistop international air tickets. The website has some sample routes and (best-case, low-season) prices to help you get an idea of what tickets might cost, and a modular "Trip Planner" you can use to customize a route, play with alternatives, get instant rough estimates online, and submit your request to a human consultant when you are ready to start making reservations.

Amadeus.net

www.amadeus.net

Operated by the Amadeus computerized reservation system. Not the website to go to for prices, but possibly the best publicly accessible website if you just want to find out what flights and connections exist on "traditional" airlines (you have to look at separate sites for most "low-fare" airlines), irrespective of price. In general, there are fewer direct international flights between fewer cities than most people assume when they start planning a trip around the world.

Ask the Pilot by Patrick Smith

www.askthepilot.com

www.salon.com/technology/ask_the_pilot

One of the joys of flying on an airliner is being able to sit back, relax, and leave the flying to someone else, with great confidence that you're in good hands. But if you want to understand what's happening in the cockpit, airline pilot and Salon.com columnist Patrick

Smith is your man. To steal another airline's slogan, Smith loves to fly, and it shows. He also loves to travel, and spends his time off and his airline-pilot travel privileges exploring destinations like West Africa rather than standard tourist haunts. He has a book (*Ask the Pilot,* Penguin, 2004) largely compiled from his columns, but I prefer the greater breadth and depth of the online archive of columns to the book.

Opodo.com

www.opodo.com

Opodo is a pan-European online travel agency founded by a consortium of major European traditional airlines (just as Orbitz.com was jointly founded by major airlines in the United States) and now owned primarily by Amadeus, the one major computerized reservation system based in Europe (just as Travelocity is owned by the Sabre CRS in the United States). Most major U.S.-based online travel agencies only sell tickets for flights originating in the United States, which makes them useless if you want to arrange flights within Europe or onward from Europe. Opodo sells tickets from any of its national sites (Opodo.co.uk in English, Opodo.fr in French, Opodo.de in German, and so forth) originating anywhere in the European Union. You might (or might not) find low-fare airlines that are cheaper, but Opodo is the best place to find out if "traditional" airlines are matching their prices, or at least to get a baseline for comparison of what tickets on traditional airlines would cost.

Skyscanner

www.skyscanner.net

Which Budget?

www.whichbudget.com

Fly LC

www.flylc.com

Buggy and incomplete but useful directories of low-fare airlines by route. Skyscanner and WhichBudget include some (although not all) low-fare airlines worldwide; FlyLC only tries to list those in Europe. Each has different gaps in coverage, so try all three. Once you get the names of airlines that might serve a route that interests you, go to the airlines' own websites to confirm they actually fly that route and to check schedules, prices, and availability.

Vayama.com

www.vayama.com

Almost all major U.S.-based online travel agencies specialize in domestic U.S. travel. Vayama.com is one of the largest U.S.-based (although actually owned, not surprisingly, by a Dutch company) online travel agencies that specializes *exclusively* in international airline tickets, mainly one-way and roundtrip consolidator tickets from and to the United

States. There are specialized agencies with lower prices to specific destinations, but Vayama.com is one of the best general starting points if you want to find out whether one-way or roundtrip consolidator tickets will be cheaper than currently available published fares for a specific, simple journey from or to the United States.

Exito Travel

6740 E. Hampden Ave, Denver, CO 80224, 800-655-4053 (U.S. only), tel. 800-670-2605 (Canada only); Skype: exitotravel; info@exitotravel.com, www.exitotravel.com

Specialists in discounted air tickets from the United States and Canada to Central and South America and the Caribbean. Exito Travel focuses on serving North Americans studying, working, and living in South America, and has discounts for more flexible tickets (long stays, open jaws, etc.) than are usually available at published fares directly from the airlines. Some of their prices are available online, but not all, and they have human consultants you can talk to on the phone. Because of the paucity of flights across the South Atlantic (Africa–South America) or South Pacific (Oceania–South America), it's often more costly to include South America on an around-the-world ticket without backtracking than as a separate side trip from North America. (Similarly, it's sometimes cheaper to include Australia as side trip from Southeast Asia, as I did on my most recent trip around the world.)

Wikipedia's List of Low-Cost Airlines

http://en.wikipedia.org/wiki/List_of_low-cost_airlines

Few low-cost airlines pay to participate in the computerized reservation systems used by mainstream online and offline travel agencies and price comparison websites. There are lots of lists of low-cost airlines, but none of them are complete or authoritative. That makes Wikipedia's compilation of rumors about low-cost airlines and where they fly especially useful: If a new low-cost airline starts up, or an existing one starts a new route, it doesn't usually take long before someone updates Wikipedia to show it. It can take longer for anyone to bother to remove a discontinued route or a defunct airline.

BY RAIL
ASIA
Duncan Peattie's Chinese Railway Timetable

www.chinatt.org

For several years dedicated railfan Duncan Peattie has been producing excellent and regularly updated English translations of the Chinese railway timetables. My only quibble is that they are in English only, not bilingual, which makes them less useful in the field for communication by pointing, or for matching the Chinese place-names with those on departure boards or station platforms. There have been times in China when I was only able to communicate my desired destination to a ticket clerk by pointing to the place name in a bilingual timetable. Peattie produces two editions, both available for download as PDF files: a free "quick reference" summary timetable of express trains between main stations, which are the only trains most foreign tourists will ever take, and a complete national timetable for sale if you are getting off the main lines. The schedules are keyed to the Quail China Railway Atlas, which Peattie also distributes in either printed or PDF format, and which can be invaluable in finding possible connections and through routes.

Indian Railways

www.indianrailways.gov.in

Indian Railways' mainline reservations and ticketing have been computerized for more than 20 years, and there's now a Web interface to Indian Railways' schedules and a ticket purchase website for foreigners. Neither is very user-friendly or reliable, however, especially if you aren't familiar with the elaborate caste system of classes of trains and accommodations, the routings and connections, or the multiple stations in many Indian cities. And seats or berths on the better trains are often available only from the quota of seats reserved for foreign tourists, which can only be booked in person at train stations or at special railway ticket offices for foreigners in the largest cities (Delhi, Mumbai/Bombay, Chennai/Madras, and Kolkata/Calcutta). The staple reference for travelers on the faster trains between main cities in India, *Trains at a Glance,* is now available online as well. The site keeps getting reorganized, unfortunately, so I can't give exact URLs with the Indian Railways' site for any of these—you'll have to search the website on your own.

Japan Rail Passes

www.japanrailpass.net

Information on Japan Rail Passes in English, Japanese, and other languages. Includes pass prices, rules, and a worldwide directory of pass sales agents. Japan Rail Passes cannot be purchased inside Japan. As in the U.K. and Australia, Japanese railroads have been broken up into separate regional companies, with similar consequences in confusion and difficulty for foreign travelers. See the website for links to the individual railroads.

Jorudan

www.jorudan.co.jp/english
Hyperdia
www.hyperdia.com

English-language route and schedule information for trains throughout Japan. Buggy and difficult to use if you don't know the different stations in a city or town, but better than anything else available. Neither of these websites actually sells tickets or is operated by any of the railroads. Hyperdia is actually operated by Hitachi, and both websites appear to be technology demonstration projects for their developers.

AUSTRALIA
Rail Australia

P.O. Box 445, Marleston Business Centre, Marleston SA 5033, Australia; tel. +61-8-8213-4592, fax +61-8-8213-4490; reservations@railaustralia.com.au; www.railaustralia.com.au

Rail Australia is the joint marketing association of all the government-owned regional railway companies in Australia. The website has details of pass options and prices, but the information about the separate railroads is complete balkanized—there's no integrated route, schedule, or price information. You can buy most passes on arrival in Australia, unlike Eurail Passes or many other visitor passes. For point-to-point tickets, especially for prices, don't waste any time here. Once you figure out which railroad you might want to ride, go directly to their own website, or phone them.

EURASIA
Poezda.net
www.poezda.net/en/web
RealRussia.co.uk
http://realrussia.co.uk/trains

Poezda.net is a technology demonstration project; RealRussia.co.uk is a travel agency. Both offer interfaces to the Russian Railways schedule database that often work better than the official Russian Railways website (listed below).

Russian Railways
http://eng.rzd.ru

The Russian Railways have recently added an English-language Web interface to point-to-point train schedules within Russia, and on some (but not all) international routes to and from Russia. It's a step in the right direction, but needs major improvement to be really useful. If you don't find what you are looking for, it's probably because you have chosen the wrong station or line (but how can a first-time visitor know which one to choose?), because the city or station name has been romanized from the Cyrillic differently than you expected, or because you are trying to check schedules too far in the future. The lack of connection information isn't as much of a problem as it would be in Western Europe, India, or China: Most of the train journeys taken by tourists in Russia are on direct trains. The only place in Russia where you are likely to have to change trains is in Moscow, where you are also likely to have to make tedious transfers between train stations, and where you'll probably want to stop over anyway if you haven't been there before.

EUROPE
BritRail

www.britrail.com

BritRail passes, point-to-point ticket sales, and (some) fare and schedule information. Website operated by ACP international as principal agents for sales of British rail tickets outside the U.K.

Eurail

www.eurail.com; sales@eurail.com

Eurail Passes are now available for direct online sales. Eurail Passes can't be sold to European citizens or residents, but can now be shipped directly to addresses in Europe for use by holders of non-European passports that don't contain resident visas or any other indications of residency in Europe. It's probably easier to buy your Eurail Pass from a local agent if there is one in your country, but if you are traveling for too long a time before you get to Europe to be able buy your pass at home and have it still be valid, or you can't find a local Eurail agent where you are, it may be worth paying for shipping to buy your pass directly from Eurail.

Eurostar

tel. 08432-186-186 (U.K. only) or +44-1233-617-575; www.eurostar.com

Eurostar trains are the Channel Tunnel ("Chunnel") passenger trains between London and Paris and London and Brussels (and some intermediate stops). Many discount prices are available only directly from Eurostar and not from other agents. You can buy tickets directly online, but be sure to arrive at the station in time to pick up your ticket from an attended ticket window as well as for customs, immigration, and security checks— Eurostar passengers are closely scrutinized and subjected to full border formalities, unlike passengers on most other international trains within the European Union.

Eurotunnel

tel. 08443-35-35-35 (U.K. only), +44-1303-282201 (U.K.), or +33-3-21002061 (France); www.eurotunnel.com

Eurotunnel trains carry road vehicles with their drivers and passengers on drive-on, drive-off rail cars through the Channel Tunnel between Folkestone, England, and Calais, France. Drivers and other vehicle passengers ride in separate cars of the trains. Passengers without vehicles use the separate Eurostar trains. Bicycles are also transported on Eurotunnel trains, but can't be booked on the website; contact Eurotunnel reservations for bicycle reservations and procedures. (As of 2011, the one-way or "single journey" Eurotunnel fare for a passenger with a bicycle was UK£16 in either direction, substantially less than the lowest Eurostar fare for a passenger without a bike.)

Rail Europe

44 S. Broadway, White Plains, NY 10601; tel. 800-4-EURAIL (800-438-7245, United States only) or 800-361-RAIL (800-361-7245, Canada only); www.raileurope.com

Provides Eurail Passes, regional and country-specific rail passes, and tickets for almost all passenger trains in Western Europe. Rail Europe represents Eurail Pass and BritRail Pass participants as well as Eurostar, although each of the three requires separate tickets or passes. The Rail Europe website is one of the best (although neither complete nor entirely reliable) sources of information on point-to-point European rail schedules and fares, which aren't available on most Eurail Pass sites.

U.K. National Rail Enquiries

www.nationalrail.co.uk; tel. 08457-48-49-50 (U.K. only) or +44-20-7278-5240

British railroads have been broken up and privatized, but jointly fund this central information service for fares and schedules on all long-distance trains. They do not sell tickets, but provide Web links and can transfer calls to ticket sales agents for the individual railroads, once you decide which railroad you want to take.

Quno.com

www.quno.com

Online travel agency specializing in direct sales of British rail tickets. Operates its own schedule, route, and fare software, so it may find different (and sometimes better) routings or prices than other agents, National Rail Enquiries, or the railways themselves, especially for journeys involving connections between different railroads. Developed by Silverrail Technologies (www.silverrailtech.com), an extremely promising U.S.-based (surprisingly, given the low profile of passenger trains in the United States) software start-up that hopes to introduce similar services for trains in other countries.

NORTH AMERICA
Amtrak

60 Massachusetts Ave. NE, Washington, DC 20002; tel. 800-USA-RAIL (800-872-7245, United States only) or +1-215-856-7953; inat5@sales.amtrak.com (sales to customers outside the United States only); www.amtrak.com

Amtrak (the National Railroad Passenger Corp.) operates almost all interstate passenger trains in the United States. International sales procedures have improved greatly in recent years. Tickets and passes can now be purchased from abroad, by phone or online, and picked up from a staffed Amtrak station on arrival in the United States. Just make sure the ticket office at that station will be open when you want to pick up your tickets or pass, as many Amtrak stations are unattended or have limited ticket office hours.

National Association of Railway Passengers (NARP)

505 Capitol Court NE, Suite 300, Washington, DC 20002-7706; tel. +1-202-408-8362, fax +1-202-408-8287; narp@narprail.org; www.narprail.org

NARP is a lobbying group for the interests of railway passengers in the United States, working to protect the small fraction of government funding for transportation that goes to Amtrak and other railroads. (Most U.S. transportation funding goes to build roads and to subsidize cars, trucks, and barges.) A small but extremely knowledgeable organization, NARP has earned the respect of rail companies and politicians alike, and Amtrak listens more and more to NARP's advice. Support for NARP is crucial to the preservation, much less expansion or modernization, of long-distance rail transportation in the United States. Regular membership dues are US$35/year, US$45/family (two people). NARP members get 10 percent off most Amtrak fares, including already-discounted fares, so NARP membership can pay for itself on a single transcontinental ticket.

VIA Rail Canada

P.O. Box 8116, Station A, Montréal, QC H3C 3N3, Canada; tel. 888-VIA-RAIL (888-842-7245, Canada only) or +1-514-989-2626; customer_relations@viarail.ca; www.viarail.ca

VIA Rail Canada operates all transcontinental passenger trains and most, but not all, other long-distance passenger trains in Canada. Individual tickets and Canrail passes can be purchased online from abroad.

WORLDWIDE
The Man in Seat Sixty-One

www.seat61.com

"The Man in Seat Sixty-One" is British railwayman Mark Smith, who shares his love of rail travel through this personal introduction to the how-tos of travel by train in countries around the world and directory of links to more detailed information about train travel in particular countries. Since the *Thomas Cook Overseas Timetable* ceased publication in 2011 after many decades as the default global passenger train information source, this is the single best place to start if you aren't sure if there are trains in the country where you will be traveling, where they go, how to get fare and schedule information, or how to buy tickets.

UrbanRail.net

www.urbanrail.net

Is there a subway/metro/underground railway/streetcar/light rail system in the city you are going to visit? This personal site of railfan and author Robert Schwandl is the place to find out. While long-distance passenger rail transport is declining in many parts of the world, urban rail is booming. Guidebooks often can't keep up with the pace of new subway and streetcar lines and entire new systems, some in places you might not expect to find them.

BY ROAD

Bus reservation systems, even when highly automated, have been poorly integrated. As the listings below suggest, that's starting to change. Ask locals about online bus schedule and fare information portals, if not functional online bus ticket agencies, in any country with a sophisticated long-distance bus network used by people of a class likely to have access to the Internet.

Agência Nacional de Transportes Terrestres do Brasil

www.antt.gov.br, https://appweb.antt.gov.br/transp/secao_duas_localidades.asp

The Brazilian National Land Transport Agency provides this search engine, in Portuguese only, to determine which bus companies are licensed to carry passengers between any two cities or towns in the country. Once you have the company names, you can look up their individual websites.

BiletPlaza.com

www.biletplaza.com

Online Turkish bus ticket agency. Buggy and in Turkish only, but better than nothing. I'm not sure I'd want to trust buying a ticket on the website unless I was fluent in Turkish, but at least you can get an idea of which bus companies serve which cities, from and to which bus stations (there are multiple bus stations in many Turkish cities), with which classes of buses, on what schedules, and at approximately what fares.

Plataforma10.com

tel. +54-11-5238-5100; www.plataforma10.com

Agents for more than 100 bus companies in Argentina and between Argentina and neighboring countries. Look for the little blue-and-white striped Argentine flag on the home page to switch from the default Spanish to English (or Portuguese). Once you find a schedule and price for a class of bus and company you like, you can buy tickets on the website, by phone, at one of the Plataforma 10 kiosks throughout Buenos Aires and at bus stations and in other locations in provincial cities and towns—or directly from the particular bus company.

The Rule of the Road by Peter Kincaid

1986, 242 pp; Greenwood Press, Westport, CT

A detailed popular historical survey (by a professor of international law) of the rules governing whether people walk, ride, and drive on the left or on the right side of the road in different places.

Which Side of the Road Do They Drive On? by Brian Lucas
www.brianlucas.ca/roadside

The most detailed and up-to-date list of which side of the road people drive on in countries and territories around the world. If you are going to have to drive on the opposite side from what you are used to, it's best to be forewarned.

BY BICYCLE
Adventure Cycling Association

www.adv-cycling.org

These days you might think "adventure cycling" would refer to extreme sports, but for this organization, the adventure is in any sort of long-distance travel by bicycle: "traveling by bike is a truly life-changing experience." Also publishes *Adventure Cyclist* magazine. Based in the United States, but provides information on bicycle travel elsewhere in the world as well.

CrazyGuyOnABike.com

www.crazyguyonabike.com

"A free website for hosting bicycle touring journals, forums, and resources." Originally developed by Neil Gunton to host his own bicycle touring journal (hence the title), it now has hundreds of accounts of past and present bicycle journeys around the world, as well as articles and information on bikes, other gear, tools and repairs, trip planning and preparation, routes, etc.

See also the bicycle travel books by Willie Weir and Dervla Murphy listed earlier under *Published Travelogues*.

BY WATER
Complete Folding Kayaker by Ralph Diaz

ISBN 0071408096; 2nd ed. 2003, 256 pp; Ragged Mountain Press/McGraw-Hill, Camden, ME

The definitive book on the only seaworthy portable boats. Includes references to many other sources of boats, equipment, and information. Opinionated, but acknowledges other points of view.

Folbot (USA) Inc.

4209 Pace St., Charleston, SC, 29405; tel. 800-533-5099 (United States only) or
+1-843-744-3483, fax +1-843-744-7783; info@folbot1.com; www.folbot.com

Manufacturers of affordable, well-engineered folding kayaks. Made in the United States, but they have sales agents around the world, and their boats pack small enough to be shipped worldwide as parcels or checked as airline luggage. Substantially less expensive than most competitors, but still seaworthy and built to last. My highest personal endorsement and recommendation (as a satisfied repeat customer who paid list price) for outstanding value and over-the-top customer service and support.

Cruise & Freighter Travel Association

P.O. Box 580188, Flushing, NY 11358; tel. 800-872-8584 (United States and Canada only) or +1-718-224-0435, fax +1-718-224-3247; info@travltips.com; www.travltips.com

Although they call themselves a membership association (US$25/year), this is mainly a travel agency specializing in passenger travel on oceangoing freighter ships. The website includes a directory of transoceanic and other large freighters that carry paying passengers, including routes and approximate trip durations and prices.

Freighter World Cruises

180 South Lake Ave., Suite 340, Pasadena, CA 91101-2655; tel. 800-531-7774 (United States only) or +1-626-449-3106; info@freighterworld.com; www.freighterworld.com

Claims to be "the largest travel agency in the world dedicated to freighter cruising." Web directory by world region of passenger-carrying freighter services, routes, and prices (including some on odd routes or at short notice for as little as US$100 per couple per day, although the norm is about twice that), as well as general information on freighter travel.

Logistics

CULTURAL AWARENESS AND ADAPTATION
The Global Soul: Jet Lag, Shopping Malls, and the Search for Home
by Pico Iyer
ISBN 0-679-77611-7; paperback 2001 (hardcover 2000), 303 pp; Vintage Departures, New York

Iyer's books are often pigeonholed as travelogues, but this is a far more profound essay than that characterization might imply. *The Global Soul* doesn't lack for insightful description of travel experiences and how they affect the external world, but its focus is on the internal changes being brought about through increased world travel, migration, multiculturalism, and "globalization": changes in our conceptions of ourselves, our identities, our places in the world, and the meaning of "home."

Intercultural Press
(a division of Nicholas Brealey Publishing)

20 Park Plaza, Suite 1115A, Boston, MA 02116; tel. 888-273-2539 (U.S. only) or tel. +1-617-523-3708; info@nicholasbrealey.com; www.interculturalpress.com; www.nicholasbrealey.com/boston/subjects/interculturalpress.html

The leading publisher and distributor in the United States of books and other materials for intercultural training, both for people going abroad from the United States and for people coming from abroad to the United States. See the website for the complete catalog, all highly recommended. Titles especially likely to be useful to long-term travelers include, among many others, *Survival Kit for Overseas Living* (a cultural rather than logistical guide), *The Art of Coming Home* (a guide to coping with "reentry shock" when you get back), *American Ways: A Guide for Foreigners in the United States* (useful for understanding how you as an American are likely to appear to foreigners you meet while traveling), and books for children to help them prepare for and cope with traveling and living abroad.

Trans-Cultural Study Guide by Volunteers in Asia

first published 1975, 2nd ed. 1987, 155 pp; Volunteers in Asia Press, 1663 Mission St., Suite 504, San Francisco, CA 94103; tel. +1-415-904-8033; info@viaprograms.org; www.viaprograms.org

This book gives no answers, only questions: it's a pocket-sized primer of relatively timeless questions to ask oneself, and local people, to help understand why and how things in a "strange" (i.e., different) place are the way they are. Excellent food for thought.

See also the listings earlier under *The Ecology of Travel and Tourism* in the *Background Reading* section, and later under *Living, Working, Studying, and Volunteering Abroad*. For the particular cultural issues of travel in countries where people are much poorer than you are, see the chapter on "Bridging the Cultural Gap" in *Ethiopia: The Bradt Travel Guide* by Philip Briggs, listed above under *Africa*.

MAPS, GUIDEBOOKS, AND GEAR

This is a selective list of some of the stores I've personally visited and shopped at. Maps are peculiarly ill-suited for online or mail ordering, since it's hard to compare them or evaluate the coverage, scale, legibility, weight, and quality without inspecting them first-hand. See the directory of IMTA members (the first listing below) for other possibilities. Like booksellers, many map dealers are in business more for love of maps and travel than for money, or make more on sales of travel gear and accessories than on maps or guidebooks.

International Map Trade Association (IMTA)

2629 Manhattan Ave., PMB 281, Hermosa Beach, CA 90254-2447; tel. +1-310-376-7731, fax +1-310-376-7287; imta@maptrade.org; www.maptrade.org

An international trade association. "IMTA members are the companies that create and sell the maps, atlases, globes, and map-related products you use." See the website for an excellent worldwide directory of specialty map retailers (many of which also sell guidebooks and other products for travelers) and map production companies.

Daunt Books for Travelers

83 Marylebone High Street (tube: Baker Street, Regent's Park, or Bond Street), London W1U 4QW, U.K.; tel. +44-20-7224-2295; orders@dauntbooks.co.uk; www.dauntbooks.co.uk

A unique bookstore concept, Daunt Books shelves all books geographically. So you can find guidebooks, maps, history, politics, art, poetry, and novels about a place (by locals and outsiders), all together. See the website for details of additional London shops in Chelsea (Fulham Road), Holland Park, Hampstead, Belsize Park, and Cheapside.

Freytag & Berndt

Kohlmarkt 9, 1010 Wien (Vienna), Austria, +1-43-1-533-8685, fax +43-1-533-8686; shop@freytagberndt.at; www.freytagberndt.com

One of the largest travel map publishers, importers, distributors, and retail map stores on the European continent. Exceptional coverage, as might be expected, for Central and Eastern Europe, but also has some of the best maps to other places worldwide, including parts of the Middle East, West and Central Asia, and Africa. The website has only a partial English-language version but the store is happy to deal with English-speaking walk-in customers and phone and email inquiries in English. The address above for mail orders is also the main shop on the pedestrian mall in the center of downtown Vienna. See the website for other retail outlets in Vienna, Munich, and elsewhere.

International Travel Maps and Books (ITMB Publishing)

12300 Bridgeport Rd., Richmond, BC V6V 1J5, Canada; tel. +1-604-273-1400, fax +1-604-273-1488; itmb@itmb.com; www.itmb.com

North America's leading publisher of maps for international travel, and a leading distributor of maps from other publishers. First-rate cartography and production. Full catalog and direct sales on the website. No longer in downtown Vancouver or easily accessible by public transit, but worth a visit to Richmond to browse their store if you're in the area with a car.

The Map Shop

6-10 Peel St., Adelaide, S.A. 5000, Australia; tel. +61-8-8231-2033, fax +61-8-8231-2373; mercator@mapshop.net.au; www.mapshop.net.au

Run by devoted cartographers and map-lovers, this may be Australia's best source of maps for travelers. Retailers, publishers, importers, and producers of customized maps. Only a fraction of their catalog is online, so email or call if you don't see what you want or aren't sure which map will be best for your purposes.

Mountain Equipment Co-Op (MEC)

130 W. Broadway (between Manitoba St. and Columbia St.), Vancouver, BC V5Y 1P3, Canada; tel. 888-847-0770 (Canada and United States only) or +1-604-876-6221; info@mec.ca; www.mec.ca

Like the REI co-op in the United States, MEC is a nonprofit, member-owned consumer cooperative. It's also one of Canada's largest suppliers of outdoor and travel gear and clothing, with stores from Vancouver to Halifax as well as mail, phone, and Web ordering. See the website or call for store locations. Sales to members only, but for C$5 you can buy a share and become a member for life.

Omni Resources Inc.

P.O. Box 2096 (1004 South Mebane St.), Burlington, NC 27216-2096; tel. 800-742-2677 (United States only) or +1-336-227-8300, fax +1-336-227-3748; inquiries@omnimap.com; www.omnimap.com

With the demise of its largest competitor since the previous edition of this book, Omni Resources has become the dominant international map distributor and importer in the United states. Carries maps produced around the world, including many unavailable anywhere else outside the countries where they are published. Sells primarily as a wholesaler to retail stores, and has only a very limited stock on display at the head office for walk-in sales, but is happy to service direct retail orders. Email or call if you can't find what you want on the website.

Recreational Equipment Inc. (REI)

Mail and Internet orders: Sumner, WA 98352-0001; 800-426-4840 (United States only),
+1-253-891-2500, fax +1-253-891-2523; service@rei.com; www.rei.com

Flagship store: 222 Yale Ave N. (just north of downtown and alongside I-5 on the west side of the highway), Seattle, WA 98109; +1-206-223-1944

Founded in 1938, REI is a nonprofit consumer cooperative (the largest in the United States), entirely owned by the members and run by a member-elected board of directors. Lifetime membership is US$20; any "profits" are distributed to the members, in proportion to their purchases, at the end of each year. Dozens of stores throughout the United States as well as mail and Internet ordering. Facilitates workshops and clinics at stores for members to share their knowledge, skills, and experience. REI emphasizes equipment for active outdoor recreation, but has one of the largest selections of travel gear in the United States, including travel packs and many brands and models of water purifiers. Check out their helpful evaluation guides and comparative specification sheets for different types of gear, available online or in their stores.

Stanfords Maps and Travel Books

12–14 Long Acre (tube: Covent Garden or Leicester Square), London WC2E 9LP, U.K.;
tel. +44-20-7836-1321, fax +44-20-7632-8928; sales@stanfords.co.uk; www.stanfords.co.uk

In business at the same location for more than a century, Stanfords probably has more maps and guidebooks on display than any other store in the world, including many that aren't readily available (or only available for mail-order or online ordering, sight unseen) in the United States. Smaller branch store in Bristol.

U.S. Geological Survey (USGS)

tel. 888-ASK-USGS (888-275-8747, United States only); www.usgs.gov; http://store.usgs.gov (online orders and free downloadable maps)

USGS National Center

   12201 Sunrise Valley Dr., Reston, VA 20192 (less than a mile, although probably not walkable, from the terminals at Washington Dulles International Airport); tel. +1-703-648-5953

U.S. Geological Survey

   Box 25046, Denver Federal Center (ask for directions to the map store at the Federal Center gatehouse; government-issued ID required for entry to the Federal Center), Denver, CO 80225; tel +1-303-236-5900

U.S. Geological Survey

   345 Middlefield Rd., Menlo Park, CA 94025; tel. +1-650-853-8300

The best starting point, although not the only mapping agency or map source, for world-wide maps published by the USGS itself and many other U.S. government agencies. Extremely helpful and user-friendly. Over-the-counter retail sales only at the three locations listed above and in Rolla, MO, and Anchorage, AK. More and more USGS maps are being made available as free downloads rather than, or sometimes in addition to, in printed form. USGS maps are also distributed by Omni Resources, ITMB (Canada), Stanfords (U.K.), and many other map stores.

WEATHER, CLIMATE, AND WHEN TO GO

World Weather Guide by E. A. Pearce and C. Gordon Smith

Hutchinson World Weather Guide
ISBN 1859863426; revised ed. 2000, 480 pp; Helicon Publishing, Oxford, U.K.

Fodor's World Weather Guide
ISBN 0-375-70349-7; 1998, 456 pp; Random House, New York

Times Books World Weather Guide
ISBN 0812918819; revised ed. 1990, 480 pp; Times Books, New York

Notwithstanding the different titles, these are all essentially the same book. Despite being out of print under all three titles, this is by far the best climate reference for world travelers. Get a secondhand copy of whichever edition you can find. Fortunately, climate change is slow enough and small enough that old copies aren't out of date: a change of a fraction of a degree in average temperature can be critical to the ecology, but doesn't affect the tables or descriptions in a book like this. Includes average daily maximum and minimum temperatures, rainfall, and humidity for each month of the year, as well as descriptions of typical weather, for hundreds of locations in even obscure and little-touristed countries around the world. Comprehensive, detailed, and invaluable.

WorldClimate
www.worldclimate.com

It's easy to find information on current weather—what the conditions are today, or what they are expected to be tomorrow. But what travelers need is different, and much harder to find: information on climate—what the typical conditions are at a particular time of year. This no-frills website has charts and tables of temperature, humidity, and precipitation from a variety of public domain (mostly government) sources.

Weatherbase
www.weatherbase.com

Historical climate data for thousands of locations worldwide, from varied sources.

Solar Eclipse Information
http://eclipse.gsfc.nasa.gov/solar.html

Compiled by eclipse researchers from NASA, with help from scientists and amateur eclipse followers around the world, the bulletins on this site are the definitive resource for would-be eclipse observers. A detailed bulletin is produced a year or more before each total eclipse of the sun, mapping the eclipse path and other data and giving details on likely observing conditions and chances of seeing the eclipse at each point.

LANGUAGES AND COMMUNICATION
Bay Foreign Language Books
Unit 3(B) Frith Business Centre, Frith Rd., Aldington, Ashford, Kent TN25 7HJ, U.K.; tel. +44-1233-720-020, fax +44-1233-721-272; sales@baylanguagebooks.co.uk; www.baylanguagebooks.co.uk

"Suppliers of language learning material in over 600 languages." Mainly a distributor to bookstores, government agencies, educational institutions, and libraries, but also sells directly to the public worldwide by mail.

Grant & Cutler (at Foyles)
113-119 Charing Cross Rd., London WC2H 0EB (tube: Tottenham Court Road), London W1F 7AY, U.K.; tel. +44-20-7734-2012, fax +44-20-7734-9272; grantandcutler@foyles.co.uk; www.grantandcutler.com

Formerly the U.K.'s largest independent foreign-language booksellers, Grant & Cutler's retail shop has been merged into the foreign-langauge section on the first floor of Foyle's main store. Language-learning materials as well as fiction and nonfiction books, periodicals, and films from around the world. See the website for their catalogs by language and topic.

Internet Language Company

11515 NE 26th Ave., Suite 201, Seattle, WA 98125; tel. +1-253-353-2761, fax +1-206-400-1156; sales@multilingualbooks.com; www.multilingualbooks.com

Language-learning and translation books (dictionaries, grammars, phrasebooks, references, textbooks, literature readers), tapes, CDs, software, and pocket-sized electronic translators.

Kwikpoint International Translators

908 King St., Ste. 300, Alexandria, VA 22314; tel. 888-KWIKPOINT (888-594-5764, United States only) or +1-703-370-5527, fax +1-703-370-5526; www.kwikpoint.com

Pocket, wallet, and passport-sized laminated cards with pictographs illustrating basic travel concepts for use in communication by pointing. Remarkably well-designed (by a touring bicyclist, naturally) and functional. There are superficially similar competitors, but these are the best, and the standard ones used (in customized versions) by everyone from the U.S. military to multinational corporations, medical professionals, and independent travelers. I find the passport size the best compromise between compactness and comprehensiveness.

Language Book Centre

131 York St., Level 1, Sydney NSW, Australia; tel. +61-2-9267-1397, fax +61-2-9264-8993; language@abbeys.com.au; www.languagebooks.com.au

This division of Abbeys Bookshop offers the largest range in Australia of language-learning and foreign-language books and materials.

LCL International Booksellers

104-106 Judd St. (tube: King's Cross and St. Pancras), London WC1H 9PU, U.K.; tel. +44-20-7837-0486, fax +44-20-7833-9452; sales.lcl@btinternet.com; www.lclib.com

Specialists in dictionaries, textbooks, grammars, and other resources for learning a wide range of languages.

Merriam-Webster's Guide to International Business Communications
by Toby D. Atkinson
ISBN 0-87779-608-4; 2nd ed. 1999, 400 pp; Merriam-Webster Inc., Springfield, MA

When you need help figuring out how to dial a phone number in another country, what goes on which lines of an address, or how to find the physical location in a foreign city corresponding to a mailing address, this is the book to look for in the library. Be sure to read the introductory chapters on "How to Get Phone Calls and Faxes Through" and "How to Make Your English More Understandable" to nonnative speakers, before you leave home. Gives detailed information on address, telephone, and other communication formats only for selected countries, mostly First World, but notes correctly that, "An awareness of the terminology and practices in these countries will help you understand those in many others."

The Other Tongue: English Across Cultures edited by Braj B. Kachru
ISBN 0-252062000; 2nd ed. 1992, 384 pp; University of Illinois Press, Urbana, IL; ISBN 0-564067-5; 2nd ed. 1996, 384 pp; Oxford University Press, New Delhi, India (distributed in the United States by South Asia Books)

That it's possible to travel the world speaking only English is due to the unique role of English as an international language. Today most people in the world who use English are not native speakers of English, were taught by nonnative speakers of English, and use English primarily to communicate with other nonnative speakers. If native speakers of English, especially monolingual ones, want to use English effectively for international communication, we need to understand and accept the variety of English dialects that have evolved and, in many cases, sunk deep local roots around the world: West African English, South Asian English, Malaysian/Singaporean English, etc. This book is a thought-provoking introduction to these issues. Academic, but quite accessible, and deliberately structured to introduce and survey the topic.

Schoenhof's Foreign Books
www.schoenhofs.com, 76A Mt. Auburn St., Cambridge, MA 02138; tel. +1-617-547-8855
Europa Books/Schoenhof's: 832 N. State St., Chicago, IL 60610; tel. +1-312-335-9677
Mail and online order fulfillment: 8124 N. Ridgeway Ave., Skokie, IL 60076, tel. 800-277-4645 (United States only), fax +1-847-676-1195; info@schoenhofs.com

A fixture in Harvard Square for more than 150 years, Schoenhof's offers "the largest selection of foreign-language books in North America," including language-learning material for over 700 languages and dialects, as well as fiction and nonfiction in 50 languages. Strong emphasis on Europe and European languages, but does cover the world.

See also the foreign-language book and periodical distributors listed earlier in the sections for each world region.

COMPUTERS, CAMERAS, AND ELECTRONIC DEVICES
B&H Photo
420 9th Ave. (between 33rd St. and 34th St., 1 block west of Penn Station), New York, NY 10001; www.bhphotovideo.com

I've bought digital cameras, audio recorders, and other gadgets from B&H both at their store in Manhattan and online. Their core market is photography and audio/video professionals, but they also stock "consumer-grade" products, and their knowledgeable staff is willing to take the time to help explain products and choices to amateurs. Unlike typical "closed box" stores, they have working product samples on display that you can touch, feel, and compare side by side before you decide to buy.

Central Computers

837 Howard St. (1 block from Moscone Center), San Francisco, CA 94103; tel +1-415-495-5888, fax +1-415-896-5888; www.centralcomputers.com

If you are going to buy an Asus netbook or tablet computer in the United States, this is the place. Online and walk-in sales in San Francisco and at four other stores in Silicon Valley; see the website for addresses. Main U.S. factory service center for Asus. Direct importer of computer parts and accessories from mainland China as well as Taiwan, with its own full-time sourcing office in Shenzhen.

DealExtreme

www.dealextreme.com

Electronic devices (including mobile/cell phones) and other gadgets and accessories such as adapters, charging cables, and replacement batteries, sourced and shipped directly from Shenzhen (mostly) and other places in China. All prices on their website include airmail shipping worldwide. You need to allow anywhere from a couple of weeks to a couple of months for delivery, but the prices are so much lower than for similar Chinese-made goods from U.S. outlets that it's well worth the wait. And some of these products such as mobile phones designed for the Chinese domestic market aren't otherwise available at all in the United States. Quality varies; check the customer reviews for the specific item before you buy. The best place to get a full set of spares and accessories, before you leave on a big trip, for any electronic devices you are bringing with you.

Dynamism.com

tel. 800-711-6277 (United States and Canada only) or +1-312-587-0402, fax +1-702-995-8539; sales@dynamism.com; www.dynamism.com

Many of the miniature computers and other electronic devices most suitable for travelers are sold only in Japan, Korea, and/or Taiwan. Dynamism.com adapts them for United States and international use (installing English-language versions of the operating system, user interface, etc.) and distributes and supports them worldwide. If "small is beautiful" and "size matters" are your computer mantras, this is the place to find your fantasy.

Safeware

6500 Busch Blvd., Suite 233, Columbus, OH 43229; tel. 800-800-1492 (United States only) or +1-614-781-1492, fax +1-614-781-0559; service@safeware.com; www.safeware.com

Computers, smartphones, iPads, and other electronic devices are fragile magnets for theft. Airlines won't accept liability for electronic devices, and even most travel insurance excludes them or limits coverage to a few hundred dollars. Safeware is the only major company providing affordable insurance for laptop computers and other portable electronic devices.

SurplusComputers.com

www.surpluscomputers.com

What's "surplus" in Silicon Valley may be just the ticket for your trip. I've bought desktop and laptop computers from these folks, and been pleased with both. Minimal service, but great value for the money. Used items I've bought have been in lightly used, near-new condition. When a call center puts new computers on every agent's desk, or a business gives all its sales people new laptops every year or two, this is the sort of outlet through which the old ones end up getting dumped at bargain prices.

MOBILE/CELLULAR TELEPHONES

GSM World—the GSM Association

www.gsmworld.com

Coverage maps, roaming agreements, and listings and links for local mobile (cellular) phone operators worldwide. The place to go to find out which of the international-standard GSM band(s) are in use in each of the countries you plan to visit, so you know which bands your phone needs to cover. (Warning: listings of new networks on GSMworld.com are sometimes premature. Always click through to the website for the local operator to verify the current status of their service.)

Steve Kropla's Help for World Travelers

www.kropla.com

A compendium of information on telephone, television, and electrical systems worldwide: What's the voltage in this country? What's the frequency? Which electrical power and telephone plug(s) are in use? Compiled as a labor of love and service to fellow travelers by corporate jet-setter Steve Kropla, with the assistance of volunteer contributors around the world.

Telestial

27 Drydock Ave, 5th Floor, Boston, MA 02210; tel. 800-707-0031 (United States only), tel. 1-800-795-252 (Australia only), tel. 0800-376-2370 (U.K. only); tel. +1-213-337-5560; support@telestial.com; www.telestial.com

Cell phones and prepaid SIMs for world travel, including both single-country SIMs (the cheapest choice for use within those specific countries), and global roaming SIMs with more expensive per-minute rates that can be used anywhere in the world (useful to have one of as a backup, even if you buy single-country SIMs in places where you stay a while). See the website for toll-free customer service numbers in other countries.

LIVING, WORKING, STUDYING, AND VOLUNTEERING ABROAD

Alternatives to the Peace Corps: A Guide to Global Volunteer Opportunities
edited by Caitlin Hachmyer
ISBN 978-0-935028-31-7; 12th ed. 2008, 148 pp; Food First Books; Institute for Food and Development Policy/Food First; 398 60th St., Oakland, CA 94618; tel. +1-510-654-4400, fax +1-510-654-4551; info@foodfirst.org; www.foodfirst.org

An excellent directory of U.S.-based domestic and international volunteer programs; also includes a few listings of programs based in the Third World, and a good bibliography of other resources.

ExpatExchange.com
www.expatexchange.com

Community website for expats around the world. A useful place to connect with foreigners already living in a place you are thinking of moving, and to find advertisements for services targeted to expats, from mail forwarding to auto shipping to insurance and banking.

Expatica.com
www.expatica.com

Netherlands-based online community website for expatriates, mainly those living in Europe or the United States. Resource guides and expat service directories and ads may be useful to those in other places as well.

The Global Citizen: A Guide to Creating an International Life and Career
by Elizabeth Kruempelmann
ISBN 1-58008-352-8; 2002, 384 pp; Ten Speed Press, Berkeley, CA; www.the-global-citizen.com

International career planning and job search advice from the former moderator of the international job message board on Monster.com. Sometimes overly optimistic, and relatively uncritical in its reviews of programs and organizations, but has lots of good suggestions on job-search tactics.

Global Exchange
P.O. Box 675, Newcastle, NSW 2300, Australia; tel. +61-2-4929-4688;
info@globalexchange.com.au; www.globalexchange.com.au; distributed by Australian Book Group; www.australianbookgroup.com.au

Publishers of guides for Australians and Aotearoa/New Zealanders living, working, volunteering, or studying overseas, and for foreigners living or working in Australia. Many of these work opportunities are based on reciprocal working-holiday schemes, in which the United States doesn't participate. (No relation to Global Exchange in the United States.)

GoAbroad.com
www.goabroad.com

Website for students from the United States considering or planning work, study, or volunteering abroad.

How to Live Your Dream of Volunteering Overseas
by Joseph Collin, Stefano DeZeraga, and Zahara Heckscher
ISBN 0-14-200071-X; 2002, 468 pp; Penguin Putnam, New York; www.volunteeroverseas.org

A superb book that should be the standard reference on the topic. Other books on volunteering abroad are mostly compilations of organizational self-descriptions. In contrast, the descriptions of specific programs in this book are based on visits to their work sites abroad and interviews with current and former participants, giving honest, critical pros and cons. Even more valuable are the sections on how to define your own goals for volunteering, find a program (or create your own) that suits them, prepare for your overseas experience, and follow through after you return. Includes a discussion of independent travel as an alternative to organized or prearranged volunteer programs. If you are thinking of volunteering abroad, start with this book.

International Volunteer Programs Association (IVPA)
P.O. Box 287049, New York, NY 10128; tel. +1-646-505-8209; www.volunteerinternational.org

"IVPA is an alliance of nonprofit, nongovernmental organizations based in North America, that are involved in international volunteer and internship exchanges." The website includes a database of programs searchable by country or world region, program type, and duration.

Peace Brigades International (PBI)
PBI International Office: Development House, 56–64 Leonard St., London EC2A 4JX, U.K.; tel. +44-20-7065-0775; www.peacebrigades.org
PBI/USA: 1326 9th St. NW, Washington, DC 20001; tel. +1-202-232-0142, fax +1-202-232-0143; info@pbiusa.org; www.pbiusa.org

PBI volunteers from around the world provide nonviolent escort services and assistance in conflict resolution in areas of violence. PBI goes only where it is invited and works primarily to support indigenous organizations seeking to resolve conflicts nonviolently. For those seeking an alternative to "conflict resolution" through military intervention or other use of force, or to acquiescence in war and repression, and willing to make a serious commitment to peace work, PBI provides an excellent opportunity to work for peace while learning about the world. See the website for contacts in other countries.

Resource Guide

*The Peace Corps and More: 220 Ways to Work, Study and Travel
in the Third World* by Medea Benjamin
ISBN 0-9711443-1-1; 3rd ed. 2003, 200 pp; Global Exchange (USA); 2017 Mission St., 2nd Floor,
San Francisco, CA 94110; tel. +1-415-255-7296, fax +1-415-255-7498; info@globalexchange.org;
www.globalexchange.org

A selective but useful directory mainly of U.S.-based nongovernmental organizations
that offer structured volunteer work opportunities in the Third and Fourth Worlds. Also
lists a few government programs and some socially responsible education and tour programs. Includes a good but equally selective bibliography. Global Exchange is an operator of "Reality Tours" from the United States, with an explicit preference, reflected in
this and their other books, toward escorted group travel rather than independent "do it
yourself" travel. (No relation to Global Exchange in Australia.)

A Practical Guide to Global Health Service by Edward O'Neil Jr., M.D.
ISBN 1-57947-772-0; 2006, 404 pp; American Medical Association; www.ama-assn.org

Written by a practicing emergency-room physician with experience as a medical volunteer in Africa and Latin America, this is the definitive guide to health-related international volunteer opportunities, particularly but not exclusively for medical professionals.
The organization O'Neil founded, Omnimed (www.omnimed.org), places mainly doctors,
but some of the other 300 organizations profiled in the book accept volunteers without
special skills. O'Neil's companion volume, *Awakening Hippocrates—A Primer on Health,
Poverty and Global Service,* also published by the AMA, addresses questions of even
more general interest and importance: if people around the world are sick mainly because they are poor, what is the obligation of someone who has taken a Hippocratic
Oath to heal the sick? And what does this mean to each of us in the First World who
benefits from global disparities of wealth and health?

Transitions Abroad
www.transitionsabroad.com

One of the most comprehensive U.S.-based resources on work, study, and living abroad.
The emphasis is on students and younger people, but the website has material of interest to all ages.

Volunteers for Peace (VFP)
7 Kilburn St., Suite 316, Burlington, VT 05401, tel. +1-802-540-3060; info@vfp.org; www.vfp.org

VFP organizes multinational groups of volunteers for constructive projects around the
world, mostly for a few weeks at a time. VFP workcamps are an excellent way to extend
one's stay in a country, meet people from other countries, and learn more about local
life than is possible for most tourist travelers.

VIA (formerly Volunteers in Asia)

1663 Mission St., Suite 504, San Francisco, CA 94103; tel. +1-415-904-8033; info@viaprograms. org; www.viaprograms.org

One of the most culturally sensitive and politically responsible U.S.-based volunteer organizations, VIA sends volunteers from the United States to teach English in several countries in Asia for periods ranging from a few months to two years, as well as operating some shorter-term educational and exchange programs. Exceptionally good predeparture preparation program.

Work Your Way Around the World by Susan Griffith

ISBN 1-85458-329-8; 12th ed. 2005, 576 pp; Vacation Work, Oxford, U.K.; www.vacationwork.co.uk

Griffith is optimistic but not totally unrealistic about what sorts of jobs, and at what wages, you can expect to find, and gives particularly apt warnings about the poor job prospects for Northern visitors in Southern countries. Read this book before you plan to finance your trip by working along the way.

See also the earlier listings for Intercultural Press under *Cultural Awareness and Adaptation* and for the *Moon Living Abroad* series under *Destination Guidebooks for Independent Travelers.*

Passports

U.S. PASSPORTS

National Passport Information Center

Passport Services Agency; U.S. Department of State; tel. 877-4-USA-PPT (877-487-2778, United States only); http://travel.state.gov/passport

The Passport Agency urges you to apply for your passport by mail, not in person, which is fine as long as you have enough time (*at least* two months, preferably three months or more) before you plan to leave. Take the application, in an unsealed envelope, together with the originals of your proof of identity and citizenship (typically a driver's license or other state photo ID card and your birth certificate, for people born in the United States) to a post office or county clerk's office that accepts passport applications. They must inspect your documents and certify that you have proven your identity and citizenship before your application can be forwarded to the National Passport Center. Applications can be sent by regular mail, but I very strongly recommend that passports and passport (and visa) applications be sent exclusively by Express Mail (not Priority Mail, registered mail, or certified mail) or by private overnight delivery services, and returned the same way, no matter how much time you have before your intended departure. At Passport Agency offices, applications are accepted in person by appointment only, on payment of rush charges, and with evidence of impending departure, such as tickets or an e-ticket confirmation printout. Call ahead to verify current requirements, locations, and hours. In-person applications are processed in order of priority of departure, and can be issued the same day if truly necessary. See the website for passport office locations.

CANADIAN PASSPORTS
Passport Canada

Place du Centre, 200 Promenade du Portage, Commercial Level 2, Gatineau (Hull sector) QC K1A 0G3, Canada; tel. 800-567-6868 (Canada and United States only) or +1-819-997-8338; www.ppt.gc.ca

Application forms and step-by-step instructions for Canadian passports are available at passport offices, Canada Post outlets, Service Canada centers, or on the Passport Canada website.

U.K. PASSPORTS
Identity and Passport Service (IPS)

Globe House, 89 Eccleston Square, London SW1V 1PN, U.K.; tel. 0300-222-0000 (U.K. only); SMS 0300-222-0222 (U.K. only); www.ips.gov.uk/passport; www.direct.gov.uk/en/TravelAndTransport/Passports

You can start the application process for a U.K. passport by completing a form on their website. A printed application will then be mailed to you to sign and return with your photographs, payment, and documentation. The Identity and Passport Service recommends that you apply for a passport at least six weeks before your intended departure, preferably longer, especially in the spring and early summer when the largest numbers of people apply for passports for summer holiday travel. All first-time adult applicants for a U.K. passport must now appear for an in-person interview at a passport office before their passport will be issued. After you submit your application, you will be contacted to schedule an interview.

IRISH PASSPORTS
Passport Office

Republic of Ireland; Dept. of Foreign Affairs; Setanta Centre, Molesworth St., Dublin 2, tel. +353-1-671-1633; Irish Life Building, 1a South Mall, Cork, tel. +353-21-494-4700 (applications from counties Clare, Cork, Kerry, Limerick, Tipperary, and Waterford only); www.foreignaffairs.gov.ie; www.dfa.ie

Irish citizens can obtain and submit passport application forms at the passport offices in Dublin or Cork, or through most post offices and Garda stations in Ireland or Irish embassies and consulates abroad.

AUSTRALIAN PASSPORTS
Passports Australia

Department of Foreign Affairs and Trade; tel. 131-232 (Australia only);
passports.australia@dfat.gov.au; www.passports.gov.au

Australian citizens can apply for a passport in person at most post offices in Australia, or at passport offices. Post offices may require advance appointments for passport application interviews, so call in advance. Normal processing time is supposedly 10 working days; expedited processing is available for an additional charge on proof of imminent departure. Application forms and instructions are available at most post offices, or on the Passports Australia website.

AOTEAROA/NEW ZEALAND PASSPORTS
Aotearoa/New Zealand Passport Office

Dept. of Internal Affairs, P.O. Box 10-526, Wellington, Aotearoa/New Zealand;
tel. 0800-22-50-50 (Aotearoa/New Zealand only) or +64-4-474-8100, fax +64-4-382-3410;
passports@dia.govt.nz; www.passports.govt.nz

Aotearoa/New Zealand citizens can request passport application forms by phone or download them from the website. Completed applications can be mailed to the passport office. Regular service supposedly takes only 10 days; in-person rush service is available at passport offices for an extra charge.

Visas

WORLDWIDE VISA AND ENTRY REQUIREMENTS
Travel Information Manual

IATA Data Publications; timatic.indp@iata.org; www.timaticweb.com;
www.iata.org/ps/publications/Pages/timaticweb-travel-requirements.aspx

This is the reference used by airlines in deciding whether you will be admitted to your destination (and thus whether to let you on the plane). Unlike most sources that list requirements only for citizens of a particular country, the *Travel Information Manual* includes information on visa, entry, and transit requirements for citizens of all countries. It's useful, and the best available *secondary* source, but should never be relied on without double-checking with each country's embassy or consulate. The print edition is sold only by subscription (€242/year as of 2011). Ask to look at a copy of the printed TIM at an airline office, or ask a travel agent to print out or email the relevant pages from the electronic edition of TIMATIC available through their computerized reservation system. The Timaticweb.com website is for paid subscribers only, but you may be able to get a brief free trial by registering, which would suffice for one-time use to check the database for all the countries you plan to visit on a big trip. Various airlines and travel agencies offer cobranded versions of Timaticweb on their websites. These come and go, but the IATA website above has links to some of them. If the URL has changed, search IATA.org for references to "Timatic."

VISA AND OTHER REQUIREMENTS FOR U.S. CITIZENS TRAVELING ABROAD

U.S. Department of State

Because visa requirements are determined by the government of the country you want to visit, the starting point in determining the entry requirements for another country is finding the nearest embassy or consulate of that country. Because all agents of foreign governments in the United States must register with the U.S. Department of State, lists of foreign diplomatic offices and officers found here are complete and definitive except in the case of governments not recognized by the United States, or of changes since the last (usually annual) update. Visa and entry requirements, however, can be changed without notice to the U.S. government, so the U.S. Department of State summaries of foreign-entry requirements are only informational, not authoritative. Some of this information is also available in print, but it changes sufficiently often that I can't recommend relying on the print versions. Get the latest revisions available on the Internet, and double-check them with the relevant embassies or consulates.

Foreign Embassies and Consulates in the United States

www.state.gov/s/cpr/rls/i

Diplomatic List

www.state.gov/s/cpr/rls/dpl

Foreign Consular Offices in the United States

www.state.gov/s/cpr/rls/fco

The Diplomatic List covers foreign embassies in Washington, D.C. Foreign Consular Offices covers all foreign consulates and other diplomatic offices elsewhere in the United States. Both include contact information (including URLs for many consular and embassy websites) and complete staff directories of all accredited diplomats, with titles.

Foreign Entry Requirements by Country

http://travel.state.gov/travel

Summaries of other countries entry requirements for U.S. citizens are included in the State Department's advisories about each country. Please don't rely on this website: verify everything with each country's own authorities. But it's useful as a starting point to refer to when contacting embassies or consulates.

U.S. Department of the Treasury, Office of Foreign Assets Control

Treasury Annex, 1500 Pennsylvania Ave. NW, Washington, DC 20220; tel. 800-540-6322 (United States only) or +1-202-622-2490; www.treas.gov/ofac

OFAC issues and enforces regulations for trade embargoes that restrict travel and tourism spending and/or imports by U.S. citizens to, from, or with listed countries and entities. Most U.S. government restrictions on travel come from OFAC, not the State Department. Warning: many of these rules affect visitors to the United States from other countries (if they have previously visited embargoed countries), not just citizens of the United States. Getting an answer from OFAC, even to a very specific question, posed in writing, as to what is or isn't allowed, has sometimes taken me as much as a year.

Embassy.org

www.embassy.org/embassies

The U.S. State Department list of foreign embassies in the United States is authoritative and comprehensive, but doesn't necessarily list their websites. Not all embassies have websites, of course, but this unofficial, commercial website has the best available collection of links to those that do. Note that it lists only embassies in Washington, D.C.; there's no information here on consulates (or their websites) in the rest of the United States, or the rest of the world.

VISA REQUIREMENTS FOR FOREIGN VISITORS TO THE UNITED STATES

U.S. Department of State

tel. +1-202-663-1225; http://travel.state.gov/visa

Outside the United States, information on travel to the United States can be obtained from any U.S. embassy or consulate, but be prepared to wait in very long lines. The State Department website has details on requirements for each type of visa as well as downloadable application forms and contact information for all U.S. embassies and consulates abroad. As a U.S. citizen, I apologize in advance to foreign visitors for what they have to go through to obtain permission from the U.S. government to visit our country, and how they are treated by customs and immigration inspectors on arrival.

VISA SERVICES

Zierer Visa Service

1650 Tysons Blvd., Suite 1350, McLean, VA 22102; tel. 800-361-6385 (United States only), +1-703-903-1400; customerservice@zvs.com; www.zvs.com

Additional offices in New York, Atlanta, Miami, Chicago, Houston, San Francisco, Los Angeles, and (of course) Washington, D.C. Commercial visa-expediting services aren't cheap, but you may have to use one if you need a lot of visas in a hurry or need a visa for a country such as China whose consulates and embassies don't accept visa applications by mail. There are others, but Zierer is a company I've used myself and can recommend.

Safety and Health

GOVERNMENT HEALTH ADVICE AND INFORMATION
Centers for Disease Control and Prevention
Traveler's Health Hotline; tel. 800-CDC-INFO (800-232-4636, United States only); www.cdc.gov/travel

Official U.S. inoculation and health recommendations for international travelers, in general and by country and region.

International Travel and Health by the World Health Organization
www.who.int/ith

The WHO is the UN-affiliated coordinating body for international public health efforts, disease prevention, and response to disease outbreaks. The WHO website includes the complete text of the WHO reference manual, *International Travel and Health*, as well as bulletins and advice on health issues for travelers in each country and region of the world.

GOVERNMENT POLITICAL AND SAFETY ADVICE AND INFORMATION
Background Notes (all countries) by the U.S. Department of State
www.state.gov/r/pa/ei/bgn

Not specifically for travelers, but provide a broader overview than the U.S. State Department's travel publications. The *Background Notes* give a more descriptive and often more enlightening (if equally opinionated) source of U.S. government information about other countries than the better-known *CIA World Fact Book*.

Bureau of Consular Affairs, U.S. Department of State
http://travel.state.gov/travel
Country Specific Information
(all countries)
Travel Warnings
(included with the *Consular Information Sheet* whenever a Travel Warning is in effect)

Useful, if biased, publications from the U.S. Department of State.

Department of Foreign Affairs and International Trade (Canada)

www.voyage.gc.ca

Canada's DFAIT publishes a detailed set of travel reports and warnings by country.

Foreign & Commonwealth Office (U.K.)

www.fco.gov.uk/en/travel-and-living-abroad

The U.K. FCO provides travel advice for more than 200 countries, including advisories on places it considers especially risky.

Australian Department of Foreign Affairs and Trade (DFAT)

www.smartraveller.gov.au

Consular advice bulletins from the Australian government can provide a useful "reality check" on the often more alarmist warnings from the U.S. government. You can subscribe on the website to get updates by email if the advice for a particular country is changed.

REGISTERING YOUR TRAVEL PLANS WITH YOUR GOVERNMENT

None of the programs listed below (for U.S., Canadian, U.K., and Australian citizens) are mandatory. But if your government knows where you are, they might be better able to assist you in a crisis, and/or advise you about emerging issues related to travel in your future planned destinations. With each of these schemes, you set up an online "account" and profile, and can then register your travel plans (countries and expected dates) online, in advance, for an entire multicountry trip or for multiple future trips. Note that these are secure websites with URLs that begin with "https" not "http."

Smart Traveler Enrollment Program (STEP)

https://travelregistration.state.gov

U.S. citizens can register their travel plans with the Department of State through this website, eliminating the need to register in person at U.S. consulates or embassies, which are sometimes the most dangerous places in a country where the U.S. government is very unpopular. If you have registered, you'll be notified automatically of new U.S. travel advisories related to your location or your intended future destinations.

Registration of Canadians Abroad (ROCA)

https://www.voyage2.gc.ca/Registration_inscription

"A registration service for all Canadians travelling or living abroad. This service is provided so that we can contact and assist you in an emergency in a foreign country, such as a natural disaster or civil unrest, or inform you of a family emergency at home."

Resource Guide

LOCATE: Registration of British Nationals Overseas

https://www.locate.fco.gov.uk/locateportal

"LOCATE is a free service provided by the Foreign and Commonwealth Office for British nationals travelling to or living outside of the United Kingdom. The details you provide when you register will help our embassy and crisis staff contact you and give you better assistance in an emergency such as a natural or manmade disaster or civil disturbance. We are encouraging all British nationals travelling and living abroad to register with us on LOCATE, even for short trips."

Online Register of Australians Overseas (ORAO)

https://www.orao.dfat.gov.au

All Australian citizens traveling or living abroad are encouraged to register their travel plans with the Department of Foreign Affairs and Trade through this website.

OTHER TRAVEL HEALTH AND SAFETY ISSUES
Association for Safe International Road Travel (ASIRT)

11769 Gainsborough Rd., Potomac, MD 20854; tel. +1-301-983-5252, fax +1-301-983-3663; asirt@asirt.org; www.asirt.org

Founded by the mother of an American medical student who was killed, with 21 other people, in a (typical) Third World bus crash, ASIRT compiles country-by-country reports on road travel safety, and works to increase awareness of road travel as the most dangerous aspect of travel. Most ASIRT *Road Travel Reports* say essentially the same thing: "Road travel is dangerous. Outside the First World, never travel by road at night." So it isn't necessary to get them for every country you plan to visit. There's useful general info on the website, though, including a pocket guide to how to say "Please drive more slowly" and similar things in many languages.

Beyond Fear: Thinking Sensibly About Security in an Uncertain World
by Bruce Schneier
ISBN 0-387-02620-7; 2003, 296 pp; Springer Verlag, New York

An exceptionally clear framework for how to evaluate travel security and safety issues. Schneier's background is in cryptography and computer security. In recent years he's applied his analytic and expository expertise to a wider range of security questions, particularly aviation security, and has served on an advisory committee appointed by the U.S. Transportation Security Administration.

City of Walls: Crime, Segregation, and Citizenship in São Paulo
by Teresa P. R. Caldeira
ISBN 978-0520221437; 2001, 504 pp; University of California Press, Berkeley

Many of our fears about travel in the cities of the South are, if we are honest with ourselves, about our conceptions of race, poverty, and the idea of "the city" itself. Caldeira is a São Paulo native who teaches in Southern California. This book is a fascinating exposition of Paulista urban geography and ethnography, but so written as to draw out the implications for other cities from Los Angeles to Johannesburg. São Paulo is one of the most interesting metropolitan areas I've ever visited, and certainly one of those least appreciated globally despite its size and significance, but not easily accessible to a visitor without a car and fluency in Portuguese. (I had the next best thing, or better: knowledgeable and generous local hosts to show me around.) I recommend this book to anyone who wants to understand their own fears of urban violent crime, wherever in the world you are headed.

Fear of Flying Clinic (FOFC)

1777 Borel Place, San Mateo, CA 94402; tel. +1-650-341-1595; office@fofc.com; www.fofc.com

The FOFC is a nonprofit organization that draws on the expertise of professionals from the Federal Aviation Administration and major airlines. Instructors include a pilot, flight attendant, airline mechanic, and air traffic controller, who explain all aspects of air flight safety procedures and airplane control systems as well as basic principles of aerodynamics. Classes include a tour of a major airline's maintenance facility and an air traffic control tower. The clinic employs a licensed behavioral therapist who works closely with fearful fliers in developing techniques to conquer their anxieties. Workshops several times a year at San Francisco International Airport. Similar programs elsewhere include the Seattle-area Fear of Flying Clinic, www.fearofflyingclinic.org.

Landmine and Cluster Munition Monitor

by the International Campaign to Ban Landmines
www.the-monitor.org

Annually updated country profiles on the extent of mining, mine casualties, and mine clearance. A must-read for anyone contemplating travel in mined areas.

Staying Healthy in Asia, Africa, and Latin America

by Dirk G. Schroeder, ScD, MPH
ISBN 1-56691-133-8; 5th ed. 2000, 230 pp; Avalon Travel, Emeryville, CA

Developed by Volunteers in Asia (listed above under *Living, Working, Studying, and Volunteering Abroad*) for its own volunteers and training programs, this book covers what to do before you go, immunization and other requirements, what to bring, what to do to avoid getting sick, and what to do if you do get sick. I'm not an advocate of unnecessary self-diagnosis or self-treatment. But when your mind is dulled by sickness and you're isolated in a place where no one speaks your language and/or there is no doctor, and you need to figure out what to do, this is the book you want to have in your backpack.

Resource Guide

Wide Awake at 3:00 a.m. by Richard M. Coleman, PhD
ISBN 0-7167-1796-4 (paperback), ISBN 0-7167-1795-6 (hardcover); 1986, 195 pp;
W. H. Freeman & Co., New York

Still the best book on jet lag, what causes it, and how to deal with it. Jet lag is a disturbance of the body's normal daily cycles of alertness, sleepiness, and other functions. Coleman is an expert on those cycles: a former director of the Stanford University Sleep Disorders Clinic and a consultant on shift work, scheduling, and jet lag to businesses, traveling athletes, and others. Honest and practical; not a "miracle cure" book, as there is no "cure" for jet lag. Clearly and entertainingly written for a lay audience.

See also Chapter 2, "Travel, Health, and Safety Guidelines" in Edward O'Neil Jr.'s *A Practical Guide to Global Health Service*, listed earlier under *Living, Working, Studying, and Volunteering Abroad* in the *Logistics* section, which includes reviews of the professional literature on travel health topics including transportation safety, deep vein thrombosis, and antimalarials.

TRAVEL MEDICINE AND IMMUNIZATION CLINICS

This is a selective list of some specialized travel health and immunization clinics I know of, have used, or have had recommended to me by others. If you have an ongoing relationship with a doctor, health care service, or health maintenance organization, you may want to consult them first. I encourage readers who have had good experiences with travel clinics not listed here, particularly those in major gateway cities and countries not listed, to let me know so that I can include them in future editions. This list is not intended to be exhaustive, and mergers and acquisitions in the health care "industry" make it impossible to keep up to date. For travel clinics in other areas, see your regular health care provider, or the worldwide directories in the following section.

Most of these clinics fall into two categories: inexpensive drop-in immunization clinics (the cheapest option if you just need immunizations, sometimes located near ports and airports to serve travelers and ship and airline crews) and more expensive specialized clinics, usually associated with teaching hospitals, that offer much more extensive (and expensive) physician consultations, advice, and background information.

UNITED STATES
Travel Medicine and Immunization Clinic
Beth Israel Deaconess Medical Center; Lowry Medical Office Building,
110 Francis St., Suite GB—basement ("T" stop: Longwood), Boston, MA 02215;
tel. +1-617-632-7740, fax +1-617-632-7626; www.bidmc.org

Services by appointment only.

Travel Medicine Clinic

Northwestern University Memorial Hospital; 676 N. Saint Clair St., Suite 900, Chicago, IL 60611; tel. +1-312-926-3155; nmpgtravel@nmh.org; www.nmpg.com/travel-medicine

Services by appointment only.

Adult Immunization and Travel Clinic

San Francisco Department of Public Health; 101 Grove St., Room 102 (Civic Center, across Grove Street from the side entrance to City Hall), San Francisco, CA 94102; tel. +1-415-554-2625; travelshots.dph@sfdph.org; www.sfcdcp.org/aitc.html

"A nonprofit, fee-for-service clinic...committed to providing convenient, knowledgeable, personalized, and cost-effective immunization services for travelers." No appointments needed for consultations and immunizations, but call ahead to confirm location and drop-in hours. Why don't public health services in other big international gateway cities provide services like this?

SFO Airport Medical Clinic

St. Mary's Medical Center, Catholic Healthcare West; Departures/Ticketing Level, International Terminal ("A" side), San Francisco International Airport; tel. +1-650-821-5601; fax +1-650-821-5662; www.stmarysmedicalcenter.org/Medical_Services/198763; www.flysfo.com/web/page/atsfo/passenger-serv/med-serv

Call for appointments and drop-in immunization hours.

CANADA
Travel Medicine Clinics

Public Health Agency of Canada
www.phac-aspc.gc.ca/tmp-pmv/travel/clinic-eng.php

Nationwide directory of public and private travel clinics and immunization facilities, with links to their websites. Not necessary complete, and does not imply government endorsement, but extremely useful.

UNITED KINGDOM
Medical Advisory Services for Travellers Abroad (MASTA)

www.masta-travel-health.com

One of the largest networks of private commercial travel health and immunization clinics in the U.K. See the website for clinic locations, hours, and procedures.

WORLDWIDE
Travel Clinic Directory

American Society of Tropical Medicine and Hygiene (ASTMH); 111 Deer Lake Rd., Suite 100,

Deerfield, IL 60015; tel. +1-847-480-9592, fax +1-847-480-9282;
www.astmh.org/source/ClinicalDirectory

The American Society of Tropical Medicine and Hygiene (ASTMH) is a professional organization for specialists in tropical medicine, hygiene, and related disciplines, mainly in the United States and Canada, but including some in other countries. A directory of all those members worldwide who wish to be listed (excluding those not providing services to the general public) is available on the ASTMH website. Some members are in individual practices, but many work at specialty travel clinics. Unfortunately, the directory listings are for individual physicians, not for clinics.

International Association for Medical Assistance to Travelers (IAMAT)
www.iamat.org
United States

1623 Military Rd. #279, Niagara Falls, NY 14304-1745; tel. +1-716-754-4883

Canada

67 Mowat Ave., Suite 36, Toronto, ON M6K 3E3, Canada; tel. +1-416-652-0137

Canada (alternate)

2162 Gordon St., Guelph, ON N1L 1G6, Canada; tel. +1-519-836-0102, fax +1-519-836-3412

Aotearoa/New Zealand

206 Papanui Rd., Christchurch 5, Aotearoa/New Zealand

IAMAT coordinates a referral network of bilingual and multilingual (mainly English-speaking) doctors around the world who have agreed to a standard schedule of fees, in U.S. dollars, for office visits and hotel or house calls for travelers. IAMAT membership and the IAMAT referral directory are free on request, but donations are encouraged. Many travelers find that it allays their fears to carry the portions of the IAMAT directory for the places they plan to visit. But it's rarely that hard to find an English-speaking doctor in the sort of big city where most IAMAT doctors practice, and in much of the world IAMAT rates are often higher than the prices IAMAT doctors, or equally qualified English-speaking doctors who treat foreign travelers, charge patients who don't mention IAMAT.

Travel Clinic Directory
International Society of Travel Medicine (ISTM); 315 W. Ponce de Leon Ave., Suite 245, Decatur, GA 30030; tel. +1-404-373-8282, fax +1-404-373-8283; Skype: istm.office; istm@istm.org; www.istm.org; www.istm.org/WebForms/SearchClinics

A professional organization of travel medicine specialists with more than 2,500 members in 75 countries. The website includes a worldwide directory of clinics, hospitals, and private practices with which members are affiliated.

Travel Insurance

Some regular insurance agents handle travel insurance, especially long-term comprehensive travel medical insurance. You can also get travel insurance from travel insurance companies, direct providers of medevac and travel emergency services, and independent travel insurance brokers and agencies that can help you compare the offerings of different insurers. Following are some of each type that I know of in the United States. (Travel insurance is generally much easier to find in other countries, and rarely marketed across international borders.) These listings are not intended as endorsements, but are just to help you get started on your own research. I've heard good and bad things about almost all of these companies. Additional travel insurance providers in the United States are listed in the member directory of the U.S. Travel Insurance Association, www.ustia.org. If you already have insurance, it may cover you while you are traveling; check the details of your existing coverage before buying additional insurance for travel.

TRAVEL INSURANCE COMPANIES

Access America

P.O. Box 71533, Richmond, VA 23286-4684; tel. 800-729-6021 (United States only), fax 800-346-9265 (United States only); customerservice@accessamerica.com; www.accessamerica.com

Coverage: Emergency medical, medevac, and trip cancellation and interruption. Supplier default coverage is limited to a few select airlines and tour operators, mainly the largest and most expensive, and excludes all companies that aren't specifically listed as covered.

CSA Travel Protection

P.O. Box 939057, San Diego, CA 92193-9057; tel. 800-348-9505 (United States only); csa@csatravelprotection.com; www.csatravelprotection.com

U.S. subsidiary of Europ Assistance, an international travel assistance and insurance company based in France. Coverage: Emergency medical, medevac, and trip cancellation and interruption.

Highway to Health

1 Radnor Corporate Center, Suite 100, 100 Matsonford Rd., Radnor, PA 19087; tel. 888-243-2358 (United States only) or +1-610-254-8700, fax +1-610-254-8797; www.highway2health.com

Coverage: Comprehensive medical, emergency medical, medevac, and trip cancellation and interruption.

International Medical Group (IMG)

2960 N. Meridian St., Indianapolis, IN 46208-4715; tel. 800-628-4644 (United States only) or +1-317-655-4500, fax +1-317-655-4505; insurance@imglobal.com; www.imglobal.com

Coverage: Comprehensive travel medical insurance. Expensive but genuinely comprehensive coverage. IMG is the primary provider of medical insurance for Peace Corps volunteers, and a leading insurer of missionaries and other U.S. expatriates living and traveling in the Second, Third, and Fourth Worlds.

Seven Corners

303 Congressional Blvd., Carmel, IN 46032; tel. 800-335-0611 (United States only) or +1-317-575-2652, fax +1-317-575-2659; cs@sevencorners.com; www.sevencorners.com

Coverage: Comprehensive medical, medevac, and trip cancellation and interruption. Plans for U.S. residents traveling abroad and for foreign visitors to the United States.

Travelex

P.O. Box 641070, Omaha, NE 68164-7070; tel. 800-228-9792 (United States only) or +1-410-308-2903; customerservice@travelexinsurance.com; www.travelexinsurance.com

Coverage: Emergency medical, medevac, trip cancellation and interruption.

Travel Guard

3300 Business Park Dr., Stevens Point, WI 54482; tel. 800-826-4919 (United States only) or +1-715-345-0505; www.travelguard.com

Coverage: Emergency medical, medevac, and trip cancellation and interruption. Unlike most travel insurers that offer at most half a dozen standard coverage packages, Travel Guard allows a fair amount of online customization (although nothing close to what ought to be possible) of which coverages you want, in what amounts.

TravelSafe Insurance

P.O. Box 7050, 40 Commerce Dr., Wyomissing, PA 19610-6050; tel. 888-885-7233 (United States only); info@travelsafe.com; www.travelsafe.com

Coverage: Emergency medical, medevac, and trip cancellation and interruption. Offers an added-cost option that repays 90 percent of any forfeited prepaid travel costs if you cancel a planned trip for any reason, which may be worthwhile if you fear you may have to cancel for some reason that wouldn't otherwise be covered (such as illness of someone not closely enough related to you for the cancellation to be covered by standard trip cancellation coverage).

World Nomads

Level 5, 24 York St., Sydney NSW 2000, Australia; tel. +61-2-8263-0400; www.worldnomads.com

Coverage: Emergency medical, medevac, and limited (US$5,000) trip cancellation and interruption. For legal reasons, coverage and prices vary by country of residence at the time of purchase, but generally similar plans designed for long-term, independent budget travel are available to anyone, anywhere in the world. Among the cheapest reputable options if you only want emergency medical and medevac coverage for long-term travel. Most services including claims processing are provided online only.

PREPAID EMERGENCY SERVICES PROVIDERS

AirMed International

1000 Urban Center Dr., Suite 470, Birmingham, AL 35242; tel. 800-356-2161 (United States only) or +1-205-443-4880, fax 866-872-8624 (United States only) or +1-205-443-4841; www.airmed.com

Services: Emergency medical transportation. AirMed offers prepaid medical evacuation services for a flat annual "membership" fee, with progressively higher rates for longer stays of more than 90 days outside your home country. AirMed owns and operates its own planes, with its own staff—which may or may not give better service than a local contractor, but may take longer to arrive from their base in the United States. AirMed only provides medevac service to members if, in AirMed's judgment, it is medically necessary.

MEDJET Assistance

3500 Colonnade Pkwy., Suite 500, Birmingham, AL 35243; tel. 800-963-3538 (United States only) or +1-205-595-6626, fax 800-863-3538 (United States only) or +1-205-595-6658; info@medjetassistance.com; www.medjetassistance.com

Services: Emergency medical transportation. For a fixed annual fee, MEDJET Assistance will provide (through contractors—they aren't an aircraft operator themselves) air ambulance transportation to the hospital of your choice, worldwide, if you are hospitalized. That's much more generous than typical travel insurance, which only covers transportation to the nearest hospital they deem suitable—not necessarily the one nearest your home—and only if *their* doctors decide it's essential. If you have insurance, but it doesn't provide for medical evacuation, this may be most comprehensive medevac add-on available. Note, however, that the standard plan doesn't cover you if you are out of your home country for more than 90 days at a time. You have to pay a substantially higher "expatriate" rate for coverage for longer stays abroad.

INDEPENDENT TRAVEL INSURANCE BROKERS

Each of these brokers offers a selection of travel insurance policies from multiple issuers.

InsureMyTrip.com

100 Commerce Dr., Warwick, RI 02886; tel. 800-487-4722 (United States only) or +1-401-773-9300, fax +1-401-921-4530; info@insuremytrip.com; www.insuremytrip.com

TravelInsuranceCenter.com

8420 W. Dodge Rd., Suite 510, Omaha, NE 68114; tel. 866-979-6753 (United States only) or +1-402-343-3699; www.travelinsurancecenter.com

Travel Insurance Services

2950 Camino Diablo, Suite 300, Walnut Creek, CA 94597-3991; tel. 800-937-1387 (United States only) or +1-925-932-1387, fax +1-484-652-5394; info@travelinsure.com; www.travelinsure.com

Money Matters

ATM LOCATORS

All of the major credit, debit, charge, and ATM card networks have Web directories of locations worldwide where their cards can be used to get cash, if everything is working. Keep in mind, though, that these directories are not necessarily complete or up to date. They're useful if you are having difficulty finding an ATM where your card will work, but are not to be relied on. The exact URLs change often, so if one of them doesn't work, search the home page of that network for "ATM locator."

Co-op Network (credit unions and cooperatives)

www.co-opnetwork.org

www.co-opfs.org/public/locators/atmlocator

Discover Card/Pulse

http://debit.discovernetwork.com/cal/search.do

MasterCard/Cirrus/Maestro

www.mastercard.us/cardholder-services/atm-locator.html

STAR System

www.star.com

Visa/Plus/Electron
www.visa.com/atms
http://visa.via.infonow.net/locator/global/

BILL RECEIVING AND PAYMENT
Paytrust (a service of Intuit)
www.paytrust.com

Many banks offer online bill payment. But for bills that come in the mail instead of online, how do you know what to pay, or when? For US$10–15 per month, Paytrust will give you a unique post office box number to use as a billing address, and scan all bills that arrive at that address so that you can view and pay them online. Popular with expats and long-term travelers, and accustomed to dealing with them. A Web service, obviously, but in my experience their telephone service and support have been excellent.

CURRENCY CONVERSION
While you are traveling, it's generally best to think in local currency, rather than to try to convert every price or transaction. But exchange rate tables and conversion tools can be useful in travel planning, especially if you are trying to interpret or compare prices that are specified in different currencies. The exchange rate tables in most newspapers list only a few First World currencies, and don't include many of the Third World currencies likely to be of interest to world travelers. Here are a couple of sources for exchange rates and conversions for a wider range of world currencies.

OANDA.com Currency Tools
www.oanda.com/currency/converter

Most other Internet travel sites use "private label" versions of the OANDA.com or XE.com (see below) currency converters. In addition to online conversions, you can generate a printable "cheat sheet" with equivalent amounts of any two currencies, such as your home currency and the currency of the country you are visiting, to carry with you for quick reference while traveling.

Pacific Exchange Rate Service
http://fx.sauder.ubc.ca

Various tools and display and print formats derived from a database of currency exchange rates maintained by the business school at the University of British Columbia, Canada. Includes printable rate sheets and tables of historical rates.

XE.com Interactive Currency Table

www.xe.com/ict

Generates a printable table of exchange rates for any currency of interest, either at the current rates or as of any desired date since 1995. Useful if you are trying to convert prices from an older guidebook (use the rate for two years earlier than the copyright date, as a rule of thumb), or if you are preparing a travel expense report and rates have changed significantly since your trip.

Consumer Protection

Your legal rights and avenues for recourse in a dispute with a travel company vary depending on what legal system(s) has or have "jurisdiction" over the transaction in question. That can be difficult to determine, and may depend on where you are, where you were at the time of the transaction, where your credit-card issuer is based, where the company with which you did business is located (before you clicked on "buy," did you check where the company that runs the website is based?), and other factors. More than one country's laws may apply to the same incident. Consumer-protection and law-enforcement agencies, leery of the potential extra work for them of policing and resolving cross-border e-commerce disputes, have been extraordinarily slow to clarify these jurisdictional ambiguities, even as they have become common problems.

UNITED STATES

American Society of Travel Agents

ASTA Consumer Affairs Department; 1101 King St., Suite 200, Alexandria, VA 22314; tel. +1-703-739-2782, fax +1-703-684-8319; consumeraffairs@asta.org; www.asta.org

Keeps records of complaints against members and offers informal assistance in mediating disputes between travelers and members. Requires members to subscribe to its code of professional ethics, and can expel members who fail to comply with its rules, fail to respond to complaints, or have too many unresolved complaints. Limited, but more effective than most industry self-regulation schemes.

California Seller of Travel Registration Unit

State of California, Office of the Attorney General, 300 S. Spring St., Los Angeles, CA 90013; tel. +1-213-897-8065, fax +1-213-897-8846; http://ag.ca.gov/travel

Travel Consumer Restitution Corp. (TCRC)

P.O. Box 6001, Larkspur, CA 94977-6001; tel. +1-415-458-3032, fax +1-415-924-2033; www.tcrcinfo.com

The protection of the California Seller of Travel Law (Business and Professions Code

Section 17550) and the TCRC is limited to purchases of travel services by California residents from businesses located in California. But anyone who sells travel to California residents must register with the state government, and list their CST registration number in all advertisements and promotional materials. You can verify a CST registration number on the CST website. "Sellers of travel" include travel agents and tour operators. Cruise lines and U.S. airlines had the lobbying clout to have themselves exempted from the registration requirement and the restitution fund, so the law provides no protection against air or cruise line bankruptcy or other default. Non-U.S. airlines are clearly subject to the CST law but have thus far ignored it. It's unclear what would happen were a Californian to make a complaint against a foreign airline under the law; were foreign airlines directly to challenge the special exemption for U.S. airlines; or were anyone to challenge the law's application to sales of international tickets as infringing the exclusive jurisdiction of the federal government over international trade. It's typical of U.S. provincialism that this law was written without regard for its international implications.

U.S. DEPARTMENT OF TRANSPORTATION (DOT)

The Department of Transportation, which is supposed to enforce federal laws affecting airlines, gives out one address for consumer complaints and another for enforcement requests, as follows.

Aviation Consumer Protection Division (C-75)

U.S. Department of Transportation, 1200 New Jersey Ave. SE,
Washington, DC 20590; tel. +1-202-366-2220; airconsumer@ost.dot.gov;
http://airconsumer.ost.dot.gov

"Where appropriate, letters and Web form submissions will be forwarded to an official at the airline for further consideration." Sounds like a big help, doesn't it? To be fair, I should note that the DOT at least counts the complaints before they forward them to the airlines, and publishes monthly reports as to the numbers and general nature of complaints against each airline. It's mostly a system for monitoring quality-of-service issues rather than real enforcement, although in theory the complaint records can be used as a basis for rule-making. I don't know anyone who's gotten a satisfactory response to a complaint filed in this way.

Office of Aviation Enforcement and Proceedings (C-70)

Assistant General Counsel for Aviation Enforcement and Proceedings, 1200 New Jersey Ave. SE,
Washington, DC 20590; tel. +1-202-366-9342; www.dot.gov/ost/ogc/org/aviation

If you think an airline has broken the law, and want the Department of Transportation to do more than count your complaint and maybe forward it to the airline, you need to make a formal complaint to this office. This is the office, for example, to which to send complaints of such fraudulent and deceptive airline practices as code sharing and labeling of "change of equipment" flights as "direct," or reports of violations by the airlines of federal truth-in-advertising laws by advertising of "half-roundtrip" prices or "one-way fares based on roundtrip travel." Airlines in the United States are exempt from most state and local consumer-protection and truth-in-advertising laws, so unless DOT takes action, these practices will continue indefinitely. Make clear that you are not asking for your letter to be passed on to the offending airline for a formulaic reply from their customer-relations department, but making a legal request that the DOT initiate an investigation and consider whether enforcement proceedings against the airline are warranted for the violation or practice in question. I'm not a lawyer, but my understanding is that the magic words to use in your letter (certified postal mail, return receipt requested) are something like, "This is a formal complaint and request for investigation and enforcement action pursuant to Title 49 U.S. Code, Section 41712." Enough sacks of mail, dear readers, and maybe DOT will get the message and start doing its job to protect consumers.

EUROPE

Air Travel Organiser's Licence (ATOL) Section

Consumer Protection Group, Civil Aviation Authority; K3 CAA House, 45–49 Kingsway, London WC2B 6TE, U.K.; tel. +1-44-20-7453-6424; advice@caa.co.uk; www.atol.org.uk

Most sales of discounted air tickets in the U.K. are covered by the ATOL consumer protection scheme. Travel agents selling tickets or packages requiring an ATOL must include their ATOL number in all advertisements and brochures. You can verify an advertised ATOL number on the ATOL website or by phone. Each ATOL licensee is required to post a bond to cover reimbursement of its customers if the agency, tour operator, airline, or other supplier of covered travel services defaults or goes out of business. ATOL fees also support a trust fund that makes up the difference in the cases where liabilities exceed the bonds. As the CAA puts it to U.K. travelers, "If it hasn't got an ATOL, don't book it at all."

European Air Passenger Rights

http://apr.europa.eu

Regulation (EC) No 261/2004 established "common rules on compensation and assistance to passengers in the event of denied boarding and of cancellation or long delay of flights." See the European Commission website for details on the rules and a link to the list by country of national enforcement bodies responsible for handling consumer complaints against airlines that fail to comply. The European Union rules apply to all flights departing *from* airports in the EU, regardless of the airline, and by flights from elsewhere *to* the EU if and only if they are operated by EU-based airlines. There is no comparable U.S. rule. So if you are flying from the United States to Europe, you are much better protected if you fly on a European airline.

Additional Resources

Hasbrouck.org

www.hasbrouck.org

My personal website, including my blog, email newsletter sign-up, updated answers to frequently asked questions about travel issues, resource guides and links, and some information about who I am (other than a traveler, travel writer, and travel consultant), and what I do when I'm not traveling or writing about travel.

PracticalNomad.com

www.practicalnomad.com

The website for this series of books from Avalon Travel, including *The Practical Nomad: How to Travel Around the World* and *The Practical Nomad: Guide to the Online Travel Marketplace.*

INDEX

HELP MAKE THIS A BETTER BOOK

All details in this book were reviewed, and facts and prices verified to the best of my ability, in 2011 before this fifth edition went to press. All things change, and I welcome your assistance in keeping this book current.

For changes between going to press and the publication of the next edition of this book, follow my blog (www.hasbrouck.org/blog) and the Practical Nomad website (www.practicalnomad.com). Internet references are especially ephemeral, so please check the website, or let me know by email, if any of the Internet or other resources in this book are no longer at the same addresses.

The information in this book is as accurate as was possible at the time it was written and revised. In an effort to be helpful, I give opinions on many matters on which others would disagree; realize that these are only my opinions. Don't take anything you read here as gospel. Be as skeptical of what you read here as you would be of any other advice. If you think I'm wrong, please write and tell me so. If something is unclear or I've left something out that you'd like explained or think should be said, or if there is something you found especially useful and want to be sure is retained, please let me know.

Please send all contributions, corrections, anecdotes, and suggestions to:

Edward Hasbrouck
c/o Avalon Travel
1700 Fourth St.
Berkeley, CA 94710 USA
nomad@hasbrouck.org
www.hasbrouck.org

DISCLAIMER

It's customary for reputable travel books to contain a disclaimer to the effect that the author accepted no "freebies" or discounts from suppliers of travel services mentioned in the work. The assumption is that free or reduced-rate transportation, accommodations, or other travel services for travel writers are given in exchange for implicit or explicit promotional consideration.

Because I can't say I received no discounts or wrote about nothing in which I have a financial interest, here's a full disclosure:

For most of my career, writing hasn't paid my rent. In this book I mention Airtreks.com, where I worked from 1998 through 2006 as a travel consultant, and with whom I still have a paid affiliation. After long and thoughtful consideration, I decided that the value of their services to you, the reader, should be more important than my fear of appearing self-serving. Feel free to ignore what I say about them if you think it motivated solely by self-interest.

As a travel agent and as a travel writer, I have sometimes received free or reduced-rate transportation (although far less than most people might think) on various airlines, more as partial compensation for having sold tickets on those airlines than in any expectation that I'll give them a favorable write-up in this book or elsewhere. I don't feel compromised: This book isn't a comparative review of airlines, and I'll let you make your own judgments about which ones to fly with. I personally choose based upon price. Were I to make recommendations, I'd pan some airlines that have given me free tickets and praise some others that I'd have to pay to fly.

I occasionally get discounts on hotels, almost always at upscale places where I wouldn't otherwise stay. I've also occasionally gotten free beds in hostels where I've been giving travel seminars—but where I would have stayed, and which I would recommend, anyway. I still recommend local hostelries of the sort that don't give discounts or pay commissions to travel agents.

I've often been given free admission to museums and other attractions, and I've eaten a lot of free lunches at travel industry events. As above, I'm not reviewing or recommending specific sites, sights, or restaurants. When I do so in my blog, I disclose any where I've been given discounts or freebies.

Finally, a few publishers gave me complimentary copies of books listed in the Resource Guide, slightly reducing the amount I spent on compiling my library of travel references. I'm grateful for their assistance. But I haven't listed any resources that I wouldn't be willing to pay for; I don't list some that I was sent for free; and my highest recommendation goes to some of those that are most expensive and for which I paid full price.

ACKNOWLEDGMENTS

Thanks to all the fellow travelers who've shared their experiences with me over the years, first and foremost Ruth Radetsky, my companion in travel, life, and love for the last 29 years and, I hope, for the rest of my life.

I've learned much from colleagues at the travel agencies where I have worked, including W. Alexander Hagen, J. P. Whitecloud, Michael Sukhenko, Hermine Craven, and Brenda Semrow. At AirTreks.com, thanks especially to Jim Pilaar, Tom Michelson, Jesse Walker-Shaw, Demos Pantelides, Aimée Miles, Cat MacLeod, Lorin Kalisky, John Taylor, David Derrick, Dan and Sarah Gamber, Annie Beug, and Glenn Talken.

The staff and volunteers at Hostelling International in San Francisco and elsewhere have been unfailingly supportive from the start, as have REI staff, fellow REI members, and others too numerous to list at hostels, bookstores, travel stores, campuses, and other venues for my talks. Readers and participants in my seminars have been a helpful sounding board and source of ideas, questions, and issues needing to be addressed. Thanks also to everyone who has sent me criticisms, updates, or suggestions. You have corrected many of my errors, and I am solely to blame for those that remain.

Thanks to the Front Porch Salon, Tom Brosnahan, Wayne Bernhardson, David Stanley, Chris Baker, Don George, Jay Campbell, Jeff Greenwald, Wendy Grossman, Aífe Murray, the late Paul Grimes, and my fellow members of the Bay Area Travel Writers and the guidebook writers email list for providing personal and professional support and encouragement.

Avalon Travel continues to justify, in their relationship with me, their longstanding reputation as a writer's publisher. Special thanks to Bill Newlin, Pauli Galin, Erin Van Rheenen, Angelique Clarke, Kevin McLain, Dave Hurst, Kari Gim, Amanda Bleakley, Mary Beth Pugh, Rosie Levy, Krista Rafanello, Stacy Johnson, Hannah Cox, Elizabeth Hansen, Jen Rios, Jodee Krainik, Sabrina Young, and Donna Galassi. Thanks also to the people in production, operations, and distribution who've helped to move this book from my hands (microphone, actually) to your hands.

John Gilmore, David Greene, the First Amendment Project, and the Computers, Freedom, and Privacy community have helped immeasurably with my recent work. Thanks also to Erik Josefsson, Jay Stanley, Barry Steinhardt, Lee Tien, Lillie Coney, Deborah Pierce, Linda Ackerman, and Robert Ellis Smith.

I owe a special debt of gratitude to all those hosts over the years whom I have failed to thank properly for their hospitality. Whether or not I ever get the chance to return your favors, may you all receive as warm welcomes, wherever you go, as so many of you have given me.